Accession no.
01019710

KT-233-128

WITHDRAWN

WITHDRAWN

C.

(

Various theoretical models in psychology and the social sciences have emphasized the social foundation of the mind and the role that social interactions play in cognitive functioning and its development. In this volume the metaphor used to capture this is *interactive minds* – a term chosen because it emphasizes social transaction and communication between minds without implying particular mechanisms or outcomes. For instance, we include in our conceptualization of interactive minds both internal and external forms of interaction with others. In addition, we emphasize that not all products of interacting minds are positive.

Besides focusing on the social foundation of cognition, *Interactive Minds* takes a life-span perspective, which is especially suitable for understanding interactive dynamics of behavior and human development. Each of the authors deals with a different topic and each presents a clear analysis of the basic dimensions of the problem. Among the issues addressed are biological-evolutionary aspects of cooperation, the role of social interaction in learning, the conceptualization of linguistic knowledge, peer problem solving, the psychological study of wisdom, gender dynamics, collaborative memory in adults and the elderly, cooperative construction of expert knowledge, and communities of practice in university study.

In the Epilogue, the implications for research and theory in various fields, including education, developmental and cognitive psychology, and cultural anthropology, are outlined.

Interactive minds

Interactive minds

Life-span perspectives on the social foundation of cognition

Edited by

PAUL B. BALTES
Max Planck Institute for Human Development and Education

URSULA M. STAUDINGER
Max Planck Institute for Human Development and Education

·1159410

LIBRARY

ACC. No. 01019710 . | DEPT.

CLASS No. 302-12 BAL

UNIVERSITY COLLEGE CHESTER

CAMBRIDGE
UNIVERSITY PRESS

Published by the Press Syndicate of the University of Cambridge
The Pitt Building, Trumpington Street, Cambridge CB2 1RP
40 West 20th Street, New York, NY 10011-4211, USA
10 Stamford Road, Oakleigh, Melbourne 3166, Australia

© Cambridge University Press 1996

First published 1996

Printed in the United States of America

Library of Congress Cataloging-in-Publication Data
Interactive minds: life-span perspectives on the social foundation of cognition /
edited by Paul B. Baltes, Ursula M. Staudinger.
    p.   cm.
    Includes bibliographical references and indexes.
    ISBN 0-521-48106-6 (hc). – ISBN 0-521-48567-3 (pb)
    1. Cognition and culture.   2. Social perception.   I. Baltes, Paul B.
II. Staudinger, Ursula M.
BF311.I564   1996
302'.12 – dc20   95-19302
                                             CIP

A catalog record for this book is available from the British Library.

ISBN 0-521-48106-6 Hardback
ISBN 0-521-48567-3 Paperback

On the occasion of his eightieth year, we dedicate this book to Ernst E. Boesch, whose work exemplifies the promise inherent in the interface between developmental, social, and cultural psychology.

Contents

vii

Contributors

Margarita Azmitia, Psychology Department, University of California, Santa Cruz, CA 95064, USA

Paul B. Baltes, Max Planck Institute for Human Development and Education, Lentzeallee 94, 14195 Berlin, Germany

Laura L. Carstensen, Department of Psychology, Stanford University, Stanford, CA 94305-2130, USA

Michael Cole, Laboratory of Comparative Development and Department of Communication, University of California, San Diego, 9500 Gilman Drive, La Jolla, CA 92093-0092, USA

William Damon, Center for the Study of Human Development, Brown University, Box 1938, Providence, RI 02912, USA

Roger A. Dixon, Department of Psychology, University of Victoria, Victoria, BC V8W 3P5, Canada

Gerd Gigerenzer, Max Planck Institute for Psychological Research, Leopoldstraße 24, 80802 Munich, Germany

Jacqueline J. Goodnow, School of Behavioural Sciences, Macquarie University, Sydney NSW 2109, Australia

Odette N. Gould, Department of Psychology, North Dakota State University, Fargo, ND 58105-5075, USA

Peter Graf, Department of Psychology, University of British Columbia, 2136 West Hall, Vancouver, BC V6T 1Z4, Canada

Hans Gruber, Institute for Educational Psychology, University of Munich, Leopoldstraße 13, 80802 Munich, Germany

Peter Hammerstein, Max Planck Institute for Behavioral Physiology, 82319 Seewiesen, Germany

Dietmar Janetzko, Center for Cognitive Science, University of Freiburg, Friedrichstraße 50, 79098 Freiburg, Germany

Wolfgang Klein, Max Planck Institute for Psycholinguistics, Wundtlaan 1, NL-6525 XD Nijmegen, The Netherlands

Markus Knauff, Center for Cognitive Science, University of Freiburg, Friedrichstraße 50, 79098 Freiburg, Germany

Gisela Labouvie-Vief, Department of Psychology, Wayne State University, 71 West Warren, Detroit, MI 48202, USA

Heinz Mandl, Institute for Educational Psychology, University of Munich, Leopoldstraße 13, 80802 Munich, Germany

Alexander Renkl, Institute for Educational Psychology, University of Munich, Leopoldstraße 13, 80802 Munich, Germany

Richard A. Shweder, Committee on Human Development, University of Chicago, 5730 South Woodlawn Avenue, Chicago, IL 60637, USA

Jacqui Smith, Max Planck Institute for Human Development and Education, Lentzeallee 94, 14195 Berlin, Germany

Ursula M. Staudinger, Max Planck Institute for Human Development and Education, Lentzeallee 94, 14195 Berlin, Germany

Robert J. Sternberg, Department of Psychology, Yale University, Box 208205, New Haven, CT 06520-8205, USA

Gerhard Strube, Center for Cognitive Science, University of Freiburg, Friedrichstraße 50, 79098 Freiburg, Germany

Franz E. Weinert, Max Planck Institute for Psychological Research, Leopoldstraße 24, 80802 Munich, Germany

Acknowledgments

This book is an outgrowth of one of the conferences that the Center of Psychology and Human Development of the Berlin Max Planck Institute for Human Development and Education organized as part of its program on life-span developmental psychology. The conference took place at the Institute in the fall of 1993. First of all, therefore, we acknowledge the generous support provided by our home institution and the Max Planck Society for the Advancement of Science.

During the journey from conference papers to book chapters, wide use was made of the very idea of this book, interactive minds. The chapters were revised in interaction with extensive reviews, which were prepared both by conference participants and by external reviewers. We thank the authors for their imaginative responses to the challenges posed by the reviews and for their continuing efforts to improve their chapters. As to the reviewers, and also on behalf of the chapter authors, we would like to acknowledge with admiration and much appreciation the scope and depth of the evaluations received. The following persons provided such reviews: Petra Badke-Schaub, Jürgen Baumert, Cynthia Berg, Manfred Bierwisch, Augusto Blasi, Rosemarie Blieszner, Jochen Brandtstädter, Robert Burgess, Laura Carstensen, Eve Clark, Willem Doise, Anders Ericsson, Peter Frensch, Jutta Heckhausen, Ravenna Helson, Theo Hermann, Robert Hoffman, Christine Howe, Reinhold Kliegl, Lothar Krappmann, Jane Lancaster, Wolfgang Lempert, Richard Lerner, Lea Light, Ineke Maas, George Maddox, Carol Magai, Jack Meacham, John Nesselroade, Fritz Oser, Alice Rossi, Wolfgang Schneider, Neil Smelser, Beate Sodian, Anna Stetsenko, Stephanie Teasley, Günter Tembrock, Dietmar Todt, Jan Valsiner, Elke van der Meer, Robert Zajonc.

Special compliments and thanks are due to our editorial and secretarial staff at the Max Planck Institute for Human Development and Education. Irmgard Pahl, Gregory Cain, and Anne Tschida assisted us ably in format editing, proof reading, and preparing the indexes. Candy Cooley, Helga Kaiser, and Ulrich Knappek provided the necessary secretarial and conference administrative support, with dedication and utmost care. This volume owes much to their generous and cooperative attitude.

This cooperative spirit extended beyond the Max Planck Institute. Our collaborative relationships with Cambridge University Press and its staff were splendid. Julia Hough, as our responsible editor, provided without fail the kind of intellectual and organizational support that authors and editors hope for but often do not receive. The production process was supported by the diligent and fast work of Mary Racine, the production editor, and Lisa Lincoln, the production controller.

Our expressions of heartfelt thanks to our colleagues and staff, however, are not meant to detract from our responsibilities as editors. Let us hasten to add, therefore, that those whom we acknowledge deserve much of the credit but none of the blame for whatever shortcomings remain in this volume. This is particularly true of the selection of topics and authors. Considering the complexity of its theme, it is perhaps not surprising that this book cannot offer definite or comprehensive coverage. Other researchers and lines of scholarship could have been involved. Despite these limitations, we are hopeful that the book, with its special emphasis on the life-span nature of interactive minds, provides new perspectives. We have aimed at assembling a good collection of what current behavioral research has to offer as it moves toward a more intensive and empirically based recognition of the role of interactive minds in the development of human cognition.

Interactive minds in a life-span perspective: prologue

Paul B. Baltes and Ursula M. Staudinger

That human behavior and development are at least in part a creation of social forces, social interaction, and social transmission is considered a truism by most, laypersons and academicians alike. Certainly, this belief is a fundamental tenet of the social and behavioral sciences. The classic thought experiment is to imagine a world in which infants are raised without social transaction and support, a world that does not contain language, artifacts, or other culturally based resources, such as reading, writing, and arithmetic. Development would be very different from what we are used to. If, in the extreme case, there were no social transactions, infants would not survive.

On a conceptual level, the social-interactive orientation toward the evolutionary and ontogenetic origins of humankind is strong enough for some social scientists to begin to invade the language of genetics as a means of communicating the pervasive and powerful role of social factors. In addition to mechanisms of "genetic inheritance," social scientists speak of mechanisms of social and "cultural inheritance" and further claim that the processes of social and cultural inheritance are associated with specific principles of organization, transmission, and dissipation (Durham, 1990).

Two other illustrations of the powerful role of interactions with others in cognitive behavior come from everyday life and the history of science. The first is a statement attributed to the philosopher Friedrich Nietzsche: "A significant person engages not only his own intelligence, but also that of his friends" (our translation). The second is based on statements made at the funeral of Wolfgang Pauli, physicist and Nobel Prize winner, known among his colleagues and students for his sharp and encompassing mind. On this occasion, other famed physicists reiterated how often they mentally invoked Pauli when contemplating a new finding or evaluating a particular interpretation: "How would Pauli think about this? How would he criticize what I have done?" When discussing the meaning of interactive minds in a later section of this prologue, we will label these two examples *external* (Nietzsche) and *internal* (Pauli) forms of interactions between minds.

1

The role of social factors in cognition: a theory–method mismatch?

Just as social-cultural forces are recognized in general by social scientists as cornerstones of the systems influencing and regulating development, so too are such forces acknowledged in the field of developmental psychology. As developmental psychologists, many of us have been "interactively socialized" to appreciate the role of social factors and to view development as essentially social in nature. Despite the existence of so-called organismic models of development (Reese & Overton, 1970), which are easily mistaken for so-called person-centered (personological) paradigms, in which most of the relevant sources of development are assumed to be located within the individual, it is difficult for developmentalists to conceive of development as a process primarily or solely driven and organized from within the organism.

This long-standing insight and commitment to the social nature of human development notwithstanding, theory and method, to paraphrase Wittgenstein, do not always (or even often) coincide in developmental work (Boesch, 1991; Cole, 1991). Because of this discrepancy between theory and method, it is not surprising that there is a continuing search for the role of the "social interactive" in developmental theory and research. One persuasive example is the enrichment and transformation of social-learning theory by cognitive dimensions in order to understand more fully the social foundation of action and thought (Bandura, 1986). Another current example of this continuous struggle for a better match between theory and method is the vigorous revisitation of early twentieth-century social constructivist scholars such as Baldwin and Piaget (Chapman, 1988; Edelstein & Hoppe-Graf, 1993), Luria (1976), and Vygotsky (1978; Wertsch, 1985). A third example is the ongoing mandate of interactionism (Magnusson & Endler, 1977; Pervin & Lewis, 1978) with its call for more explicit consideration of interactive and transactional conceptions in various fields of psychological inquiry. A further illustration of this perdurable search for a better representation of collective and social-interactive perspectives in psychology is the recent stream of "postmodern" (Neimeyer, Neimeyer, Lyddon, & Hoshmand, 1994) efforts to articulate reality as social construction. Finally, there are the recent debates about collectivism versus individualism (Miller & Prentice, 1994; Smelser, 1995; Triandis, 1990) as central theoretical and metatheoretical concepts in delineating individual as well as cultural differences. Certainly, researchers in these fields argue that more attention must be paid to social-interactive paradigms.

On the surface, then, the fundamental role of social forces and social processes in the evolutionary and ontogenetic origins of behavior and the human mind is clearly and widely acknowledged. Yet, as behavioral and social scientists explore the empirical basis of this fundamental orientation and as they attempt to look beyond the surface and unravel the processes involved in mindful behavior and human development, the task becomes more difficult. Often the conceptual message is lost on the way to the forum. The translation of the intellectual agenda into scientific evidence continues to be incomplete. According to some social and cultural psychologists (Cole, 1991), for instance, the nonsocial person-centered research paradigms persist in the study of cognition even when the fundamental role of context is obvious (see also Greeno, Chi, Clancey, & Elman, 1993, for recent debates on this issue). In a similar way it has been argued (e.g., Shotter, 1990) that Bartlett's early work on "contextualized" memory (1923), which was social-interactive in theoretical and empirical orientation, disappeared in his later research (Bartlett, 1932), which inaugurated the so-called cognitive revolution in psychology (cf. Neisser, 1967).

The scientific survival of person-centered, nonsocial paradigms seems to have been enhanced by the advent of neurobiology with the concomitant belief in genetically controlled and brain-based hardwiring of information processing. Paradigms of molecular genetics, of course, are not in themselves nonsocial. In many ways, this would be counter to the very meaning of biology as a science. On theoretical and empirical grounds, genetic programs and brain-related structures do reflect the social-cultural basis of evolution and the role of microenvironments (see, e.g., Edelman, 1992; Magnusson et al., in press, for a review from a developmental point of view). However, the use of molecular-genetic and neurobiological approaches in empirical research often seduces cognitive psychologists into assuming, if only tacitly, that the basic structure of the mind is invariant.

In light of this theoretical background and dynamic, the present volume aims at strengthening the social-interactive orientation of the study of mind and cognitive development and achieving a greater match between theory and empirical methods. In this effort, this book does not stand alone. During the past decade, and especially recently, several volumes and stimulating review chapters have had similar goals (e.g., Bar-Tal & Kruglanski, 1988; Bornstein & Bruner, 1989; Cohen & Siegel, 1991; von Cranach, Doise, & Mugny, 1992; Forman, Minick, & Stone, 1993; Levine, Resnick, & Higgins, 1993; Light & Butterworth, 1992; Resnick, Levine, & Teasley, 1991; Rogoff, 1990; Rogoff & Lave, 1984; Sternberg & Wagner, 1994; Wozniak & Fischer, 1993).

A unique feature of this volume is that it places social-interactive approaches to cognition within the framework of the life-span view of human development (P. Baltes, 1987; P. Baltes, Reese, & Lipsitt, 1980; Brim & Wheeler, 1966; Elder, 1975, 1994; Kohli, 1978; Mayer, 1986; Riley, 1987; Sørensen, Weinert, & Sherrod, 1986). We argue that life-span theory and research may provide a fruitful way to understand and organize questions about the role of social transaction in cognition and cognitive development. In addition, we aspire to make explicit the kind of methodological paradigms that are appropriate to the analysis of the social foundation of cognition. Therefore, we asked the chapter authors to delineate as clearly as possible the kind of research paradigms needed to study social-interactive phenomena. Our metaphor for these research paradigms is "interactive minds." However, beyond proposing this term as a theme, we did not require the authors to develop their texts around this conception. On the contrary, we left it open to them to choose whatever conceptual language they preferred.

Interactive minds: why a new metaphor?

Initially we considered employing one of the concepts already in the literature, such as shared knowledge, mutual knowledge, society of mind, situated cognition, collective mind, collaborative cognition, distributed cognition, or collaborative memory (e.g., Levine et al., 1993, for a review; Bar-Tal & Kruglanski, 1988; Bornstein & Bruner, 1989; Minsky, 1986; Salomon, 1993). For three interrelated reasons, we decided against this and identified *interactive minds* as an important new concept.

Directional openness of performance outcome

First, we searched for a term that while clear in its social-interactive orientation and intellectual commitment, was unbiased as to the direction or valence of performance outcome. Although we believe that the overall consequences of social interactions in cognition and cognitive development (over multiple tasks and contexts as well as ontogenetic time) are in general performance-enhancing, we are equally convinced, and there is much research literature to support this view, that not all conditions of social interaction improve performance (e.g., Bond & Titus, 1982; Hill, 1982; Stroebe, Diehl, & Abakoumkin, 1992). People may not effectively interact with each other for motivational reasons, distraction due to attentional load, differences in level of functioning, whether due to differences in talent or knowledge, or incompatibilities in styles of problem solving. Moreover, there are issues associated with the proper sequencing and combination of social transactions with person-centered phases of activity in the problem-solving process. Finally, there are differences in the nature of cognitive tasks that vary in the degree to which performance enhancement or performance debilitation through interactive minds can be expected (Staudinger, Chapter 10, this volume). In our view, the concept of interactive minds is open to these variations in processes and outcomes.

There are also genetic arguments for directional openness of performance outcomes associated with social transactions. The evolutionary-psychological approach to the study of mind (Barkow, Cosmides, & Tooby, 1992; Buss, 1995; Gigerenzer, Chapter 11, this volume) can be used as an example. It emphasizes that the genetic shadows of past brain evolution are not entirely functional today. Earlier adaptations of human–environment transactions, due to their space- or context-boundedness, may have involved brain-related dispositions that in today's world are dysfunctional. The gains and losses that accrue from social transactions, then, can have their basis both in evolution-based genetic predispositions and in the constellations of performance factors that define a given social transaction during ontogenesis and microgenesis of intellectual performance.

Search for a good metaphor

Second, we sought a concept with good metaphorical properties. Metaphors have been shown to be powerful regulators and modulators of theoretical efforts, in psychology at large (Leary, 1990) as well as in cognition and cognitive development in particular (Gigerenzer, 1991; Sternberg, 1990a). Metaphors not only characterize and condense the core of theoretical efforts, they are also potent mental representations or schemata that guide what we study, how we study it, and why we study it. Often, metaphors are powerful because, as memory and attentional cues, they operate at subconscious levels and with a high degree of selective automaticity (Ortony, 1993).

What about the role of metaphors in the study of mind? Is there an existing metaphor that propels one to think immediately about the social-interactive nature of cognitive functioning? A first source is Sternberg (1990a). He distinguished among seven prominent metaphors in the study of the mind and intellect: the geographic, the computational, the biological, the epistemological, the anthropological, the sociological, and the systems metaphors.

For the topic of interactive minds from a psychological point of view, three of these metaphors and their intellectual traditions are especially relevant. They are the *epistemological* metaphor (Piaget) and its lineage, including Piagetian social constructivism (e.g., Chapman, 1988; Edelstein & Hoppe-Graf, 1993); the *sociological* metaphor, where in developmental psychology Bakhtin and Vygotsky are historical rallying figures (e.g., Bakhtin, 1990; Sigel & Vandenberg, 1994; Vygotsky, 1978; Wertsch, 1991); and the *anthropological* metaphor, perhaps most evident in modern strands of cultural psychology (e.g., Boesch, 1991; Cole, 1991; D'Andrade, 1995; Shweder, 1991). In the research traditions associated with these three metaphors, we are likely to find the historical, theoretical, and empirical prologues to and expositions of the intellectual agenda of this book.

Since Sternberg's writings, and perhaps in addition to the "brain" metaphor in cognitive psychology, at least one further metaphor has captured center stage in the psychological study of cognition and cognitive development: the *evolutionary psychological* metaphor (Barkow et al., 1992; Buss, 1995; Gigerenzer, Chapter 11, this volume; Klix, 1993). Because the conceptual meaning of this metaphor is intrinsically tied to evolution, we do not expect it to carry the entire argument for the study of the social foundation of mind. However, we would like to underscore its relevance to the topic at hand. While the evolutionary psychological way of thinking recognizes and is fundamentally based on the important role of neurobiology, it makes explicit that the "social nature of the mind" is genetically built into the human genome and, therefore, must be considered as one attempts to assess and interpret cognitive functioning. It is here where social-cultural and biological-genetic perspectives meet: Co-evolution of genes and culture provides a new window on the neurobiological study of mind (see also Cavalli-Sforza & Feldman, 1981; Cosmides & Tooby, 1989; Durham, 1990; Gigerenzer, Chapter 11, this volume).

Individuals as units of conception

There was a third reason for finding a new metaphor. Although we had identified at least three metaphors (the epistemological, sociological, and anthropological) that speak to the role of social interaction in the evolution and ontogenesis of mind, and the social constructivist might have been able to offer us a further alternative, we continued our search. Why?

None of the metaphors just described is specifically focused on social-cognitive interaction. Moreover, the two metaphors closest to and most explicit in their social orientation in evolution and ontogenesis, the sociological and anthropological ones, lie outside the field of psychology. Because the theme of this book is interactive minds and the psychology of cognition and cognitive development, and we wanted to stimulate psychological research that is more social interactive, we decided not to use sociological or anthropological terms as our metaphorical guideposts. A similar concern could have been expressed regarding the social-constructivist view had we decided to pursue its metaphorical line of conceptualization.

We would like to add a few words about this decision grounded in science-theoretical considerations. Among psychologists, there is a perhaps unfortunate resistance (see Cole, 1991; Shweder, 1991) to linking psychological endeavors to the conceptual voices of sociology and anthropology, even while acknowledging the fundamental importance of the theoretical orientations and conceptual agendas of these disciplines. Psychology seeks a unique location in the spectrum of behavioral and social sciences, with its own person- and behavior-centered concepts and empirical-experimental methods of inquiry. The basic units for psychological theory and research are individuals and their mind-based resources, even when studied at different levels of aggregation (Lazarus, 1995). Following this seeming preference of psychologists, we looked for a metaphor that makes explicit the individual-level focus of psychology, but at the same time suggests the social characteristics of mind.

In sum, we chose the term *interactive minds* for three reasons: (1) to keep open the outcome directionality (valence) of social interaction, (2) to coin a metaphor with effective imagery involving social interaction and transaction, and (3) to preserve the unique psychological emphasis on individuals as the constituent basis for interaction. We hope that the term has a future, that it encompasses the work of researchers involved in diverse topics, such as group processes in cognition, social mind, shared cognition, socially situated cognition, social cognition, cooperative cognition, distributed cognition, and collaborative memory. Like these terms, *interactive minds* is meant to communicate that the interaction among minds is fundamental to the psychological understanding of cognition, in both cognitive and developmental psychology.

Moreover, we are hopeful that the term carries enough mental imagery that it automatically evokes thinking about the social nature of cognition and cognitive development and, therefore, stimulates the design and application of social-interactive research paradigms. Encouraging such research endeavors and exploring whether novel paradigms are necessary for translating social-interactive approaches to the study of the mind into empirical inquiry are among the major issues of this book. Eventually, this concerted effort might help to reduce the putative mismatch between theory and method in the psychological study of the social foundation of mind.

Interactive minds: definition and some issues

Good metaphors are meant to be largely self-explanatory in their conceptual direction. Yet in terms of the specifics involved, they are supposed to be flexible. In this vein, we do not intend to offer a psychological microtheory of the structure and function of interactive minds in this book. Rather, our focus is on using the interactive-minds orientation as a heuristic, as a means by which research questions are framed, by which methods are chosen and created, and by which observations are evaluated. The specific implementation of the orientation is left to individual researchers and their particular emphases. Because of this heuristic perspective, we have refrained from offering a precise definition of *interactive minds*, but some definitional attempt is necessary to delimit our intended scope.

Definition of interactive minds

What territory do we wish to cover with our conception of interactive minds? The following statement characterizes our conceptual map. *Interactive minds* implies that the acquisition and manifestation of individual cognitions influence and are influenced by cognitions of others and that these reciprocal influences between minds contribute to the activation and modification of already available cognitions as well as to the generation (development) of new ones.

The specific interactions and their results can be characterized by different perspectives and criteria. For instance, the interaction of minds can vary along the dimensions *internal–external, proximal–distal, explicit–implicit, unidirectional–bidirectional*, or *immediate–delayed*, and the resulting effects on cognitive manifestations can be *facilitative, neutral*, or *debilitative.*

This definition of interactive minds, at least for the purpose of the present psychology-oriented book, suggests some boundary conditions. We as *psychologists* focus on individuals as units, but what are individual units? Is it necessary that the interaction always involve the presence of persons? Typically, one would argue yes. At the same time, psychology also studies mental representations, and these can be organized to reflect coherent knowledge about personal entities (e.g., parents, children, spouses, friends, the various voices of one's conscience, protagonists in biographies). We are inclined to include such internal transactions with mental representations of other persons (e.g., inner dialogues) in our conceptual territory of interactive minds. This seems meaningful also because the origins and emergence of these mental representations of other persons most likely involved at one point some form of person-to-person contact.

Gray zones emerge when we consider entities such as computers constructed to simulate human behavior as, for instance, in chess playing or in modern versions of virtual reality, or when we consider mental representations of good and bad persons, and of other goals and goal structures that are defined on a societal level. In principle, if *social scientists* and *humanists* were to use the term *interactive minds*, it is likely that they would be inclined to extend their views beyond the mind as an individual entity and to include mental representations of "artifacts" and "societal and collective action sources" in their consideration (see also Cole, Chapter 2, this volume). In the present context, with its focus on psychological phenomena, we lean toward being more restrictive and delimit interactive minds to situations in which the partner is externally present or internally represented in a person-centered manner. This limiting definition, however, is not necessarily shared by all the authors of this volume.

We are not prepared to assert that *all* cognitions have social foundations or social-interactive properties. It is possible to imagine cognitions (such as sensory and perceptual categories) whose evolutionary and genetic origins as well as ontogenetic manifestations lie predominantly or even solely in nonsocial mechanisms of the acquisition and refinement of information (Klix, 1993).

Interactive minds: some issues and questions

Beyond such a general definition of interactive minds, we do not pursue nor can we offer a more precise theoretical account. What we do want to communicate in this prologue, however, are the kinds of questions researchers may want to consider as they forge their own approach to the study of interactive minds. Table P.1 offers such a listing. It summarizes the questions we collected

Table P.1. *Interactive minds in the study of cognition and cognitive development: some issues*

Issue 1: Ontogenetic (proximal) vs. evolutionary (distal) sources of interactive minds
How do ontogenetic and evolutionary sources interact?
Is evolutionary preparedness based on past adaptivity always facilitative?
Are cultural evolution and transmission another form of inheritance?

Issue 2: The basic nature of interaction between minds during ontogenesis
Are there cognitions without social-interactive contribution?
Can interactive minds be reduced to social stimulation, or are they constitutive of cognition?
Are there differences in the composition and directionality of interactive systems at different stages of life?
When does the ability develop to represent others mentally as partners in internal dialogues?
Which factors and life experiences generate individual differences in the use of interactive minds?

Issue 3: The form and function of interactive minds
Dynamics of social interaction include dominance vs. cooperation vs. competition vs. conflict.
Knowledge and skills can be distributed across people and subgroups.
Minds can interact once and also sequentially.
Interactive minds include concurrent, as well as retrospective and prospective (internal), interactions.
Knowledge is represented at different levels.
A single mind has limitations (capacity, incompatibility) as a carrier of knowledge.

Issue 4: The nature of interactional outcomes
Interactive minds are a criterion of truth and of the unknown.
Is the collective mind more than the sum of the parts?
Qualitative vs. quantitative outcomes must be distinguished.
Gains and losses have to be determined for the individual contributors and the overall outcome.
Outcomes can be analyzed with regard to the individual or the collective.

Issue 5: Interactive minds: new methodologies and research paradigms
What are the units of analysis: individual, dyad, group?
Is the focus of analysis on the process or the product?
Individual and interactive activities can be analyzed in sequence.
Are there generalizable recommendations or only function- and domain-specific ones?
Do we need "truly" new methodologies or just a reallocation of weights involving existing empirical paradigms?

as we planned this book, identified topics, and searched for persons we wanted to invite as conference participants and chapter authors.

In the table, we distinguish among five general issues that we also presented as an opening framework to the authors. The first concerns the relationship between ontogenetic (proximal) and evolutionary (distal) sources of interactive minds. What is their relationship and dynamic? What is primarily due to genetic evolution? Is genetically based preparedness always facilitative and synergistic when it comes to present-day cognitions and their ontogeny? How can one characterize the co-evolution of genes and cultures and their respective mechanisms of inheritance, interaction, transmission, and so forth? The chapters by Cole, Hammerstein, Gigerenzer, Labouvie-Vief, and Klein are particularly instructive on this set of questions (see also Durham, 1990).

The second issue concerns the role of interactive minds during the ontogenesis of cognitions. Aside from the often véhement disagreements about the role and nature of gene–environment relationships, differences exist among developmental scholars' basic theoretical postures concerning interactive minds and the role of social context. Depending on their theoretical orientations, some researchers prefer to view social-interactive processes in the acquisition and manifestation of cognitions as mere social stimulation, as part of the context that gives directionality and goal structures; others view social interaction as constitutive to cognition, as a generative-organizing system that links minds together in the production of new cognitions. In the extreme case of viewing cognition as a part of collective minds, cognitive processes and products can be seen as multipersonal in the sense that the cognitions involve more than what a single mind can carry and express. A special issue of *Cognition* (Greeno et al., 1993; see also the Epilogue, this volume) illustrates these various assumptions and demonstrates that the position taken on these issues is more than a matter of empirical truth. It is a metatheoretical issue, that is, a matter of how truth is constructed. Similar conclusions can be drawn from work on language development (see Klein, Chapter 3, this volume).

From our point of view, an especially intriguing question deals with the ontogeny of mental representations associated with other persons as significant "organizational structures" or "node points" in memory. As mentioned in our discussion of the meaning of interactive minds, we include in our conception internal interactions with others on the representational level. In life-span theory, external and internal transactions with significant others such as parents and other socialization agents play an important role in the process of "internalization," a process considered critical in most developmental theories (e.g., Lawrence & Valsiner, 1993; Wertsch, 1991). For this reason, the role of so-called significant others has become a cornerstone in life-span research and theory.

Building on the study of mental representations of persons and personal attributes, as well as mental schemata associated with action settings (e.g., Baldwin, 1992; Schank & Abelson, 1977; Wyer & Srull, 1986), it would be important from a life-span perspective to investigate the storage and processing patterns associated with "significant others" (parents, friends, teachers, work colleagues, famous personages, etc.) that people acquire, transform, and use as they develop from children into adults and subsequently into seniors.

What are the associated memory structures, the degree of complexity, as well as the contextual conditions in which these mental representations of persons are activated, for instance at encoding or recall, or during problem solving? What rules guide the internal transactions among one's primary self and these "significant others" that function as part of the internal interactive game "between minds"? Who, during the life course, is added as a significant other, who is eliminated, and what are their specific functions?

The third issue included in Table P.1 concerns the form and function of interactive minds. The statements and questions associated with this issue amplify the many possibilities of form and function. In terms of antecedents, correlates, and consequences, interactive minds can reflect the many forms and dynamics of social communication and social exchange: dominance, cooperation, competition, conflict, and interference. As expectations about the minds of others become critical, questions about intersubjectivity play a critical role. In psychology, this point is perhaps most persuasively argued by social-developmental constructivists (Edelstein & Hoppe-Graf, 1993).

In addition, variations in form and function can involve differentiation in the sequencing and joining of separate bodies of procedural and factual knowledge available to the minds in interaction. The time dimension is important in still another respect. On the one hand, prospective interactions, that is, the anticipation of social interactions, for example, have been found to be effective with regard to the promotion and prevention of inferential error (Osborne & Gilbert, 1992). Research on life review, on the other hand, has suggested that past interactions, or, better, the reconstruction of past interactions, contribute to the concurrent knowledge and judgment about fundamental life problems (e.g., Staudinger, 1989) and the meaning of life (Wong & Watt, 1991). It should be added here that life review very often is also conducted in interactional settings (e.g., Meacham, 1995).

In other instances, the essence of interactive minds follows from the limitations of individual minds, including the incompatibility of knowledge and skills required for a particular solution, such as when high-level, polylanguage-based knowledge must be brought together to reach desired outcomes. From a life-span perspective, one illustration is the coupling of cognitions resulting from interactions among members of different generations and age structures of the life course, each with a common but also unique set of contextual experiences and associated cognitive resources. Furthermore, there are questions associated with the way in which collections of minds (such as a given society) arrange for role differentiation and forms of distributed knowledge. Cross-cultural research on self-categorization, for example, has shown that in the United States internal features of the self, such as traits, attributes, and attitudes, are critical to self-definition, whereas in Japan social roles, duties, and obligations, that is, attributes that connect the self to the larger world, are more crucial (e.g., Markus & Kitayama, 1994; Triandis, 1990).

The fourth issue listed in Table P.1, the nature of interactional products, illustrates the pluralism and functional richness of interactive-mind outcomes. Fundamental questions in the study of the mind concern the prerequisites for effective interaction. The issues listed here also highlight whether products of interacting minds represent more than the sum of the parts, that is, more than the additive product of the cognitions that individuals generate on their own. The evaluation of outcomes can be rather different depending on whether quantitative or qualitative criteria are applied. The multifunctionality of inter-active minds is highlighted by the fact that many instances of knowledge and judgment do not involve shared goals, procedures, and outcomes. Rather, when minds interact, distinct intentions, differences in desired outcomes, and variations in individual- as well as in collectivity-based outcomes are often involved. Because of this differentiation of interactional outcomes, there are questions of method. For instance, what levels and criteria of social-interactive assessment should be considered as we study the nature of interactional out-comes? How are they combined to form a systemic view?

The last observation leads to the fifth issue, which concerns methodology and research strategies. One important aspect is the appropriate unit of analy-sis (individual, dyad, group, collectivity) and the possible joint, multivariate, and structural consideration of such units. Granott (1995), for instance, has conducted microdevelopmental research on the co-construction of knowledge in adults who attempted to solve a mechanical robot problem in teams. She demonstrated that the information provided by a dyadic (social ensemble) approach to analysis is different from that obtained by an individual-unit level of analysis (see also von Eye & Kreppner, 1989). Methodological questions also concern issues of process versus product assessment, including the search for the effectiveness of collaborative versus individual components in the social-interactive and sequentially ordered script of problem solving.

Not the least of these are questions of content- and domain-specificity. Is it possible to advance general principles of interactive minds, or are they always bound by function-, task-, context-, and person-specificities? That some specificities, in addition to general principles, are involved is easily argued on the basis of life-span research. Interacting minds involving different age groups (as in mother–child transactions or social transactions in nursing homes between staff and elderly residents) display rather different patterns of trans-actions depending, for instance, on shared or conflictual expectations about the goal of interaction, the respective levels of competence, attributed role functions of the interacting partners, as well as questions of relative power (M. Baltes & Silverberg, 1994; Carstensen, 1993).

Two local research examples as precursors

We mentioned that the unique contribution of the present volume to the study of the social foundation of the mind, in addition to the introduction of the interactive-minds metaphor, is based on its life-span developmental approach. Before we characterize the life-span orientation in psychology and the reasons for our decision to use this approach as a forum for a book on interactive minds, we point to some more local reasons for our interest in the topic of interactive minds.

Some of our recent life-span work at the Berlin Max Planck Institute seemed to suggest that we suffered from the same kind of theory–method mismatch alluded to earlier. We were increasingly troubled by the conclusion that despite our basic theoretical commitment to life-span human development as a social and cultural enterprise, we had not yet implemented to any significant degree the implications of the view of human ontogenesis as inherently social-interactive. The challenge that led us to consider social-interactive perspectives more rigorously originated primarily from two research agendas.

Psychology of wisdom

The first was research on the *psychology of wisdom*, one of the topics that scholars interested in adult development and aging have proffered as an illustration of positive aspects of human aging (Clayton & Birren, 1980; Sternberg, 1990b). As we attempted to specify the concept of wisdom, we reached the conclusion that wisdom is inherently a *collective* body of knowledge and skills (P. Baltes & Smith, 1990; P. Baltes, Smith, & Staudinger, 1992; Smith, Chapter 9, this volume; Staudinger, Chapter 10, this volume).

A cultural-anthropological analysis of the concept of wisdom revealed that for several millennia wisdom has been seen as something that transcends the reach of any one individual (P. Baltes, 1993, 1995). An exception is the early religion-based view of wisdom as a deity (Lady Wisdom). However, as soon as wisdom moved from heaven to earth in the cultural history of wisdom (Rice, 1958), it became a widely shared position that individuals could not single-mindedly represent the kind of coalition between mind (knowledge) and character (virtues) that was necessary for wisdom to emerge. Apparently, for wisdom to emerge and to be instantiated, social discourse and social representations in a variety of bodies of knowledge ranging from proverbs to legal documents were essential.

Furthermore, as we examined manifestations of wisdom and naive-subjective theories of wisdom (Clayton & Birren, 1980; Holliday & Chandler, 1986; Sowarka, 1989; Staudinger & P. Baltes, 1994), the social-interactive quality of wisdom also came to the foreground. Many manifestations of wisdom are other-oriented and include interpersonal qualities, such as advice seeking and advice giving. In addition, the acquisition of wisdom has been assumed to be fundamentally tied to excellent mentorship by others and long-term interpersonal apprenticeship.

The view of wisdom as a collectively held and collectively activated body of knowledge and skills was further supported by empirical data. Perhaps not surprisingly in retrospect, we obtained fairly low levels of wisdom-related performance in our initial empirical work (see Staudinger, Chapter 10, this volume, for an overview). These low levels, obtained even with carefully selected individuals such as persons nominated as wise, were based on think-aloud responses to life dilemmas collected with individual-centered paradigms.

One conclusion we drew was that we were victims of a theory–method mismatch. As a result of our insight into the collective nature of wisdom and other lines of argument (see Staudinger, Chapter 10, this volume), we attempted to translate these theoretical considerations into methods of empirical inquiry that reflected the notion of interactive minds (Staudinger & P. Baltes, 1995). Specifically, research participants, after they were confronted with life dilemmas, were asked to engage in internal and external dialogues with others before responding to the wisdom tasks. And, indeed, these social-interactive conditions (both internal and external) led to higher performances.

Models of successful aging

The second area that demonstrated to us the important and underdeveloped role of social-interactive research encompassed models of successful life-span development (P. Baltes & M. Baltes, 1990; Staudinger, Marsiske & P. Baltes, 1995). The specific theoretical challenge was to formulate *models of successful aging* (P. Baltes, 1993; P. Baltes & M. Baltes, 1990; M. Baltes & Carstensen, in press; Rowe & Kahn, 1987). As one moves through life and explores conditions of developmental optimization, such as the conditions provided by society as a general network of development-enhancing factors, one is impressed by two conclusions. Both speak to the important role of socially constructed and social-interactive resources in the construction and regulation of life-span development.

One conclusion to emerge from this inquiry into the optimizing conditions of human ontogenesis is that what we observe as contexts for human development is the result of a long process of social-cultural evolution, of history-based production of resources (including genomes), and of the social-interactive transmission of these resources to subsequent generations. What strikes life-span researchers as they compare resource constellations across the ages of the life course (infancy, childhood, adolescence, adulthood, old age) is that the age-specific support contexts of optimization seem to differ markedly in their power and degree of investment.

The cultures of childhood, youth, and early adulthood have a long history and refinement, and they appear to reflect a good synergy between biology and culture as well as major and largely efficacious commitments in terms of resource allocation (P. Baltes & Graf, in press). In the case of aging and old age, however, we witness a kind of cultural lag, a social production deficit regarding the availability of development-enhancing support contexts (Riley & Riley, 1989). Because long life is a fairly recent phenomenon, there has been no long-standing cultural effort or tradition to develop age-friendly and age-stimulating social environments. Thus, life-span scholars and gerontologists tend to argue that we do not yet have a well-developed "culture of old age" (P. Baltes & M. Baltes, 1992).

There is a second conclusion about the optimizing conditions of old age that amplifies the important role of social transactions. As one moves into the later phases of life, the primary resource for advances in levels and maintenance of functions is not biology but culture. For researchers on aging, the insight that the biology of aging is not a "good friend" of old age is paramount (P. Baltes & Graf, in press; Finch, 1990). Contrary to childhood and adulthood, it appears that in old age the biology of the organism blocks advances in functioning. Of course, biological resources continue to represent the foundation for behavior in old age as well. But the dominant direction of this biological foundation in old age is decline and loss of function. Most likely this is largely so for evolutionary reasons. Evolutionary selection pressure was not invariant across age. Rather, in evolution a negative correlation between selection pressure and age is assumed to have operated (Finch, 1990). As a consequence, the benefits of evolution-based genetic selection are focused on the first half of life up to reproduction. If progress is to occur during the last part of life, this progress has to be anchored essentially in culture, including the social-interactive components and socially mediated artifacts of culture.

The study of aging, then, has resulted in the widely shared recognition of the commanding importance of the role of cultural and social factors. In childhood, not the least because of biologically based potential for growth (Rutter, 1987; Staudinger et al., 1995; Thelen, 1992), the dominant pattern of behavioral development is one of advance, that is, positive change in adaptive capacity. In work on old age, and especially in the search for conditions of optimal and successful aging, the social-interactive and intergenerational context is brought to the fore in a radical manner. Part of this as yet underdeveloped culture of old age is a lack of adequate social resources and social support.

In fact, the issue is not only one of a lack of development-enhancing social resources. There is also the question of effectiveness when social resources are present. For instance, some work shows that the nature of social interactions in old age, when and if they occur, might even be dysfunctional in a "normative" sense. Social interactions and transactions involving the elderly often proceed from the very social expectation of aging deficits and thereby may contribute to further decline on the part of the elderly.

One telling example is observational work by Margret Baltes and her colleagues on the social world of old age in the context of bodily self-care and related behaviors (M. Baltes, 1995, in press). This research is aimed at observing and quantifying social transactions between older persons and their social partners. It has consistently demonstrated that social transactions between elderly persons and their social partners follow a "dependence-support and independence-ignore script." Whatever the behavior (be it dependence or independence) older persons displayed, it was discounted in ensuing social transactions. Instead, the predominant response from the social environment was congruent with the notion that older persons were inherently dependent and therefore required dependence-supportive social reactions. Their independent behaviors were largely ignored or responded to as if they were dependent and help-seeking.

In our research on the psychology of wisdom and on models of successful aging, then, we became convinced of the necessity for more rigorous consideration of social-interactive conditions. We developed a commitment to explore the kinds of steps necessary to introduce a social-interactive component into theories of and research on adult development and aging, and to translate our theoretical account into more appropriate methods of empirical inquiry (see also Dannefer, 1992). We were excited to find similar developments and lines of reasoning about a possible theory–method mismatch in other fields of psychology. At this point, and as a complement to our empirical research efforts, we decided to host the conference on which this book is based.

Life-span psychology as an organizational framework

We have argued that one of the two major reasons for publishing this book was to explore the degree to which a life-span approach to the study of human development is useful in organizing the psychology of interactive minds. In the following, we shall pursue this proposition in more detail. What are some of the specific theoretical perspectives of life-span theory and the mutual contributions that can result from joining the two orientations, life-span theory and the study of interactive minds?

Propositions of life-span psychology

Life-span work on human development in psychology dates back to the two monumental volumes, *Philosophische Versuche über die menschliche Natur und ihre Entwicklung*, by Tetens (1777). In these volumes, published more than two centuries ago, Tetens outlined the critical role of social factors in the creation of human development (P. Baltes, 1983; Groffmann, 1970; Reinert, 1979), including the close interplay between social-cultural development and individual development. Especially during the last decades of the twentieth century, life-span psychology has recaptured this emphasis and evolved into a metatheory containing a family of guiding propositions or principles about the nature of ontogenesis and about empirical research strategies for implementing the life-span developmental research agenda (P. Baltes, 1987; see also the 12 volumes of the series *Life-Span Development and Behavior* published between 1978 and 1985 by Academic Press and subsequently by Erlbaum). The *Life-Span* series comprises a large number of chapters in which life-span and life-course perspectives are applied to a variety of topics in psychology and the social sciences.

Some of the perspectives expressed in life-span theory and research are highly consistent with arguments about the role of social and cultural factors in human behavior advanced by other research traditions such as cultural psychology (see also Boesch, 1991; Cole, Chapter 2, this volume). Among the perspectives on life-span theory in psychology is a concerted commitment to *contextual, social-interactive*, and *dialectical* approaches as well as to recognizing and making explicit the close connection between ontogenetic and cultural-evolutionary change (P. Baltes, 1987; Dixon & Lerner, 1988; Lerner, 1986; Riegel, 1973, 1976). Although in their presentation as a conceptual gestalt, these propositions have been advanced as prototypical of life-span psychology, as individual propositions they are not specific to it. On the contrary, and as mentioned before, contextualism and social interactionism, for instance, have become theoretical guideposts in other developmental specialties as well (Bronfenbrenner & Ceci, 1994; Cole, 1991; Lerner, 1991).

Table P. 2 summarizes some of the key propositions of life-span developmental psychology (P. Baltes, 1987), and as we briefly define these propositions, we offer illustrations of the way this framework might be helpful for a concerted effort to study interactive minds.

The first proposition, that human development extends across life from conception into old age, hints at the variety of contexts and social transactions in which cognitive development and cognitive functioning are embedded. Interactive partners include at one point in time as well as in sequence such persons as parents and kin, peers, teachers, colleagues, friends, life companions, marriage partners, human-services professionals, and staff in care institutions. As to the study of interactive minds, a life-span view provides a first look at the sequencing and patterning of social contexts and their relative salience at different points in the life course. We need to consider the reciprocal and sequential nature of each of these transactions as argued so persuasively by Bell (1968) for the case of child development (see also Azmitia, Damon, Dixon & Gould, Chapters 5, 7, and 8, respectively, this volume).

The notion of the multidimensionality of development and of the multidirectionality of developmental trajectories suggests the perspective that at any given time in the life course, developmental outcomes can be both positive and negative in the sense of multifunctionality. The quality and effectiveness of interactions, for instance, can vary between clusters of individuals (e.g., parents vs. peers), and interactive functioning in earlier states may in-

Table P.2. *Summary of theoretical propositions characteristic of life-span developmental psychology*

Concept	Proposition
Life-span development	Ontogenetic development is a lifelong process. No age period holds supremacy in regulating the nature of development.
Multidimensionality/ multidirectionality	Development is multidimensional, and considerable diversity is found in the directionality and functionality of changes that constitute ontogenesis, even within the same domain.
Development as gain/loss	The process of development is not a simple movement toward higher efficacy, such as incremental growth. Rather, through life, it always consists of the joint occurrence of gain (growth) and loss (decline).
Plasticity	Much intraindividual plasticity (within-person modifiability) is found in psychological development. The key developmental agenda is the search for the range of plasticity and its age-associated constraints.
Historical embeddedness	How ontogenetic (age-related) development proceeds is markedly influenced by the kinds of sociocultural conditions existing in a given historical period and by the way these evolve.
Contextualism as paradigm	Any particular course of individual development can be understood as the outcome of the interactions (dialectics) among three systems (spatial and temporal contexts) of developmental influences: age-graded, history-graded, and non-normative.

Source: After P. Baltes (1987).

volve protective and risk conditions for later phases of the life course. Implied in the notion of multidirectionality is also the view that at different stages of life interactive minds exhibit varying dynamics in terms of such characteristics as bonding, connectedness, conflict, and separation (M. Baltes & Silverberg, 1994). Consider, for instance, the changing role of autonomy and independence in parent–child relationships as children grow older and later as adults may become, from a functional point of view, the caregivers of their own parents; or consider the structure and function of social networks that as convoys (Kahn & Antonucci, 1980) generate a matrix of interactive minds across the life course.

The third proposition, development as simultaneity of gain and loss, stresses the view that development is never pure advance or decline. For instance, as children acquire the recognition and production of their mother tongue, they experience some recognition and production losses regarding sounds not contained in their primary language (see Klein, Chapter 3, this volume). Similarly, as suggested by clinical developmentalists (Noam, Powers, Kilkenny, & Beedy, 1990; Vaillant, 1990), gains and losses are associated with various degrees of interdependencies as children grow into mature adults and have to modify and transform their established conceptions of identity and associated scripts of interactive minds. These examples of gain–loss relationships during human development illustrate that the outcomes of interactive minds are rarely unidirectional. Multifunctionality (M. Baltes, 1995) is the rule rather than the exception.

The fourth proposition, the search to understand the range and limits of plasticity, fosters inquiry into the role of social factors in the regulation of human development. In addition, it focuses on the "zone" or "norm of reaction" of possible development (P. Baltes, 1987; Lerner, 1984). In which way can and do interacting minds optimize the activation of latent potential? Where do we find a lack of social resources and scripts for interactive minds? To what degree are social transactions conditions of interference and inhibition? To what degree do earlier states in the life span involving the structure and functioning of interactive minds represent conditions of enrichment or inhibition for later functioning? And to what degree are dysfunctions or lacking abilities compensated for by the interaction between minds (Dixon & Bäckman, 1995; Wegner, Erber, & Raymond, 1991)? Here questions of educational and clinical psychology meet those of developmental and cognitive psychology (Cicchetti & Cohen, 1995; Staudinger et al., 1995).

The last two propositions, historical embeddedness and contextualism, make the strongest case for the role of individual, social, and cultural context. These propositions inform us of the need not only to focus on context but to consider contexts of human development along spatial and temporal dimensions. The focus on age-graded, history-graded, and non-normative (idiosyncratic) conditions (P. Baltes, Reese, & Lipsitt, 1980) of the ontogenetic matrix of influences shown in Table P.2 is but one example of such a perspective. Historical embeddedness and contextualism also alert psychologists to the significance of interdisciplinary work. As we engage the concept of interactive minds in psychology, it is useful to recognize the concepts, methods, levels of analysis, and kind of data that neighboring disciplines use as they approach the study of interactive minds and social transaction (see also Hammerstein, Cole, Klein, Chapters 1, 2, and 3, respectively, this volume).

The propositions listed in Table P.2 are fairly abstract and they are likely to communicate more to life-span researchers than to cognitive psychologists. We need to move, therefore, to more specific demonstrations of the usefulness of a life-span orientation to the study of interactive minds. What is special in the arguments advanced in life-span theory regarding contextualism and the role of social-cultural factors and their implications for the study of interactive minds?

Life-span research: toward an organization of contexts and interactive patterns

In our view, life-span theory contains innovative potential regarding the way cognitive researchers might organize and pursue evidence in the psychological study of the social foundation of mind. If one considers the substantive territory of life-span psychology, that is, individual development from birth to death and the fact that lifelong development operates across extended periods of time and various life contexts, the metatheoretical emphases of life-span theory on the intersystemic connections between cultural evolution and ontogenesis, between contextual, social-interactive, and dialectical approaches, take on a new gestalt.

Rather than to acknowledge social transactions on a case-by-case, piecemeal basis, the field of life-span development points to overall structures, as well as to interconnections that reflect how and in which contexts minds interact in the production and regulation of human development. A life-span point of view, then, not only suggests that it makes little sense to conceptualize developing individuals within acontextual and socially noninteractive ways, but that it is necessary to embrace a contextualistic view of behavior. Life-span theory offers specific information on the organization of social transactions and their associated contexts. The family of concepts associated with life-span theory (including the arguments for multidimensionality, multidirectionality, multifunctionality, the gain–loss dynamic, the search for the range of plasticity, and the recognition of historical and ontogenetic embeddedness) provide a special window on the matrix and ontogenetic system of interactive minds.

To revisit and amplify: As individuals move through life, they encounter a series of fairly predictable social contexts with distinct characteristics, task demands, and social scripts. Consider the various roles that individuals occupy as they develop within a family and kinship network from birth to old age: infant, child, adolescent, adult, spouse, parent, grandparent, relative, etc. (Kreppner & Lerner, 1989). As soon as one contemplates the life-span story of role-associated settings, one's attention is drawn to structural properties of the interactive-mind agenda. In addition, not only the individual life course within the family system, but also the nexus of other life-span contexts needs consideration (Dannefer, 1984, 1992; Hetherington & P. Baltes, 1988). Thus, individuals not only interact with members of their family system; they also interact with peers, teachers, friends, and colleagues at work, and with other constellations of persons they encounter in everyday life. These interactions do not occur at random but in the specific contexts that form their worlds and niches of life-span development (see also Azmitia, Goodnow, Smith, Chapters 5, 6, and 9, respectively, this volume).

As we extend our view to the structure and sequence of the life course, then, a rich spectrum of territories with their particular geographies of social partners, life tasks, forms, and functions of interactive minds emerges. Table P.3 organizes the general territory of life-span human development by providing two concrete examples. In the middle column, using the concept of developmental tasks (Havighurst, 1948), we summarize some of the main life tasks and life contexts that individuals are required to manage over time. In the rightmost column, the focus is on one concrete life-span theory, that of Erikson (1968). Both examples illustrate how developmental topics and contexts define the structure and sequence of the life course. As we consider the settings associated with this life-span agenda, it is likely that cognitive interactions among individuals will be essential in defining the rate, level, direction, and functionality of outcomes.

The listing of settings and life tasks in Table P.3 also exemplifies systematic changes in the number of interacting partners, the functions of social interactions, and task demands. Cole (Chapter 2, this volume), for instance, suggests age-related changes in the proportion of internal and external partners involved in mind interactions over the life course. Early in development, most mind interactions are external, that is, person-to-person. With increasing age and cognitive development, internal interactions with social partners at the representational level will increase. Eventually in old age, with a decreasing number of social network members, internal transactions with others become more and more dominant. Another example of life-span-related changes involves the nature of everyday tasks and problem solving. Berg and Calderone (1994), for instance, reported that the interpretation of and means of solving everyday problems differ across the life span. Starting at midlife, people characterize everyday tasks as higher in interactive-minds saliency.

Life-span thinking, if applied systematically, may offer specifications beyond a substantively and temporally ordered taxonomy of contexts, themes, and goals of cognitive functioning. One further illustration of specificity that follows from life-span thinking is the question of the relative influence of interacting partners on one another in defining goals and achieving strategies of problem solving (see Dixon & Gould, Smith, Staudinger, Strube et al., Mandl et al., Chapters, 8, 9, 10, 13, and 14, respectively, this volume). Both sequentially and concurrently, as individuals move through life, they are likely to occupy different roles: as learner, teacher, parent, mentor, worker, leader, model, patient. It is challenging to analyze how individuals develop in order to manage such diverse role relationships. Morality, as one aspect of interpersonal regulation, is one potentially fruitful construct for this kind of analysis

Table P.3. *Developmental contexts that define the structure and sequence of the life course*

Life stage	Developmental task (example: Havighurst)	Developmental theme/outcome (example: Erikson)
Infancy (birth to 2 years)	Social attachment Maturation of sensory and motor functions Sensorimotor intelligence and primitive causality Object permanence Emotional development	Trust vs. mistrust/hope
Toddlerhood (2 to 4 years)	Elaboration of locomotion Fantasy and play Language development Self-control	Autonomy vs. shame/willpower
Early school age (4 to 6 years)	Sex role identification Early moral development Group play Development of self-esteem	Initiative vs. guilt/ purpose
Middle school age (6 to 12 years)	Friendship Self-evaluation Concrete operations Skill learning Team play	Industry vs. inferiority/ competence
Early adolescence (12 to 18 years), later adolescence (18 to 22 years)	Physical maturation Formal operations Emotional development Membership in peer groups Heterosexual relationships	Identity vs. identity confusion/fidelity
Early adulthood (22 to 34 years)	Autonomy from parents Sex role identity Internalized morality Career choice	
Middle adulthood (34 to 60 years)	Marriage Childbearing Work Lifestyle	Intimacy vs. isolation/ love
	Nurturing of marital relationship Management of household Child rearing Management of career	Generativity vs. stagnation/care

Table P.3. *(cont.)*

Life stage	Developmental task (example: Havighurst)	Developmental theme/outcome (example: Erikson)
Later adulthood (60 to 75 years)	Promoting intellectual vigor Redirecting energy toward new roles Accepting one's life Developing a point of view about death	Integrity vs. despair/ wisdom
Very old age (75 years until death)	Coping with physical changes of aging Developing a psychohistorical perspective Traveling uncharted terrain	

(see Damon, Chapter 7, this volume). Where the question of interactive minds is concerned, these role structures and systemic relationships are far from unidirectional and harmonious. On the contrary, a key feature of life-span change in roles, role allocation, and role efficacy is competitiveness and involves structural conflict and transitional tension (see Labouvie-Vief, Goodnow, Chapters 4 and 6, respectively, this volume).

As a further example of specification, consider the goals defined in Erikson's theory. For each of the eight stages of Erikson's model, the presence of significant others is relevant. Interactions with primary care givers co-determine the sequelae of bonding and attachment; same-sex and other-sex peers are critical social partners in the formation of identity and intimacy during adolescence and early adulthood. Spouses, professional colleagues, and members of older generations most likely represent the primary social forces in the acquisition and refinement of generativity. As mentioned before, it is likely that with increasing age the relative number of mentally coded partners and their interactive consequences increases. At least in informal conversations, adults report frequent internal dialogues with select significant others such as mentors or life companions. Moreover, it is probable that with increasing age the selection of social partners is shaped more by emotional than by informational aspects of social exchange, as proffered by Carstensen (1992) in her life-span theory of social selectivity. In old age, an intriguing question concerns the degree to which reversals in the relative power of the persons involved in interactive patterns are necessary to optimize the management of finitude.

In the present volume, the authors present selections from this contextual and temporally ordered landscape of life-span development to highlight the many instantiations of interactive minds and to illustrate how experiences in one domain may affect those in others. We are also aware of the fact that this effort is but one preliminary step, but we hope to have accentuated the potential gains that the study of interactive minds in cognition and cognitive development within the contextual and conceptual landscape provided by life-span considerations may yield. What we have not accomplished yet is the empirical demonstration of the interconnections among these domains of functioning, both concurrently and sequentially. Nor have we addressed questions dealing with the relative influence of these interactive mind patterns on one another, what other scholars have called interdependence of minds (Goodnow, Miller, & Kessel, 1995; Markus & Kitayama, 1991). When is there positive and cumulative transfer? When do earlier patterns stand in the way of new adaptive demands in the sense of negative transfer? How do people manage, for instance in the case of illness or advanced old age, the transition from egalitarian minds, from independence and autonomous functioning, to situations of dependence or dependent social embeddedness (M. Baltes & Silverberg, 1994)? These and similar questions are beyond the scope of this book and await further inquiry.

Many of the examples given from a life-span perspective are not new, of course. One might argue that work in cognitive psychology, social psychology, or developmental psychology illustrates similar issues. It is our impression, however, that work in cognitive or social psychology is not aimed at grasping the larger world of social-cognitive interactions in an effort that is explicitly integrative. Thus, some research programs are oriented toward understanding interactive minds in the context of teacher–student collaborations, and others in peer interactions. Some focus on group problem solving in the context of work environments, and still others seek to describe and explain collaborative memory among elderly spouses. We hope that a consideration of the contexts and structural sequences of life-span development offers one, albeit only one, integrative framework that organizes the social world and thereby provides a new view on what some might think are old themes. In the final analysis, of course, it is the mutual enrichment among fields of inquiry that is likely to advance the study and understanding of the whys, hows, and wherefores of interactive minds.

Organization of the book

We begin with some critical reflections on the scope of the topics covered in this volume that are also meant to stimulate others to expand on the present effort. It is perhaps too easy simply to refer to the problem of pragmatic limitations. In other words, because the topic of interactive minds is so complex, it is not surprising that the book cannot offer a comprehensive overview. We made choices, and in so doing, we intentionally or unintentionally selected from a larger pool of potential authors and research approaches.

As we reflect on our choices, we are particularly impressed with three shortcomings. We now believe that it would have been desirable to include in the theoretical overview section a more sociologically oriented chapter on the structure and distribution of knowledge on a societal level of analysis and representation (e.g., Douglas, 1986; Moscovici, 1976; Smelser, 1995). It might also have been profitable to include a chapter on the role of modern information technology. Because of this new technology, many current aspects of interactive minds involve computers rather than persons, and this will most likely increase in the future. Finally, we would now include a chapter on the psychopathology of interactive minds. Such a chapter would have demonstrated more explicitly the gain–loss dynamic of interactive minds. But, we are sure, there are other missing connections and perspectives depending on personal inclinations and research preferences.

Despite these limitations, we are hopeful that the chapters in this book offer new insights and a good demonstration of what current work on interactive minds and a life-span perspective has to contribute to a better understanding of the social foundation of cognition and cognitive development. The 14 chapters of the book are grouped into three parts: general theoretical framework, research on various age periods in life-span development, and illustrations of research in cognitive, educational, and organizational-industrial psychology. This organization is not meant to imply an exclusive focus of the chapters on each of these areas. In our view, however, these are their primary emphases.

The four chapters in the first part, which provides the general theoretical framework, establish the interdisciplinary backdrop for a life-span perspective on interactive minds. In his chapter on the evolution of cooperation, Peter Hammerstein supplies knowledge and insight from evolutionary biology. Michael Cole represents cultural psychology and makes a persuasive argument for the "socialness" of cognition. Wolfgang Klein, as a linguist, specifies the social features of one of the central means of social interaction, that is, language. This part is rounded off by the chapter of Gisela Labouvie-Vief, who uses gender to demonstrate how deeply rooted and pervasive cultural influences modulate the structural and functional nature of mind, and how this gender-based dynamic frames specific forms of internal and external dialogue.

The second part, presenting research on ontogenetic development and the role of interactive minds at different points in the life course, is the centerpiece of the book. Our emphasis is on periods of life beyond childhood. In our view, research and theory on interactive minds in infancy and childhood have been very well covered in a number of other recent volumes (e.g., Bornstein &

Bruner, 1989; Cohen & Siegel, 1991; Forman et al., 1993; Light & Butterworth, 1992; Rogoff & Lave, 1984; Wozniak & Fischer, 1993).

When selecting the research represented in this part, we were guided by the wish to identify developmental studies that deal with topics of cognition and social cognition and show substantial ecological validity (cf. Poon, Rubin, & Wilson, 1989; Sternberg & Wagner, 1986), such as peer interactions in the context of school performance (Margarita Azmitia), the development of rules for everyday collaboration in family settings (Jacqueline Goodnow), the setting and pursuit of moral goals (William Damon), memory for stories (Roger Dixon and Odette Gould), planning about life (Jacqui Smith), and knowledge and judgment about fundamental life problems (Ursula Staudinger). We believe that one of the strengths of the interactive-minds perspective is that it brings the laboratory and everyday life phenomena more closely together.

The third part contains contributions from outside developmental psychology proper. Although many areas of psychology other than those selected could have been considered, cognitive, educational, and work-related psychology seemed of foremost importance to the theme of the book – that is, life-span perspectives on the social foundation of cognition. In this part, examples are provided for the application of the interactive-minds perspective to various areas of life development. One application concerns university education (Heinz Mandl, Hans Gruber, and Alexander Renkl); another, knowledge engineering and artificial intelligence (Gerhard Strube, Dietmar Janetzko, and Markus Knauff). A third involves what happens when the idea of interactive minds is introduced into the study of logical reasoning (Gerd Gigerenzer) and the study of thinking styles (Robert Sternberg).

The Epilogue is a special feature of this book. It is not written by one author; rather we asked several noted scholars from different fields of psychology to comment on the chapters from their disciplinary perspectives. Peter Graf reflects on the significance of the volume for cognitive psychology. Laura Carstensen highlights perspectives from social developmental psychology. Franz Weinert comments on issues of educational psychology. And Richard Shweder relates concepts, methods, and issues from cultural psychology to the chapters. These authors seem to agree that the book is timely and that the contributions selected from a life-span perspective point to new avenues of thinking, empirical inquiry, and theoretical organization. At the same time, the Epilogue gives testimony to the many conceptual and empirical challenges that remain uncompleted.

References

Bakhtin, M. (1990). *Mikhail Bakhtin: Creation of prosaics* (G. S. Morson & C. Emerson, Trans.). Stanford, CA: Stanford University Press.

Baldwin, M. W. (1992). Relational schemas and the processing of social information. *Psychological Bulletin*, *112*, 461–484.

Baltes, M. M. (1995). Dependency in old age: Gains and losses. *Current Directions in Psychological Science*, *4*, 14–19.

Baltes, M. M. (in press). *The many faces of dependency in old age*. New York: Cambridge University Press.

Baltes, M. M., & Carstensen, L. L. (in press). The process of successful ageing. *Ageing and Society*.

Baltes, M. M., & Silverberg, S. B. (1994). The dynamics between dependency and autonomy: Illustrations across the life-span. In D. L. Featherman, R. M. Lerner, & M. Perlmutter (Eds.), *Life-span development and behavior* (Vol. 12, pp. 41–90). Hillsdale, NJ: Erlbaum.

Baltes, P. B. (1983). Life-span developmental psychology: Observations on history and theory revisited. In R. M. Lerner (Ed.), *Developmental psychology: Historical and philosophical perspectives* (pp. 79–111). Hillsdale, NJ: Erlbaum.

Baltes, P. B. (1987). Theoretical propositions of life-span developmental psychology: On the dynamics between growth and decline. *Developmental Psychology*, *23*, 611–626.

Baltes, P. B. (1993). The aging mind: Potential and limits. *Gerontologist*, *33*, 580–594.

Baltes, P. B. (1995). *Wisdom*. Manuscript in preparation.

Baltes, P. B., & Baltes, M. M. (1990). Psychological perspectives on successful aging: The model of selective optimization with compensation. In P. B. Baltes & M. M. Baltes (Eds.), *Successful aging: Perspectives from the behavioral sciences* (pp. 1–34). New York: Cambridge University Press.

Baltes, P. B., & Baltes, M. M. (1992). Gerontologie: Begriff, Herausforderung und Brennpunkte [Gerontology: Concept, challenges, and issues]. In P. B. Baltes & J. Mittelstraß (Eds.), *Zukunft des Alterns und gesellschaftliche Entwicklung* [The future of aging and societal development] (pp. 1–34). Berlin: de Gruyter.

Baltes, P. B., & Graf, P. (in press). Psychological aspects of aging: Facts and frontiers. In D. Magnusson et al. (Eds.), *Individual development over the lifespan: Biological and psychosocial perspectives*. Cambridge: Cambridge University Press.

Baltes, P. B., Reese, H. W., & Lipsitt, L. P. (1980). Life-span developmental psychology. *Annual Review of Psychology*, *31*, 65–110.

Baltes, P. B., & Smith, J. (1990). The psychology of wisdom and its ontogenesis. In R. J. Sternberg (Ed.), *Wisdom: Its nature, origins, and development* (pp. 87–120). New York: Cambridge University Press.

Baltes, P. B., Smith, J., & Staudinger, U. M. (1992). Wisdom and successful aging. In T. Sonderegger (Ed.), *Nebraska Symposium on Motivation* (Vol. 39, pp. 123–167). Lincoln: University of Nebraska Press.

Bandura, A. (1986). *Social foundations of thought and action: A social cognitive theory*. Englewood Cliffs, NJ: Prentice-Hall.

Barkow, J. H., Cosmides, L., & Tooby, J. (Eds.). (1992). *The adapted mind: Evolutionary psychology and the generation of culture*. New York: Oxford University Press.

Bar-Tal, D., & Kruglanski, A. W. (Eds.). (1988). *The social psychology of knowledge*. Cambridge: Cambridge University Press.

Bartlett, F. C. (1923). *Psychology and primitive culture*. Cambridge: Cambridge University Press.

Bartlett, F. C. (1932). *Remembering: A study in experimental and social psychology*. Cambridge: Cambridge University Press.

Bell, R. Q. (1968). A reinterpretation of the direction of effects in studies of socialization. *Psychological Review*, *75*, 81–95.

Berg, C. A., & Calderone, K. S. (1994). The role of problem interpretations in understanding the development of everyday problem solving. In R. J. Sternberg & R. K. Wagner (Eds.), *Mind in context* (pp. 105–132). New York: Cambridge University Press.

Boesch, E. E. (1991). *Symbolic action theory and cultural psychology*. Heidelberg: Springer.

Bond, C. F., Jr., & Titus, L. J. (1982). Social facilitation: A meta-analysis of 241 studies. *Psychological Bulletin*, *94*, 265–292.

Bornstein, M. H., & Bruner, J. S. (Eds.). (1989). *Interaction in human development*. Hillsdale, NJ: Erlbaum.

Brim, O. G., Jr., & Wheeler, S. (1966). *Socialization after childhood: Two essays*. New York: Wiley.

Bronfenbrenner, U., & Ceci, S. J. (1994). Nature–nuture reconceptualized in developmental perspective: A bioecological model. *Psychological Review, 101*, 568–586.

Buss, D. M. (1995). Evolutionary psychology: A new paradigm for psychological science. *Psychological Inquiry, 6*, 1–30.

Carstensen, L. L. (1992). Social and emotional patterns in adulthood: Support for socioemotional selectivity theory. *Psychology and Aging, 7*, 331–338.

Carstensen, L. L. (1993). Motivation for social contact across the life-span: A theory of socioemotional selectivity. In J. Jacobs (Ed.), *Nebraska Symposium on Motivation* (Vol. 40, pp. 205–254). Lincoln: University of Nebraska Press.

Cavalli-Sforza, L. L., & Feldman, M. (1981). *Cultural transmission and evolution: A quantitative approach*. Princeton, NJ: Princeton University Press.

Chapman, M. (1988). *Constructive evolution: Origins and development of Piaget's thought*. New York: Cambridge University Press.

Cicchetti, D., & Cohen, D. J. (Eds.). (1995). *Developmental psychopathology* (Vols. 1 and 2). New York: Wiley.

Clayton, V. P., & Birren, J. E. (1980). The development of wisdom across the life span: A reexamination of an ancient topic. In P. B. Baltes & O. G. Brim, Jr. (Eds.), *Life-span development and behavior* (Vol. 3, pp. 103–135). New York: Academic Press.

Cohen, R., & Siegel, A. W. (Eds.). (1991). *Context and development*. Hillsdale, NJ: Erlbaum.

Cole, M. (1991). Cultural psychology: A once and future discipline? *Nebraska Symposium on Motivation, 38*, 279–335.

Cosmides, L., & Tooby, J. (1989). Evolutionary psychology and the generation of culture, Part II. Case study: A computational theory of social exchange. *Ethology and Sociobiology, 10*, 51–97.

D'Andrade, R. (1995). *The development of cognitive anthropology*. Cambridge: Cambridge University Press.

Dannefer, D. (1984). Adult development and social theory: A paradigmatic reappraisal. *American Sociological Review, 49*, 100–116.

Dannefer, D. (1992). On the conceptualization of context in developmental discourse: Four meanings of context and their implications. In D. L. Featherman, R. M. Lerner, & M. Perlmutter (Eds.), *Life-span development and behavior* (Vol. 11, pp. 84–111). Hillsdale, NJ: Erlbaum.

Dixon, R. A., & Bäckman, L. (Eds.). (1995). *Compensation for psychological defects and declines: Managing losses and promoting gains*. Hillsdale, NJ: Erlbaum.

Dixon, R. A., & Lerner, R. M. (1988). A history of systems in developmental psychology. In M. H. Bornstein & M. E. Lamb (Eds.), *Developmental psychology: An advanced textbook* (2nd ed., pp. 3–50). Hillsdale, NJ: Erlbaum.

Douglas, M. (1986). *How institutions think*. Syracuse, NY: Syracuse University Press.

Durham, W. H. (1990). Advances in evolutionary culture theory. *Annual Review of Anthropology, 19*, 187–210.

Edelman, G. M. (1992). *Bright air, brilliant fire: On the matter of the mind*. New York: Basic Books.

Edelstein, W., & Hoppe-Graf, S. (1993). *Die Konstruktion kognitiver Strukturen: Perspektiven einer konstruktivistischen Entwicklungspsychologie* [The construction of cognitive structures: Perspectives of a constructivist developmental psychology]. Bern: Huber.

Elder, G. H., Jr. (1975). Age differentiation and the life course. *Annual Review of Sociology, 1*, 165–190.

Elder, G. H., Jr. (1994). Time, human agency, and social change: Perspectives on the life course. *Social Psychology Quarterly, 57*, 4–15.

Erikson, E. (1968). Life cycle. In *International encyclopedia of the social sciences* (pp. 286–292). New York: Macmillan & Free Press.

Finch, C. E. (1990). *Longevity, senescence, and the genome*. Chicago: University of Chicago Press.

Forman, E. A., Minick, N., & Stone, C. A. (1993). *Contexts for learning.* New York: Oxford University Press.

Gigerenzer, G. (1991). From tools to theories: A heuristic of discovery in cognitive psychology. *Psychological Review, 98,* 254–267.

Goodnow, J. J., Miller, P. J., & Kessel, F. (Eds.). (1995). *Cultural practices as contexts for development* (New Directions for Child Development, No. 67). San Francisco: Jossey-Bass.

Granott, N. (1995, March). *How is knowledge co-constructed? A microdevelopmental view.* Paper presented at the Biennial Meeting of the Society for Research in Child Development. Indianapolis, IN.

Greeno, J. G., Chi, M. T. H., Clancey, W. J., & Elman, J. (1993). Situated action. (Special issue) *Cognitive Science, 17.*

Groffman K. I. (1970). Life-span developmental psychology in Europe. In L. R. Goulet & P. B. Baltes (Eds.), *Life-span developmental psychology: Research and theory* (pp. 54–68). New York: Academic Press.

Havighurst, R. J. (1948). *Developmental tasks and education.* New York: McKay.

Hetherington, E. M., & Baltes, P. B. (1988). Child psychology and life-span development. In E. M. Hetherington, R. M. Lerner, & M. Perlmutter (Eds.), *Child development in life-span perspective* (pp. 1–19). Hillsdale, NJ: Erlbaum.

Hill, G. W. (1982). Group versus individual performance: Are $N + 1$ heads better than one? *Psychological Bulletin, 91,* 517–539.

Holliday, S. G., & Chandler, M. J. (1986). Wisdom: Explorations in adult competence. In J. A. Meacham (Ed.), *Contributions to human development* (Vol. 17, pp. 1–96). Basel: Karger.

Kahn, R. L., & Antonucci, T. C. (1980). Convoys over the life course: Attachment, roles, and social support. In P. B. Baltes & O. G. Brim, Jr. (Eds.), *Life-span development and behavior* (Vol. 3, pp. 253–286). New York: Academic Press.

Klix, F. (1993). *Erwachendes Denken: Geistige Leistungen aus evolutionspsychologischer Sicht* [Thinking comes to life: Cognitive performance from an evolutionary psychology perspective]. Heidelberg: Spektrum Akademischer Verlag.

Kohli, M. (Ed.). (1978). *Soziologie des Lebenslaufs* [Sociology of the life course]. Darmstadt: Luchterhand.

Kreppner, K., & Lerner, R. M. (Eds.). (1989). *Family systems and life-span development.* Hillsdale, NJ: Erlbaum.

Lawrence, J. A, & Valsiner, J. (1993). Conceptual roots of internalization: From transmission to transformation. *Human Development, 36,* 150–167.

Lazarus, R. S. (1995). Emotions express a social relationship, but it is an individual mind that creates them. *Psychological Inquiry, 6,* 253–265.

Leary, D. E. (Ed.). (1990). *Metaphors in the history of psychology.* New York: Cambridge University Press.

Lerner, R. M. (1984). *On the nature of human plasticity.* New York: Cambridge University Press.

Lerner, R. M. (1986). *Concepts and theories of human development* (2nd ed.). New York: Random House.

Lerner, R. M. (1991). Changing organism–context relations as the basic process of development: A developmental contextual perspective. *Developmental Psychology, 27,* 27–32.

Levine, J. M., Resnick, L. B., & Higgins, E. T. (1993). Social foundations of cognition. *Annual Review of Psychology, 44,* 585–612.

Light, P., & Butterworth, G. (Eds.). (1992). *Context and cognition: Ways of learning and knowing.* Herfordshire: Harvester Wheatsheaf.

Luria, A. R. (1976). *Cognitive development: Its cultural and social foundations.* Cambridge, MA: Harvard University Press.

Magnusson, D., & Endler, N. S. (Eds.). (1977). *Personality at the crossroads: Current issues in interactional psychology.* Hillsdale, NJ: Erlbaum.

Magnusson, D. L., et al. (Eds.). (in press). *Individual development over the lifespan: Biological and psychosocial perspectives.* Cambridge: Cambridge University Press.

Markus, H. R., & Kitayama, S. (1991). Culture and the self: Implications for cognition, emotion, and motivation. *Psychological Review, 98*, 224–253.

Markus, H. R., & Kitayama, S. (1994). A collective fear of the collective: Implications for selves and theories of selves. *Personality and Social Psychology Bulletin, 20*, 568–579.

Mayer, K. U. (1986). Structural constraints on the life course. *Human Development, 29*, 163–170.

Meacham, J. A. (1995). Reminiscing as a process of social construction. In B. K. Haight & J. D. Webster (Eds.), *The art and science of reminiscing: Theory, research, methods, and applications* (pp. 37–48). Washington, DC: Taylor & Francis.

Miller, D. T., & Prentice, D. A. (1994). The self and the collective. *Personality and Social Psychology Bulletin, 20*, 451–453.

Minsky, M. L. (1986). *The society of mind*. New York: Simon & Schuster.

Moscovici, S. (1976). *Social influences and social change*. London: Academic Press.

Neimeyer, R. A., Neimeyer, G. J., Lyddon, W. J., & Hoshmand, L. T. (1994). Review: The reality of social construction. *Contemporary Psychology, 39*, 459–463.

Neisser, U. (1967). *Cognitive psychology*. New York: Appleton-Century-Crofts.

Noam, G. G., Powers, S. I., Kilkenny, R., & Beedy, J. (1990). The interpersonal self in life-span developmental perspective: Theory, measurement, and longitudinal case analyses. In P. B. Baltes, D. L. Featherman, & R. M. Lerner (Eds.), *Life-span development and behavior* (Vol. 10, pp. 59–104). Hillsdale, NJ: Erlbaum.

Ortony, A. (Ed.). (1993). *Metaphor and thought* (2nd ed.). New York: Cambridge University Press.

Osborne, R. E., & Gilbert, D. T. (1992). The preoccupational hazards of social life. *Journal of Personality and Social Psychology, 62*, 219–228.

Pervin, L. A., & Lewis, M. (Eds.). (1978). *Perspectives in interactional psychology*. New York: Plenum.

Poon, L. W., Rubin, D. C., & Wilson, B. A. (Eds.). (1989). *Everyday cognition in adulthood and late life*. New York: Cambridge University Press.

Reese, H. W., & Overton, W. F. (1970). Models of development and theories of development. In L. R. Goulet & P. B. Baltes (Eds.), *Life-span developmental psychology: Research and theory* (pp. 115–145). New York: Academic Press.

Reinert, G. (1979). Prolegomena to a history of life-span developmental psychology. In P. B. Baltes & O. G. Brim, Jr. (Eds.), *Life-span development and behavior* (Vol. 2, pp. 205–254). New York: Academic Press.

Resnick, L. B., Levine, J. M., & Teasley, S. D. (Eds.). (1991). *Perspectives on socially shared cognition*. Washington, DC: American Psychological Association.

Rice, E. F. (1958). *The Renaissance idea of wisdom*. Cambridge, MA: Harvard University Press.

Riegel, K. F. (1973). Dialectical operations: The final period of cognitive development. *Human Development, 16*, 346–370.

Riegel, K. F. (1976). The dialectics of human development. *American Psychologist, 31*, 689–700.

Riley, M. W. (1987). On the significance of age in sociology. *American Sociological Review, 52*, 1–14.

Riley, M. W., & Riley, J. W., Jr. (Eds.). (1989). The quality of aging: Strategies for interventions. *Annals of the American Academy of Political and Social Sciences* (Vol. 503). Newbury Park, CA: Sage.

Rogoff, B. (1990). *Apprenticeship in thinking: Cognitive development in social context*. New York: Oxford University Press.

Rogoff, B., & Lave, J. (Eds.). (1984). *Everyday cognition: Its development in social context*. Cambridge, MA: Harvard University Press.

Rowe, J. W., & Kahn, R. L. (1987). Human aging: Usual and successful. *Science, 237*, 143–149.

Rutter, M. (1987). Resilience in the face of adversity: Protective factors and resistance to psychiatric disorder. *British Journal of Psychiatry, 147*, 598–611.

Salomon, G. (Ed.). (1993). *Distributed cognitions: Psychological and educational considerations.* New York: Cambridge University Press.

Schank, R. C., & Abelson, R. P. (1977). *Scripts, plans, goals, and understanding.* Hillsdale NJ: Erlbaum.

Shotter, J. (1990).The social construction of remembering and forgetting. In D. Middleton & D. Edwards (Eds.), *Collective remembering* (pp. 120–138). Newbury Park, CA: Sage.

Shweder, R. A. (1991). *Thinking through cultures.* Cambridge, MA: Harvard University Press.

Sigel, I. E., & Vandenberg, B. (1994). Voice and context. *Psychological Inquiry, 5,* 344–353.

Smelser, N. (1995). *Georg Simmel Lectures at the Humboldt University.* Stanford, CA: Center for Advanced Study of the Behavioral Sciences.

Sørensen, A. B., Weinert, F. E., & Sherrod, L. (Eds.). (1986). *Human development and the life course: Multidisciplinary perspectives.* Hillsdale, NJ: Erlbaum.

Sowarka, D. (1989). Weisheit und weise Personen: Common-Sense-Konzepte älterer Menschen [Wisdom and wise persons: Common-sense concepts of elderly people]. *Zeitschrift für Entwicklungspsychologie und Pädagogische Psychologie* [Journal of Developmental and Educational Psychology], *21,* 87–109.

Staudinger, U. M. (1989). *The study of life review: An approach to the investigation of intellectual development across the life span.* Berlin: Edition Sigma.

Staudinger, U. M., & Baltes, P. B. (1995). *Interactive minds: Enhancing wisdom-related performance.* Unpublished manuscript. Berlin: Max-Planck-Institut für Bildungsforschung.

Staudinger, U. M., & Baltes, P. B. (1994). Psychology of wisdom. In R. J. Sternberg et al. (Eds.), *Encyclopedia of intelligence* (Vol. 2, pp. 1143–1152). New York: Macmillan.

Staudinger, U. M., Marsiske, M., & Baltes, P. B. (1995). Resilience and reserve capacity in later adulthood: Potentials and limits of development across the life span. In D. Cicchetti & D. Cohen (Eds.), *Developmental psychopathology: Risk, disorder, and adaptation* (Vol. 2, pp. 801–847). New York: Wiley.

Sternberg, R. J. (1990a). *Metaphors of mind: Conceptions of the nature of intelligence.* New York: Cambridge University Press.

Sternberg, R. J. (Ed.). (1990b). *Wisdom: Its nature, origins, and development.* New York: Cambridge University Press.

Sternberg, R. J., & Wagner, R. K. (Eds.). (1986). *Practical intelligence.* New York: Cambridge University Press.

Sternberg, R. J., & Wagner, R. K. (Eds.). (1994). *Mind in context.* New York: Cambridge University Press.

Stroebe, W., Diehl, M., & Abakoumkin, G. (1992). The illusion of group effectivity. *Personality and Social Psychology Bulletin, 18,* 643–650.

Tetens, J. N. (1777). *Philosophische Versuche über die menschliche Natur und ihre Entwicklung* [Philosophical perspectives on human nature and its development]. Leipzig: Weidmanns Erben & Reich.

Thelen, E. (1992). Development as a dynamic system. *Current Directions in Psychological Science, 1,* 189–193.

Triandis, H. C. (1990). Cross-cultural studies of individualism and collectivism. In J. J. Berman (Ed.), *Nebraska Symposium on Motivation* (Vol. 37, pp. 41–143). Lincoln: University of Nebraska Press.

Vaillant, G. E. (1990). Avoiding negative life outcomes: Evidence from a forty-five year study. In P. B. Baltes & M. M. Baltes (Eds.), *Successful aging: Perspectives from the behavioral sciences* (pp. 332–355). New York: Cambridge University Press.

von Cranach, M., Doise, W., & Mugny, G. (Eds.). (1992). *Social representations and the social bases of knowledge.* Lewiston, NY: Hogrefe & Huber.

von Eye, A., & Kreppner, K. (1989). Family systems and family development: The selection of analytical units. In K. Kreppner & R. M. Lerner (Eds.), *Family systems and life-span development* (pp. 247–269). Hillsdale, NJ: Erlbaum.

Vygotsky, L. S. (1978). *Mind in society: The development of higher psychological processes.* Cambridge, MA: Harvard University Press.

Wegner, D. M., Erber, R., & Raymond, P. (1991). Transactive memory in close relationships. *Journal of Personality and Social Psychology, 61,* 923–929.

Wertsch, J. V. (1985). *Vygotsky and the social formation of mind.* Cambridge, MA: Harvard University Press.

Wertsch, J. V. (1991). *Voices of the mind: A sociocultural approach to mediated action.* Cambridge, MA: Harvard University Press.

Wong, P. T. P., & Watt, L. M. (1991). What types of reminiscence are associated with successful aging? *Psychology and Aging, 6,* 272–279.

Wozniak, R. H., & Fischer, K. W. (Eds.). (1993). *Development in context: Acting and thinking in specific environments.* Hillsdale, NJ: Erlbaum.

Wyer, R. S., & Srull, T. K. (1986). Human cognition in its social context. *Psychological Review, 93,* 322–359.

Part I

General theoretical framework

1 The evolution of cooperation within and between generations

Peter Hammerstein

Abstract

This chapter explores the basic explanatory patterns that evolutionary biologists use in their contemporary studies of cooperation. The scope of these explanatory patterns is discussed and illustrated with a variety of examples from the animal world. Furthermore, recent developments in the conceptual architecture of evolutionary theory are reviewed. These developments have fundamentally changed our understanding of cooperation and have provided new analytical tools – for example, evolutionary game theory. This theory has been used to show that "common interest" in many cases does not lead to the evolution of cooperation. In contrast, "common genes" provide a fairly solid argument in favor of the evolution of some cooperation. Outside the primate world, there is surprisingly little evidence for cooperation based on reciprocation. But there are a great number of examples involving animals in which cooperation takes the form of trade between unequal partners who often belong to different generations. The chapter ends with a discussion of how psychology can learn from biology and yet avoid the pitfalls of flat biologism.

Introduction and conceptual background

In 1543, Nicolaus Copernicus published his famous work *De revolutionibus orbium coelestium*, in which he founded the heliocentric view of our solar system. We are all familiar with the important turning points in the history of physicists' interpretation of the world. However, some crucial turning points in the history of biological thought have not yet received the same degree of public attention. This is particularly true of a major change in how biologists have interpreted animal behavior in social interactions from an evolutionary point of view.

Earlier this century, the majority of zoologists (e.g., Lorenz, 1966) attempted to explain social behavior functionally in terms of its advantage to the

I wish to thank the Wissenschaftskolleg zu Berlin for its generous support. I also thank Robert Burgess, Gerd Gigerenzer, Heribert Hofer, Ineke Maas, Ronald Noë, Jonathan Waage, Rolf Weinzierl, Wolfgang Wickler, and several anonymous referees for their valuable comments.

35

species, population, or other aggregates above the level of the individual. In this approach, the phenomenon of cooperation among members of the same species was thought to be a simple consequence of the idea that natural selection molds the behavior of animals so as to improve the performance of the species or other higher-order units of evolution. However, two insights gained from empirical and theoretical work shook this classical view of social life. First, the more facts became available about how animals actually behave in their natural environment, the more it became clear that in most species the scope of cooperation is surprisingly limited: Whenever it is advantageous to the individual (in the sense specified later), animals tend to steal (e.g., Barnard, 1984; Borgia, 1985), cheat (e.g., Adams & Caldwell, 1990; Dominey, 1980; Møller, 1988; Taborsky, 1994; Trivers, 1985), dominate or desert a partner (e.g., Alatalo, Carlson, Lundberg, & Ulfstrand, 1981; Rohwer & Rohwer, 1978), monopolize local resources instead of sharing them (Brown, 1964; Brown & Orians, 1970; Kummer & Cords, 1991), kill a conspecific (e.g., Packer & Pusey, 1984; P. F. Wilkinson & Shank, 1977), and overexploit the local environment (e.g., van Alphen & Visser, 1990). Second, the mathematical theory of evolution lends very little support to the idea that species performance is crucial to the functional analysis of social behavior. Biological theoreticians have shown that under most circumstances natural selection operates more effectively at the level of individual organisms than at the level of populations or other higher units. This means that when individual success can be improved at the expense of species welfare, this decrement of welfare will not strongly influence the direction of evolution. Unless very special conditions are met, it seems therefore more appropriate to ask why cooperative animal behavior is beneficial to the individual than to ask what its group or species benefits are.

This well-founded methodological individualism has dramatic consequences for the biological view of social life. It deprives us of the otherwise more desirable romantic view of harmonious nature, very much like Copernicus deprived us of the tempting thought that the earth is the center of the universe. Interestingly, the founder of evolutionary theory, Charles Darwin, had already based his major thoughts on methodological individualism, but many of his general statements are somewhat ambiguous in this regard. Fisher (1930) and Haldane (1932) were perhaps the first evolutionary biologists who expressed very clearly a firm distaste for species benefit arguments. However, it took a long time until their visionary statement led to research activities that finally laid the solid foundation of methodological individualism in evolutionary biology (e.g., Boorman & Levitt, 1972, 1973; Hamilton, 1964; Maynard Smith, 1976; Williams, 1966).

Once biologists learned to avoid high levels of aggregation (e.g., the species level) when defining their "units of selection," methodological individualism was challenged once again by scientists who started "disaggregating" the individual. The ethologist Richard Dawkins (1976, 1982), for example, suggested that the gene was the relevant unit of selection. He was a provocative advocate of the (somewhat exaggerated) idea that "if adaptations are to be treated as 'for the good of' something, that something is the gene" (1982, p. vi). Dawkins conceived of the individual simply as a "survival machine" in support of its genes. From his point of view, cooperation of the genes in an organism is to be treated as a problem like that of cooperation among individuals in a population. In this sense he foreshadowed a growing field of modern research that deals with intragenomic conflict.

Intragenomic conflict can indeed play an important role if one tries to unravel mysterious properties of organisms. Consider, for example, the complicated process of meiosis, by which cells of sexually reproducing diploid organisms achieve a reduction of the number of their chromosomes. This process initiates the production of eggs and sperm, each of which carries only half the original set of chromosomes. Ideally, this process could be organized as follows: The diploid cell would divide once and pass half the chromosomes to one daughter cell and the remaining half to the other daughter cell. In reality, however, the cell first doubles the number of chromosomes and then undergoes two consecutive reduction divisions. Hurst (1993) compared this strange process to the walk of a drunken person who tends to make first one step backward and then two steps forward. Zoologists have always wondered about this detour on the way toward chromosome reduction.

Now, what is the evolutionary logic of "drunken" meiosis? To understand this logic it is important to consider the following metaphor: Genes enter little "boats" (egg or sperm) that will carry them into new organisms before the "ship" (the organism) on which they have traveled so far sinks (dies). The more little boats a gene enters compared with its competitors, the higher will be its relative representation in the next generation of organisms. This means, however, that rare genes can have a selective advantage if they disturb in their own favor the procedure of how genes are distributed over the little boats. Thus, at the genetic level, an evolutionary force acts against cooperation of the genes during and after meiosis.

Although this evolutionary force against genetic cooperation was known even before Dawkins wrote his book on the "selfish gene," it took a long time until biologists started interpreting the mysterious organization of meiosis as a defense mechanism against genes that fail to cooperate during reduction division. Haig and Grafen (1991) interpret the "drunken behavior of the cell" during meiosis as a means to prevent genes from disturbing the process of meiosis in the "selfish" way described earlier. Genes with toxic effects on their own cell's sister cell during reduction division would "shoot themselves in the foot," that is, they would be destroyed by the toxin of copies of themselves that were produced by the mysterious duplication process. If Haig's evolutionary interpretation of meiosis is correct, then evolution has produced a mechanism that limits the scope for noncooperative genes in an organism. This redirects our attention to the organismic level and helps us to understand why in general there is no need to adopt a more "reductionist" approach if we study animal cooperation.

From a Darwinian point of view, interacting organisms seem to be "players" in an "evolutionary game." Competition among organisms is the driving force behind adaptive evolutionary change. A new trait is favored by natural selection not because it is good, but because it is better than others. Maynard Smith (1982) therefore suggested that models from game theory should be applied to the evolutionary study of animal interaction. This approach provides an important theoretical "backbone" for the study of conflict and cooperation that also supports many of the arguments presented in this chapter. Evolutionary game theory deals mainly with equilibrium states of selection processes. Its standard approach is to search for an evolutionarily stable strategy (ESS). An ESS is a strategy that will be maintained in a population despite the forces of mutation and selection. The property of evolutionary stability always relates to a given environment. Therefore, one can use this concept in a meaningful way only when changes in the environment are slow compared with the adaptation process in question. It would be a misunderstanding to think that the concept of evolutionary stability is based on the idea that evolution stands still forever.

In this context it is also necessary to specify the biological use of the term *strategy*. It is not assumed that animals make any cognitive choice of strategy in the sense of classical game theory of the economics literature. Strategies are considered to be behavioral programs that are genetically transmitted from generation to generation. The individual simply performs an inherited strategy. Natural selection provides the mechanism of choice instead. A priori it is not clear at all whether or not this noncognitive choice mechanism would produce results that resemble rational economic decisions. However, a look at the mathematical foundation of evolutionary game theory (Hammerstein & Selten, 1994) shows that the evolutionary process and the process of rational decision making both come to a halt at points that share the characteristic of a Nash equilibrium. A Nash equilibrium (Nash, 1951) is a "list" containing a strategy (behavior program) for every player (interacting individual) of a game (competitive social situation) with the following property: If everybody else behaves according to the specified list of strategies, then no player would have a payoff incentive to deviate unilaterally from his or her strategy on that list.

Interacting animals in their natural environment should therefore appear to a human observer *as if* their actions were chosen by a decision process that satisfies the main criterion for economic rationality. This can be taken as an indication that major parts of economic theory are relevant to biological evolution and perhaps even more relevant to biology than to human economics. It is indeed tempting to state the following "rationality paradox." Humans typically claim a "monopoly" on rational decision making when they compare themselves with the animal world. However, from the literature in social psychology and experimental economics (e.g., Casscells, Schoenberger, & Grayboys, 1978; Gigerenzer, 1991; Kahneman, Slovic, & Tversky, 1982; Tyszka, 1983), we know that actual human decision processes deviate systematically from the principles of economic rationality. Paradoxically, we learn from contemporary biology (Krebs & Davies, 1993) that animals often behave as if they had taken a course in rational economic decision making and applied it to their individual lifetime reproductive success. Courses in economic decision making do not have the reputation of enhancing the cooperative tendencies of their students in later life. However, under many circumstances the logic of economics does suggest cooperative action, as we shall see in the remainder of this chapter. In this sense, biologists should perhaps not trade in the term *economic behavior* for the more catchy term *selfishness* that various authors have used as a caricature or with a taste for the sensational.

Finally, a question that is crucial for evaluating the basic concepts used throughout this chapter must be asked: How safe are the theoretical grounds on which economic interpretations of animal behavior are based? Critics of evolutionary game theory would point to a fundamental problem of the neo-Darwinian picture of evolution. Strategies are complex traits that depend on more than one gene. When traits are encoded by more than one gene, the direction of evolutionary change is not always the one that Darwin would have indicated. In such cases, the complex genetics underlying a phenotypic trait may constrain phenotypic evolution so strongly that no principle from optimality theory or game theory can be used to characterize evolutionary equilibrium states of a population in a given environment.

At first glance this critical insight seems to strongly undermine our thinking in behavioral ecology. However, a new approach to organismic adaptation called the "streetcar theory of evolution" (Hammerstein, in press) shows the weakness of this criticism. In this theory, no dogmatic assumption is made about the "selfishness" of biological entities. Neither the gene nor the organism is a priori considered to be a "unit of selection," and no assumptions are made about what it is that evolution optimizes, at what level of biological organization optimization would occur, and whether it would occur at all. The mechanistic process of evolution is described by selection equations that simultaneously capture the phenotypic and the genotypic scenario. It is assumed that the evolving traits are encoded by several genes and that recombination takes place between these genes. The only restrictive assumption of the streetcar theory is one about the "well-behaved" mechanics of inheritance, since it assumes the rules of Mendelian genetics (with fair meiosis) to hold. This assumption is typically made in models of population genetics.

A streetcar comes to a halt at various temporary stops and starts moving after new passengers come aboard. Eventually it reaches a final stop, where it stays for much longer. An evolving population resembles a streetcar in the sense that it may reach several temporary (genotype frequency) equilibria that depend strongly on the genetic architecture, before it reaches a final equilibrium that has higher stability properties and is mainly determined by selective forces at the phenotypic level. The important new passengers at temporary stops are mutants that "enter the population" and cause new evolutionary change. Final stops have the property that no new passenger (mutant) would cause the streetcar (population) to move away from this stop unless the environment changes or the passenger affects the basic mechanics of inheritance. Mathematical theorems about these final stops show that they necessarily satisfy the game-theoretic conditions mentioned earlier (this statement holds for a wide range of assumptions). Therefore, the process of natural selection leads in the long run to phenotypic adaptation, although the evolutionary path toward adaptation may include a non-Darwinian "detour."

Cooperation based on common interest

Common interest is perhaps the simplest reason for the evolution of cooperation. When a female and a male mate and she produces an offspring, this offspring contributes to the Darwinian fitness (lifetime reproductive success) of both parents. Since fitness is the evolutionary measure of success, it seems at first glance almost obvious that both parents should have an incentive to care for the offspring if a great deal of care is needed to raise, say, a brood successfully. In many birds this is indeed the case. Parental behavior plays such an important role and is so energy- and time-consuming for these birds that one parent can hardly compensate for the partner's care if the other parent dies or deserts. In some animal species it seems as if females even copulate with several males in order to ensure the parental effort of more than one partner (Davies, 1991). (Note that here and in the remainder of this chapter, the expression "in order to" does not relate to an actual goal that an animal has in mind. Rather, "in order to" should be understood as shorthand for the following statement: The behavior in question has certain consequences that are crucial for its maintenance by the evolutionary process.)

An example of male recruitment for parental care via additional copulations was given by Davies (1990, 1992), who argued that in the dunnock (*Prunella modularis*) some females actively escape from "mate-guarding" dominant males in order to copulate with another subordinate male. This in turn causes the subordinate male to participate in parental care together with the dominant male and the female – a polyandric situation. The subordinate's evolutionary incentive for care, in this example, is created by the share of paternity that the female offers to him. In another bird, the purple martin (*Progne subis*), dominant males invite subordinate males to their territory in order to attract more than one female (Morton, Forman, & Braun, 1990). In this case the dominant male would not be able to look after a second female's offspring. The evolutionary solution to this problem is to "share" the second female with the subordinate and let him care for her young. In this polygynous case it is in the dominant's own interest to let the subordinate copulate with the second female in order to ensure his parental cooperation. Clearly, this argument holds only as long as the dominant male sires some of the young.

There are also other ways for male birds to mate with more than one female even if their parental activity is mainly restricted to one mother's brood. In the pied flycatcher (*Ficedula hypoleuca*), some males mate with one female and search actively for another female while hiding their "marital state" (Alatalo et al., 1981). The second female then finds herself in the awkward situation of being deserted by her mate when she starts caring for her offspring. Her reproductive success is negatively affected by this male's behavior because she will raise fewer young during this season. Conversely, the few young she raises increase his reproductive success so that he has an evolutionary benefit from cheating.

The last example shows how careful one has to be with the expression "common interest in animals." In the context of parental behavior, only at first glance does it seem as if both parents of a joint brood simply have a common interest in the success of their brood. The crucial point here is that the evolutionary measure of success is lifetime reproductive success and not the number of surviving offspring from a single clutch of eggs. In most animals it seems as if a female would increase her future reproductive output if she could pass on the burden of parental care to a male. Among bony fishes, for example, females typically are ever-growing organisms with an egg production capacity that relates to their body size. If the female doesn't care for the young, she can "invest" the saved resources in her own growth and thus increase her egg production capacity. Conversely, if a male deserts, he can use the saved time and resources to mate with other females and to increase his competitive ability if this plays a major role in gaining access to a female. For these reasons, one would expect an evolutionary conflict between the sexes over parental investment.

The biological facts are that evolutionary conflict over parental investment is rarely resolved in a way that we would call "fair" in anthropomorphic terms. Screening the entire animal kingdom, we find that if parental care takes place at all, it is most often the case that one sex deserts and leaves the mating partner behind with the offspring. An exception to this trend consists of birds with biparental care. In most animal species, cooperation between the sexes starts with the search for mates and ends with copulation. One might perhaps suspect there to be a hidden division of reproductive labor between the sexes. One sex may look after the young and the other might perform a less obvious but equally important task related to reproduction. However, in many species no such task division can be found. Even more surprising, screening the entire animal kingdom once again for all species with uniparental care, we find that in a majority of cases females take the burden of "looking after the offspring." They also produce the eggs – an activity that typically (though not in all parts of the animal kingdom) requires a far greater effort than the production of sperm. This comes close to saying, "The female does it all."

Why is there so little cooperation between the sexes? Trivers (1972) argued that the female has a greater interest in the offspring because of her higher investment in gametes (eggs as opposed to sperm). This argument is fragile because it has the flavor of committing the so-called Concorde fallacy (Dawkins & Carlisle, 1976). Past investment is not a good reason for accepting future losses. Another idea put forward by Trivers is that the female knows rather well who her offspring is but "pater semper incertus." This argument is weak because "pater semper incertus" implies not only that a male has less to lose from desertion, but *also* that there will be less to gain from extra copulation with other females (Maynard Smith, 1977, 1978). Finally, there is the spatial association between an individual and the fertilized egg. When the fertilized egg is still located in the female's body, the male often has the first opportunity to desert. Game-theoretic models (Dawkins & Carlisle, 1976; Hammerstein, 1995) show that this easily puts the female in a weak strategic position in the evolutionary game. Biological examples with external fertilization and a spatial association between the male and the fertilized eggs provide a test for this line of reasoning. This is often the case in those bony fishes that have spawning territories defended by a male. The female "deposits" her eggs in his territory, and he is spatially associated with the fertilized eggs because he has to maintain the territory in order to attract further mating partners. In this case game-theoretic considerations would suggest that evolution should cause males to care for the eggs. Male parental care is indeed more typical than female care in bony fishes with external fertilization (Clutton-Brock, 1991; Maynard Smith, 1978; Ridley, 1978). In some pipefish and in all sea horses the males even possess a "brood pouch" as a morphological adaptation to their parental behavior (Vincent, 1990; Vincent, Ahnesjö, Berglund, & Rosenqvist, 1992). The female lays her eggs directly into the male's pouch.

To complete this section, it must be emphasized that "to care or not to care" is not a full description of what males can potentially do with regard to a female's offspring. There are various examples in which males actively undermine female brood care. In the Serengeti lion (*Panthera leo*), for example, when new males take over a pride, they have a tendency to systematically kill the cubs of all nursing mothers if these cubs were fathered by other males (Bertram, 1975; Packer & Pusey, 1984). This shortens the time span until the female becomes sexually receptive again. The same kind of infant killing is also reported for many animal species, including several primate species

(Hausfater & Hrdy, 1984). Furthermore, even females may kill each other's infants. In house mice (*Mus musculus*), cooperatively breeding females occasionally kill another mother's young as long as they can identify them as not being their own progeny (König, 1994).

Cooperation between genetic relatives

Why does an individual's own offspring play such a central role in evolutionary reasoning? It seems to be due to the high degree of genetic similarity between parent and offspring. If a phenotypic trait leads to a high rate of reproduction of individuals carrying the trait, then this trait itself will increase in frequency because of the genetic relatedness between parent and offspring. Suppose now that instead of producing its own offspring, an animal helps its parents to raise more brothers and sisters than they would be able to bring up without help. The parents then have an increased reproductive success, whereas the helper probably decreases his or her own reproductive success by refraining from attempts to reproduce. This is an altruistic act because it causes a fitness benefit to the receiver and a fitness cost to the donor. However, because of the genetic relatedness between donor and receiver, the genetic material that codes for help is transported into the next generation via the receiver.

This indirect gene transfer via genetic relatives makes it possible for kin-directed altruistic behavior to evolve. In a famous publication, Hamilton (1964) explored the conditions for the evolution of altruism between genetic relatives. He found that the conditions for its evolution in the preceding helping context are provided by a very simple inequality,

$$\frac{b}{c} > \frac{r_{\text{donor to own offspring}}}{r_{\text{donor to recipient's offspring}}}, \tag{1}$$

where r is the coefficient of genetic relatedness between the organisms indicated by the subscripts, b is the benefit to the receiver, and c is the cost to the donor. Here both cost and benefit are measured in terms of offspring produced. Inequality (1) relates to Hamilton's concept of inclusive fitness. Inclusive fitness is a weighted sum of the behavioral effects on the number of one's own offspring and those of relatives, with the coefficients of genetic relatedness used as weights.

The simple inequality (1) of kin selection theory plays a role in the theory of social evolution that resembles to some extent the role of the simple formula $E = mc^2$ in Einstein's theory of relativity. Like the tip of an iceberg, this formula indicates a major breakthrough in evolutionary theory that helps to understand the most advanced forms of animal cooperation. These are found in the social insects (ants, bees, wasps, and termites). Advanced forms of cooperation in these insects (Wilson, 1971, 1975) involve a reproductive division of labor in the sense that many individuals never reproduce themselves and instead help their mother with raising brothers and sisters, as well as maintaining and defending the colony (eusociality). Charles Darwin was rather worried about the existence of sterile castes of workers in social insects because he did not immediately see through which mechanism evolution could have shaped the highly adaptive behavioral and morphological adaptations of these castes. Hamilton's kin selection theory has resolved Darwin's problem, and inequality (1) or similar more elaborate principles have become a key element in all convincing explanations of eusociality.

In bees, ants, and wasps, the genetic relatedness between sisters can (but need not) reach the high value of $\frac{3}{4}$, whereas that of mother and daughter is only $\frac{1}{2}$. The unusual haplodiploid system of genetic inheritance in hymenopteran insects allows for such effects. It must be emphasized, however, that (1) can be satisfied even if the genetic relatedness between the donor and the recipient's offspring is substantially smaller than that between the donor and its own offspring. This is an obvious property of Hamilton's inequality. As trivial as this insight may be, it has often been overlooked in popular textbook chapters on social insects, where authors shared a passion for the right-hand side of (1) and based their thoughts on the empirically fragile assumption of a high degree of genetic relatedness between the donor and the recipient's offspring. Gadagkar (1991) showed very convincingly the drawbacks of this passion, and he foreshadowed the new trend of evolutionary research on insect sociality: a passion for dealing with the left-hand side of (1), that is, for demonstrating that $b \gg c$. A look at conditional life tables is informative. The probability of surviving as a helper "at home" may be far greater than in a breeding attempt that involves "leaving home." In this case, the lost opportunities of breeding, c, are small for a helper. If, in addition to this, the effect of helping, b, on the helper's mother's reproduction is strong, then b can be far greater than c.

The insect societies under consideration have properties that suggest a "major step in evolution." The distinction between sterile and reproductive individuals in an ant colony, for example, resembles that between somatic cells and cells of the germ line in an organism. It is therefore tempting to conceive of a colony of the most advanced social insects as a superorganism that is composed of individual organisms instead of cells (Hölldobler & Wilson, 1990). Superorganisms are not free of internal conflict, but the same can be said about normal organisms in which different parts of the genome have conflicting "interests." As long as one keeps this restriction in mind, it seems in many cases fruitful to treat the superorganism approximately as if it were a unit of selection far above the individual. This is perhaps an exception to the rule of methodological individualism stated in the introduction. However, the earlier caveat about internal conflict means that one should never completely forget about methodological individualism even in the context of superorganisms. Various authors (e.g., Seger, 1991) have come up with stronger warnings than this against abandoning methodological individualism. They express very skeptical views about the superorganism concept. It should be emphasized here that the debate about superorganisms is mainly a semantic one. Everybody uses the same basic theory anyway, regardless of the taste for terms.

Hamilton's theory for the evolution of altruistic behavior makes it possible to understand the extreme cases of morphological specialization (the equivalent of differentiated body tissue) found in certain castes of workers. In the termite *Nasutitermes exitiosus*, for example, members of the sterile soldier caste have a head that is shaped like a water pistol. The soldiers use this structure as a defense mechanism in order to spray toxic substances at enemies. In *Myrmecocystus* ants some workers have a morphological specialization of the abdomen that makes it almost impossible for them to move and that transforms them functionally into "living honey casks." The colony uses these casks for storing food (Wilson, 1971).

Kin selection theory also plays a major role outside the world of social insects. It explains, for example, why in many birds, such as the Florida scrub jay (*Aphelocoma coerulescens*; Woolfenden & Fitzpatrick, 1984), some of the young stay with their parents and help this breeding pair to feed their young. This behavior resembles that of an insect worker with the exception that young birds will eventually make breeding attempts on their own. Over his or her lifetime an individual then acts first as a helper and may receive help from others at a later stage. A more extreme case with great similarity to insect societies is known in mammals. The naked mole rat lives in large underground colonies in which only one pair (the "queen" and the "king") seems to reproduce for a considerable length of time. Most individuals in these colonies probably never reproduce themselves.

The logic of repeated evolutionary games

How much scope is there for cooperation between genetically unrelated individuals of the same species? Let us consider the best-known example of a "classical" game – the prisoner's dilemma (Luce & Raiffa, 1957). If unrelated animals had to play a "single-shot" prisoner's dilemma game, generation after generation, then evolution would in the long run program them to "play" the noncooperative strategy. This is the only Nash equilibrium and the only evolutionarily stable strategy (ESS) of this game. Are there ways to escape from this evolutionary trap? In the human world, the possibility of signing a binding contract before playing the prisoner's dilemma game would lead to a cooperative solution. This requires an institution that imposes sanctions against breach of contract. In the original story of the prisoner's dilemma one could imagine a court of the underworld to play the role of this institution. However, in the world of nonhuman animals one can hardly imagine the possibility of signing binding contracts. In this regard there seems to be a wider scope for cooperation in human societies than in the nonhuman world.

The other well-known way to escape from the noncooperative trap of the prisoner's dilemma is to look at the repeated version of this game in which the same two individuals go through a sequence of interactions with a nondeterministic end. Axelrod and Hamilton (1981) argued that the strategy "tit for tat" is an ESS for this repeated game. To play tit for tat means to start cooperatively in the first period and then to imitate in all subsequent periods the opponent's behavior of the last period. Theoreticians did not unanimously accept the analysis of Axelrod and Hamilton. Selten and Hammerstein (1984) showed that tit for tat indeed fails to satisfy the conditions for an ESS. Their result was confirmed several times in the subsequent literature (e.g., Boyd & Lorberbaum, 1987; Foster & Young, 1990).

Most recently, Nowak and Sigmund (1993) have analyzed a repeated prisoner's dilemma game in which mistakes occur at a low frequency. They come to the conclusion that tit for tat is not even evolutionarily stable against all strategies with a one-step memory. In their extremely restricted universe of strategies, a fairly different solution, which they named "Pavlov," turns out to be evolutionarily stable. A Pavlov player cooperates if and only if both players opted for the same alternative in their previous move. This means that the Pavlov player repeats his or her former move after receiving one of the two higher payoffs of the game, but switches behavior if "punished" by receiving one of the two lower payoffs.

Perhaps it is the theoretical confusion about what to expect as an ESS that has hindered empirical biologists to come up with any convincing piece of evidence for cooperation in a repeated prisoner's dilemma. Another reason for this lack of evidence could be that this game has a fairly artificial structure with simultaneous moves of the players in each period. Therefore, it is worth mentioning that as early as 1971 (i.e., before the origin of evolutionary game theory) Trivers had suggested a slightly different and biologically more plausible scenario when he introduced the concept of "reciprocal altruism." He looked at a model of cooperation in which two players act in an alternating sequence of moves. The player (animal) whose turn it is to act has the decision between altruistic or nonaltruistic behavior. One can imagine animals to perform the altruistic act conditional upon the other animal's behavior in the past. This conditional altruism would be protected against exploitation, and it would ensure that the partner has an incentive for cooperation. Long-term reciprocity explains the short-term altruism of an animal. From a lifetime perspective this short-term altruism does not look altruistic any more.

Is there more empirical content in the story of reciprocal altruism than in the story of tit for tat? Since Trivers wrote his seminal paper on reciprocity, biologists have spent 20 years "hunting" for good examples. To summarize the results of this search, only a few cases of reciprocal altruism have been identified and most of them did not convince the scientific community. Trivers himself mentioned the interspecific cooperation of a cleaner fish and its customer (another fish that gets cleaned) as an example. A cleaner fish not only purges its customer's skin from parasites. It may also act as a "living toothbrush" that cleans the mouth of its potential predator from the inside. Why does the customer not swallow it? Is it the expectation that the cleaner will be needed again when the customer pays his future visits to the "cleaning station"? There is probably a more immediate reason not to kill the cleaner, because this animal may not have finished its "job" at the moment of toothbrushing. Therefore, it does not seem to be the long-term repeated interaction that causes the evolution of the predator's biting inhibition. Furthermore, the cleaner's behavior does not have the flavor of altruism; nor does it seem to be conditional on the customer's previous cooperation. If the customer does not cooperate, its living toothbrush dies immediately and there is absolutely no possibility for further cooperation.

Perhaps the only convincing (nonprimate) example of reciprocation in repeated interactions was found by G. S. Wilkinson (1984) in his studies of female vampire bats. These bats search for blood every night and sometimes fail to obtain their "meal." If this happens two nights in a row, an individual comes close to the starvation point. It is therefore not astonishing that an unsuccessful individual starts begging for blood from other individuals in the roost. This often causes a well-fed individual to "donate blood" by regurgitation. Wilkinson showed that a female who had already received a donation later regurgitated, with particularly high probability, when the original donor was in need of blood.

In primates subtle patterns of coalition and alliance formation (van Hooff & van Schaik, 1992) have been described that seem to require a remarkable degree of "social intelligence" (Cheney & Seyfarth, 1990). At least in this part of the animal kingdom we find evidence for reciprocity (De Waal, 1992; Dunbar, 1988). When primates cooperate, this may be for reasons of hunting or defense against predators. However, in many cases they cooperate by supporting each other in agonistic interactions with members of their own species. This seems to be a major if not the main theme in primate cooperation (Harcourt, 1989).

Various studies have shown that there is a positive correlation between the amount of time two animals of a given primate species spend grooming and the amount of support they give each other in agonistic interactions with conspecifics (e.g., Dunbar, 1980; Smuts, 1985; Strum, 1983). Vervet monkeys, for example, actively solicit partners for aid when they are facing an opponent in an agonistic encounter. Seyfarth and Cheney (1984) performed an experiment to find out whether previous grooming activities increase the chance that the groomed individual will show signs of interest in helping the groomer in case of such an emergency. Using a tape recorder, they imitated the groomer's solicitations for aid. The results of this study showed that the tendency to pay attention to the call decreases with the time that elapsed between the last grooming act and the solicitation for aid. It was not shown, however, that help really would have been extended. Furthermore, it is very difficult to estimate the costs and benefits of grooming in primates. This was discussed, for example, by Goosen (1981) and Harcourt (1992), who drew a picture of grooming in which the hygienic effects of this activity do not play any major role. Most cases of primate grooming take place in a complex social context – a context that requires more explanatory sophistication than that offered by the simple model of reciprocal altruism.

One general point of criticism should also be mentioned here. Unlike ants or flatworms, primates are not the mechanistic little robots that simple evolutionary models deal with. Their cognitive abilities make it difficult – as in humans – to find out what properties are genetically transmitted. It also seems very likely that cognitive and communicative abilities of primates, and some other mammals, add new dimensions to the scope for cooperation. Imagine a group of chimpanzees hunting a red colobus monkey (one of their favored prey items in Taï National Park). The red colobus is much lighter than a chimpanzee and can jump from tree to tree via small branches that would not carry the hunting individuals. From this point of view it is easy for the red colobus to escape. However, since the chimpanzees seem partially able to plan cooperative hunting activities, they can send interceptors to some trees and chase the colobus into their arms from the other side (Boesch, 1994).

Chimpanzees eat colobus monkeys alive and do not seem to care about their pain and screaming. They are not much less cruel to conspecifics. Jane Goodall (1986) has given us impressive reports of what she conceived of as warlike behavior in chimpanzees. Huntingford (1989) suggested using the less anthropomorphic term *group fighting* instead of *war*, but this seems to me a minor semantic issue. Males of one group may kill many members of a neighboring group, probably in an attempt to "steal" their females and to take over their territory. Their raids are made by two or more individuals and remind us of the unpleasant fact that cooperation in primates is often directed against conspecifics. Cooperation of this kind is a prerequisite for tribal fight or war.

Trade between unequal partners

Cooperation often takes place between a dominant and a subordinate animal. In such cases the dominant typically controls access to important resources or to mating partners. This control enables the dominant animal to trade in limited access to these "goods" for help from the subordinate. In a bird called pukeko (*Porphyrio porphyrio*), for example, territorial males accept younger males in their mating territories. This has the disadvantage for the territorial animal that the younger will father some of the offspring produced in his territory. However, it has the positive effect that the younger participates (in his own interest and probably with no incentive to cheat) in defense against other males. The subordinate therefore helps to maintain a sizable territory. This positive effect seems to override the losses due to intraterritorial mating competition.

This interpretation is elaborated by Craig (1984). He demonstrated quantitatively that the trade is indeed beneficial to both the territory owner and the subordinate. He noticed that two neighboring territory owners are in a situation similar to the prisoner's dilemma. In order to avoid intraterritorial competition for mates, both neighbors would be well advised not to recruit a younger "assistant." However, if only one of them does recruit, he will be able to "push his neighbor against the wall" and increase his own territory. This makes it important for the neighbor to also recruit a younger male. In the end both territorials are worse off than they could have been without assistants because they now share the original territories with younger males. The game-theoretic logic forces them into this behavior, which is not Pareto optimal.

Biological trade can be more subtle than in the case of the pukeko. Reyer (1984, 1990) showed for the African kingfisher (*Ceryle rudis*) that breeding pairs of this bird may recruit two kinds of sexually mature males as "helpers at the nest." First, their own young may stay with them for a season and help feed their brothers and sisters instead of attempting to breed on their own. So far this is only the standard story of cooperation between overlapping generations due to kin selection. However, to his great surprise, Reyer also found male helpers that were not genetically related to the breeding pair. He revealed in a long-term field study the hidden ultimate causes of this cooperation. Unrelated helpers increase their chances of becoming future mates of the females that receive the help. They trade in current help for future mating success.

Gaining access to mates can also be part of a more obvious trade. In many insects, for example, males present a "nuptial gift" to a female if they want to copulate with her. Furthermore, the size of the gift often determines the amount of sperm transferred. A way of cheating here is to "wrap" the gift with cheap materials that make it look more impressive than it really is. This can lead to the extreme case where the entire gift consists of the wrapping, as seems to be the case in balloon flies (Kessel, 1955; Oldroyd, 1964). It is a deal and not just "courtesy" when male animals offer their "box of chocolates." Unfortunately, evolution also seems to have generated very rude forms of male mating behavior. In certain species some males try to gain access to females by forced copulations (e.g., R. Thornhill, 1980). This is an extreme form of noncooperation between the sexes.

Returning to the discussion of trade, it is possible to think of a variety of "goods" that can be traded. In mutual interactions between ants and other insects (their "cattle"), the ant receives nutrients and provides protection against predators in return (e.g., Seibert, 1992). A nondomesticated African bird, called the honeyguide (*Indicator indicator*), cooperates with humans in foraging activities (Isack & Reyer, 1989). The honeyguide searches for a beehive with its precious nutrients, but it has difficulties in reaching them. It therefore indicates the location of the hive to humans, who are better at solving this problem. Humans use their techniques to gain access to honey and the bird eats what is left over. There are perhaps many other cases of animal trading that have not yet been discovered because some of the relevant goods of a trade are located in the animal's brain. It is very interesting in this regard to read the reports on groups of African elephants in which old females are treated very well by younger group members (Moss, 1988). When they get ill, for example, they receive extensive care by younger elephants, and when they die this care seems to a human observer like the ceremony of a funeral. After a certain age, females no longer reproduce and appear to go into menopause. What might be the evolutionary logic that causes younger elephants to treat them well? The most plausible hypothesis is that their value to younger group members is the knowledge that they have accumulated over a lifetime. One could imagine, for example, that in the case of a drought they would be able to find a water hole that nobody else in the group knew about. Unfortunately, it is difficult to obtain nonanecdotal evidence in support of this "wisdom effect" in elephants.

Concluding remarks: the relation between biology and psychology

The history of animal behavior research is full of examples where authors have "burned their fingers" when they tried to describe their ideas about animals by concepts taken from the human world. There seems to be a temptation caused by a great variety of superficial similarities between *some* aspects of traits in *certain* nonhuman organisms and something we know about the human world. For example, many ant species have a social organization that looks to us like a "structured society," and in a figurative sense they may have "cattle," "plantations," and an "army." Termites are so skilled as house builders that they construct "sky scrapers with air conditioning." Greylag geese (*Anser anser*) behave as if they had been educated by a Catholic priest in that they are (almost) monogamous. Even in botany one can find superficial similarities. The tobacco plant acts as a "chemical factory" producing one of nature's most powerful "insecticides" called nicotine. All this does *not* mean that the organization of human behavior strongly resembles that of an ant, termite, or goose or that the organization of a DDT factory has much in common with a tobacco plant.

Therefore, I emphasize that biological studies of animals and plants are conducted mainly to understand the variety of phenomena in the nonhuman world. In the context of cooperation, these studies have led to a number of evolutionary patterns of explanation, some of which have been outlined and illustrated in this chapter. It is impressive to see how much insight can be gained by asking the question of why it is beneficial in terms of lifetime reproductive success to cooperate (or not) under given environmental conditions. There is a hidden assumption underlying this approach – namely, that the environmental conditions that we study are characteristic of those under which evolution has molded the trait under investigation. Furthermore, there is the hidden assumption that traits are appropriately defined so that they have some genetic basis.

If one tries to undertake evolutionary studies of human behavior, two complications arise that admittedly make this a very difficult task. First, we no longer live under the circumstances that were characteristic of our evolution. Second, because of cultural input and the complexity of our mental mechanisms, there is no simple relationship between genotypes and observable behavior. However, these difficulties are technical rather than fundamental. According to the biological understanding of life, evolution must have "shaped" the inherited architecture of the human mind. Ideally, we would therefore want to undertake a "time machine" excursion into the past and identify the conditions under which human mental mechanisms evolved in the Pleistocene. This is perhaps a caricature of the research program of "evolutionary psychology" that was advertised very convincingly by Barkow, Cosmides, and Tooby (1992). To this interdisciplinary program biology can contribute knowledge about mechanisms of the evolutionary process, and psychology can provide knowledge of how to deal with the information-processing mechanisms of the human mind. There would be corresponding advantages to both disciplines if they were to pursue the goals of evolutionary psychology jointly. Biologists would gain more insights about the structural organization of behavior, and psychologists would better understand the functional design of the mind.

A major lesson to be learned from biology is that our mind was originally designed to cooperate only when no other action would lead to higher individual success in the complicated social games humans play. However, this is not to advocate the absurd idea that our evolved minds are mainly predisposed toward ruthless behavior that is selfish in a very narrow, everyday sense. There are two important reasons for this, namely, (a) that altruistic acts toward genetic relatives are beneficial due to kin selection and (b) that biological payoff is defined as reproductive success over the entire life span. The second reason needs further explanation. If we assume, for example, that our ancestors lived in tribal communities that sometimes engaged in intertribal fights, then the expectation of future group defense of the local community would create a certain payoff incentive for an individual to cooperate with other group members long before any fight broke out. Here the expectation of future cooperation can open the door for behavior toward nonrelatives, which is altruistic from a "myopic" point of view and not based on reciprocal altruism. The altruism helps to keep alive and in good condition partners that will be needed later when they have to cooperate unconditionally because it *then* pays to cooperate anyway. The same expectation can enhance the scope for kin-directed altruism beyond the limits set by Hamilton's formula (1).

This kind of reasoning also applies to phenomena that have little or nothing to do with fighting. An individual may, for example, help others now and increase his or her survival probability if those who receive this help are important for a trade that will take place in the future. This idea relies heavily on an unequal distribution of needs, knowledge, or physical abilities, since in a homogeneous world there would be no reason for a trade. Note also that the traded commodity can be immaterial if, for instance, knowledge is transferred between interacting minds. This was mentioned earlier with regard to the cooperation between older and younger elephants, but humans clearly are better examples of the intergenerational "trade" of wisdom. Unfortunately, if evolution has taught humans to play their 'social games" well, communication between generations should include acts of cheating and manipulation. In many primate species, older individuals are dominant and exert a great deal of control over social partners. Wherever we find similar dominance patterns in humans, older individuals can strongly manipulate the information flow between generations in their own favor. For example, some of the less gifted university professors may act vigorously against the acceptance of a new theory even if it is fairly obvious that the new theory has far more explanatory power than the older one. Probably, this behavior has little to do with any kind of "search for truth" or with "wisdom" and should be viewed instead as an attempt to "remain in control" of social processes. Many of us have experienced how this can hold up new developments in science.

In the same vein, social rules about inbreeding avoidance can be discussed. In a nonegalitarian society we should expect these rules to depend on evolved behavioral tendencies of the rule makers, that is, of powerful individuals (Alexander, 1979). Most likely there is an evolved tendency to maintain power and wealth. Therefore, N. W. Thornhill (1990) claimed that cousin marriages can lead to new concentrations of wealth that threaten the powerful positions of rulers in stratified societies. On the basis of a cross-cultural study, she found strong indication that this can explain why rules against cousin marriages exist.

Note that the key element in Thornhill's evolutionary explanation is not the avoidance of inbreeding depression, that is, lower survival rates for inbred offspring. Her study is mentioned here as an example of how careful one must be in identifying the way in which biology "comes into play" in human studies.

However, in order not to push Thornhill's argument too far, it has to be taken into account that the avoidance of strong inbreeding (i.e., incest between brothers and sisters, mothers and sons, or fathers and daughters) seems to have a more direct biological basis. Degler (1991) describes the history of this thought in his discussion of the Westermarck effect. Looking at human development, Westermarck (1891) suggested that adults should have a reduced tendency to have sex with partners with whom they lived in close proximity for a long time during childhood. This resembles a proximate biological mechanism for incest avoidance. However, it should also be mentioned that biological theory would not predict incest avoidance under all ecological and social circumstances. Moreover, there are conditions under which incestuous mating would be beneficial (in evolutionary terms) to one sex, but not to the other (Hammerstein & Parker, 1987). If mating takes place under such conditions, it can hardly be interpreted as a cooperative act.

The desire for sex is perhaps the most obvious consequence of the fact that our minds have been "manufactured" by the evolutionary process. Yet in France – not known as a culture with strong sex aversion – the government has repeatedly been concerned about low birthrates. Clearly, our contraceptive measures undermine the reproductive effect of sex, which shows how easily our mental mechanisms can be uncoupled from their original evolutionary function – an almost trivial statement that many scientists have made before. However, it is less well known that a female's reproductive physiology may also strongly control the process of whose sperm fertilizes her eggs. Baker and Bellis (1993) interpret the physiological processes associated with female orgasm as a means of exerting this control, particularly in the context of "extrapair copulation." Their data are not as solid as one would wish, but there are theoretical reasons to expect that they at least point in the right direction. If Baker and Bellis are correct, women have a very strong position in the evolutionary game of interacting sexes.

During the second half of this century, the institutions of marriage and the family went through a number of systematic changes in industrialized societies. There is a centrifugal force acting within families that seems to be related to the central role of individual success in evolutionary theory (Burgess, 1994). This force has created a growing number of female-single-parent households. Lancaster (1989) analyzed female reproductive behavior under the assumption that there are evolved female tendencies to adjust reproductive behavior to changes in the environment (see also Burgess & Draper, 1989). Lancaster lists a number of conditions under which to expect female-single-parent households. One such condition is that men have very limited access to resources, so that they are unable to provide sufficient support for spouse and children. This can drive the human "mating system" into a state in which women have a number of male partners sequentially and no long-lasting relationship with the same man. Lancaster's way of analyzing human mating systems has much in common with the way in which Davies (1991) analyzes such systems in animals.

When it comes to the "game" between parents and their children, the methodological individualism of evolutionary theory makes it easy to explain why most humans invest more time and resources in their own progeny than in the children of others. However, one partner in a couple may not even invest in his or her own offspring. As we have seen earlier, there can be significant gains from deserting one's offspring and mate if one looks at this phenomenon from a lifetime perspective. The unpleasant evolutionary logic (if it applies) is that the deserting individual creates more children with other partners than it loses from not providing care.

Even when both parents participate in parental behavior, there is still a conflict between parents and offspring concerning the amount of care: Children want to get more than parents are willing to give, and they want to get more than their brothers and sisters – an experience probably shared by most readers of this chapter. The evolutionary logic of this parent–offspring conflict was revealed by Trivers (1974), who related it, roughly speaking, to the fact that every child is genetically more related to him- or herself than to his or her present and future brothers and sisters. Once children are old enough to be independent of parental care, they may actually become "better behaved" and partly support younger brothers and sisters, particularly when the father is absent and the mother has to engage efficiently in economic activities. This is probably the case in many human cultures (Burgess, 1994). It is easy to imagine that such kin-directed support "costs" little and produces major benefits to those who receive support – a situation like that of "helpers at the nest" in birds.

Let us finally address the question of how evolution has acted on basic patterns of information processing in "interacting human minds." From a biological point of view we would expect to find a set of context-dependent mechanisms rather than a universal one. This is a consequence of the idea that evolution occurs only in small steps. A computer example may help to illustrate this point. Suppose that natural selection acts on the design of a computer program. Whenever there is pressure for change, natural selection can only "patch" the old program instead of inventing a more elegant new design – a phenomenon often observed in the development of operating systems. Correspondingly, logical mistakes and biases in human reasoning may strongly depend on the context in which this reasoning takes place. Cosmides and Tooby (1992) argued that as far as cheater detection in social interactions is concerned, human reasoning can be very logical, whereas it may be much less so in another context. This is in accord with the idea that our primate ancestors "trained" their cognitive capabilities mainly in complex social situations in which their success depended strongly on the ability to cooperate without being exploited by others.

References

Adams, E. S., & Caldwell, R. L. (1990). Deceptive communication in asymmetric fights of the stomatopod crustacean, *Gonodactylus bredini*. *Animal Behaviour, 39*, 706–716.

Alatalo, R. V., Carlson, A., Lundberg, A., & Ulfstrand, S. (1981). The conflict between male polygamy and female monogamy: The case of the pied flycatcher, *Fidecula hypoleuca*. *American Naturalist, 117*, 738–753.

Alexander, R. D. (1979). *Darwinism and human affairs*. London: Pitman.

Axelrod, R., & Hamilton, W. D. (1981). The evolution of cooperation. *Science, 211*, 1390–1396.

Baker, R. R., & Bellis, M. A. (1993). Human sperm competition: Ejaculate manipulation by females and a function for the female orgasm. *Animal Behaviour, 46*, 887–909.

Barkow, J. H., Cosmides, L., & Tooby, J. (Eds.). (1992). *The adapted mind*. New York: Oxford University Press.

Barnard, C. (Ed.). (1984). *Producers and scroungers: Strategies of exploitation and parasitism*. London: Croom Helm.

Beretram, B. C. R. (1975). Social factors influencing reproduction in wild lions. *Journal of Zoology, London, 177*, 463–482.

Boesch, C. (1994). Chimpanzees–red colobus monkeys: A predator–prey system. *Animal Behaviour, 47*, 1135–1148.

Boorman, S. A., & Levitt, P. R. (1972). A frequency-dependent natural selection model for the evolution of social cooperation networks. *Proceedings of the National Academy of Sciences, U.S.A., 69*, 2711–2713.

Boorman, S. A., & Levitt, P. R. (1973). Group selection on the boundary of a stable population. *Theoretical Population Biology, 4*, 85–128.

Borgia, G. (1985). Bower quality, number of decorations and mating success of male satin bowerbirds (*Ptilinorynchus violaceus*): An experimental analysis. *Animal Behaviour, 33*, 266–271.

Boyd, R., & Lorberbaum, J. P. (1987). No pure strategy is evolutionarily stable in the repeated prisoner's dilemma. *Nature, 327*, 58–59.

Brown, J. L. (1964). The evolution of diversity in avian territorial systems. *Wilson Bulletin, 76*, 160–169.

Brown, J. L., & Orians, G. H. (1970). Spacing patterns in mobile animals. *Annual Review of Ecology and Systematics, 1*, 239–262.

Burgess, R. L. (1994). The family in a changing world. *Human Nature, 5*, 203–221.

Burgess, R. L., & Draper, P. (1989). A biosocial theory of family violence: The role of natural selection, ecological instability, and coercive interpersonal contingencies. In L. Ohlin & M. H. Tonry (Eds.), *Crime and justice: An annual review of research* (Vol. 11, pp. 59–116). Chicago: University of Chicago Press.

Casscells, W., Schoenberger, A., & Grayboys, T. (1978). Interpretation by physicians of clinical laboratory results. *New England Journal of Medicine, 299*, 999–1000.

Cheney, D. L., & Seyfarth, R. M. (1990). *How monkeys see the world: Inside the mind of another species*. Chicago: University of Chicago Press.

Clutton-Brock, T. H. (1991). *The evolution of parental care*. Princeton, NJ: Princeton University Press.

Cosmides, L., & Tooby, J. (1992). Cognitive adaptations for social exchange. In J. H. Barkow, L. Cosmides, & J. Tooby (Eds.), *The adapted mind* (pp. 163–228). New York: Oxford University Press.

Craig, J. L. (1984). Are communal pukeko caught in the prisoner's dilemma? *Behavioral Ecology and Sociobiology, 14*, 147–150.

Davies, N. B. (1990). Dunnocks: Cooperation and conflict among males and females in a variable mating system. In P. B. Stacey & W. D. Koenig (Eds.), *Cooperative breeding in birds: Long-term studies of ecology and behavior* (pp. 455–485). Cambridge: Cambridge University Press.

Davies, N. B. (1991). Mating systems. In J. R. Krebs & N. B. Davies (Eds.), *Behavioural ecology* (pp. 263–294). Oxford: Blackwell Scientific.

Davies, N. B. (1992). *Dunnock behaviour and social evolution.* Oxford: Oxford University Press.

Dawkins, R. (1976). *The selfish gene.* Oxford: Oxford University Press.

Dawkins, R. (1982). *The extended phenotype.* Oxford: Freeman.

Dawkins, R., & Carlisle, T. R. (1976). Parental investment, mate desertion and a fallacy. *Nature, 262,* 131–133.

Degler, C. N. (1991). *In search of human nature.* New York: Oxford University Press.

De Waal, F. B. M. (1992). Coalitions as part of reciprocal relations in the Arnhem chimpanzee colony. In A. H. Harcourt & F. B. de Waal (Eds.), *Coalitions and alliances in humans and other animals* (pp. 233–258). Oxford: Oxford University Press.

Dominey, W. J. (1980). Female mimicry in male blue gill sunfish – a genetic polymorphism? *Nature, 284,* 546–548.

Dunbar, R. I. M. (1980). Determinants and evolutionary consequences of dominance among female gelada baboons. *Behavioral Ecology and Sociobiology, 7,* 253–265.

Dunbar, R. I. M. (1988). *Primate social systems.* London: Croom Helm.

Fisher, R. A. (1930). *The genetical theory of natural selection.* Oxford: Oxford University Press.

Foster, D., & Young, H. P. (1990). Stochastic evolutionary game dynamics. *Theoretical Population Biology, 38,* 219–232.

Gadagkar, R. (1991). Demographic predisposition to the evolution of eusociality: A hierarchy of models. *Proceedings of the National Academy of Sciences, U.S.A., 88,* 10993–10997.

Gigerenzer, G. (1991). How to make cognitive illusions disappear: Beyond "heuristics and biases." In W. Stoebe & M. Hewstone (Eds.), *European review of social psychology* (pp. 83–115). New York: Wiley.

Goodall, J. (1986). *The chimpanzees of Gombe: Patterns of behavior.* Cambridge, MA: Harvard University Press.

Goosen, C. (1981). On the function of allogrooming in Old-World monkeys. In A. B. Chiarelli & R. S. Corruccini (Eds.), *Primate behaviour and sociobiology* (pp. 110–120). Berlin: Springer.

Haig, D., & Grafen, A. (1991). Genetic scrambling as a defence against meiotic drive. *Journal of Theoretical Biology, 153,* 531–558.

Haldane, J. B. S. (1932). *The causes of evolution.* London: Longman.

Hamilton, W. D. (1964). The genetical evolution of social behaviour. Parts 1 and 2. *Journal of Theoretical Biology, 7,* 1–16, 17–52.

Hammerstein, P. (in press). Darwinian adaptation, population genetics and the streetcar theory of evolution. *Journal of Mathematical Biology.*

Hammerstein, P. (1995). *Evolutionary game theory.* Oxford: Oxford University Press.

Hammerstein, P., & Parker, G. A. (1987). Sexual selection: Games between the sexes. In J. W. Bradbury & M. B. Andersson (Eds.), *Sexual selection: Testing the alternatives* (pp. 119–142). Chichester: Wiley.

Hammerstein, P., & Selten, R. (1994). Game theory and evolutionary biology. In R. J. Aumann & S. Hart (Eds.), *Handbook of game theory with economic applications* (Vol. 2, pp. 929–993). Amsterdam: North-Holland.

Harcourt, A. H. (1989). Social influences on competitive ability: Alliances and their consequences. In V. Standen & R. A. Foley (Eds.), *Comparative socioecology* (pp. 223–242). Oxford: Blackwell Scientific Publications.

Harcourt, A. H. (1992). Coalitions and alliances: Are primates more complex than non-primates? In A. H. Harcourt & F. B. de Waal (Eds.), *Coalitions and alliances in humans and other animals* (pp. 445–471). Oxford: Oxford University Press.

Hausfater, G., & Hrdy, S. B. (Eds.). (1984). *Infanticide: Comparative and evolutionary perspectives.* New York: Aldine.

Hölldobler, B., & Wilson, E. O. (1990). *The ants.* Heidelberg: Springer.

Huntingford, F. A. (1989). Animals fight, but do not make war. In J. Groebel & R. A. Hinde (Eds.), *Aggression and war* (pp. 25–34). Cambridge: Cambridge University Press.

Hurst, L. D. (1993). Drunken walk of the diploid. *Nature, 365*, 206–207.

Isack, H. A., & Reyer, H. U. (1989). Honeyguides and honcy gatherers: Interspecific communication in a symbiotic relationship. *Science, 243*, 1343–1346.

Kahneman, D., Slovic, P., & Tversky, A. (Eds.). (1982). *Judgment under uncertainty: Heuristics and biases*. Cambridge: Cambridge University Press.

Kessel, E. L. (1955). Mating activities of balloon flies. *Systematic Zoology, 4*, 97–104.

König, B. (1994). Components of lifetime reproductive success in communally and solitarily nursing house mice – a laboratory study. *Behavioral Ecology and Sociobiology, 34*, 275–283.

Krebs, J. R., & Davies, N. B. (1993). *An introduction to behavioural ecology* (3rd ed.). Oxford: Blackwell Scientific.

Kummer, H., & Cords, M. (1991). Cues of ownership in long-tailed macaques, *Macaca fascicularis*. *Animal Behaviour, 42*, 529–549.

Lancaster, J. (1989). Evolutionary and cross-cultural perspectives on single-parenthood. In R. W. Bell & N. J. Bell (Eds.), *Sociobiology and the social sciences* (pp. 63–72). Lubbock: Texas Tech. University Press.

Lorenz, K. (1966). *On aggression*. New York: Harcourt, Brace, & World.

Luce, R. D., & Raiffa, H. (1957). *Games and decisions*. New York: Wiley.

Maynard Smith, J. (1976). Group selection. *Quarterly Review of Biology, 51*, 277–283.

Maynard Smith, J. (1977). Parental investment: A prospective analysis. *Animal Behaviour, 25*, 1–9.

Maynard Smith, J. (1978). *The evolution of sex*. Cambridge: Cambridge University Press.

Maynard Smith, J. (1982). *Evolution and the theory of games*. Cambridge: Cambridge University Press.

Møller, A. P. (1988). False alarm calls as a means of resource usurpation in the great tit, *Parus major*. *Ethology, 79*, 25–30.

Morton, E. S., Forman, L., & Braun, M. (1990). Extrapair fertilizations and the evolution of colonial breeding in purple martins. *Auk, 107*, 275–283.

Moss, C. (1988). *Elephant memories: Thirteen years in the life of an elephant family*. London: Elm Tree.

Nash, J. F. (1951). Non-cooperative games. *Annals of Mathematics, 54*, 286–295.

Nowak, M., & Sigmund, K. (1993). A strategy of win-stay, lose-shift that outperforms tit-for-tat in the prisoner's dilemma game. *Nature, 364*, 56–58.

Oldroyd, H. (1964). *The natural history of flies*. New York: Norton.

Packer, C., & Pusey, A. E. (1984). Infanticide in carnivores. In G. Hausfater & S. B. Hrdy (Eds.), *Infanticide: Comparative and evolutionary perspectives* (pp. 31–42). New York: Aldine.

Reyer, H. U. (1984). Investment and relatedness: A cost/benefit analysis of breeding and helping in the pied kingfisher (*Ceryle rudis*). *Animal Behaviour, 32*, 1163–1178.

Reyer, H. U. (1990). Pied kingfishers: Ecological causes and reproductive consequences of cooperative breeding. In P. B. Stacey & W. D. Koenig (Eds.), *Cooperative breeding in birds* (pp. 529–557). Cambridge: Cambridge University Press.

Ridley, M. (1978). Paternal care. *Animal Behaviour, 26*, 904–932.

Rohwer, S., & Rohwer, F. C. (1978). Status signalling in Harris sparrows: Experimental deceptions achieved. *Animal Behaviour, 26*, 1012–1022.

Seger, J. (1991). Cooperation and conflict in social insects. In J. R. Krebs & N. B. Davies (Eds.), *Behavioural ecology: An evolutionary approach* (pp. 338–373). Oxford: Blackwell Scientific.

Seibert, T. F. (1992). Mutualistic interactions of the aphid *Lachnus allegheniensis* (Homoptera: Aphididae) and its tending ant *Formica obscuripens* (Hymenoptera: Formicidae). *Annals of the Entomological Society of America, 85*, 173–178.

Selten, R., & Hammerstein, P. (1984). Gaps in Harley's argument on evolutionarily stable learning rules and in the logic of "tit for tat." *Behavioral and Brain Sciences, 7*, 115–116.

Seyfarth, R. M., & Cheney, D. L. (1984). Grooming, alliances and reciprocal altruism in vervet monkeys. *Nature, 308*, 541–543.

Smuts, B. B. (1985). *Sex and friendship in baboons*. New York: Aldine.

Strum, S. C. (1983). Use of females by male olive baboons (*Papio anubis*). *Americal Journal of Primatoloty*, *5*, 93–109.

Taborsky, M. (1994). Sneakers, satellites, and helpers: Parasitic and cooperative behavior in fish reproduction. In P. J. B. Slater, J. S. Rosenblatt, C. T. Snowdon, & M. Milinski (Eds.), *Advances in the study of behavior* (Vol. 23, pp. 1–100). San Diego, CA: Academic.

Thornhill, N. W. (1990). An evolutionary analysis of rules regulating human inbreeding and marriage. *Behavioral and Brain Sciences*, *14*, 247–293.

Thornhill, R. (1980). Rape in Panorpa scorpionflies and a general rape hypothesis. *Animal Behaviour*, *28*, 52–59.

Trivers, R. L. (1971). The evolution of reciprocal altruism. *Quarterly Review of Biology*, *46*, 35–57.

Trivers, R. L. (1972). Parental investment and sexual selection. In B. Campbell (Ed.), *Sexual selection and the descent of man* (pp. 139–179). Chicago: Aldine.

Trivers, R. L. (1974). Parent–offspring conflict. *American Zoologist*, *14*, 249–264.

Trivers, R. L. (1985). *Social evolution*. Menlo Park, CA: Benjamin-Cummings.

Tyszka, T. (1983). Contextual multiattribute decision rules. In L. Sjöberg, T. Tyszka, & J. A. Wise (Eds.), *Human decision making* (pp. 243–256). Bodafors: Doxa.

van Alphen, J. J. M., & Visser, M. E. (1990). Superparasitism as an adaptive strategy. *Annual Review of Entomology*, *35*, 59–79.

van Hooff, J. A. R. A. M., & van Schaik, C. P. (1992). Cooperation in competition: The ecology of primate bonds. In A. H. Harcourt & F. B. de Waal (Eds.), *Coalitions and alliances in humans and other animals* (pp. 357–389). Oxford: Oxford University Press.

Vincent, A., Ahnesjö, I., Berglund, A., & Rosenqvist, G. (1992). Pipefishes and seahorses: Are they all sex role reversed? *Trends in Ecology and Evolution*, *7*, 237–241.

Vincent, A. J. C. (1990). *Reproductive ecology of seahorses*. Unpublished doctoral dissertation. University of Cambridge.

Westermarck, E. A. (1891). *The history of human marriage*. London: Macmillan.

Wilkinson, G. S. (1984). Reciprocal food sharing in the vampire bat. *Nature*, *308*, 181–184.

Wilkinson, P. F., & Shank, C. C. (1977). Rutting-fight mortality among musk oxen on Banks Island, Northwest Territories, Canada. *Animal Behaviour*, *24*, 756–758.

Williams, G. C. (1966). *Adaptation and natural selection*. Princeton, NJ: Princeton University Press.

Wilson, E. O. (1971). *The insect societies*. Cambridge, MA: Harvard University Press.

Wilson, E. O. (1975). *Sociobiology: The new synthesis*. Cambridge, MA: Harvard University Press.

Woolfenden, G. E., & Fitzpatrick, J. W. (1984). *The Florida scrub jay*. Princeton, NJ: Princeton University Press.

2 Interacting minds in a life-span perspective: a cultural-historical approach to culture and cognitive development

Michael Cole

Abstract

This chapter takes as its central premise that as a result of the process of enculturation, human minds come to interact indirectly in/through the cultural medium they share. Following the lead of cultural-historical psychologists representing several national traditions, culture is conceived of as the uniquely human environment consisting of the residue of the activity of prior generations, existing in the present in the form of artifacts, aspects of the physical world that have been transformed by their inclusion in goal-directed human actions. The implications of this view are traced from birth to old age in a manner designed to highlight the affinity between cultural-historical and life-span approaches to cognitive development.

In this chapter I explicate the role of culture in the way that human minds interact over the life span. In doing so, one of my major goals is to explore what I perceive to be close affinities between the cultural-historical approach to development that I have been working with and the contextualist, life-span approach proposed by such scholars as P. B. Baltes (1987), Dixon (1985), Featherman and Lerner (1985), and Labouvie-Vief (1981). I will discuss these affinities in the last section of the chapter after presenting some of the considerations that have led me to identify them.

Cultural-historical ideas about culture and mind

The core premise of the cultural-historical approach to psychology is that there is an intimate connection between the special environment that human beings inhabit and the fundamental, distinguishing qualities of human minds.

The special quality of the human environment is that it is suffused with the behavioral adaptations of prior generations in external form. This premise, which can be found in the writings of cultural-historical psychologists from many national traditions, is captured well by John Dewey (1938, p. 39):

> In a word, we live from birth to death in a world of persons and things which is in large measure what it is because of what has been done and transmitted from previous human activities. When this fact is ignored, experience is treated as if it were something which goes on exclusively inside an individual's body and mind. It ought not to be necessary to say that experience does not occur in a vacuum. There are sources outside an individual which give rise to experience.

In their early work on this subject, the Russian cultural-historical psychologists expressed this idea by writing that the special morphology of behavior and mind of the human creatures who inhabit a cultural environment is the ability to mediate their actions through artifacts and to arrange for the rediscovery of these forms of mediation by the next generation (Luria, 1928; Vygotsky, 1929, 1978).

Although the Russian cultural-historical psychologists, like many of their contemporaries (e.g., Bergson, 1911/1983), spoke of mediation through tools, they were thinking not only of hammers and needles, but of signs, symbols, and language. All mediators are double sided; they partake of and constitute the borders between the individual and the social, what is "in the mind" and what the mind is in.

The centrality of mediation to human cognition is relevant to this book's emphasis on interacting minds because the cultural-historical approach to mental actions emphasizes that as a result of the process of enculturation, human minds come to interact *in*directly, in/through the cultural medium they share. Hence, understanding how the cultural medium structures the interaction of minds is crucial for comprehending the relationship between culture and cognitive development.

My exploration of the application of these ideas to understanding changes in the ways that minds interact over the life span will proceed as follows. First, I will characterize what I understand to be crucial properties of the cultural medium within which human beings develop and minds interact. Next, I will propose a few skeletal principles as guides in thinking about how age-graded differences in the relation of humans to the cultural medium can be expected to shape the nature of interaction. Finally, I will provide a series of examples, generally well known in the literature of child and adult development, that illustrate how culture enters into the process of cognitive change at different stages of the life span.

The nature of the cultural medium

Following Dewey, Bergson, and the Russian cultural-historical psychologists, I conceive of the cultural medium as the uniquely human environment consisting of the entire ensemble of transformations of the physical environment accumulated by a social group in the course of its historical development. Those transformations exist in the present in the form of artifacts, aspects of the physical environment that have been transformed by their inclusion in goal-directed human activity.[1]

Essential to this view of culture is that artifacts are simultaneously ideal (conceptual) and material. At first this idea may strike the reader as absurd because we are used to thinking of artifacts as solid objects and not as embodying ideality. A hammer is a very material object. However, hammers and all other artifacts are ideal in that they embody in coded form the essential constraints on interactions of which they were previously a part and that they mediate in the present. What differentiates a word such as *language* from, say, a table are the forms and the relative prominence of their material and ideal aspects. No word exists apart from its material instantiation (as a configuration of sound waves, hand movements, writing, or neuronal activity), whereas every table embodies an order imposed by thinking human beings. D'Andrade made this point when he wrote that "material culture – tables and chairs, buildings and cities – is the reification of human ideas in a solid medium" (1986, p. 22).

Levels of artifacts

Following Wartofsky (1979), I find it useful to distinguish artifacts with respect to what might be called levels of organization. The first level refers to *primary artifacts* as objects directly used in production (as examples, Wartofsky gives "axes, clubs, needles, bowls"; modern examples include computers, telecommunications networks, and mythical cultural personages). The second level, *secondary artifacts*, consists of representations of both primary artifacts and modes of action using primary artifacts. Wartofsky refers to secondary artifacts as "reflexive embodiments." Secondary artifacts play a central role in memory and communication, preserving and transmitting modes of action. It is at the level of secondary artifacts that we find the most obvious connection with what is discussed as schemas or cultural models in contemporary anthropological approaches to culture and cognition (see later).

Wartofsky also distinguished a third level, *tertiary artifacts*, that constitutes relatively autonomous "worlds" with their own "rules, conventions, and outcomes." Wartofsky was thinking of tertiary objects connected with perception and art, such as dramatic productions and games, but the category is more generally useful for it corresponds to any activity setting with its own standing rules, conventions, and outcomes – that is, all of the everyday activity settings populated by developing human beings. There is also a kinship between the notion of tertiary artifacts and social institutions, a major source of structuration of human thought and action.

Patterning of artifacts in the cultural medium

The early Russian cultural-historical theorists articulated the principle of artifact-mediated action, but culture is more than a random accumulation of artifacts and associated actions. There is structure in the cultural medium, but the task of specifying how much structure has so far eluded anthropologists.

Some anthropological circles tend to think of culture as a uniform, patterned ensemble of shared beliefs, values, symbols, tools, and so forth that people share in common. This "configurational" approach is greatly influenced by the work of Franz Boas and his students in anthropology (see Bok, 1988, or Stocking, 1968, for excellent summaries of Boas's work), as well as by the cross-cultural psychologists who study "cognitive style" (Berry, 1976).

There is no doubt that culture is patterned, but there is also no doubt that it is far from uniform and that its patterning is experienced in local, face-to-face interactions that are locally constrained and, hence, heterogeneous with respect to "culture as a whole." Consequently, anyone interested in the question of culture and cognition must be concerned with the effective units of culture vis-à-vis mind: They are to be located somewhere between the "perfectly patterned whole" and the "random collection of artifacts."[2]

In one well-known attempt to characterize the effective units of culture, Geertz proposed that "culture is best seen not as complexes of concrete behavior patterns – customs, usages, traditions, habit clusters – . . . but as a set of control mechanisms – plans, recipes, rules, instructions (what computer engineers call 'programs') – for governing behavior" (1973, p. 44). Significantly (because these mechanisms might seem to be located entirely inside people's heads and therefore might seem entirely ideal), Geertz continues in a manner that links up neatly with the notion of artifact mediation that is central to the cultural-historical approach:

> The "control mechanism" view of culture begins with the assumption that human thought is basically both social and public – that its natural habitat is the house yard, the marketplace, and the town square. Thinking consists not of "happenings in the head" (though happenings there and elsewhere are necessary for it to occur) but of traffic in what have been called, by G. H. Mead and others, significant symbols – words for the most part but also gestures, drawings, musical sounds, mechanical devices like clocks. (1973, p. 45)

A complementary notion of structured ensembles within the overall medium of culture is offered by Roy D'Andrade, who suggests the term *cultural schemas* to refer to units that organize entire sets of conceptual-material artifacts. In D'Andrade's terms,

> typically such schemas portray simplified worlds, making the appropriateness of the terms that are based on them dependent on the degree to which these schemas fit the actual worlds of the objects being categorized. Such schemas

> portray not only the world of physical objects and events, but also more abstract worlds of social interaction, discourse, and even word meaning. (1984, p. 93; original in italics)

D'Andrade (1990) refers to intersubjectively shared cultural schemas as cultural models. Such models are used to interpret and guide action in a wide variety of domains, "including events, institutions, and physical and mental objects" (p. 108).

An especially important class of cultural schemas that has been the object of intense investigation in recent years is that of a "script," an event schema, embodied in narratives, as the basic organizer of both culture and cognition (Bruner, 1986; Nelson, 1981, 1986). Nelson refers to scripts as "generalized event schemas" that serve to specify the people who participate in an event, the social roles that they play, the objects that are used during the event, the sequences of actions required, the goals to be attained, and so on.

Once people have even a crude idea of what the appropriate actions associated with going to a restaurant are, they can enter the flow of the particular event with partial knowledge, which gets enriched in the course of the event itself, facilitating later coordination. "Without shared scripts," Nelson writes, "every social act would need to be negotiated afresh" (1981, p. 109). Nelson also points out that children grow up within events controlled by adults and hence within adult scripts. In this sense, she remarks, "The acquisition of scripts is central to the acquisition of culture" (1981, p. 110).

Jerome Bruner (1990) elaborates on the notion of generalized event representation by extending the analysis of scripts (which apply to relatively short-term, local events) to narratives (which are sequences of scripts with their own structuring resources). If it were not for such narrativized framing, he writes, "We would be lost in a murk of chaotic experience and probably would not have survived as a species in any case" (p. 56).

Putting scripts and schemas in context

It is obvious that scripts and schemas do not float around in a void. The uses to which a table is put, or the meaning of a word, are not invariant in our daily lives. Thought cannot be reduced to its artifactual representation. Rather, uses to which the artifacts are put, their instrumentality, their meaning (none of which can be completely reduced to the other) depend on the context in which they are embedded.

A useful approach to the notion of context for our present purposes is one that sees the level of everyday activity (the kinds of activity mediated by scripts, à la Nelson) as a localized kind of individual/cultural/social medium that mediates between the macro and micro levels of psychological and sociological analysis. Wentworth (1980, p. 92) provides a useful definition of context in this spirit: "The context is the world as realized through interaction and the most immediate frame of reference for mutually engaged actors. *The context may be thought of as the situation and time bounded arena for human activity. It is a unit of culture."*

I can summarize my basic points about the cultural medium as follows. Culture's most elementary constituents are artifacts, dual material/ideal mediators that connect/constitute mind and world. In their role as mediators of human action, artifacts are variously configured to serve as resources for constructing joint activity, for coordinating human beings with the world and each other. They do not determine activity; they provide resources for constructing activity. From this perspective, a basic unit of analysis for the study of interacting minds is persons acting in a context – that is, joint, mediated activity (Lektorsky, 1984; Rogoff, 1990; Wertsch, 1985, 1991). Wozniak (1986) and Valsiner (1988) refer to this position as a "co-constructivist" developmental theory.

Under what conditions do interacting minds meet?

If minds interact through culture as systems of artifacts, and if no two people totally share the culture they all draw upon, how is it possible for there *ever* to be a "meeting of minds"? How do they, in Wentworth's terms, come to share the same context?

Emile Durkheim, whose views are similar in many respects to those of the Russian cultural-historical psychologists, put the problem quite distinctly. He provided an "answer-in-principle" that highlights the question of interacting minds in an especially clear fashion:

> In fact, if left to themselves, individual consciousnesses are closed to each other; they can communicate only by means of signs which express their internal states. If the communication established between them is to become a real communion, that is to say, a fusion of all particular sentiments into one, common sentiment, the signs expressing them must be themselves fused into one single and unique resultant. . . . It is by uttering the same cry, pronouncing the same word, or performing the same gesture in regard to some object that they become and feel themselves in unison. . . . Individual minds cannot come in contact with each other except by coming out of themselves; but they cannot do this except by movements. (Durkheim, 1915/1965, p. 262)

The key to producing moments of common understanding, communion, and fusion when minds interact, according to Durkheim, is coordination around the products of prior coordinated actions and reactions – for example, coordination through artifacts. To ensure that the necessary degree of coordinated movement occurs, cultures provide for situations called rituals, mediated by symbolic artifacts and arranged in sequences corresponding to scripts and schemas. In rituals, the mind is embodied or materialized in an obvious way, just in case someone did not get the idea. Referring to the necessary properties of coordination, Durkheim declared that "when this homogeneity is once established and these movements have taken a stereotyped form, they serve to symbolize the corresponding representations" (1915/1965, p. 263). But what about individual minds? Under what conditions can we say that two individual minds have interacted in such a way that one mind can be said to "have met" the other?

Before the time that he encountered Vygotsky and became an advocate of cultural-historical psychology, Alexander Luria proposed a methodology for knowing what another person is thinking that provides an experimental model of the conditions under which two minds can "meet." As described by Luria (1979), he was seeking to provide an objective experimental method that would improve upon the Jungian and Freudian uses of free association as a way of probing the unconscious, preverbal mind. He had little faith that the responses he obtained to his stimulus words were from either the unconscious, the preverbal mind, or the dissembling mind. And he did not know how to tell the difference.

He called the method the "combined motor method." The crux of the method was for the subject to begin by learning to execute two independent motor actions simultaneously in response to a signal (a sound). One action was to push down a button; the other was to hold the other hand perfectly still between two metal plates. This skill took some time to accomplish, but it eventually led to stable button-pushing and stable hand-holding behavior. When stability was achieved, the tone was replaced by someone speaking words. After a bit of perturbation, stability was again achieved. This complex, well-coordinated system of interaction served as the baseline for the manipulation to follow.

Among the words presented as stimuli to push/hold still, the experimenter then placed "forbidden words," words that it was believed the subject would not want to reveal special knowledge about. (In some cases these words were derived from everyday life cases where someone was suspected of hiding something – a crime or a socially undesirable family background; in other cases, the hidden words had been induced by hypnosis, but the experimenter did not know what they were.) Luria's insight was that the experimenter can claim to read the subject's mind if, and only if, the publicly shared activity, whereby the experimenter sets up a system that the subject must coordinate with, is *selectively* disrupted. If a criminal's smoothly organized system of coordinations is disrupted *only* by the word *handkerchief* and a handkerchief played a central role in the crime, we have firm evidence that the investigator and the criminal are sharing the same thought.

Luria was, to be sure, relying on the fact that he was dealing with adults and a set of highly simplified cases over which he had control. This is not the usual situation in real life, where people's behavior is not so finely coordinated. But the essential condition he specified for knowing other minds – selective disruption of ongoing, artifact-mediated, joint activity – remains crucial.

The conditions for minds to interact can now be summarized. The interaction of minds occurs in the medium of culture. That medium is a heterogeneously structured accumulation of the products of past adaptations of the group that have survived into the present as the means by which people interact with each other and the physical world.

In everyday life, as already mentioned, a certain degree of coordination is achieved through shared, scripted activities, their "standing patterns" of acceptable behavior, and norms, all of which are aspects of structure in the medium of culture. Schegloff (1991) and others also emphasize the added importance of the moment-to-moment contingencies of face-to-face interaction in the cultural medium. Minds can be said to interact when two or more people achieve sufficient coordination to allow for the selective disruption of artifact-mediated joint activity.

Changing interactions of minds from birth to old age

For understanding how culture influences the changing ways in which minds interact over the course of the life span, it is essential to keep in mind that human ontogeny is constituted of processes operating simultaneously at the phylogenetic, cultural-historical, and microgenetic (moment-to-moment) levels of structuration. Each of these "genetic domains" (Wertsch, 1985) is characterized by its own scale of temporality, with time generally "moving faster" as we move down the scale.

This heterochrony of the genetic domains constituting human development is, I believe, an important factor in determining how the human mind is created in the cultural medium that sets up a uniquely human relationship between past, present, and future. With the important exception of periods of catastrophic cultural dislocation, changes associated with the individual human life span are rapid compared with changes in the cultural medium. The consequent differences among individuals in relation to the cultural medium associated with different chronological ages, combined with social divisions of labor, are important in shaping how minds interact at different points in the life span.

The interaction of minds at the birth of a child

The need to inquire into the ontogenetic status of the minds that interact is well illustrated when babies first emerge from the womb. When one baby in a group of babies in a nursery begins to cry, other babies are likely to cry, a phenomenon known as "contagious crying" (Martin & Clark, 1987). Such crying is believed to be a primitive precursor of empathy, the sharing of another's feelings. It might be considered a "precultural" form of interaction.

The matter is quite different when the baby is face to face with its parents. In this case, the parents' contributions to the interaction are mediated through culture. Their interpretive processes play a controlling role in the interaction and whether or not it will be said that a meeting of minds has occurred. To parents, a baby is not a "natural," meaningless object. They interpret the infant's properties in terms of existing cultural categories.

When middle-class American mothers are asked to interact with their newborns, they are likely to carry on animated "discussions" as if their babies were really conversing with them (Brazelton, Kozlowski, & Main, 1974). Kaluli (Papua New Guinea) parents, by contrast, assume their babies have no understanding so that attempting to communicate with them is useless (Ochs & Schieffelin, 1984).

A phenomenon observed by British pediatrician Aiden Macfarlane (1977) illustrates cultural mediation of initial parent–child interactions in a manner that provides a kind of model for thinking about how cultural and phylogenetic influences interact in shaping both the baby's characteristics and the process of cultural mediation. To make clear the point of this example, first consider Figure 2.1a, which presents in schematic form five different time scales operating simultaneously at the moment when parents see their newborn for the first time. The vertical ellipse represents the scripted events immediately surrounding birth, which occurs at the point marked by the vertical line.

At the top of the figure is what might be called "geological time," or the history of the earth. The bottom four time lines correspond to the "developmental domains" (Wertsch, 1985) that according to the cultural framework espoused here, simultaneously serve as major constraints for human development. The second line represents phylogenetic time, the history of life on earth, a part of which constitutes the biological history of the newborn individual. The third line represents cultural-historical time, the residue of which is the child's cultural heritage. The fourth line represents ontogeny, the history of a single human being that is the usual object of psychologists' interest. The fifth line represents the moment-to-moment time of lived human experience, the event called "being born" (from the perspective of the child) or "having a baby" (from the perspective of the parents) in this case. Four kinds of genesis are involved: phylogenesis, culturogenesis, ontogenesis, and microgenesis, each "lower" level embedded in the level "above it."

When considering the moment of birth we are reminded that not one but at least *two* ontogenies must be involved; at a minimum one needs a mother and a child interacting in a social context for the process of birth to occur and for development to proceed. These two ontogenies are coordinated in time by the simultaneous structuration provided by phylogeny and cultural history (Figure 2.1b).

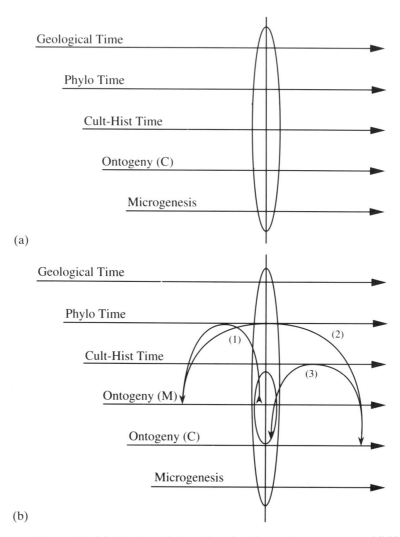

Figure 2.1. (a) The five kinds of time in effect at the moment a child is born (marked by the vertical line). "C" denotes child. (b) How culture is converted from an ideational/conceptual property of the mother into a material/ interactional organization of the baby's environment. Note that there are two ontogenies included, the mother's and the baby's. The curved lines depict the sequence of influences: (1) The mother thinks about what she knows about girls from her (past) cultural experience; (2) she projects that knowledge into the child's future (indicated by remarks such as "She will never be a rugby player"); and (3) this ideal/conceptual future is then embodied materially in the way the mother interacts with the child. "M" denotes mother; "C," child.

The behaviors of adults as they first catch sight of their newborn child and categorize the child as male or female reveal the way in which the mother's and child's ontogenies are coordinated under constraints provided by a combination of phylogeny, cultural history, and the mother's ontogenetic experience. The parents almost immediately start to talk about and to the child. Their comments arise in part from phylogenetically determined features (the anatomical differences between males and females) and in part from cultural features they have encountered in their own lives (what they know to be typical of boys and girls in their culture). Typical comments include the invocation of scripted events such as "I shall be worried to death when she's eighteen" or "She can't play rugby" (said of girls) (Macfarvane, 1977). Putting aside our negative response to the sexism in these remarks, we see that adults interpret the phylogenetic-biological characteristics of the child in terms of their own past (cultural) experience. In the experience of English men and women living in the 1950s, it could be considered "common knowledge" that girls do not play rugby and that when they enter adolescence they will be the object of boys' sexual attention, putting them at various kinds of risk. Using this information derived from their cultural past and assuming cultural continuity (e.g., that the world will be very much for their daughter as it has been for them), parents project a probable future for the child.[3] This process is depicted in Figure 2.1b by following the arrows: mother seeing the baby → (remembered) cultural *past* of the mother → (imagined) cultural *future* of the baby → adult treatment of the baby in the *present*.

Two features of this system of transformations are essential to understanding the contribution of culture in constituting development. First, and most obviously, cultural mediation introduces a clearly nonlinear element into human interaction; culturally defined *future* circumstances become ontogenetically experienced *current* conditions of the child's experience based on the ontogenetically *past* cultural-historical circumstances of the parent. Second, if less obviously, we see the way in which the parents' (*ideal*) recall of their past and (*ideal*) imagination of their child's future becomes a fundamentally important *material* constraint organizing the child's life experiences in the present, a process illustrating the dual material/ideal nature of all artifacts. This rather abstract, nonlinear process of transformation is what gives rise to the well-known phenomenon that even adults totally ignorant of the real gender of a newborn will treat the baby quite differently depending upon its symbolic/cultural "gender." Adults literally create different material forms of interaction based on conceptions of the world provided by their cultural experience when, for example, they bounce "boy" infants (those wearing blue diapers) and attribute "manly" virtues to them while they treat "girl" infants (those wearing pink diapers) in a gentle manner and attribute beauty and sweet temperaments to them (Rubin, Provezano, & Luria, 1974; see also Labouvie-Vief, Chapter 4, this volume).

Macfarlane's example also motivates the special emphasis placed on the social origins of higher psychological functions by cultural-historical psychologists (Cole, 1988; Rogoff, 1990; Valsiner, 1988; Vygotsky, 1987; Wertsch, 1985). As the example demonstrates, human nature is social in a sense different from the sociability of other species. Only a culture-using human being can "reach into" the cultural past, project it into the (ideal/conceptual) future, and then "carry" that future "back" into the present to create the sociocultural environment of the newcomer.[4]

Generalizing the lessons of the first meeting

These examples may strike the reader as only tangentially related to the question of interacting minds. After all, the child has virtually no knowledge of the culture into which he or she is born, and it might also be claimed that the neonate is essentially "mindless." However, I want to argue that these first meetings already suggest important factors that we must consider as we trace the ways in which minds interact in the decades of human life to come. For one thing, the earliest forms of postnatal human interaction orient us to the fact that in talking about the ways that minds interact, we must take account of the ontogenetic status of the interactants. The newborn is both biologically immature and culturally naive. How the infant mind interacts with others will depend crucially on who those others are, their degree of enculturation, and the particular cultural beliefs they acquire. By the same token, at the other end of the life span, the mind of a 90-year-old, with an enormous store of cultural knowledge, will interact very differently with another 90-year-old than with a 50-year-old or a 5-month-old. Some of these differences will result from diverse relationships to the cultural medium, others to biological properties of the individuals, still others to their social roles and attendant power relationships of the interactants vis-à-vis each other, which in turn are intertwined with culture.

Early in life, when children are physically immature and have yet to accumulate a cultural-historical past, when their lives, as we say, "lie before them," it is the more powerful adults who structure children's experience in terms of their expectations for their future. (Recall Nelson's observation that children grow up inside of adult scripts.) Assuming the 70-year life span of many people living in industrialized countries in the late twentieth century, biological maturation and cultural appropriation proceed more or less "hand in glove" until individuals reach their late twenties or early thirties. Then the directionality of phylogenetic and cultural-historical factors contributing to development begins to separate; culturally organized experience continues to accumulate while the biological substrate of mind begins to weaken, requiring reorganization of mental life (P. B. Baltes, 1987). The social roles that one plays and the contexts in which they are played may expand or begin to contract, depending on one's place in the social order (Sørensen, Weinert, & Sherrod, 1986).

Because the ways in which the process of interacting minds changes across the life span will depend on the interplay of all of these factors, it is obviously impossible to provide a comprehensive account of the processes at work. However, it is possible to illustrate the way in which they operate in a series of examples taken from different ages.

Getting on a schedule

In the earliest weeks after birth, children and caretakers must become coordinated in such a manner that the adults are able to provide enough resources to accommodate the newcomers. Children must be drawn into society, just as they must engage their caretakers and draw into themselves the cultural resources accumulated by society if they are to continue to develop. In this process, there is an intricate interplay between the initial characteristics of children and the sociocultural environment into which they are born. This initial synchronization becomes the "carrier wave" for the neonate mind to begin interacting with surrounding minds.

One obvious component of this process of coordination involves getting the baby to sleep on a schedule that meshes with the adult activity cycle. Another component is feeding, which must be coordinated with the sleep cycle. There are wide cultural differences in how these coordinations are achieved (Super & Harkness, 1982). Among children in the United States, where most people live by the clock and infants are encouraged to sleep through the night as soon as possible, there is a marked shift toward the adult day–night cycle a few weeks after birth. There is also pressure for meals to be scheduled at the convenience of adults. By contrast, Kipsigis (Kenyan) infants, who sleep with their mothers and spend their days strapped to their mothers' backs, spend much of the day napping while their mothers go about their work. At night, they may be found snoozing on their mothers' backs while they are dancing or conversing with their neighbors, and feeding takes place more or less on demand. In each case, children rather quickly adjust to the adult schedule.

For my present purposes, such cultural differences are unimportant. What is important is that in each case the meshing of the sleep and feeding cycles with the daily rhythms of adult life increases the overall coordination between infants and their caretakers, making a "meeting of minds" through selective discoordination possible.

The major signal of serious discoordination is, of course, crying. Cries carry a small amount of differential information. Adults from many cultures can distinguish between a hunger cry and a cry induced by a painful stimulus. However, in order to assess the source of the infant's distress in a more fine-grained fashion, the caretaker must have a detailed knowledge about the baby's regular daily rhythm.

A new kind of meeting? The emergence of social smiling

Between the ages of $2\frac{1}{2}$ and 3 months, several different lines of development, which have been proceeding more or less independently, converge around the phenomenon of social smiling (Emde, Gaensbauer, & Harmon, 1976). The development of this seemingly simple behavior illustrates the intricate way in which different lines of development must relate to each other for a transition to a qualitatively new level of development to occur.[5] Maturation of the visual system enables a new level of visual acuity and a new ability to analyze the visual field. Babies can focus their eyes on, and direct their smiles to, people. Their smiles, which until this time have born no contingent relationship to others, now come under the control of the social behavior of their parents. As a consequence, smiling, to this point a seemingly unrelated behavior, is transformed. With the advent of social smiling, there is a new form of interaction among minds.

This contrast is quite apparent to the adult participants. Before the advent of social smiling, one encounters descriptions such as the following: "I don't think there is interaction . . . They are like in a little cage surrounded by glass and you are acting all around them but there is not interaction" (Robson & Moss, 1970, pp. 979–980). After the advent of social smiling, the following behaviors emerge:

> His eyes locked on to hers, and together they held motionless. . . . This silent and almost motionless instant continued to hang until the mother suddenly shattered it by saying "Hey!" and simultaneously opening her eyes wider. . . . Almost instantly the baby's eyes widened. His head tilted up. His smile broadened. (Stern, 1977, p. 3)

At this point the "culture" part of the mechanism by which minds interact is still carried entirely by the adult. It is manifested in the way that the adult interprets the baby's behavior. Note that the transformation from reflex to social smiling takes place only if there is proper feedback from the infant's caretakers. Without appropriate feedback, as occurs in the case of some blind children, social smiling does not develop. (See Cole & Cole, 1992, pp. 170ff for additional discussion of this point.)

From primary to secondary intersubjectivity

Colin Trevarthan (1980) refers to the kind of coordinated turn taking and emotional sharing illustrated in the preceding example as *primary intersubjectivity*. As part of a new biosocial-behavioral reorganization of life between the ages of 6 and 9 months, babies become considerably more mobile.

They can move away from the immediate presence of watchful adults, so they can no longer rely on the adults to help them complete their actions and to rescue them from their mistakes in the same manner as before.

Both babies and caretakers must accommodate the uncertainties of their increasing separation as babies begin to move about on their own. Caretakers arrange the environment so that babies are likely to encounter no harm, and they keep a watchful eye (or ear) open for something amiss. Babies anticipate trouble, too. They keep an eye on their caretakers' responses to the things they do, becoming openly wary of strange events and people because they are not sure what unfamiliar adults will do.

At about this same time, they begin to interact with others in a new and more complex way that Trevarthan calls *secondary intersubjectivity*, the hallmark of which is that the infant and the caregiver can now share understandings and emotions that refer beyond themselves to objects and other people. An interesting indicator of this ability at 6 to 9 months is the interaction of minds called *social referencing*, when babies check their mother's reactions to an uncertain event or an unfamiliar person and respond in terms of her emotional evaluation as evidenced by her facial expression (Campos & Stenberg, 1981).

An indication of secondary subjectivity that is crucial for the ability to interact with another mind through an artifact manifests itself within a short time in the form of pointing. When 12-month-olds see a remote-controlled car roll past, they point at it and then look to see how the mother reacts to it. Within a few months they look at the mother to see if she is looking at the car (e.g., to see whether they and the mother have noticed this unusual event in common) and *then* point to it. Here we see the earliest evidence of joint mediated activity; the car is now mediating the child's interactions with the mother (Butterworth, 1991).

The emergence of language

Thus far the role of culture in cognitive development has been a relatively "external" one. Children find themselves in an environment that is organized according to the cultural patterns of their social group, embodied in scripted activities with which they have become coordinated. The beginnings of language, however, bring about a fundamental reorganization of children's minds and their relations to their sociocultural environment. Before the advent of language, if children can be said to understand their actions, that understanding is implicit (Karmiloff-Smith, 1992). Beginning with the appearance of early words, and accelerating rapidly between (very roughly) 18 and 30 months of age, children manifest a new mode of behavior, mediation through artifacts in the material form of patterns of sound (or motions of the hands, in the case of the deaf).[6]

According to the cultural-historical contention, the advent of language has profound effects on both the nature of mind and the ways in which minds can interact. Before the advent of language, children could be said to be "in culture"; with the appropriation of language, culture ceases to be external to the children and becomes a part of their basic psychological processes, reorganizing them in the process. Vygotsky and his colleagues referred to all sorts of conventional signs, language, counting systems, mnemonic techniques, charts, maps, drawings, and the like as "psychological tools." As such, they manifest the basic property of all tools: "By being included in the process of behavior, the psychological tool alters the entire flow and structure of mental functions" (Vygotsky, 1981, p. 137).

Before the flowering of language, one can trace the development of thinking and the development of language as more or less separate threads. There is, in Vygotsky's phrase, a "pre-linguistic" phase in the development of thought and a "pre-intellectual" phase in the development of language (babbling, cooing, etc.). The unique characteristic of human development, he maintained, is that these two lines of development become interwoven, as a result of which "thinking becomes verbal and speech intellectual" (Vygotsky, 1987, p. 112).[7]

Many manifestations of the changes in cognition accompany the acquisition of language-mediated behavior. One is *symbolic play*, whereby objects and events are treated in an "as if" manner in which the conventional meanings are held in suspension and manipulated. Before the advent of language, interactions among peers are generally transitory and fleeting. But 3-year-olds can coordinate with one another using a variety of primary and secondary artifacts, embedded within the tertiary artifact called "pretending to have a tea party." At the same time, children acquire the ability to think about other people's mental states, or beliefs, as indicated in tasks where children must understand that others may entertain a false belief (Astington, 1993).

Despite their differences, each of these cases is symptomatic of the new way in which minds can interact once children's actions are mediated through the artifactual system of language. The strings of artifacts (words) that children exchange with others mean that interactions are no longer restricted to the here and now. They have the power to invoke objects and events remote in time and space; the cultural past and future enter into present interactions in a new, and uniquely human, way.

Interacting minds in middle childhood

Among the many phenomena that I might choose to illustrate the special character of how culture and cognition construct each other in middle childhood, I have chosen a phenomenon first highlighted by Piaget: the fact that during middle childhood children spend significant amounts of time in age-graded groups without direct adult supervision.

I take the crux of the issue to be the following. In infancy and early childhood, by virtue of the fact that parents, grandparents, or older siblings are present in the settings where children find themselves, discoordinations and conflicts in their interactions with age-mates are repaired by the concrete intervention of society. What changes occur so that children can regulate their interpersonal interactions without direct adult intervention? Piaget's well-known answer was that children came to be able to govern their behavior by social rules, for which the prototype was to be found in rule-based games (Piaget, 1965).

Rule-based games are a model of society for children in two closely related respects, Piaget argued. First, "Games with rules are social institutions in that they remain the same as they are transmitted from one generation to the next and they are independent of the will of the individuals who participate in them" (Piaget & Inhelder, 1969, p. 119). Like other social institutions – language, for example – games provide an already existing structure of rules about how to behave in specific social circumstances.

Second, like all social institutions, rule-based games can exist only if people agree to mediate their behavior through them. To play a game such as hopscotch or baseball, children must learn to subordinate their desires and behavior to a socially agreed-upon system. In Piaget's view, it is through the give and take of negotiating plans, settling disagreements, making and enforcing rules, and keeping and breaking promises that children come to develop an understanding that social rules provide a structure that makes possible *cooperation* with others (Piaget, 1965).

Piaget's characterization of games as social institutions has all the properties we have come to expect of cultural artifacts; they make possible the interaction of people in coordinated systems of activity. "It seems obvious," Piaget wrote,

> that individual operations of intelligence and operations making for exchange in cognitive cooperations are one and the same thing, "the general conditions of actions" to which we have continually referred being an interindividual as well as intraindividual coordinator. (Piaget, 1967, p. 360)

From a cultural-historical perspective, rule-based games are tertiary artifacts of a new order. They do not directly model everyday events, but rather create qualitatively new, non–everyday events, within which minds (and bodies) interact. Subsequently, everyday events will come to be interpreted in terms of, and mediated by, these non–everyday artifacts.

There are certainly other attainments of middle childhood that would lead us to assume that minds begin to be able to interact with each other in new ways. For example, insofar as children attend school and acquire the ability to read and write, interaction through print, which breaks the boundaries of the here and now, becomes possible. It is also in middle childhood that children come to be trusted with complex chores, indicating that their parents can trust them to "behave themselves" (or at least hold them accountable if they do not).

Adolescence

Common to both cultural-historical and Piagetian theory is the belief that the transition from childhood to adulthood corresponding to the stage of adolescence in modern industrialized societies entails the acquisition of a new mode of thought.[8] According to Inhelder and Piaget, this new mode of thought is the ability to think in terms of formal operations. They contrast concrete and formal operations in the following way:

> Although concrete operations consist of organized systems (classifications, serial ordering, correspondences, etc.), [children in the concrete operational stage] proceed from one partial link to the next in step-by-step fashion, without relating each partial link to all the others. Formal operations differ in that all of the possible combinations are considered in each case. Consequently, each partial link is grouped in relation to the whole; in other words, reasoning moves continually as a function of a "structured whole." (Inhelder & Piaget, 1958, p. 16)

Inhelder and Piaget speculated that an essential social condition promoting the development of formal operations was the fact that the transition from childhood to adulthood entails a shift in the responsibility that people have for seeing that activities go well. No longer can individuals rely on more capable others to see that things are done right; they must see to it themselves.

Vygotsky ascribes the underlying change in thinking associated with the transition to adulthood to a shift from "thinking in complexes" to "thinking mediated by genuine concepts." In terms reminiscent of Inhelder and Piaget, he wrote, "What distinguishes the construction of the complex [from 'genuine concepts'] is that it is based on connections among the individual elements that constitute it as opposed to abstract logical connections" (Vygotsky, 1987, p. 136).

A great deal of contemporary evidence indicates that formal operational thinking, or thinking in true concepts, is relatively rarely encountered, even in societies that explicitly seek to teach their use (Cole & Cole, 1992, chap. 16). This evidence caused Piaget (1972) to conclude that while all normal people attain formal operations, "they reach this stage in different areas according to their aptitudes and their professional specializations (advanced studies or different types of apprenticeship for the various trades): the way in which these formal structures are used, however, is not necessarily the same in all cases" (p. 10). In other words, a lawyer might think in a formal manner about legal cases, but not when sorting the laundry, or a baseball manager might employ formal operational thinking to choose his batting lineup, but fail to do so in the combination-of-chemicals task.

I find the "density of knowledge plus new responsibilities" explanation of the conditions that promote the appearance of formal operations quite congenial. According to this view, different societies arrange for their young people to gain deep knowledge in a restricted number of domains; no one is an expert at doing everything. When deep knowledge is associated with responsibility for action, it creates the cultural conditions that promote the kind of systematicity embodied in formal operational tasks. Such thinking appears to be, by and large, specific to the activities where the proper conditions hold.

The most promising suggestion I have seen for a universal domain in which people achieve something akin to formal operations comes from Erik Erikson's (1968) ideas about identity formation, which hinge on a new way of thinking about the self in relationship to society. Erikson believed that adolescents face the task of incorporating their new sexual drives and the social demands placed on them into a fully integrated and healthy personality. He called this integrated state "identity," which he defined as "a sense of personal sameness and historical continuity" (Erikson, 1968, p. 17).

What makes Erikson's ideas germane to this discussion is that he saw adolescent identity formation as involving more than the individual personality. To forge a secure sense of self, adolescents must resolve their identities in both the individual and the social spheres or, as Erikson (1968) put it, establish "the identity of these two identities" (p. 22). He explained the thought processes involved in the following passage:

> In psychological terms, identity formation employs a process of simultaneous reflection and observation, a process taking place on all levels of mental functioning, by which the individual judges himself in the light of what he perceives to be the way in which others judge him in comparison to themselves and to a typology significant to them; while he judges their way of judging him in the light of how he perceives himself in comparison to them and to types that have become relevant to him. (pp. 22–23)

Although Erikson's description of the kind of thinking required to achieve an integrated sense of identity may seem unnecessarily convoluted, this passage is worth careful study because it corresponds closely to Piaget's descriptions of formal operational thinking.

Erikson's core idea is that adolescents engage in an identity-forming process that depends on (1) how they judge others, (2) how others judge them, (3) how they judge the judgment processes of others, and (4) their ability to keep in mind social categories ("typologies") available in the culture when making judgments about other people.

Note that it is not enough to take only one or two of these elements into account – say, how you judge others using social categories of importance to you. Rather, you must simultaneously consider both your own and other people's judgments, plus the perspective of society (embodied in the linguistic categories used to formulate the judgments). It is this latter quality that clearly implicates culture in the way that formal operations change the nature of the way that minds interact. Not any form of systematicity will do; rather, it is systematicity in terms of culturally shared categories that is the crucial factor.

As a consequence of the ability to think systematically about the self in relation to others and cultural categories, a new way in which minds can interact emerges, one based entirely on talk outside the context of action – talk mediated by social norms and conventions.

The reorganization of mental life in adulthood

The affinity between cultural-historical and life-span approaches to mind first impressed me when the publishers of *The Development of Children* (Cole & Cole, 1992) asked us to include a brief chapter on adulthood and aging. I noted that those theorists who thought of development in largely biological terms, or in terms of cognitive universals, did not see development as a lifelong process, but those who believed culture to be important in development proposed developmental stages following adolescence.

Freud, in good Darwinian style, believed that development ceases after adolescence because once young people reach the genital stage and complete the process of sexual reproduction, they have fulfilled their fundamental bio-logical role – to ensure the continuation of the species. To be sure, adults must care for their offspring until they are sufficiently mature to repeat the cycle, but Freud did not attribute any particular developmental significance *for the parents* to the activities of parenting.

In Piagetian theory, formal operations are the logical end point of develop-ment because they provide a comprehensive logical apparatus that allows a person to maintain a state of cognitive equilibrium. Piaget (1967) recognized that pure logic is an insufficient basis for mature action, pointing out that some of the less attractive aspects of teenage behavior result from adolescents' new discovery of the power of logic, which leads them to act "as though the world should submit itself to idealistic schemes rather than systems of reality" (p. 64). Experience brings about a more realistic balance between the adolescent's newfound powers of systematic thinking and the messiness of life. "Just as experience reconciles formal thought with the reality of things," Piaget wrote, "so does effective and enduring work, undertaken in concrete and well-defined situations, cure dreams" (1967, pp. 68–69).

However, this coming to terms with reality did not imply *developmental* change for Piaget; in his view, there existed no stage of thought beyond formal operations. At best, he believed, changes after adolescence represent a process of consolidation and an increase in judgment about how to employ one's – fundamentally unchanged – cognitive resources.

By contrast, Erikson's theory, in which culture plays an important role, assumes that just as childhood development proceeds through the resolution of conflicts associated with the "main tasks" of each age period, so too adult-hood development is propelled by the need to resolve crises associated with each of its main tasks. Like many recent students of adult development, Erikson sees an important transition period in the late thirties, when, if they are healthy, people achieve the stage of *generativity*. This is a time when people begin to reconsider their life paths and, in George Vaillant's (1977) terms, to take "responsibility for the growth, leadership, and well-being of one's fellow creatures, not just raising crops or young children" (p. 202).

In recent years there have been a number of efforts to elaborate life-span approaches in order to extend and refine theories such as those proposed by Piaget and Erikson, by documenting the changes in modes of thought that are likely to take place in adulthood. A dominant concern of those building on Piagetian theory is to demonstrate the emergence of a new set of cognitive abilities that grow out of (or in parallel with) formal operations (Alexander & Langer, 1990; Fischer, Kenny, & Pipp, 1990). One way to interpret these continuing changes is that people in their twenties and thirties develop the ability to relate one abstract system to another and, eventually, to think about entire systems of abstract relations (Fischer et al., 1990). While I do not doubt that such higher-order formal systems thinking is possible under some cultural circumstances, especially if one has pencil and paper in hand, I do doubt the general significance of such elaborations on the basic logic of creating hierar-chies of logical closed systems outside the realm of science.

I find more congenial suggestions put forward by scholars such as Kegan (1982) and Labouvie-Vief (1992; see also Chapter 4, this volume), who argue, in the spirit of Piaget's remarks quoted earlier, that, as people grow older, they can think not only within abstract systems, but about them. This thinking about, contra Piaget, does lead to qualitative changes in thought processes. In Labouvie-Vief's view, for example, adults

> move away from the earlier hierarchical model and establish a way of thinking in which the two poles of mental functioning are seen as interactive and as dialectically related. As a result of the process, such categories as objective and subjective, self and other or self and society, and mind and body are no longer in dualistic opposition. Instead, the individual understands that each mutually affects the other, mutually defining and deepening each other. (1994, pp. 206–207)

In Labouvie-Vief's view, a particularly important result of this new form of thinking is that the reintegration of logic and emotion and, with them, aspects of the self associated with traditionally oppositional gender roles, becomes possible. This reintegration creates the foundations of a lifelong develop-mental process that she associates with Erikson's notions of generativity in adulthood.

An important factor contributing to the kinds of reorganization of thinking discussed by Labouvie-Vief and others is that in adulthood one begins to review old events from a new generational perspective. A simple example transpired in my family while I was in the process of writing this chapter. A middle-aged friend of my wife's told her about the extreme stress she felt because her 35-year-old daughter's husband had left her and her early preteenage children for a younger woman. Her grandchildren refused to talk to their father even when forced to spend time with him in accordance with the separation agreement. The father was initiating legal steps to gain custody of the children in the hope of regaining their love. My wife's friend said that she was simply sick with the pain she felt for her daughter and her grandchildren.

My wife, herself a grandmother now, reflected on how angry she used to get when her mother expressed similar emotions with regard to events in either her or her sister's life. Viewed from the perspective of a daughter, a mother's expression of pain ("I am so upset that your husband is unemployed I can hardly sleep") is easily interpreted as coercion and disapproval. Experiencing the same event from the other side of the generational divide provides a wholly different way of thinking about such matters.

Coming from a cultural-historical perspective, I too believe that lifelong development is the expected pattern. In my own thinking I have linked this difference to the basic principles on which a cultural-historical approach rests: the need and ability of human beings to live in an environment suffused with the accumulated artifacts of past generations. The key point was made by Labouvie-Vief:

> Whether or not aging is adaptive, therefore, cannot be judged at a level of simple biological reductionism. Even though aging does bring a reduction in biological resilience, aging organisms may have evolved new structures that increase the coping efficiency of the population as a whole. (1981, p. 215)

The gain–loss dynamic: developmental trade-offs in old age

As Labouvie-Vief (1981) points out, the child developmentalist suffers from the fact that, in the early years of life, development seems to be a matter of "conjunctive, cumulative continuity." The child grows larger, has more elaborated brain circuitry, inhabits a broader range of contexts, acquires more knowledge, engages in more complex forms of social interaction, and so on. With the intertwined threads of development all flowing in the same direction, ferreting out their distinctive contributions is made extremely difficult. This circumstance is one of the major motivations for comparative work, where biological abnormalities and cultural differences (e.g., whether or not children start school at the age of 7 years) provide an opportunity partially to unravel the tangled web of development.

Although the data are not unequivocal, the growth of biological capacities to the age of approximately 30 and their subsequently slow decline appear to follow the course of change described metaphorically by many psychologists over the years: From birth through puberty and a few years more, the tide of life rises, sometimes with a rush, sometimes with a smooth, imperceptible advance along the beach. At some vaguely definable time, the high-water mark is reached, and the tide slowly retreats (Katchadourian, 1987). A similar story appears adequate to describe those intellectual capacities referred to as "fluid" and believed to depend heavily on biological factors (Horn & Donaldson, 1980). This pattern of rise and decline can also be seen in the social domain: Infants begin life confined entirely to contexts where they can be watched over and protected by parents; the range of contexts where the growing person can act as an independent agent grows steadily into middle age; then the contexts for independent action begin to shrink, until life ends as it began, with the elderly person dependent on others and capable of acting only within a restricted range of contexts.

On the other hand, as Paul Baltes has pointed out, aspects of intellectual and social change suggest both the qualitative rearrangement of psychological processes and discontinuities in experience. Qualitatively new forms of thinking arise from the fact that "crystallized," "pragmatic" abilities increase while "fluid," "mechanical" abilities decrease, requiring people to reorganize their thinking to maintain their effectiveness as they grow older (P. Baltes, 1987, 1993). This changing balance among mental resources interacts with the social discontinuities in an individual's life, such as retirement or the loss of a spouse, that bring about dramatic changes in the contexts of a person's everyday activities.

When we take into consideration the complex psychological trade-offs entailed by changes in the biological, cognitive, and social domains, the picture of adulthood as a period of stability followed by a gradual decline often fails to correspond to a particular individual's actual experience of psychological change. Instead of a general feeling of gradual decline, what emerges from studies of adult development is an intricate, shifting mosaic in which gradual change and predictable experiences are mixed with sudden, unexpected events – new insights, conceptual reintegrations – and triumphs mixed with disappointments, loss of power, and decline. Even as one's physical powers decrease, the accumulated experiences of a lifetime, the "crystallized" and "pragmatic" aspects of cognition, provide adults with resources for dealing with life that are completely beyond the reach of the young. This same, changing dynamic has an inevitable impact on the ways in which minds interact, making more difficult the coordination necessary for knowing what other people are thinking.

With respect to people roughly one's own age, the longer one lives, the rarer it is to meet other people who share knowledge of one's past, including the cultural artifacts that have coordinated the interactions of one's mind with others. This situation is exacerbated in modern-day nursing homes, in which people are exposed to strangers for whom their past is only a story. In these conditions, it is perfectly understandable that people would bring treasured objects with them "to make a sparse environment richer, not only in meaning but also in the proportion of the encapsulated environment that could respond to them" (Lawton, 1990, p. 640).

The difficulties of interacting with younger minds are of a related kind. Elderly people think in terms of a long time span in which the trajectory of various kinds of events is well mapped. Assuming cultural continuity (which individuals always assume, whatever the reality), this stable vision of the flow of life from the past also gives them an unusual grasp of the "future" of the younger people with whom they interact. The younger person, of course, cannot see this "future." In an important sense, then, the old and young live in different worlds, rendering difficult, if not impossible, the meeting of minds.

This was equally true earlier in life, of course, where the meeting of minds was simply papered over by the overpowering ability of adults to define the reality of the children whose lives they were arranging. But with the aged we have reversed perspectives of seeing development from the point of the older, not the younger, individual. This perspective reveals a contradiction in the way that minds interact during old age, namely, that the cognitively more knowledgeable person is now the socially and biologically less competent person, whose dependence is the source of myriad and complex interpersonal uncertainties (M. Baltes & Wahl, 1992).

At the same time, the aged confront their own futures with no more certainty than the young, a fact that speaks to the similarity of the developmental processes at all ages. This point was made by the novelist Milan Kundera (1988), who expresses it far better than I could:

> We leave childhood without knowing what youth is, we marry without knowing what it is to be married, and even when we enter old age, we don't know what it is we're headed for: the old are innocent children of their old age. In that sense, man's world is a planet of inexperience. (p. 100)

Culture in development: toward a synthetic view

I have pursued two goals in this chapter. The first was to sketch ways in which the interaction of phylogenetic and cultural-historical contributions to ontogeny shape the ways whereby minds can be said to interact over the life span. In doing so, I have sought to illustrate how principles of development evident early in ontogenesis retain their relevance into adulthood and old age. My second goal has been to suggest that the cultural-historical approach I have sketched here, which heretofore has been applied primarily to childhood, fits well with life-span approaches to development such as that promoted by Paul Baltes. Thinking of culture as history in the present, both views assert that "the processes of individual development are governed both by principles of ontogenesis and by factors associated with the concurrent process of biocultural change" (Baltes, 1987, p. 619).

As Paul Baltes (1987) emphasizes, such an approach is inherently interdisciplinary, requiring analysis not only at the psychological but also at the cultural and social levels. In this regard, I find encouraging the affinities between the cultural-historical approach I have been espousing and the life-span/life-course treatments of development in the work of sociologists such as Buchmann (1989) and Kohli (1986). Kohli (1986, p. 272) speaks of the life course as a social institution.

> It socializes in two ways: It regulates the movement of individuals through their life in terms of career pathways and age strata, and it regulates their biographically relevant actions by structuring their perspectives for movement through life. It has thus a double impact: on the social positions in their sequential organization, as well as on the symbolic horizons within which individuals conceive of themselves (and of others) and plan their actions. In other words, *it has a material as well as a symbolic aspect.* (Emphasis added)

The affinity between this view and my earlier discussion of the ways in which artifacts are organized in terms of cultural models and scripts is made even clearer by Buchmann (1989), whose monograph on the entry into adulthood is titled *The Script of Life in Modern Society*.

These kinds of affinities give me hope that a synthetic, truly life-span approach to human development that treats human beings as phylogenetically evolved creatures interacting in the medium of culture is within our grasp.

Notes

1 To quote the Russian epistemologist Evald Ilyenkov, "The world of things created by man for man, and, therefore, things whose forms are reified forms of human activity . . . is the condition for the existence of consciousness" (1977, p. 94).

2 Another important source of heterogeneity with respect to the cultural medium is that it is heterogeneously distributed across any population. This point has been emphasized by Ted Schwartz (1978, 1990), who explores the way in which knowledge is distributed differentially across persons, generations, occupations, classes, religions, institutions, and so on. Schwartz argues that culture is necessarily a distributed phenomenon insofar as it is brought to bear, and acquired, in everyday interactions among people, no two of whom share all of the culture of the group to which they belong.

3 Writing about the special temporal quality of culturally mediated human thought, White remarks that "this world of ideas comes to have a continuity and a permanence that the external world of the senses can never have. It is not made up of the present only, but of a past and a future as well. Temporally, it is not a succession of disconnected episodes, but a continuum extending in both directions, from infinity to infinity" (1942, p. 372).

4 This analysis also shows how culture contributes to both continuity and discontinuity in individual development. In thinking about their babies' futures, these parents are assuming that the "way things have always been is the way things will always be," a purely artificial form of continuity that allows people to "project" the past into the future, thereby creating a stable interpretive framework that is one of the important elements of psychological continuity.

This assumption, of course, is wrong whenever there are conditions of cultural change following the birth of the child. As but a single example, in the 1950s, American parents who assumed that their daughter would not be a soccer player at the age of 16 would have been correct. But in 1990, a great many American girls play soccer. In addition, as life-span developmental psychologists emphasize, unique historical events (a war, a depression) may provoke great discontinuity in development (Featherman & Lerner, 1985).

5 As a way of dealing with the resulting complexities of tracking the dynamic system of development over time, in prior publications I have sought to provide a framework that understands developmental change as the emergent synthesis of several major "factors" or "aspects" of human life interacting over time (Cole, 1992; Cole & Cole, 1992). The heuristic device I have adopted is to analyze developmental change in terms of the social, biological, and cultural factors that give rise to a sequence of qualitative rearrangements in the organization of experience and behavior that Emde and his colleagues referred to as a "bio-behavioral shift" (Emde et al., 1976). Cole and Cole (1992) expanded on this idea, referring to "bio-social-behavioral shifts" because, as the work of Emde et al. showed, every biobehavioral shift involves changes in the relations of individuals to their social world.

6 According to Piaget, the flowering of language during this period is the consequence of a reorganization of mind in which children become capable of representing the world, i.e., of representing it to themselves mentally. Current evidence (see Karmiloff-Smith, 1992, for a review) indicates that children are capable of nonpropositional, analogue forms of representation considerably earlier. In Karmiloff-Smith's terms, it is the *redescription* of these early forms of representation into language that concerns me here.

7 In his descriptions of the qualitative transformations in mind brought about by the acquisition of language, Vygotsky displays his affinity to contextualist worldviews, as described by Pepper (1942). In Pepper's terms, the fusion of phylogeny and cultural history brought about by the acquisition of language is an emergent, qualitatively distinct, new form of mind in relation to (interwoven with) the world.

8 According to my reading of the evidence, adolescence as a recognized, distinctive life stage exists under social conditions where there is a marked gap between the biological capacity for sexual reproduction and changes in social status associated with the capacity for cultural reproduction (Whiting, Burbank, & Ratner, 1986). In societies characterized by relatively simple technological means of production, where biological maturity occurs relatively late by the standards of modern industrial societies, there may be no commonly acknowledged stage of development equivalent to adolescence. Similarly, there may be some such stage recognized for one part of a society and not for others, associated with such factors as gender (adolescence appeared to be a strictly male phenomenon in ancient Greece) and social class (Modell & Goodman, 1990).

References

Alexander, C., & Langer, E. (Eds.). (1990). *Higher stages of human development: Perspectives on adult growth*. New York: Oxford University Press.

Astington, J. (1993). *The child's discovery of the mind*. Cambridge, MA: Harvard University Press.

Baltes, M. M., & Wahl, H. W. (1992). The behavior system of dependency in the elderly: Interactions with the social environment. In M. Ory, R. P. Abeles, & L. Lipman (Eds.), *Aging, health, and behavior* (pp. 83–106). Beverly Hills, CA: Sage.

Baltes, P. B. (1987). Theoretical propositions of life-span developmental psychology: On the dynamics between growth and decline. *Developmental Psychology, 23*, 611–626.

Baltes, P. B. (1993). The aging mind: Potential and limits. *Gerontologist, 33*, 580–594.

Bergson, H. (1911/1983). *Creative evolution*. New York: Henry Holt.

Berry, J. (1976). *Ecology and cultural style*. New York: Sage-Halstead.

Bok, P. (1988). *Rethinking psychological anthropology*. New York: W. H. Freeman.

Brazelton, T. B., Koslowski, B., & Main, M. (1974). The origin of reciprocity: The early mother–infant interaction. In M. Lewis & L. Rosenblum (Eds.), *The effect of the infant on its caregiver* (pp. 49–76). New York: Wiley.

Bruner, J. S. (1986). *Actual minds, possible worlds*. Cambridge, MA: Harvard University Press.

Bruner, J. S. (1990). *Acts of meaning*. Cambridge, MA: Harvard University Press.

Buchmann, M. (1989). *The script of life in modern society*. Chicago: University of Chicago Press.

Butterworth, G. (1991). The ontogeny and phylogeny of joint visual attention. In A. Whitten (Ed.), *Natural theories of mind* (pp. 223–232). Oxford: Blackwell.

Campos, J. J., & Stenberg, C. R. (1981). Perception, appraisal, and emotion: The onset of social referencing. In M. E. Lamb & L. R. Sherrod (Eds.), *Infant social cognition: Empirical and social considerations* (pp. 273–314). Hillsdale, NJ: Erlbaum.

Cole, M. (1988). Cross-cultural research in the socio-historical tradition. *Human Development, 31*, 137–151.

Cole, M. (1992). Context and modularity. In L. T. Winegar & J. Valsiner (Eds.), *Children's development in social context* (pp. 5–32). Hillsdale, NJ: Erlbaum.

Cole, M., & Cole, S. (1992). *The development of children* (2nd ed.). New York: Scientific American Books.

D'Andrade, R. (1984). Cultural meaning systems. In R. A. Shweder & R. A. LeVine (Eds.), *Culture theory: Essays on mind, self, and emotion* (pp. 88–132). New York: Cambridge University Press.

D'Andrade, R. (1986). Three scientific world views and the covering law model. In D. Fiske & R. A. Shweder (Eds.), *Meta-theory in the social sciences* (pp. 19–41). Chicago: University of Chicago Press.

D'Andrade, R. (1990). Some propositions about relations between culture and human cognition. In J. W. Stigler, R. A. Shweder, & G. Herdt (Eds.), *Cultural psychology: Essays on comparative human development* (pp. 65–129). New York: Cambridge University Press.

Dewey, J. (1938). *Experience and education*. New York: Macmillan.

Dixon, R. (1985). Contextualism and life-span developmental psychology. In R. L. Rosnow & M. Georgoudi (Eds.), *Contextualism and understanding in behavior science* (pp. 125–144). New York: Praeger.

Durkheim, E. (1915/1965). *The elementary forms of religious experience*. New York: Free Press.

Emde, R. N., Gaensbauer, T. J., & Harmon, R. J. (1976). *Emotional expression in infancy: A behavioral study. Psychological Issues Monograph Series, 10* (1, Serial No. 37). New York: International Universities Press.

Erikson, E. H. (1968). *Identity: Youth and crisis*. New York: Norton.

Featherman, D. L., & Lerner, R. M. (1985). Ontogenesis and sociogenesis: Problematics for theory and research about development and socialization across the lifespan. *American Sociological Review, 50*, 659–676.

Fischer, K., W., Kenny, S. L., & Pipp, S. L. (1990). How cognitive processes and environmental conditions organize discontinuities in the development of abstractions. In C. Alexander & E. Langer (Eds.), *Higher stages of human development: Perspectives on adult growth* (pp. 162–190). New York: Oxford University Press.

Geertz, C. (1973). *The interpretation of cultures*. New York: Basic.

Horn, J. L., & Donaldson, G. (1980). Cognitive development in adulthood. In O. G. Brim & J. Kagan (Eds.), *Constancy and change in human development* (pp. 445–529). Cambridge, MA: Harvard University Press.

Ilyenkov, E. V. (1977). The problem of the ideal. In *Philosophy in the USSR: Problems of dialectical materialism* (pp. 71–99). Moscow: Progress.

Inhelder, B., & Piaget, J. (1958). *The growth of logical thinking from childhood to adolescence*. New York: Basic.

Karmiloff-Smith, A. (1992). *Beyond modularity: A developmental perspective on cognitive science*. Cambridge, MA: MIT Press.

Katchadourian, H. (1987). *Fifty: Midlife in perspective*. New York: Freeman.

Kegan, R. (1982). *The emerging self: Problem and process in human development*. Cambridge, MA: Harvard University Press.

Kohli, M. (1986). Social organization and subjective construction of the life course. In A. B. Sørensen, F. E. Weinert, & L. R. Sherrod (Eds.), *Human development and the life course: Multidisciplinary perspectives* (pp. 271–292). Hillsdale, NJ: Erlbaum.

Kundera, M. (1988). *The art of the novel.* New York: Grove.

Labouvie-Vief, G. (1981). Proactive and reactive aspects of constructivism: Growth and aging in life-span perspective. In R. M. Lerner & N. A. Busch-Rossnagel (Eds.), *Individuals as producers of their development: A life-span perspective* (pp. 197–230). New York: Academic.

Labouvie-Vief, G. (1992). A neo-Piagetian perspective on adult cognitive development. In R. J. Sternberg & C. A. Berg (Eds.), *Intellectual development* (pp. 197–228). New York: Cambridge University Press.

Labouvie-Vief, G. (1994). *Psyche and eros: Mind and gender in the life course.* New York: Cambridge University Press.

Lawton, M. P. (1990). Residential environment and self-directedness among older people. *American Psychologist, 45,* 638–640.

Lektorsky, V. A. (1984). *Subject, object, cognition.* Moscow: Progress.

Luria, A. R. (1928). The problem of the cultural development of the child. *Journal of Genetic Psychology, 35,* 493–506.

Luria, A. R. (1979). *The making of mind.* Cambridge, MA: Harvard University Press.

Macfarlane, A. (1977).*The psychology of childbirth.* Cambridge, MA: Harvard University Press.

Martin, G. B., & Clark, R. D. (1987). Distress crying in neonates: Species and peer specificity. *Developmental Psychology, 18,* 3–9.

Modell, J., & Goodman, M. (1990). Historical perspectives. In S. S. Feldman & G. R. Elliott (Eds.), *At the threshold: The developing adolescent* (pp. 93–132). Cambridge, MA: Harvard University Press.

Nelson, K. (1981). Social cognition in a script framework. In J. H. Flavell & L. Ross (Eds.), *Social cognitive development* (pp. 97–118). Cambridge: Cambridge University Press.

Nelson, K. (1986). *Event knowledge: Structure and function in development.* Hillsdale, NJ. : Erlbaum.

Ochs, E., & Schieffelin, B. (1984). Language acquisition and socialization: Three developmental stories and their implications. In R. A. Shweder & R. A. Levine (Eds.), *Culture theory* (pp. 276–320). Cambridge: Cambridge University Press.

Pepper, S. (1942). *World hypotheses.* Berkeley: University of California Press.

Piaget, J. (1965). *The moral judgment of the child.* New York: Free Press. (Original work published 1932)

Piaget, J. (1967). *Biology and knowledge.* Chicago: University of Chicago Press.

Piaget, J. (1972). Intellectual evolution from adolescence to adulthood. *Human Development, 15,* 1–12.

Piaget, J., & Inhelder, B. (1969). *The psychology of the child.* New York: Basic.

Robson, K. S., & Moss, H. A. (1970). Patterns and determinants of maternal attachment. *Journal of Pediatrics, 77,* 976–985.

Rogoff, B. (1990). *Apprenticeship in learning.* New York: Cambridge University Press.

Rubin, J. Z., Provezano, F. J., & Luria, Z. (1974). The eye of the beholder: Parents' view on sex of newborns. *American Journal of Orthopsychiatry, 44,* 512–519.

Schegloff, E. A. (1991). Conversation analysis and socially shared cognition. In L. B. Resnick, J. M. Levine, & S. D. Teasley (Eds.), *Socially shared cognition* (pp. 150–171). Washington, DC: American Psychological Association.

Schwartz, T. (1978). The size and shape of a culture. In F. Barth (Ed.), *Scale and social organization* (pp. 215–252). Oslo: Universitetsforlaget.

Schwartz, T. (1990). The structure of national cultures. In P. Funke (Ed.), *Understanding the USA: A cross-cultural perspective* (pp. 110–149). Tubingen: Gunter Narr Verlag.

Sørensen, A., Weinert, F. E., & Sherrod, L. R. (Eds.). (1986). *Human development and the life course: Multidisciplinary perspectives.* Hillsdale, NJ: Erlbaum.

Stern, D. (1977). *The first relationship.* Cambridge, MA: Harvard University Press.

Stocking, G. (1968). *Race, culture, and evolution*. New York: Free Press.

Super, C. M., & Harkness, S. (1982). The infant's niche in rural Kenya and metropolitan America. In L. L. Adler (Ed.), *Cross-cultural research at issue* (pp. 47–55). New York: Academic.

Trevarthan, C. (1980). The foundations of intersubjectivity: Development of interpersonal and cooperative understanding in infants. In D. Olson (Ed.), *The social foundations of language and thought* (pp. 316–342). Norton: New York.

Vaillant, G. (1977). *Adaptation to life*. Boston: Little, Brown.

Valsiner, J. (1988). Ontogeny of co-construction of culture within socially organized environmental settings. In J. Valsiner (Ed.), *Child development within culturally structured environments: Vol. 2. Social co-construction and environmental guidance in development* (pp. 283–297). Norwood, NJ: Ablex.

Vygotsky, L. S. (1929). The problem of the cultural development of the child. *Journal of Genetic Psychology, 36*, 415–434.

Vygotsky, L. S. (1978). *Mind in Society*. Cambridge, MA: Harvard University Press. (Original work published 1930)

Vygotsky, L. S. (1981). The development of higher forms of attention in children. In J. V. Wertsch (Ed.), *The concept of activity in Soviet psychology* (pp. 189–240). Armonk, NY: Sharpe.

Vygotsky, L. S. (1987). Thinking and speech. In R. W. Rieber & A. S. Carton (Eds.), *The collected works of L. S. Vygotsky: Vol. 1. Problems of general psychology* (N. Minick, Trans.) (pp. 39–285). New York: Plenum. (Original work published 1934)

Wartofsky, M. (1979). *Models*. Dordrecht: D. Reidel.

Wentworth, W. M. (1980). *Context and understanding*. New York: Elsevier.

Wertsch, J. V. (1985). *Vygotsky and the social formation of mind*. Cambridge, MA: Harvard University Press.

Wertsch, J. V. (1991). *Voices of the mind*. Cambridge, MA: Harvard University Press.

White, L. (1942). On the use of tools by primates. *Journal of Comparative Psychology, 38*, 432–435.

Whiting, J. W. M., Burbank, V. K., & Ratner, M. S. (1986). The duration of maidenhood. In J. B. Lancaster and B. A. Hamburg (Eds.), *School age pregnancy and parenthood* (pp. 273–302). Hawthorne, NY: Aldine de Gruyter.

Wozniak, R. H. (1986). Notes toward a co-constructive theory of the emotion–cognition relationship. In D. J. Bearison & H. Zimiles (Eds.), *Thought and emotion: Developmental perspectives* (pp. 39–64). Hillsdale, NJ: Erlbaum.

3 Essentially social: on the origin of linguistic knowledge in the individual

Wolfgang Klein

> The mind, that ocean where each kind
> Does straight its own resemblance find.
> Yet it creates, transcending these
> Far other worlds and other seas,
> Annihilating all that's made
> To a green thought in a green shade.
> Andrew Marvell

Abstract

Ever since Hermann Paul and Wilhelm Wundt, there has been a debate on whether language should be seen as a social or an individual phenomenon. While it is clear that there are many social aspects of language – for instance, its use for communicative purposes – the dominant view among linguists as well as psychologists seems to be that linguistic knowledge is a matter of the individual mind. On the basis of arguments from language acquisition, this chapter defends an opposing view that can be condensed in a simple thesis: The individual's linguistic knowledge has both a genetic and a social source. But the former is not specific to language. Whatever is specific to language is social. In this sense, the individual's linguistic knowledge does not merely have social aspects – it is socially constituted.

Introduction

Within that chorus of mental capacities whose harmonies and dissonances constitute the human mind, language plays a primary as well as a secondary role. It is secondary because language crucially depends on the presence and functioning of other mental capacities, partly shared with other species, such as perception, memory, the capacity to develop associations, various types of reasoning, and perhaps others; in a way, language is parasitic on these capaci-

I wish to thank the participants of the conference "Interactive Minds" for a lively and useful discussion and Paul Baltes and five anonymous reviewers for very helpful comments on an earlier draft of this chapter.

ties of the mind. It is primary, first, because the language capacity is unique to the human mind. It has occasionally been claimed that other species possess the linguistic faculty as well. Bees, monkeys, and dolphins have been mentioned in this connection. But as long as this claim is put forward only by human beings and not by representatives of these species themselves, we probably need not take it too seriously. It is also primary because it is the language capacity that renders possible all "higher forms" of cognition, as well as that particular kind of interaction between members of a species, that we feel to be characteristic of human beings. We may be able to imagine a "mind" without language, but surely not a human mind without language. We may imagine a society without language, but surely not a human society. In that sense, the language capacity is not only a social phenomenon, it is an *essential social* phenomenon: What is social with humans is based on language. It is quite a different question, though, whether this capacity is an essentially social phenomenon. Is it a genetically transported gift of nature to our species that allows us to act together in a particular way, such as the capacity to walk erect or to use our 10 fingers, or does language in some way *result* from the interaction of minds? This is the question that I address in this chapter.

It is not a trivial question. Most linguists would be inclined to say that there is something deeply social in language. But first, such a view is vague, and second, not all linguists share it. Noam Chomsky, for example, probably the best-known linguist of our day, explicity denies that language's communicative and hence social function is particularly relevant to the nature of the human language capacity. It is a part of our genetic endowment, just as the hands, the liver, or the cerebellum are; and just like other parts of our genetic endowment, language may serve social functions, though it is not socially constituted. We may use our hands to hit or to caress someone; but the anatomy and physiology of the human hand is not, or at least not in an essential way, the result of hitting and caressing.

It is not a new question, either. In fact, one may say that the major ways of conceptualizing the object of linguistic investigation center around the question of whether this object is a "social phenomenon" or an "individual phenomenon." This is briefly illustrated in the following section. In the third section, I sort out several understandings of what "essentially social" means with regard to language. The fourth and main section of this chapter is devoted to the ontogenesis of language and the relative weight of social versus genetic factors in this process. The final section is devoted to some general conclusions.

An old debate

It is with a peculiar mixture of admiration and condescension that the modern linguist tends to look at what the nineteenth century achieved in the field of language studies: admiration, because a great deal of the "lexicon-proof" knowledge about the world's major languages – that knowledge which you expect in a reliable encyclopedia – we owe to the work of nineteenth-century scholars; condescension, because it is felt that the real job has still to be done – to uncover the general principles behind all of these empirical facts and findings. This attitude is not entirely false; our predecessors showed a certain preference for little facts compared with big theories, and this balance has definitely shifted. But a mere characterization of that period as the age of hunting and gathering in linguistics would not do justice to it. The title of Hermann Paul's influential *Principien der Sprachgeschichte*, one of the master-pieces of nineteenth-century linguistics, is quite telling: It was the *principles* of historical linguistics – meaning any systematic study of language – he was after, not individual facts. Paul's book first appeared in 1880, was reprinted several times, and soon was translated into English and other languages. To the fourth edition of 1909, Paul added a new preface, which starts as follows:

> In the first place, the reader will expect from this new edition a discussion of the first volume of Wundt's "Völkerpsychologie" [i.e., the volume dedicated to language]. I am sorry to say that, despite many stimulating details that this work contains, my attitude with regard to the main points cannot be but negative. . . .
>
> The opposition between Wundt and me has not so very much to do with the fact that I adopted Herbart's psychology . . . whereas Wundt relies on his own system. . . . There is a much deeper and broader gap that separates us and that cannot be bridged in any way, and this is a consequence of our respective positions toward the so-called "Völkerpsychologie."
>
> As the general title of his great work indicates, Wundt places Völker-psychologie side by side with individual psychology. . . . According to him, language change is a change in the collective mind (*Volksseele*), rather than a change in the individual mind (*Einzelseele*). The problem that for me is at the very heart of the investigation, the question of how individuals interact among each other, is no issue for Wundt. . . . I do not believe that this can lead to a full understanding of linguistic development.[1] (p. v)

What exactly is the target of this attack? This is best explained by a citation from Wundt's (1900) book – in fact, the first paragraph:

> Psychology in the usual and general meaning of this term tries to inves-tigate the facts of immediate experience, as presented to us by subjective consciousness, in their origin and their mutual relationship. In this sense, it is *individual psychology*. It completely dispenses with an analysis of those phe-nomena that result from the interaction of a multitude of individuals. Pre-cisely for this reason, it is in need of a complementary perspective which we assign to *Völkerpsychologie*. Accordingly, the task of this subdomain of psy-chology is the study of *those psychic processes on which the common develop-ment of human communities and the origin of joint mental products of general validity is based*.[2] (p. 1)

Wundt elaborates on this idea, but the basic point is perfectly clear: There is the individual mind, and it is the task of "Individualpsychologie" – psychology in the common sense of the word – to study the properties of this individual mind with the methods of experimental psychology. But there are also psychological facts beyond the realm of the individual – those phenomena that result from the mental interaction of many individual minds. These facts constitute the "collective mind" (*Volksseele*); and the "joint mental products of general validity" are, as Wundt says, primarily "language, myth, custom" (*Sprache, Mythos, Sitte*). The origin, development, and characteristic properties of, for example, the religious beliefs, scientific ideologies, moral norms, or legal systems shared by some group of people transcend the individual mind. Consequently, they cannot be adequately studied by the experimental methods of individual psychology, as initiated by Fechner and Wundt himself. The range of these methods is confined to what Wundt calls elementary processes of consciousness (*elementare Bewußtseinsprozesse*). This does not exclude particular apects of language use from being studied with experimental methods, such as articulatory processes, sound perception, or word recognition – in short, all those low-level processes that occur in the individual. But the way in which a language categorizes and encodes time and space, marks plurality or definiteness, or expresses reference to persons, objects, and events – all of this goes beyond what the individual mind does when using language in a particular situation, and hence is beyond the methods of experimental psychology, at least the methods available in Wundt's days. But it is these features that characterize language, and not the individual use made of it by a particular person on a particular occasion. Language, as Wundt understands it, is *essentially social*, and its individual side is marginal. It is not the individual mind that creates, to use the words of Andrew Marvell, "Far other worlds and seas," but the collective mind or, as one might say as well, the joint activity of many individual minds.

The linguist Hermann Paul (1880) sees no point in this notion. He explicitly states that linguistics is a part of psychology – but of individual psychology:

> [*It is a*] *fact of fundamental importance, always to be kept in mind, that all purely psychological reciprocal action exclusively occurs within the individual mind. Any interrelation among minds is indirect, mediated by physical means.* It is as it is; there can only be individual psychology, not to be paralleled by a *Völkerpsychologie*, or whatever you may call it.[3] (p. 12s)

In other words, all mental phenomena, and in particular language, are in the individual mind. There is interaction between individual minds, but this interaction is merely physical, and thus not a matter of psychology. Wundt was a psychologist. In fact, he is often considered to be the founding father of modern psychology. Paul was a linguist. But it appears to me that in modern psychological thinking, Paul's view has become the dominant one. But is he right? And how is this in modern linguistic thinking? I shall leave the first question open for the moment and return to it below.

As for the second question, twentieth-century linguistics shows a very mixed picture. This is not the place for a detailed discussion, but in a nutshell, linguistic thinking in this century has been dominated by two fundamentally different ways to conceptualize its object – language.

There is, first, the structuralist tradition, usually traced back to Ferdinand de Saussure, according to which the core object of linguistic investigation is an abstract social system, a *fait social*, the *langue*, more or less shared by the individual speaker. Language is social is beyond the individual. What is individual, is (a) the *faculté de langage*, that is, the innate capacity to learn and to use a language to some extent, and (b) the singular use made of it on a particular occasion for specific purposes (the *parole*). This tradition dominated the first half of our century and is still strong, in more or less varied forms, among many linguists.

The second tradition is the one initiated mainly by Noam Chomsky in the 1950s. In this "generative view," it is the knowledge of the individual that constitutes the core object of linguistic investigation. In an oft-quoted passage, Chomsky (1965) writes:

> Linguistic theory is concerned primarily with an ideal speaker-listener, in a completely homogeneous speech-community, who knows its language perfectly and is unaffected by such grammatically irrelevant conditions as memory limitations, distractions, shifts of attention and interest, and errors (randomly or characteristic) in applying his knowledge of the language in actual performance. (p. 3)

The object of linguistic investigation is the knowledge of the individual speaker. The question whether this knowledge serves interactive purposes or, more important, whether it comes about by interaction is not of central concern, if it is interesting at all. Note, however, that Chomsky also assumes that there is something like "the language of a community" that is perfectly reflected in the individual speaker's mind. Hence, there is a social entity called language, but only its reflex in the individual is of real interest to linguists. In later work, this position is somewhat radicalized. In Chomsky (1985) a distinction is made between "external language" and "internal language." The latter is (basically) the grammatical knowledge of the individual speaker, and the former is some ill-defined and ontologically doubtful entity, hardly accessible to serious scientific investigation. Not all authors in this tradition are that radical. In fact, most authors in either this or the structuralist tradition hardly ever take an explicit stand on this issue. Sometimes, they express some more or less ritual commitment to a particular position. But it does not really affect their concrete work. In other words, the issue is not settled, and although there may be some tilt toward the "individualistic" position, opinions among linguists differ.

In what follows, I will not try to deepen this picture, but return to the core question: Is language genuinely social, or, in Wundt's terms, does it belong to the "collective mind," or is it just a matter of the individual mind?

What is a "genuinely social entity"?

What does it mean to say that the linguistic knowledge of the individual is a social phenomenon? I think this question can be understood in at least four ways – with respect to functionality, (cultural and social) relativity, (partial) storage, and ontogenesis. These will be discussed in turn.

Functionality

Language serves social functions.[4] It allows the individual to express thoughts, feelings, and wishes, as well as to transmit these to others. It makes it possible to coordinate actions in a maximally flexible way; without language, joint human action would be reduced to the coordination principles of an anthill. It also makes it possible to create and apply systems of legislation or infinitesimal calculus, to play chess or video games, to build a Porsche 911 or the neutron bomb, to think up value-added tax and to impose it on people. In a word, language is at the very heart of all social and cultural achievements of humankind. In that sense, language is not only a social phenomenon; it is the basis of all societal behavior.

That should make the linguist proud to deal with such a distinguished subject of research. But does it also mean that language in itself is socially constituted? If we had no hands, probably all of the achievements just mentioned would be impossible, too. Nevertheless, we would not say that hands are in any significant sense "socially constituted." They are part of our genetic endowment and serve social functions. But they are not brought about by the interaction of the individual with other individuals. In much the same sense, one might argue that language is part of the individual's genetic endowment, just like memory or perception. Metaphorically speaking, language is "an organ of the brain" that permits us to behave socially and to create a culture, or cultures. But it is not brought about by interaction with other minds.

There is one crucial difference, though: Hands and feet, memory and perception are there from birth, and although their development is not entirely independent of the interaction of the individual with other individuals, this interaction seems to influence their properties only to a minimal extent. They grow naturally, and although we can intervene in this process by, for example, bandaging the feet of girls or by taking memory-training classes, they would also grow without this intervention. Language does not grow within the human mind without interaction with other minds. But this concerns the *ontogenesis* of language in the individual, a point to which we will return shortly.

Cultural and social relativity

There is not one, worldwide language, but many languages. They share a number of properties, but they also vary in some respects – from society to society, from culture to culture.[5] In fact, there is also considerable linguistic variation within a society or culture. This variation affects all aspects of linguistic knowledge, as outlined in the following subsections.

Pragmatics. Languages have very different forms of address, different ways to perform particular speech acts such as making promises, offending people, or telling stories; they have different rules of verbal politeness, and so forth.

Semantics. Languages exhibit very different ways of conceptualizing spatial and temporal relations and of encoding them by linguistic means. In the Indo-European languages, for example, each finite sentence inevitably includes a time marking that comes with the verb form, irrespective of whether the speaker wants to mark time or not; many languages encode spatial relations relative to the position of the speaker, as reflected in deictic words such as *here, there, left, right*; other languages do not have such a "deictic rooting" of spatiality, and so on.

Syntax. Depending on the language, the finite verb may be at the end of the sentence, between subject and object, or at the beginning; some languages have all possibilities. In German, it is in the second position in the main clause and in the final position in the subordinate clause. Some languages have case marking, while others don't, and those that have case marking sometimes use the same forms for all nouns; others vary from noun to noun. In English, the object is placed after the finite verb, in German before or after the verb, and in French after the verb when it is lexical and before the verb when it is an (unstressed) pronoun; and so on.

Phonology. Although the repertoire of clearly distinguishable sounds that can be produced by the articulatory organs are within a definable biological range, and although the acoustic features exploited to that purpose over all the languages in the world are quite limited, the individual use made of these possibilities varies from language to language.

Lexicon. This is perhaps the domain that exhibits the greatest range of variation. There is no word that is used in all languages of the world, with the possible exception of *Coca Cola*; but even that is pronounced differently.

All of this variation does not preclude common features – linguistic universals. But it is clear that whenever languages differ with respect to some property, this property cannot be innate: It must have been learned from the social environment during language acquisition.[6] But again, this is a matter of ontogenesis, to which we will return in a moment.

Do social and cultural variation as such show that language is socially constituted? We could imagine that due to some political or social development, all languages might die out except Chinese (or Spanish, the most expansive language these days). Then variation across languages would disappear. Would the fact that only one language was left substantially change the nature of this language? If the notion of language as socially constituted is dependent on the existence of variation, the answer should be yes. But even then, it cannot be innate that a book should be called *shu*, or that perfectivity has to be marked by adding the particle *le* to the nonfinite verb. All of these properties have to be learned from the social environment, and hence by social interaction. In other words, although the social and cultural variation that we observe across languages could be accidental and hence not constitutive for the nature of language, the social interaction that typically, though perhaps not necessarily, leads to this variation, again, is not. But this is a matter of the ontogenesis of language.

Partial storage

One problem with Wundt's notion of the collective mind and its possible emanations is their doubtful ontological status. Where is the collective mind, if not in the brain of the individual? Where is language, if not in the heads of those who are able to speak and understand it? Exactly this problem was one of Paul's major concerns, and this concern equally applies to the Saussurian notion of *langue* in the sense of a *fait social*, the core notion of structural linguistics. What we have, what we can put our hands on, is the *linguistic knowledge of the individual speaker*, as stored in the speaker's brain cells. Exactly this is what is meant by the Chomskyan notion of *linguistic competence*. Chomsky and his followers do not say that linguistic competence is part of the brain: It is a mental, not a physical, entity. When you look into the individual speaker's brain, you cannot see language. But somehow it must be stored there, and it is the only place where it is stored. The linguist's major tasks are to study the nature of this knowledge, the principles that govern it, and the way in which it gets to where it is stored.

Wundt and Saussure were well aware of the somewhat dubious ontological status of their notions, as well of the empirical problems in investigating them. Their point was simply that there is a difference between language, on the one hand, and whatever a particular speaker knows of it, on the other. Equating these two things would have been as absurd to them as equating algebraic topology with what a particular person knows about it. Although there is no place where algebraic topology is to be found except in the minds of people who think about it, no one would confuse the study of algebraic topology with the study of what some particular person at some particular time knows about it. No individual speaker knows the English language in its entirety. All entries in *Webster's* belong to the English language. There is no one on earth who knows all of them. The same point can be easily made for syntactic constructions, as well as for pragmatic knowledge about the use of English in specific communicative situations. What we find in the individual speaker's mind is not the English language but that particular knowledge of the English language that the individual in question happens to have learned and has stored there. This knowledge is always selective, and the storage in the brain is always partial. Hence, it makes perfect sense to distinguish clearly between the individual's linguistic knowledge, or linguistic competence, on the one hand, and language itself, on the other. That both normally do not collapse is not a matter of philosophy; it is simply an empirical fact. In one word, language *transcends* the individual mind; it belongs to the "collective mind," and in this sense, it seems "genuinely social."

But is the empirical fact that the individual's knowledge of language is only partial in any way constitutive of what we understand by language? We could easily imagine that one of the many languages in New Guinea is spoken by only a few speakers whose knowledge is more or less the same, or even entirely the same. Would we then say that, under these particular circumstances, language is no longer essentially social but simply a matter of the individual mind? Probably not. It seems therefore that, on the one hand, we must clearly distinguish between language itself and whatever the individual knows about it, but, on the other hand, the mere fact that this knowledge is normally selective and incomplete is not the defining criterion for the social constituency of language. Chomsky's notion of the "ideal speaker-hearer who lives in a homogeneous speech community and knows its language perfectly well" is an idealization and as such as unrealistic as any idealization. But unless one is interested in those particular aspects of language from which it explicitly abstracts away, I do not think that it does not do justice to the explicandum of linguistics.

Summing up the discussion so far, I believe that factors such as the functionality of language, its usual cultural and social variation, as well as the normal discrepancy between language and what an individual speaker knows about it, constitute important social dimensions of language. But I am not convinced that they are constitutive for that particular faculty which distinguishes our mind – or our minds – from that of all other species. This leaves us with one last factor – the way in which linguistic knowledge comes about.

Ontogenesis

We do not know how humankind came to language, or language to humankind. The issue excited and still excites so much speculation that I will here obey article 2 of the Societé linguistique de Paris, which, when it was founded in 1866, explicitly forbade any discussion of this question. Let us suppose, therefore, that at least one language exists already, English, and that it is partially stored in the minds of its speakers. How did this knowledge in an individual speaker, say Queen Elizabeth, come about? First, there must be a biological component in the ontogenesis of language. Queen Elizabeth's horses did not learn English, although they may have heard almost as much as she did. Second, there must also be some external stimulus from the social environment. Even a member of the royal family would not learn English if locked in a room from birth, without any verbal contact with human society. But this fact as such is perhaps not too revealing. A child raised in complete darkness from birth could never learn to see; similarly, a child who gets no speech input could never learn a language. In much the same way as it would seem strange to say that the characteristics of the human visual system – compared with those of the fly, for example – are derived from what catches the child's eye, it would be strange to assume – one might argue – that linguistic knowledge derives from the verbal behavior of the child's social environment. The relative weight of innate and environmental factors in the ontogenesis of linguistic knowledge needs some more detailed examination, to which we turn in the next section.

Biological and social sources of linguistic knowledge in the individual

The thesis

To Herodotos, we owe the story of the Egyptian king Psammetikh, who wanted to know what the mother tongue of humankind was. To that end, he let some children grow up without any verbal contact, and since the first recognizable production of one of the children resembled the Phrygian word for bread, *bekos*, it was decided that Phrygian was the first human language.

The experiment had a clear design, a clear hypothesis, and a clear outcome. It met all standards of scientific experimentation. It was also clearly asocial, and this for two reasons – first, because of the way in which the children were treated and, second, because of the way in which Psammetikh, or his linguistic advisers, thought about the ontogenesis of linguistic knowledge: It is entirely innate, and what is innate is not some universal feature of language but one full language – humankind's first and initial language. If there is any *social* component in the ontogenesis of language, then its only role is to distort what was originally there. In one sentence, linguistic knowledge need not be acquired; it is there at birth.

Two and a half thousand years later,[7] no one would want to repeat, or at least would not dare to repeat, Psammetikh's experiment, and no one would believe that one full language, not even English, is there at birth. Still, the notion remains that the individual's linguistic competence is predominantly innate, and that the role of social factors – the relative share of the linguistic environment in which the child grows up in his or her eventual linguistic knowledge – is a comparatively minor one. I believe this view is false. More precisely, I would like to defend the following radical hypothesis: The individual's linguistic knowledge has a genetic as well as a social source. But the former is not specific to language; whatever is specific to language is social.

One problem with this thesis is that the term *social* is not entirely clear. In the next section, I will explain what I have in mind.

Genetic and experiential transmission of knowledge

Nature has provided us with two ways to transmit information – by means of the genetic code, and whatever is perceived by our sensory organs and further processed by the brain. I shall call the former genetic transmission and the latter experiential transmission. Genetic transmission is a relatively stable process, robust, and with limited possibilities of variation. We know of no way in which acquired information could be genetically transmitted. Experiential transmission is less robust, but much more flexible. In particular, it allows one to transfer information gained from experience to some other individual, and thus to increase the amount of knowledge available to oneself, as well as to the collective mind – if there is a collective mind. All of this is not new, but it should be kept in mind in what follows.

The use of a language in a particular social situation is the most important way to transmit information from the mind of one individual to the minds of other. In fact, this is nothing but a somewhat circuitous way of saying that minds interact with each other. So far, we have talked only about the experiential transmission of some information of whatever sort *by means of language*. But how is the individual's linguistic knowledge itself transmitted – genetically or experientially? I can now restate my general thesis as follows: Both the genetic and the experiential transmission of information play a role in the ontogenesis of the individual's linguistic knowledge; but whatever is specific to linguistic knowledge comes from other minds via experiential transmission.

This hypothesis is at variance with what many linguists believe. Given the present state of knowledge on the ontogenesis of language, it can be neither proved nor refuted at this point. Still, there are some arguments in favor of it, to which I will now turn.

What determines language acquisition?

We all have acquired a language during the first years of our life – our first language. Most of us have learned another language as well. This may have happened in various ways, and the transitions between these ways are gradual. There are children who are exposed to more than one language right from the beginning; others start to learn a second language with a delay of some years, while the first language is still being acquired; in still other cases, the acquisition of a second – or even a third or fourth – language begins when the acquisition of the first language is completed, which is normally the case during puberty, perhaps earlier. In this latter case, the second language is most often learned by explicit teaching in the classroom, which usually does not lead to perfect mastery, in contrast to the acquisition of the first language and early acquisition of the second language, both normally learned "in the natural way," that is, by everyday exposure to speakers of the language to be learned. In short, there is not *one* way to gain linguistic knowledge but many, and if we want to understand the ontogenesis of linguistic knowledge, this variability has to be taken into account. In each of these cases, the acquisition of a language is a very complex process that in the case of both child and adult extends over many years and whose course and final outcome depend on a number of interacting factors. In any event, however, there are three major components that are necessarily present.

First, the learner must have a particular *language learning capacity*, which is part of his or her genetically transmitted endowment – the species-specific *language faculty*. In psycholinguistics, it is common to call this faculty of our brain the *language processor*, a term that I will use here. The language learning capacity is nothing but the language processor in its application on new material.

Second, the learner must have *access* to this new material, that is, to utterances from the language to be learned. In the beginning, all this material is new to the learner; after a while, he or she already has some knowledge of the language to be learned and can use this knowledge to process new material. In other words, the learning process is an accumulating one; it increases linguistic knowledge by exploiting linguistic knowledge, and this partly explains why this process usually takes that long.

Third, the learner must have a reason, a *motivation*, to apply his or her language processor to the new material. This motivation can vary widely. The motive to learn the first language is probably the need of social integration – "Become a member of that society in which you have to live." The motive for acquiring a second language may also be the need for social integration; but more often, it is simply the wish to make oneself understood for limited purposes, or – in the classroom – the need or wish to please one's parents with good marks. Although the various types of motivation are in many ways crucial for the course and especially the final result of the acquisition process, I will not consider them here. Moreover, I will only concentrate on language acquisition outside the classroom, that is, on the acquisition of linguistic knowledge by interaction with the social environment, since this is the point in which we are interested here.

This leaves us with two essential components – the language processor, on the one hand, and the input from the social environment, on the other. Both crucially contribute to the way in which linguistic knowledge is built up in the individual. A simple picture would now be to say that whatever the former contributes is genetically transmitted, and whatever the latter contributes is experientially transmitted. In fact, the situation is somewhat more complex. To show this, we must have a somewhat closer look at these two components.

Language processor. The way in which the language processor works at some particular time depends on two factors: biological determinants and the knowledge already available at that point in time.

Biological determinants include, first, several *peripheral organs*, notably the entire articulatory apparatus from the larynx to the lips, and second, the entire auditory apparatus (for simplicity's sake, I ignore written language here, whose acquisition is usually a derived process, anyway). Second, they include some parts of *central processing in the cortex*, such as memory, higher-level aspects of perception, and some parts of cognition. I shall try to sort out what precisely these latter aspects of cognition are and in what way they interact. It is open to what extent particular aspects of reasoning, for instance, are indispensable for the acquisition and use of linguistic knowledge; the fact that, for example, children with specific brain impairments can learn language shows that there is some independence, but it is unclear how far this independence goes. What is more important is the possibility that, as has been claimed by some authors, there might be a specific "language module" in the human brain – a part of the cortex that is responsible only for language, or some parts of language. This is the Chomskyan position that considers language to be something like a "mental organ" that interacts with, but is in principle independent of, other higher cognitive faculties. We shall return to this point later.

Both peripheral and central biological determinants, as well as their interaction, are innate; whatever they contribute to language, it is genetically transmitted information. Both also change in the course of life, and this is probably a major reason for the normally lower success of adults who try to learn a new language (although surely not the only reason). As with most biological determinants in the human body, the ones necessary for language can be trained to some extent, and in this indirect way social factors may affect them. But for present purposes, we may simply say that they constitute the "genetic contribution to the linguistic knowledge in the individual."

The biological determinants set, as it were, the frame within which the process of language acquisition may occur. This process is not instantaneous; it extends over many years, and during this time, the knowledge available to the learner constantly changes. This knowledge includes minimally[8] two major components that are relevant.

The first is the learner's *world knowledge* at a given point in time that allows him or her to break down the more or less continuous stream of sound that emanates from the social environment and hits the ears, to isolate bits and pieces of it, and to give meaning to these.

The second is the learner's *language-specific knowledge* of the language to be learned, the acquisitional process always being stepwise: Once you have learned some bits and pieces, you are able to access further parts of the input; for example, without having learned some phonological distinctions, it is impossible to approach some aspects of morphology. Hence, the entire process is an accumulative one: Linguistic knowledge is increased by using linguistic knowledge, up to a point where nothing new can be detected in the input.

This point is particularly important. The language processor itself is not just a biological component of our cortex, whose function is determined by genetically transmitted information. This is only the case at the initial point where the learner has not been exposed to any input as yet. At any later point, the language processor itself is changed by permanent interaction with the input, hence with experientially transmitted information. What is this latter information?

Input. How does the learner get access to the language of his or her social environment? If we exclude language learning in the classroom, in which the learner is often not directly faced with language itself, but rather with a more or less appropriate description of it, then the primary input is the physical speech signal – sound waves hitting the eardrums, which should make some sense. For the learner, this stream of noises is not yet segmented into phonemes, morphemes, words, sentences. In fact, this is the first task that has to be solved, and if there were only sound waves as input, this task would be insoluble. Suppose someone locked you into a room and played Inuktitit to you, for days, weeks, even years – you would not learn it, any more than you would be able to learn Chinese just by regularly listening to shortwave radio programs in Chinese. The creation of linguistic knowledge in the speaker's mind requires a second type of input – all the accompanying information, gestures, actions, and the entire situational context that eventually allows the speaker to break down the sound stream into smaller entities and to give them a meaningful interpretation. In other words, the input actually consists of two connected sources of information – the *sound stream* and the entire *parallel information*. Both of these are experientially transmitted – information that stems from other speaking and acting minds. Without those two types of experiental information, and without the learner's interpretive processes that brings them together, no acquisition of a particular language is possible.

I believe what has been said so far is fairly obvious, at least at the level of generality at which it has been discussed. Obvious, too, are the consequences to be drawn for our general hypothesis. First, whatever a speaker knows about a particular language stems from his or her interpretation of the sound stream produced by other people *and* the actions that go with this production of sounds. The input is not just a sort of trigger for a biological process – it is meaningful actions in social context. Second, only at the initial stage is the individual's language processor exclusively based on genetically transmitted information. Then the language processor itself changes due to whatever has been processed from experientially transmitted information.

Taken together, both conclusions would clearly justify the claim that the ontogenesis of linguistic knowledge in the individual is indeed socially consti-tuted, and in that sense, linguistic knowledge is *essentially social*. There are two possible objections. First, one might argue that a substantial part of the indi-vidual's linguistic knowledge is not acquired at all, and hence does not have to be acquired. Second, it is an empirical issue to what extent the function of the language processor is indeed accumulative, that is, a stepwise analysis of the input. I will briefly address these two objections in the following section.

Problems

To what extent is the mind's learning capacity itself affected by the learning process? Clearly, there are some purely biological prerequisites. Without memory, language learning would be difficult, as it would be without the capacity for sensory perception. All of these capacities are not specific to language, however. Moreover, as was argued earlier, these biological determi-nants do not suffice, except to start with. Further processing systematically exploits the knowledge that is available after a while due to prior steps in acquisition. The fact that this knowledge is crucial is best illustrated by an example.

One of the most salient rules of German syntax – in fact, the basis of German word order regularities – concerns the position of the finite verb. The finite verb consists of two components – a lexical component and the finite component proper. These may be separated into two word forms, as in *hat gegessen*, where *hat* is the finite component and *gegessen* the lexical compo-nent; it may also be projected into one word, as in the more or less synony-mous *aß*.[9] The basic rules of German say that the lexical component is regularly sentence-final, whereas the finite component changes its position according to sentence type: It is in the second position in declarative main clauses, in the initial position in yes–no questions and imperatives, and in the final position (even after the lexical verb) in subordinate clauses. If both components are fused to one form, such that the positional constraints are at variance, it is the finite component that wins. Almost everything in German word order is based on these regularities; if they are not learned, there is little chance to learn German syntax. This is different in English, in fact, in all languages; hence, these regularities cannot be innate knowledge and must be learned from input analysis. To achieve this, the learner must be able to identify what the finite component of the verb is. The only way to identify this component is by its inflectional morphology. Hence, the learner must first know the German verb morphology – not necessarily the complete paradigm, but enough to identify the finite verb. In contrast with English, this task is not precisely what one would call easy. (Mark Twain's famous remarks about German highlight the point.) In particular, German finite verbs – as well as uninflected words – can end in extremely complex consonant clusters, for example *-ltst* (as in *hältst* or *schmilzt*) or *-rgst* (as in *wügst* or *verbirgst*). Sometimes even a well-educated German has problems identifying a finite verb form as such (e.g., *wüscht*). Decomposing such a consonant cluster is an extremely difficult phonological problem for both first and second language learners. But if the necessary phonological knowledge is not available, the morphological problem cannot be solved, and as a consequence, the fundamental rule of German word order cannot be acquired.

I do not think, incidentally, that this *essentially accumulative nature of learning* is peculiar to the acquisition of linguistic knowledge. Very often, our capacity to learn something simply depends on previous knowledge, and the highly normal, natural, and automatic acquisition of linguistic knowledge in the individual is only a special and particularly complex instance of this general principle – with the peculiarity that the information so processed comes from "other minds."

Whatever is acquired is acquired with step-by-step analysis of the sound stream and parallel information, and this is not accidental. But is it really necessary that all components in the mature speaker's linguistic knowledge be acquired? It could well be that part of the speaker's linguistic knowledge is there right from the beginning.

This is indeed the key assumption of acquisition researchers who work in the "generative paradigm." It leads to an interesting, because simple, theory of language acquisition. Basic parts of the structure are right there, and only some open slots, so to speak, must be filled by input analysis. This general idea has been worked out in some detail in the so-called parameter-setting approach. It basically says (I will not go into any detail here; see, e.g., Weissenborn, Goodluck, & Roeper, 1992) that there is a "peripheral part" of linguistic knowledge, which has to be learned by input analysis, and a "core part," which is universal, genetically transmitted, but contains at birth some "open parameters" with a limited number of options. All the child has to do is to choose one of the options, and this is done based on specific cues from the input.

Researchers in this framework do not agree on what these parameters are, and so it is difficult to evaluate the empirical merit of this idea. But independent of that problem, it is beyond dispute that only those components of linguistic knowledge can be genetically transmitted that are common to *all* languages. No one is born to learn Tagalog or Twi; every newborn can learn any language. Hence, whatever distinguishes Latin from Chinese, for example, must be experientially transmitted. This includes:

1. the entire vocabulary,
2. the entire morphology,
3. the entire syntax to the extent to which it is covered in descriptive grammars, and
4. most (if not all) of phonology

– in a word, practically everything. This does not necessarily exclude the possibility that, on some abstract level, there are also some universal properties. But if this is the case, then it remains to be shown that these universal properties go in any way beyond the constraints on perception, memory, pattern processing, and higher functions of cognition that are characteristic of the human mind in general.

At this point, the empirical evidence is too weak to settle this issue. Personally, I believe that it is possible to find such universal constraints on what constitutes general linguistic knowledge. But I see little reason to believe that these constraints go in any way beyond general, not field-specific constraints of the human mind. Until evidence to the contrary is given, however, a theory that operates with only general constraints on the human mind rather than with a specific "language module," characterized by independent mental principles, makes the more powerful generalizations, and is therefore preferable – until evidence to the opposite is given.

Conclusion

The core conclusion is straightforward: Linguistic knowledge of the individual requires a genetic disposition; only the human mind is apt to learn language. Whatever linguistic knowledge the speaker eventually has stored in his or her brain is experientially transmitted; it is information that stems from other minds – sound waves emitted by them in connection with actions performed by them. There is no factual evidence whatsoever that components of linguistic knowledge in the individual are genetically transmitted – above and beyond general constraints on the structure and functioning of the human mind. Linguistic knowledge is essentially *social*. It is *essentially* social. It is brought about by the interaction of the individual mind with other minds. This view has not really been proved. It could still be falsified. But given what we presently know about language and the human mind, it is by far the simplest view compatible with the facts.

In the introduction, it was pointed out that language is in two ways unique among the capacities of the human mind: First, no other species has it, and second, it is what renders possible all "higher forms" of cognition, as well as that particular kind of interaction among members of a species that we feel to be characteristic of human beings. What does this picture of language imply for what we understand by "specifically human cognition" and "specifically human interaction"? The idea of language being essentially social does not mean that there is no "biological component" in language. After all, no other species has it. It rather means that the human mind has a fairly general, genetically transmitted disposition on which the interaction with other minds superimposes a very specific structure, the individual's linguistic knowledge. Once brought about as a *product* of such a process, language becomes a *means* – the essential means – of transmitting information from other minds to whatever is in the individual mind at birth. Let me briefly illustrate this with two examples.

The first concerns one of the fundamental categories of human cognition – space. The way in which the human mind conceptualizes space partly depends on our genetic endowment – our capacity to see, hear, and experience, on the one hand, and the capacity to remember what we have seen, heard, and experienced in previous actions, on the other. Human space, to the extent to which it is biologically constituted, is roughly characterized by three essential features:

1. It consists of smaller entities (subspaces, places), for which a twofold structure is defined:
2. a topological structure such that places can be contained in other places, in the environment of other places, or be adjacent to other places;
3. an order structure such that places are ordered with respect to each other in three dimensions – vertical, transverse, and horizontal.

There is good reason to assume that all human beings share these properties of space. But the way in which, for example, the average European conceptualizes space goes far beyond this. For example, we *define* the three dimensions as "up–down," "front–back," "left–right" by projecting our body asymmetries on them: Up is where the head (normally) is, and down is where the feet (normally) are; front is where we look to, and back is the opposite direction; left is where most people have their weak hand, and right is the opposite direction (or in whatever other way this body asymmetry is defined). Such a superimposed structure is culture-specific. It must be learned from other people in the social environment; other cultures impose very different structures on the "biological space" (see, e.g., Klein, 1994; Levinson, 1993). Similarly, culture-specific knowledge may allow us to introduce a *metric* into the basic space – a systematic way of indicating distances between places, and so on. We will not follow this up here – the basic point should be clear: The way in which the human mind conceptualizes space has a universal component, shared by all normal members of our species due to genetically transmitted properties of our body and our mind. It also has a culture-specific component, brought about by the experiential transmission of information from one mind to the other. The main instrument of this transmission is language, in itself brought into the individual's head by experiential transmission.

The second example concerns a peculiarity of human interaction. Animals kill other animals, but rarely beyond the immediate need for survival. Sometimes, they even kill members of their own species. But again, when it happens, it is usually for quite evident biological reasons, such as survival of the individual, the "individual's genes," or sometimes the immediate social community. This is also found among humans, and the extent as well as the way in which it is evaluated varies from culture to culture. But we do more. One peculiarity of human interaction is the fact that we kill each other systematically, far beyond immediate biological need. The reason is normally a strong belief system – nationalism, religion, some kind of ideology. The convictions that constitute these belief systems are not genetically transmitted – they are brought about by intensive interaction between minds. Probably, these belief systems could not be created by human minds and transmitted to other human minds if they were not linked to genetic components of our brain. But they far exceed our "biological nature." Our genes may tell us to survive, but they do not tell us to die and to kill in this world in order to survive in another. They tell us to defend our progeny, but they do not tell us to defend our faith or our flag and to kill those who have a different faith or flag. Murder may be biological; mass murder is always social.

The particular form and the relative weight of the universal, genetically transmitted components of the human mind, on the one hand, and the more specific experientially transmitted additional structures brought about by the interaction between minds, on the other, may vary considerably across different aspects of human cognition and human behavior, and so do the opinions of researchers in this area. Since Darwin published *The Descent of Man* in 1871, the balance on the average seems to have gone toward the former, the biological component. I think the case of language, and maybe also the two examples given earlier, illustrate that a great deal in the mind of the individual is genetically transmitted but is shaped even more by the interaction among minds.

Notes

1 "Von der neuen Auflage wird man vor allem eine Auseinandersetzung mit dem ersten Bande von Wundts Völkerpsychologie (Leipzig 1900, ²1904) erwarten. Leider kann ich mich diesem Werke gegenüber, so viele Anregungen es auch im einzelnen bringt, doch in den Hauptpunkten nur ablehnend verhalten. . . .

"Der Gegensatz zwischen Wundt und mir beruht nicht so sehr darauf, daß ich mich an die Psychologie Herbarts angelehnt habe . . . während Wundt sein eigenes System zugrunde legt . . . eine viel tiefere und breitere Kluft trennt uns, die sich auf keine Weise überbrücken lässt, in Folge der beiderseitigen Stellung zur sogenannten Völkerpsychologie.

"Wundt stellt, wie schon der Gesamttitel seines grossen Werkes zeigt, die Völkerpsychologie neben die Individualpsychologie. . . . Die Veränderungen der Sprache erfolgen nach ihm durch Veränderungen in der Volksseele, nicht durch solche in den Einzelseelen. Das Problem, welches für mich im Mittelpunkt der Untersuchung steht, die Frage, wie sich die Wechselwirkung der Individuen untereinander vollzieht, ist für Wundt überhaupt kein Problem. . . . Auf diese Weise kann meiner Überzeugung nach kein volles Verständnis der Sprachentwicklung gewonnen werden."

2 It should be stressed that this translation is very approximate and misses a great deal of the original flavor; a more accurate translation would require many comments on the choice of terms.

The original passage is as follows: "Die Psychologie in der gewöhnlichen und allgemeinen Bedeutung dieses Wortes sucht die Tatsachen der unmittelbaren Erfahrung, wie sie das subjektive Bewußtsein uns darbietet, in ihrer Entstehung und in ihrem wechselseitigen Zusammenhang zu erforschen. In diesem Sinn ist sie *Individualpsychologie*. Sie verzichtet durchgängig auf eine Analyse jener Erscheinungen, die aus der geistigen Wechselwirkung einer Vielheit von Einzelnen hervorgehen. Eben deshalb aber bedarf sie einer ergänzenden Betrachtung, die wir der *Völkerpsychologie* zuweisen. Demnach besteht die Aufgabe dieses Teilgebiets der Psychologie in der Untersuchung *derjenigen psychischen Vorgänge, die der allgemeinen Entwicklung menschlicher Gemeinschaften und der Entstehung gemeinsamer geistiger Erzeugnisse von allgemeingültigem Wert zugrundeliegen*" (italic phrases spaced in original).

3 "[Es ist eine] *Tatsache von fundamentaler Bedeutung, die wir niemals aus dem Auge verlieren dürfen, daß alle rein psychische Wechselwirkung sich nur innerhalb der Einzelseele vollzieht. Aller Verkehr der Seelen untereinander ist nur ein indirekter, auf physischem Wege vermittelter.* Es bleibt also dabei, es kann nur eine individuelle Psychologie geben, der man keine Völkerpsychologie oder wie man es sonst nennen mag gegenüber stellen darf" (italic phrases spaced in original).

4 The literature on the social functions of human language is vast, and what can be done here is merely to allude to some of these functions. Clark (1992), for example, gives a good impression of this dimension of language.

5 The study of the culture-specific variability of language has a long tradition in linguistics, represented by names such as Humboldt, Sapir, and Whorff. Gipper (1972) gives a good survey of this work. A representative recent investigation in this tradition is Lucy (1992).

6 This does not mean, of course, that biological processes of reproduction exclude variation. In fact, Darwinism is based on this notion. What I mean is simply that language-specific properties, such as those mentioned earlier, cannot be innate: It cannot be innate that a rose is called "rose," that the determiner follows the noun, or that unvoiced stops are aspirated.

7 Despite these ethical obstacles to empirical research, the investigation of language acquisition has made some progress within this time. Slobin (1986–1991) gives an excellent survey of empirical and theoretical issues.

8 I say "minimally" because in second language acquisition, there is another type of available knowledge that influences the way in which the learner approaches the input – that is, first language knowledge. The new language is perceived in the light of old knowledge, and this leads to the various kinds of (positive and negative) transfer in second language acquisition.

9 In English, the situation is very similar with *has eaten* and *ate*, except that the word order rules are quite different. Therefore, I have chosen the German examples.

References

Chomsky, N. (1965). *Aspects of the theory of syntax*. Cambridge, MA: MIT Press.

Chomsky, N. (1985). *Knowledge of language*. New York: Praeger.

Clark H. (1992). *Arenas of language.* Chicago: University of Chicago Press.

Gipper, H. (1972). *Gibt es ein sprachliches Relativitätsprinzip?* [Is there a linguistic relativity principle?]. Untersuchungen zur Sapir-Whorf-Hypothese [Studies on the Sapir-Whorf hypothesis]. Frankfurt (Main): Fischer.

Klein, W. (1994). Keine Känguruhs zur Linken. Über die Variabilität von Raumvorstellungen und ihren Gebrauch in der Sprache [No Kangaroos to the left: On the variability of spatial concepts and their use in language]. In H.-J. Kornadt, J. Grabowski, & R. Mangold-Allwinn (Eds.), *Sprache und Kognition* [Language and cognition] (pp. 163–182). Heidelberg: Spectrum.

Levinson, S. (1993). *Language and cognition: The cognitive consequences of spatial description in*

Guughu Yimidhirr. Unpublished manuscript, Forschungsgruppe Kognitive Anthropologie (Research group cognitive anthropology), Max Planck Institute of Psycholinguistics, Nijmegen.

Lucy, J. (1992). *Language diversity and thought: A reformulation of the linguistic relativity hypothesis*. Cambridge: Cambridge University Press.

Paul, H. (1880). *Principien der Sprachgeschichte* [Principles of historical linguistics] (4th ed., 1909). Halle: Niemeyer.

Slobin, D. (1986–1991). *The cross-linguistic study of language acquisition* (Vols. 1–3). Hillsdale, NJ: Erlbaum.

Weissenborn, J., Goodluck, H., & Roeper, T. (Eds.). (1992). *Theoretical issues in language acquisition*. Hillsdale, NJ: Erlbaum.

Wundt, W. (1900). *Die Sprache* [Language] (2 vols., 2nd ed. 1904). Leipzig: Engelmann.

4 Knowledge and the construction of women's development

Gisela Labouvie-Vief

Abstract

This chapter suggests that interactive minds can be studied at several levels of analysis, which all are embedded and interrelated. Collective representations of the mind are translated into internalized models and self-structures that are regulated and maintained through specific patterns of interaction – and these, again, support specific mental models. The relationship between mind and gender as it has been historically construed and as it is being transformed in contemporary thought as well as in the lives of contemporary research participants is used as an illustration. Specifically, the traditional dualistic model of the mind is shown to imply a specific view of hierarchical and competitive relationships that are encoded by symbolizing some dimensions of the mind as "masculine," others as "feminine." These encodings further engender specific social processes within which individuals acquire identities veering toward either the masculine or the feminine pole. How these encodings are negotiated and sometimes transcended in individual development is demonstrated via an empirical review of literature on gender differences in achievement and achievement-related feelings, as well as coping and defense processes.

Recent reformulations of theories of the mind, as well as the selves who embody this mind, are introducing a new metaphor of how two polarities of mind and self are to relate. If the old metaphor is based on a dualistic opposition of subject and object, mind and body, or reason and emotions, the newly emerging metaphor, in contrast, is that of a mutually enriching dialectic among separate but complementary aspects. Central to both of these models is the question of how to organize two modes of thinking and ways of speaking: a definitional language of logos in which reality is cast in terms of agreed-upon decontextualized and objective principles, and an organismic language in which experience is inherently tied to subjective time-, context-, and person-bound feelings (see Bruner, 1986; Epstein, 1990; Labouvie-Vief, 1994).

The emergence of such a new language of relationship is itself a dialectical process. On the one hand, it depends on the availability of broad collective representations or epistemes (Foucault, 1975) that form embedding structures

109

or templates for individual representations of the nature of knowledge. On the other hand, such epistemes also offer the starting point for critique and transformation in the course of individual development. That adulthood is the locus of such transformative processes is a cornerstone of many views of adult development (e.g., Dabrowski, 1970; Kegan, 1982; Kohlberg, 1984; Labouvie-Vief, 1994; Loevinger, 1993).

In my own work (e.g., Labouvie-Vief, 1982, 1990, 1994), I have suggested that the ability to engage in such transformation hinges on the degree to which the individual is able to reunite the duality of languages of mind and self. Following our public ways of speaking, these languages become dualistically and oppositionally structured in early development when the individual is concerned with acquiring mastery of the rules and symbol systems of a culture. At this juncture of the life span, knowledge comes to be understood as certain and structured by outer, objective processes. But in later life, many individuals discover – as have many contemporary philosophers – that so-called objective knowledge structures already embody a language of subjective processes that, though hidden from conscious view, has exerted a powerful influence. Out of this recognition the unique opportunity arises of reintegrating these languages of objective knowledge and subjective desire as they are allowed to engage in a dialectical interchange.

I suggest that such reformulations entail complex, multilevel ramifications as to the interaction of minds. First, dualistic models of the mind imply a view of how different components of the mind interact. Since that interaction is framed in terms of opposition and conflict among different mental faculties or structures, dualistic models thus encode competitive and hierarchical relationships between different aspects of mind and self *within any one person*. Second, these codes are not merely intrapersonal, but also mirror interpersonal modes of interaction that are also derived from the model of hierarchy and competition. Thus, they point beyond intrapersonal processes to more *collective representations* of which intrapersonal models are an internalized version. Finally, I suggest that such representations are specifically maintained by *interpersonal interactions* of which they are a mirror: They are based on implicit visions of an interpersonal world in which some individuals *possess* more desirable qualities of mind and self (such as agency, logic, and rational control), while others are attributed the less desirable qualities (such as being at the mercy of context and desire). Thus, who is said to possess more or less desirable aspects of the mind is regulated through systems of prescriptions of which our models of the mind ultimately are a particularly sophisticated codification.

To discuss the interweaving of these multiple meanings of the concept of interaction and mind, I review theory and research relating to mind and gender. The gendering of the mind, and the attributions of mental processes it generates, offers a particularly rich arena to discuss interacting minds, because the interweaving of internalized and private models, public discourses, and social regulative processes is extremely pervasive and richly documented in many cultures (see Labouvie-Vief, 1994). The discussion of this interweaving is structured around two major sections. In the first section, I begin with a historical and philosophical overview showing that the concept of a divided mind has always encoded specific forms of interaction. These interactions were modeled after hierarchical power and gender relations and incorporated such relations by symbolizing some faculties as *masculine*, others as *feminine*. While at first, such gendering was not related to the forms of social interaction that engendered it, more recent discussions have made this dialectic more explicit. As a result, modern theories of mind and self are gradually explicating the dynamic between collective models, social constraints, and intraindividual representations.

While the first section of the chapter is primarily theoretical in focus, the second section is empirical and reviews research to suggest that the divided model of the mind is related to two prototypical, masculine and feminine forms of development as reflected in gender differences in achievement, achievement-related feelings, and coping strategies. The chapter concludes with the suggestion that changing concepts of the nature of the mind are intricately interwoven with changing concepts of gender and gender relationships.

Models of mind as models of interaction

Self as subject, other as object

The notion that the mind is to be arranged along a polarity of processes or functions has a long and distinguished history. It is so broad as to cut across virtually all of our cultural heritage; indeed, it may well constitute an extremely pervasive aspect of the thought, myth, ritual, and symbolic life of many cultures (e.g., Labouvie-Vief, 1994; Neumann, 1954; Ortner, 1974). It suggests that there are two distinct ways or modes in which we talk about and experience reality (see Bruner, 1986; Epstein, 1990). In one of those modes, we approach reality in a definitional, objective way in which what is real depends on agreed-upon, collectively standardized frameworks or systems of knowledge. In the other mode, in contrast, what we experience as real is based on an inner reality of imagination, intention, subjective experience, and psychological causality. As a consequence, reality is divided into the realm of the immanent and embodied (earth, body, temporal and sensuous processes), on the one hand, and the transcendent and eternal (mind and spirit, sky and heaven, universal and timeless processes), on the other.

While there is much agreement that the mind is best represented as some combination of these two polarities, there has been much debate over how this relationship is to be described. Since the two modes of knowing often appear to partake in a paradoxical and antagonistic relationship (see Hofstadter, 1980; Labouvie-Vief, 1994), theories have often viewed the two within a competitive model rather than a cooperative one. In those views, it was a primary aspect of mature mental functioning that it could exert rational control over unruly instincts. Occasionally, as in the romantic philosophy of Rousseau, that rationalist hierarchy was inverted by the assertion that reason, far from ensuring harmony, corrupts an inborn innocence. Even in those romantic views, however, the basic core image of conflict and competition was not transcended. Rather, it was merely turned upside down while retaining core competitive images: those of control, sub- and superordination, and hierarchic organization.

In the intellectual tradition of Western civilization, that hierarchical model was first explicitly elaborated in classical Greek culture. Although Greek dualism itself underwent significant modifications in the millennia to follow, it still offers a prototype by which to study core features of hierarchical models of mind and self. The Greek philosophers (see Collingwood, 1945) were engaged in forging a new language with which to speak about the nature of what we now would call mental activity, and in this first attempt to draw basic distinctions, dualisms emerged in a still unselfconscious and quite concrete way. This is evidenced quite clearly in the work of Plato, who presents a culmination of the Greek efforts to formulate a new view of the mind and self.

To writers before Plato, inner, mental activities such as thinking, intending, planning, or resolving inner conflict were most often described in terms of outer rather than inner processes such as divine, mythic, and organismic happenings (e.g., Donald, 1991; Labouvie-Vief, 1994; Onians, 1954; Simon, 1978). For this language of action, bodily, and interpersonal processes the Greek philosophers began to substitute a language of a self no longer primarily identified with its bodily processes and concrete actions, but of a mental self who could direct and control those enactive processes. The new language of the mind culminated in Plato's work, and it offered a language of a self as the agent and author of those actions rather than a passive sufferer of them.

The result was a sharp dualism in which the mental world of universal truths was dissociated from the bodily world of organismic, emotional, and imaginative processes. The new concepts of mind and self were based on such oppositions as mind versus body, self versus other, objective truth versus subjective inclination. Thus, as mythos became differentiated from logos, it also became subordinated to it. The two poles were arranged vertically, with the mental pole superior, and the bodily, organismic one inferior. As a consequence, the wise and mature person was a transcendent self who aimed at universal and objective truths while purging himself of the contaminations of bodily, organismic existence.

In postmodern critiques of classical dualism, of course, we have come to realize that dualistic models already embody assumptions about subjective processes, even while they assert that knowledge must be isolated from such processes. Because at the center of knowledge there are already centers of subjectivity and desire (e.g., Bernstein, 1991; Habermas, 1984), a number of more recent writers (e.g., Foucault, 1985; Labouvie-Vief, 1994; Lloyd, 1984; Schott, 1988) have attempted to analyze the notion of desire that animated that dualism.

Indeed, the dualism articulated in Greek philosophy did not really sever the mental world from that of subjectivity and desire. A case in point is Plato's discussion of the relationship between knowledge and love or desire in the *Symposium*. Agathon, one of the speakers, claims that desire or love is the prime motivator of all creative activity. It is at the basis of science and art, indeed all activity whether sacred or profane. Desire is what animates abstract knowledge; it is "the creative power by which all living things are begotten and brought forth" (Plato, 1961, p. 549). This notion, in effect, is quite similar to more modern views of the relationship between knowing and desiring: Piaget (1980), for example, proposed that emotions and affects represent the energetic and motivational side of knowledge, weaving the two into a seamless fabric.

On closer examination, however, the result is not at all a symmetrical structure. The association of knowledge and desire was uniquely shaped after the layered model of reality, as is revealed in Dotima's famous doctrine of the different levels of love. Here, spiritual love between men who create ideas, and the material love resulting in procreation, are contrasted. Plato says:

> Those whose creative instinct is physical have recourse to women, and show their love in this way, believing that by begetting children they can secure for themselves an immortal and blessed memory hereafter forever; but there are those whose creative desire is of the soul, and who long to beget spiritually, not physically, the progeny which it is the nature of the soul to create and bring to birth. . . . If you ask what that progeny is, it is wisdom and virtue in general. (209b; quoted in Keller, 1985, p. 24)

Thus, in actuality, Plato's model (and more generally, the Greek view; see Foucault, 1985) implied a strong valuation of forms of desire, parallel to the hierarchy of forms of knowledge. It is significant, too, that the equation drawn uses the specific metaphor of sexual reproduction. Sexual reproduction, Plato asserts, is a less valuable form of procreativity, since the generative function of the mind takes ascendancy over the inferior generative processes of the body.

In differentiating bodily and mental forms of procreativity, each with their own forms of desire, Plato joins a pervasive symbolic equation. And even though the aim of his philosophy was to substitute an objective logos language of universal knowledge, that language remained deeply permeated with the myth and symbolic imagery of his contemporaries. Indeed, as I suggest elsewhere (Labouvie-Vief, 1994), there are exact parallels between the new language of logos and the language of mythos it claimed to supersede. The vertical model of the mind is supported by an elaborate imagery of hierarchical control. Good and evil, strong and weak, "up" and "down" – all are dimensions of reality that provide pervasive metaphors and that speak of the idealization of power, strength, control, and domination as aspects of the new transcendent self.

However, while these agentic forms of subjectivity and desire were very much part of the constitution of the transcendent subject, the dualistic model could not effectively integrate the less agentic forms – those dealing with passivity, suffering, surrender, and being the object of desire rather than its agent. These forms were split off from the sense of self, and projected instead onto the other who was part of a relationship. Foucault (1985) comments on this asymmetry of desiring subject and desired object. Discussing views of sexual relationships, he notes that whether in homosexual or heterosexual love, such relationships followed a sharply asymmetrical model, based on an opposition between activity and passivity. These asymmetries

> were seen as being of the same type as the relationship between a superior and a subordinate, an individual who dominates and one who is dominated, one who commands and one who complies, one who vanquishes and one who is vanquished. Pleasure practices were conceptualized using the same categories as those in the field of social rivalries and hierarchies: an analogous agonistic structure, analogous oppositions and differentiations, analogous values attributed to the respective roles of the partners. And this suggests that in sexual behavior there was one role that was intrinsically honorable and valorized without question: the one that consisted in being active, in dominating, in penetrating, in asserting one's superiority. (Foucault, 1985, p. 215)

The issue was that to delight in and to be a subject of pleasure did not pose a theoretical problem. But to be an object of another's desire presented a difficulty, which was resolved by projecting these object qualities onto partners in interaction. A particularly pervasive aspect of this split is that different forms of desire, as well as their corresponding forms of knowledge, were associated with masculinity and femininity. How close this association was is evident in Plato's quote discussed earlier. It was also a major element of Aristotle's description of reproductive physiology. This model was an attempt, in fact, to map the duality of Plato's model of the mind onto issues of reproduction. Believing, like other Greek philosophers, that matter was of lower importance than spirit, Aristotle argued that this was evident in processes of sexual reproduction. He theorized that the woman contributed the more primitive and material principle to the embryo, but denied that the man's contribution also was of a material sort. Instead, he held that the masculine contribution was more spiritual and "divine." This superiority of the masculine principle was derived from the belief that the male principle is active, the female principle passive.

According to Neumann (1954; see also Bettelheim, 1962; Labouvie-Vief, 1994), Plato's equation between mental and bodily forms of procreativity appears to be typical of human symbolic life in general. As cultures develop a language of the spatial separation of mind and body, these layers also become associated with different processes of generation. That basic model provided a core structure for theories of mind, as well. It was carried over into the Enlightenment era and even into modern times (see Keller, 1985; Labouvie-Vief, 1994; Lloyd, 1984; Schott, 1988), and has divided mind and desire in terms of two hierarchical poles. These poles, rather than engaging in dialectical interchange, were organized by a single symbolic and narrative framework: One pole represented victory, activity, perfection, strength, and masculinity, the other subjugation, passivity, imperfection, weakness, and femininity.

The tendency to frame models of the mind as a single pole of which the second pole is merely a degradation or inversion thus pervades both views of knowledge and those of desire. As Lacqueur (1990) has argued, correlated with such models is a one-sex view of desire, which structures the conceptualization of desire right down to notions of sexual anatomy. Thus, female anatomy is conceived of as a hollow, negative space, characterized by passivity and simply receiving (male) life force. In contrast, male anatomy is viewed as positive, active, creative, and truly generative. More generally, these metaphors have been adopted directly or indirectly by many psychological theorists who view male desire as active and intrusive, but female desire as passive and receptive (e.g., Erikson, 1951; Freud, 1925/1963). But perhaps most significantly, this dualism is extended to notions of mind and self, as well. Thus, the male is viewed as the desiring subject, the representer who renders the woman as an object of his desire. Femaleness, in turn, is constituted out of its being the object of masculine desire: the woman is the one gazed upon and acted upon, the one represented, the other to the desiring and willful self (Beauvior, 1974; Benjamin, 1988; Lloyd, 1984).

The co-construction of subject and object in interaction

Dualistic positions have accepted the polarity of active versus passive as unproblematic and self-evident, assuming that passivity is a lack of activity in a simple, one-dimensional relationship. That relationship is deemed as purely formal and as existing outside and independent from the interpersonal context that it describes. Instead, differences in the constitution of self were assumed to reflect *outside* forces, whether these be understood as formal causes, such as biological differences in endowment, or mythic ones, such as divine processes. In more modern models of the mind, that assumption has been challenged with the notion that formal relationships are also an expression of specific forms of interpersonal relating. Accordingly, the experience of self as agent and subject, or self as object to others' agency will reflect a relational dialectic through which different forms of consciousness can mutually create each other.

Such a process of mutual creation was first described by Hegel (1807/1977) in his famous description of the master–slave relationship and the forms of consciousness it supports. Hegel proposed that becoming conscious always requires the presence of another, an intersubjective rather than merely subjective awareness. The self, recognizing that the object of desire is a being independent of the self, tries to overcome that otherness by overcoming the other. But if successful, that struggle creates a distortion of the consciousness of both self and other. One individual takes on the position of the master, whose self-consciousness is distorted by the very subjection that sustains it. The other individual takes on the self-consciousness of the slave, whose consciousness of servitude maintains the free consciousness of the master.

Hegel's analysis is very similar to Sartre's (1943/1958) comparison between the consciousness of looking and of being looked at. For Sartre, the subject is the one who looks; but for the one looked at by the subject, the experience is not of a subject or agent, but rather of an "objectified self," a "self-for-others." The self is transformed from a transcendent consciousness into a degraded one. The self becomes objectified, and this brings with it a series of unique feelings such as shame, which involves the awareness of being an object to another. The self becomes an objectification of the other's gaze.

Both Hegel's and Sartre's analyses introduce a relational component into the dialectic of subject and object. Thus, they realize that the awareness of self as subject and self as object constitute each other. At the same time, however, they adhere to the ancient notion that ultimately it is the transcendent, agentic self that is the more valuable one. Thus, for Hegel, the other is merely a vehicle for the self's self-certainty, while for Sartre, the self is a self who refuses to be known as an object. In both cases, as Benjamin (1988) argued, the self remains primarily defined by self-interest.

A number of recent writers have commented on this basic "egocentric" bias in many psychological theories. For example, this narcissistic, egocentric self is at the core of Freud's theory of development. As Greenberg and Mitchell (1984) note, for Freud the primary goals of the individual are selfish and need-oriented: maximization of pleasure and minimization of pain. The other, who significantly is called the "object," is relatively nonintrinsic and accidental to that goal:

> All of the most important psychic processes are produced by excesses or deficiencies or gratification; the object is merely the vehicle through which gratification is either obtained or denied. In the earliest developmental epochs in Freud's system, the infant is essentially autistic and the libido lacks any attachment to objects apart from the ego itself. The object in Freud's theory remains temporally secondary and always functionally subordinate to the aims of drive gratification. (Greenberg & Mitchell, 1984, p. 136)

Piaget's (1965) theory, too, accords the other a problematic status. It does not assume that the primary form of relatedness is to other selves, but to a world of material objects. That bias is seen most clearly in Piaget's account of infant knowledge. Here we see infants exploring, and interacting with, inanimate objects. How, then, does the self come to relate to others? Piaget thinks that relationships to others are possible once the child has reached a certain level of cognitive sophistication. For example, once the sensorimotor child acquires the ability to conceive of the object as something outside and independent of the self, Piaget argues, the child can develop feelings of attachment and dependence. Years later, the individual is able to cognitively construct the logical necessity of a social dimension to knowledge. That realization comes when the child becomes aware that knowledge is not something given from the gods, but something that is co-constructed cooperatively among a group of individuals equal in power. Thus, mutuality comes to be an epistemological problem, rather than a primary fact of human existence.

As Benjamin (1988) notes, indeed, models of the self rarely grant the other the same kind of agentic and subjective status that is accorded to the self. For example, in many psychodynamic views of the self, that other is exemplified by the mother whose primary role is seen as supporting and mirroring the self, molding herself to his (or her) every need; but there is no equal emphasis on the healthy consequences of the mother asserting her own will and subjectivity. However, there now is growing recognition that models of the mature self should be based on the notion of a dialectical balance, in which a tension between the two polarities is maintained. According to that view, both of these tendencies – the self as willful agent and the self as passive recipient and sufferer of others' agency – are polarities that the mature individual can negotiate and draw upon.

Kohut's (1977) formulation of a theory of the self, for example, can serve as a prototype of such a bipolar self. Kohut proposes that one of the self-poles is based on willful self-interest; this grandiose-exhibitionistic self seeks to be admired and idealized by others, and can form the basis of the development of self-esteem, ambitions, strivings for success and creative expression, and a "masculine" style. The other pole is the idealizing self that sees not only the self but also the other as a positive center of striving and initiative. This "feminine" pole seeks to identify with and idealize others as sources of values and feelings.

Kohut suggests that mature development is based on a tandem transformation of these two poles. Grandiosity and narcissism are transformed into self-directedness and creativity, while the idealization of others is transmuted into mature love and the ability to idealize and value others. In reality, however, development often bifurcates in less optimal ways. Thus, one pole can develop into grandiosity, exploitiveness, devaluation of others, and lack of empathy, while the other can lead to excessive dependency and overinvesting in and overidealizing others (Blatt & Schichman, 1983; Kohut, 1977; Westen, 1985; Wink, 1991).

These separate tendencies can come to interface through a process of mutual exchange and constraints. The process by which complementary selves are thus defined in relation is referred to as "projective identification." The term was first introduced by Melanie Klein (Segal, 1974), who attempted to describe how the infant can cope with extremely negative affects such as rage and fear. She suggested that the infant does so by externalizing the "bad" and projecting it onto others; this process allows the infant to gain control over the other and to avoid painful feelings of separation or anger.

Since Klein's early work, the concept has been widely elaborated (see Goldstein, 1991; Zinner, 1989) and applied to many other situations, including marital interaction patterns. Here, too, the emphasis is on the externalization of parts of the self that are felt to be unacceptable and frightening, though they may be neutral or positive in another (such as a person of the opposite sex). Once projected onto the other, the self then can maintain contact with the abandoned self-parts in an indirect, interactional way; indeed, projective identification allows the self to feel at one with the recipient of the projection. Thus, the blurring of the boundaries between self and other allows the person to maintain a sense of closeness.

Another aspect of projective identification is that the person projects acts in such ways as to evoke the projected qualities in the person on whom they have become projected. In this way, self and other continue to define each other in relation, in ways that allow both to split off the projected parts and to experience them through the other. Goldstein (1991) comments on this process:

> For example, a husband maintains a desired image of himself as aggressive and competitive by projecting his unwanted passive and helpless qualities onto his wife. This is ideal for the wife, who is able to maintain her desired image of a passive and helpless woman by projecting her competitive and aggressive qualities onto the husband. Thus, the projective identifications are mutually rewarding and complementary. (p. 159)

Elsewhere, I have suggested (Labouvie-Vief, 1994; see also Gilligan, 1982; May, 1980) that such bifurcated patterns are the basis of the cultural construction of gender, in which culture assigns different domains of competencies to men and women. The boy's or man's sense of self is dependent on his identification with agency-mind-spirit, whereas he needs to disidentify with passivity, feeling, and organismic limits. However, since mind and agency are the domains more valued culturally, the male can derive a positive sense of self-worth from this process of partial identification, since he is able to idealize himself through the ideals of culture. But for the woman, such positive self-identity remains extremely problematic. Indeed, she is encouraged to surrender her claim to consciousness and knowledge, a major source of positive self-identification. Thus, the female's main source of identification remains negative, since she carries the devalued aspects of culture. As a result, where the core masculine experience is that of enhancing and inflating one's sense of agency and competence (Kohut's grandiose-narcissistic self), the core feminine experience is that of surrendering such claims to others (Kohut's idealizing self). Girls begin quite early to relinquish a sense of their agency and desire to relational needs. Instead, these strivings become disconnected and repudiated as the "other," the bad or dreaded self. That disavowed self is then idealized in men and experienced vicariously in relationship. Boys, on the other hand, are encouraged from an early age to strive for and claim those accomplishments as their own, while repudiating their own sense of weakness, dependency, and helplessness.

In sum, I have suggested in this section that models of the mind imply specific views of interaction. In particular, I suggest that an emphasis on the knower as agent has created some knowers as agent-less objects to those agents. However, this bifurcation is specifically engendered in interpersonal settings where faculties are attributed differentially to individuals of different power status and/or biological sex. As a result of such processes of projective identification, individuals come to selectively express one polarity of mental functioning, while constraining interactions with others in such a way that the suppressed functions can be experienced indirectly through others.

The creation of feminine development

The relational construction of self-as-object

The notion that cultural models of knowledge have different though complementary effects on the self-identification of men and women has recently become the focus of much theoretical and research attention. Whereas development has traditionally been associated with increases in abstract thought, individuality, independence, and self-confidence, the claim is that this form of development describes only one form of experience, a form more associated with the masculine (see e.g., Belenky, Clinchy, Goldberger, & Tarule, 1986; Gilligan, 1982). In contrast, women have often experienced their development as renunciation, surrender, and victimization – a loss of voice, a process of silencing (Bem, 1993; Brown & Gilligan, 1992; Duby & Perrot, 1992/1993; Lerner, 1993). This silencing of women is a historical reality, since women have left few direct records of their own experience. Such silence has often been taken as evidence of women's biological limits, but as they have begun to gain greater access to educational and economic resources, their silence has become interrupted with attempts to speak their own experience and to examine the lenses through which they have been represented.

One such lens consists of myths, stories, and artistic representations that pervade cultural constructions of gender. In such representations, the duality of willful agency and rational control versus helplessness and passivity is narratively and iconically translated into the dialectic of heroic conquering versus surrender and descent (see Chinen, 1992; Gilligan, 1982; Labouvie-Vief, 1994; May, 1980). Thus, one polarity is idealized, even inflated, as "masculine": It is based on an imagery of rising, light, and sun, and it symbolizes such psychological qualities as leadership, rational self-control, self-assertiveness, individuality, and willfulness. The other polarity, in turn, is degraded and devalued: Its imagery is based on falling, being conquered and surrendering, and of engulfment in dark spaces, and it symbolizes suffering, powerlessness, and entrapment in unconscious processes. Thus, the idealization and inflation of the masculine and the devaluation of the feminine are considered "normal." Indeed, the pattern of inflation of the masculine and suppression of the feminine is not only considered normal; it forms the very basis on which the relationship is built – even the basis of erotic attraction and desire.

Such representations form a general narrative structure within which individuals impart meaning to the structure of their lives. How pervasive such narrative templates are has been examined in women's autobiographies (e. g., Benstock, 1988; Heilbrun, 1988; Heller, 1990). Traditional autobiographies center on the pursuit and nurture of love relationships with men. In such biographies, women do not themselves undergo a heroic quest, but subordinate their quest to that of a male actor. The role of the woman is to renounce assertiveness and striving for individuality, to sacrifice her own agency to that of her man, to inspire him, to serve as a vehicle rather than an agent. Even if a quest for her own independence becomes the focus of the narrative, the results are often tragic and testify to the dire consequences of women's abandoning traditional narrative structure: At best, women end their quest when they marry, or they continue their quest to fall victim to illness, madness, or suicide. Thus, whereas the prototypical masculine form of self is based on the heroic wrenching away of agency from others, the complementary image of development as renunciation, surrender, and victimization is one that pervades women's experience.

This sense of renunciation is also apparent in psychological research dealing with aspects of feminine experience, such as women's representations of their intellectual and creative development. Until early this century, philosophers and psychologists believed that women were biologically unequipped for heightened intelligence, creativity, or moral judgment. However, more recent research has pointed out a complex process by which, as part of their adopting a culturally prescribed role of femininity, women begin to surrender a sense of themselves as thinkers and creators. Even though in early childhood, girls *surpass* boys on most measures of school achievement, as they grow into adolescence and into adulthood, girls' superiority over boys begins to decline, and they tend to fall behind boys. As they grow older, girls are often found to retreat from achievement-related challenges, and in adulthood, differences in achievement between men and women remain profound (e.g., Brown & Gilligan, 1992; Eccles, 1984; Kaufmann & Richardson, 1982; Maccoby & Jacklin, 1974; Tomlinson-Keasey, 1993; Tomlinson-Keasey & Blurton, 1992).

Indeed, just as Freud (1925/1963) suggested, the process of socialization in woman may require that they turn against themselves and actively suppress evidence of superior intellectual achievement and so-called masculine emotions such as assertiveness and willfulness. The resulting uniquely feminine conflicts have been widely discussed in biographical and literary research. Heilbrun (1988), in *Writing a Woman's Life*, shows that highly creative women learn to experience their superior powers as dangerous and split off from the self. She argues that women learn to identify such striving as anger or egotism. Shameful of the creative strivings that lead to such labeling, extraordinary women are engaged in a constant struggle to suffocate their strong selves, to hide them apologetically. Indeed, Heilbrun argues that, well into this century, it remained impossible for women to admit in their own autobiographical narratives claims of achievement, admissions of ambition, or the realization that their own accomplishments may be more than mere luck or the result of others' generosity.

Psychological studies also suggest that these feelings of shame and discounting of their achievement persist well into the present day. Evidence about these achievement conflicts began to accumulate after Terman's 1925 study of gifted children (Terman & Oden, 1925, 1947, 1959). Although as children, the boys and girls in the group showed small differences in intelligence, adolescence brought a rather sharp decline in IQ scores for girls. In a similar vein, the later educational and employment history of girls, unlike that of boys, shows little of their early promise. Recent research continues to describe the conflicts of women over their achievement. Kerr (1987), for example, shows that gifted girls begin to downgrade and relinquish ambitious career goals as they grow up. These women come to deny that they are gifted or special, and instead of proud displays of self-exhibition one finds a "cheerful insistence on normality" (see also Tomlinson-Keasey, 1993).

Such findings suggest that, for a girl or woman, her agentic and intellectual strivings are experienced differently than for a boy or man: She is less likely to find them mirrored, and as a result to feel them to be "real" and to emanate from her own center. This conclusion is also upheld by research examining the relationship between actual intellectual performance and one's self-concept about these performances. Men and boys are more likely than girls to evaluate their performance positively in situations of performance achievement (e.g., Dweck & Bush, 1976; Martin & Nivens, 1987; Roberts, 1991; Roberts & Nolen-Hoeksema, 1989). That is, they are likely to overestimate their ability initially and remain unaffected by negative evaluations. In contrast, women underestimate their performance and are more strongly affected by others' feedback. These patterns may be especially strong in gender-stereotyped areas such as math or science, where girls are especially likely to disclaim their sense of agency, even though they may outperform boys (AAUW, 1992; Byrne, Shavelson, & March, 1992; Yee & Eccles, 1988).

The work of Gilligan (Brown & Gilligan, 1992; Gilligan, 1982, 1990; Gilligan, Lyons, & Hanmer, 1990) and others also shows that girls who early in adolescence were confident and outspoken, become increasingly confused and silent about what they know. They come to doubt that what girls and women know and experience has value in the adult world: because it too often "brings a message of exclusion – stay out; because it brings a message of subordination – stay under; because it brings a message of objectification – become an object of another's worship or desire, see yourself as you have been seen over centuries through a male gaze . . . keep quiet and notice the absence of women and say nothing" (Gilligan, 1990, p. 26).

Such relinquishment of a proud sense of self-confidence primes the girl for emotional experiences of shame, depression, and powerlessness that are not equally prevalent in the boy. More generally, such core emotional experiences are related to different core senses of self as evidenced in gender-related coping and defense strategies. Cramer (1979) found that such differences increase with development. As they move through high school, males increasingly externalize conflict, while females increasingly use defenses that internalize conflict, turning aggression and assertiveness inward. In her most recent research (Cramer, 1990), "turning against others" remains a stereotypically masculine coping style, while women are more likely to use "turning against the self" defenses. These aspects were also found in our own research on adult coping and defense styles (Diehl, Coyle, & Labouvie-Vief, in press; Labouvie-Vief, Hakim-Larson, & Hobart, 1987): Women were more likely to utilize defenses of turning against the self and of self-blame and self-doubt, while men were more likely to rely on coping and defense strategies in which emotions are externalized and/or intellectualized.

Beyond the gendered mind

Along with rejecting the self as sufferer and nonrational thinker and celebrating the self as rational agent, our past epistemologies have projected the less desirable polarity outward and thus constructed femininity as a less desirable and mature state of being. However, dissatisfaction with this narrative of mind as the heroic conqueror who subdues the nonrational self has grown to almost universal proportions in the past 30 years or so (for a summary, see Labouvie-Vief, 1994). As faith in the power of logos has become criticized, many contemporary views of the mind have begun to return to the dimensions of mind and self abandoned by the classical view. Emotion and intuition, time and process, variability and disorder, all the elements that previously were devalued as feminine have come to the forefront of philosophical discussions (for a review, see Labouvie-Vief, 1994).

Since traditional models and narratives were based on an imagery of gender, such a process of reevaluation also implies a reconsideration of the meanings of masculinity and feminity. The first theorist to propose such a reevaluation was Jung (e.g., 1954), who suggested that changes in the valuation of the masculine and the feminine constitute the essense of mature adult development, those changes are often associated with midlife. Jung suggested that this period brings a search for the self, accompanied by a "turning inward" (see also Neugarten, 1968); energies that previously had been invested in the pursuit of outer goals became withdrawn, and the individual focused those energies toward an examination of his or her inner life in an attempt to rebalance the life structure. In this process, Jung argued, the individual engaged in a profound restructuring of such epistemological categories as rational–nonrational, mind–body, and self–other – the very categories that are being reevaluated in contemporary culture.

Jung's theory (see Whitmont, 1969) specifically suggested that in defining reality exclusively by the dimensions of logos, past epistemologies had failed to account for a dimension of human experience just as critical: that of myth, narrative, and similar symbolic forms that constitute important expressions of inner experience. In his insistence that a full theory of the life span must integrate this dimension of mythos, Jung also anticipated a major contemporary movement by tying these epistemological changes to gender. One major way in which midlife renewal happens is that an individual confronts the images he or she holds of the masculine and the feminine. Jungians (see Daugherty, 1992; Young-Eisendrath & Wiedemann, 1987) believe that the split-off elements are usually encountered most profoundly in the contrasexual images; but now, the individual has to begin realizing that these are inner constructions and unrecognized behavior patterns that must be reclaimed and integrated into the self's thinking and acting.

Jung's view of changes in gender evaluations thus ties them to midlife and is rooted in the view that strong gender polarization is normative at earlier parts of the life span. Nevertheless, Jung's theory also embodies the perspective that the traditional devaluation of the feminine and overevaluation of the masculine constitutes a distorted view of development that tragically can limit the full potential of women and men alike. Thus, it suggests that both culturally and individually, the polarities need to be integrated in such a way that the masculine emphasis on mind and transcendence is moderated by an equal emphasis on body and immanence.

Jung's proposals have had a revolutionary impact on such fields as myth and religion, art and literature, and, more indirectly, philosophy and psychology. The wide-ranging analysis of the kinds of symbolic structures that underlie our notions of the rational have become an almost universal aspect of contemporary thought across many disciplines. In all of those, a reexamination of notions of gender has become a core undertaking, attesting to the fact that part and parcel of defining new models of the mind involves attempts to break out of the constraints of past narratives.

One area in which such a rewriting of lives is apparent is in literary studies of how women represent their own experience. While past narratives of women's development suggest that female protagonists envisioned their lives as dwarfed and muffled (Heilbrun, 1988; Pratt, 1981), many contemporary woman writers attempt to write new stories that entail new visions of womanhood (Smith, 1993).

Such a rewriting of lives is also evident from psychological research on men's and women's lives. In the lives of men, this process often requires that the previously devalued feminine principle be upgraded, a process that can lead through a crisis often experienced as threatening and confining as men feel overwhelmed by an intrusion of the feminine, perceived as domineering and hostile (Gutmann, 1987). Jaques (1965) argued that, for men, this transition is essentially an experience of depression and disempowerment, as warded-off feelings of vulnerability and helplessness, symbolized as feminine, are encountered and processed. Similarly, Levinson and co-workers (Levinson, Darrow, Klein, Levinson, & McKee, 1978) found that in this period a man confronts how inner constructions of the feminine (and the correlated meaning of masculinity) have limited his life structure and narrowed his dream. One man at midlife, for example, wanted to write novels, but was limited by his sense that such creative activities somehow were feminine. Yet, eventually, he was able to integrate these split-off feelings into his self and go on to a successful new career as a novelist. Both Jaques and Levinson suggest that such reinterpretations of gendered meanings eventually lead to a transformation and release of creative power, priming the individual for complex and integrative forms of creativity. On a perhaps more mundane level, psychological research has noted that, as they age, men become less stereotyped in terms of masculine and feminine attributes and interests (Lowenthal, Thurner, & Chiriboga, 1975; Sinnott, 1977; Vaillant, 1976).

In the lives of women, however, a reevaluation of gendered polarities of the mind is not as likely to be experienced as diminishment and depression. Instead, one often observes a sense of heightened energy as, in Gutmann's (1987) parlance, women move from a world of confinement to one of daring openness, of a release from their earlier interiority. Many authors concur that women's later life brings a liberation from the confinement of traditional sex roles (e.g., Helson & Moane, 1987; Helson & Wink, 1992; see also Cooper & Gutmann, 1987; Haan, 1981, 1985).

One question is whether the notion of midlife changes is more of an ideal than a reality. As the literature suggests, the transformation of later life creativity in either gender constitutes an ideal rather than a statistical norm, since only few and extraordinary individuals are able to break out of the confines of their youthful adaptations. As far as women are concerned, it is perhaps better to state that a woman's reclaiming of her authority constitutes a unique task around which her later life appears to be organized. Thus, her conflicts and her sense of self may be focused around the inner struggle about empowering herself as creator. However, only some women may resolve this struggle, because there have been and continue to be pervasive cultural conditions that discourage women from reaching toward full development of their potentials. If we reach back far enough historically, evidence of this release of creative energy is extremely rare. Instead, as Virginia Woolf (1929) noted in *A Room of One's Own*, and as Heilbrun (1988) reiterated in *Writing a Woman's Life*, one is much more impressed with the degree to which women's creative voices were silenced. However, as Heilbrun notes, in more recent generations of women writers – for example, Virginia Woolf and Sylvia Plath – one finds that the inner conflicts about achievement and creative expression are sharply and poignantly articulated. Even so, they often cannot be integrated, and rather than a sense of breaking out of confines one finds a sense of consuming envy, hopelessness, and despair. Similarly, studying gifted women, Tomlinson-Keasey (1993; Tomlinson-Keasey & Blurton, 1992) notes that, paradoxically, a woman's awareness of her superior skills may often diminish rather than enhance her adulthood, weighing her down with a sense of failure and discouragement rather than a freeing of energy (see also Veroff, Reuman, & Feld, 1984).

For men, in turn, the major obstacle to successful transformation may consist in a retreat from the depressive crisis mentioned earlier. Jaques (1965), for example, believes that the midlife reexamination forms a crisis that, though it is confronted by all adults, is not necessarily resolved successfully by all. Instead, they may retreat from the crisis and form more and more rigid forms of adaptation, either defensively bolstering their sense of power through increasing ruthlessness, or defending against grandiosity through self-effacing weakness. In a similar vein, Gutmann notes that many men he studied have not fully integrated a sense of femininity. As a result, they seem to be haunted by a sense of diminishment vis-à-vis the feminine, of feeling disempowered by women they have come to experience as dangerously powerful and domineering.

Jung and researchers to follow assumed that changes in gender polarization are primarily related to those surrounding midlife. There is some justification for that assumption, because much research suggests that midlife, in general, may be a period where individuals reorganize their thinking so as to be less dualistic and to be better able to integrate contrasts and contradictions (for a review, see Baltes & Smith, 1990; Labouvie-Vief, 1994). Nevertheless, this

view still adheres to the notions that early development implies strong normative pressures toward sex role specialization and does not take into account the
dramatic cultural changes that have occurred in sex role definition. Normative
pressures seem to have changed dramatically for more recent cohorts and are
apparent in religion, literature, art, as well as in philosophy and psychology.
Thus, one would expect that, in the future, decreases in sex role specialization
would be related not only to age, but also to generational or cohort membership. Currently, however, we still know little about how age and cohort
membership interact in producing changing patterns of gender polarity across
the life course.

Conclusions

I have suggested that one important domain of the interaction of minds is that
of gender. But the dimension of gender also highlights the fact that interactive
minds are not always engaged in exchanges of mutual support, aimed at
enhancing each others' development. Rather than following cooperative
patterns, I have reviewed evidence that gendered patterns of interaction are
often structured according to hierarchical rules, rules that ultimately limit the
potential of both men and women.

The competitive structure of gender, I have suggested, is deeply embedded
in our traditional theories of mind. In idealizing logos, such models have been
based on a masculine symbolic structure: a structure idealizing heroic quests in
which the hero rises victoriously over dimensions deemed feminine – relationship, body, and immanence. Such representations have formed the cultural
template that guides identification of individuals as masculine. While for men
that template prescribed notions of heroic agency and rising above others, for
women it has implied that they identify themselves as objects to others'
agency, rather than as independent agents themselves. The resulting conflicts
about agency and authority are vividly expressed in women's conflicts about
these self-domains.

Contemporary culture has begun to reevaluate the nature of the mind,
stressing the fact that it is always related and embodied. Basic to such a
reevaluation, I have argued, is that men and women break out of the gendered
representations and carve out different ones that suggest new possibilities of
interaction. Rather than using core metaphors of control and competition, we
can employ metaphors of playful cooperation. Indeed, Lakoff (1987) suggests
the metaphor of a dance, and notes:

> Try to imagine a culture where arguments are not viewed in terms of war,
> where no one wins or loses, where there is no sense of attacking or defending,
> gaining or losing ground. Imagine a culture where an argument is viewed as a
> a dance, the participants are seen as performers, and the goal is to perform in
> a balanced and aesthetically pleasing way. (pp. 4–5)

References

American Association of University Women (1992). *The AAUW Report. How schools short change girls.* AAUW Educational Foundation. Washington, DC.

Baltes, P. B., & Smith, J. (1990). Toward a psychology of wisdom and its ontogenesis. In R. J. Sternberg (Ed.), *Wisdom: Its nature, origins, and development* (pp. 87–120). New York: Cambridge University Press.

Beauvoir, S. de (1974). *The second sex.* New York: Vintage.

Belenky, M. F., Clinchy, B. M., Goldberger, N. R., & Tarule, J. M. (1986). *Women's ways of knowing.* New York: Basic.

Bem, S. L. (1993). *The lenses of gender.* New Haven, CT: Yale University Press.

Benjamin, J. (1988). *Bonds of love: Psychoanalysis, feminism, and the problem of domination.* New York: Pantheon.

Benstock, S. (Ed.). (1988). *The private self: Theory and practice of women's autobiographical writing.* Chapel Hill: University of North Carolina Press.

Bernstein, R. J. (1991). *Beyond objectivism and relativism: Science, hermeneutics, and practice.* Philadelphia, PA: University of Pennsylvania Press.

Bettelheim, B. (1962). *Symbolic wounds: Puberty rites and the envious male* (rev. ed.). New York: Collier.

Blatt, S. J., & Schichman, S. (1983). Two primary configurations of psychopathology. *Psychoanalysis and Contemporary Thought, 6,* 187–254.

Brown, L. M., & Gilligan, C. (1992). *Meeting at the crossroads: Women's psychology and girls' development.* Cambridge, MA: Harvard University Press.

Bruner, J. (1986). *Actual minds, possible worlds.* Cambridge, MA: Harvard University Press.

Byrne, B. M., Shavelson, R. J., & March, H. W. (1992). Multigroup comparisons in self-concept research: Reexamining the assumptions of equivalent structure and measurement. In T. M. Brinthaupt & R. P. Lipka (Eds.), *The self: Definitional and methodological issues* (pp. 172–203). Albany: State University of New York Press.

Chinen, A. B. (1992). *Once upon a mid life: Classic stories and mythic tales for the middle years.* New York: Tarcher.

Collingwood, R. G. (1945). *The idea of nature.* Oxford: Oxford University Press.

Cooper, K. L., & Gutmann, D. L. (1987). Gender identity and ego mastery style in middle-aged and post–empty nest women. *Gerontologist, 27,* 347–352.

Cramer, P. (1979). Defense mechanisms in adolescence. *Developmental Psychology, 15,* 476–477.

Cramer, P. (1990). *The development of defense mechanisms: Theory, research, and assessment.* New York: Springer.

Dabrowski, K. (1970). *Mental growth through positive disintegration.* London: Gryf.

Daugherty, N. (1992). *Unfolding Neumann's map: Imagining masculine archetypal wholeness.* Thesis presented to the Chicago Jung Institute, Evanston, IL.

Diehl, M., Coyle, N., & Labouvie-Vief, G. (in press). Age and gender differences in strategies of coping and defense across the life span. Psychology and Aging.

Donald, M. (1991). *Origins of the modern mind: Three stages in the evolution of culture and cognition.* Cambridge, MA: Harvard University Press.

Duby, G., & Perrot, M. (Eds.). (1992–1993). *A history of women in the West* (Vols. 1–4). Cambridge. MA: Harvard University Press.

Dweck, C. S., & Bush, E. (1976). Sex differences in learned helplessness: Part 2. The contingencies of evaluative feedback in the classroom; and Part 3. An experimental analysis. *Developmental Psychology, 14,* 268–276.

Eccles, J. (1984). Sex differences in achievement patterns. *Nebraska Symposium on Motivation, 39,* 97–132.

Epstein, S. (1990). Cognitive-experiential self-theory. In L. A. Pervin (Ed.), *Handbook of personality: Theory and research* (pp. 165–191). New York: Guilford.

Erikson, E. H. (1951). *Childhood and society.* New York: Norton.

Foucault, M. (1975). *The order of things*. New York: Vintage.
Foucault, M. (1985). *The history of sexuality: Vol 2. The use of pleasure*. New York: Random House.
Freud, S. (1925/1963). Some psychological consequences of the anatomical differences between the sexes. In P. Rieff (Ed.), *Sexuality and the psychology of love* (pp. 183–193). New York: Macmillan.
Gilligan, C. (1982). *In a different voice*. Cambridge, MA: Harvard University Press.
Gilligan, C. (1990). Teaching Shakespeare's sister: Notes from the underground of female adolescence. In C. Gilligan, N. P. Lyons, & T. J. Hanmer (Eds.), *Making connections* (pp. 6–29). Cambridge, MA: Harvard University Press.
Gilligan, C., Lyons, N. P., & Hanmer, T. J. (Eds.). (1990). *Making connections*. Cambridge, MA: Harvard University Press.
Goldstein, W. N. (1991). Clarification of projective identification. *American Journal of Psychiatry, 148*, 153–161.
Greenberg, J. R., & Mitchell, S. A. (1984). *Object relations in psychoanalytic theory*. Cambridge, MA: Harvard University Press.
Gutmann, D. (1987). *Reclaimed powers: Toward a new psychology of men and women in later life*. New York: Basic.
Haan, N. (1981). Common dimensions of personality development: Early adolescence to middle life. In D. Eichorn, N. Haan, J. Clausen, M. Honzik, & P. Mussen (Eds.), *Present and past in middle life* (pp. 117–153). New York: Academic.
Haan, N. (1985). Common personality dimensions or common organizations across the life-span? In J. M. A. Munnichs, P. Mussen, E. Olbrich, & P. G. Coleman (Eds.), *Life-span and change in a gerontological perspective* (pp. 17–44). New York: Academic.
Habermas, J. (1984). *The theory of communicative action: Vol 1. Reason and the rationalization of society*. Boston: Beacon.
Hegel, G. W. F. (1807/1977). *Phenomenology of spirit* (A. V. Miller, Trans.) Oxford: Oxford University Press.
Heilbrun, C. (1988). *Writing a woman's life*. New York: Ballantine.
Heller, D. A. (1990). *The feminization of quest-romance: Radical departures*. Austin: University of Texas Press.
Helson, R., & Moane, G. (1987). Personality change in women from college to midlife. *Journal of Personality and Social Psychology, 53*, 176–186.
Helson, R., & Wink, P. (1992). Personality change in women from the early 40's to the early 50's. *Psychology and Aging, 7*, 46–55.
Hofstadter, D. R. (1980). *Gödel, Escher, Bach: An eternal golden braid*. New York: Vintage.
Jaques, E. (1965). Death and the midlife crisis. *International Journal of Psychoanalysis, 46*, 502–514.
Jung, C. G. (1954). *The psychology of transference* (R. F. C. Hull, Trans.). Princeton, NJ: Princeton University Press.
Kaufman, D. R., & Richardson, B. L. (1982). *Achievement and women: Challenging the assumptions*. New York: Free Press.
Kegan, J. (1982). *The evolving self*. Cambridge, MA: Harvard University Press.
Keller, E. F. (1985). *Reflections on gender and science*. New Haven, CT: Yale University Press.
Kerr, B. A. (1987). *Smart girls, gifted women*. Columbus, OH: Ohio Publishing.
Kohlberg, L. (1984). *Essays on moral development: Vol. 2. The psychology of moral development*. San Francisco: Harper & Row.
Kohut, H. (1977). *The restoration of the self*. New York: International Universities Press.
Labouvie-Vief, G. (1982). Dynamic development and mature autonomy. *Human Development, 25*, 161–191.
Labouvie-Vief, G. (1990). Wisdom as integrated thought: Historical and developmental perspectives. In R. J. Sternberg (Ed.), *Wisdom: Its nature, origins, and development* (pp. 52–86). Cambridge: Cambridge University Press.

Labouvie-Vief, G. (1994). *Psyche and Eros: Mind and gender in the life course.* New York: Cambridge University Press.

Labouvie-Vief, G., Hakim-Larson, J., & Hobart, C. (1987). Age, ego level, and the life-span development of coping and defense processes. *Psychology and Aging, 2*, 286–293.

Lacqueur, T. (1990). *Making sex: Body and gender from the Greeks to Freud.* Cambridge, MA: Harvard University Press.

Lakoff, G. (1987). *Women, fire and dangerous things.* Chicago: University of Chicago Press.

Lerner, G. (1993). *The creation of feminist consciousness.* New York: Oxford University Press.

Levinson, D. J., Darrow, C. N., Klein, E. B., Levinson, M. H., & McKee, B. (1978). *The seasons of a man's life.* New York: Ballantine.

Lloyd, G. (1984). *The man of reason: "Male" and "female" in Western philosophy.* Minneapolis: University of Minnesota Press.

Loevinger, J. (1993). Measurement of personality: True or false. *Psychological Inquiry, 4*, 1–16.

Lowenthal, M. F., Thurner, M., & Chiriboga, D. (1975). *Four Stages of life.* Washington, DC: Jossey-Bass.

Maccoby, E. E., & Jacklin, C. N. (1974). *The psychology of sex differences.* Stanford, CA: Stanford University Press.

Martin, V., & Nivens, M. K. (1987). The attributional response of males and females to noncontingent feedback. *Sex Roles, 16*, 453–462.

May, R. (1980). *Sex and fantasy: Patterns of male and female development.* New York: Norton.

Neugarten, B. L. (1968). The awareness of middle age. In B. L. Neugarten (Ed.), *Middle age and aging* (pp. 93–98). Chicago: University of Chicago Press.

Neumann, E. (1954). *The origins and history of human consciousness.* Princeton, NJ: Princeton University Press.

Onians, R. B. (1954). *The origins of European thought : About the body, the mind, the soul, world, time, and fate.* Cambridge: Cambridge University Press.

Ortner, S. (1974). Is female to male as nature is to culture? In M. Z. Rosaldo & L. Lamphere (Eds.), *Woman, culture, and society* (pp. 67–88). Stanford, CA: Stanford University Press.

Piaget, J. (1965). *The moral judgment of the child.* New York: Free Press.

Piaget, J. (1980). *Experiments in contradiction.* Chicago: University of Chicago Press.

Plato (1961). Symposium (M. Joyce, Trans.). In E. Hamilton & H. Cairns (Eds.), *Plato: Collected dialogues* (pp. 845–919). Princeton, NJ: Princeton University Press.

Pratt, A. (1981). *Archetypal patterns in women's fiction.* Brighton, Sussex: Harvester.

Roberts, T. (1991). Gender and influence of evaluations on self-assessments in achievement settings. *Sex Roles, 109*, 297–308.

Roberts, T., & Nolen-Hoeksema, S. (1989). Sex differences in reactions to evaluative feedback. *Sex roles, 21*, 725–747.

Sartre, J.-P. (1943/1958). *Being and nothingness* (H. E. Barnes, Trans.). London: Methuen.

Schott, R. M. (1988). *Cognition and eros: A critique of the Kantian paradigm.* Boston: Beacon.

Segal, H. (1974). *Introduction to the work of Melanie Klein.* New York: Basic.

Simon, B. (1978). *Mind and madness in ancient Greece.* Ithaca, NY: Cornell University Press.

Sinnott, J. D. (1977). Sex-role inconstancy, biology, and successful aging. *Gerontologist, 17*, 459–463.

Smith, S. (1993). *Subjectivity, identity, and the body: Women's autobiographical practices in the twentieth century.* Bloomington: Indiana University Press.

Terman, L. M., & Oden, M. (1925). Mental and physical traits of a thousand gifted children. *Genetic Studies of Genius* (Vol. 1). Stanford, CA: Stanford University Press.

Terman, M. L., & Oden, M. (1947). The gifted child grows up. *Genetic Studies of Genius* (Vol. 4). Stanford, CA: Stanford University Press.

Terman, M. L., & Oden, M. (1959). The gifted group at mid-life. *Genetic Studies of Genius* (Vol. 5). Stanford, CA: Stanford University Press.

Tomlinson-Keasey, C. (1993). Tracing the lives of gifted women. *American Psychological Association Esther Katz Rosen Lecture presented to the American Psychological Association 101st Annual Convention*, August 20, Toronto, Canada.

Tomlinson-Keasey, C., & Blurton, E. (1992). Gifted women's lives: Aspirations, achievements, and personal adjustment. In J. Carlson (Ed.), *Cognition and educational practice: An international perspective* (pp. 151–176). Greenwich, CT: JAI.

Vaillant, G. E. (1976). Natural history of male psychological health. *Archives of General Psychiatry, 33,* 535–545.

Veroff, J., Reuman, D., & Feld, S. (1984). Motives in American men and women across the adult life span. *Developmental Psychology, 20,* 1142–1158.

Westen, D. (1985). *Self and society: Narcissism, collectivism, and the development of morals.* New York: Cambridge University Press.

Whitmont, E. C. (1969). *The symbolic quest: Basic concepts of analytical psychology.* Princeton, NJ: Princeton University Press.

Wink, P. (1991). Self- and object-directedness in adult women. *Journal of Personality, 59,* 769–791.

Woolf, V. (1929). *A room of one's own.* London: Harcourt, Brace, Jovanovich.

Yee, D. K., & Eccles, J. S. (1988). Parent perceptions and attributions for children's math achievement. *Sex Roles, 19,* 317–333.

Young-Eisendrath, P., & Wiedemann, F. (1987). *Female authority.* New York: Guilford.

Zinner, J. (1989). The implications of projective identification for marital interaction. In J. Scharff (Ed.), *Object relations family therapy* (pp. 155–173). Dumone, PA: Aronson.

Part II

Research on ontogenetic development

5 Peer interactive minds: developmental, theoretical, and methodological issues

Margarita Azmitia

> Collaboration operates through a process in which the successful intellectual achievements of one person arouse the intellectual passions and enthusiasms of others, and through the fact that what was at first expressed only by one individual becomes a common intellectual possession instead of fading away into isolation.
>
> From an interview by John-Steiner (1985, p. 187)

Abstract

The cognitive potential of peer interactive minds has long been the subject of scholarly interest and research. Yet we are still far from developing a theory of peer interactive minds across the life span. This chapter raises some issues that will have to be addressed as we move toward constructing such a theory. The first part of the chapter presents a summary of contemporary research on the processes and outcomes of peer interactive minds in childhood and adolescence. Special attention is paid to how negotiation processes, the nature and difficulty of the task, and the relationship between the collaborators influence the processes and outcomes of peer interactive minds. The second part highlights the merits of linking work focusing on childhood and adolescence with that on adulthood and old age. It is argued that while this linkage is desirable, it will be challenging to construct given the differences in tasks, procedures, and, to an extent, research questions that have motivated research carried out on different periods of the life span. The final section of the chapter raises theoretical and methodological issues that currently confront the field. These issues include integrating the products of social and individual activity, rethinking our methodologies for assess-

This chapter benefited from discussions with Ryan Montgomery, Jakob Linnet, and the participants of the "Interactive Minds" conference. Lothar Krappmann, in particular, helped me refine my thinking and provided detailed comments on several drafts of the chapter. I am also grateful to Bill Damon, Barbara Rogoff, Stephanie Teasley, and two anonymous reviewers for their helpful comments and suggestions. Only I, of course, am to blame for any errors or misconceptions that remain in the manuscript. Some of the research reported here was supported by a postdoctoral fellowship from the Spencer Foundation and faculty research grants from Florida International University and the University of California at Santa Cruz. Correspondence concerning this chapter should be sent to Margarita Azmitia, Psychology Department, University of California, Santa Cruz, CA 95064.

133

ing knowledge construction and revision, and devoting more attention to the pace and pattern of cognitive development.

The potential synergy of peer interactive minds has been the subject of scholarly debate for many centuries. Whether concerning adolescents in Socrates' ancient Greek Academy, contemporary children collaborating on a school project, two grandmothers solving a moral dilemma, or a team of scientists creating and testing a theory, the age-old question remains: How do peers create intellectual synergy and cognitive development? By cognitive development I mean both adding to and revising our knowledge and strategies. Considerable research (for reviews, see Gilovich, 1991; Kuhn, 1991) has shown that revising our knowledge or abandoning old views is especially difficult, regardless of whether we are talking about scientific theories or social stereotypes. Knowledge revision is difficult because we tend to ignore or devalue information that is inconsistent with our beliefs. Peers can help us revise our knowledge by focusing our attention on information that we would not otherwise consider and forcing us to question or explain our views.

The first goal of this chapter is to review work that addresses processes and outcomes of peer interactive minds in childhood and adolescence. Because the work on childhood and adolescence has proceeded relatively independently from research on adulthood and old age, the second goal is to suggest potential linkages between these two bodies of work. The final goal is to highlight some of the methodological and theoretical challenges that currently confront research on peer interactive minds. To foreshadow my conclusion, I will propose that although the past two decades have brought considerable advances, many challenges remain, both in theory construction and in the application of our findings to classrooms, work places, and other environments of daily living.

Before proceeding with the first goal, it may be useful to review the many ways that peers can influence knowledge acquisition and revision. First, their influence may be at the motivational or affective level, increasing each other's willingness to attempt difficult tasks and reducing frustration when the work becomes too challenging. Second, peers may observe and imitate the behaviors and strategies of others. Third, a more expert peer might tutor a novice. Not only does the novice increase his or her knowledge, but through teaching the expert also refines his or her understanding and learns to communicate it effectively. Fourth, peers can engage in lively discussions and negotiations that may result in mutually shared and potentially higher levels of understanding (Azmitia & Perlmutter, 1989; Winegar, 1988). In this chapter, I devote special attention to this fourth notion of peer interactive minds.

Because most researchers have focused on a single age group or a limited age period (e.g., childhood, adolescence, adulthood), we currently lack models of peer interactive minds across the life span. When I began writing this chapter, I had the overambitious goal of proposing a life-span model of peer interacting minds. Many months later, I had the more modest aim of simply setting forth some candidate processes and issues that may frame this life-span model. In particular, I will propose that understanding how age-related changes in communicative, metacognitive, and negotiation skills work together to influence the processes and outcomes of collaborations between peers may provide the foundation for this life-span model. Because my research has focused on childhood and adolescence, I will devote more attention to these periods. Staudinger (Chapter 10, this volume) provides a fine review of the work on peer interactive minds in adulthood.

One of the many lessons that we have learned while researching peer interactive processes and outcomes is that context matters. Context effects may include cultural differences (Ellis & Gauvain 1992; Tharp & Gallimore, 1988), societal or institutional norms and prescriptions for social interaction (Perret-Clermont, Perret, & Bell, 1991), the nature of the relationship between collaborators (Nelson & Aboud, 1985; Goodwin, 1993), and the characteristics of the task or the setting (Cooper, Ayers-Lopez, & Marquis, 1982; Ellis & Rogoff, 1986). Because of space limitations, I will focus only on some aspects of the relational and task contexts. In particular, my discussion of the relational context targets the processes and outcomes of the interactive minds of friends and acquaintances, and my proposals about task effects mostly address the role of task difficulty.[1]

The chapter is organized as follows. First, I review research on peer interacting minds in childhood and adolescence. I pay special attention to how age-related changes in negotiation skills affect the dynamics and products of peer collaboration. I also consider how the difficulty of the task and the nature of the relationship between the collaborators (i.e., friends vs. acquaintances) moderate these processes and outcomes. Second, I make some suggestions about what researchers studying peer interactive minds at different points of the life span can learn from each other's work. Finally, I offer some thoughts on theoretical and methodological issues that currently confront the field.

Peer interactive minds in childhood and adolescence

In an earlier piece of work, Marion Perlmutter and I (Azmitia & Perlmutter, 1989) sketched a developmental framework for studying social influences on cognition. Because this chapter elaborates on that framework, I will first summarize its main points. We suggested that children's task performance depends on their skill level relative to the difficulty of the task, and that the impact of social input on their performance and, more broadly, their cognitive growth also depends on these variables. For example, when children's skill level is very low, they may be able to follow simple directions and imitate behaviors, but may not be able to see how these behaviors facilitate problem solving. Difficult tasks might also absorb so much of their attention and thinking that sustained and meaningful social interaction is precluded. As will be discussed, it is possible that young children often find themselves in this situation, thus accounting for the fragility of peer interacting minds and their cognitive outcomes during the preschool years (see Brownell & Carriger, 1991; Verba, in press). As their communicative, collaborative, metacognitive, and negotiation skills increase during middle childhood and adolescence and become more routinized or automatic, individuals may be less hampered by task difficulty and derive greater benefits from peer collaborative problem solving.

Our model also addressed the mechanisms through which social interaction leads to the creation and revision of knowledge. Like others before us, we proposed that imitation, conflict and its negotiation, tutoring or apprenticeship, and co-construction (i.e., the elaboration and integration of the perspectives of the different collaborators into a mutually shared view) can mediate the cognitive outcomes of peer collaboration. However, we took issue with the practice of pitting the effects of one mechanism against those of another in order to decide which is the best mechanism of facilitation, because this practice can obscure the possibility that each mechanism might facilitate a specific kind of cognitive change. For example, imitation might be sufficient for adding knowledge or strategies, but conflict, negotiation, and co-construction may be necessary for revising knowledge or abandoning old strategies in favor of better tools. An additional reason for our reservations about this competitive strategy was that it draws attention away from the possibility that different mechanisms may be salient at different points of the life span. We speculated, for example, that during the preschool years, imitation may be the most powerful mechanism for promoting knowledge acquisition because children's limited interactive skills constrain their ability to sustain collaborative dialogues, coordinate views, or resolve conflicts (see Hartup, 1983; Selman, 1980). As children hone their collaborative and negotiation skills, other mechanisms of facilitation may become salient, although imitation will still be an important mechanism of knowledge construction (but perhaps not of knowledge revision).

In framing our developmental model, we devoted special attention to discussing how age-related changes in children's and adolescents' metacognitive skills influenced processes, mechanisms, and outcomes of peer interacting minds. We were especially interested in these metacognitive skills because they are key elements of knowledge construction and revision, as they allow individuals to allocate cognitive resources effectively to both the task and the collaboration, to plan, implement, and monitor a problem-solving strategy, and to evaluate the proposed solution for the problem.

Although Garton (1992) agreed with our view that age-related changes in metacognitive skills have implications for the processes and outcomes of peer

interactive minds, she quite rightly faulted us for not devoting sufficient attention to the influence of age-related changes in children's and adolescents'
communicative skill. She suggested that it is important to consider these
changes not only because discourse is one of the pathways through which
metacognitive skills are constructed, but also because age-related changes in
communicative skills affect the process of negotiation and co-construction of
knowledge (for a similar argument, see also Berkowitz, Oser, & Althof, 1987;
Miller, 1987; Piaget, 1965; Rubtsov, 1981; Selman, 1980; Wertsch, 1978).

In this chapter, I address Garton's criticism by discussing age-related
changes in two aspects of communication – conflict and its negotiation – that
influence collaboration and knowledge construction and revision. I pay special
attention to conflict negotiation processes because they figure prominently in
Piaget's (1965) and Vygotsky's (1978) theories, which have dominated child
developmental work on peer interactive minds. I will focus on two aspects of
negotiation – the negotiation and renegotiation of problem-solving roles and
that of knowledge. To contextualize the impact of age-related changes in these
two dimensions of negotiation, I will first describe their role in age-related
changes in the ability to initiate, maintain, and repair social interaction and
collaborative problem solving.

Age-related differences in collaborative skills

Collaborative skills include all the tools that allow us to engage in social
interaction and create a shared understanding of our task and our roles and
goals. It is not enough to start a dialogue. This dialogue must be moved along
and repaired when confusions, misunderstandings, or conflicts ensue. Similarly, we must monitor each other's actions, anticipating movements, offering
assistance, or "backing off" when our partner appears to have matters under
control or assistance would not be welcome. Finally, we must also keep in
mind the goals of the collaboration so that we can accomplish them or change
them if they no longer seem tenable or a better alternative emerges.

Before reviewing the specific age-related changes in collaborative skills, it is
important to point out that even though our ability to collaborate increases
with age, collaboration is challenging across the life span. All of us would
probably agree with the proposal that it takes considerable time and effort to
build and maintain a truly collaborative interaction, and even more time and
effort to build a truly collaborative *relationship* (see Hinde, 1979). One of the
biggest challenges is that, like any other relationship, this collaboration must
evolve and grow, as otherwise, it would become stagnant and unfulfilling
(Fogel, 1993). Because most of our work on peer interactive minds in childhood and adolescence has focused on interactions (as opposed to relationships), except for a brief section on collaborations between friends, I too will
be focusing on peer interactions over one or a small number of sessions.

Before 2 years of age, children are able to coordinate their actions and goals with another peer at only a rudimentary level, and even then they do so infrequently. Often, successful interaction depends on the presence of a supportive context, such as an adult who facilitates communication and coordinations between the infants (Rogoff, 1990) or a task that requires cooperation, provides many clues to its solution, or is more open-ended, such as symbolic play (Hartup, 1983; Verba, 1993, in press).

Around 2 years of age, however, there is a dramatic shift in children's ability to sustain interactions. In particular, they begin to engage in reciprocated play and to collaborate to solve simple problems, particularly those that do not depend heavily on discussion or require children to take on more than one role (Brownell & Carriger, 1991; Tomasello, Kruger, & Ratner, 1993). Brownell and Carriger suggest that this shift in children's ability to establish a shared understanding may be mediated, at least in part, by the growth of symbolic and representational skills. Children's increasing mobility, exposure to other children, and communicative skill also contribute to these changes in peer interaction and collaborative problem solving.

Although preschoolers are more skilled than infants or toddlers at managing interaction and creating a shared understanding, their skills are fragile and are often tied to specific familiar contexts. For example, numerous scholars have detailed the synergy of peer interactive minds during play. During play, young children create scenarios, negotiate and coordinate complex roles, justify their views, flexibly shift the discourse and interaction toward new goals, and, on occasion, compromise (Corsaro, 1985; Garvey 1987; Verba, in press). However, young children's ability to coordinate their behaviors during collaborative problem-solving tasks is more limited. Although they can share resources and take turns, preschoolers are often unable to explain their views, repair breakdowns in interaction and understanding, and refrain from attempting to dominate the problem-solving process, a tendency that is also reflected by their frequent reliance on unilateral conflict resolution strategies such as blocking and insistence (Azmitia, 1988; Miller, 1987; Selman, 1980).

Garvey (1987) suggests that these difficulties may be due, at least in part, to the fact that problem solving requires that peers focus their actions and attention toward a specific, single goal, that is, the solution of the problem. Because play allows flexible alteration of goals, children may avoid breakdowns by redefining their aims whenever they encounter an obstacle. The fragility of peer interactive minds during the preschool years may also be due to difficulties in resisting distraction, coordinating joint attention, or shifting attention to other strategies or dimensions of the problem (Cooper & Cooper, 1984; Ellis & Siegler, in press).

It is important to point out, however, that although during the preschool years collaborative problem solving can be fragile, the degree to which limitations in communicative and interactive skills will affect peer interactive minds depends on the nature of the problem and its difficulty. For example, collaborations involving pairs of experts proceed more smoothly and are more resistant to disruption than those involving pairs of novices (Azmitia, 1989). Children are also better able to sustain collaboration when the task is familiar or when it provides feedback that supports a particular view more than another (Rogoff, 1990).

During middle childhood, peers become increasingly able to initiate, maintain, and repair collaboration and achieve a shared understanding of their problem-solving roles and goals. Also, cognitive gains following the collaboration are evident over a wider range of tasks. A variety of explanations have been offered to account for these improvements in the processes and outcomes of peer collaborative minds. These explanations include general proposals concerning development, such as declines in egocentrism (Piaget, 1965), or suggestions targeting more specific processes or abilities, such as an increased understanding of fairness and reciprocity (Youniss, 1980), improvements in the regulation of their own and others' affect to reduce frustration and increase task enjoyment (Hartup, in press), and advancements in perspective taking such that collaborators recognize the need to justify their positions and reach mutually agreeable resolutions of conflicts (Hartup, in press; Miller, 1987; Selman, 1980).

However, once again the task context influences the processes and outcomes of peer interactive minds. If the task is too difficult, it may absorb all the individuals' processing resources, thus increasing the fragility of collaboration (Azmitia & Perlmutter, 1989; Ellis & Rogoff, 1986). An additional reason for the difficulty children may have in maintaining collaboration and a shared understanding in very difficult tasks is that their frustration and anxiety may lead to hostility and to defensiveness or rigidity in perspectives. Given this unpleasant state of affairs, children may prefer to withdraw from the interaction and work by themselves. However, because of the developmental changes discussed in the preceding paragraphs, these task difficulties will decrease as children progress through the middle childhood years.

Forman (1992) and Selman (1980) have suggested that it is not until early to middle adolescence that the impact of task difficulty (and task context) on peer interacting minds becomes attenuated due to dramatic growth in communicative, collaborative, and metacognitive skills. Put more simply, on average, adolescents are able to achieve a shared understanding of the collaboration and the task across a wider variety of situations. Bos (1934) and Forman and McPhail (1993) have provided detailed analyses of two key processes that can facilitate knowledge acquisition and revision. First, partners can elaborate on each other's perspectives and work to integrate their positions and build a joint understanding of the problem (i.e., co-construct the solution). Second, partners can challenge each other's reasoning, justify their challenges, and attempt to resolve their differences (i.e., conflict and negotiation). Subsequent research has shown that in late childhood and early adolescence, conflict is more likely to lead to knowledge acquisition, revision, and generalization than to co-construction (Kruger, 1993).

It is important to point out, however, that neither co-construction nor conflict and its negotiation necessarily lead to better solutions or higher levels of understanding. Indeed, like collaborating adults, at times adolescents co-construct a new *misunderstanding* of the problem (Forman & McPhail, 1993; Levin & Druyan, 1993). Regardless of its accuracy, however, this new understanding reflects the synergy of interacting minds, as it is often impossible to isolate the contributions of each adolescent. Bos notes:

> The same things happen in cases where, in lively exchange of thoughts, adults discuss a problem. Through the interpretation of the other, which is rejected by us, we arrive at ideas, which in turn are taken over, eventually are further elaborated, and thereby lead to a result. Whom shall we give credit for the solution? It was fortunate that our young candidates did not bother about the authorship and after intensive collaboration simply declared that they had worked out the problems *together*. (1934, p. 364)

Despite these age-normative changes in adolescents' skills, it is the case that many adolescents are unable to create and transform knowledge during collaboration, and that even when they do, not all adolescents display these discoveries at a later time (e.g., subsequent interactions, their next project, an exam, or an individual posttest). Some of this variability reflects individual differences in cognitive skills and knowledge about a domain. These variations may also reflect differences in the ability and willingness of collaborators to negotiate and renegotiate collaborative roles and construct a shared understanding of the task or problem. I will return to this issue later, when I distinguish between the potential and the reality of children's and adolescents' interacting minds. For now, I want to focus on the age-related changes in negotiation processes that mediate knowledge construction and revision. I first discuss role negotiations and renegotiations and then knowledge construction and revision.

Age-related differences in the negotiation and renegotiation of roles

Role negotiations and renegotiations maintain and repair social interaction. As mentioned, these processes are also linked to the cognitive outcomes of peer interactive minds. For example, individuals who make joint decisions and coordinate their problem-solving activities make greater cognitive gains than those who do not (Rogoff, 1990; Tharp & Gallimore, 1988). Also, the acquisition of competence by novices during collaborations with more expert partners is mediated by the renegotiation of problem-solving roles such that the novices gradually increase their participation in the task until they become capable of solving the problem independently (Vygotsky, 1978).

Role negotiation and renegotiation can be especially problematic for pre-schoolers because they frequently experience difficulty sharing, compromising, and balancing the demands of the task with the demands of managing the collaboration. Negotiating problem-solving roles may also be challenging for children, adolescents, or adults with limited collaborative experience or who prefer to work on their own. Although there certainly is wide within-culture variability, it is generally the case that U.S. schools and universities emphasize individual work. However, even though individuals in U.S. society may have limited opportunities to collaborate in academic contexts, from an early age they collaborate in games, relationships, and social interactions. The collaborative and negotiation skills acquired in these contexts may be transported to academic settings, such as when children transport the turn-taking strategies from games into the classroom. However, transporting these strategies into the classroom is not enough; they must be adapted to the characteristics of academic problem solving. For example, unlike games, relationships, and social interactions, in which roles are often familiar and routinized, this is usually not the case for academic tasks. Also, while even young children are able to establish problem-solving roles, what is tricky, and consequently shows significant improvements with age, is (1) renegotiating roles during the course of collaboration and (2) establishing a style of interaction wherein individual contributions or strict accounting of turns are deemphasized in favor of a joint goal.

I base these two suggestions on the results of a series of studies in which my student colleagues and I (Azmitia, 1989; Azmitia & Linnet, 1995; Azmitia, Lopez, Conner, & Kolesnik, 1991; Azmitia & Montgomery, 1993) have been studying ontogenetic and microgenetic changes in children's and young adolescents' ability to negotiate and renegotiate mutually agreeable problem-solving roles with acquaintances. Across all the age groups (4 to 11 years of age) and tasks (copying models, writing, isolating causal variables), most collaborators initially adopted a "let's take turns" strategy. However, the ability to adhere to this strategy increased with age. Age-related differences in the ability to sustain this strategy were especially evident in collaborations that involved partners with different skill levels, such as experts and novices.

The nature of the task may have contributed to the fragility of this egalitarian collaboration strategy. In particular, preschoolers had more difficulty sustaining turn taking in tasks that provided clear feedback about each participant's competence level, such as reproducing designs or copying Lego models. Within minutes, preschool-age experts attempted to persuade their more novice partners to allow them to take control of the task. Although initially the novices accepted their secondary roles (thus achieving a shared understanding of roles and goals), as their competence increased they attempted to renegotiate their roles to increase their participation. Their expert partners typically resisted their renegotiation attempts, the novices persisted, and often the collaboration disintegrated into a battle of wills and disruptive behaviors such that either the task was not completed, one child withdrew from the interaction, or both, as illustrated in the following example from a task in which children were building a copy of a Lego house:

> Novice: You gotta let me help. You said you would.
>
> Expert: I will, after I finish this [the door].
>
> Novice: [Sighs, sits back, crosses arms around chest, and frowns. Twenty-two seconds later, takes some blocks and begins building a section of the model [correctly]. After the section is completed, he hands it to the expert.] I built this for our house.
>
> Expert: [Looks over.] I'm the builder, you find Legos [for me] when I tell you, OK? Give me a yellow two-dot.
>
> Novice: I wanna be a builder too. She [experimenter] said work together. My window is good [points to model and back to section he built].
>
> Expert: Well, it's not going on my house [moves copy of model out of the reach of the novice].
>
> Novice: [Starts shaking the table, making it impossible for expert to continue building.]
>
> Expert: Stop it! If you don't quit it we won't get finished. I'm almost done with the door.
>
> Novice: [Stops shaking the table, observes the expert until he finishes the door.] My turn! My turn!
>
> Expert: It's not time for your window yet.
>
> Novice: But its the only thing [left] . . . and the roofs but the window goes first [points to model]. How about I do the window and you [do] the roofs? Here [offers roof pieces].
>
> Expert: You'll mess it up [the window]. I gotta do it.
>
> Novice: No, I know how. See [points to his completed window]? It's the same [points to model].
>
> Expert: [Looks] Well, you don't know how to put it on.
>
> Novice: Yeah I do!
>
> Expert: If you want me to use your window you gotta let me put it on.
>
> Novice: [Sighs, puts head down on arms, and disengages from the interaction. Eighteen seconds later, starts pelting the expert with Legos, and when the expert lifts his hands to protect himself from the Legos, he quickly reaches over and smashes the copy of the Lego house to pieces.]

One might assume that the attempts at role renegotiation made by novices were ineffective because their negotiation strategies were unilateral (e.g., insisting, grabbing, avoiding, blocking). As evident in the preceding example, however, this hypothesis is untenable because novices often used non-egocentric strategies such as justifying their position, bartering, or proposing a compromise (see Selman, 1980). It is possible that these nonegocentric strategies failed to persuade the experts because any renegotiation would have entailed their giving up resources or power. Moreover, because the experts had the skill to complete the task independently, they had little to gain from agreeing to renegotiate the problem-solving roles. Possibly, if the experts had had a stronger motivation for relinquishing control, such as realizing that time was running out and the task was far from complete, or their partners alluded to the obligations of friendship, they would have been more responsive to the role renegotiation attempts made by the novices.

A small pilot study that explored role renegotiation in pairs of experts and novices who were close friends revealed that friendship was a more powerful motive for persuading the expert to renegotiate the problem-solving roles than time constraints, perhaps because preschoolers have a limited understanding of time. However, although novices who alluded to the obligations of friendship were more likely to persuade their partners than novices who alluded to efficiency or time pressures, their success was short-lived. Soon, the experts reasserted their dominance. In many cases, what ensued was a pattern in which the novice reminded his or her friend about their agreement, the expert honored the agreement for a short time, and then regained control of the task, at which point he or she was chastised by the novice, and so on and so forth until the task was completed or time expired. It is possible that this inability to sustain more egalitarian roles even when collaborating with friends may reflect preschoolers' understanding of the goals of a collaborative problem-solving task. In particular, experts might have viewed the goal of solving the problem as more important than the goal of solving it together, even when their partner was a close friend. This suggestion receives some support from an additional pilot study in which we emphasized in our instructions that collaboration was more important than task completion. In this situation, experts still took control of the task and resisted the requests for role renegotiation of their novice partners. It appears then, that if one wants to promote more egalitarian problem-solving roles during the preschool years, one should avoid pairing children whose skills differ substantially or use tasks in which the discrepancy in the skills of the partners is not so obvious.

During middle childhood and early adolescence, peer collaborators became more capable of adhering to the turn-taking strategy and negotiating and renegotiating their problem-solving roles even when feedback from the task made it obvious that their expertise differed dramatically. However, it was still the case that expertise affected role negotiations, since, at least initially, experts took a leadership role in the task. This leadership role may have been essential to keep the problem-solving process on track. Pozzy, Healy, and Hoyles (1993) found that groups in which someone initially took the lead in coordinating the planning and decision making were able to collaborate and learn more effectively than those in which no one took the lead or was allowed to do so. Groups in which there was no leader were less effective because either many avenues were pursued and abandoned, or collaborators were unable to agree on which plan to follow. Especially pertinent to my point that successful collaborations require flexibility in roles over time, Pozzy and others found that the most successful groups were those in which the leader relinquished control once the plan was in place and group members had negotiated acceptable roles. We have observed a similar result in our studies.

In particular, collaborations between experts and novices during middle child-hood and early adolescence are more successful than those between expert and novice preschoolers because the experts, and especially girls, are more open to increasing the role of the novice once he or she exhibits increased understanding and skill.

In the case of these older peers, nonegocentric strategies such as justifica-tions and a willingness to compromise were more successful for role negotia-tion than egocentric strategies, such as insistence, threatening, grabbing, or blocking. On the surface, this statement might seem to contradict my earlier point that nonegocentric, collaborative negotiation strategies do not necessar-ily increase the success of negotiations. However, I think that the age-related increase in the effectiveness of these strategies was due, at least in part, to an increase in expert children's and adolescents' willingness to listen to and consider the justifications, bargains, and compromises offered by their novice partners. Thus, and it should not come as a very surprising conclusion, the success of role renegotiation strategies is not independent of the receptivity of partners to renegotiate the problem-solving roles even though such renegotia-tion may result in their giving up some of their resources or power.

Older children's and young adolescents' openness to role renegotiation may have stemmed from age-related increases in the understanding of social con-ventions, reciprocity, and fairness (see Youniss, 1980). For example, they often yielded when their partner alluded to the rules of the task (e.g., "She [the researcher] said we were supposed to work together"), a type of justification that was seldom effective when used by preschoolers.[2] Age-related increases in successful role renegotiation may also have been due to age-related improve-ments in the ability to monitor the negotiation process and switch strategies or drop the issue if success appeared unlikely. Dropping the bid for renegotiation before the partner becomes too frustrated and aroused may repair the interac-tion and increase the probability that the renegotiation bid will work if intro-duced at a later time. We saw ample evidence of this increased flexibility in role negotiation and renegotiation by the late elementary school years (10 or 11 years of age). Teasley and Roschelle (1993) have noted a similar pattern when collaborators are exchanging ideas and opinions about a task, which suggests that this flexibility and adaptiveness of negotiation extends beyond role renegotiation to the renegotiation of knowledge.

Finally, in addition to their greater mutuality and flexibility in role negotia-tion, older collaborators also appeared to have a more relaxed approach to turn taking. Preschoolers had aimed for strict equality: They kept track of each other's contributions by counting block placements and impeding placements when someone was trying to extend his or her turn. They also kept a running commentary about the division of labor and often reminded each other about what they had agreed upon. Eight- and 11-year-olds, in contrast, negotiated the division of labor at the start of the session and subsequently paid less attention to each other's specific contributions; the division of labor became an issue only when one of the partners seriously violated a previous agreement or attempted to renegotiate it. Finally, older children and young adolescents were also more likely than younger children to talk about the goals of the task. For example, they discussed whether the experimenter's relatively vague exhortation to "work together" meant cooperate, divide the labor, or simply try to do the task as efficiently as possible, even if this meant that the more competent partner would do all the work and the less competent partner would act as gopher and cheerleader. Their discussion of the goals might suggest that these older children and young adolescents were more aware of the need to establish a shared understanding of the goals of the task. These shared goals not only sustained and repaired collaboration, but also increased the probability that these collaborations would lead to the joint creation and revision of knowledge.

Age-related differences in the negotiation and renegotiation of knowledge

Peer collaborative processes can provide insights not only into how collaborators negotiate their roles and the goals of the task, but also into the processes of knowledge construction and revision (see Miller, 1987; Rubtsov, 1981). Scholars representing a broad theoretical spectrum (e.g., Gottman, 1983; Miller, 1987; Piaget, 1965; Rogoff, 1990; Selman, 1980; Van Eemeren, Grootendorst, & Kruiger, 1984; Vygotsky, 1978; Youniss, 1980) converge in suggesting that negotiations will succeed and affect individuals' knowledge only if the negotiators enter into the process in "good faith," that is, with the goal of finding a joint solution to the problem. Although these cooperative argumentation processes are evident by toddlerhood, they show considerable development across childhood and adolescence (see Miller, 1987, for a lengthier discussion of this issue). One major developmental shift, which occurs during elementary school years, involves the ability to operate on the reasoning of others and create a joint understanding of a problem.

Numerous researchers (e.g., Azmitia & Montgomery, 1993; Berkowitz & Gibbs, 1985; Berkowitz et al., 1987; Kruger, 1992; Tolmie, Howe, Mackenzie, & Greer, 1993) have demonstrated that peers who engage in transactive dialogues, that is, dialogues in which they operate on each other's reasoning, are more likely to increase their conceptual understanding. These dialogues can take the form of coordinating ideas into a general theory or rule that is then applied and tested (e.g., Tolmie et al., 1993) or resolving disagreements and evaluating the merits of contrasting approaches to the problem (e.g., Azmitia & Montgomery, 1993; Berkowitz & Gibbs, 1985; Kruger, 1992).

Drawing on Piaget (1965), Berkowitz and Gibbs (1983, 1985) suggested that when peers operate on each other's reasoning, they become aware of contradictions and inadequacies in their thinking. This awareness promotes internal disequilibrium, the resolution of which results in cognitive growth. Although transactive dialogues have largely been investigated from a neo-Piagetian perspective, they can also be investigated within Vygotsky's framework, which has the advantage of focusing attention on how transactive dialogues create knowledge (Forman & McPhail, 1993).[3]

Because Piaget (1965) believed that the capacity to engage in transactive discussion and reasoning is attained only during the formal operational period, early studies of the relation between transactive dialogues and cognitive development (e.g., Berkowitz & Gibbs, 1983) were focused on adolescents and young adults. Recently, however, Kruger (1992) and Berkowitz and Gibbs (1985) have explored transactive dialogues in younger children. Although their results suggest that peer interacting minds create transactive dialogues long before the formal operational stage, it is the case that younger (elementary school–aged) children produce not only fewer but different kinds of transacts than adolescents and adults. Children's transactive dialogues consist largely of representational transacts, which tend to be paraphrases of their partner's reasoning. Adolescents' and young adults' transactive dialogues, in contrast, contain a high proportion of operational transacts, which transform and challenge their partner's thinking. Because operational transacts are associated with greater conceptual change than representational transacts, Berkowitz and Gibbs (1985) and Berkowitz and others (1987) suggest that at least in tasks that tap reasoning skills, collaborations between adolescents or young adults may have a greater developmental potential than those between younger children.

Berkowitz and others' (1987) framework represents one of the few attempts to map developmental changes in peer interacting minds across the life span. They propose that despite large individual differences (see also Dimant & Bearison, 1991), during adolescence and adulthood operational transactive dialogues increase in density and become vehicles for the synthesis of well-documented conceptual frameworks or scientific theories. (The final stages in their theory probably represent the potential of peer interactive minds; it is especially unlikely that many individuals will reach their final stage, *ideal discourse.*)

At this ideal stage, dialogue is focused on developing the best position, without concern for personal views, power, or status. Because few individuals are able to keep these concerns in check, the capacity to create and maintain ideal discourse may be a defining feature of wisdom. However, while an individual might have the capacity to create ideal discourse, he or she would need a wise partner to actually instantiate it. That is, as argued earlier, an individual's strategies, no matter how sophisticated, will not succeed in the absence of a receptive partner. Hence, to create and maintain ideal discourse both partners need to keep their personal views, power, or status in check so as to develop the best possible theory or position.

Berkowitz and others' (1987) model provides a useful framework for capturing age-related changes in transactive dialogues. It now remains to be demonstrated empirically that these transactive processes lead to specific cognitive outcomes. Studies that link transactive dialogues to cognitive *outcomes* are rare, in part because of the current emphasis on the importance of focusing on developmental *processes*. While I agree that process analyses are essential for constructing a theory of peer interactive minds across the life span, it is equally important to consider the outcomes of such peer dialogues. Perhaps outcomes have fallen in disfavor among many developmental psychologists because they have been perceived as static, unchanging entities. However, outcomes need not be conceptualized as static entities, but rather as what individuals can do in a particular moment given the status of their knowledge and the characteristics of the situation in which they are asked to apply it. Without doubt, their knowledge continues to change and expand as a result of both individual and social encounters with tasks or problems.

To develop practical applications of our findings, we must consider both outcomes and processes of peer interacting minds. Effective peer collaborative programs are surprisingly difficult to implement or reproduce in schools and universities, and thus unless we can explain in detail how to create processes and outcomes, many teachers will not be receptive to our proposals. In the following section, I will highlight some of the differences between the potentials and the realities of peer interacting minds, to explore the issue of practical application further.

From potential to reality

As our understanding of peer interactive minds grows, it is reasonable to ask ourselves whether our findings generalize beyond the relatively controlled problem-solving contexts or tasks we have tended to study. This question is especially relevant given the considerable interest of educators in using our findings to engineer peer collaborative and tutoring programs in schools and universities. Over the past decade, numerous scholars have made suggestions for developing such programs. These suggestions have included the creation of motivational frameworks for collaboration (e.g., Slavin, 1987), the forms of peer interaction that are best suited for different kinds of tasks and cognitive gains (e.g., Damon, 1984; Palincsar & Brown, 1984; Rogoff, 1990), and the kinds of concepts that are most likely to benefit from peer interactive minds (Phelps & Damon, 1989). Although their proposals have often met with success, discussions and evaluations of the resulting programs often fail to mention the wide variability within and across classrooms in the processes and outcomes of peer interactive minds. Moreover, we seldom admit that while we know what kinds of peer interactive minds promote cognitive development, many of us are not yet sure of how to replicate these interactive minds in the "wilds" of the classroom without completely restructuring the schools.[4] I now turn to some factors that lead to this variability and may pose obstacles for creating and maintaining the synergy of peer interactive minds.

One problem with our models is that we have conceptualized the negotiation of roles and knowledge too romantically (see Krappmann & Oswald, 1987). For example, following Piaget (1965), our models often assume that at least by middle childhood or adolescence, peers will adhere to principles of reciprocity and equality. The reality is that, across the life span, peer negotiations during collaborative problem solving (or in other arenas, for that matter) are often Machiavellian – that is, motivated by power and self-interest more than by the desire to find the best solution (see Krappmann & Oswald, 1987, for a lengthier discussion of this issue). The negotiation process is also affected by the social status of the collaborators. Even in the laboratory, it is often the case that an expert will maintain the status quo by deferring to a novice partner with higher social status. During informal conversations with these experts, some told us that they saw the collaboration as an opportunity to interact and potentially develop a relationship with a more popular peer who would not otherwise be open to an extended interaction. Other experts explained that they had deferred to the more popular novices because they were afraid of the consequences of challenging them. For example, one boy told us he worried that if he did not let his partner "run" things during our laboratory task, his partner would tell others not to play with him when they returned to the classroom. Taken together, these disclosures by experts suggest that we need to consider that processes and outcomes of peer interactive minds are embedded within the larger context of peer relationships.

The processes and outcomes of peer interactive minds also depend on the meaning that collaborators attribute to the task. While our laboratory research suggested that by middle childhood most children were capable of collaborating effectively with a peer, when we studied these same children's and adolescents' collaborations and role negotiations in the classroom (Azmitia & Linnet, 1995) we observed numerous power struggles and breakdowns that interfered with problem solving and task completion. Interestingly, some of the children and adolescents who had viewed working together and exploring a variety of perspectives as more important than task accuracy in the laboratory were more concerned with task accuracy in the classroom. When we queried them informally about these situational differences, they pointed out that while their performance in our laboratory tasks would not show up in their report cards, their performance in the classroom would. Thus, we must also consider how individuals' personal stakes in the outcome of the problem-solving process influence their willingness or ability to display their collaborative and negotiation competencies.

A final problem is that our models of the links between negotiation and cognitive development are too simple. For example, perhaps spurred on by finding positive correlations between transactive negotiations and cognitive growth, we have often assumed a causal connection between them. However, this is an empirical question that must be addressed by future work. The positive correlations between some aspects of dialogues and cognitive growth may have also led us to assume that "more is better," but our current models do not have a way of accounting for the common finding that progress, or insight, occurs during one dramatic moment during which the timing and process is indistinguishable from other transactive negotiations. We also have a poor understanding of why ideas and issues that were unresolved during interaction influence the subsequent posttest performance of individuals. Consider the following negotiation between two 11-year-olds who were trying to decide which pizza ingredients, if any, had led to the death of a subset of diners:

> C1: So it has to be onions and green olives
> C2: Yeah, onions but it can't be green olives. See, this dead one doesn't have it [points to dead one].
> C1: That doesn't matter, it [green olives] just has to be in the dead but not in the alive. See, no green olives, no green olives, no green olives [points to alive].
> C2: But it has to be in all of them [the dead]. Otherwise they wouldn't all die. What killed this one then? [points to dead diner that didn't eat green olives].
> C1: The onions, see, they [dead] all have onions.
> C2: Well, I'm writing just onions.
> C1: And green olives. Onions *and* [emphasizes] green olives.
> C2: Let's just go on to the next one.
> C1: Ok. [Whispers:] But it was onions and green olives.

Although Child 2 was unconvinced during the negotiation, his performance in a subsequent individual posttest indicated that he understood that an ingredient did not have to be in all the pizzas consumed by the dead diners to be a causal factor. Piaget's followers would not be puzzled by this finding, because they would propose that this conflict provoked an internal disequilibrium that Child 2 subsequently resolved on his own. However, this explanation suffers from circularity, as at present we lack the tools to measure internal disequilibrium. Perhaps a different way of looking at this delayed effect on knowledge revision is to ask what motivated Child 2 to reconsider his position. As will be seen in the next section, one possibility is that because these adolescents were close friends, the respect of Child 2 for Child 1 may have led him to puzzle over his friend's position after the problem-solving interaction had ended. This added opportunity for reflection increased the potential that Child 2 would recognize the validity of his partner's argument, thus abandoning his less adequate belief. This explanation, of course, will also suffer from circularity until we are able to devise a way to test it empirically. It does appear, however, that, at least in some situations, by early adolescence the interacting minds of friends can be more powerful contexts for change than those of acquaintances.

The interacting minds of friends

To date, we know very little about the dynamics and cognitive products of different peer relationships, and, in particular, acquaintanceship and friendship. This gap in our knowledge is unfortunate, because, as Moss suggests, "It is evident that different relationship contexts fundamentally will affect collaborative cognitive endeavors with respect to participants' motivations for engaging in joint activity and how responsibility is shared during interaction" (Moss, 1992, p. 118).

There are several features of friendship that may promote the negotiation and renegotiation of roles and knowledge. First, conversations between friends are characterized by greater mutuality than collaborations between acquaintances (see Gottman, 1983; Hartup, in press), which may indicate that friends are more attuned to each other's needs and goals and are thus better able to establish a shared understanding. Second, because friends trust each other, they may be more willing than acquaintances to expose their views and challenge each other (Nelson & Aboud, 1985; Shantz & Hobart, 1989). Third, because friends have great respect for each other, they might attend closely to each other's points, thus increasing the possibility of influence (Hartup, in press). Finally, because friends are concerned with equality and fairness they may put greater effort into negotiating and renegotiating roles and meaning.

Up until recently, most research on the developmental affordances of friendship focused on socioemotional development. There are several reasons for this state of affairs. First, Piaget (1965) and Vygotsky (1978), the most influential theorists on research on peer learning, did not elaborate on the cognitive affordances of different peer relationships. Researchers following in their footsteps have thus focused on assessing the impact of factors that play a role in Piaget's and Vygostky's models, such as expertise, power, and onto-genetic constraints. Second, up until recently researchers were in search of universal processes and outcomes of peer interacting minds. Third, the dynamics of children's friendships are not well understood, and given the tremendous variability that is already inherent in peer interactive minds, researchers may have been reticent to introduce yet another wild card into the equation. Finally, as Damon (1990) observed, teachers often assume that children or adolescents will not work effectively with friends. Because research on peer interacting minds has often been driven by educational considerations, our laboratory tasks have modeled the classroom – that is, explored collaborations between acquaintances.

Increasingly, however, researchers interested in cognitive development (e.g., Azmitia & Montgomery, 1993; Berndt, Perry, & Miller, 1988; Ellis &

Gauvain, 1992; Hartup, in press; Nelson & Aboud, 1985; Newcomb, Brady, & Hartup, 1979) have explored the processes and outcomes of the interactive minds of friends. Their findings are mixed. Some (e.g., Azmitia & Montgomery, 1993; Hartup, in press; Nelson & Aboud, 1985) have found that collaborations between friends lead to greater equality in roles, more transactive discourse, and larger increases in knowledge than collaborations between acquaintances, but others (e.g., Berndt et al., 1988; Newcomb et al., 1979) have failed to find differences in the processes and outcomes of the collaborations of friends and acquaintances. After reviewing these studies, Ryan Montgomery and I speculated that the nature of the task and its difficulty may mediate differences in the processes and outcomes of the collaborations of friends and acquaintances. In particular, it appeared that studies that yielded support for the cognitive advantage of working with a friend had employed challenging tasks or tasks that drew heavily on metacognitive skills such as planning, monitoring, and evaluating evidence.

To test these speculations, we carried out a study of young adolescents' (11-year-olds) collaborations on problems of isolating causal variables (e.g., which pizza ingredients, if any, caused the death of some of the members of a group of diners, and an adaptation of Kuhn & Brannock's, 1977, plant problem, which asks individuals to look at an array of healthy and sick plans and isolate the variable(s) that are responsible for keeping the plants healthy). We chose the isolation of variables problem because the mature understanding of causality figures prominently in theories of cognitive development. Also, age-related differences in the ability to isolate causal variables have received considerable attention by Kuhn and her colleagues (for examples of this work, see Forman & Cazden, 1985; Kuhn, 1991; Kuhn, Amsel, & O'Loughlin, 1988). Because they have provided detailed descriptions of the microgenetic processes through which individuals acquire an understanding of causality, we could use their descriptions to identify the peer discourse events that would provide a window into the negotiation of knowledge and its potential internalization into the individual minds of collaborating peers.

As predicted, we found that adolescents who collaborated with a friend exhibited greater pretest to posttest change than adolescents who collaborated with an acquaintance. When we analyzed the videotaped collaborations, we found that friends were more likely than acquaintances to justify their proposals, work collaboratively, engage in transactive discussions of task concepts and solutions, and evaluate their outcomes. Although all these discourse and interaction features were positively correlated with problem-solving accuracy during both the collaboration and posttest sessions, only the correlation between transactive conflicts and problem-solving accuracy was statistically significant.

These findings were mediated by task difficulty. In particular, the differences between friends and acquaintances regarding transactive dialogues and

task performance were significant only in the most difficult isolation of variables problems. Further analyses of the interactions revealed that, in the more
difficult problems, the collaborations of acquaintances tended to disintegrate.
For example, adolescents often became absorbed in the task and began to
work individually and produce self-directed (private) speech. There was also
an increase in power struggles and conceptual conflicts characterized by unilateral negotiation strategies, such as insistence, physical blocks, or verbal
aggression. Most pairs of friends, in contrast, were able to sustain and repair
the collaboration in these difficult circumstances. They maintained their partner's involvement by asking questions, offering encouragement, and making
statements to the effect that "We're in this together" or, as one girl told her
partner, "They [the experimenters] are trying to trick us, but we'll show 'em."
During conceptual conflicts, they justified their positions, were receptive
to criticism and to their partner's proposals, and refrained from personal
attacks.

Although one could argue that these differences in the collaborations of
friends and acquaintances reflect differences in their social and cognitive
competencies, the adolescents were randomly assigned to the friends or acquaintances conditions, and subsequent analyses revealed no differences in
the pretest scores of the two groups. I suggest that it is more likely that the
differences in collaboration processes and outcomes reflect variations in adolescents' motivations to achieve a shared understanding of their roles, goals,
and the task, as well as the ease with which they could achieve such understanding. For example, adolescents' respect for their friends and eagerness to
work with them may have led them to work harder at repairing the collaboration and resolving conflicts of roles or ideas. It is also possible that due to their
longer interaction history, the interaction routines of friends were more automatized, and thus they were able to maintain the collaboration even when the
problem made high demands on their cognitive resources. These speculations
require further scrutiny. I hope, however, that I have succeeded in making a
case for exploring further the influence of relationships, task difficulty, and
other contextual variables on peer interactive minds. An important goal for
the future is to not treat these relationships as monolithic – friendship and
acquaintanceship relationships vary dramatically, and not all friendships have
the positive qualities that I have described.

I do not want to leave the reader with the impression that in order to
maximize the synergy and cognitive outcomes of children's and adolescents'
interactive minds, we should try to ensure that they collaborate with their
friends. Collaborating with an acquaintance might allow individuals to stretch
their skills in the service of accommodating to the interactive and cognitive
skills of an unfamiliar partner (see Rogoff, 1990). Moreover, because in both
childhood and adulthood there is a decline in the incidence of negotiations

among close friends and romantic partners (Clark, 1984; Krappmann, personal communication, October 1993), this factor will have to be taken into account in our models about the relation between negotiation and cognitive development. It is possible that this decline in negotiations is domain-specific (e.g., confined to duties and responsibilities). It seems likely that negotiations about knowledge, ideas, and values remain an active component of friendships. If such were not the case, the relationship would not evolve, and over time, individuals would feel bored and stifled and search for new, more exciting relationships (see Fogel, 1993).

Peer interactive minds across the life span

Peer interactive minds in adulthood have been explored extensively in research on group problem solving in social psychology (for reviews, see Levine & Moreland, 1990, and Levine & Resnick, 1993) and on collaboration and knowledge construction in work settings (e.g., Goodwin, 1993; Hutchins & Paley, 1993; Suchman, 1993). The interactive minds of adults have also been studied by researchers interested in jury decision making (e.g., Hastie & Pennington, 1991) and by developmental psychologists interested in the role of dialogue in promoting moral and cognitive development (e.g., Berkowitz & Gibbs, 1983; Dimant & Bearison, 1991), creativity (e.g., Czikszentmihalyi & Sawyer, in press; John-Steiner, 1985), and wisdom (Staudinger, Chapter 10, this volume). Although space considerations prevent me from summarizing this literature, Staudinger (Chapter 10, this volume) provides an excellent introduction to this work. My goal for this section is merely to argue for the need for cross-fertilization of research on peer interactive minds in childhood and adolescence as well as in adulthood and old age.

As mentioned earlier, work on children and adolescents has proceeded relatively independently from work on adults and the elderly. Given this state of affairs, one might ask what researchers studying peer collaborative cognition at different points of the life span could learn from each other's work. I suggest that those of us who have focused on childhood and adolescence would do well to take note that we have to study both interacting minds and solitary reflection. Staudinger (Chapter 10, this volume), for example, found that adults who were allowed a few minutes of solitary reflection following their discussion with a peer gave more sophisticated solutions to uncertain life situations than adults who worked alone or participated in peer discussions but were not allowed these moments of solitude before the posttest. Perhaps we have lost sight of the importance of solitary conscious or unconscious activity for cognitive growth as a result of the contemporary emphasis on the social construction of knowledge. Individual posttests are not enough. We have to explore the genesis and ontogenesis of knowledge longitudinally, trying to, as

Staudinger (Chapter 10, this volume) suggests, capture the delicate balance between interactive and solitary activities.

Csikszentmihalyi and Sawyer's (in press) interviews with professionals who were nominated as unusually creative by their peers also suggest that it might be useful to study informal discussions of issues or problems in which children and adolescents are not constrained by the demands of generating a tangible product, because this "cognitive play" seems essential for the genesis and ontogenesis of knowledge. We also need to increase our understanding of the situatedness (see Suchman, 1993) of peer interactive minds, paying greater attention to the fact that our task and the participants' interaction processes are embedded in a larger cultural setting that influences task solutions and collaboration dynamics.

In addition, we should move beyond relying exclusively on analyses of verbal processes to studying other ways in which peer interactive minds communicate and learn from each other. Hutchins and Paley (1993), for example, have shown how incorporating actions and nonverbal messages into the analyses can help us not only to illuminate dimensions of knowledge construction and revision that talk does not capture, but also to contextualize the meaning of the talk. Finally, because tolerance for ambiguity and flexibility in considering alternatives may be one of the hallmarks of adulthood, and perhaps the major difference between children's and adults' interactive minds, we must begin to study other types of tasks, especially problems with ill-formed or, at the very least, multiple solutions. Even in adulthood, however, flexibility and tolerance of ambiguity is not guaranteed. Indeed, truly sophisticated problem solving that takes into account ambiguities and what is within the realm of possibility may be a defining feature of wisdom (Baltes, 1993).

Scientists studying peer interactive minds in adulthood and old age might emulate the work on childhood and adolescence insofar as they pay more attention to age-related changes in the processes and outcomes of peer interactive minds. There are both improvements and declines in communicative, metacognitive, and negotiation skills over adulthood (see Baltes, 1993), but at this point we do not know how these normative and non-normative developmental changes influence the processes and products of peer interactive minds. An interesting question is whether one compensatory strategy for remaining productive and creative is to enlist the collaboration of others, and thus, in some cases older adults may benefit more from collaboration than younger adults. If so, the benefits of collaboration would be greater in older than younger adulthood. But this is an empirical question, and because my knowledge of peer interactive minds in adulthood is limited, I am reticent to speculate further. I end with some issues that challenge our future understanding of the processes and outcomes of peer interactive minds, regardless of whether one studies children, adolescents, or adults.

Peer interactive minds: theoretical and methodological issues

Despite our progress in understanding the processes and outcomes of peer interactive minds, we currently face several obstacles that make it difficult to create a life-span developmental theory of peer collaborative cognition. First, as mentioned earlier, one challenge is that the work on children and adolescents for the most part has proceeded independently from the work on younger and older adults. Often, different questions, methodologies, and problems characterize research on early and later parts of the life span. Thus, it will not be easy to link the findings together. Second, regardless of which part of the life span we focus on, the formulation of powerful concepts and mechanisms for the co-construction of cognition has not been accompanied by empirical documentation of how the social discourse becomes the internal discourse that leads to knowledge construction and revision. It is not that such documentation has not been attempted. Rather, we are still hampered by our inability to look inside minds to explain the puzzle that even in cases where partners appear to have the same amount of knowledge before the collaboration, the same discourse events promote cognitive growth in some individuals but not in others.

I will suggest that part of the problem is that we need to rethink our pretest–collaboration–posttest designs such that they are adapted to the slow, nonlinear pace of cognitive development. As mentioned, we should also consider whether our fascination with peer interacting minds may have led us to underestimate the contribution of solitary work and reflection to cognitive development, or at least to fail to recognize that cognitive development requires both social interaction and solitary reflection.[5] Finally, concerning an issue that I will not discuss further because I cannot offer a solution, we need to develop more sensitive measures of our research participants' knowledge and competencies. For example, our current penchant for assessing mastery or knowledge from the products of pretest, interactive, and posttest sessions may over- or underestimate the competence of our participants. We often also make the incorrect assumption that if individuals are exposed to a more sophisticated, well-justified view, they will recognize its import and revise their own thinking, or alternatively, if their partner's view is less sophisticated, they will challenge it and through the process of explaining their objections, increase their confidence in their own beliefs. The fact is that we still know very little about the impetus for knowledge construction and revision during and following social interaction.

In this concluding section, I shall focus on two questions: Where are we now? Where do we go from here? The good news is that the past few decades of research and application have been quite stimulating. Through detailed (and exhausting) observation of peer collaborative processes, we have identified some of the features of peer interactive minds that promote cognitive growth and linked these features to both individual and social-contextual developmental processes. We have also gained a better understanding of how some contextual and cultural factors will affect the ability and willingness of peers to collaborate and co-construct cognition. Our work has made an impact on educational practices all over the world, such that peer learning has become quite popular in school and university classrooms. The bad news is that I believe we have not made as much progress as we think, particularly in our understanding of the relation between specific collaborative processes and specific cognitive products.

Our lack of progress is not due to a lack of powerful mechanisms or metaphors – for example, co-construction, internalization, appropriation, and transactive discussion – but rather at least partly to our failure to specify these mechanisms at both the theoretical and empirical level. Lawrence and Valsiner's comment concerning the limitations of our current treatment of internalization can also be applied to our other mechanisms:

> This general concept of internalization is not sufficient for elaborated theoretical use, nor is it helpful in deriving empirical research methodologies. To go beyond generalities, it is necessary to specify what "materials" are imported from society into the intra-personal world of any individual and *in what ways* it operates. (1993, p. 151)

In his commentary on Lawrence and Valsiner's paper, Wertsch (1993) makes a radical proposal: If we really want to understand the cognitive outcomes of social interaction, we need to stop using metaphors such as internalization, which imply a dualism between the social and the individual. He suggests that we substitute the concept of mastery for internalization and focus our efforts on mapping how the performance of individuals changes over the course of a social interaction and beyond (e.g., during future individual or collaborative encounters with the problem or task). Although Wertsch's points are well taken and his proposal useful, focusing on analyzing the mastery process is not enough. After all, this is the approach that the majority of scholars following Vygotsky's sociocultural tradition have taken over the past few years, and as I contend, we are still far from understanding the transformations through which social interaction promotes cognitive development. Moreover, if we focus on measuring changes in performance, are we tapping into competence? Does it matter? Although I cannot answer these questions at present, I suggest that we need to consider them. If we do decide to go the "task performance equals mastery" route, then we need to gain a better understanding of how contextual and developmental factors influence the processes and outcomes of peer interactive minds and use our findings to develop a well-specified theoretical model. In addition, as mentioned, we should reconsider our current ways of assessing mastery or knowledge.

I have been one of the proponents of the advantages of the pretest–collaboration–posttest design for assessing the cognitive outcomes of peer interactive minds. As mentioned earlier, upon reflection I have come to recognize that there are several problems with this design. First, it is often the case that improvements in children's and adolescents' performance during the collaboration fail to materialize in the posttest. Rogoff, Radziszewska, and Masiello (in press) have proposed that the finding that gains observed during the collaboration session do not generalize to the individual posttest is not surprising because the collaboration and the posttest represent different social contexts. They add that it is unreasonable to assume that posttest performance is the best characterization of the "true inner state" of our participants, and suggest that following the collaboration, we should assess their participation in a variety of social and individual contexts to get a better estimate of conceptual change. The points of Rogoff and her colleagues are well taken. Their strategy is quite compatible with Wertsch's proposal and enhances it by introducing sociocultural considerations into performance assessments. Yet this strategy does not take us much beyond describing how individuals develop mastery in a variety of contexts. Our task is still to explain these changes in mastery, and I am not sure that observations or detailed descriptions of contexts and processes of participation will yield the explanations that we need. (But of course, I must admit that at the moment I cannot offer an alternative approach.)[6]

An additional problem with the posttest design is that it is based on the assumption that we have a grasp of the pace of development and thus know when we should measure it – that is, when to administer the posttest and how much change to expect. In a series of studies, Christine Howe and her colleagues (Howe, Tolmie, & Rodgers, 1992; Tolmie et al., 1993) have explored children's, adolescents', and young adults' co-construction of understanding in the domain of physics. Their work is unique (but see Phelps & Damon, 1989) in that they administer more than one posttest following the collaboration session. What initially intrigued me about their findings was that they demonstrated that the cognitive benefits of the collaboration did not materialize immediately. In the first posttest, peers who had engaged in transactive discussions showed a similar level of mastery than those who had not engaged in these types of dialogues. In the posttest that was administered 2 months later, however, peers who had engaged in transactive dialogues showed significantly more sophisticated understanding of physics than those who had not. Howe and her colleagues proposed that this delayed effect may index the time that it takes individuals to re-equilibrate their cognitive structures or to reflect on the understanding that they co-constructed during the collaboration and put it into practice.

In the context of an electronic discussion sponsored by the Laboratory of Comparative Human Cognition (San Diego, California), Steve Draper, one of Tolmie and Howe's colleagues, pointed out in jest that their data suggest that the process of fermentation may provide the new metaphor for cognitive development. That is, the products of peer interactive minds may need to ferment for a while before they are incorporated into existing cognitive structures and begin to guide performance (see also Staudinger, Chapter 10, this volume). This fermentation process is not necessarily conscious, but at some point it passes a threshold into awareness. While the fermentation metaphor may prove to be another theoretically powerful but empirically useless construct, it is worth pursuing. To track the fermentation process empirically, we need to carry out longitudinal research. The value of carrying out such research is illustrated by the contributions that Deanna Kuhn and her colleagues (e.g., Kuhn, 1991; Kuhn, et al., 1988; Kuhn & Phelps, 1979) have made to mapping microgenetic changes in the scientific reasoning of individuals. An important contribution of their research is to show that change is not linear; that is, it is subject to false starts, regressions, and resistance to change. In many cases, individuals also fail to realize the significance of their findings, thus ignoring potential insights or solutions (Kuhn & Phelps, 1979).

Carrying out longitudinal studies of peer interactive minds, both in terms of including multiple collaborative sessions and a series of posttests spaced over several months, is not the only (and perhaps even best) solution for linking the processes and cognitive products of peer collaboration, but it is at least an alternative that is worth pursuing. Without stronger and better specified theoretical and measurement models, however, even this alternative may fail to help us make significant progress in our understanding of peer interactive minds. One of our biggest challenges, and the one that I would like to explore in my future work, is understanding enough about tasks, collaboration processes and outcomes, and their developmental patterns so that we can create the situations in which peer interactive minds produce, revise, and appropriate knowledge in both the laboratory and in the "wilds" of the classroom, the work place, or any environment of daily living.

Notes

1 I would be the first to admit that we also need to address how the nature of the task influences peer interactive minds. This is a particularly relevant issue if we consider that different processes and mechanisms are associated with different kinds of cognitive outcomes (cf. Damon, 1984). Unfortunately, discussing this issue with the depth that it requires must be left for another chapter as my agenda for this chapter is already quite full.

2 This strategy, however, was often effective when paired with a threat to tell the experimenter that the child was not following his or her instructions to work together.

3 Piaget's and Vygotsky's frameworks are not as far apart as they are often portrayed in the literature. Process analyses are quite common in contemporary research that follows from Piaget's theory, and researchers in the Vygotskian tradition are increasingly considering the role of ontogenetic constraints in negotiation. Moreover, there is a growing trend to integrate both approaches to generate a tighter framework for conceptualizing the cognitive products of peer collaboration.

4 Of course, one solution to this problem *is* to restructure the schools (e.g., Tharp & Gallimore, 1988). However, mounting evidence suggests that the change brought about by restructuring is

remarkably difficult to sustain, and that over time the institutions often revert to their initial state. Moreover, most of us do not have the experience or resources needed to restructure the schools.

5 Of course, there is no such thing as a solitary mind; the individual always hears the "voices" of others who have influenced his or her thinking and problem-solving competencies (see Wertsch, 1991). By solitary reflection I simply mean thought that occurs when one is by oneself.

6 Perhaps I am hesitant to accept Rogoff and others' proposal because I think that, by adopting it, one searches only for the contextual impetus for developmental change and thus pays insufficient attention to the role of the cognitions and motivations of individuals in promoting development.

References

Azmitia, M. (1988). Peer interaction and problem solving: When are two heads better than one? *Child Development, 59*, 87–96.

Azmitia, M. (1989, April). *Constraints on learning through collaboration: The influence of age, expertise, and interaction dynamics.* Paper presented at the biennial meetings of the Society for Research in Child Development, Kansas City, KS.

Azmitia, M., & Linnet, J. (1995). Elementary school children's conflicts with friends and acquaintances. Unpublished manuscript.

Azmitia, M., Lopez, E. M., Conner, S., & Kolesnik, K. (1991, July). *Children's negotiation of collaboration and learning.* Paper presented at the biennial meetings of the International Society for the Study of Behavioral Development, Minneapolis, MN.

Azmitia, M., & Montgomery, R. (1993). Friendship, transactive dialogues, and the development of scientific reasoning. *Social Development, 2*, 202–221.

Azmitia, M., & Perlmutter, M. (1989). Social influences on children's cognition: State of the art and future directions. In H. W. Reese (Ed.), *Advances in child development and behavior* (Vol. 22, pp. 89–144). New York: Academic.

Baltes, P. B. (1993). The aging mind: Potential and limits. *Gerontologist, 33*, 580–594.

Berkowitz, M. W., & Gibbs, J. C. (1983). Measuring the developmental features of moral discussion. *Merrill-Palmer Quarterly, 29*, 399–410.

Berkowitz, M. W., & Gibbs, J. C. (1985). The process of moral conflict resolution and moral development. In M. W. Berkowitz (Ed.), *New directions for child development: Peer conflict and psychological growth* (pp. 71–84). San Francisco: Jossey-Bass.

Berkowitz, M. W., Oser, F., & Althof, W. (1987). The development of sociomoral discourse. In W. M. Kurtines and J. L. Gewirtz (Eds.), *Moral development through social interaction* (pp. 322–352). New York: Wiley.

Berndt, T. J., Perry, T. B., & Miller, K. E. (1988). Friends' and classmates' interactions on academic tasks. *Journal of Educational Psychology, 80*, 506–513.

Bos, M. C. (1934). Experimental study of productive collaboration. *Acta Psychologica, 3*, 315–426.

Brownell, C. A., & Carriger, M. S. (1991). Changes in cooperation and self–other differentiation during the second year. *Child Development, 61*, 1164–1174.

Clark, M. S. (1984). Record keeping in two types of relationships. *Journal of Personality and Social Psychology, 47*, 549–557.

Cooper, C. R., Ayers-Lopez, S., & Marquis, S. (1982). Children's discourse during peer learning in experimental and naturalistic situations. *Discourse Processes, 5*, 177–191.

Cooper, C. R., & Cooper, R. G. (1984). Peer learning discourse: What develops? In S. Kuczaj (Ed.), *Children's discourse* (pp. 77–97). New York: Springer.

Corsaro, W. M. (1985). *Friendship and peer culture in the early years.* Norwood, NJ: Ablex.

Czikszentmihalyi, M., & Sawyer, K. (in press). Creative insight: The social dimension of a solitary moment. In R. J. Sternberg & J. E. Davidson (Eds.), *The nature of insight.* Cambridge, MA: MIT Press.

Damon, W. (1984). Peer education: The untapped potential. *Journal of Applied Developmental Psychology, 5,* 331–343.

Damon, W. (1990). Social relations and children's thinking skills. In D. Kuhn (Ed.), *Perspectives on teaching and learning thinking skills: Contributions to Human Development* (pp. 95–107). Basel: Krager.

Dimant, R. J., & Bearison, D. J. (1991). Development of formal reasoning during successive peer interactions. *Developmental Psychology, 27,* 277–284.

Ellis, S., & Gauvain, M. (1992). Social and cultural influences on children's collaborative interactions. In L. T. Winegar & J. Valsiner (Eds.), *Children's development within social context: Vol. 2. Research and methodology* (pp. 155–180). Hillsdale, NJ: Erlbaum.

Ellis, S., & Rogoff, B. (1986). Problem solving in children's management of instruction. In E. C. Mueller & C. R. Cooper (Eds.), *Process and outcome in peer relationships* (pp. 301–325). New York: Academic.

Ellis, S., & Siegler, R. S. (in press). The development of problem solving. In *Handbook of Perception and Cognition.*

Fogel, A. (1993). *Developing through relationships: Origins of communication, self, and culture.* Chicago: University of Chicago Press.

Forman, E. A. (1992). Discourse, intersubjectivity, and the development of peer collaboration: A Vygotskian approach. In L. T. Winegar & J. Valsiner (Eds.), *Children's development within social context: Vol. 2. Research and methodology* (pp. 143–160). Hillsdale, NJ: Erlbaum.

Forman, E. A., & Cazden, C. B. (1985). Exploring Vygotskian perspectives in education: The cognitive value of peer interaction. In J. V. Wertsch (Ed.), *Culture, communication, and cognition: Vygotskian perspectives* (pp. 323–347). Cambridge: Cambridge University Press.

Forman, E. A., & McPhail, J. (1993). Vygotskian perspective in children's collaborative problem solving activity. In E. A. Forman, N. Minick, & C. A. Stone (Eds.), *Contexts for learning: Sociocultural dynamics in children's development* (pp. 213–229). Oxford: Oxford University Press.

Garton, A. F. (1992). *Social interaction and the development of language and cognition.* Hillsdale, NJ: Erlbaum.

Garvey, C. (1987, April). *Creation and avoidance of conflict.* Paper presented at the biennial meetings of the Society for Research in Child Development, Baltimore, MD.

Gilovich, T. (1991). *How we know what isn't so: The fallibility of human reason in everyday life.* New York: Free Press.

Goodwin, C. (1993, November). *Seeing as a situated phenomenon.* Paper presented at the NATO sponsored workshop Discourse, Tools, and Reasoning: Situated Cognition and Technologically Supported Environments, Lucca, Italy.

Gottman, J. (1983). How children become friends. *Monographs of the Society for Research in Child Development, 48* (3, Serial 201).

Hartup, W. W. (1983). Peer relations. In E. M. Hetherington (Ed.) & P. H. Mussen (Series Ed.), *Handbook of child psychology: Vol. 4. Socialization, personality, and social development* (pp. 103–196). New York: Wiley.

Hartup, W. W. (in press). Cooperation, close relationships, and cognitive development. In W. M. Bukowski, A. F. Newcomb, & W. W. Hartup (Eds.), *The company they keep: Friendships and their developmental significance.* New York: Cambridge University Press.

Hastie, R., & Pennington, N. (1991). Cognitive and social processes in decision making. In L. B. Resnick, J. M. Levine, & S. D. Teasley (Eds.), *Perspectives in socially shared cognition* (pp. 308–327). Washington, DC: American Psychological Association.

Hinde, R. A. (1979). *Towards understanding relationships.* New York: Academic.

Howe, C., Tolmie, A., & Rodgers, C. (1992). The acquisition of conceptual knowledge in science by primary school children: Group interaction and the understanding of motion down an incline. *British Journal of Developmental Psychology, 10,* 113–130.

Hutchins, E., & Paley, L, (1993, November). *Constructing meaning from space, gesture, and talk.*

Paper presented at the NATO sponsored workshop Discourse, Tools, and Reasoning: Situated Cognition and Technologically Supported Environments, Lucca, Italy.

John-Steiner, V. (1985). *Notebooks of the mind.* New York: Harper.

Krappmann, L., & Oswald, H. (1987, April). *Negotiation strategies in peer conflicts: A follow-up study in natural settings.* Paper presented at the biennial meetings of the Society for Research in Child Development, Baltimore, MD.

Kruger, A. C. (1992). The effect of peer and adult–child transactive discussions on moral reasoning. *Merrill-Palmer Quarterly, 38,* 191–211.

Kruger, A. C. (1993). Peer collaboration: Conflict, cooperation, or both? *Social Development, 2,* 165–183.

Kuhn, D. (1991). *The skills of argument.* Cambridge: Cambridge University Press.

Kuhn, D., Amsel, E., & O'Loughlin, M. (1988). *The development of scientific thinking skills.* New York: Academic.

Kuhn, D., & Brannock, J. (1977). Development of the isolation of variables scheme in experimental and natural experiments' contexts. *Developmental Psychology, 13,* 9–13.

Kuhn, D., & Phelps, E. (1979) A methodology for observing development of a formal reasoning strategy. In D. Kuhn (Ed.), *New directions for child development: Intellectual development beyond childhood* (pp. 45–58). San Francisco: Jossey-Bass.

Lawrence, J. A., & Valsiner, J. (1993). Conceptual roots of internalization: From transmission to transformation. *Human Development, 36,* 150–167.

Levin, L., & Druyan, S. (1993). When sociocognitive transaction among peers fails: The case of misconceptions in science. *Child Development, 63,* 1571–1591.

Levine, J. M. & Moreland, R. L. (1990). Progress in small-group research. *Annual Review of Psychology, 41,* 585–634.

Levine, J. M., & Resnick, L. B. (1993). Social foundations of cognition. *Annual Review of Psychology, 44,* 585–612.

Miller, M. (1987). Argumentation and cognition. In M. Hickmann (Ed.), *Social and functional approaches to language and thought* (pp. 225–249). San Diego, CA: Academic.

Moss, E. (1992). The socioaffective context of joint cognitive activity. In L. T. Winegar & J. Valsiner (Eds.), *Children's development within social context: Vol. 2. Research and methodology* (pp. 117–154). Hillsdale, NJ: Erlbaum.

Nelson, J., & Aboud, F. (1985). The resolution of social conflict between friends. *Child Development, 56,* 1009–1017.

Newcomb, A. F., Brady, J. E., & Hartup, W. W. (1979). Friendship and incentive condition as determinants of children's task-oriented social behavior. *Child Development, 50,* 878–881.

Palincsar, A. S., & Brown, A. L. (1984). Reciprocal teaching of comprehension-fostering and comprehension-monitoring activities. *Cognition and Instruction, 2,* 117–175.

Perret-Clermont, A. N. Perret, J. F., & Bell, N. (1991). The social construction of meaning and cognitive activity in elementary school children. In L. B. Resnick, J. M. Levine, & S. D. Teasley (Eds.), *Perspectives on socially shared cognition* (pp. 41–62). Washington, DC: American Psychological Association.

Phelps, E., & Damon W. (1989). Problem solving with equals: Peer collaboration as a context for learning mathematics and spatial concepts. *Journal of Educational Psychology, 4,* 639–646.

Piaget, J. (1965). *The moral judgement of the child.* New York: Basic.

Pozzi, S., Healey, L., & Hoyles, C. (1993). Learning and interaction in groups with computers: When do ability and gender matter? *Social Development, 2,* 222–241.

Rogoff, B. (1990). *Apprenticeship in thinking: Cognitive development in social context.* New York: Oxford University Press.

Rogoff, B., Radziszewska, B., & Masiello, T. (in press). Analysis of developmental process in sociocultural activity. In L. Martin, K. Nelson, & E. Tobach (Eds.), *Cultural psychology and activity theory.* Cambridge: Cambridge University Press.

Rubtsov, V. V. (1981). The role of cooperation in the development of intelligence. *Soviet Psychology, 19,* 41–62.

Selman, R. L. (1980). *The growth of interpersonal understanding.* New York: Academic.

Shantz, C. U., & Hobart, C. J. (1989). Social conflict and development: Peers and siblings. In T. J. Berndt & G. W. Ladd (Eds.), *Peer relationships in child development* (pp. 71–94). New York: Wiley.

Slavin, R. E. (1987). Developmental and motivational perspectives on cooperative learning: A reconciliation. *Child Development, 58,* 1161–1167.

Suchman, L. (1993, November). *Centers of coordination: A case and some themes.* Paper presented at the NATO sponsored workshop Discourse, Tools, and Reasoning: Situated Cognition and Technologically Supported Environments, Lucca, Italy.

Teasley, S. D., & Roschelle, J. (1993). Constructing a joint problem space: The computer as a tool for sharing knowledge. In S. P. Lajoie & S. D. Derry (Eds.), *Computers as cognitive tools* (pp. 229–258). Hillsdale, NJ: Erlbaum.

Tharp, R., & Gallimore, R. (1988). *Rousing minds to life.* Cambridge: Cambridge University Press.

Tolmie, A., Howe, C., Mackenzie, M., & Greer, K. (1993). Task design as an influence on dialogue and learning: Primary school work with object flotation. *Social Development, 2,* 183–201.

Tomasello, M., Kruger, A. C., & Ratner, H. H. (1993). Cultural learning. *Behavioral and Brain Sciences, 16,* 495–552.

Van Eemeren, F. H., Grootendorst, R., & Kruiger, T. (1984). *The study of argumentation.* New York: Irvington.

Verba, M. (1993). Construction and sharing of meanings in pretend play. In M. Stanback & H. Sinclair (Eds.), *Pretend play among 3-year-olds* (pp. 1–29). Hillsdale, NJ: Erlbaum.

Verba, M. (in press). Beginnings of collaboration in peer interaction. *Human Development.*

Vygotsky, L. S. (1978). *Mind in society.* Cambridge, MA: Harvard University Press.

Wertsch, J. V. (1978). Adult-child interaction and the roots of metacognition. *Quarterly Newsletter of the Institute for Comparative Human Development, 2,* 15–18.

Wertsch, J. V. (1991). *Voices of the mind.* Cambridge: Cambridge University Press.

Wertsch, J. V. (1993). Commentary. *Human Development, 36,* 168–171.

Winegar, L. T. (1988). Children's emerging understanding of social events: Co-construction and social process. In J. Valsiner (Ed.), *Child development within culturally structured environments: Vol. 2. Social co-construction and environmental guidance in development* (pp. 3–27). Norwood, NJ: Ablex.

Youniss, J. (1980). *Parents and peers in social development.* Chicago: University of Chicago Press.

6 Collaborative rules: how are people supposed to work with one another?

Jacqueline J. Goodnow

Abstract

To occasions of shared action, from conversations to intellectual teamwork or household divisions of labor, people bring expectations about what each person should contribute, about appropriate forms of control, delegation, and reward, and about the distribution of credit or blame. This chapter takes as its major aim the analysis of such expectations, bringing out the form they take and demonstrating research formats that make it feasible to answer questions about the strength of various expectations and the course of their development. Of particular relevance, it emerges, are the links between expectations and the definition of the relationship (e.g., a relationship of equals or nonequals, of people in "exchange" or "communal" relationships to one another). Most of the examples are drawn from studies of household divisions of labor: divisions between parents and children, or between adult partners. The general principles, however, are relevant to all occasions when people work together on a problem or when what one person does influences what others do.

The term *collaborative* in the title signals my interest in a particular set of interactive situations: a set in which people work together on a task or in which the work of one person is part of the work of a unit. Into that set one may place the work of a household, a research group, a classroom, a firm, or a factory. I make the specification because all situations are in some sense "interactive" or "social." Even in experimental settings that appear to call for an individual to work alone, other people are involved. They may give rise to the problem, define the task, set boundaries or the time allowed, provide resources, place limits on the approaches we may use, create the history for what we do. We need then to offer some specification of what distinguishes one "interactive" or one "social" situation from another.

I am happy to acknowledge several debts: to the Australian Research Council for financial support; to several colleagues who have worked with me on "collaborative rules" (Jennifer Bowes and Pamela Warton especially); to Peggy Miller, who has taught me to think about narratives and conversations as forms of collaborative work; and to the organizers and members of the Berlin conference, who challenged me to think in a new way about some old issues.

163

The term *rules* signals my interest in the question: What ideas do people hold about the way one person's work or activity should be coordinated or interwoven with that of another? Those ideas or expectations may be of several kinds. To any collaboration, for instance, we bring ideas about what each person should do (both how much and what part of the work). Less obviously, we also bring ideas about possible delegation; reasonable rewards; appropriate divisions of credit and blame; proper styles of control, supervision, or mentoring; acceptable and intolerable ways of joining in, turning down a request, or negotiating points of difference.

Not signaled in the title is the particular research route that my colleagues and I have been pursuing in order to understand the nature and sources of such expectations. We decided early on that we would concentrate on the way work was expected to be done rather than follow what are coming to be relatively well-trodden paths: exploring who actually does what in any joint effort and the circumstances under which people working together are more effective than people working alone. That decision presented two challenges. The first was to lay out a number of expectations. We needed specific ideas rather than general referrals to "fairness" or "rightness." We also needed to go beyond the obvious appeal of exploring ideas about how much each person should do. The second challenge was to find ways of thinking about change and variation. How are ideas about collaboration acquired? Do they vary with the individual's age, gender, ethnicity, socioeconomic status, vested interests, or cohort? Do they display life-span development? What conceptual frameworks might accommodate the forms that change and its correlates take?

We are far from having met those challenges in full. We have, however, found a particularly rich content area to use as a base. This is the area of household work. It is not, as I shall note later in the chapter, the only area we have used as a base. It is, however, the base we have used most often and the base for most of the studies I shall draw from throughout this chapter. The choice, I should say from the start, has taught us something about the ideas that social scientists hold about expected divisions of labor: expected territories and ownerships of knowledge. Some of my cognitive colleagues, for instance, have difficulty in accepting any form of "everyday thinking" as a respectable part of cognitive science. Even when they are able to stretch the definition of "social cognition" to cover an interest in parents' models of development (e.g., Goodnow & Collins, 1990), they boggle at including the "trivia" of household work. Developmental psychologists see the topic as more respectable but often regard it as a move into "moral development" (the research deals with "the way work is supposed to be") or "sociology" or "family studies." Sociologists, in turn, take the topic for granted – for them it has complete respectability – but some clearly find it strange that we spend so much of our time on the ideas that people hold rather than concentrating on overt behaviors or carefully scaled measures of satisfaction and discontent.

I hope to show that household work has numerous virtues as an area in which to explore the nature and sources of collaborative rules – rules that can then be looked for and explored in other settings. I hope also to show how studies based in this area can be used to meet two goals: to bring out the methods, the paradigms, by which one may explore the social aspects of cognition, and to link specific research studies to general questions and conceptual frameworks related to development over the life span.

The chapter has six sections. The first lays out the background to my interest in ideas about the way work of any kind proceeds and to the anchoring of empirical research in one particular work setting: households where people are involved in family or couple relationships. The second and third discuss the particular expectations we have explored and the methods we have used to describe them – methods that can be extended to other forms of work and to a variety of ages or social groups. The first of this pair concentrates on ideas about what each person should do – both the amount and the kind of work, with an emphasis on the latter. This is the expectation for which I can report the largest set of empirical studies. The second of the pair reports the analysis of further expectations – ideas about reasonable rewards and sanctions, acceptable methods of control or monitoring, and appropriate styles of work or negotiation.

The next three sections form a trio of extensions. It is all very well to demonstrate that people hold a variety of expectations about the way household work should proceed. To go beyond this, we need first to indicate that the analysis of ideas is helpful in bringing a fresh look to the analysis of what people do. In this respect, we have differentiated among the ways in which work is shared between adult partners or assigned to children, and among the ways in which people signal to one another what their expectations are.

Next, we need to indicate how the concepts and methods developed for the analysis of work in households can be extended to other settings where people work together or where what one person does is interwoven with the actions of others. The extensions outlined involve teaching (see Mandl, Gruber, & Renkl, Chapter 14, this volume), analyses of expert–novice interactions (see Azmitia, Chapter 5, this volume; Strube, Janetzko, & Knauff, Chapter 13, this volume), and the way people collaborate in telling stories (see Dixon & Gould, Chapter 3, this volume).

Finally, we need to locate a theoretical framework that will cover variations among individuals and change over the life span or across historical time. The framework I propose is drawn from theories that consider the ideas that individuals hold as essentially shared with others: as "social representations" (e.g., von Cranach, Doise, & Mugny, 1992) or as "cultural models" (e.g., D'Andrade & Strauss, 1992). These models encourage us to think about individuals and societies as holding multiple views of events. Age, for instance, can be seen as involving gains or losses. Care of the aged can be seen as a community or a family obligation, as a duty or as an expression of love. Changes in the salience of one view over another may then be prompted by several factors – by a shift, for instance, in relationships, vested interests, or responsibilities. The critical point is that change in any set of ideas is always viewed by way of comparison with alternative views that are not invented de novo but are already held. Using these theories as a general base, I shall propose that change may be regarded as a shift in the domain to which expectations are referred and from which rules or legitimations are drawn. What was once perceived or framed as a simple question of gender ("men's work, women's work"), for instance, is now often perceived or framed as a question of fairness, preference, or practicality. The principles (e.g., fairness) are not new, but there has been a change in what the principle is seen as covering or implying. Such a view may well be applied to a number of other areas of change over the life span or across historical time.

Theoretical and empirical background

I begin by noting the sources of my interest in ideas about "good" cognitive performances and the potential of concentrating on tasks where the work of two or more people is interwoven. That note is then followed by an outline of the reasons for selecting, as a base for empirical research, a particular content area: the contributions to household work made by children or by adults, with an emphasis on the ideas that people hold about the way work should proceed.

The significance of ideas about what performance should be like

I have for some time been interested in two particular aspects of cognition. The first has to do with the way the ideas we hold as individuals are related to the ideas held by others. When, for instance, do we appropriate or resist the views of events that others – friends, families, colleagues, schools, "opinion makers" – present to us? The other aspect has to do with a particular set of ideas that people may share. These are the ideas that people hold about "good" cognitive performance.

The second aspect is an interest that began for me with the need to account for differences among cultural groups in their scores on tests designed to measure intelligence. Cultural differences in test scores, I proposed, often stemmed from differences in what are regarded as the "smart" or "intelligent" actions to take when faced with a task. That proposal led me first of all to recognize the extent to which "cognitive values" (Goodnow, 1990b) are embedded in most Western achievement and laboratory tasks. When we evaluate test performances, for instance, we often give special approval to performances that are fast, contain no redundancy, are done without help, and are as well "elegant," "original," or in "good style," even when these qualities are not required to solve a problem (Goodnow, 1976; Goodnow, 1990b; Goodnow, Knight, & Cashmore, 1985). That recognition led in turn to my becoming aware that cognitive values provide a way of specifying two often amorphous concepts in the developmental literature. One of these is *social context*. This notion could be defined in terms of the prevailing ideas about optimal, tolerable, and unacceptable performances. The other is *acculturation* or *enculturation*. This could be described as the acquisition of the group's prevailing ideas. In effect, cognitive development could be regarded as involving the acquisition of not only capacity or knowledge but also a set of ideas about what one should use one's capacity or knowledge for and how the use should proceed.

Surprisingly, there is relatively little material on the nature and sources of such values, even though they set the stage for negative judgments of people in later life (their "slowness" is inevitably seen as a sign of deficit) or of people who hold a different set of values ("the pedestrian bourgeoisie" usually gathers little praise from academics). One explicit discussion of implicit values is contained in Bourdieu's provocative analysis of "distinction," essentially an analysis of what is regarded as "good form" or "good taste" in activities ranging from the presentation of food to students' essays (Bourdieu, 1979). Another is contained within accounts of conversation as a "communication game" governed by a number of rules, ranging from turn taking to the expectation that each party will respect the value of speaking in ways that are brief, relevant, and in line with the other's understanding. (The term *communication game* is from Higgins, McCann, and Fondacaro, 1982, who provide a summary of Grice's well-known arguments on such values as brevity and relevance).

How could one extend the conceptual and empirical analysis of cognitive values? My first approach explored judgments about "good" productions by way of asking teachers and children to evaluate children's drawings (Goodnow, Wilkins, & Dawes, 1986). This content area, however, limited the questions I could ask. My second approach consisted of turning to tasks where people work together or where what one person does influences what the other does. Occasions such as these seemed to offer scope for a wider variety of judgments. The critical problem, however, was to find a specific kind of collaborative task: one that would turn the promise into reality.

The selection of household tasks as a substantive base

Where is one to find a substantive content area that provides a rich and varied base for exploring the nature and sources of the ideas people hold about the way a performance or a piece of work should proceed? Broadly speaking, three substantive bases stand out so far in the study of collaborative or overlapping contributions to a task or a performance. One of these has to do with language. The tasks are typically various kinds of communication tasks, with variations occurring in features such as the extent to which speakers use a common referent or draw on similar sets of inferences (e.g., Kraus & Fussell, 1990). A second has to do with the nature of learning or problem solving. These tasks typically call for group problem solving or the combination of experts and novices on an assigned task or in the course of classroom interactions. Azmitia (1988; Chapter 5, this volume) covers a number of such tasks. Others are to be found in the work of Rogoff and her colleagues (e.g., Rogoff, 1990) and Perret-Clermont and her colleagues (Perret-Clermont, Perret, & Bell, 1991), as well as in Forman, Minick, and Stone (1993). The third content area has to do with interpersonal relationships. Here the tasks typically involve observations of the way people persuade others to adopt their point of view or the way they negotiate a compromise (e.g., Falbo & Peplau, 1980; Scanzoni, 1978; Smetana, 1988). The people interacting vary less in their expertise than they do in the length or the expected future of their relationship to one another, in their bargaining power, or in the degree of control they have over the agenda.

Each of these lines of research contains tasks or forms of work that met some of my needs. None, however, seemed to meet all my specifications. I needed a content area that would (a) enable me to ask both about the expectations people held concerning the way collaborative work should proceed and about the way the work proceeded in practice; (b) be meaningful to adults and children, allowing me to gain a sense of the meanings that children might acquire and whether or not they acquired them; (c) allow some room for a lack of agreement – a divergence of viewpoints – as well as for consensus; (d) allow for the impact of relationships between the people involved; and (e) provide a place for considering how affects (satisfaction and discontent) arise. That meant a further requirement: The expectations would need to matter; people would need to care about violations of what they expect. Finally, the content area should allow me to explore a variety of expectations that would be relevant beyond the immediate task and work setting.

I can no longer reconstruct the moment when it occurred to me that household tasks met my criteria. At an earlier point, I had been impressed by the extent to which mothers in two cultural groups in Australia – Anglo-Australian and Lebanese-Australian – differed in their views about children's household jobs (Goodnow, Cashmore, Cotton, & Knight, 1984) and had mentally tagged the difference as interesting. I then began, however, to read the literature on household tasks, keeping an eye open for concepts and methods that might be useful.

I started with analyses of children's work contributions (Goodnow, 1988). I next began to read about couples, predominantly as background for a study of adults who depart from stereotyped divisions of work by gender (Goodnow & Bowes, 1994). In collaboration with Jacqui Smith, I am now reading about the extent to which, at the upper end of the life span, work can again move from parent to child. In the section on building a theoretical framework I will comment on the relative lack of connection among these three literatures. For the moment, it will be sufficient to say that at all parts of the life span, the major theme has been the analysis of what people do. The minor theme has been the analysis of the meanings that work and its patterns have for people. That minor theme is increasingly gaining recognition as a critical gap in the understanding of household work (e.g., Ferree, 1990), but a great deal is yet to be uncovered. In effect, exploring the expectations people of various ages and in various relationships (e.g., parent or partner) held about the way household work should proceed promised to add to our understanding of both this particular form of collaborative action and collaborative action in general.

With several colleagues, I have now completed a series of studies on expectations about the way work contributions to a household should proceed. Most of these studies have now appeared in print or are under review. In effect, the papers are available and I can, accordingly, set aside the details. The best single source is a relatively detailed overview (Goodnow, in press). Within this series of studies, the samples are relatively varied. Some of the studies involve preadolescent children; some involve adolescents and young adults; some involve parents; one concentrates on couples who *do* share the work of a household. The main limitation is that, with one exception (Goodnow et al., 1984), the samples are all from one ethnic group (though they are more diverse in socioeconomic status). This ethnic background is often referred to in Australia as *Anglo-Australian*, a term meaning that the people are monolingual English speakers whose parents were also monolingual English speakers and whose country of origin – one or more generations back – was likely to be England, Ireland, Scotland, or Wales. We are in the process of widening that ethnic base, but we needed first a sample where we felt we would be able to grasp the nuances because we are members of it. The methods are also relatively varied. We have most often used interviews, but within these have embedded a variety of methods: open-ended questions, rating scales, sorting tasks.

I shall bring the several studies together by ignoring their chronological order and by concentrating instead on what we have learned about expectations and principles with regard to four aspects of collaborative or contingent work: expectations about (a) what each should do (with an emphasis on kind rather than amount), (b) appropriate rewards and sanctions (Is money, for instance, an acceptable reward for the work that children do? How should blame be distributed if a delegated task is not done?), (c) appropriate forms of control, regulation, or monitoring (Who, for instance, has the right to set the standards or agenda? What is an acceptable way to check that a delegated task has been done?), and (d) the spirit or style of work and negotiation (Should your work, for instance, be ideally in the form of a cheerful gift rather than an enforced tribute? What are the implications of doing something as "a favor"?).

I shall take each of these areas of expectation in turn, with the most attention given to the first. As I proceed, there will emerge a further indication of the methods used, as well as the pervasive impact of ideas about the nature of relationships on the way work proceeds. Issues of trust, respect, fairness, coercion, equality, the avoidance of "commercialism," and strict exchange or servant-like status surface regularly as underlying the distinctions made between one job and another or one way of proceeding and another.

A first set of rules: what each should do

The literature on work contains one general statement of what expectations might be: "from each according to capacity." That well-known definition of a just world seemed a possible starting point. We suspected that other principles were also involved. What they were, however, was an open question.

We began also by noting that expectations about what people should do are of two kinds. Some are *expectations of amount* – for instance, that each person will do "a fair share" or that a division of work will be "50:50." Others are *expectations of kind* – what particular jobs one or the other person should do. We decided to concentrate on the latter type of expectation, a decision prompted in part by the sense that feelings of discontent seemed often to be attached to particular jobs and in part by the responses of mothers in our first pilot interviews: "What particular jobs are you talking about?"

Finally, we developed early in the series of studies an attachment to a particular method: asking about *the movability of a job*. Could this job be set aside? Could it be moved to someone else? If so, to whom and under what circumstances? If not, why not? There are good conceptual grounds for asking, in the analysis of any performance, about the extent to which an activity or a viewpoint is seen as fixed or changeable. In addition, a question about moveability brought out an important aspect of expectations, encouraging us to persist with this approach in our first study (Goodnow & Delaney, 1989).

More specifically, we have:

1. *Asked mothers, "If X did not do this job, would you ask another child (brother or sister) to do it, would you insist or wait until X could do it, or would you do it yourself?"* The answers brought out an interesting distinction among tasks and the first of a number of principles that went beyond capacity. The task distinction is between family-care jobs (e.g., setting the table) and self-care jobs (e.g., making one's bed, putting away what one has used). Family-care jobs are easily moved from one child to another. Self-care jobs are seldom moved, except as a favor (often to the family – e.g., when "We're all in a hurry

today"). More often, the mother would "take back the job," a phrase suggesting that it is hers in the first place, on loan to a child (Goodnow & Delaney, 1989).

The distinction between the two kinds of job is based on a rule that we have now seen in operation over and over again. We have come to give it the name of "causation" (Goodnow & Warton, 1991). Colloquially, if you created a problem, a mess, a need for a job to be done, then the job of fixing, cleaning up, or repairing is yours. You ask others to do it only under special circumstances. What is more, the expectation that others will clean up after you is likely to generate a particular resentment among people who are not paid to do so (although even paid staff may resent your leaving an "unnecessary" mess or an "avoidable" problem). For people who are not paid, expecting that they will clean up after you implies that they occupy the position of a hired hand or a service/servant status, an implication incompatible with the way they see themselves when they are members of a couple or a family.

2. *Asked parents, "How would you feel about asking a partner or a teenaged son/daughter to do the following jobs?"* And why would this be so? Answers in this case were limited to some given options (e.g., would ask without second thoughts; would have second thoughts but would ask; wouldn't ask, would do it myself; Goodnow, Bowes, Warton, Dawes, & Taylor, 1991). This question added still further to the factors considered in any distribution of work. The explanations parents offered covered the inevitable references to competence ("They can't do it"; "They don't know how"; "They can't do it the way I want it done"). The answers also covered, however, references to efficiency, to the extent to which the request is likely to encounter resistance (noted as a major factor in dealing with teenagers), and to the extent to which a request would generate ill feeling (would generate a gain in labor but a cost to the relationship). Involving someone else on a task can clearly involve the presence of a variety of considerations. We shortchange ourselves if we think of collaborative work or guided participation as based only on assessments of competence or on a principle such as "from each according to capacity."

3. *Asked children of several ages to group jobs into those which, on a busy day, they could ask someone else in the family to do and whether they could ask a mother, a father, a sister, or a brother to do each of four jobs:* set a table, make the child's bed, clean a bathtub or basin, wash a car (Goodnow et al., 1991). Children showed a very clear awareness of the difference between asking someone to take over a self-care job (e.g., making my bed) and asking for a task outside self-care (e.g., setting the table). They also made it clear that generation was a guiding dimension for some job distributions (requests for setting the table seldom went to parents), while gender was the guiding dimension for others (requests for bathroom jobs could go more easily to mothers and sisters than to fathers or brothers; the reverse was true for washing a car).

In effect, what may be moved from one person to another is a function not only of the job, but also of who that person is and what their relationship is to you.

4. *Asked adults who share household work which jobs they share and which they do not* (Goodnow & Bowes, 1994). Some jobs turn out not to be shared because they are the specialty of one or the other of the partners, sometimes with a sense of territoriality attached (in the words of one man, "I prefer her to stay out of my kitchen"). Two jobs that more often carry the connotations of "should not be shared" again invoke the rule of "causation" – ironing and washing cars. There were, among our sample of sharing couples, those in which one or the other person made these jobs a specialty. In about 40% of the couples, however, these jobs were done on the basis of "to each his or her own." Each ironed his or her own clothes, cleaned his or her own car. The reasons offered were of the order: "I use the car most"; "It's my car"; or "I'm the one who likes to wear things that need ironing – why should anyone else pick up the tab?" Such rationales were practically never offered for a task such as cooking (references to special diets or special dishes that require unusual amounts of time or effort were the exceptions).

5. *Kept track of references to amount.* Our sharing couples spoke as if they had read Clark (1984) on the avoidance of strict scorekeeping within close relationships. They spoke of keeping work "roughly equal," but they avoided rosters and explicitly rejected any exact matching of what each did as "not part of a relationship." The one case of rosters was for a couple who found them useful at the beginning of a new pattern of sharing but dropped them as soon as "we knew what each other was doing." By and large, these are couples who are committed to being "fair," who feel able to speak up when they feel things are "getting too far from being even," and whose greater concern is not with the total overall amount of work but with the amount of disliked jobs that are done. In the words of one man, "Fairness for us means that no one person gets stuck with all the jobs we both dislike." With jobs often divided on the basis of preference, it is predominantly the *disliked jobs* (if they are not eliminated or turned over to a paid worker) that attract a concern with the amount that each partner does (Goodnow & Bowes, 1994).

We have by no means exhausted the use of possible distributions of an activity as a way of locating the ideas that underlie phrases such as "my job" or "your job" and of determining the fixedness or the flexibility with which ownership is regarded. To take one example, we have concentrated so far on the perceptions of the person interested in seeking help or making a request. We have not yet considered the perceptions of the person who is on the receiving side of help: the person who encounters offers of assistance or of some "takeover" of what they usually do. In such circumstances, what are the activities we happily divest ourselves of? What counts as "interference" or as a resented takeover? With Jacqui Smith, I have begun to read about the potentially negative consequences of receiving help. With her, I have also begun to explore the response of adults in several age groups to occasions of unsolicited help or unwanted advice – occasions likely to round out the picture gained so far of expectations as to who should do what kinds of work or what parts of a job.

Further rules: incentives, controls, styles

For each of three further content areas, I shall note the form that the main studies have taken and draw out the major results. Placing these further rules into a single set may seem an unwarranted compression. Space, however, is an issue. In addition, the number of studies we have so far completed is smaller than the set for expectations of what each should do.

Incentives: appropriate rewards and sanctions

To any work setting, people bring ideas about the amounts and kinds of reward (praise, thanks, bonuses, promotion, reciprocal favors) that particular actions should attract from others. People also bring ideas about the reasonableness of attaching various amounts and kinds of negative response (from disapproval or blame to penalties of various kinds) to particular actions. In both cases – rewards and sanctions – it is easy to note that people often vary in their ideas as to what should happen. The question is whether we can pin down the nature of these variations and some of the conditions under which they occur.

Our primary exploration of rewards and sanctions has been by way of research on two topics, one directed toward parents' ideas about acceptable and unacceptable connections between *money* and children's household jobs, the other by way of asking children and adolescents about *blame* in situations we have labeled as involving the "delegation" of work. Imagine, we say, that you have asked a sibling to do for you a job that you normally do. Your brother or sister agrees (we choose families where this is a real person), but the job is not done. Who should be blamed? Who should "get into trouble"? How much blame should go to each person?

Money in connection with children's household jobs. Our interest has been predominantly in the appropriateness of money as a reward – that is, with expectations about kind rather than amount. From our explorations of this topic, I shall bring out four points. The first is that our results confirm Clark's (1984) proposal that people are cautious about the use of money in what are regarded as communal relationships (those marked by the expectation that people will be more responsive to the needs of the other than to any strict reciprocity). To take one example, almost all of our Australian mothers responded negatively to the question: Can one child pay another (a brother or sister) to do his or her task? Almost always, the explanation given was that such a practice would be incompatible with "being a family" (Goodnow, 1987). (Teenagers, however, tell us that the practice occurs more often than parents know about.) The minority view was either a lack of concern "because the arrangement wouldn't last" or acceptance on the grounds that it would "teach them about bargaining."

The remaining points emerge from a more structured study in which we asked parents to rate how acceptable they find various kinds of connections between money and jobs. For each connection, parents reported whether their position was one of the following: "completely comfortable with it," "O.K. but not my first choice," "O.K. as a last resort," and "under no circumstances." The connections to be rated ranged from a tight contingency between money and jobs ("so much for each job completed") to no ties at all ("money and jobs are kept quite separate from one another"). In between these two extremes were several gradations, covering such possibilities as money for extra but not regular jobs or increases for a job especially well done (Warton & Goodnow, 1995).

One of the primary findings of this study was similar to evidence obtained when investigating the question of what may be asked of others: All jobs are not alike. In this case, the main distinction was between "regular" jobs and "extra" jobs. Most parents approved of paying for extra jobs but not for regular jobs (the jobs "they should do anyway").

The next point to be noted had to do with the way approvals often reflect the combination of principles that are to some degree incompatible with one another but are nonetheless all endorsed by parents. On the one hand, for instance, the majority of our parents considered that ideally money and jobs should be kept separate. Children should be willing to work without being paid, and some money should come to them as a right. On the other hand, the majority of parents also felt that "nothing is for nothing." In their words, "If children are receiving money, they should be doing something in return." The variations among parents – and among occasions for the same parent – depend on which of these principles (both part of an "Anglo" culture) is made salient by particular circumstances (Goodnow & Warton, 1992a). The child who happily does his or her jobs, for instance, helps parents to feel that money is irrelevant. The child who resists, who violates the expectation that "everyone should contribute something to the unit," is more likely to make salient the principle of "nothing for nothing."

The final point is related to method. It is tempting to infer principles from what people do; that is, to make usage the basis for inferring ideas about what is acceptable or not. People may find acceptable, however, many practices that they themselves do not follow. Moreover, the best test of whether a rule is important may consist of what people avoid – what they *do not* or *will not* do.

For these reasons, we have found it best to present options in terms of acceptability rather than usage. It did indeed turn out that acceptability often differed from practice. Moreover, the clearest picture of differences among parents came from analyzing not the approvals but the disapprovals – options that attracted the response "under no circumstances." The strongest agreement among these parents, for instance, occurred in their rejection of a piecework practice: specific amounts of money for specific jobs (Warton & Goodnow, 1995).

The distribution of blame. In contrast to the large amount of research on the distribution of rewards, there has been little exploration of the distribution of blame (or of any negative outcomes), in large part because the study of accountability has strongly focused on the individual's intentions or ability to foresee consequences. Considering situations that involve two or more people involves what lawyers term "indirect" or "vicarious" responsibility (e.g., Hart & Honoré, 1985). Suppose, for instance, that you have not directly caused some unfortunate event to occur but your agent has done so. To what extent are you to be held liable? And should the degree of your liability be altered by your having taken steps to see that your agent knows what should be done and does it?

Any collaborative or team activity, any delegation of responsibility, raises the same issues. The procedure we have used is to ask about delegation situations within the family. Suppose, we said, you have asked a brother or sister (again a real person, and one close in age to the subject) to do a job for you that you normally do. If the job is not done, is it fair that you get into trouble? When the question is asked as baldly as this, 80% to 90% of our 8-, 11-, and 14-year-olds assert that this is not fair: "They are the ones who forgot," "who didn't do it." In effect, only the principle of direct causation is invoked. The minority position, increasing only slightly with age, is that this is fair, "because it is still your job"(Warton & Goodnow, 1991). A more sophisticated position emerges, however, when we ask if it is the first person's responsibility to check (most agree that this is so) and then give our informants four poker chips with the request: "Use these to show me how much of the blame should go to *X* and how much to you. You can divide them so that it is all to one of you and none to the other, or 3 and 1, or half and half. How would you divide them?" The sample covers 14- and 18-year-olds, but there are no signs of age changes.

When we simply ask the question and provide no information about circumstances, the dominant pattern is one of an equal distribution to the one who asks and the one who agrees. We can, however, move that modal pattern toward more blame to the one who agrees if we now add that the asker has checked on whether the job has been done or has given a reminder. There are still outliers who give all the blame to the one who agreed (on the grounds that "they are the ones who forgot" – a causation argument) or the one whose job this normally is (on the grounds that it "was their job in the first place"). The modal pattern, however, shifts toward less blame to the asker than to the person who agreed to do the tasks (Goodnow & Warton, in press). That shift makes ideas about the distribution of blame appear more similar to the equity notions that appear in studies of the distribution of rewards. It also makes one wonder about the degree of agreement between everyday ideas about indirect responsibility and the ideas that are embodied in law. The law – at least in some countries – specifies that liability in vicarious responsibility is independent of the effort taken to see that one's agent acts responsibly (Hart & Honoré, 1985). The everyday view, at least up to the age of 18 years, appears to lean toward regarding degrees of liability as relative and as unevenly distributed between the direct and the indirect cause of the final outcome.

Control, supervision, monitoring

To any work setting, people bring expectations about who should be in charge of what, and what represents reasonable or unreasonable supervision. The challenge is again to find ways of specifying these ideas, with a particular eye to the ideas that are likely to invite a lack of consensus, a sense of dissatisfaction, or a need for negotiation.

We have found useful three lines of exploration. One is to ask about the reasonableness of expecting to be reminded. Even 8-year-olds agree that they should not need to be reminded to do "their" jobs, although they also report that they very often are reminded and suggest that a failure to be reminded by a member of the family is an unfriendly act (Warton & Goodnow, 1991).

The second line of exploration consists of asking about the setting of standards. A difference in standards turns out to be the difficulty most frequently reported by couples who share household work (Goodnow & Bowes, 1994). The interesting question then has to do with whether people live with the difference, move toward a compromise, or accept an arrangement in which jobs go to whoever has the higher standards (an outcome that, in some accounts of negotiation, is seen as stemming from high investment reducing one's bargaining power). Our sharing couples generally prefer the first two solutions to the third, largely on the grounds that letting standards settle the issue can often result in a departure from a reasonable degree of equality. The issue of standards, however, remains the source of tension most frequently reported by sharing couples.

The third approach consists of asking about reasonable and unreasonable ways to follow through after delegation (Goodnow & Warton, 1992b). Among 14- and 18-year-olds, almost all agree that if they ask someone else to do a job for them, the other's agreement is not the end of the asker's responsibility. The asker should check that the work has been done and, if necessary, provide a reminder. The delicate area concerns how one checks or gives a reminder. There is consensus on the need, within the family, to proceed in a way that avoids negative attributions – implying that the other is lazy, forgetful, incompetent, or inferior. Both males and females agree on this score. Females, however, often see, in paid work settings, the same need to consider the face and the feelings of the other that applies within the family. Fewer males do so. Paid work is more likely to be seen as a setting where one should expect that those who pay will check directly and openly and will accept no excuses for a job not being done (Goodnow & Warton, 1992b). Whether this reflects a difference in gender socialization, or in the kinds and durations of part-time positions that young males and young females are likely to experience, we cannot tell from these data. We can, however, say firmly that asking about the monitoring of a delegated job is a highly viable way of exploring ideas about the distribution of control in any joint activity.

The style of negotiation

The style of negotiation is strongly highlighted in the interviews on household work. What matters is not only the work that is done, but also the spirit or style with which it is done or an issue is raised. We know, for instance, that adults can live comfortably with a variety of ways of raising and discussing an issue. For some, "a few quiet words" represents the ideal. Others are quite comfortable with longer and more open discussions, often accompanied by a certain degree of volatile emotion (e.g., "We both rant and rave a bit and then get down to the real issue"). What matters to each couple is that they find a way of proceeding that is within the limits of what each regards as a "reasonable" or "good" relationship (Goodnow & Bowes, 1994).

If we orient ourselves again to questions of method, how can we explore ideas about spirit or style? And what are the main points that these methods have yielded?

The main approach we have used so far consists of exploring what people designate as "good" or "low" moments, and "reasonable" or "unreasonable" ways to proceed. I have already noted – in the section on control and monitoring – our use of questions about "reasonable" and "unreasonable" ways to proceed after delegating a job. The exploration of "good" and "low" moments took place with reference to children's household jobs. We asked mothers to describe for us both a "good moment" and a "low moment" with regard to children's household contributions, and to tell us what the moment had meant to them (Goodnow & Delaney, 1989). The low moments occurred when mothers felt they had been assigned a low, typically servant status, most frequently by their work being unnoticed (a response that makes one invisible) or by being expected to clean up after others (an expectation that violates the principle of causation mentioned earlier – "your stuff, your mess, your problem – your job"). In contrast, the good moments occurred when a child acted without being reminded and in a way that showed an awareness of others – an awareness, for instance, of a parent's or a sibling's fatigue, pleasure, pressure of time, or past generosity. What makes these moments good is that what is being offered is not the result of nagging or reminding. Instead, the action is self-regulating. Moreover, the implied relationship is not one in which the mother plays the part of a watchful manager with a careless or unwilling helper. Instead, there is the implication of what has been called by anthropologists a "gift relationship" (e.g., Titmuss, 1971). The ideal, for mothers, is clearly one of work that is cheerfully volunteered and thoughtfully chosen – in effect, a gift rather than an enforced tribute.

In less systematic fashion, we have also noted the ways in which people express their reluctance to do a specific piece of work, paying particular attention to the openness with which reluctance is expressed or recognized. When parents are referring to their teenage children, for example, reluctance is often openly recognized (Goodnow et al., 1991). When adult partners are referring to each other, the situation is more complex. The intransigence of teenagers may be accepted as part of their nature. Unwillingness on the part of adults who are supposed to care for one another, and to regard each other as equals, is apparently another matter.

The tension that hidden unwillingness can create is at the core of Backett's (1982) analysis of a Scots sample of couples. Among these couples, pleas of incompetence (e.g., "I don't know how," "You do it so much better," "I just don't see what needs to be done") were often a disguise for unwillingness, a disguise often recognized but accepted as a lesser evil than a confrontation with unwillingness. These couples avoided any open departure from what Backett (1982) terms the ideal of "voluntarism" (the view that, in a fair relationship, people will be "willing if asked" or will certainly not expect of others what they themselves would hate to do). At a certain point in our interviews with Australian adults, we also began to feel that the facade of voluntarism was carefully maintained. (It needs to be remembered that these adult subjects were volunteers, a status likely to reduce the incidence of couples or families for which the level of conflict is regarded as a problem.) In fact, we began to wonder when we would hear open expressions of unwillingness, of refusal. They did occur frequently, however, in a particular group – among couples who *do* share work and who feel secure in the conviction that they are doing their share. Among these couples a man or woman would often say quite freely, "There are some things I *won't* do," and would respond to statements about "not knowing how" with a certain degree of amusement (Goodnow & Bowes, 1994).

All told, we have learned a great deal about the importance of the relationship to the definition of what is regarded as an appropriate spirit or style. The topic nonetheless remains one that strongly calls for further exploration. We need to know, for instance, how far a particular spirit or style is insisted upon, and what that insistence means to both parties. (I have in mind, for instance, a father who – to the great resentment of his teenaged children – said regularly, "If you can't do it with a good grace, I'd rather you didn't do it at all.") We are also in need of data with regard to the ways in which people use a reluctant style as a way of avoiding work, and the ways in which they signal the spirit with which they have made a work contribution. How, for instance, do people signal that what has been done is a favor, should not be taken for granted, and should not be regularly requested?

And what do people do?

In the section on appropriate styles, we have begun to mingle comments about the ideas people hold with comments about what they do, primarily by reference to the words people use to frame an issue and the ways by which they signal or assert unwillingness.

It may appear as if we have little interest in what people do, and it is true that we have often used what people do (or don't do) primarily as a route into the discovery of underlying expectations. Expectations and assumptions, our argument has run, deserve particular attention because they influence action, help account for satisfaction and discontent, and provide a way of pinning down changes over time and differences among people. Expectations are also so far in short supply in analyses of collaborative actions – for instance, among the analyses that developmentalists offer for children learning how to perform tasks with adult help (e.g., Rogoff, 1990) or of adults learning what a job involves (e.g., Chaiklin & Lave, 1993). In most analyses of collaboration, it might be said, describing the practice seems to take precedence over describing the individual's changing understanding of the practice (Lave, 1993). The same imbalance appears to occur in accounts of household work, an area well supplied with analyses of what people do, especially in the form of the time spent in various activities, but less well supplied with analyses of the meanings that various jobs or ways of working hold for people.

Nonetheless, it is clear that any full account of collaboration or interaction must consider the way in which the work *does* proceed. Let me then note some of the particular ways in which we have considered what happens in practice, paying particular attention again to methods and results that are extendable to other work settings.

In a first form of concern, we have noted the patterns that couples adopt when they blur or bend divisions of work based on gender – patterns such as the adoption of nonstereotyped specialties, of "fluid shifts" (jobs are done by whoever is available or feels like doing them), or "to each his or her own" (e.g., "I wash my car and iron my clothes, and you do yours"; Goodnow & Bowes, 1994). The specification of such patterns, we have proposed, is a necessary step beyond accounts in terms of hours or percentages of the work. It is useful to be able to describe a pattern as a "50:50" or an "80:20" arrangement, as well as to know how any percentage is played out.

In a second bite at the question of what people do, we have noted the ways in which children come to be involved in household tasks, as reported by mothers and oriented toward the mother's actions (Goodnow & Delaney, 1989). We came to place mothers into four groups. In one, the mother's approach was "managerial." She assigned tasks, expected them to be done on a regular basis, and followed through when a task was not done. In a second group, the mother aimed at a managerial approach but was clearly unsuccessful, because she was either inconsistent or outmaneuvered by the children. In a third, the mother did not see herself as a delegating manager. The children "did not really do any work" ("work" was the mother's domain). The children were expected, however, "to be willing if asked," to be appreciative, and to "keep things tidy," not to "undo" what the mother had done. The fourth style was one we termed "let the tide rise." Work was allowed to accumulate until someone's threshold was reached (not necessarily the mother's), and everyone then joined in a "blitz."

There are undoubtedly other ways of describing how children come to be involved. These groupings, however, provide a base for describing differences among families. They provide as well a potential base for describing the nature of conflict. Conflict over household jobs has long been noted as frequent where children are concerned, especially around adolescence. We would now see it as useful to break down conflict in terms of the usual style of involvement. A managerial style, for instance, may allow some negotiation in terms of efficiency or the need for the work to be done. In contrast, being willing if asked frames the problem in moral terms. An example is a mother, answering a question about what she says or might say when a child's work is being left undone fairly regularly, who described herself as saying, "What's the matter? Don't you want to help?" That way of framing a child's involvement leaves little room for negotiation. Guilt now hangs heavy in the air.

Still with an eye to what children do, a group of us at Macquarie University are exploring the impact of the sex of both a child and a sibling on the extent to which children are involved in sex-typed tasks (boys doing "boys' jobs," girls doing "girls' jobs," defined by a difference in the frequency within the sample of these jobs being done by boys and girls in the 8- to 14-year-old range; Antill, Goodnow, Cotton, & Russell, 1995). What happens, we have asked, when we consider families with two children in this age range: both boys, both girls, or one of each? We had hoped to find that sex typing is diminished when the children are of the same sex, the "appropriate" gendered pair of hands sometimes being unavailable. To our regret, the effect of a sibling's sex has turned out to be small. Instead, the impact of gendered availability appeared strongly in another form. We had been looking for a "modeling" effect (a positive correlation between what a parent does and what a same-sex child does). What we found, when correlations occurred, was that these were negative in direction. Work that a parent does may become less rather than more available for a child's involvement. It is as if the parent's involvement says, "I'm already doing this; find something else." In effect, we were back to the issue of the demarcation or availability of work, but this time in the form of what is available after some pieces of work are already "taken" by others.

It will be clear by now that I am consistently intrigued by the words that people use to frame an issue, to present an argument, or to account for the way they proceed. That attraction is part of an interest in whether negotiations between adults are described as a matter of "a few quiet words" or as "battles," and in the variety of ways in which people use the word *fair* (Goodnow & Bowes, 1994).

That attention to words – to the way aspects of work are represented – is also part of an interest in the way parents speak to children about the work they do. The results on this score are intriguing. The pilot interviews led us to ask mothers, after they had just described a good or a low moment, if they had any "favorite sayings" or any "special ways" of acting when a low moment came up. One of the surprises was the frequency with which these Anglo-Australian mothers described themselves as using what we came to call "drama" or "theater." They described themselves, using Australian terms, as "having a rant and rave," "chucking a mental," "turning on my fishwife act," "slamming the door in grand style." In Australian society, it is "Mediterranean types" (immigrants from Italy or Greece) who are often described as "dramatic." It was as if these mothers had all read dramaturgical accounts of social interactions or – as a colleague, Gabriele Oettingen, has suggested – ethological accounts of "display" behavior.

The further surprise was the use of indirect speech. Developmental theories of compliance and/or internalization stress the importance (at least for long-term effects) of parents offering clear rationales for what they wish children to do. How then were we to account for the frequency with which parents (most of the reports are from mothers, but the phenomenon occurs among fathers also) made statements that were far from clear? Why do parents say to young children that this is "not a hotel, guesthouse, cafeteria, laundromat," that "I'm not running a taxi service," or that "you must think this is the back side of the moon" (i.e., an area no one ever sees)? Why do they say, "Were you born in a tent?" when what they want a child to do is to close a door left open? Indirect speech, it turns out, is not a phenomenon limited to Australian families. Judith Becker (1988) has observed a similar phenomenon in U.S. families. We both have some ideas as to why indirect speech is common – what expectations and feelings give rise to it – but we are far from any strong test of these (Becker & Goodnow, 1992). The phenomenon, however, is striking. It certainly needs to be considered in any account of how children come to acquire the understand-ing of work that parents presumably expect them to acquire.

In sum, we have not ignored the actual performance of collaborative ac-tions, or contributions to shared tasks, even though we set as our primary target the analysis of expectations, assumptions, and distinctions among pieces of work that people bring to any task. In the process, some ways of describing the actual nature of collaborative actions have emerged that hold promise as ways of enriching the analysis of overt behaviors and the links among ideas, actions, and feelings, not only for household work but for collaborative work in any setting. At this point, however, our choice of emphasis continues to fall on the task of delineating ideas and of finding ways to turn questions into researchable forms and theoretical frameworks within which to place changes and variations in the ideas held.

Extensions beyond households

Up to this point, I have allowed the dissection of expectations to be anchored only in analyses of household tasks. I have also allowed the issue of methods to dominate the issue of theoretical frameworks. The time has come, however, to redress the balance.

A first step toward building a general framework consists of extending the analysis of collaborative rules beyond households. If the notion of collabora-tive rules is to have general value, it must apply to other situations. I will outline some particular extensions, all of which have to do with the set of expectations that was first emphasized (expectations about the kind of work each person should or should not do) but that is a limit of convenience rather than necessity.

As a start, I shall turn to an extension we are already in the process of making, with Pamela Warton taking the main responsibility. This is to the area of teaching. This extension began when we asked teachers what they deleted from the work they normally did, after their teachers' union (in the course of a labor dispute) recommended that they work to rule – that is, do only what was specifically written into their list of duties (Warton, Goodnow, & Bowes, 1992). That study brought out the importance of distinctions between the parts of a job that are regarded as essential or mandatory, and those that are regarded as extra or discretionary. That useful distinction, however, did not pin down what did or could happen to the discretionary parts. They could be dropped altogether, deferred, or passed to someone else (e.g., parents could take over field trips). To narrow those possibilities and focus on what can and cannot be passed to others, Pamela Warton is now asking academics which parts of their work – marking, tutorials, lectures, student consultation – they feel can be turned over to others, and what the conditions are that make this form of delegation comfortable, tolerable, or unacceptable. Such distinctions among parts of a job (another form of distinctions based on demarcation and moveability) are clearly relevant to decisions in any work setting.

As a further extension, I draw attention to the tasks that psychologists often use for exploring expert–novice interactions, tasks often referred to as based on Vygotskian theory and often presented as an analogue to apprenticeship in everyday life. In these experimental tasks, an expert is asked to help a novice solve a problem. The interaction regarded as most conducive to learning on the part of the novice is one in which the expert withdraws support as the novice gains competence, with the novice then becoming self-regulating. The format, I have noted (Goodnow, 1990b), assumes willing teachers and eager learners. It is also one that is typically analyzed as if differences in capacity were the only issue. The assumption is made that experts should and will withdraw from the field as novices gain skill. Novices, for their part, should and will increase their commitments as they gain competence. In a sense, "If they can, they should." In everyday life, however, apprenticeship situations may not proceed along such clear-cut lines. The expert may be reluctant to hand over responsibility; the apprentice may not be eager to take over (Azmitia, Chapter 5, this volume; Goodnow, 1990a, 1990b). In effect, thinking about a variety of collaborative rules encourages one to ask at least two questions. How did psychologists come to place such a single-minded emphasis on differences in competence as the deciding factor in interactions involving teaching and learning? In practice, when do various departures occur from the rule that developmentalists imply, a rule that says, "If you can hand on this skill, or take over this task, you should do so"?

The final extension I shall make is to expectations about the telling of stories. I noted at the start that in the area of language attention has already been given to questions about who does what (e.g., in the form of turn taking) and about the nature of shared understanding. Talk is also an area where we know that people hold expectations about each other's obligations, obligations that range from Gricean rules (be brief, be relevant, etc.) to the special obligation of women to fill in silences or smooth out awkward spots.

The phenomenon I wish to draw attention to, however, is one highlighted by Peggy Miller's analysis of the everyday stories people tell about themselves or others, stories about what happened to me today or what *X* did. For the stories told by a group of African-American parents (a group much given to everyday narratives), Miller has distinguished among stories that are about children, with children, and around children. She has also commented that the experience of listening to a story that is about you but is being told by someone else in your presence may signal a particular status – that of a "child" (Miller, 1992). Moreover, she tells me, that same implication – the other as "not fully competent" – applies in the case of people feeling they have the right to tell the story of another person's illness (physical or mental).

There are clearly occasions when one is happy to have someone else tell one's story (the other may, in fact, be able to present it in a way that the conventions of modesty or personal trumpet blowing do not encourage if one tells the story oneself). At the same time, there are also many occasions when having one's story told by another is the cause of discomfort and/or resentment. The story may be yours by virtue of your having been the chief actor. The story may also be of the kind you regard as private, or it may have been told to the other in confidence. One of the actions that makes a "poor friend," children say, is when others use the disclosure you made to them in friendship as a way to gain the friendship of another (Goodnow & Burns, 1985).

In related fashion, there are occasions when we feel discomfort or annoyance on observing one person "correct" another's story. To use an anecdote, an elderly relative of mine regularly corrected the somewhat embellished accounts of shared experiences that her spouse was given to. The corrections were made in the name of accuracy ("That's not quite the way it was"), but they left the storyteller, and the listeners, uncomfortable. We clearly hold expectations about the proper balance between accuracy and telling a "good story," that is, proper in relation to the setting. We also clearly hold expectations about appropriate prompts, questions, interruptions, and corrections. Just as we may learn a great deal about the norms of task interactions by considering the implications of my job/your job, I propose, we may well learn from considering the implications of my story/your story. At the least, considering "shares of the story" in even a cursory way makes it clear that expectations about the way contributions should be made are far from being limited to the domain of household work. In short, we can carry the analyses of household work over to other forms of work, and we need not be limited to accounts of household work in the search for a helpful theoretical framework.

Toward a theoretical framework and a life-span perspective

It would be regrettable if I ended with only a specification of the expectations that people bring to the work they do and a demonstration of the methods we may employ to bring out the nature and impact of these expectations. We also need a procedure of accounting for the way ideas are acquired in the first place or come to change. In effect, we need a developmental theory both for conceptual reasons and for the life-span focus of this volume. Moreover, we need a particular kind of developmental theory. It will, for instance, have to be one that can be used across the life span, taking account of change in adults as well as among children and asking how the events or the ideas held at one point in the life span are linked to those held at other times. To add a further requirement, the sources considered as the bases of change will need to go beyond biological or physical factors. Instead, there will need to be a clear place for changes in conditions such as social position, social identity, relationships with others, and the resources or constraints that accompany some general social "climate."

For several reasons, it is unlikely that analyses of household work per se will yield an adequate theoretical framework. In this section, I shall outline my reasons for this and then present what I see as a viable possibility – namely, a framework drawn from the analysis of "social representations" or "cultural models." The final comments will then extend that framework by proposing a specific form of change – change in the domain to which an issue is referred and from which legitimations or accounts are drawn. The specific example is the shift away from the referral of household work to the domain of gender ("men's work," "women's work"; see also Labouvie-Vief, Chapter 4, this volume) and the increasing occurrence of referrals to domains such as competence, practicality, justice, self-respect, and the definitions of "a good relationship."

Possible frameworks from the literature on household work

Why make the statement that a conceptual framework covering life-span changes in ideas about joint efforts, collaborative ventures, or divisions of labor is not likely to spring well formed from the literature on household work alone? The reasons are threefold. First, this literature is in general not oriented toward questions of development. Second, it is "age segregated," with little overlap between discussions of what happens at different ages, and – by and large – it displays a greater concern with accounting for inertia than for change. Third, it gives greater attention to structural conditions and "resources" than to the ideas people hold about work.

Age segregation in analyses of household work. Household work is a topic that turns up in analyses of several parts of the life span. There are studies related to children's household contributions, to divisions of labor between adults during various phases of their relationship as a couple (this is the biggest set of studies), and to divisions between generations when parents are elderly.

Across these literatures, however, there is little cross-referencing and little integration of models or methods. To take but one example, studies of the possible movement of work from elderly parents to younger members of the family are concerned with the substitutability of people (e.g., work moves first to daughters – especially if they are unmarried – then to daughters-in-law, and then possibly to sons; Johnson & Troll, 1992; Qureshi & Simons, 1987). Substitutability (in the form of ideas about the moveability of various pieces of work or as a model for describing the pattern of work) does not appear in the childhood literature at all. In fact, it was a model I had felt the need to "invent" for the analysis of ideas about children's work (e.g., Goodnow et al., 1991; Goodnow & Delaney, 1989).

A stronger concern with inertia than with change. One of the major debates within analyses of household work has centered around the unexpectedly small impact of women's increased involvement in paid work on the number of hours that their partners spend on household work. Both equity theory and economic theory (the latter arguing for spheres of work as interconnected, with change in one inducing change in the other) have led to the expectation of change. The contrast between this expectation and the data have given rise both to the general sense of a "major puzzle" (England & Farkas, 1986) and to detailed studies such as Hochschild's (1989) close account of a small set of couples, a superb analysis of the ways in which stereotyped patterns persist even when the public rhetoric is one of "sharing." There is, it is true, no shortage of analyses that ask about variations in the pattern of work (mainly variations in the amount that each family member does) as a function of differences in age, length of a relationship, education, socioeconomic status, the relative hours of paid work, or the relative income of husband and wife. By implication, these correlates suggest that individuals will change their involvement in household work when some of these circumstances change. In short supply, however, are analyses of the way individuals come to shift their involvement in household work – a shortage that was one reason for our collecting a sample of couples who *were* sharing household work, with many of them changing from an earlier conventional pattern of household division of labor (Goodnow & Bowes, 1994).

"Meanings" as a minor theme. To a psychologist, perhaps especially to one interested in cognition, most of the literature on household divisions of labor seems driven by theories that Ferree (1990) has described as emphasizing "resources." There are, for instance, repeated analyses of the extent to which the hours committed by a man or a woman to paid work are correlated with the hours each commits to household work. The results are highly variable (Baxter, 1990, provides one summary).

Increasingly, the argument is emerging that such variable results, along with the "major puzzle" I have noted, call for less attention to resources and more attention to the "meanings" that work holds for people. Ferree (1990) is one such voice. The argument is also to be found in other sources – for example, in Hood's (1986) and Finch's (1983) analyses of the implicit contracts that each partner sees as existing in a marriage (in the words of one man we interviewed, "I didn't get married to make beds"), in Lein's (1984) concern with the reasons women offer for returning to paid work, and in Yeandle's (1984) attention to the extent to which the "reference frames" for returning to work (e.g., the family's need for money, the woman's pleasure in getting out of the house, the lack of disruption to caring for the family) are shared by both partners. By and large, however, my reading of the literature on adult household work patterns, which comes predominantly from sociology, is in line with Ferree's (1990) view that resource theories have been dominant over attention to meanings.

If analyses of household work, in themselves, do not offer an ideal developmental framework for the analysis of collaborative rules – a framework that gives meanings and changes in meanings a central place – where can we turn? The type of theory I currently find best suits my needs is that referred to earlier as "social representations" (e.g., van Cranach et al., 1992) or "cultural models" (e.g., D'Andrade & Strauss, 1992). The next section outlines the essentials of that type of theory (see also Cole, Chapter 2, this volume) and brings out its potential as a way of viewing change over the life span.

A general theoretical framework

Is there a theoretical position into which we can fit the results we have generated and that also holds particular promise as a way of looking at both life-span change and the nature of shared understanding? There is, in fact, no need to invent new theories to cover such issues. There is a body of theory already available, one that has already been concerned with the nature and sources of shared ideas. Most of this conceptual analysis has been carried out with reference to the development of shared understanding among members of a large social group (members of a culture or subculture). It can, however, be readily extended to cover the development of shared understanding within smaller groups such as families, work teams, classrooms, or members of an experimental dyad. Most of this conceptual analysis has also been carried out with reference to topics outside the meanings given to household work. The concerns have more often been with the ideas people hold about the nature of intelligence, of madness, of proper ways to teach or bring up children, and of differences between men and women. Ideas about the nature of household work, or of work in any form, can however be readily included under the same rubric.

One approach within this body of theory is to be found under the label of "intersubjectivity," a term emphasizing the mutual understanding of meanings that people come to acquire or negotiate as they live together or work together on a task (e.g., Perret-Clermont et al., 1991). The emergence of such mutual understanding, and the difficulties that arise when it does not exist are central concerns in analyses at the University of Neuchâtel of interactions between tester and testee in psychometric situations and between teacher and pupil in classroom settings. In the words of one report, "Knowledge and cognitive competence are dependent on each interactor's representation of the role of his partner, of what knowledge is about, of the common task, and of the setting in which the encounter takes place" (Schubauer-Leoni, Perret-Clermont, & Grossen, 1992).

A slightly different but overlapping framework is to be found in accounts of shared ideas as "social representations" (e.g., von Cranach et al., 1992; Goodnow & Warton, 1992a), as "cultural models" (e.g., D'Andrade & Strauss,

1992), as "consensus models" (e.g., Romney, Weller, & Batchelder, 1986), or as "cultural representations" (e.g., Lüscher, 1995). Like positions emphasizing intersubjectivity, these accounts have pointed to the importance of shared ideas for effective communication and for the regulation of social life. They contain, however, a more explicit concern with occasions where agreement does not occur. They have also moved more directly toward specifying the several qualities that shared ideas or shared knowledge may have.

I am partial to these views because they offer an alternative to regarding the ideas that people hold as based only on each individual's own direct experience, a basis that accounts of cognitive development have often regarded as sufficient. They are also directly relevant to any analysis of the shared as well as unshared knowledge and understanding that interactive or collaborative settings inevitably highlight, and have particular potential for scholars interested in life-span development.

At the risk of ignoring differences among a variety of positions, let me draw together several accounts of shared ideas, by way of outlining the qualities of ideas that have been highlighted. I list these qualities in seriatim fashion. It might be noted, however, that in a sense the first quality (that ideas are not evenly shared or completely agreed on by all) is the starting point, with the others arising as ways of accounting for a lack of complete agreement or consensus. I have also described the qualities in terms of the way ideas occur within a social group (the usual emphasis), with some additional comments added on occurrence within an individual.

In brief, shared ideas, knowledge, or understanding are likely to be:

1. *Not evenly shared.* Some ideas are likely to yield more agreement than others. Even the ideas that are widespread, however, are not likely to be shared with equal understanding or equal commitment by all. In an alternative phrasing, knowledge or understanding is likely to be "socially distributed" rather than being held equally by all members. The research implication of this proposition is that one begins to ask, What is the nature of the distribution? Who is closest to the majority view? Who are the outliers and in what specific ways do they differ from the majority?

2. *Multiple.* No culture or social group is likely to contain only one view on an issue. There will be more than one view, for instance, of how to achieve a just social system, how to bring up children or to educate them, and how household tasks should be allocated. The research implication is that we need to pay attention not only to the modal view, but also to its alternatives and their status (the extent to which they are treated with respect, scorn, or embarrassment).

3. *Contested.* A certain degree of competition is usually present between alternative viewpoints. It will not be sufficient then simply to document the presence of more than one view. The further phenomenon to be alert for is the nature of the tension between viewpoints: the nature of the contest between them or of the criticism each offers of the other. To take an example from Quinn's (1992) analysis of the household domain, what degree of conflict is experienced – in public debate and within the individual – between the ideas of "wifely duty" and "human dignity"? To take another that I

find equally intriguing, why do young adults speak with such negative affect – with a kind of amazed horror – about mothers who "let themselves be treated like servants" or fathers who "didn't even know their way to the kitchen"? More is involved than any simple acceptance of multiple viewpoints.

4. *Differentially insisted upon.* We are under pressure to take the group's views on some issues (D'Andrade, 1981). On others, we are allowed to be different, or even encouraged to be individual and original. The phenomenon to account for is then not so much consensus or agreement, but the occurrence of "acceptable disagreement" (Goodnow, 1995), and of negotiation over differences that one or both parties see as needing some resolution.

5. *Changing over time.* Change over time is expected. The critical issues have to do with describing the nature of change and how change comes about. Two suggestions stand out (they are particularly present in accounts of social representations). In one of these, change comes about through some general events in society. At times of dissatisfaction, for example, with formal medicine, the strength of alternative views increases. Change also occurs by way of the drift, into everyday views, of formal theory, providing a new vocabulary and a new way of interpreting events. One famous example consists of the drift, into everyday vocabulary and interpretations, of words and phrases from psychoanalytic theory: neurosis, unconscious, id, ego, superego, repression, Freudian slip. Of equal interest, I suggest, is the absorption of terms and meanings that began in legal and feminist theory – new terms such as *sexist*, and new meanings for terms such as *discrimination* or *chauvinist*.

The second type of suggestion for the occurrence of change looks to shifts in some particular characteristics of the individual, such as age or social position. Age brings with it differences in exposure to various issues or in the capacity to understand particular interpretations of an event. Social position is more complex. Let me offer some examples. My view of who is responsible for a child's progress in school will vary as a function of whether I am a teacher or a parent. My view of job negotiations will vary as a function of whether I am employer or employee, supervisor or supervisee, in a "position of trust" or in a position that is carefully monitored or regularly checked, in a position where change means a move away from disadvantage or a loss of privilege. My view of what I should do within the household will vary as a function of my becoming – as an adolescent or an adult – newly engaged in activities outside the house. Throughout, the selection of a viewpoint is part of "who I am" and/ or part of maintaining an image of oneself that is reasonably positive. As an individual's circumstances change so do these aspects of identity or position, and along with these changes, there comes a shift in the viewpoints one now sees as reasonable or uses to interpret events. From this perspective, no new viewpoint is invented. There is a change, however, in the extent to which the individual now appropriates or endorses one rather than another of the viewpoints that are available within the culture or within his or her own repertoire for interpreting events.

A return to the meanings of household work

I have outlined the essentials of positions that emphasize knowledge or mean-ings as shared in various degrees, and that offer a basis for considering either historical or individual change in the ideas that people hold. As a final step, let me now put the meanings of household work and a life-span perspective more firmly into that general picture.

To start with, one may view any part of the life span as involving a change in social position. Children change in their competence, in the extent to which they make particular demands from others, and in the extent to which they see a continuation of the "same old tasks" as implying that they are still children (the last possibility is suggested by Shanahan, Elder, & Conger, 1993). Adults also change in their level of competence (e.g., in how much they need to rely on others) and in the demands made on them by themselves or others. Each such change may alter the demand to find a way of making sense of what is happening (to oneself or to others) and the attractiveness of one available interpretation over others.

This much is a part of the general theory of social representations. Mugny and Carugati (1989), for instance, use this aspect of social representation theory to account for differences between parents with young children and parents with children in school in the extent to which they endorse school-based definitions of intelligence. What is added by analyses of ideas about household work is an argument for a specific form of change. In essence, ideas about household work highlight change in the form of *a shift in the domain to which an issue is referred and from which rules or legitimations are drawn.*

That proposal starts from the recognition that household work attracts multiple representations – that is, referrals to more than one domain. The work may, for instance, be referred to the domain of gender. This is "men's work," this is "women's work." No further legitimation may be felt to be needed, although the referral may be bolstered by assertions of differences in natural competence or comments on history and universality. Work may also be referred, however, to other domains – may be framed as a question of fairness, justice, practicality, or the maintenance of a "good relationship."

The second step in my proposal is the notion that change over the life span or across time may be usefully regarded as a change in the dominant domain of referral and legitimation. What evidence do we have for this statement?

In support of the argument are first of all the occasions where gender is explicitly rejected as a sufficient base for the allocation of work. Among our "sharing" couples, for instance, we heard with surprisingly high frequency the statement: "I don't see why I should do it *just because* I'm a man" or "*just because* I'm a woman." Over half of the people we interviewed made com-ments along these lines. Their discussion of what was fair or just might not go further than this statement (this was far from being a highly politicized sample), but they were firm on maleness or femaleness being an insufficient basis for determining what they should do, especially if they did not enjoy the job.

Gender did appear at times in the form of referrals to the past treatment of women as unfair ("Women have had a poor deal for centuries" or "My mother, poor woman, did *everything*"). More often, however, the referrals were to the present: to fairness, to the need to avoid "resentments" that can undermine a relationship, to preferences, and to practicality ("It's just a matter of getting things done").

These are couples, however, who have moved well away from conventional gender demarcations. (They were, in fact, nominated by others as doing things "differently.") Perhaps referrals to gender are still the basis of decision and legitimation in more conventional samples. Let me turn then to a sample of parents (mothers and fathers) reporting on what they would comfortably assign to a teenaged son or daughter, what they would think twice about, and why they would feel either way (Goodnow et al., 1991). This group was deliberately drawn from a sample regarded as politically conservative (most of the couples were also "lower middleclass" in socioeconomic status). Nonetheless, explicit references to gender ("That's a boy's job" or "That's a girl's job") were rare. They accounted, in fact, for only 3% of all explanations offered, despite the fact that there were still gender differences in what the children did.

In this latter sample, what replaces any reference to "boys' jobs" versus "girls' jobs"? Many of the explanations were to differences in competence or in willingness. Competence helps sustain gender differences. Willingness ("All you get is a long argument") or rather unwillingness can work in either direction. In this group, it undercut the assignment of work to either teenager. Undercutting references to gender, and differences in the work done, was also a high frequency of justifications in terms of what we have called "causation." In the words of one mother, "Mark makes his bed; Mark sleeps in it, Mark makes it." In effect, the justice of assignments based on who created the need for the work or "whose stuff this is" argues against what was – one generation earlier – standard practice among these Anglo-Australians: Girls made their own beds and those of others. That practice is not only no longer followed by most of this ethnic group; it is also seen as "unfair" or as "useless to expect." Even if parents see a gender-based request as still "reasonable," the children will often not do so, especially if the request violates some other principle (e.g., "not my stuff," "I didn't use it") that they wish to have upheld or that interferes with some other activity they wish to pursue.

One other legitimation is of interest with regard to children's household jobs. This consists of referrals to "the need to know." It is no longer the case, these Anglo-Australian mothers point out, that children move directly from living at home to living as part of a couple. In between, there is likely to be a period of "flatting," sharing space with a group of peers. Boys then have a "need to know" that is seen as not existing in earlier times (times sometimes referred to as "moving from mother's care to wife's care"). One might easily argue that household skills can be learned when needed (an argument we have been offered more often by Lebanese-Australian mothers; Goodnow et al., 1984). The interesting phenomenon is that practicing how to meet future needs is regarded by many Anglo-Australian mothers as a reasonable way to proceed and a reasonable argument to offer their children. Times have changed, they point out to their children. And household practices now need to change to fit the new world.

My comments up to this point have had to do with the nature of change rather than its sources. *What could produce such changes in the domain to which a topic is referred and from which legitimations are drawn?* An optimal account of change would take note of the fact that change does not occur in a single step, as well as the way that each step is potentially influenced by various conditions. Among the sharing couples we interviewed, for instance, over half had started with a conventionally gendered pattern. For them, the first step toward change usually took the form of a discontent with the old pattern. The next step involved making a change. The third step consisted of maintaining the change or modifying it as circumstances changed. Each step could be influenced by multiple factors: a change in the hours of paid work, an increase or decrease in the number of people living at home, a shift in the health status of one or both partners, a sense that everything had become "too much." At each step along the way, however, a contributing factor was the way in which the issues of work and a change in the pattern were framed and justified to oneself and one's partner. The justifications could vary. Among them, for example, were references to need ("I can't cope"), fairness ("We're both working the same hours, so how come I'm the only one who's busy on Saturdays?"), the protection of leisure time ("We get through it faster if we both do it"), the importance of caring ("I like to see her relaxing after a hard day"), and simple dislike ("I loathe washing cars and you don't mind it so much").

The choice of a specific referral is undoubtedly influenced by what each partner finds convincing and reassuring. We have not explored directly how a specific choice comes to be made (we suspect that referrals are both multiple and fluid). We did, however, ask couples directly about the importance to them of several factors (own experience as a child, the women's movement, the examples of friends). The individual's own history was the factor most often endorsed (Goodnow & Bowes, 1994). Either one's parents shared the work or – the power of negative example – their pattern was one that the next generation vowed to avoid ("My mother wore herself out"; "My father couldn't even make a cup of coffee").

As observers, however, we see several conditions outside the family that provide a changing framework. First, for paid work, there has been a great deal of media attention to the illegality of job allocations on the basis of gender. The wrongness of discrimination on the basis of sex has become part of everyday discourse. This is certainly an area where the insufficiency of "just because I'm a woman or a man" has been well aired.

Second, for household work, the women's movement has offered alternative descriptions of what women do, both by references to the unfairness of a "second shift" or a "double day" and by framing the position and work of women as a form of "oppression." In our samples, we have rarely seen *oppression* taken up as a specific term. It does appear, however, to be one contribution to the discomfort, often accompanied with a touch of scorn, that many women expressed when referring to their traditional mothers ("How could they have let themselves in for that?"). We had thought this attitude might be specific to our Australian samples. It was with special interest then that we read an account by Gullestad (1984) of working-class women in Norway (women in couple relationships). On her second time in the community – 8 years after the first round of interviews – Gullestad was impressed by the extent to which the women spoke in terms of the importance of "sharing" and "togetherness," as well as by the gap they perceived between themselves and older women who "did everything" and "put up with everything." The household work one does has now become an issue not only of practicality, competence, and justice, but also of self-respect.

In sum, the nature of change may be specified as a shift in the domain to which a problem is referred and from which legitimations are drawn. I have made that argument in terms of the views expressed, and the phrases used, by people commenting on their own lives. Let me now round out the argument by noting (a) that formal analyses of household work reflect a similar change and (b) that the issue of referral to a domain is to be found in analyses outside the area of household work.

The first part of that argument is prompted by noting a change in the placement of articles on household divisions of labor. Traditionally, articles on the distribution of household tasks have appeared in journals of "marriage and the family" or journals about "sex roles." My own submissions to developmental journals have several times attracted reviewers – fortunately in the minority – who recommended submission to "family" journals. During the past 5 years, however, articles on the division of household tasks have begun to appear not only in developmental journals but also in journals concerned with justice. Williamson and Clark's (1989) article, appearing in a special issue of *Social Justice Research*, is one example of that recategorization. Okin's (1989) book title – *Justice, Gender, and the Family* – makes it particularly explicit.

The second part of the argument – the general significance of referrals to a domain – could involve me in a wide-ranging set of references. I shall restrict myself to three. One is the work of Lawrence (1988) on the decisions that magistrates make when dealing with cases such as shoplifting or driving under the influence of alcohol. The first step toward decision making, she finds, consists of referring the particular case to one of several possible domains: For shoplifting for instance, these domains may refer to the need of the individual for help or the need of society for protection. That first referral then influences the evidence that is noticed and the weight given to various factors. The second example comes from Gigerenzer's contribution (Chapter 11) to this volume. Gigerenzer proposes that a basic step in all thinking or problem solving consists of the question: To what domain shall I refer this problem? What kind of a problem is this? He has also pointed to the way the choice of a domain influences the kind of information to which one becomes alert. The third example comes from Habermas (1979), who has argued that the choice of a domain (Habermas considers referrals to morality, technology, custom, or aesthetics) influences the kind of evidence we turn to or are persuaded by, and can be at the heart of difficulties in communication. I may see an issue as a moral question; you may see it as a matter of economic cost. All three proposals imply that change need not take the form of inventing a new category or a new domain. Instead, change may often take the form of an old category being extended to cover a new case, of an existing domain being seen as embracing a phenomenon not previously seen as belonging to it. That kind of change may clearly occur at any part of the life span.

   These comments on change represent the end of my argument. To reduce it to its essentials, there is value in asking about the ideas people hold concerning the way work should proceed when they combine with others on a task or when their work is part of the work of a unit. There is value in grounding questions about those expectations within a substantive area such as household tasks (an area that combines an interest in the nature of the work and of the interactive relationship). There is value also in grounding the questions we ask and the way we interpret results within a view of ideas as social representations or cultural models – positions that orient one toward an awareness of ideas as unevenly shared, differentially endorsed, usually balanced by an alternative or minority view, often contested, and inevitably changing over time. The gains lie not only in our understanding of a particular work setting (households). They lie also in the development of concepts and methods that can be applied to a variety of collaborative or interactive situations and that help us understand the nature of differences among individuals, among collaborative settings, and across time.

References

Antill, J. K., Goodnow, J. J., Cotton, S., Russell, G. (1995). Family structure and the gendered differentiation of household tasks. Macquarie University. Unpublished manuscript.
Azmitia, M. (1988). Peer interaction and problem solving: when two heads are better than one. *Child Development, 59*, 87–96.
Backett, K. (1982). *Mothers and fathers: A study of the development and negotiations of parental behaviour.* London: Macmillan.

Baxter, J. (1990). Domestic labour: Issues and studies. *Labour and Industry, 3,* 112–145.

Becker, J. A. (1988). The strength of parents' indirect techniques for teaching preschoolers pragmatic skills. *First Language, 8,* 173–182.

Becker, J. A., & Goodnow, J. J. (1992). "What's the magic word"? "Were you born in a tent"? – The challenge of accounting for parents' indirect uses of speech with children. *Newsletter of the Laboratory of Comparative Human Development, 50,* 517–522.

Bourdieu, P. (1979). *Distinction: A social critique of the judgment of taste.* London: Routledge & Kegan Paul.

Chaiklin, S., & Lave, J. (Eds.). (1993). *Understanding practice.* Cambridge: Cambridge University Press.

Clark, M. S. (1984). Record keeping in two kinds of relationships. *Journal of Personality and Social Psychology, 47,* 549–557.

D'Andrade, R. G. (1981). The cultural part of cognition. *Cognitive Science, 5,* 179–195.

D'Andrade, R. G., & Strauss, C. (1992). *Human motives and cultural models.* Cambridge: Cambridge University Press.

England, P., & Farkas, G. (1986). *Households, employment and gender: A social, economic and demographic view.* New York: Aldine de Gruyter.

Falbo, T., & Peplau, L. (1980). Power strategies in intimate relationships. *Journal of Personality and Social Psychology, 38,* 618–628.

Ferree, M. M. (1990). Beyond separate spheres: Feminism and family research. *Journal of Marriage and the Family, 52,* 866–884.

Finch, J. (1983). *Married to the job: Wives' incorporation in men's work.* London: Allen & Unwin.

Forman, E. M., Minick, N., & Stone, C. A. (Eds.). (1993). *Contexts for learning.* New York: Oxford University Press.

Goodnow, J. J. (1976). The nature of intelligent behavior: Questions raised by cross-cultural studies. In L. Resnick (Ed.), *The nature of intelligence* (pp. 169–188). Hillsdale, NJ: Erlbaum.

Goodnow, J. J. (1987, April). *The distributive justice of work.* Paper presented at the biennial meeting of the Society for Research in Child Development, Baltimore.

Goodnow, J. J. (1988). Children's household work: Its nature and functions. *Psychological Bulletin, 103,* 5–26.

Goodnow, J. J. (1990a). The socialization of cognition: What's involved? In J. Stigler, R. Shweder, & G. Herdt (Eds.), *Culture and human development* (pp. 259–286). Chicago: University of Chicago Press.

Goodnow, J. J. (1990b). Using sociology to extend psychological accounts of cognitive development. *Human Development, 33,* 81–107.

Goodnow, J. J. (1995). Acceptable disagreement across generations. In J. Smetana (Ed.), *Parents' socio-cognitive models of development* (New Directions in Child Development, Vol. 66, pp. 51–64). San Francisco: Jossey-Bass.

Goodnow, J. J. (in press). From household practices to parents' ideas about work and interpersonal relationships. In S. Harkness & C. Super (Eds.), *Parents' cultural belief systems.* New York: Guilford.

Goodnow, J. J., & Bowes, J. M. (1994). *Men, women, and household work: Couples illustrating change.* Sydney: Oxford University Press.

Goodnow, J. J., Bowes, J. M., Warton, P. M., Dawes, L. J., & Taylor, A. J. (1991). Would you ask someone else to do this task? Parents' and children's ideas about household work requests. *Developmental Psychology, 27,* 817–828.

Goodnow, J. J., & Burns, A. (1985). *Home and school: Child's eye views.* Sydney: Allen & Unwin.

Goodnow, J. J., Cashmore, J., Cotton, S., & Knight, R. (1984). Mothers' developmental timetables in two cultural groups. *International Journal of Psychology, 19,* 193–205.

Goodnow, J. J., & Collins, W. A. (1990). *Development according to parents.* London: Erlbaum.

Goodnow, J. J., & Delaney, S. (1989). Children's household work: Differentiating types of work and styles of assignment. *Journal of Applied Developmental Psychology, 10,* 209–226.

Goodnow, J. J., Knight, R., & Cashmore, J. (1985). Adult social cognition: Implications of parents' ideas for approaches to development. In M. Perlmutter (Ed.), *Social cognition. Minnesota Symposia on Child Development* (Vol. 18, pp. 287–324). Hillsdale, NJ: Erlbaum.

Goodnow, J. J., & Warton, P. M. (1991). The social basis of social cognition: Interactions about work and lessons about relationships. *Merrill-Palmer Quarterly, 37*, 27–58.

Goodnow, J. J., & Warton, P. M. (1992a). Contexts and cognitions: Taking a pluralist view. In P. Light & G. Butterworth (Eds.), *Contexts for learning* (pp. 151–177). Oxford: Oxford University Press.

Goodnow, J. J., & Warton, P. M. (1992b). Understanding responsibility: Adolescents' views of delegation and follow-through within the family. *Journal of Social Development, 1*, 89–106.

Goodnow, J. J., & Warton, P. M. (in press). Shades of blame: The distribution of responsibility after delegation. *Journal of Moral Education.*

Goodnow, J. J., Wilkins, P., & Dawes, L. (1986). Acquiring cultural forms: Cognitive aspects of socialization illustrated by children's drawings and judgments of drawings. *International Journal of Behavioral Development, 9*, 485–505.

Gullestad, M. (1984). *Kitchen-table society: A study of family life and friendships of young working-class mothers in urban Norway.* Oslo: Universitetsforlaget.

Habermas, J. (1979). *Communication and the evolution of society.* London: Heineman

Hart, H. L. A., & Honoré, A. M. (1985). *Causation in the law* (2nd ed.). Oxford: Oxford University Press.

Higgins, E. T., McCann, C. D., & Fondacaro, R. (1982). The "communication game": Goal-directed encoding and cognitive consequences. *Social Cognition, 1*, 21–37.

Hochschild, A. (1989). *Second shift: Working parents and the revolution at home.* New York: Viking.

Hood, J. C. (1986). The provider role: Its meaning and measurement. *Journal of Marriage and the Family, 48*, 349–359.

Johnson, C. L., & Troll, L. (1992). Family functioning in late life. *Journal of Gerontology, 47*, 566–572.

Kraus, R. M., & Fussell, S. R. (1990). Mutual knowledge and communication effectiveness. In J. Gelegher, R. A. Kraut, & C. Egido (Eds.), *Intellectual teamwork: Social and technological foundations of cooperative work* (pp. 111–146). Hillsdale, NJ: Erlbaum.

Lawrence, J. A. (1988). Making just decisions in magistrates' courts. *Social Justice Research, 2*, 155–176.

Lave, J. (1993). The practice of learning. In S. Chaiklin & J. Lave (Eds.), *Understanding practice* (pp. 3–32). Cambridge: Cambridge University Press.

Lein, L. (1984). *Families without villains.* Lexington MA: Heath.

Lüscher, K. (1995). *Homo interpretans*: On the relevance of perspectives, knowledge, and beliefs in the ecology of human development. In P. Moen, G. Elder Jr., & K. Lüscher (Eds.), *Lives in context: The ecology of human development* (pp. 563–598). Washington, DC: American Psychological Association.

Miller, P. (1992). Narrative practices and the social construction of self in childhood. *American Ethnologist, 17*, 292–311.

Mugny, G., & Carugati, F. (1989). *Social representations of intelligence.* Cambridge: Cambridge University Press.

Okin, S. M. (1989). *Justice, gender, and the family.* New York: Basic.

Perret-Clermont, A.-N., Perret, J. F., & Bell, N. (1991). The social construction of meaning and cognitive activity in elementary school children. In L. B. Resnick, J. M. Levine, & S. D. Teasley (Eds.), *Perspectives on socially shared cognition* (pp. 41–62). Washington, DC: American Psychological Association.

Quinn, N. (1992). The motivational force of self-understanding: Evidence from wives' inner conflicts. In R. G. D'Andrade & C. Strauss (Eds.), *Human motives and cultural models* (pp. 90–126). Cambridge: Cambridge University Press.

Qureshi, H., & Simons, K. (1987). Resources within families: Caring for elderly people. In J. Brannen & G. Wilson (Eds.), *Give and take in families* (pp. 117–135). London: Allen & Unwin.

Rogoff, B. (1990). *Apprenticeship in thinking*. Oxford: Oxford University Press.

Romney, A. K., Weller, S. C., & Batchelder, W. H. (1986). Culture as consensus: A theory of culture and informant accuracy. *American Anthropologist, 88*, 313–332.

Scanzoni, J. (1978). *Sex roles, women's work, and married conflict*. Lexington, MA: Heath.

Schubauer-Leoni, M. L., Perret-Clermont, A.-N., & Grossen, M. (1992). The construction of adult–child intersubjectivity in psychological research and in school. In M. Von Cranach, W. Doise, & G. Mugny (Eds.), *Social representations and the social bases of knowledge* (pp. 69–77). Bern: Huber.

Shanahan, M. J., Elder, G. H., Jr., & Conger, R. D. (1993, April). *Adolescent work in rural America: Ecological variations in social development*. Paper presented at the biennial meeting of the Society for Research in Child Development, New Orleans.

Smetana, J. G. (1988). Adolescents' and parents' conceptions of parental authority. *Child Development, 59*, 321–335.

Titmuss, R. (1971). *The gift relationship*. New York: Vintage.

von Cranach, M., Doise, W., & Mugny, G. (Eds.). (1992). *Social representations and social bases of knowledge*. Bern: Huber.

Warton, P. M., & Goodnow, J. J. (1991). The nature of responsibility: Children's understanding of "your job." *Child Development, 62*, 156–165.

Warton, P. M., & Goodnow, J. J. (1995). Money and children's household jobs: Parents' views of their interconnections. *International Journal of Behavioral Development, 18*, 335–350.

Warton, P. M., Goodnow, J. J., & Bowes, J. A. (1992). Teaching as a form of work: Effects of teachers' roles and role definitions on working to rule. *Australian Journal of Education, 36*, 170–180.

Williamson, G. L., & Clack, M. S. (1989). The communal/exchange distinction and some implications for understanding justice in families. *Social Justice Research, 3*, 77–103.

Yeandle, S. (1984). *Women's working lives: Patterns and strategies*. London: Tavistock.

7   The lifelong transformation of moral goals through social influence

William Damon

Abstract

This chapter examines the growth and transformation of moral goals in the course of a person's life. It begins by presenting theoretical and methodological considerations in the study of moral goals. It then presents a model of social influence and moral development. The purpose of the model is to explicate the ways in which a person's characteristics, such as natural dispositions and social experience, interact with new social experiences to form and transform the individual's moral goals throughout life.

The chapter examines three expressions of morality that occur at different periods in the life span: (a) the early emergence and later elaboration of empathy and sympathy; (b) the learning of moral concepts during childhood; and (c) the formation and sustenance of moral commitment during adulthood. These three sets of phenomena differ in many ways: They make their initial appearances at different periods of life; they vary widely in their behavioral implications; and the first two occur in practically all children, whereas the third occurs only in certain subsets of people. Yet, despite these apparent differences, similar processes of social influence and goal formation are implicated in all three. Drawing on data collected in recent years by a number of investigators, including the author and his colleagues, the chapter analyzes the ways in which multiple processes of social influence contribute to a person's moral goals for each of these disparate cases. The chapter concludes with a discussion of the dynamic interrelations between social influence, moral goals, moral behavior, and the development of self-identity.

During the past 20 years, I have on many occasions revisited the question of how people acquire moral beliefs, goals, and commitments. My initial research program in this area examined children's moral beliefs at the very early ages when they begin expressing their moral ideas verbally (Damon, 1977, 1980). As part of this investigation, I also explored the extent to which children were guided by the ideas they expressed. Following this work, I became interested in how children's moral ideas are connected to their social experience, not only in the sense of how their beliefs might influence both their judgments and their actions (Damon & Hart, 1988; Damon & Killen, 1982). Integrating other

198

research on children's early moral emotions, I attempted a comprehensive statement about how children's moral growth reflects a dynamic interplay of cognitive, affective, and behavioral development in an evolving context of social relationships and personal goals (Damon, 1988). In a recent study with Anne Colby, we used this framework to analyze moral development at the adult end of the life span (Colby & Damon, 1992). The subjects for this case study were a group of highly committed "moral exemplars."

Each of the topics that I have examined – the learning of moral concepts during childhood, the elaboration of moral emotions and other early pro-social reactions, and the display of deep moral commitment in adulthood – has interested me in its own right, at least in part because each has such clear implications for the quality of our individual and collective moral lives. Yet in addition to the compelling social and personal issues that each topic represents, I also have found a common theme among them, one defined by my search as a developmental psychologist for general processes of moral growth. It is this common theme that I shall focus on in this chapter.

The common theme is the manner in which a person's characteristics interact with the social world to transform the person's moral goals. This theme is not limited to the three topics that I have noted: My conviction is that similar interactive processes underlie practically all instances of moral growth. The framework that I propose here is intended as a general depiction of individual moral change through social influence. In my research to date, I have not had a chance to examine empirically more than a few types of moral development. But because the three topics that I discuss in this chapter vary so greatly in their behavioral particulars, I shall take them as a reasonable starting point in assessing the framework's general utility for describing progressive change across the spectrum of human morality.

Models of moral development

What should we look for in a general account of moral development? In some ways, *though not in all*, we should look for the same features that any satisfactory account of psychological development must have. First, it must explain the contrasts between different age periods that have been widely reported and confirmed in longitudinal and cross-sectional research (Damon, 1988; Rest, 1983). Second, it must account for short-term learning that can be readily induced by assorted interventions, experimental or otherwise (Blasi, 1983). Third, it must include processes that can explain the enormous variety of behavioral and cognitive changes displayed in different social and cultural settings (Shweder, Mahapatra, & Miller, 1987). These are general features required by any psychological account of developmental change.

But due to the particularities of the moral domain, an account of moral development requires certain components not needed for explanations of other areas of psychological growth. Three special components are critical when analyzing moral development.

First, any account of moral development begins with presuppositions about how to distinguish moral from nonmoral concerns. Not just any human rule, regularity, value, standard, or belief can legitimately be called moral. It is important to make this distinction, since genuinely moral concerns have a developmental course with special features not found in other sorts of concerns (Damon, 1988). This is not the place for a philosophical treatise on the distinction between the moral and the nonmoral. Suffice it to say for now that I, like many others who study morality, include in my analyses of moral development the categories of justice, benevolence, social responsibility, honesty, liberty, rights, and harm (e.g., see Shweder et al., 1987). I exclude, among other things, the concerns that Max Weber, and others in his footsteps, have called custom, convention, and personal interest (Turiel, Killen, & Helwig, 1987).

Second, moral beliefs are more directly derived from the actual social conditions in which they operate than are many other intellectual beliefs or affective functions. Morality in any form – individual or collective – has an intrinsic social component; variation among moral beliefs always reflects variation in social experience. Models of change that de-emphasize social influence (e.g., the biological maturation models currently in vogue throughout the field) are insufficient when it comes to moral growth. Yet biological processes are central to moral growth: There are key natural dispositions that direct early moral reactions and set parameters for later social influence. Any model of moral growth must define the interplay between natural moral dispositions such as empathy and the social influence that transforms these dispositions into stable systems of moral obligation.

Third, human morality subsumes many diverse cognitive, affective, and behavioral processes. As some examples, morality includes *both* reflection *and* habit, *both* reasoning about hypothetical moral problems *and* conduct in real situations, *both* emotional responses *and* intellectual appraisals. It is not likely that they all grow concomitantly with one another. There may be great differences in the patterning of changes both within and between individuals so that, for example, person A might be strong on reflection but not on habit, person B may be just the opposite, person C may be strong (or weak) on both, and all three people may periodically change the way in which they coordinate the two. This is why it is essential to take account of all the operative distinctions if we are to understand morality in its full complexity.

All of these general and specific characteristics of moral change have been recognized in social science and philosophy. All of the available developmental models can be adapted to deal with them. But most models seem stretched beyond their boundaries when confronted with such phenomena, despite the user's agility in theoretical accommodation. The ultimate but as yet unrealized goal is to create an account of moral development that incorporates all the particular characteristics of morality coherently within its own framework – and that does so in accord with its conception of development as a whole and without violation to any of its fundamental assumptions.

Each of the major contending models of moral development has certain strengths and limitations in its conception of change processes. Piagetian and cognitive-developmental models offer useful descriptions of age differences among populations of children that Western scientists have studied. But these models have been constrained in their analysis of change processes by their characterization of social influence as external to cognitive belief systems. In such models, social influence is conceived as a process of invasion rather than as an integral part of the belief system. External influence is seen as setting the person into internal conflict – "disequilibration," in Piaget's term – which is then resolved through individual reflection and cognitive change. As a consequence of the invasion metaphor, the individual is viewed as fundamentally apart from the social world, and the question of how communication between the two comes about becomes problematic. This is especially true in early life, when children have few communication skills and, as Piaget emphasized, assimilate most new information to their established habitual reactions (see Damon & Colby, 1987, for a more detailed account of the way in which social influence is characterized in Piaget's equilibration model).

Social-psychological models are sometimes better equipped to recognize the dynamic interplay between individual and social influence, but they lack developmental accounts of how individuals acquire and maintain their longstanding patterns of thought and conduct (e.g., Gollwitzer, 1993; Moscovici, 1977). Perhaps the strongest contributions toward integrating social and developmental processes have been made by recent adaptations of Vygotskian theory (Wertsch, 1981, 1985). Because Vygotskian approaches start with the assumption that human knowledge is organized through social interaction from the start, they have been able to capture the ways in which individuals are guided by communicative processes. Even in this perspective, though, there still remain questions of how individuals maintain continuities of thought and action over time. The Vygotskian perspective has not been particularly concerned with the legacy that social participation leaves on the individual. What does a person bring away from a social experience? How does that legacy affect the person's next social engagement? In short, what, and how, do people *learn* from the social settings that surround them? There also remain questions of how individuals themselves affect the social world that influences their own development. The social transformation of the individual is only half the story of behavioral change. Throughout their development, individuals can alter their families, cultures, and societies. It is important in any developmental account to preserve the individual's proactive engagement within all the matrices of social influence that contribute to the individual's development.

Goal transformation through social influence

The model that I use to discuss moral change has some features in common with the cognitive-developmental and social-psychological approaches, as well as recent writings within the Vygotskian tradition (see Rogoff, 1989, 1993; Wertsch, 1981, 1985), the life-span approach, and certain European writings on goal theory (e.g., Baltes, 1987; Gollwitzer, 1993). The model's primary focus is on the moral goals that persons acquire, and revise, in the course of their lifetimes. By "moral goals" I mean the kinds of "unequivocal behavioral orientations" that some European social psychologists have referred to as "goal intentions" (Gollwitzer, 1993). In my usage, therefore, the term *moral goal* refers to broad interests and commitments that emanate from values, principles, and reactions that reflect the moral concerns that I have noted earlier. A moral goal implies a dedication to achieving a just or benevolent state of affairs. At times a moral goal may be linked to a specific outcome or center on a particular course of action, but usually a moral goal also transcends any particular outcome or act. It is an enduring commitment to moral values and principles rather than an attempt to accomplish a discrete deed.

As an analytic strategy, a focus on moral goals provides more comprehensive access to moral development than does a focus on either moral judgment or moral action. The advantage over purely cognitive strategies is that a focus on moral goals examines the incorporation of a new system of motives rather than merely the acquisition of new knowledge. The core assumption of a moral goals model is that new perspectives are shaped collaboratively (or sometimes antagonistically) in the course of continual negotiations between persons. This means that all new ideas owe their shape to some type of interaction between external guidance and internal belief. The assumption is that moral goals are developed in communication with others, through processes that combine social influence with active personal engagement. The focus on goals, therefore, offers a more compelling starting point than the cognitivist assumption that ideas are formed by individuals "figuring out" the way the world works by observing reality.

The model proposes that the conditions for developmental change are created by social influences that trigger a reformulation and eventual consolidation of moral goals. This process – *the transformation of goals through social influence* – is the foundation of moral development throughout the life span. This process results in a building of commitments toward justice, caring, truthfulness, and other concerns of rights, responsibility, and benevolence.

Beyond its role in encouraging a person to form lifelong commitments to moral goals, social influence also guides the formation and transformation of strategies that are designed to achieve these broad goals – the "implementation intentions" that psychologists have studied since the turn of the century (see Gollwitzer, 1993, on the studies of Ach and his followers). These strategies are directed toward particular outcomes, many of which are ephemeral and context-bound. Although important for the course of day-to-day events, such strategies do not in themselves constitute enduring moral goals. The subject of this chapter is the development of the person's broader moral goals rather than the particular implementation strategies that the person constructs from moment to moment.

To support the development of moral goals, social influence must trigger the reevaluation of a person's current capacities; it must also guide the further elaboration of these capacities. There are many types of social influence through which people try to alter one another's behavior. If one has sufficient power, for example, one may simply try to tell another what to do and possibly even what to think. And even beyond unilateral power assertion, there are other, more subtle forms of coercion, persuasion, cajoling, attitude adjustment, reasoning, and so on.

But for long-term developmental change in a person's orientation, many of these social influence strategies are ineffective. Coercion, for example, works only as long as the power assertion remains in effect. Once removed, there is a drift (or a rush) away from the enforced position. For more permanent change, the person must participate actively in the transformation. Moreover, for genuine growth, there must be an extension of a capacity that the person has already partially worked out. Development, alone among all the possible changes in a person's psychological states, draws on the following social influence conditions:

- A collaborative (or antagonistic) relationship between persons having alternative perspectives
- An initial – though only partial – match of goals between the parties
- An initial – and partial – mismatch of goals, in which the goals of the influencing parties constitute an extension of the goals of the parties being influenced
- Active participation of each party in joint transactions
- An extended period of such transactions, during which the parties first become engaged in actions that reflect joint goals and then become increasingly engaged in activities reflecting goals not initially shared
- Accompanying such transactions, rich and frequent communications about the goals and strategies, as well as about the values underlying the goals and strategies
- A structure of guidance providing a bridge from matched to mismatched goals
- A mutual receptivity to direction and feedback
- An exchange of concerns and capacities, culminating in developmental alterations of perspectives
- An adoption of new or broadened goals, usually modified in a manner that

can be coherently integrated into the person's prior perspective (even as that perspective changes to accommodate the new goals)
- An eventual adoption of new strategies for pursuing the new goals, again with whatever modifications are needed to assimilate these strategies into the person's developing perspective

The developmental transformation of goals is a gradual process, occurring over months and sometimes years of communication. It may begin in a small way, as when one person induces another to entertain a new idea or to adopt a new behavior. But long-term, permanent growth does not begin until the latter person's goals are affected. For this to occur, the first person's rationale for the idea or behavior must be accepted. Through this route, not only a discrete action but an entire social perspective is eventually transferred.

According to the goal transformation account, negative as well as positive social influences can play a part in the growth of moral goals. Negative social influences occur when pressure is brought to bear on a person by intense assertions of values that the person rejects. When a social engagement presents values that a person has determined to be illegitimate, the person's resistance can lead the person toward a transformation, elaboration, or strengthening of his or her moral goals.

A person's moral goals play a primary role in shaping the person's social behavior and self-identity. Moral goals are a powerful subset of the long-term goals around which most lives are organized. Perhaps more than any other type of personal goal, moral goals often attain the status of a binding commitment that lasts throughout an entire life. To a greater or lesser degree, most people eventually try to reconcile their moral goals with their other personal goals. When this reconciliation is complete, as I discuss later, one finds a unity between morality and self, as well as a tenacious commitment to moral action.

Empathy, sympathy, and the development of pro-social behavior

I begin with empathy for three reasons. First, empathic reactions are among the first moral tendencies that appear in life – in fact, they appear so early and so universally that they force us to consider the role of natural dispositions in the formation of moral goals. Second, empathy is an emotion with strong ties to both thought and behavior. When considering a topic such as interacting minds, it is important to remember that emotions are an integral part of the interactive mix, both on the mental and on the interpersonal level: Empathic responding is an unambiguous example of this. Third, the development of empathy is a lifelong affair, drawing on every cognitive, affective, and behavioral system that brings about the growth of the person's moral goals in general.

Emotional proclivities toward pro-social behavior appear so early that psychologists now believe them to be inborn (Kagan, 1984). The most unambiguous of such proclivities is a cluster of emotional reactions known as *empathy* and *sympathy*. These interpersonally oriented affective states create in the child a sense of shared responding that links the child psychologically to others. In the course of empathic and sympathetic reactions, the child's own emotional comfort is affected, either positively or negatively, by his or her perception of another person's well-being. These emotional reactions provide the child with a motivated reason to care about another person's welfare, to aid the other, and to keep the other from harm (Strayer & Shroeder, 1989). They also give the child affectively charged reasons to avoid hurting the other through violent acts.

The developmental roots of empathy and sympathy begin very early in life. Although it is a matter of speculation whether true empathy or sympathy can be found in newborns, psychologists have identified reactions that certainly represent early precursors (Campos, Campos, & Barrett, 1989). One such reaction is the infant crying response called "contagion" (Piaget, 1951). In nurseries and neonatal wards, 2- or 3-day-old infants have been observed crying at the sounds of other infants' crying (Damon, 1983). Without any physical pain of their own, infants emit matched vocal signs at the sound of another's distress (see also Azmitia, Chapter 5, this volume).

Contagious crying may be caused by the infant's perceptual confusion of itself with others in combination with the infant's tendency to reproduce its own behavior. A circular pattern may be triggered, in which the infant repeats the crying response that it mistakenly takes as its own. Yet, even if only attributable to this sort of egocentric confusion, contagious crying indicates an initial disposition toward spontaneously responding with a sign of distress to another's discomfort. At the very least, this disposition represents a precursor to both empathy and sympathy.

Although related, empathy and sympathy are different in important ways. Eisenberg (1989) has proposed the following distinctions between the two constructs:

> We define *empathy* as the sharing of the perceived emotion of the other. Specifically, it is an affective state that stems from the apprehension of another's emotional state or condition and that is congruent and quite similar to the perceived state of the other.
> *Sympathy* . . . we define as an emotional response, stemming from another's emotional state or condition, that is not identical to the other's emotion but consists of feelings of sorrow or concern for the other's welfare. (pp. 2–3)

Such a distinction suggests that empathy and sympathy do not have identical influences on children's social conduct. In empathy, a child shares another's feelings, but the child's primary concern may remain on the experience of the self. Children, for example, may resent those who cause them to feel the same unpleasant things that they are feeling. In such cases, empathy would not necessarily trigger other-oriented behavior: A plausible alternative response would be to dissociate the self from the other and to stop empathizing. Empathy may provide the emotional substance behind a desire to care for another, but it does not in itself fully establish that desire. Sympathy, on the other hand, implies a direct concern for the other and not an absolute sharing of feelings. This means that sympathy inevitably has an altruistic orientation. Its affective demands can be satisfied only through pro-social action or through resistance to antisocial action. While sympathy may at times draw on empathy for its emotional substance and charge, of the two emotions it is the one more strongly directed toward helping and not harming the other.

Empathy and sympathy provide good examples of transformations that change moral emotions into moral goals during the course of development. Hoffman (1984) has described a sequence in which the "global empathy" of the newborn becomes transformed into effective systems of thought and action. Initially, the newborn may feel discomfort at signs of another's distress, but the newborn often cannot draw clear boundaries between the feelings of self and other: hence, the phrase "global empathy." As an example, Hoffman cites observations such as the following:

> At nine months, Hope had already demonstrated strong reactions to other children's distress. Characteristically, she did not turn away from these distress scenes, though they apparently touched off distress in herself. Hope would stare intently, her eyes welling up with tears if another child fell, hurt herself, or cried. At that time, she was overwhelmed with her emotions. She would end up crying herself and crawling quickly to her mother for comfort. (pp. 12–13)

Such reactions are common, but they are also erratic and unconnected with action. For these emotional responses to become linked with effective action – such as helping others in appropriate ways – children must acquire specific goals that direct their actions in predictable ways. For most children, this process begins late in infancy (Hoffman, 1984). At this time, the infant's previously undifferentiated feelings of discomfort at another's distress grow into feelings of genuine concern for particular others. In short, the infant's empathic reactions increasingly become channeled into sympathetic feelings for people that the infant cares about. The infant begins to realize that other people are independent beings who have their own happy or unhappy feelings.

Further, the infant becomes aware that people can affect one another's feelings either positively or negatively – that is, people can upset one another through harsh communications or can relieve one another's distress through kind communications. All of this awareness is learned directly, through the active experience of communicating with one's caregivers and peers. The communicational channels that make this learning possible have been described as a fundamental "intersubjectivity" that prepares the infant for receiving cognitive, linguistic, and emotional messages from others as early as birth (Trevarthen, 1992).

Although the infant becomes aware of, and concerned about, the needs and feelings of particular others, the infant is rarely able to act appropriately in response. Hoffman cites an observation of a 1-year-old who showed empathic concern for a crying playmate. The empathic child brought his own blanket to comfort the crying child, unaware that this blanket would mean nothing to someone else. By early childhood, children develop a firmer sense of how to respond to another's distress. As Hoffman and others have documented, 6-year-olds can be remarkably astute about directing their efforts in a manner that recognizes another's particular needs. By the end of childhood, most children have acquired generalized altruistic intentions. Their empathic and sympathetic responses become broadened to include those whom they have never met, such as starving children in distant countries.

The transformation of empathy into sympathetic concerns, helping goals, and altruistic intentions, requires the growth and integration of social-cognitive capacities, such as perspective taking, which are elaborated through processes of social interaction. In the course of social interactions, other people express their own needs. When these expressions take a form that the child can grasp – and is motivated to grasp – the child discovers that the needs of the other differ from the needs of the self. Evocative expressions of others' needs that are both understandable and highly motivating leave the most lasting influence. Such expressions have a transformative effect on the child's broad goals and commitments, as well as on the strategies that the child uses to achieve these goals. Both effects can occur throughout the life span, in adulthood as well as in infancy, as I shall show in my discussion of adult moral commitment.

This process can vary greatly across individuals. Some children quickly become able, accurately and consistently, to share other perspectives emotionally and cognitively. Some, in contrast, seem unwilling or unable to do so, and others do so in erratic or distorted ways. Young delinquents, for example, have been observed to show surprise at the notion that they should care at all about the harm they cause others – "After all, she isn't me!" one youth was quoted saying (Damon, 1988). In cases where violent youngsters do express empathic sentiments, these sentiments are often wildly misplaced. One youth with a long history of mayhem was heard worrying about the pain that pine trees might feel when they are cut down to serve as Christmas trees (Damon, 1988).

Such failures and distortions of empathy become apparent long after birth and are attributable to maladaptive patterns of social influence. For example, an adolescent who becomes part of a violent street gang may show empathy with fellow gang members while acting with great cruelty to those on the outside. A shift in allegiance within the gang can then alter the youth's pattern of empathic responding, so that a once-befriended colleague suddenly becomes a target for anger rather than an object of empathy. When the child's social world is unpredictable, hostile, and dangerous, the child's natural empathic reactions have little opportunity to be guided into a reliable pattern of moral goals and pro-social behavior. Instead, the reactions may continue in an infantile mode of erratic impulses that are unconnected to any sustained concerns for other people or helpful actions that recognize the particular needs of particular others.

Early empathy and sympathy are, in a sense, universal "natural events" that provide a foundation for the formation of altruistic goals and intentions. Life provides people with other such natural events, not all of which are universal or inborn. For example, a serious illness or physical handicap, even when incurred late in life, may predispose a person toward empathic responding. But not all children turn their empathic reactions into moral goals, just as not all afflicted adults turn their bout with illness into a more charitable orientation. Both children and adults are continually influenced by their past and present social experience, and this experience transforms them. Some transformations set the stage for further developmental acquisitions, whereas others turn into stable goals that persist over time and influence the course of the child's future social behavior (Caspi, Bem, & Elder, 1989). In this sense, as Michael Cole (Chapter 2, this volume) writes, the child's developing characteristics constitute a kind of "second nature" that is built on a dynamic interplay between natural events and social influence.

The acquisition of moral concepts in childhood

I turn now to some data from a series of studies that I conducted with young children who were just learning ideas about fairness (see Damon, 1977, 1980, 1988; Damon & Killen, 1982). The experiments varied in their specific procedures, but the general idea was to construct in the laboratory a "real-life" distributive justice situation. The experiments posed children the task of dividing among themselves (and a younger child previously removed from the situation) a reward for making bracelets. Children were agemates, either 4, 6, 8, or 10 years old, and the reward was 10 candy bars. The experimental situations all had built into them conditions that encouraged children to consider issues like merit, gender, special need, and age in their discussions. In some versions of the experiment, we focused on the children's conduct and actual choices during the group debate. In other versions, we focused on their moral reasoning several weeks before and after the experiment.

These experiments followed a paradigm established in Geneva by Doise and Mugny, except that we were looking for socially induced changes in the realm of fairness, rather than in the area of physical or spatial conservation (see Doise & Mugny, 1984). For the present purpose, I shall extract two findings from our experiments. The first reveals a change in behavioral choice that was frequently triggered by the experimental encounter, the second a change in the children's reasoning about fairness.

Table 7.1. *Number of subjects constructing equal and unequal distributions at each of four age levels and at each of three choice points*

| | Choice point | | | | | |
| | Before group session | | At start of group session | | At end of group session | |
Age	Equal	Unequal	Equal	Unequal	Equal	Unequal
4	7	29	6	30	15	21
6	19	17	22	14	24	12
8	22	14	32	4	36	0
10	28	8	34	2	36	0

The first finding can be read from Table 7.1, which shows a bidirectional movement toward equal solutions. This movement was associated with both age and the progress of the group debate. The age trend is simply that older children construct more equitable solutions than do younger children, at all of the three choice points in the debate. In addition, however, *within* each age there was a progressive increase in equitable solutions from the first choice point to the second to the third. In other words, at all ages, the longer the children spend in the group, the more likely they are to opt for equality. As can be seen from Table 7.1, the two trends toward equality (age and choice point) reinforce each other, so that all 72 of the oldest children chose equality by the end of the group session.

Equality is one of the fundamental elements of justice, but it is not the only, the best, or the most sophisticated way of dealing with a fairness conflict. Many of the older children in this study showed, both before and after the group sessions, that they often preferred other considerations over simple equality: considerations like merit (extra "pay" for extra work or talent), benevolence (inequality in the service of special need or deprivation), and so on. Only the children in the lower middle section of this age range – the 6-year-olds – preferred equality as a general solution to all sorts of problems. The youngest children, like the older ones, tended more toward unequal than equal solutions, although, in their case, equality was eschewed in favor of self-preference rather than merit or need.

Why, then, did equality have such an appeal for children of all ages in this experimental situation? To answer this we must look beyond the parameters of justice reasoning to the demands of the group. Our situation was one in which agreement was necessary: The children could not get any of the candy bars until they had reached a consensus among themselves about how to split them up. In such a situation, equality is an excellent way to reach agreement. By definition, it is a perfect leveler of differences. In an equal solution, a person's full "deserving" may not be recognized; yet no one's claims are ignored to any great degree. This is why it works in a group even where none of the group's members finds it wholly satisfactory.

In this study, the accomplishment of the older children was to anticipate this quickly, often (temporarily) setting aside their other beliefs about fairness in the process. Many of the younger children also came to recognize this, although it took some exposure to the peer debate to get them there. As might be expected, the younger children did not always manage to figure out in the course of one peer debate what the older children could quickly anticipate. Whereas all of the older two groups eventually reached consensus through equal solutions, 8% of the 6-year-old groups and 22% of the 4-year-old groups never reached any consensus at all, despite unlimited time and the risk of walking away without any candy.

My main interest, though, was neither in those children who had already learned how to deal quickly and efficiently with such a situation nor in those who clung to old ways without learning how to resolve the situation. Rather, it was in that sizable group of children who changed their approach in the face of pressing group demands. What were the developmental implications of such a change? Did it show learning? Was it a precursor of genuine growth in social competence? If so, growth of what sort? Was it merely learning new group manipulation strategies or did it have something to do with moral change, despite the pragmatic nature of the goals that triggered it?

Here I refer briefly to a second set of findings, from an experiment designed around these particular questions. This was a training-study version of the preceding situation, complete with pretest, two posttests, and two experimental control groups (one of which was a nontreatment group; the other hypothetically went through a similar-sounding situation with an adult).

The gist of the findings were as follows: (a) A majority of children placed in the peer debate situation showed some advance in their reasoning about justice by the time of the posttests; (b) the proportion of children who changed in the course of the actual peer encounter was significantly greater than those who changed in either of the two control groups; (c) the nature of the effected change was an increase in the percentage of statements above the reasoning mode, rather than a holistic shift in judgment;[1] and (d) children who engaged in conflictual interactions with their peers were the least likely to change, whereas groups of children who accepted each other's statements positively were more likely to change, particularly when this happened at the lower age levels.

In prior writings, I have had some trouble explaining this pattern of results from a developmental perspective. The trend toward equality as a behavioral choice seemed connected more with situational than with individual factors, particularly since this choice did not always reflect the typical judgmental preferences of the subjects. As for the reasoning changes induced by the group debate, developmental theory would more likely predict conflict to be positively associated with change than to be inversely related, as we found. The relation between change and children's tendencies to accept one another's ideas reciprocally would seem to fit with an imitation theory of learning. Yet we can also tell that the changes we observed were not simple repetitions of ideas that the children had heard. Rather, the posttest responses often included notions never explicitly expressed during the group encounter.

What is needed to account for these findings is a theoretical view showing how social influence guides the child's active construction of judgment and choice. A goals model provides one such theoretical view. But note that even this view must be modified to deal with peer influences of the sort observed in the present situation. When the influencing party is another child, the induced perspective (or even perspectives) may be new to both parties rather than a substitution of one party's for the other's. This requires us to note that in some cases of social guidance, new goals may be *jointly* discovered rather than transmitted. As I shall discuss later, this is also true in the case of adults who are still expanding their moral ideas and commitments.

A transformation-of-goals model includes a variety of negotiation procedures, ranging from inducement and eventual substitution of one party's goals for another's to co-discovery of new ideas that may lead to new perspectives and goals. This is why a transformation-of-goals model is useful in thinking about the results of this experiment. Certainly our situational parameters – the most prominent of which was group pressure – guided children toward their moral choices. This guidance influenced particular responses to a particular event (equality as a means of reaching consensus now) rather than shaping children's general moral orientations. The older children's greater readiness to anticipate and accept such guidance indicates that (a) there is a lesson to be learned in such peer confrontations, and (b) they had learned at least a good part of this lesson during their own social histories.

In fact, there was more than one "lesson" for the children in this encounter. One lesson certainly was the usefulness of equal distribution in resolving differences within a group. This was in large part a practical lesson, a procedure for getting out of the situation with a share of the reward. But it also had moral implications. For the youngest children, it may have introduced the notion of equal treatment to their moral repertoires. For the older ones, it likely triggered a process of moral reflection that produced some judgmental change. In this case the lesson may have been procedural in another sense; that is, given this particular kind of situation, it is better to distribute the rewards equally even though in other situations it is important to bring in other concerns such as equity or merit. It is important to note that, particularly among the older children, the experimental intervention did not lead to a generalized tendency to use an equality solution to distribution problems.

In this experiment we see individual construction fostered, guided, but not quite directed by social influence. For some children, the peer debate experience forced a choice that posed for them a new possibility – equality of treatment. For others, it gave them a chance to hear and discuss other alternatives, some of which they would ultimately consider more morally satisfying than equality, though in the end they would choose equality as a way to resolve the current situation. For still others (a large 44% minority), the situation provided no grounds for enhancing their moral reasoning in any detectable way. The situation was the same for all children and certainly had an impact, yet registered differently on the moral consciousness of different individuals. So, at least in this peer-type learning experience, the direction of change is only in part socially determined.

The tendency for change to follow from accepting rather than conflictual interactions does suggest that those children more open to guidance were the ones who profited most by it. The scaffold was available, but the child had to be willing to grow within it. The group's direction structured the choices of its participants but did not absolutely determine them. Similarly, it made possible some eventual shifts in moral perspective, but did not define the exact nature of these shifts. Nor did it produce these shifts in all participants. We see here a process of co-construction that relied on an integration of social guidance with individual initiative.

The development of deep moral commitment

I turn now to a study recently completed by Anne Colby and myself (Colby & Damon, 1992) of how deeply committed individuals – "moral exemplars" – develop their moral commitments. The exemplars, and the criteria for their selection, were chosen from an extensive nominating process involving 20 distinguished moral philosophers, scholars, theologians, and religious leaders from a wide variety of ideological persuasions. The selection criteria included (a) a sustained commitment to moral principles showing a generalized respect for humanity; (b) a disposition to act in accord with one's moral principles, implying also a consistency between the means and ends of one's actions; (c) a willingness to risk one's self-interest for the sake of one's principles; (d) a characteristic of inspiring others to moral action; (e) a dedicated responsiveness to the needs of others; and (f) a sense of humility about one's own importance relative to the world at large. Our nominators identified 86 living Americans who meet all of these criteria, and we arranged to interview 23 of these people. The final sample included about equal numbers of women and men, a broad mix of racial, ethnic, and socioeconomic backgrounds, and a wide range of religious and political orientations.

The interview consisted of an extensive set of questions about the moral exemplar's personal experiences and beliefs. We probed for events and influences that may have shaped the exemplar's character, critical life decisions that the exemplar has made, and the exemplar's feelings and thoughts during these critical decisions. Below, I describe one of the exemplars from our study and quote from her interviews. ("AC" in the quoted sections is Anne Colby; "VD" is Virginia Durr, the subject.) I have selected sections that illustrate the process of moral goal transformation through social influence.

Virginia Foster Durr is a white woman from a prominent family in Montgomery, Alabama. She was 84 at the time of our interview. As a young child, she, like most upper-class white children in the southern United States at the time, was very close to the family's black servants and their children but was separated from them as she grew older. Although she questioned this segregation to some degree at the time and during a number of later incidents, she held the prevailing views on segregation until she was in her thirties.

It was not until later when she married Clifford Durr and moved to Washington, D.C., that her perspective on race relations began to change. While there, she became involved in New Deal politics and was a very active member of the Women's Democratic National Committee. Her primary interest lay in the right to vote, which had been denied blacks as well as many women and poor whites through the imposition of a poll tax. She was closely connected socially to many of the important political figures of the day. For example, her sister was married to Hugo Black, who ran for the U.S. Senate and was later a very important member of the U.S. Supreme Court and instrumental in the move toward desegregation on the national level.

When Senator Joseph McCarthy and his associates began their anti-Communist campaign in the early 1950s, the Durrs had to leave Washington because of Clifford Durr's refusal to sign a loyalty oath. They moved from Washington to Colorado, where they encountered further trouble when Virginia signed a letter protesting certain aspects of U.S. policy in the conduct of the Korean War. She refused to recant, and her husband was fired from his job as a result. This was an act of considerable import, since the Durrs had three small children and very little money at that time. After Clifford Durr lost his job in Colorado, the Durrs went back to Alabama, where they lived with his parents, which was a source of great anguish to Virginia, given the great differences between the two generations of Durrs on political and moral ideology. The Durrs spent the rest of their professional lives in Alabama fighting segregation and running a law office that defended primarily poor blacks.

I now quote from the very beginning of Virginia Durr's interview to illustrate the way in which her social experiences interacted with her values, beliefs, and character to result in the developmental path she took:

> AC: Now, before I start asking the questions that I came with, I would like to hear a little bit more about your experience of not having made choices, as you put it. Maybe you could just talk about that a little bit. You've mentioned that a couple of times . . .

VD: You make, I suppose you make choices every day of your life. But the thing is, as far as the decisions I made concerning my part say in the racial struggle in the south, it wasn't a decision, it was something that grew over a period of years and one thing led to another. But I never (like Paul on the road to Damascus, was it?) thought that I saw a revealing light and just all of a sudden saw the light. But it was over a period of a number of years that I began to change my feelings. And the same thing was true really about the – well in a way, it was true about so many things. I changed as things happened. Rather, things happened and I changed because they happened.

Later in the interview she says:

VD: And actually I don't think that I really had much change in my attitude at all until I got to Washington in 1933. By that time I was thirty years old. . . . The thing that really changed me, I think, was the fact that I got into the Women's Democratic National Committee as a volunteer. You see, at that time, this is one of the things about being Southern that is also – even if you get to be a friend, you're exploiting them, blacks, all the time. My husband wasn't making but $6,500 a year, but we had a cook which I paid, I think, $12 a week to, and I had a nurse and I had a yard man, someone to do the laundry and the nurse made $12 or $15 a week. But the thing was that I had time to go in and be a volunteer at the Women's Division of the Democratic National Committee and that I'd gotten to be very devoted to the Roosevelts by that time. And in the Democratic Committee I met black women on an equal basis. So that was my first meeting with black women on a totally equal basis. And Mrs. Roosevelt was there a lot. But the thing was, D.C. was segregated. People don't remember now that the District of Columbia was as segregated as Alabama. Woodrow Wilson had done it. I don't think it was ever segregated after the Civil War until he came in and he segregated everything. All the government buildings were segregated and D.C. was segregated. And ah, so there was a movement started to desegregate the District of Columbia and this Mrs. [?] who was a black woman whose husband had been a judge, and she brought the suit. She went into some lunch place and they wouldn't serve her and these two young lawyers were with her and they took her case to the courts and it was won. So segregation was abolished in D.C. And so you see, I saw it done in the District of Columbia. But, of course, I saw it done with the backing of the Supreme Court and the backing of the Justice Department, the backing of Mrs. Roosevelt, the Democratic Committee, and so on and so forth.

AC: So that experience really changed you?

VD: Well that did change me a great deal. And then the Democratic Women started this fight against the poll tax because the southern women didn't vote because of the poll tax. Course the poor whites didn't vote, and the blacks didn't vote at all and only about ten or twelve percent of the people were eligible. And, so I got into that struggle and then that brought me in contact with a lot of black men and women, and so many people and that also was very enlightening. But there again, I had the backing of Mrs. Roosevelt and had the backing of the White House actually. But it took years and years for it to go through.

AC: When you were spending so much energy on the fight against the poll tax, what was driving that do you think, from your point of view? What was really the energy behind it inside you?

> VD: I thought the right to vote was something that everybody ought to
> have.

One advantage of using goal theory to explain change in this manner is that it avoids the fruitless cognition–affect split that has plagued other developmental explanations. A goal is an affectively charged motivator but is also part of an entire intellectual perspective. This is why genuine goal substitution, whether in childhood or adulthood, takes some time to achieve. Goal substitution entails a gradual transformation, through social influence, of one's perspective or one's actions in the social world. As such, it drives development on the cognitive and affective fronts together.

Implicit in the broadening of goals during the adult years is a further elaboration of the capacity for empathy and sympathy that began in the early months of life. Deeply committed adults like Virginia Durr continually discover new objects of empathic concern. As they acquire new concerns, they develop broader moral goals and forge new strategies for achieving these goals. The continual discovery of new objects of empathic concern indicates a capacity to remain open to information and influence from others. Certainly in the case of Virginia Durr, we see a history of openness to input from others. Her emerging goals were not self-initiated, but they do reflect what we might call an "active receptiveness" to social influence on her part.

The active receptiveness that we found has two noteworthy characteristics. First, the very fact of its existence signifies a potential for significant moral growth even late in life. Second, this was not a blanket receptiveness toward just any sort of influence. Witness, for example, Durr's equally strenuous resistance of the pressures to yield to the McCarthy people or to go along with the prevailing racial views of her friends in Alabama. She played an active role in choosing the social influences that would help shape her new moral goals.

It is also important to emphasize that at each step in her evolving moral engagement with the civil rights movement, Virginia Durr actively chose to move forward rather than to withdraw. Consequently, the direction and shape of her moral growth was co-constructed by a continual interplay between Virginia and her chosen community. The social influences in Durr's life cannot be understood without knowing what she herself brought to the process.

A transformation-of-goals model does not presuppose a form or direction of change. In many cases, people follow paths that are better described as corruption than development. Social pressures are complex and multidirectional. Which of the various pressures are most salient and the nature of their influence depends very much on the individual's cognitive framework for interpreting morality and on his or her character and values. This framework, of course, is built up through a history of social influences, but is particular to the individual and also no doubt borrows from the individual's natural dispositions. In the case of Virginia Durr, her prior cognitive framework certainly predisposed her to be more susceptible to some influences than others.

The integration of self and moral goals

What, then, are the reasons behind the remarkable depth, intensity, and scope of our exemplars' moral experience? I believe that a central reason lies in the close relation between self and morality that exemplars establish. Over the course of their lives, there is a progressive uniting of self and morality. Exemplars come to see morality and self as inextricably intertwined, so that concerns of the self become defined by their moral sensibilities. The exemplars' moral identities become tightly integrated, almost fused, with their self-identities. One businessman and social reformer expressed this sense of fusion during an interchange in one of our interviews with him:

> *When you think about these [moral] goals and values and so on, how do these relate to your sense of who you are as a person and your identity?*
>
> Well, it's one and the same. Who I am is what I'm able to do and how I feel all the time – each day, each moment. . . . It's hard for me to separate who I am from what I want to do and what I am doing.

Now, self and moral goals can be coordinated in any number of ways in a person's life. Self-goals can be segmented from moral ones, as when we apportion our paychecks into amounts dedicated to ourselves and amounts dedicated to charity. The two goals can stand in opposition to each other, as when someone jumps in front of a bus to save a child or, reciprocally, as when cheating someone to improve one's own lot. Or they can be united. In this last case, there is the sense that one's most powerfully motivating goals derive directly from one's moral convictions. Consequently, in serving morality one serves oneself. In this manner, one identifies oneself largely as an agent of one's moral goals.

Most people connect self-goals and moral goals to some degree – as when, for example, they act altruistically toward their children or other loved ones. But most people also experience some degree of conflict between what they most want to do and what they feel would be best to do from the moral point of view. Although they may want to do the right thing, they also want other things that clash with their moral goals. A unity between self and morality is far from typical, although it can be approached. Moral exemplars do so, and this is the key to the extraordinary range and depth of their moral commitments.

The co-occurrence of unified goals, effective social action, and a sense of certainty that we found in our moral exemplars was not coincidental. Rather, it follows from a more general principle in the relation between moral judgment and conduct: Where there is perceived concordance between self and morality, there will follow direct and predictable links between judgment and conduct, as well as great certainty in the action choices that result. Goals are a central component of self. When moral and personal goals are united, moral goals become central to the self. The general principle operates most clearly in the cases of highly moral individuals; but it also applies generally in the course of normal human behavior and development.

In a previous developmental analysis of self-understanding, I have described periods in childhood and adolescence when concepts of morality and self become joined (Damon, 1984; Damon & Hart, 1986, 1988). Early in life, morality and self are separate conceptual systems with little integration between them. When children refer to who they are or what they are like, they typically make no reference to their moral goals or beliefs. Instead, they focus on the surface features of their physical, active, social, or psychological selves. Children often speak about what is fair and what they would (or even should) do as wholly separate affairs. They will strongly affirm their desire to be fair with their friends, but this desire bears little implication for their self-concept: They do not think of themselves as persons who are fair or not fair (instead, they define themselves by their physical features, likes and dislikes, activities, family identities, and so on). Their moral concerns do not translate into concerns about who they are. This segregation is resolved toward the end of childhood, when in fact children do begin thinking about themselves in terms of how kind, just, and responsible they are.

When children begin to define themselves even to some small degree by their moral inclinations, a closer link between their moral interests and their self-interest is created. This leads to a bit more predictability between children's moral judgment and their conduct. We have evidence for this both from our own studies of children's sharing behavior and from other research on moral development during childhood and adolescence. In experimental studies, for example, children become more likely with age to do what they say they should do. They show greater consistency between their actions and beliefs, even when they are tempted to act selfishly, cheat, or otherwise violate their moral codes.

For most people, of course, moral interests and self-interests become linked only up to a point. There remain prominent schisms between morality and the self after childhood and, indeed, all throughout life. The resolution of the two at the end of childhood remains only partial: In our self-concept study, only two adolescents showed a tendency to define their identities *primarily* in terms of their moral beliefs. The self-concept study went only through late adolescence, so a stronger developmental trend toward integration might have been discovered by an extension of the study into adulthood. But it is safe to conclude that a true uniting of morality and the self remains a rare event, confined to exemplary individuals such as those participating in our study. In most people, the relationship between the two varies from relative separation to relative integration. Moreover, the extent of unity is an aspect of personality growth that derives more from a person's sense of self than from the nature of the person's moral beliefs.

I would argue, therefore, that morality and the self grow closer together during the course of normal development but still remain relatively uncoordinated for most (but not all) individuals. What is more, it is not possible to gauge the extent to which an individual has integrated the two simply by focusing on his or her moral judgment. This is because a person's moral judgment does not determine the place that morality occupies in the person's life. To know this latter key quality, we must know not only how the person views morality, but also how the person understands the self in relation to his or her moral beliefs. People with substantially similar moral beliefs may differ in their personal identification with those moral beliefs. Those for whom morality is central to their personal identities may be powerfully motivated by their moral beliefs and goals. People who define themselves in terms of their moral goals are likely to see moral problems in everyday events; and they are also likely to see themselves as necessarily implicated in these problems. From there it is a small step to taking responsibility for the solution. Others may have equally elevated notions of the good but may consider these notions to be peripheral to many of their own life engagements and therefore feel no particular sense of personal responsibility for action.

This is not to claim that the nature of one's moral conceptions is unimportant for self-identity, one's sense of responsibility, or moral conduct. Certainly there are conceptual moral positions from which it becomes practically impossible to deny one's personal responsibility on critical occasions. For example, a sincere moral belief in the sanctity of life makes it very difficult for a person to ignore the pleas of a person whose life is being threatened. Many moral positions resist separation from a sense of responsibility: They can only be segregated from the self (or separated from their action implications) through rationalization and/or distortion of the facts in the case.

Nevertheless, even though the nature of one's moral beliefs may place limits on how one places morality within the frame of one's personal life, there is still considerable variation possible within these limits. In other words, moral beliefs in themselves may bear *some* implications for how they are to be used in one's personal life, but these implications cannot cover every circumstance, and at best they offer only partial solutions to real-life problems. At worst, they can be ignored or denied. This is true at the most elevated reaches of moral judgment, as well as at the less sophisticated levels. In the end, moral behavior depends on something beyond the moral beliefs in and of themselves. It depends on how and to what extent the individuals' moral concerns are important to their sense of themselves as persons. For some strongly committed people, these concerns are of absolute and undeniable importance to their sense of who they are. But the reason for this lies less in the nature of their moral concerns than in the way they integrate these concerns with their sense of self.

The integration of moral and personal goals joins together the various intellectual and active ways in which one can respond to a moral event. The self-reflective judgment lends support and perspective to the moral response, and the moral response lends substance and shape to the self-reflection. This makes a powerful combination. Moreover, the integration facilitates the key developmental process of goal transformation. It facilitates this process by creating coherent systems of action and reflection that *at the same time* bolster and challenge one's moral commitments. Neither moral nor personal goals alone could accomplish this. When the two combine, moral commitments can be kept alive in the most literal sense – that is, they not only endure but keep growing. This is what accounts for the capacity of some people to continue revising and expanding their moral goals throughout life.

Note

1 This indicates the slow rate of change. It is my belief that developmental change is slow because it involves a change of goals as well as cognition. But the experimental change was not trivial. Although in itself the experimental effect was small, previous research (Damon, 1980) has shown that such changes normally lead to major shifts in subsequent years.

References

Baltes, P. B. (1987). Theoretical propositions of life-span developmental psychology: On the dynamics between growth and decline. *Developmental Psychology, 23,* 611–626.

Blasi, A. (1983). Moral cognition and moral action: A theoretical perspective. *Developmental Review, 3,* 178–210.

Campos, J. J., Campos, R., & Barrett, K. (1989). Emergent themes in the study of emotional development. *Developmental Psychology, 25,* 8–32.

Caspi, A., Bem, D., & Elder, G. (1989). Continuities and consequences of interactional styles across the life course. *Journal of Personality, 57*(2), 376–406.

Colby, A., & Damon, W. (1992). *Some do care: Contemporary lives of moral commitment.* New York: Free Press.

Damon, W. (1977). *The social world of the child.* San Francisco: Jossey-Bass.

Damon, W. (1980). Patterns of change in children's social reasoning: A two-year longitudinal study. *Child Development, 53,* 831–857.

Damon, W. (1983). *Social and personality development.* New York: Norton.

Damon, W. (1984). Self-understanding and moral development from childhood to adolescence. In W. Kurtines & J. Gewirtz (Eds.), *Morality, moral behavior, and moral development* (pp. 114–147). New York: Wiley.

Damon, W. (1988). *The moral child.* New York: Free Press.

Damon, W., & Colby, A. (1987). Social influence and moral change. In W. Kurtines & J. Gewirtz (Eds.), *Moral development through social interaction* (pp. 71–104). New York: Wiley.

Damon, W., & Hart, D. (1986). Stability and change in children's self-understanding. *Social Cognition, 4,* 102–118.

Damon, W., & Hart, D. (1988). *Self-understanding in childhood and adolescence.* New York: Cambridge University Press.

Damon, W., & Killen, M. (1982). Peer interaction and the process of change in children's moral reasoning. *Merrill-Palmer Quarterly, 28,* 347–367.

Doise, W., & Mugny, G. (1984). *The social development of the intellect.* New York: Pergamon.

Eisenberg, N. (1989). Empathy and sympathy. In W. Damon (Ed.), *Child development today and tomorrow* (pp. 137–155). San Francisco: Jossey-Bass.

Gollwitzer, P. M. (1993). Goal achievement: The role of intentions. *European Review of Social Psychology, 4*, 141–185.

Hoffman, M. L. (1984). Interaction of affect and cognition on empathy. In C. E. Izard, J. Kagan, & R. B. Zajonc (Eds.), *Emotions, cognition, and behavior* (pp. 1–41). Cambridge: Cambridge University Press.

Kagan, J. (1984). *The nature of the child*. New York: Basic.

Moscovici, S. (1977). *Social influence and social change*. New York: Basic.

Piaget, J. (1951). *Play, dreams, and imitation in childhood*. New York: Norton.

Rest, J. (1983). Morality. In P. Mussen (Ed.), *Handbook of child psychology* (pp. 556–629). New York: Wiley.

Rogoff, B. (1989). *Apprenticeship in thinking*. New York: Oxford University Press.

Rogoff, B. (1993). Guided participation in cultural activity by toddlers and caregivers. *Monographs of the Society for Research in Child Development, 58*(8), 1–182.

Shweder, R., Mahapatra, M., & Miller, J. (1987). Culture and moral development. In J. Kagan & S. Lamb (Eds.), *The emergence of morality in young children* (pp. 1–83). Chicago: University of Chicago Press.

Strayer, J., & Shroeder, M. (1989). Children's helping strategies: Influences of empathy, emotions, and age. In N. Eisenberg (Ed.), *Empathy and related emotional responses* (pp. 85–107). San Francisco: Jossey-Bass.

Trevarthen, C. (1992). The self born in intersubjectivity: An infant communicating. In U. Neisser (Ed.), *Ecological and interpersonal knowledge of the self* (pp. 32–52). New York: Cambridge University Press.

Turiel, E., Killen, M., & Helwig, C. C. (1987). Morality: Its structure, functions, and vagaries. In J. Kagan & S. Lamb (Eds.), *The emergence of moral concepts in young children* (pp. 155–244). Chicago: University of Chicago Press.

Wertsch, J. (1981). *The concept of activity in Soviet psychology*. Armonk, NY: Sharpe.

Wertsch, J. (1985). *Vygotsky and the social formation of mind*. Cambridge, MA: Harvard University Press.

8 Adults telling and retelling stories collaboratively

Roger A. Dixon and Odette N. Gould

Abstract

Adults of all ages frequently tell or retell stories collaboratively, that is, in conversational or interactive settings. Although there is a growing literature on aging-related changes in a variety of aspects of performance in storytelling or story-retelling, very little research has been conducted on aging and the interactive features of such activities. Cognitive collaboration is of intrinsic theoretical interest to psychologists interested in aging, for it is not only a common condition of performance, but a potential means by which some individual-level, aging-related decline could be compensated. We summarize our recent research on collaborative storytelling, in which younger and older married couples described a recent vacation, and on collaborative retelling of narratives, for which some evidence of compensation related to interactive experience was inferred. We conclude that interactive approaches to cognitive aging have considerable promise.

Telling and retelling stories are complex cognitive activities frequently pursued in a variety of contexts by children, adolescents, and adults of all ages. A story may be generated from a complex of declarative knowledge, episodic memory, and, of course, imagination. Similarly, stories may be told with a complex of motivations and purposes, including amusing a listener or oneself, informing an audience, or presenting oneself socially. There is but a fuzzy boundary between telling and retelling a story, and the distinction is not presently of particular theoretical import. Briefly, however, the distinction may be described as follows. Whereas *storytelling* is a term often used to refer to the process of generating a narrative to represent verbally an activity or event, whether previously experienced or fictional, story-retelling more often refers to the process of generating a narrative that represents a previously

The authors appreciate the helpful comments of Hubert Sydow and two anonymous reviewers on an earlier version of this chapter. Roger Dixon also acknowledges support for the research projects described herein from the Natural Sciences and Engineering Research Council of Canada and from the Canadian Aging Research Network (CARNET).

221

experienced verbal representation of an activity or event. Thus, generating a narrative to represent a true or fictional autobiographical event is storytelling, whereas generating a narrative to represent a magazine news item or a novel one has read, or even a story one has recently heard, are examples of story-retelling. Despite such minor differences, telling and retelling stories are similar in many ways. Notably, both depend prominently on cognitive processes such as memory and result in generated narratives.

Considering the universe of stories that are told or retold, some are imparted through the medium of writing and others are offered orally. One may tell (in writing) the story of one's day in a diary, or a series of impressions and events in a letter. Written stories may be told rather factually, as in a newspaper article, or deliberately fictionalized as in a novel. Story writers may have an intended audience (or readership), but the audience rarely participates in the actual writing of the story. The audience for story writers is typically more distal (than immediate), although it may eventually be quite large. Nevertheless, in principle, stories may be written individually or interactively, with the latter occurring either through a sequence of individual-based productions or entirely interactively among the authors at the time of production.

In this chapter we are concerned with oral storytelling. Telling a story orally may take forms, and have purposes, similar to those of story writing. One may describe an event of the day or from the distant past, elaborating or even confabulating about it. One may tell about a favorite vacation, retell a news story previously read or heard, or repeat a joke or humorous anecdote. Written stories, whether published or not, have a certain permanence and will present the same objective characteristics (e.g., words and sentences) to each successive reader as long as the paper and print survive. Oral stories typically do not have this kind of permanence. Nevertheless, once told, stories do not simply cease to exist; they may be remembered and retold, perhaps even frequently, as circumstances arise. Storytellers typically have an immediate audience and, in frequent circumstances, an interactive audience. Consider a story being told about a vivid previous family event. Some individuals in the audience may have participated in that event or heard previous representations, and therefore have something to offer in its telling. They may, for example, through both verbal and nonverbal cues, influence the direction the storytelling takes. This implies that oral stories may be more likely to mutate (both on-line and over time) than their more permanent written counterparts. Notably, more than one individual may actually share the activity of storytelling, whether sequentially or interactively.

Overall, it is safe to assert that telling and retelling stories is a common cognitive activity for adults, one that may have both individual (e.g., knowledge, memory, and motivation) and interactive (e.g., process characteristics such as social cooperation, sharing the cognitive load, and strategy implementation) aspects. The products of storytelling may vary in a variety of ways (e.g., cohesion, accuracy, comprehensiveness) as a function of these individual and interactive aspects. Finally, these individual and interactive aspects may vary developmentally. As they do in so many ways, older adults may differ from younger adults in the individual characteristics they bring to a storytelling episode, in the interactional processes in which they engage, and therefore in characteristics of the stories actually told. Our focus in this chapter is on selected processes and products of the collaborative oral expression of stories, and how these relate to adult cognitive development.

Oral storytelling: soliloquy and colloquy

As noted earlier, oral storytelling may often be conducted interactively. Unlike written storytelling, an audience is typically present as the telling unfolds. Listeners may become participants through subtle influences or direct contributions to both the process of storytelling and the content of the story being told. In this section we elaborate on these features of oral storytelling, especially as they pertain to our research program on developmental issues in collaborative telling and retelling of narratives by adults. One preliminary note on terminology: Although the term *storytelling* may refer to both oral and written expressions of a narrative, as we use it in the remainder of this chapter it refers to the oral medium.

Soliloquy and colloquy: an analogy with music performance

Although individuals qua individuals may engage in storytelling in the context of a (relatively) passive audience or in solitude, storytelling often occurs in conversational or interactive settings. That is, a narrative may be produced individually, with few if any direct contributions from others, or interactively, with regular and perhaps integral contributions from more than one individual. Even a soliloquy – a relatively unattended and private storytelling – may occasionally be at least marginally interactive. From storytellers in ancient cultures and keepers of oral histories to modern raconteurs and stand-up comedians, narrators may practice their craft in the context of an audience that may subtly or directly influence the direction, content, quality, and elaboration of a given narrative (Livo & Rietz, 1986; Mergler & Goldstein, 1983; Yates, 1966). To the extent, of course, that a storytelling episode is influenced, shared, or conducted by more than one individual, it is less a soliloquy than a colloquy. Similarly, a presumed colloquy can have elements or embedded episodes of soliloquy. In everyday life, then, stories one hears or tells may have elements that range from individual or socially isolated narrative processes to integrally interactive and conversational storytelling.

Although the everyday context of telling or retelling stories is frequently a social or interactive one, psychological research on the life-span development of narrative performance has focused on a more individualized context. For example, in research on cognitive development from early to late adulthood (a field referred to as "cognitive aging") it is the rare study indeed that considers, much less addresses, the interactive or socially embedded nature of much everyday cognitive activity (Dixon, 1992; Staudinger, Chapter 10, this volume). A standard research practice – one that has indeed been methodologically and theoretically fertile – has been for an individual to perform a specified language processing task in the relative isolation of a laboratory, with perhaps only a computer and well-trained (read: reserved and purposely script-following) experimenter also in the room. The extent to which this situation reflects that of everyday life – or to which the observations of an individual in solitude represent the performance of an individual in everyday social interaction – is unknown, and perhaps unknowable. It is, however, of both theoretical and practical interest (Bronfenbrenner, 1977; Herrmann, Johnson, McEvoy, Hertzog, & Hertel, in press; Neisser & Winograd, 1988).

We may suppose, however, that there are differences both in how well and in what manner a soliloquy versus a colloquy is accomplished. Let us consider an analogy with music performance. Some – but perhaps not much – storytelling activity fits the analogy of a solo classical music performance. One may practice passage by passage, constructing competence in performing the piece, and then perform it in the same way one practices it, with little input from the quietly but raptly attentive audience. Similarly, in the performance of a classical music score for a group – for example, a duet, quartet, or orchestra – the way in which one practices in solitude or in a group should fit precisely into the piece as actually performed by the group. (The group practice sessions are, of course, likely to be quite interactive, but each individual has an objectively available part to play, and the range of interpretation of that part is relatively constrained.)

In contrast, much everyday storytelling might follow more closely an analogy with some forms of contemporary jazz. In a contemporary jazz chart there are indeed some parameters known to all participants – for example, the key(s), the time signature(s), or even particular chord progressions or melodic hooks. But in a performance of a given piece there are often portions that are substantially improvisational. The chart gives the underlying rules, but the performer selects and plays a "story" that may vary from one performance to the next. In fact, what one actually plays may be quite dependent on what other members are producing on-line or have just contributed.

The magnificence of a classical symphony – consider the better examples of Mozart, Beethoven, or Mahler – is that the individual parts – previously written, scrupulously scripted, and painstakingly rehearsed – fit together in a sensitive, predictable, and wholly satisfying fashion. Although less generally appreciated, the supreme beauty of modern jazz – consider the post-traditional work of Miles Davis, Sun Ra, or the Art Ensemble of Chicago – is that it is often deeply interactive, occasionally emergent, but also sensitive and entertaining. Whereas performing a play or reading a speech may share features with classical music performance, everyday interactive storytelling and retelling may share considerable features with some contemporary jazz performance.

Collaboration in cognition: a preview

In the remainder of this chapter we summarize (a) our reasons for attending to cognitive performance in interactive situations, (b) our own interest in examining the development of such forms of cognition throughout adulthood, and (c) highlights from our recent research in the area of collaborative storytelling and story-retelling. First, we note that most of the research conducted on telling or retelling stories in adulthood has been conducted at the individual level of analysis. That is, especially in research on remembering and retelling narratives, the focus has been consistent with traditional individual-based experimental psychology. Therefore, we explore the background and characteristics of research on collaboration in retelling stories. Second, in more recent work on collaborative telling or retelling of stories, researchers are attending not only to the veridicality (or accuracy) of the story, but also to many other aspects of the products and processes of the interaction. The latter focus takes on special meaning in understanding developmental differences in how effectively groups of different ages and compositions collaborate on complex cognitive problems.

In the next section, we discuss these two central issues in somewhat more detail, attending to their application to life-span cognitive development. Following the discussion of these two issues, the remainder of the chapter is devoted to summarizing briefly a set of recent studies in which we have addressed the questions of how – and how well – younger and older adults collaborate in telling and remembering stories. The highlights from these studies are designed to illustrate our initial approach to investigating interactive cognitive functioning in adults.

Collaborative (re)telling of stories and cognitive aging

In life-span developmental research, the quantity and quality of both correct and other information produced in a storytelling (or story-retelling) episode is of theoretical interest – as are, of course, the processes through which such information is generated. Although there is relatively little research comparing adults on how they tell stories about natural or personal events, there is considerably more on how well they remember stories with which they are presented by researchers. In this research, younger adults (performing as individuals) typically remember (on average) more correct information from the original narratives or expository texts than do older adults (e.g., Hultsch & Dixon, 1990; Zelinski & Gilewski, 1988). Observed exceptions may be due to individual differences factors such as domain-specific cognitive skills and life experiences (e.g., Dixon & Bäckman, 1993a). There is a growing body of research in story remembering and retelling on the issue of the amount and value of other qualitative features of the recall protocols of adults of all ages. The results of this research are less clear-cut than those pertaining directly to memory. A crucial issue – and one that has obtained a smattering of empirical support – concerns the extent to which older adults might be producing alternative yet legitimate and valuable varieties of information.

Although not producing as much actual recall of the original story as younger adults, the older adults, through default or by choice, may generate information that (a) contributes uniquely to the retelling of the original narrative or (b) reflects an alternative but legitimate style of storytelling (e.g., Adams, 1991; Adams, Labouvie-Vief, Hobart, & Dorosz, 1990; Dixon & Bäckman, 1993a; Mergler & Goldstein, 1983). If either (a) or (b) is the case, theories of decline in cognitive aging, as supported by story recall data, might have to be adjusted such that the losses evident in actual recall performance are offset to some extent by apparent gains in other aspects of the product or process of retelling the narrative. Although of considerable theoretical interest, both the content and style with which stories are told or retold, as well as other features of the process through which the retelling occurs, are rarely studied directly. One paradigm through which a more direct examination of these issues can be conducted is that in which individuals work together to accomplish the task.

Why study collaborative cognitive aging?

Frequently, observers from a variety of perspectives have noted that a substantial proportion of everyday remembering (and other cognitive) activity occurs in a social context. Other individuals in the social context may play roles ranging from passive listeners to conversational interactants to active collaborators. We use the term *collaborative cognition* to refer to that cognitive activity that occurs in the context of more than one individual, where the activity is (a) typically directed at an identifiable set of tasks, (b) usually in pursuit of common goals, and (c) performed cooperatively (in some fashion). We have suggested elsewhere that as active external (human) cognitive aids, collaborators may be useful in promoting cognitive performance and may serve a compensatory function for individuals who have experienced aging-related cognitive decline (Dixon, 1992). Specifically, individuals who have experienced injury- or aging-related decrements in fundamental mechanisms that contribute to remembering performance (e.g., speed of processing, neurological integrity) may be able to compensate by combining their available resources with collaborators. In this way, they may produce more information as a group than would individuals, a case that would be similar to, but not a pure example of, compensation (Bäckman & Dixon, 1992; Dixon & Bäckman, 1993b).

Collaborative cognition occurs frequently in multiple situations, such as when scientific colleagues attempt to solve a thorny methodological problem in an experiment they are designing or analyzing, when family groups or lineages attempt to reconstruct stories from their shared past, or when strangers attempt to solve negotiation or navigation problems (Dixon, 1992). Theorists as varied as Vygotsky (1978) and Greeno and Moore (1993) have argued that such cognition in collaborative situations should be investigated further. Indeed, reflecting an active debate in the cognitive sciences between the symbolic approach (Vera & Simon, 1993) and the situational approach, Greeno and Moore (1993) have claimed that cognitive activities should be considered carefully as interactions between agents and both physical systems and other agents (see also Lave & Wenger, 1991; Resnick, Levine, & Teasley, 1991). From this perspective, a considerable portion of cognition is situated action, and this portion has been underrepresented in the cognitive developmental literature.

The sequence (or, loosely put, logic) of the premises and implications of the present approach to research on collaborative cognition in adulthood is depicted in Figure 8.1. Many of these premises are based on previous theoretical and empirical work on cognition in group situations (e.g., Clark & Stephenson, 1989; Middleton & Edwards, 1990; Resnick et al., 1991; Steiner, 1972). Four especially pertinent points may be abstracted from this body of work. First, whatever the theoretical approach, it is fair to say that much of everyday collaborative cognition is directed at remembering narratives broadly considered (e.g., news events, personal or shared stories, and autobiographical events). Second, the retelling of these narratives is conducted through a conversation that also takes the form of a narrative. Therefore, for research purposes, such conversational narratives are convertible to protocols, which can be coded for the presence of a variety of both story recall statements and conversation-based statements. Third, contributions to these conversations, like individual-based recall, may vary systematically in both the quantity of information recalled and the quality or pattern of the information produced. It is not known, for example, how the collaborative retelling of stories would compare with the individual level of performance in terms of either recall or nonrecall statements. Fourth, some of the activities, individuals, or statements occurring in a collaborative situation may variously promote or detract from the goals of the task or group. That is, collaborative groups may experience *process gain* or *process loss*, terms used to refer to the fact that group performance may not be a simple multiple of individual performance (Hill, 1982; Steiner, 1972). Although there are many complications in estimating optimal

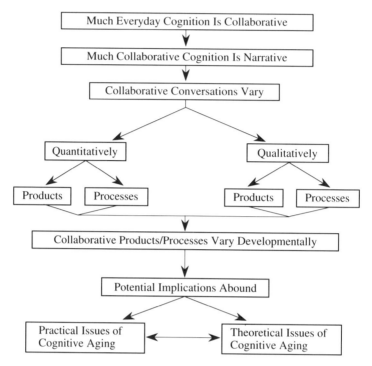

Figure 8.1. Linkages among the premises and goals of research on collaborative cognition and aging.

productivity for a group cognitive process, some tasks (e.g., those easily divisible) and individuals (e.g., those performing consistently at high levels) promote near-optimal group performance. In contrast, other tasks (possibly less well-structured tasks such as narrative recall) and individuals (e.g., social loafers) result in lower-than-optimal levels of group performance. Further research is required to determine the best way to evaluate how close to the optimal level group performance is for telling and retelling stories, as well as how best to promote higher levels of group performance.

Objectives of research on collaborative cognition

We alluded earlier to our assumption that the paradigm of collaborative cognition may provide some unique information about both products and processes of cognitive functioning. One example of particular interest in cognitive aging is that the process of collaboration may produce observable on-line evidence of metacognitive activities that drive or direct the process of solving some cognitive problems. In fact, the use of strategies may be evident either directly or indirectly in the protocols because the communicative situation makes it necessary to make at least some of them explicit to the collaborating partner(s). In this way, the conversational transcripts may be used as think-aloud protocols to score for the presence of indicators of both productive strategies and counterproductive statements or activities. What promotes process gain and process loss, as well as what is associated with improvement or collaborative group differences, may be evident upon close inspection of the conversations.

In addition to this specific interest, however, there are several general objectives to be met in research on life-span collaborative cognition. The basic objective is to create an opportunity in a controlled setting for collaborative cognitive functioning. At its simplest, more than one person is present in the same room at the same table solving the same problem – together. Once this is accomplished, indicators of performance at both the individual and interactive "levels" can be developed. These may very well differ in their details from one cognitive task to another, but the general classifications of interest may apply across a wide range of tasks. As will be summarized later, we have also found it useful not only to characterize the qualitative aspects of the collaboration in a summational form, but to represent the dynamic character of cooperative interactions, much as one would a conversation or a music score.

A related concern is to focus on how well collaborative groups perform (we refer to such measures as product variables) and how they do whatever they do (process variables). Because there is such little precedent in cognitive aging research, initial objectives have been more descriptive than explanatory. For example, to what extent can and do younger and older adults use collaborators to perform complex cognitive tasks? At the outset of our research, it was conceivable that some individuals might never connect with their group, that the group members might not collaborate at all or interact quite ineffectively. More theoretical questions are presently being posed in some quarters. One that we have found of particular interest has concerned whether there is some evidence for compensation (broadly conceived) by older collaborating adults. More specifically, is there evidence that collaborating groups of older adults might be conducting themselves differently than younger counterparts, and could this difference be related to an effort to overcome individual-level aging-related cognitive decline?

We turn now to some highlights of research we have conducted in collaborative cognitive aging. We begin with a study on collaborative storytelling, in which the task for married couples was to tell a story about a vacation taken together. Following this, we describe briefly several studies on collaborative retelling (remembering) of stories previously heard. In the first case, of course, the original narrative (the actual vacation) varies between couples, so veridicality (i.e., correct recall) is not an issue. Instead, the content and the process of storytelling are of interest. In the second case, we have naturally controlled the original narrative being retold, so veridicality is also of concern. Thus far, we have attempted to illustrate why such research is of interest in the field of cognitive development. In the next section we highlight how such research can be accomplished and what the results may mean for theories of cognitive aging.

Collaborative storytelling by younger and older married couples

Studying the characteristics of speech produced by older adults is not a particularly new field of research (e.g., Kemper, 1988; Ryan, 1990; Ryan, Giles, Bartolucci, & Henwood, 1986). Indeed, some research has been conducted in which conversations (e.g., Boden & Bielby, 1983; Coupland & Coupland, 1990) or even narrative production or storytelling (e.g., Cooper, 1990; Kemper, Rash, Kynette, & Norman, 1990; Pratt, Boyes, Robins, & Manchester, 1989) have been used to examine adult age differences in speech. Some age-related stylistic and content differences have been noted. For example, older dyads may produce structurally similar conversations but employ aspects of the personal past more frequently than do younger dyads (Boden & Bielby, 1983). Older storytellers may also produce narratives that have a classic and pleasing (to the listener or reader) hierarchical structure (Kemper et al., 1990; Pratt & Robins, 1991). Older adults may also tend to produce narratives that have more elaborative content, that is, statements only indirectly relevant to the theme. These may include inferences and personally relevant commentary (e.g., Gould, Trevithick, & Dixon, 1991) or even prolonged off-target speech (e.g., Gold, Andres, Arbuckle, & Schwartzman, 1988).

In a recent study, we investigated three major aspects of stories produced by collaborating younger and older married couples (see Gould & Dixon, 1993, for details of the methods and results). The three aspects were (a) the structure of the narrative, (b) the content of the story produced, and (c) the interactive process of collaborative storytelling. In order to study collaborative storytelling, each couple was interviewed separately and invited to work together in describing an event or activity in which they had both participated. We asked the couples to tell us about a vacation trip they had taken together. This choice of topics had the advantages of (a) being mutually experienced objective events that were not strictly age-related, (b) evoking (probably) interesting or even pleasant autobiographical memories, and yet (c) being both sufficiently in the remote past and multifarious such that the storytelling was not likely to be a rote recitation of facts. It had the possible disadvantages of (a) being differentially dated by the younger and older couples, and (b) differing in a number of content-related features. Each couple was tested as a unit, with their storytelling videotaped for later transcription and scoring.

We examined several variables within each of three categories: the structure of the stories, the content of the stories, and the process of storytelling. With regard to structure, we observed that older adults spoke more slowly, using more words per clause than younger couples, but the two groups did not differ in a number of structural characteristics such as the presence of subordinate and digressive passages. That is, for collaborative storytelling no evidence was observed for age-related off-target or elaborative productions. They also did not differ in the degree of correct chronological sequencing of events embedded in their vacations. Interestingly, however, the older couples tended to situate events in relative time (e.g., the sightseeing occurred before lunch), whereas the younger couples were more likely to describe events in a specific temporal location (e.g., the sightseeing occurred at 10:30 a.m.). Whereas the differences in rate and words per clause can be understood as reflecting well-known individual aging-related decrements (in speed and word finding, respectively), the structures of the stories produced were similar in many other critical respects. This indicates some preservation of storytelling performance, at least at the couple level of analysis. The different preferences for temporally locating events may reflect either memory losses or a preference for structuring stories so as not to include details that arguably contribute more specificity than entertainment value to the story. Given our data, it is impossible to decide among these two alternatives, but it is notable that they harken back to the fundamental issue raised earlier – that is, whether to interpret age differences in terms of aging-related decrements or (more positively) preferences and interests.

We rated the content of the stories produced in two major ways. First, although the stories were all about a vacation, in the process of describing such an event different categories of topics may be addressed. Our analyses of the topics produced in the vacation stories revealed that younger couples produced a greater proportion of topics concerned with itinerary and event descriptions, whereas older couples produced a greater proportion of topics concerned with descriptions of people and places. Second, the overall content of the stories was rated with respect to subjective quality. Older couples tended to produce a greater proportion of topics rated as subjective than did younger couples, who produced a greater proportion of objective topics. Could these differences once again reflect a tendency for the older couples to concentrate on producing entertaining stories, rather than on the objective verbatim facts of schedules that so occupied the younger couples? No firm answer to this question is available, but it is a theoretically intriguing possibility noted also by previous researchers (e.g., Kemper, Kynette, Rash, O'Brien, & Sprott, 1989; Smith, Rebok, Smith, Hall, & Alvin, 1983). In fact, one older couple specifically noted that they were focusing on the highlights in order to maximize the entertainment value of the overall story.

Finally, we focused some attention on selected aspects of the interactive processes in which the couples engaged as they collaborated in telling the stories. The styles with which the younger and older couples told their stories were somewhat different. Younger couples appeared to share the give-and-take of topic description more completely than older couples. Indicative of more intense involvement in the minutia of the stories was the finding that younger couples produced more backchanneling statements (such as "uh huh" and "mmhm"), which have the function of expressing ongoing attention and interest. Turn taking by the older couples, in contrast, occurred at a more global level, in that the individuals seemed to produce alternating, longer monologues. It may be less cognitively demanding to both maintain vigilant interest in what one's partner is saying and prepare or store ideas for future discussion.

There are, of course, many influences on collaborative style and effectiveness, age being but one of them. Also of interest is the length and quality of the association, as well as the "age" and frequency of rehearsal of the story being told. Although not definitive, our research on collaborative storytelling is consistent with a further consideration of the hypothesis that even with individual-based, aging-related cognitive declines, older couples may enact narratives with positively valued intentions such as maximizing generality of interest and entertainment value while minimizing the cognitive demands of the collaboration and the memory demands of the task. How would older collaborating adults perform on tasks that are more constrained, such as retelling stories they have just heard?

Collaborative remembering and retelling of narratives

The amount of research conducted in collaborative remembering of narratives is quite substantial (e.g., Edwards & Middleton, 1986; Hyman, 1994; Perlmutter, 1953; Stephenson, Clark, & Wade, 1986). One of the prominent theoretical issues addressed in this research is whether successively larger groups recall more information – or more accurately – than individuals or smaller groups. Put simply, it is consistent with the long-standing concern of one area of social cognitive psychology, specifically, whether $N + 1$ heads perform better than N (Hill, 1982). The arenas in which this question has practical implications range from pedagogy to jurisprudence. Reflecting a popular (but not uncontroversial) trend in educational practice, one issue is whether groups are effective contexts for learning and performance. Pertaining to an enduring problem in applied cognitive psychology and jurisprudence, another issue is whether the veridicality and comprehensiveness of eyewitness reports can benefit from – or be imperiled by – discussion or collaboration.

These issues apply, as well, to research in collaborative cognition and aging, but are perhaps less dominating ones. Of more immediate concern are issues such as whether (a) older adults can in fact collaborate effectively in complex remembering tasks, (b) older adults' performance improves with the addition of collaborators, (c) composition or membership of the groups plays a role in performance, (d) older groups perform in the same manner (or process) as younger groups, and (e) there is evidence that older groups may be using the resources of members selectively such that they compensate for individual-level cognitive decline. Research on collaborative cognition and aging is relatively recent, and only selected issues have been addressed (e.g., Cavanaugh et al., 1989; Dixon, 1992; Gould et al., 1991; Staudinger, Chapter 10, this volume).

In this section, we summarize several studies we have conducted. Details of these studies are available elsewhere (e.g., Dixon, 1992, in press; Dixon & Gould, 1994; Gould et al., 1991). The general objective of these studies was to explore performance on narrative remembering tasks by younger and older individuals in collaborative situations. To accomplish this, we first created a situation in which there was an opportunity for same-age adults to collaborate on remembering a story. That is, unlike the standard individual-level paradigm, more than one individual was present in the same room, and they were invited to work together in recalling an auditorily presented story. As mentioned earlier, an initial purpose was to investigate the extent to which younger and older adults can and do use collaborators to perform complex cognitive tasks.

The fact and the figurative

In terms of overall remembering performance, one expectation was that younger individuals would perform better than older individuals. This was based on extensive literature on discourse memory and aging (Dixon & Bäckman, 1993a; Hultsch & Dixon, 1990; Zelinski & Gilewski, 1988). The more challenging question was whether younger or older adults would benefit more (or equally) from the presence of collaborators. For example, would older groups of two (unacquainted dyads or married couples) perform as well as parallel younger groups of two? There was no specific literature on which to base an expectation pertaining to this issue, but because communicative skills are often preserved in later life (Ryan, 1990; Ryan et al., 1986) – and communicative skills may be related to collaborative effectiveness – the hypothesis that older adults would benefit disproportionately from collaborators was considered. In our first studies with unacquainted collaborators, we observed that younger and older adults benefited equivalently from the presence of collaborators, but that younger individuals and groups remembered more information than older parallel units (Dixon, in press; Dixon & Gould, 1994).

Recall that we have focused some attention on the quality and variety of information produced in collaborative cognition protocols, not simply on the quantity of verbatim recall. Crucial issues in this regard are: (a) What is the

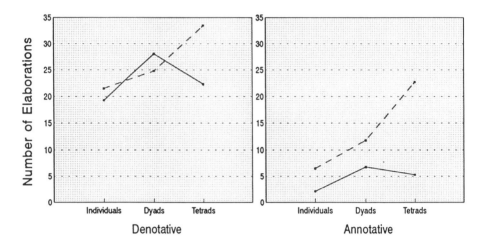

Figure 8.2. Pattern of elaboration production by younger (solid curves) and older adults (dashed curves) performing as individuals, dyads, and tetrads. (Adapted from Gould, Trevithick, & Dixon, 1991.)

balance between recall and other information produced; and (b) can the nonrecall information be usefully categorized into productive and nonproductive statements? There is not yet enough information available to judge whether there is a typical or objectively ideal balance, partly because work on the categorization of statements (and the processes they may represent) is only beginning (e.g., Adams, 1991).

In a series of analyses reported in Gould et al. (1991), we examined the elaborations produced by individuals, dyads, and tetrads collaborating on remembering and retelling a narrative. We divided all elaborations into two general categories: (a) denotative elaborations, or consistent statements based on information from the story or from world knowledge relevant to the content of the story, and (b) annotative elaborations, or statements based on evaluations and interpretations of the content of the stories or personal experience relevant to the stories. As shown in Figure 8.2, we observed that the number of denotative elaborations was high for individuals and that it increased similarly across group size for both younger and older adults. In contrast, the number of annotative elaborations was relatively low and increased more across group size for older than for younger adults. What could this mean?

Denotative elaborations are conceptually close to gist recall, clearly a form of productive performance, and younger and older adults produce them similarly in all group size conditions. Regarding annotative – the more personal and evaluative – elaborations, two contrasting arguments could be made. Such elaborations, if produced excessively, could be viewed as tangential, irrelevant, or even harmful to the task of remembering a story. In contrast, if produced judiciously they could be viewed as enriching the storytelling and perhaps even as referencing story information in terms of personal experience (e.g., Boden & Bielby, 1983; Reder, 1982; Smith et al., 1983). The profile of elaborations in this study led the authors to conclude that they were more likely positive contributors to the retelling of the story, even though they would not be counted as actual recall statements.

In sum, the results of this study confirmed the principal expectation that older unacquainted adults could successfully collaborate on a complex cognitive task (for more information, see Dixon, in press; Dixon & Gould, 1994). In addition, in a result clearly friendly to an interpretation that older adults – even groups of older adults – may intend to produce qualitatively different kinds of information in their stories, the analysis of elaborations suggests that an important goal may have been overall cohesiveness or entertainment (Gould et al., 1991). How well would well-acquainted groups coordinate their efforts and abilities? This we sought to investigate in studies of collaborative story remembering and retelling in married couples.

Communication during collaborative remembering

In subsequent studies we examined young and old unacquainted dyads and young and old well-acquainted married couples collaborating on a story-remembering task (for details see Dixon & Gould, 1994; Dixon, Hunt-Matheson, & Meers, 1993). We selected one variety of naturally occurring experienced collaborative groups, married couples. Our assumption was that such groups frequently work together in solving complex cognitive problems, many of which bear a resemblance to retelling narratives such as those we used in our experiment (Wegner, Erber, & Raymond, 1991). Our first two major research interests were similar to those of the first study. Specifically, we were interested in whether there were age differences in absolute levels of recall performance and in some indicators of processes of interaction.

One important qualification of the comparisons being made in this experiment should be noted. Our major comparison was between the age of couples, and age is obviously confounded with dyadic experience. That is, we compared younger and older couples who varied also in length of marriage. (Although a complete design would have been preferable, it was not practical. Whereas it is possible to find older couples who have been married for only a few years, (a) in this cohort these couples would likely have been married to somebody else for a lengthy period, thus introducing additional contaminants, and (b) it is not possible to find younger couples who have been married for lengthy periods equivalent to that of older couples.) Our initial approach to this problem was to address the issue of couple expertise directly by examining each individual's knowledge and agreement with his or her partner on selected issues. As expected, we observed that younger and older married couples exhibited a similar level of "couple expertise."

In two successive studies we found evidence that older married couples might perform as well as younger married couples, even in quantity of information actually recalled. This, of course, is a theoretically intriguing result (Dixon, in press; Dixon & Gould, 1994; Dixon et al., 1993). To understand how such results might occur – that is, how older married couples might accomplish the somewhat unprecedented task of performing at the same level as younger counterparts – we compared some aspects of the communication styles of younger and older unacquainted dyads and married couples. Unlike the previous studies, however, our goal in this study was to examine explicitly the process through which the dyads and couples performed the collaborative remembering and retelling task (see Gould, Kurzman, & Dixon, 1994, for details). Thus, after the conversations were transcribed, each statement was coded into one of four categories. These categories were collected into two classifications, story-related statements and conversation-related statements. The two categories in the story-related statements were (a) individual story-based productions, which consisted of correctly recalled information and story-based inferences produced by an individual, and (b) collaborative story-based productions, which consisted of correct recall framed as a dialogue between the partners. The two categories in the conversation-related statements were (a) task discussion productions, which were statements alluding to the task itself rather than the story, and (b) sociability and support productions, which contained personal criticisms, references to one's own experience, and statements of agreement with the partner.

A count of the percentages of each of these categories of statements revealed that all four groups (i.e., younger and older dyads and couples) produced protocols in which about 55% to 60% of the statements were individual story-based productions. Collaborative story-based productions constituted between 15% and 20% of the statements produced by all groups. However, whereas younger and older married couples' statements included nearly 20% task and strategy discussion, younger and older unacquainted dyads' task statements constituted only about 10%. Instead, the latter groups seemed to produce greater proportions of sociability and support statements. Charting the appearance of statements from each of these categories across the conversations revealed the dynamic quality of these differences. A schematic representation of the process from the first to the third portion of the conversations is presented in Figure 8.3. As can be seen in the figure, for all groups individual-based story-related statements predominated in the initial one-third of their interactions (between 60% and 70%, with no other category greater than 20%). By the final one-third of the conversations, however, individual story-based statements had declined, in most cases, to less than 40% of the total

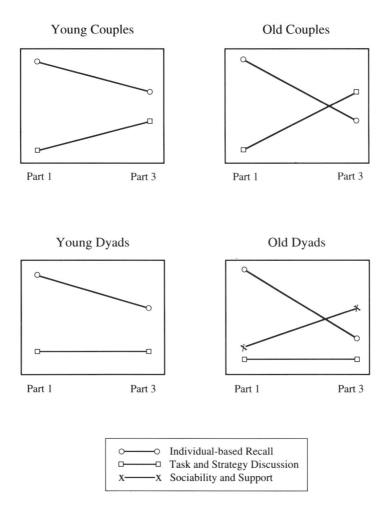

Figure 8.3. Communication during collaborative tasks: dynamic patterns for four groups. (Adapted from Gould, Kurzman, & Dixon, 1994.)

statements in that segment. Increasing for the younger and, especially, the older married couples (to over 40%) were task and strategy-based discussion statements (and no other category). Increasing for the older dyads (to over 40%) were sociability and support statements.

In sum, all couples and dyads began with a spurt of recall of information from the narrative – and very little else. As the session continued, however, and recall began to decline, older couples produced more statements about the task (e.g., strategies for improving performance), whereas older dyads offered more statements of social support. Whereas the trend for younger couples was similar to (but lower than) that of older couples, younger dyads did little to compensate for declining recall performance. This dynamic analysis of interactive remembering allows us to identify a potentially theoretically interesting phenomenon worthy of further investigation. Specifically, the pattern of results may be consistent with an effort to compensate for declining individual-level recall, especially by older couples. The older dyads are arguably less productive in their efforts, but they too demonstrated some effort to replace their declining recall production with something. Instead of strategic comments designed to further their performance, however, the older dyads concentrate on socializing with their partners, and perhaps on helping each other feel comfortable with what is being said and how well they have already done. It is conceivable that the long-term married couples are experienced enough with each other that they can bypass the sociability concern and concentrate on strategic efforts to improve their performance. Unacquainted dyads, of course, do not have the luxury of such knowledge and so concentrate on other aspects of the interaction. Of course, getting to know one's partner, as well as that partner's cognitive abilities, may be an important step in effective collaboration, at least for unacquainted older adults. From this perspective, then, it may be important to examine interactive remembering dynamically, as well as summationally, in future research.

Conclusion

We have begun to explore whether younger and older adults can collaborate effectively in complex cognitive tasks such as telling stories about multifarious previously experienced events and retelling recently heard narratives. In the first study this effectiveness was demonstrated for younger and older married couples, in the sense that coherent stories were produced with a variety of similar structural and content features. In the second study – on collaborative remembering of stories – we observed some age differences (in favor of younger adults) in remembering performance that were presumably balanced by age differences (in favor of older adults) in other relevant domains of performance. Differences in performance between the two age groups could be the result of (a) preexisting poorer individual- and couple-level cognitive skill by (say) the older adults, (b) aging-related declines in cognitive performance at either the individual or couple level, or (c) age-related differences in the goals and values of storytelling and story remembering. As in some research on cognitive aging at the individual level, this ambiguity is introduced because a wide range of response variables – including, but not limited to, quantitative measures of accuracy – were collected and considered relevant, if not productive.

We noted in the section on the collaborative retelling of stories that, in a number of ways, older married couples were not disadvantaged compared with younger married couples in overall quantity of information remembered.

One might surmise that a reason for such a robust (and unusual in the cognitive aging literature) result is that the couples were advantaged with respect to experience with cognitive collaboration. That is, they may have been able to use their unique and shared resources to compensate for individual-level cognitive decline (Dixon, 1992, in press; Gould et al., 1994). In general, older married couples appeared to produce statements designed to boost or maintain remembering performance. This strategy, increasing across time as individual-level remembering performance decreased, is consistent with a compensatory interpretation. There are, however, several limitations to the idea that couples may use experience as a compensatory mechanism. Collecting even more direct evidence that this is the mechanism the older adults were using would be valuable. It is possible (but unlikely) that older long-term married couples are better individually at memory tasks than other older adults, and that their group performance reflects merely superior individual memory skills; this can be explored in future studies (Dixon, in press). In addition, it is important to learn how to relate specific strategic statements to whether or not they promote further gains in performance.

Our research has explored the extent to which younger and older adults collaborated effectively in complex cognitive tasks pertaining to telling and retelling stories. For groups differing in age, size, and collaborative experience, differences and similarities in how and how well they performed were observed. The roles of factors such as gender and other operational definitions of collaborative experience deserve further study. Cognition in collaborative situations appears to be both a common expression of cognitive skills in everyday life and a skill for which older adults may not be as disadvantaged as they are in individual laboratory settings.

References

Adams, C. (1991). Qualitative age differences in memory for text: A life-span developmental perspective. *Psychology and Aging, 6*, 323–336.

Adams, C., Labouvie-Vief, G., Hobart, C. J., & Dorosz, M. (1990). Adult age group differences in story recall style. *Journal of Gerontology: Psychological Sciences, 45*, P17–P27.

Bäckman, L., & Dixon, R. A. (1992). Psychological compensation: A theoretical framework. *Psychological Bulletin, 112*, 259–283.

Boden, D., & Bielby, D. D. (1983). The past as resource: A conversational analysis of elderly talk. *Human Development, 26*, 308–319.

Bronfenbrenner, U. (1977). Toward an experimental ecology of human development. *American Psychologist, 32*, 513–531.

Cavanaugh, J. C., Dunn, N. J., Mowery, D., Feller, C., Niederehe, G., Frugé, E., & Volpendesta, D. (1989). Problem-solving strategies in dementia patient–caregiver dyads. *Gerontologist, 29*, 156–158.

Clark, N. K., & Stephenson, G. M. (1989). Group remembering. In P. B. Paulus (Ed.), *Psychology of group influence* (pp. 357–391). Hillsdale, NJ: Erlbaum.

Cooper, P. V. (1990). Discourse production and normal aging: Performance on oral description tasks. *Journal of Gerontology: Psychological Sciences, 45*, P210–P214.

Coupland, N., & Coupland, J. (1990). Language in later life. In H. Giles & W. P. Robinson (Eds.), *Handbook of language and social psychology* (pp. 451–468). New York: Wiley.

Dixon, R. A. (1992). Contextual approaches to adult intellectual development. In R. J. Sternberg & C. A. Berg (Eds.), *Intellectual development* (pp. 350–380). Cambridge: Cambridge University Press.

Dixon, R. A. (in press). Collaborative memory in adulthood. In D. J. Herrmann, M. K. Johnson, C. L. McEvoy, C. Hertzog, & P. Hertel (Eds.), *Basic and applied memory research: Theory in context.* Hillsdale, NJ: Erlbaum.

Dixon, R. A., & Bäckman, L. (1993a). Reading and memory for prose in adulthood: Issues of expertise and compensation. In S. R. Yussen & M. C. Smith (Eds.), *Reading across the life span* (pp. 193–213). New York: Springer.

Dixon, R. A., & Bäckman, L. (1993b). The concept of compensation in cognitive aging: The case of prose processing in adulthood. *International Journal of Aging and Human Development, 36,* 199–217.

Dixon, R. A., & Gould, O. N. (1994). *Story recall by adults in collaborative situations.* Manuscript submitted for publication.

Dixon, R. A., Hunt-Matheson, D. A., & Meers, D. E. (1993, November). *Are there cognitive benefits to long-term marriage?* Paper presented to the Gerontological Society of America, New Orleans.

Edwards, D., & Middleton, D. (1986). Joint remembering: Constructing an account of shared experience through conversational discourse. *Discourse Processes, 9,* 423–459.

Gold, D., Andres, D., Arbuckle, T., & Schwartzman, A. (1988). Measurement and correlates of verbosity in elderly people. *Journal of Gerontology: Psychological Sciences, 43,* P27–P33.

Gould, O. N., & Dixon, R. A. (1993). How we spent our vacation: Collaborative storytelling by young and old adults. *Psychology and Aging, 8,* 10–17.

Gould, O. N., Kurzman, D., & Dixon, R. A. (1994). Communication during prose recall conversations by young and old dyads. *Discourse Processes, 17,* 149–165.

Gould, O. N., Trevithick, L., & Dixon, R. A. (1991). Adult age differences in elaborations produced during prose recall. *Psychology and Aging, 6,* 93–99.

Greeno, J. G., & Moore, J. L. (1993). Situativity and symbols: Response to Vera and Simon. *Cognitive Science, 17,* 49–59.

Herrmann, D. J., Johnson, M. K., McEvoy, C. L., Hertzog, C., & Hertel, P. (Eds.). (in press). *Basic and applied memory research: Theory in context.* Hillsdale, NJ: Erlbaum.

Hill, G. W. (1982). Group versus individual performance: Are $N + 1$ heads better than one? *Psychological Bulletin, 91,* 517–539.

Hultsch, D. F., & Dixon, R. A. (1990). Learning and memory in aging. In J. E. Birren & K. W. Schaie (Eds.), *Handbook of the psychology of aging* (3rd ed., pp. 258–274). San Diego, CA: Academic.

Hyman, I. E., Jr. (1994). Conversational remembering: Story recall with a peer versus for an experimenter. *Applied Cognitive Psychology, 8,* 49–66.

Kemper, S. (1988). Geriatric psycholinguistics: Syntactic limitations of oral and written language. In L. L. Light & D. M. Burke (Eds.), *Language, memory and aging* (pp. 50–76). Cambridge: Cambridge University Press.

Kemper, S., Kynette, D., Rash, S., O'Brien, K., & Sprott, R. (1989). Life-span changes to adults' language: Effects of memory and genre. *Applied Psycholinguistics, 10,* 49–66.

Kemper, S., Rash, S., Kynette, D., & Norman, S. (1990). Telling stories: The structure of adults' narratives. *European Journal of Cognitive Psychology, 2,* 205–228.

Lave, J., & Wenger, E. (1991). *Situated learning: Legitimate peripheral participation.* New York: Cambridge University Press.

Livo, N. J., & Rietz, S. A. (1986). *Storytelling: Process and practice.* Littleton, CO: Libraries Unlimited.

Middleton, D., & Edwards, D. (Eds.). (1990). *Collective remembering.* Newbury Park, CA: Sage.

Mergler, N., & Goldstein, M. D. (1983). Why are there old people? Senescence as biological and cultural preparedness for the transmission of information. *Human Development, 26,* 72–90.

Neisser, U., & Winograd, E. (1988). *Remembering reconsidered: Ecological and traditional approaches to the study of memory*. New York: Cambridge University Press.

Perlmutter, H. V. (1953). Group memory of meaningful material. *Journal of Psychology, 35*, 361–370.

Pratt, M. W., Boyes, C., Robins, S., & Manchester, J. (1989). Telling tales: Aging, working memory, and the narrative cohesion of story retellings. *Developmental Psychology, 25*, 628–635.

Pratt, M. W., & Robins, S. L. (1991). That's the way it was: Age differences in the structure and quality of adults' personal narratives. *Discourse Processes, 14*, 73–85.

Reder, L. M. (1982). Elaborations: When do they help and when do they hurt? *Text, 2*, 211–224.

Resnick, L. B., Levine, J. M., & Teasley, S. D. (Eds.). (1991). *Perspectives on socially shared cognition*. Washington, DC: American Psychological Association.

Ryan, E. B. (1990). Normal aging and language. In R. Lubinski (Ed.), *Dementia and communication* (pp. 84–97). Philadelphia: Decker.

Ryan, E. B., Giles, H., Bartolucci, G., & Henwood, K. (1986). Psycholinguistic and social psychological components of communication by and with the elderly. *Language and Communication, 6*, 1–24.

Smith, S. W., Rebok, G. W., Smith, W. R., Hall, S. E., & Alvin, M. (1983). Adult age differences in the use of story structure in delayed free recall. *Experimental Aging Research, 9*, 191–195.

Steiner, I. D. (1972). *Group process and productivity*. New York: Academic.

Stephenson, G. M., Clark, N. K., & Wade, G. S. (1986). Meetings make evidence? An experimental study of collaborative and individual recall of a simulated police interrogation. *Journal of Personality and Social Psychology, 50*, 1113–1122.

Vera, A. H., & Simon, H. A. (1993). Situated action: A symbolic interpretation. *Cognitive Science, 17*, 7–48.

Vygotsky, L. S. (1978). *Mind in society: The development of higher psychological processes*. Cambridge, MA: Harvard University Press.

Wegner, D. M., Erber, R., & Raymond, P. (1991). Transactive memory in close relationships. *Journal of Personality and Social Psychology, 61*, 923–929.

Yates, F. A. (1966). *The art of memory*. Chicago: University of Chicago Press.

Zelinski, E. M., & Gilewski, M. J. (1988). Memory for prose and aging: A meta-analysis. In M. L. Howe & C. J. Brainerd (Eds.), *Cognitive development in adulthood: Progress in cognitive development research* (pp. 133–158). New York: Springer.

9 Planning about life: toward a social-interactive perspective

Jacqui Smith

Abstract

Life planning involves thinking about the possible future purpose, content, and course of an individual's life. It encompasses the choice of overarching life goals, guiding aphorisms, and long-range timetables, as well as the dynamic processes related to devising ways to attain, maintain, monitor, and update these goals and schedules (cf. P. L. Berger, B. Berger, & Kellner, 1967; Brim, 1992; Rawls, 1971). Knowledge about planning a life is an aspect of cognition that is socialized, applied, and challenged throughout the life span. An individual might use such knowledge to plan his or her own life, to construct and guide the life plans of others (e.g., as a parent or mentor), or to participate in the co-development of joint life plans. Theory and research on topics relevant to future anticipation and long-range planning about life are fragmented in the psychological literature and tend to focus on individual-level phenomena. In life-span developmental psychology, for example, there is a long tradition of investigating the selection of personal life goals and life tasks during adulthood. However, even in this field, relatively little attention has been paid to the social-interactive aspects of life goal selection and planning, and to the fact that individual goals most often have to be synchronized with the desires and plans of others. A central aim of this chapter is to integrate discussion of social-interactive processes associated with planning about life (e.g., interpersonal negotiation, persuasion, conflict resolution, joint anticipation, and prediction of uncertainties) into a life-span developmental framework. A catalogue of questions about life plans, planning, and planners is proposed, focusing on possible developmental changes in (a) beliefs about what aspects of life it is acceptable to plan, (b) options and expectations about individual versus joint plans and planning activities, (c) the availability of planning assistance and guidance, (d) expectations about the span of life that it is possible to plan

The ideas in this chapter were developed in the context of projects on expertise, wisdom, and life-span cognition conducted at the Max Planck Institute for Human Development and Education. I gratefully acknowledge valuable comments and insights in response to an earlier draft provided by Paul B. Baltes, Jochen Brandtstädter, William Fleeson, Peter Graf, Jacqueline Goodnow, Michael Marsiske, and John Meacham. Correspondence concerning this chapter should be addressed to Jacqui Smith at the Max Planck Institute for Human Development and Education, Lentzeallee 94, 14195 Berlin, Germany (e-mail: smith@mpib-berlin.mpg.de).

242

in advance, and (e) aspects of interpersonal relationships linked to effective versus ineffective planning.

There is a large and varied literature describing the ways individuals deal with events in everyday life. A major emphasis in this literature has been on adaptation and coping after an event has occurred. Many events, however, are considered in advance. Some degree of thought is given to how events might unfold: People think about future emotional states, about possible best and worse scenarios, and about possible consequences of actions. Furthermore, people sometimes weigh the value of simply letting things happen in their lives against the desire to direct and have some control over their own future. The present chapter brings together what is known, and what remains to be asked, about the forms that such *active anticipation* takes and the conditions that influence its occurrence. Some of the background material comes from a literature dealing with anticipation on short-term, assigned tasks, a literature often labeled as the experimental study of planning (e.g., Hayes-Roth & Hayes-Roth, 1979) or action strategies (e.g., Frese & Sabini, 1985; Gollwitzer, 1990). The larger share, however – and the emphasis of this review – has to do with decisions and strategies intended to shape the lives of individuals. Anticipations about the future developmental life paths of individuals are part of everyday ongoing activity, they have repercussions outside the laboratory, they can involve much affect, and they inevitably involve social and interpersonal interactions. The term *life planning* is coined to capture the essence of such active future anticipation.

Life planning involves thinking about the possible future content, course, and purpose of an individual's life (Smith, in press). Engaging in such future anticipation serves to reduce uncertainty, motivate behavior, and enhance an individual's sense of well-being. Evidence for different aspects of life planning can be found in everyday understanding and conversations about life matters (e.g., Schank & Abelson, 1977; Stein, 1988; Wilensky, 1983), in judgments about the life choices and life course of oneself and others (e.g., Cantor & Kihlstrom, 1989; Heckhausen & Schultz, 1993, 1995; Smith & P. B. Baltes, 1990a, b; Smith, Dixon, & P. B. Baltes, 1989), in reflections about the future self (Brandtstädter & Greve, 1994; Markus & Cross, 1990; Raynor & Entin, 1982), in behavior patterns and attributions (Cantor & Kihlstrom, 1987), and in future projections of groups and organizations (Locke & Latham, 1984).

In planning about life, one couples decisions about what one would like to see happen in the future (i.e., personal goal setting) with strategies for deciding, communicating, and determining how, when, and whether these things will in fact occur. In relation to thinking about one's own life, planning might be stimulated by such questions as: What do you want to be when you grow up? What will you do when you finish your education? What plans do you have for building a family? What do you see happening in the next 5 to 10 years in terms of your job? What will you do when your parents can no longer care for themselves? What plans do you have for your retirement? These and similar questions characterize anticipatory life planning. Thoughts about one's life plan might also be stimulated (or challenged) by unexpected events (e.g., personal illness, political change).

Although most researchers agree that the origin, content, and contexts of life plans have general social bases (P. L. Berger, B. Berger, & Kellner, 1967; Cantor & Kihlstrom, 1989), a central focus in the planning literature to date has been on describing associated cognitive activity at the individual level – in particular, research about the individual's reported life goals, decision making, and planning strategies. The social-interactive content and consequences of individual cognitions about life planning have been examined to a lesser degree.

A central goal of this chapter is to suggest new research directions and questions about life planning derived from a social-interactive (interactive-minds) perspective. One could ask, for example, whether an individual's preferred developmental goals and associated plans *include others as co-actors* (either indirectly or directly) and examine the conditions under which plans that explicitly include others are more successful than those that are ego-centered. Individuals think not only about themselves; they also think about significant others in their lives and *construct life plans for others*. Moreover, they attempt (more or less successfully) to *convince others to follow* these plans either by dialogue or by deliberately setting up (or closing off) environmental structures that guide the other's life choices in a prescribed direction. So, for instance, parents make plans for their children's futures (Goodnow & Collins, 1990), mentors create scenarios about the future development and potential of their students or protégés (Kram & Isabella, 1985; Levinson, 1978), and individuals reflect about the future goals and direction of new relationships (C. E. Berger, 1993). On a macro level, community leaders, politicians, managers, and administrators devise institutional plans that create opportunity structures for and place constraints on the future lives of others (e.g., Mintzberg, 1994).

Further, from a social-interactive perspective, one could ask whether the goals and plans reported by an individual were indeed *self-initiated* or rather *designed solely by specific others*, or developed as *the result of joint efforts*. Individuals do not always think alone about the future. There are many instances where plans about life and the future first arise through the interaction, discussions, and negotiations of two or more persons. Couples discuss, develop, and revise (often heatedly and over long periods) plans for children, family management, and partnership goals (Ickes, 1985). Plans associated with the arrival of a new baby evolve over the 9 months before birth, often requiring rapid revision at birth and increased attention to details in the days, months, and years thereafter (Russell, 1983). Within companies and institutions, executive managers, union members, and colleagues collaborate to develop future (often conflicting) plans, which have an impact not only on the larger system, but also on the careers of individuals (Hickson, 1987; Levine, Resnick, & Higgins, 1993; Menaghan, 1991).

An additional goal of this chapter is to imbed a social-interactive viewpoint on questions about life plans, planners, and planning into a life-span perspective (P. B. Baltes, 1987). Whereas there have been recent proposals to extend the study of individually centered planning in a life-span context (see Lachman & Burack, 1993, for recent proposals relating planning to theories of control and self-efficacy), calls for a tripartite integration of planning-related research into a life-span and a social-interactive perspective have yet to be realized (e.g., Goodnow, 1987; Levine et al., 1993). In developmental psychology, interest has focused primarily on the ontogenesis of individual-level cognitions related to planning, in particular, everyday planning skills (Rogoff, 1991; Scholnick & Friedman, 1993), temporal and future orientation (e.g., Brandtstädter & Wentura, 1994; Radowski, 1979), goal and life task selection (e.g., Brandtstädter, 1993; Brandtstädter, Wentura, & Greve, 1993; Pervin, 1989b), and the function and nature of future goals, dreams, and strivings in adult development (Cantor & Zirkel, 1990; Levinson, 1978; Markus & Cross, 1990).

An underlying theme in the various sections in this chapter will be the proposal that both the cognitive activities and social interactions involved in life planning may change over the life span. Before outlining this theme in more detail and describing research about plans, planners, and planning across the life span, I will first briefly review the planning literature to clarify differences between descriptions of planning for single events (e.g., a solution to an assigned problem) and planning about life.

Conceptions of planning

Differences between single-event planning and life planning

The word *plan* as both a noun and a verb is used in many different ways both in common language and in the psychological literature (Scholnick & Friedman, 1987, 1993). As a noun, plan has been used to refer to (a) something involved in the anticipation of future behavior (e.g., a scheduler; Hayes-Roth & Hayes-Roth, 1979), (b) something that regulates behavior (e.g., a procedure or template; e.g., Newell & Simon, 1972), and (c) a way of storing information about the world (e.g., a diagram or program; e.g., Schank & Abelson, 1977). Used as a verb, there is general agreement that processes associated with *planning* are goal-directed, voluntary, and intended.

Planning activities can occur at many levels of behavior, from a micro to a meta level (Wilensky, 1983). At all levels, two prime categories of processes are associated with planning: The first involves the generation, selection, and coordination of goals, and the second includes strategies for implementing decisions and actions to obtain these goals. These processes are supported by an extensive knowledge system (e.g., Schank & Abelson, 1977).

Much theory and experimental research on planning in psychology has focused on micro-level, single-event, and short-term contexts, and has described planning activities designed to solve a specified problem. Work within the cognitive science perspective best illustrates this approach (e.g., Hayes-Roth & Hayes-Roth, 1979; Riesbeck & Schank, 1989; Schank & Abelson, 1977; Scholnick & Friedman, 1987; Wilensky, 1983). Cognitive researchers strive to understand the knowledge and processes involved in (a) problem representation, (b) goal selection and organization, (c) strategy activation and execution, and (d) outcome evaluation. For this purpose, they typically examine planning problems and tasks for which all (or almost all) parameters are known and for which there is an accepted best solution, so that experimental manipulations can be introduced and hypotheses about processes tested. In some laboratories, this approach has been extended to investigate everyday instances of planning (e.g., to get to work on time or to complete shopping errands) that involve remembering (or implementing) standard "scripts" for concrete event and action sequences (cf. Rebok, 1989; Schank & Abelson, 1977; Scholnick & Friedman, 1987). There are also life-span studies within this approach that focus on describing the developmental changes in problem representation, planning, and decision-making strategies (e.g., Friedman, Scholnick, & Cocking, 1987).

How do general models of planning for micro-level and everyday single events differ from planning about life? Table 9.1 provides a general comparison of planning in these two contexts.

The most obvious difference between the two contexts is that the goals and domains of life planning are typically more complex, abstract, vague, and open-ended. While models of life planning encompass the same components as models of general planning (i.e., the generation, selection, and coordination of goals and strategies for implementing decisions and actions to obtain these goals), the components are likely to have far less certainty of definition and to involve more complexity.

Another obvious difference between a life plan and an everyday plan is the time frame involved. Whereas an everyday plan may specify a concrete sequence of decisions and actions to quickly reach a goal, more often than not the outcome of life planning is a vague intention (cf. P. L. Berger et al., 1967; Brim, 1992; Rawls, 1971). A life plan evolves over an extended period of time, increasing in clarity of final goal(s) and precision of detail. Thus, at different points in the evolutionary process, an individual's life planning strategy might well be characterized as "muddling through" or "straight down the middle."

A further important difference between everyday planning and life planning

Table 9.1. *Comparison of the attributes of everyday and laboratory planning tasks and life planning*

	Planning in everyday and laboratory problem-solving tasks	Planning about life
Goals	Usually a single goal	Usually multiple, highly complex goals
	Goal specified (or easily found)	Goal has to be created (often a complex task alone to find the goal)
	Goal is exact, concrete	Goals tend to be vague, abstract
	Priority setting easy for plans with multiple goals; goal compatibility high	Priority setting difficult for plans with multiple goals; high goal conflict and incompatibility
	Goal achievement equals solution and completion of the task; a closed problem and static target	Goal achievement usually opens new goals; an open problem and a running target
	Goals are "cool," i.e., relatively little emotional involvement or motivational investment; possibly high immediate costs of failure but minimal long-term costs	Goals are "hot," i.e., high emotional and motivational investment; high long-term costs of failure (e.g., in terms of self-esteem)
Knowledge	Mostly complete (routine script)	Imperfect (many scenarios)
Time	Usually short-term	Usually long-term
	Highly limited or constrained	Somewhat flexible
	Low variability	High variability
Resources	Required resources known and usually available at the beginning	Required resources not always known and not necessarily available (often a case of concurrent acquisition)
Actions	High controllability	Low controllability
	Relatively simple; hierarchically arranged	Highly complex; sequence unclear
	Often detailed anticipation of "plan of action" before action begins	Frequent reconstruction of vague "plan for action"
	Low error rate	High error rate
	Fast error recognition and quick recovery from errors	Often slow recognition of errors and slow recovery
	Relatively little external feedback required during plan enactment	Active search for external feedback
Actors	Usually single planner; single memory but may involve managing others	Usually more than one planner provides input (groups, family, mentor)

is that the outcome of the latter cognitive activity is likely to have substantially greater long-term repercussions. While the efficiency of planning for the completion of an errand (e.g., Hayes-Roth & Hayes-Roth, 1979) or the organization of a dinner menu (e.g., Byrne, 1977) may produce short-term frustration or happiness, planning to begin parenthood and to raise a child can have lifetime implications. As outlined in the next section, life plans may also be more intimately linked to social, interpersonal, and emotional dimensions of the self compared with everyday plans (Cantor & Kihlstrom, 1989).

Theoretical conceptions of life plans

The idea that individuals engage in planning about life and construct an overall life plan and that these activities are intimately part of a shared social-cultural knowledge system has been an important element of many developmental theories. It has been best developed, however, in the theories of Rawls (1971), P. L. Berger et al. (1967) and, more recently, Brim (1992). These theories have several aspects in common – most important, the proposal that planning is based on and requires a general and shared system of social knowledge. There is also some agreement in terms of (a) the purpose of engaging in planning about life (i.e., uncertainty reduction, self-regulation, and enhancement of well-being), (b) the basis for expecting some overall commonalities in the content of life plans, and (c) the proposal that individuals may differ. Because each theory makes specific suggestions about social interactions relevant to planning that will be elaborated in subsequent sections about plans, planners, and planning, each will be considered here in some detail.

Exposition of the ideal life plan. Rawls (1971) proposed that individuals have an overarching life plan (plan for the whole life) that provides a framework for and guides all instances of planning (subplans) for specific life tasks and life phases. Plans relate to the broad range of human desires and needs: "personal affection and friendship, meaningful work and social cooperation, the pursuit of knowledge and the fashioning and contemplation of beautiful things" (p. 425). He contended that the overarching life plan is geared toward the attainment of satisfaction and a share of the common goods of a social group:

> Each individual has a rational plan of life drawn up subject to the conditions that confront him. This plan is designed to permit the harmonious satisfaction of his interests. It schedules activities so that various desires can be fulfilled without interference. It is arrived at by rejecting other plans that are either less likely to succeed or do not provide for such an inclusive attainment of aims. . . . Plans differ since individual abilities, circumstances, and wants differ; rational plans are adjusted to these contingencies. A man is happy when he is more or less successful in the way of carrying out his plan. (p. 93)

Behind Rawls's ideas was a general theory about the nature of the fundamental social contract underlying the organization of societal institutions and individuals within a society. In essence, he assumed that persons within a society, in their relations to each other, recognize certain rules of conduct and cooperation and, for the most part, agree about the desirability of the primary social goods of the society and about a *socially just* distribution of these common goods. Primary goods, or things that "a rational man . . . would prefer more of rather than less" (Rawls, 1971, p. 92), include rights and liberties, opportunities and powers, income and wealth, and a sense of self-respect (i.e., a sense of one's own worth and a confidence in one's abilities).

Rawls (1971) also described several other aspects of life plans. First, he commented on the time frame and lack of certainty involved in planning about life:

> A plan will . . . make some provision for even the most distant future and for our death, but it becomes relatively less specific for later periods. . . . We must not imagine a rational plan is a detailed blueprint for action stretching over the whole course of life. It consists of a hierarchy of plans, the more specific subplans being filled in at the appropriate time. (p. 410)

Further, he specified some important processes: "Planning is in part scheduling" (p. 410), involving, for example, the allocation of basic resources of time and energy to activities, and the resolution of conflicting desires.

Following his view of individuals as rational thinkers, Rawls (1971) assumed that persons would adjust their plans and expectations about their individual share of primary goods in accord with their own situation. Here, he particularly mentioned personal abilities and motives: "Plans must fit the requirements of human capacities and abilities, their trends of maturation and growth" (p. 424); and, in line with the Aristotelian principle of motivation, he added that "humans take more pleasure in doing something as they become more proficient at it, and of two activities they do equally well, they prefer the one calling on a larger repertoire of more intricate and subtle discriminations" (p. 426).

Does everyone have a life plan? Here Rawls (1971) pointed to the power of social influence: "The question of what to do with our life is always there, although some societies force it upon us more obviously than others and at a different time of life. The limit decision to have no plan at all, to let things come as they may, is still theoretically a plan that may or may not be rational" (p. 413). Moreover, given the general facts of *social interdependency*, he argued that societies will encourage and support certain kinds of plans more than others. "The plans of individuals need to be fitted together so that their activities are compatible with one another and they can all be carried through without anyone's legitimate expectations being severely disappointed" (p. 6). In essence, Rawls asserted that the execution of the plans of individuals should lead to the achievement of social ends in ways that are efficient and consistent with justice. Here, he points to important dimensions relevant to a social-interactive approach: namely, that plans of individuals necessarily interlock and that social-interaction processes play a significant role in arriving at positions of coordination, agreement, and compromise that afford a just distribution of the common goods.

The socially synchronized life plan. P. L. Berger and his colleagues' (1967) descriptions of planning about life specifically illustrate the ways in which the plurality of social experience might be manifested in the everyday life of individuals. They pointed out that even though decisions and long-term plans are part of the private sphere of an individual's social life, they nevertheless touch on and require knowledge of larger social institutions, knowledge of sources of assistance and advice.

Their conception encompasses the idea that there are many possible life biographies for an individual to select among – a fact that on the one hand creates a sense of freedom but, on the other, can also lead to frustration (especially if the individual perceives factors in his or her situation that limit or inhibit this sense of freedom). In making a selection, individuals refer to (a) their repertoire of "packaged knowledge about life careers" (P. L. Berger et al., 1967, p. 74), which is part of the general social knowledge system and (b) their knowledge of their position in the map of society. Using this information, the individual calculates the probability that one or another biography could become reality:

> Thus a factory worker has a fairly realistic notion of the typical life career of a lawyer, even if his contacts with the social world of lawyers have been minimal or nonexistent. While the factory worker knows that he is unlikely to fill this particular biographical role, he can imagine without much difficulty how he might have done so if his life had taken another turn at some specific junctures. (p. 70)

They suggest that individuals have a map of society within which they can locate their own life course and future projects. As a function of anticipatory socialization, individuals have much factual knowledge about future careers that are realistic and plausible for themselves. At the same time, P. L. Berger et al. considered that there is a certain resistance to reliance on "package" knowledge in regard to thinking about and evaluating one's own life. Individuals, they suggested, search for a distinctive style, yet often simply adopt an alternative package (i.e., nonconformists are really conformists).

Planning involves what P. L. Berger and his colleagues (1967) call "multi-relational synchronization" (p. 71), that is, the coordination of the multiplicity of social relations within which one is embedded, and the different timetables associated with one's own many developmental careers (e.g., family, work, finances). The individual's life plan is the total of all the relevant timetables, their grand sum, and their integrative meaning. Further they suggested that planning presupposes "in order to" motives rather than "because of" motives. As such, the meanings of everyday life derive from future plans rather than past events: This requires considerable effort in terms of thinking in long-term time spans, controlled delay of gratification, and coping with concomitant frustrations. Planning requires projections not only in terms of time, but also in terms of space. The map that an individual is faced with involves a vast amount of data. P. L. Berger et al. also note that in modern times life planning has become a value in itself, and a large proportion of family conversations relate to creating, revising, and verifying the life plan of individual members and the group. For most young and middle-aged adults, the focus of a life plan is one's job – other aspects of planning revolve around and depend on the job, according to P. L. Berger et al.

Like Rawls, they also considered that the life plan becomes a primary source of identity and a source of life meaning: "In long-range planning, the individual not only plans *what* he will do but he plans *who* he will be" (p. 73). In this respect, for closely linked individuals (family, partner), projects, planned careers, and planned identities largely overlap. "As the individual plots the trajectory of his life on the societal map each point in his projected biography relates him to the overall web of meanings in the society" (p. 76).

Further, P. L. Berger et al. (1967) argued that it is important to distinguish between an overall life plan that is likely to be open-ended and somewhat vague, and more detailed concrete life decisions (subplans) that are nevertheless connected as means to an end:

> Regardless whether the life plan is fully articulated or only vague, there is a certain amount of frustration associated with it: if definite, then doubt can arise over the relevance of separate decisions and subplans, if vague, then there may be anxiety because of an inability to articulate desires. Further, since planning is long-term it necessarily brings with it the requirement for being able to delay gratification – to wait and postpone. (p. 73)

The importance of a life plan for personal development. Brim (1992) considered the concept of life plans in the context of his general model of human nature and ambition. He posited three things that underlie individuals' thoughts and plans about their life direction: (1) a basic drive for growth and mastery, (2) the preference to live in a way that is characterized as a level of just manageable difficulties (not too hard, and not too easy), and (3) strategies involved in managing to achieve this level by adjusting to successes and failures. Planning for the achievement of a balance between winning and losing, Brim contended, is one of the main sources of happiness and a sense of personal well-being.

Brim (1992) proposed that individuals develop plans because they are for the most part purposeful in their efforts to deal with their lives;

"Almost always what we are doing has a plan and a timetable" (p. 4). He goes on to say:

> We have images of our life course, of where we expect to be and what we expect to be doing at times in our future. These images of future life may be fuzzy. They may never come true. Nevertheless, we do have long-range goals and timetables for reaching them; and when taken all together they are a life plan, such as it is. As we succeed or fail, we revise time and time again. With experience and some abbreviations and perhaps a few diagrams, we can lay out this plan on a single page – a life plan at a glance – in its hundredth revision. (p. 4)

The central components of life plans and purposive actions for Brim (1992) are (a) desired goals; (b) indications of aspirations – ideal, minimum, realistic; (c) the relevant timetables associated with the goals; (d) means and strategies for achieving the goals; and (e) monitoring, to check for disparities between our original plans and reality. It is in terms of this final aspect that Brim focused somewhat more on the social-interactive aspects of planning about life. He described the social contexts in which individuals receive (or don't receive) information and feedback about the status of their plans and whether they are winning or losing. This information, Brim proposed, is not always obvious or open:

> All societies have customs about *who* gets *what* kinds of knowledge and *when* in life they get it. The cultural wisdom is passed out according to age, gender, and occupation. . . . Distribution mechanisms are in the family, schools, mass media, and the market place. Keeping such knowledge secret gives some individuals power and status over others. Sometimes, we do not tell others that they are losing, for fear of hurting them. Sometimes it is also difficult to find out that one is winning – especially when our competitors do not want to let on that we perhaps have the edge over them. This is captured in the saying, never let them see you sweat. (p. 60)

A life-span perspective. The conception of life planning adopted in this chapter rests on several assumptions: (a) that individuals have access to a knowledge system about life matters containing information relevant to thinking about the future (Schank & Abelson, 1977); (b) that the use of this knowledge system is socialized, shaped, and challenged throughout the life span (P. B. Baltes & Smith, 1990; Smelser & Erikson, 1980; Smith, Dixon, & P. B. Baltes, 1989); and (c) that although individuals may be able to recognize and evaluate ideal life plans (cf. Rawls, 1971) and planning processes (as a function of shared social knowledge and socialization processes), typical instances of life and future planning reflect individual and situational variations that may or may not match the ideals (Baron, 1985; Smith et al., 1989). It is proposed that these variations and approximations can be related to multiple factors including developmental phase (e.g., age and present life task), cultural values, situational expectations and constraints, personal dispositions and motives, together with intellectual ability, expertise, and resources.

Specific background to this approach to studying life planning comes from descriptions and models of plans, planning, and planners found in the areas of cognitive science, social and organizational psychology, and life-span development (Smith, in press). Cognitive science approaches, especially those of Schank and his colleagues (Schank & Abelson, 1977; Hammond, 1989; Riesbeck & Schank, 1989; Wilensky, 1983) have focused on describing the structure of plans, plan understanding, and planning processes associated with general world and social knowledge. One important offshoot of this approach is work dealing with adaptive and interacting planning processes apparent in conversation structures and narratives (Alterman, 1988; Bruce & Newman, 1978; Schegloff, 1991). Social psychologists provide hypotheses about the consequences of plan construction and processing of future scenarios for emotional and personal well-being, motivation, and self-regulation (Johnson & Sherman, 1990; Srull & Wyer, 1986) and suggest frameworks for evaluating the social-interactive processes involved in making and implementing decisions (e.g., Janis & Mann, 1977; Read & Miller, 1989).

Hypotheses about the possible differences between planners and context-by-planner interactions can be derived from life-span developmental theory. Clearly in childhood and adolescence, differences relate to the ontogenesis of social knowledge, future perspectives, and the understanding of self (e.g., Flavell & Ross, 1981; Mischel & Patterson, 1978). Adult planners may also differ, for example, in terms of expertise and knowledge of life tasks (e.g., Cantor & Kihlstrom, 1989; Featherman, Smith, & Peterson, 1990), life goal structures and motives to engage in future planning (e.g., Brandtstädter & Wentura, 1994; Brandtstädter & Renner, 1990; Brim, 1992), as well as personal life history and intellectual capacity (e.g., P. B. Baltes, 1991; P. B. Baltes, Smith, & Staudinger, 1992). The contributions of each of these areas will be outlined in the sections on plans, planners, and planning.

Research on plans, planners, and planning: room for a life-span developmental and social-interactive (interactive-minds) perspective?

The preceding short review of general conceptions of planning and theories of life planning sets the stage for dealing with the central goals of this chapter, namely, to ask whether a social-interactive and a life-span perspective to considering aspects of life planning would open new questions and provide further insight. Three areas are considered: (a) research on the life goals and tasks included in life plans, (b) proposals about differences between planners, and (c) suggestions about planning strategies. In the scope of this chapter, it is not possible to provide a comprehensive review of all research relevant to plans, planners, and planning. Rather, the present focus is on the possible relevance of a life-span developmental and social-interactive approach.

The social content of plans: research on life goals and life tasks

There is a long history of research in developmental, social, and personality psychology into the personal values and life goals that feature in individual's self-narratives, self-perceptions, and self-motivation structures (e.g., Braithwaite & Scott, 1991; Frese & Sabini, 1985; Pervin, 1989a). In general, there is considerable overlap in findings about the particular themes and domains that characterize the values, life goals, and tasks of individuals, and agreement that the overall purpose of goal setting relates to personal well-being, satisfaction, and a sense of mastery (as described by Rawls, 1971, and Brim, 1992). This overlap is not surprising: It reflects social consensus and shared knowledge about desirable life events, personal qualities, and developmental trajectories (e.g., Hagestad & Neugarten, 1985; Heckhausen, Dixon, & P. B. Baltes, 1989). There is much diversity, however, in the general theoretical label used to characterize this activity.

Table 9.2 summarizes central researchers and their respective labels. In addition, Table 9.2 provides a global indication of (a) whether the author specifically proposed changes across the life span, (b) the method of data collection, and (c) the examples of the life goals and life tasks reported. For the purpose of highlighting one of the central points of this chapter about a social-interactive perspective, these examples have been roughly divided into two categories: those goals indirectly versus directly involving others. This categorization opens the way for new questions (discussed later) about life goals and life tasks.

Do the various researchers listed in Table 9.2 describe the goals associated with life planning? To begin, consider Rokeach's (1968) proposals concerning the enduring beliefs about specific modes of conduct (instrumental values) and end states of existence (terminal values) that underlie individual and group attitudes and belief systems. His theory and method has had considerable impact and has been used widely in social and developmental research. There is a clear match between his *terminal values* and the goals of life plans described by Rawls (1971), P. L. Berger et al. (1967), and Brim (1992). Similarly, the life and developmental tasks outlined by Erikson (1959), Bühler (1968), Havighurst (1961), and Cantor and Kihlstrom (1987) match with the idea that there should be individual and age-related differences as a function of person–environment contingencies.

The definitions of Little (1983), Emmons (1989), Klinger (1977), and McAdams (1985) also all suggest planning processes. Take, for example, Little's (1983; Palys & Little, 1983) *personal project*, which he defined as a set of interrelated acts extending over time that is intended to maintain or attain a state of affairs foreseen by the individual. The personal project represents, according to Little, those important things that individuals think about, plan for, carry out, and sometimes but not always achieve. McAdams's (1985)

Table 9.2. *Overview of definitions of life goals and themes: examples of proposed goals that would involve others indirectly and directly*

Author	Label	Method	Developmental change	Involves others indirectly	Involves others directly
Maslow (1943)	Hierarchy of needs	Theory	?	Self-actualization	Belongingness
Erikson (1959)	Developmental tasks	Theory/interview	Yes	Integrity	Intimacy, generativity
Bühler (1968)	Life's basic tendencies	Interview/scale	Yes	Self-limiting adaptation	Love and family
Morris (1956)	Ways to live	Vignette scale	Yes	Cultivate self-knowledge	Concern for others
Havighurst (1961)	Developmental life tasks	Theory	Yes	Occupation	Marriage, establish family
Cantor and Kihlstrom (1987)	Life tasks	Checklist/questionnaire	Yes	Get good grades	Make friends
Schank and Abelson (1977)	Life and interpersonal themes	Theory	?	Personal qualities, physical sensations	Love, lifestyle, professional ambitions
Levinson (1978)	A "dream"	Interview	Yes	Occupation	Family
McAdams (1985)	Imago	Interview/text analysis	Yes	Agentic (e.g., teacher)	Communion (e.g., lover)
Markus and Nurius (1986)	Possible selves	Structured interview	Yes	Competent self	Lonely self

Table 9.2. (*cont.*)

Author	Label	Method	Developmental change	Involves others indirectly	Involves others directly
Allport et al. (1960)	Basic interests and values	Scale	?	Theoretical, aesthetic	Social, political
Rokeach (1968)	Terminal values	Scale	?	Wisdom, happiness	Family security, friendship
Brandtstädter et al. (1989)	Developmental goals	Checklist scale/probes	Yes	Status/superiority in job	Marital stability
Kuhlen (1959)	Life goals	Checklist	Yes	Be good housewife	To marry, get or stay in job
Wadsworth and Ford (1983)	Personal goals	Structured interview/grid	Yes	Personal growth	Family and social life
Ford and Nichols (1987)	Human goals	Questionnaire	?	Happiness, cognitive productivity	Belongingness, social responsibility
Rapkin and Fischer (1992a)	Life goals	Checklist scale	Yes	Stability, safety, security	Reliance on services
Klinger et al. (1980)	Current concerns	Structured interview	?	(Individually defined)	(Individually defined)
Little (1983)	Personal project	Structured interview	?	(Individually defined)	(Individually defined)
Emmons and King (1988)	Personal strivings	Structured interview	?	Make good impression	Make new friends

imago, defined as an idealized and personified image of the self, encompasses needs, interpersonal styles, and motives and attempts to combine a description of both agency and communion (intimacy, generativity) themes within an individual's life. For Klinger (1977), a *current concern* encompasses the state of the organism between commitment to a goal and either attainment or disengagement from the goal. The range of potential concerns is great and might change frequently, but one could image that there would be patterns of recurrence and some coherence in choice of concerns guided by overarching life goals and plans. This is precisely what Emmons (1989) suggested with his concept of *personal strivings* (which he defined as idiographically coherent patterns of goal strivings) and it also underlies Markus's definition of *possible selves* (e.g., Markus & Ruvolo, 1989). The notion of possible selves is consistent with the general definition of a plan as a sort of diagram: Possible selves are defined as specific representations of one's self in future states and circumstances that serve to organize and energize one's action. Levinson's (1978) proposal that individuals develop a *dream* or *imagined possibility* about their desired future personal identity and life purpose is also captured in present notions of life plans.

While the conceptions all relate to the notion of life planning, there are differences in terms of whether proposed goals and themes are life-phase-specific or not. So, for example, the *life tasks* of Cantor and Kihlstrom (1987) presently center on young adulthood, while the goals described by Rapkin and Fischer (1992a,b) relate to late adulthood. Rokeach's (1968) values and Brandtstädter's (1993; Brandtstädter, Renner, & Baltes-Götz, 1989) research, on the other hand, relate to all of adulthood and old age, but not necessarily childhood. The goals also vary in terms of their implied time span (e.g., current life tasks and current concerns may have a shorter time frame than ways of life or terminal values and may not readily be linked to a broader and more global life plan) and perceived idiographic quality (the interests of some researchers are in developing individual case histories rather than in considering possible similarities in development of planning about life).

Open questions and new directions. From this brief overview of research on life goals and life tasks, it is clear that (a) individuals do think about and set goals for their future life, (b) there is considerable consensus about the range of desirable life goals and tasks, and (c) there is still room to ask more questions about the *social content* of the goals and tasks selected by individuals at different life periods. Furthermore, one could ask *how often individuals set goals with others in mind*. The suggested categorization of goals in Table 9.2, according to whether they directly or indirectly involve others, could be one step in this direction. Few researchers so far have paid attention to this aspect of goal selection (exceptions include M. M. Baltes & Silverberg, 1994; Brandtstädter, 1993; Carstensen, 1992). Brim (1992, p. 15) added two further dimensions that could be used to classify the implied social content of individual life goals – namely, whether a choice implies *competitive versus cooperative interactions* with others and the environment and whether it entails *selfish versus unselfish* motives.

From a social-interactive perspective, it would be possible and perhaps enlightening to pose the following questions about life goals and tasks. Each question could also be extended by asking whether the answer might change as a function of the developmental and life phase of the individual, and hypotheses could be developed to predict conditions under which the planning strategies implied would successfully reduce uncertainty, motivate activity, and/or enhance personal well-being.

1. When individuals nominate personal goals and tasks that to be completed must directly involve others (e.g., the goal to get married), do they think in social-interactive (interactive-minds) terms?
2. How often do individuals set personal goals with others in mind (either directly or indirectly)?
3. Do individuals vary in their preferred ratio and commitment to life goals that directly versus indirectly involve others?
4. Is it easier to plan for solo or joint ventures?

In some cases, it may be possible to obtain an answer to the first question from existing data sets. Those researchers who use open interviews, for example, could determine whether or not subjects embedded their goal nomination in the context of a narrative explanation about the role(s) of significant others in their proposed goal. Various researchers (refer to Table 9.2) have used checklists or written short reports for obtaining goal nominations that do not allow for an analysis of narrative or explanative context. They often complemented this procedure, however, with more in-depth questions about personal emotions linked to the goal, perceived distance from attainment, importance, commitment, perceived controllability, time and effort investment, and, in some cases, diary and event recordings of experiences relevant to personal goals in everyday situations (e.g., Cantor & Fleeson, 1994). With these procedures, it would be relatively easy to also include probe questions addressing issues about social interaction.

Another technique that might be used to investigate social-interactive aspects of goal setting involves assessing initial and developed concordance in the ideas and thoughts of co-actors. Such techniques have been frequently used in research mapping the course of marital relationships and therapist–client interactions. So, for example, initial mismatches in partners' reported marital and relationship goals and plans may converge or diverge over time as a function of interpersonal interaction (Berscheid, 1985; Brandtstädter, Baltes-Götz, & Heil, 1990; Kelley et al., 1983). Successful therapy outcomes may be predicted, according to Beutler and Bergan (1991), by an initial (or progressively developed) concordance in life values between therapist and client.

Questions 2 and 3 can be easily linked to life-span developmental theories (e.g., Erikson, 1959; Smelser & Erikson, 1980) that propose changes from ego-centered thinking and self-regulation to a more interpersonal, intergenerational, and social orientation (e.g., life tasks of intimacy and generativity). In later life, there may be changes in preferred ratios of more self-focused versus other-focused goals as a function of health constraints, availability of co-actors, and emotional needs and concerns about maintaining autonomy (M. M. Baltes & Silverberg, 1994; Carstensen, 1993).

Question 4 was suggested by research showing that goals of moderate difficulty are the most motivating compared with goals that are too easy or too difficult (Brim, 1992). It could be argued that goals defining joint ventures with others involve an increased level of complexity and uncertainty due to the necessity of coordinating each actor's contributions. Of course, perceived ease or relative difficulty is likely to be interpreted differently as a function of the individual's experience, motives, and expertise. Cantor, Norem, Niedenthal, Langston, and Brower (1987), for example, have reported differences in indicators of planning ease for the two most salient tasks of college students, namely, making friends and getting good grades. Plans for achievement situations were more detailed and rich in alternatives (indicating greater knowledge and perceived control) compared with plans for interpersonal situations, which were more open and vague (see also Cantor & Fleeson, 1994). Nurmi, Pulliainen, and Salmela-Aro (1992) found that, with increasing age (from 19 to 71 years), individuals reported more interest in planning for things over which they thought they had little control (namely, their own health) and less interest in aspects of life over which they considered they had much control. Further, the choice of, and attributions about, goals more or less directly involving others is likely to be especially influenced by social expectations about *who should plan what, when, and with whom* (Goodnow, 1987), an idea to be further discussed next.

Research on planners: age, expertise, individual differences, and the appropriateness of joint ventures

When one begins to consider aspects of life planning from a developmental and social-interactive perspective, it becomes difficult (if not impossible) to separate questions about the content of life goals and plans from questions about planners. How do planning processes change with age or cohort? Are there variations in understanding and use? Are there experience and expertise differences among adult planners? Do the tasks and the time frames of plans change with age and/or cohort?

For the most part, the literature has focused on planner differences associated with cognitive development in childhood (e.g., Rogoff, 1991), social intelligence (Cantor & Kihlstrom, 1987), expertise (Featherman et al., 1990;

Locke & Latham, 1984), social role and accountability (Tetlock, 1992), gender (Goodnow, 1987), and personal disposition (Frese, Stewart, & Hannover, 1987). In most cases the planner, regardless of age or expertise, works alone. Some recent work, however, has begun to consider the benefits and existence of pairs and teams of planners: in medical teams (Engeström, 1992; Tuckett, Boulton, Olson, & Williams, 1985), families (Goodnow & Collins, 1990), educational settings (Resnick, Levine, & Teasley, 1991; Rogoff, 1991; Suchman, 1987), groups and organizations (Galegher, Kraut, & Egido, 1990; Hickson, 1987; Kram, 1985; Larson & Christensen, 1993). There are also suggestions (e.g., Goodnow, 1987) that it is important to consider social expectations about what tasks can (or should) be planned together, by whom, and when. Previous findings and proposals will be briefly reviewed with a focus on issues that could be viewed from a social-interactive perspective.

Children as planners. As in most other areas of cognitive performance that rely on world and social knowledge, older children are more proficient in understanding and making plans than are young children (Brown & DeLoache, 1978; Chalmers & Lawrence, 1993; Friedman et al., 1987; Rogoff, 1991; Scholnick & Friedman, 1993). Specific differences observed vary with task complexity. So, for example, while preschool children might set adequate goals in preparation for a shopping trip, they are easily distracted from these goals during the actual trip (Hudson & Fivush, 1991). Similarly, Gardner and Rogoff (1990) reported that even though 4-year-olds, like 7-year-olds, planned in advance how they would approach a maze task, the preparation of the younger children broke down on complex mazes and under testing-the-limits situations calling for attention to accuracy and speed.

By 5 years of age, most children understand the notion of planning for everyday routines (Kreitler & Kreitler, 1987) and can devise plans and strategies to fill in time in a task requiring delay of gratification (Mischel & Patterson, 1978). In telling a story, 5-year-olds include goal–action–outcome episodes in temporally ordered sequences indicating their understanding of the role of plan scripts in listener comprehension (Stein, 1988; Trabasso, Stein, Rodkin, Munger, & Baughn, 1992). Three-year-olds, in contrast, tell stories that include unrelated descriptions of actions, objects, characters, and states. Mischel and Patterson (1978) reported that, by age 10, many children are able to distinguish between the intentional and informative aspects of plans, and realize that having a plan is not the same as implementing it. Older children have a better sense of time and space, and are more able to deal with complex hypothetical thoughts.

An important question in relation to understanding the development of children's planning is to know whether performance benefits or changes as a function of collaboration with or guidance from others. Rogoff (1991) has reported an impressive program of research dealing with this question and based on the idea that children serve an *apprenticeship* in the domain of social knowledge. In terms of learning how to plan, she found that children benefited more from the guidance of adults and expert peers than from collaboration with unskilled peers (Radziszewska & Rogoff, 1988, 1991), and that benefits were especially clear when the children were allowed to interactively take some responsibility for task completion during practice (Gauvain, 1992; Gauvain & Rogoff, 1989). Through such *guided participation* (Rogoff, 1991) or apprenticeship in dealing with intellectual and imaginary everyday problems, children's ideas and planning strategies are socialized by those in their social environment.

To what extent are aspects of life planning also evident in childhood and adolescence? Evidence is reported in several studies that children and adolescents certainly think about their future roles in life and, at least by late adolescence, are aware of the importance and difficulties of planning in advance for a path toward achieving these goals. Russell and Smith (1979; Smith & Russell, 1984), for example, asked 7-, 10-, and 15-year-olds what they planned to do when they grew up and left school. The responses of children at each age level reflected gender-related adult life goals and opportunities. Whereas younger children also included more fantasy-like goals among their future dreams (e.g., to be a spaceman), the adolescents' future goals represented a broad range of realistic possibilities. Boys and girls were also asked to describe how their peers of the opposite sex would respond to the question. Here most children (but girls especially) accurately produced the range of future goals that the sexes had generated separately. Girls were pictured by the children as having a more restricted range of future choices than boys (a situation that actually existed in the wider community at the time of the research). Dreher and Oerter (1987), Nurmi (1991, 1993), Evans and Poole (1991), and Pulkkinen (1982) similarly report that the life goals of adolescents focus on the domains of education, future occupation, material gains, and beginning a family or partnership. Girls are more likely to express conflicts between career and family goals (e.g., Pulkkinen, 1982), and few adolescents nominate goals that they expect to be realized after age 30 (Nurmi, 1989).

Differences among adults. The literature on planning skills in adulthood and old age is strewn across a wide range of sources. In relation to everyday tasks and laboratory problems, there are reports that older adults are not as proficient as young adults (Chalmers & Lawrence, 1993; Denney & Denney, 1973) but benefit from working with others or using external aids (Adams & Rebok, 1982–1983; Chalmers & Lawrence, 1993). A different picture regarding aging-related decline is obtained on planning tasks that require planners to use their personal experiences, knowledge of life, or occupational expertise (Smith & P. B. Baltes, 1990b; Smith, Staudinger, & P. B. Baltes, 1994). Here, having more domain-specific experience and being older can have benefits. With regard to life planning, Smith and P. B. Baltes (1990b; Smith, Staudinger, & P. B. Baltes, 1994) have reported that commentaries from older adults about life dilemmas of late adulthood were rated as showing greater wisdom-related knowledge than commentaries from young adults. Older managers (often operating in a committee context) frequently make more pragmatic and realistic suggestions about future company directions than young executives (Birren, 1980; Bromley, 1969). Prognoses of older clinicians based on intuition acquired during years of professional practice often prove to be just as accurate (if not better outcome predictors) as the laboriously developed proposals of young colleagues (Dowie & Elstein, 1988). Clearly, there are individual differences. Indeed, Featherman et al. (1990) reported that even within one professional group (namely, engineers), individuals with similar managerial positions showed different degrees of flexibility and reflection in planning tasks.

Adults, like children, do not plan alone. Indeed there may be even stronger pressures to plan together with others in socially interactive contexts during adulthood. Adults are expected to work productively together *with* others and *for* others. There are normative expectations regarding the socialization of younger generations (primarily family) and expectations regarding caregiving (Hagestad & Neugarten, 1985). All of these contexts fall within the realm of individuals' plans about life.

Within families, parents hold views about the goals and qualities they would like to see their children obtain (e.g., Goodnow & Collins, 1990). LeVine (1988) has described these goals as ordered within a hierarchy characterized at the lower level by aspects of physical health and survival, at the middle level by material possessions and resources (a good job, self-supportive), and at higher levels by more cultural and aesthetic values (sociable, happy, honest, intelligent). Plans are made for each level of goal, with more or less precision, depending on environmental hazards and opportunites. Realization of these plans, of course, depends on the cooperation and understanding of family members about their role in these *joint ventures* and acceptance on the part of co-actors that some players may take a leading or directing role while others should conform (Goodnow, 1987; Goodnow & Collins, 1990). Family disputes often revolve around negotiations about the need to maintain or revise these underlying plans (see Goodnow, Chapter 6, this volume).

Within the workplace and the community, there are also expectations that individuals collaborate in planning for common future goals (Hickson, 1987). New (and especially young) members of a work team are selected according to the complementary skills and social coherence that they might contribute to the group. Processes of socialization rapidly ensure that new members learn the rules and their place in assisting with the maintenance and implementation of group plans (Levine & Moreland, 1991). Whereas in educational settings an individual's expertise is tested and rewarded, in applied settings and organizations the belief that more heads are better than one often calls for what Engeström (1992) has termed *interactive expertise* (see also Tuckett et al., 1985). So, for example, management teams and networks spend long hours jointly determining guidelines, bargaining zones, and timetables, as well as making predictions about chances and conditions of success and failure of future ventures (Hickson, 1987). Actual success or failure often depends on the extent to which each member of the team accepts joint responsibility for implementing and upholding the planned procedures.

Older professionals are expected not only to work in (or lead) teams but also to foster younger colleagues. The *mentorship* process (like the system of guided participation outlined by Rogoff, 1991) is perhaps a prototype context in adulthood where individuals engage in jointly planning about life. As described by Levinson (1978) and elaborated by Kram (1985) and Phillips-Jones (1982), mentorship involves the development of plans about career growth and direction, as well as personal identity. The content of a (younger) individual's particular life plan is nurtured, socialized, and sometimes even devised by the mentor. Mentors are also usually responsible for creating an environment that allows the life plans of their protégé(s) to be realized. Thus, mentors arrange – via sponsorship, coaching, selective protection, and the provision of challenging work – for the careers of their protégés to be enhanced (Kram, 1985). At the same time, mentors offer role modeling, counseling, confirmation, and friendship, which help the less experienced colleague to develop a sense of professional identity and competence (Levinson, 1978).

The mentoring relationship also has a characteristic trajectory that is related to the various phases of forming, implementing, realizing, and redefining a life plan (Levinson, 1978). As the career plans of the protégé reach a stage of fruition, the role of the mentor in the planning process changes. There is less need or desire (on the part of the protégé) for intensive guidance, direction, and protection. The outcome is often feelings of anger, loss, and anxiety as the pair of individuals enters the separation or redefinition phase of the relationship (Kram, 1985). While the jointly devised plans may continue, the close personal relationships may not.

Further questions. This overview of planner characteristics and implications can perhaps be summarized by two observations. On the one hand, there is a central theme that individuals of all ages often work together with others to plan about life matters. On the other hand, and perhaps best represented in the work on mentor–protégé planning, there is the notion that there are also situations where joint ventures reach a point where they are no longer productive or appropriate. These observations point to a further question that would need to be taken into consideration with regard to a social-interactive perspective on life planning – namely, *what social and cultural expectations are there about who should plan what, when, and with whom?*

While there are many situations where expectations favor teamwork, joint (or democratic) decisions, or at least the idea that *two heads are better than one*, there are also contexts where individuals are expected to *stand on their own two feet*, to work alone, and to take responsibility for planning their own future. Indeed there may even be sanctions when individuals violate these expectations. Whereas, at entry levels in a career, independent thinkers are often viewed as arrogant upstarts who would not fit in with the group, at mid-level executive and professional career stages, individuals who do not demonstrate the capacity to initiate plans and take a leading role in planning procedures may not be favored for further promotion (Derr, 1980).

Expectations about what and who should plan together versus alone may be linked not only to social and situational contexts but also to the age, perceived experience, and capacities of the individual, as well as to the life cycle of the relationship between individuals. Research into parents' belief systems have revealed particular age-linked expectations and timetables about when children should/could act alone and think for themselves on various tasks (Goodnow & Collins, 1990). Across the family life cycle, parent–child beliefs about who might/should take a leading role in deciding future goals and acting on these decisions change: Middle-aged offspring, for example, may initiate and direct many of the late life plans of their aged parents (Troll, 1994). Some areas of thought and control over one's life plans may, however, never be surrendered, even in very old age. While older parents might allow their middle-aged child to plan for and arrange health care, housing, and financial matters, plans for arranging the final testament and perhaps even processes of dying may remain the secret and private domain of the parents.

Within interpersonal relationships, mutual understanding is developed over the history of the relationship about what may be planned and decided together versus alone, and how third parties might also be involved in planning processes (C. E. Berger, 1988, 1993; Duck & Pond, 1989). Interactions in initial friendships and partnerships may require intensive periods of planning future goals and activities together, so that the life themes and narratives of the relationship are defined and perceived as being the joint possession of the separate actors (Duck, 1993). In long-standing relationships, there may be more division of labor with regard to who plans and has responsibility for what and when. Indeed, the inability of long-standing partners to take initiatives about future goals and make decisions on behalf of and in the interests of their partner may, in some instances, be viewed as a sign of immaturity or maladaptive functioning (Bradbury & Fincham, 1991).

Expectations about planning for the future together versus alone are also likely to differ across cultures. Turnbull (1985), for example, has argued that compared with many tribal cultures, every phase of the human life cycle in modern-day Western cultures is characterized by socialization practices and belief systems that favor individual values and goals over social interaction or community goals. Western children and adolescents, he argued, are encouraged to look and strive toward being independent and self-assertive in adulthood. Adults, on the other hand, "quickly come to resent adulthood and the demand that it imposes upon us to work to *support ourselves* instead of being supported by others; as though that were an infringement of our individual freedom" (p. 173). Old age and the last phase of the life cycle, Turnbull proposed, represent the negative consequences of a cultural value system geared for independence rather than mutuality and reciprocity of action. Individuals in this period of life must fight against the social stigma "associated with inutility, incompetence, and dependence" (p. 227). Older adults are "expected to retire from action (some would say from interference) in a future that is not theirs" (p. 232).

A research program to investigate social and cultural expectations about who should plan what, when, and with whom would gain much from a life-span approach and would contribute much to our understanding of current research about life goals, personal timetables, and future orientations. It may be, for example, that Nurmi's (1989) finding reported earlier that adolescents' plans only reached to age 30, and various other reports (e.g., Radowski, 1979) that the future plans of older adults were either nonexistent or span days and months rather than years, reflect cultural values and expectations more than was previously supposed.

Planning: managing interpersonal activities, dimensions, and strategies

Most models of planning processes have been developed in the context of laboratory problem-solving tasks or in relation to language comprehension and narrative production (Hammond, 1989; Hayes-Roth & Hayes-Roth, 1979; Schank & Abelson, 1977; Wilensky, 1983). The lists of process components thus reflect the structures and basic operations of individual knowledge systems. Interest focuses on how plans are stored and retrieved from memory.

Some researchers have suggested that these processes could also be explored at a group level of cognition (e.g., Larson & Christensen, 1993). For example, it is possible to consider the source and sequence of information retrieval within a group of decision makers or planners (e.g., does the memory of one problem solver serve as a cue for another), transfer and storage of information within a group, and discussion about individual variations in plan scripts.

A social-interactive approach would serve to broaden proposals about planning processes and to place them in a context outside the private sphere of individual cognition and into the sphere of interpersonal relationships. Borrowing concepts from applied settings (Locke & Latham, 1984; Mintzberg, 1994) and social psychology, it would be possible to consider planning processes as *activities, strategies, and dimensions of interpersonal relationships* associated with the following:

1. goal management (e.g., goal and partner selection, priority and agenda setting, conflict negotiation, monitoring),
2. time management (e.g., time allocation and investment, and timing of actions),
3. resource management (allocation of effort, skills, information, and materials [property, money]),
4. action management (scheduling, coordination, and feedback), and, of course,
5. people and relationship management (tactics and style of interaction).

There are many questions that could be asked about interpersonal processes related to each of these management areas. Two general questions serve as illustration:

1. What dimensions of relationships facilitate and hinder planning processes and the attainment of goals?
2. Is there a mutual development of planning processes and relationships over time?

Research from organizational and applied settings describing the *multiissue, multiparty negotiations* of plans has pointed to time and the development of mutual understanding as important ingredients in successful outcomes. Differences between good versus poor negotiators and planners appear to center on aspects of goal, time, and action management (especially setting clear agendas and schedules but flexible deadlines), and interaction management (fostering understandin, mutual consideration, and the reconciliation of conflicting preferences; Aldag & Fuller, 1993). Deciding issues of information management and responsibility for control over time are also critical aspects of planning strategies in large groups. In addition, it is often the case that different arrangements of social interactions (e.g., division into subgroups) are needed over the course of planning and plan implementation.

Mutual understanding is rare and must be strived for. Conflict, on the other hand, is seen as an important dynamic in either facilitating or hindering planning processes over time. Conflicts may arise within each of the five management areas noted earlier. Wilensky (1983), in his cognitive model of individual planning processes, focused on managing goal overlaps and conflicts. He suggested that we generally do not deal with one goal at a time as we try to understand or create plans, but rather with many goals. He nominated two central dimensions of goal conflicts: (a) ownership (individual vs. group), and (b) goal interactions (e.g. favorable-goal overlap or concord versus unfavorable-goal conflict and competition). An unfavorable relationship between goals poses the danger that they will fail or be altered, postponed, or abandoned. In a situation of goal conflict, the planner may have to decide which goal has priority: In a situation of competition, the problem is to determine the opponent's strategy and work on a counterplan (e.g., antiplan).

Wilensky suggested four general metaprinciples for resolving conflicts and setting priorities: Don't waste resources, achieve as many goals as possible, maximize the value of the goals achieved, and avoid impossible goals.

Janis and Mann (1977) considered the consequences of conflict in relation to the areas of action and interaction management. According to their model, conflict engenders feelings of stress, uncertainty, and tension that might either hinder or facilitate the quality of vigilant decision making and the nature of planning processes. So, for instance, individuals may respond with inertia, change to a new course of action (escape), defensively avoid action, become hypervigilant (initiate panic-driven reactions), or respond with adaptive vigilance.

Outlook: new methods and new questions

Although this chapter has focused on advancing a social-interactive approach to studying life planning across the life span, this does not necessarily mean that a socially oriented perspective is better than individual-oriented approaches. Rather, the purpose has been simply to suggest that a mirroring from one to the other can open new images, as well as point to new questions and new methods of data collection and analyses. It may not always be possible, or even sensible, to adopt a social-interactive approach. Some aspects of life need an individual to be the planner, and they remain the private domain of the individual; others call for a social-interactive planning approach and may fail, or be considered ineffective, if individuals try to act as if they were alone.

A catalogue of questions. Throughout this chapter, sets of questions were posed to illustrate various aspects of a social-interactive perspective on life planning. Table 9.3 summarizes some of these questions together with some of the proposed methods that were discussed.

Central questions relate to the social content (e.g., inclusion/recognition of others in plans) and the social-interactive context of both planners (e.g., expectations about making plans with and for others) and planning activities (e.g., social interaction strategies involved in evolving, negotiating, implementing, and coordinating individual and group plans). Some of these questions require methods centered on individual knowledge and perceptions; others focus on observations of planning in pairs and groups. When integrated with a life-span approach, it becomes clear that there are many questions in the area of life planning that are still to be investigated.

Planning a life is an aspect of cognition that is socialized, updated, applied, and challenged throughout the life span. From childhood, we are socialized to plan for our future life – to develop personal goals and decide on how to achieve them, to develop scenarios about what we want to do and be. Many

Table 9.3. *Some examples of a social-interactive approach to life planning: questions and methods*

Question	Example of method[a]
Personal goals: How often do individuals set goals with others in mind (directly or indirectly)?	Analysis of life planning and goal description narratives for mention of others
	Probes to determine whether significant others are actually involved in goal setting or are specifically considered when goals are selected
	Comparison of partners'/individual group members' descriptions of goals and explanations of goal-setting procedures
When are joint planning ventures appropriate?	Prototype study of situations, age groups, and relationship types in which collaborative planning is considered appropriate, helpful, necessary, etc.
What are the dynamics of interpersonal relationships in the evolution of a plan? Do these dynamics facilitate or hinder life planning?	Microlongitudinal analysis of perceptions of, e.g., plan "ownership," planning leadership, resolution of partner goal conflicts

[a] Others in text.

social institutions are built on the idea of life planning – for example, investing in the future, saving for the future, ensuring security, and structuring points where life-planning decisions have to be made. Some individuals and groups appear to be more successful than others in using planning strategies to reduce uncertainty, motivate activity, and/or enhance personal well-being.

What lies behind variations in using planning strategies? Are there critical inputs and constraints to the development of expertise in this domain? Or are differences in planning outcomes more a function of effective versus ineffective social interactions? Not all pairs and groups are characterized by mutual understanding, cooperation, and coordination. Individuals in a group may act in parallel rather than together, or may focus on blocking the efforts of others rather than facilitating them.

Effective planning together may require not only shared knowledge but also a shared sense of responsibility for the time, effort, and investment in planning activities (Schlenker, Britt, Pennington, Murphy, & Doherty, 1994) and a shared sense of accountability for the outcome (Tetlock, 1983, 1992). These two dimensions (responsibility and accountability) may, in the end, be the deciding factors in determining whether people enter into joint planning ventures or act alone. Indeed, even on an individual level, these dimensions may also play a role in an individual's decision to take life as it comes or to engage in processes of active anticipation and develop a life plan.

References

Adams, C. C., & Rebok, G. W. (1982–1983). Planfulness and problem-solving in older adults. *International Journal of Behavioral Development, 16*, 271–282.

Aldag, R. J., & Fuller, S. R. (1993). Beyond fiasco: A reappraisal of the groupthink phenomenon and a new model of group decision processes. *Psychological Bulletin, 113*, 533–552.

Allport, G. W., Vernon, P. E., & Lindzey, G. (1960). *Study of values: Manual for a scale for measuring the dominant interests in personality*. Boston: Houghton Mifflin.

Alterman, R. (1988). Adaptive planning. *Cognitive Science, 12*, 393–421.

Baltes, M. M., & Silverberg, S. B. (1994). The dynamics between dependency and autonomy: Illustrations across the life span. In D. L. Featherman, R. M. Lerner, & M. Perlmutter (Eds.), *Life-span developmental behavior* (Vol.12, pp. 42–91). Hillsdale, NJ: Erlbaum.

Baltes, P. B. (1987). Theoretical propositions of life-span developmental psychology: On the dynamics between growth and decline. *Developmental Psychology, 23*, 611–626.

Baltes, P. B. (1991). The many faces of human aging: Toward a psychological culture of old age. *Psychological Medicine, 21*, 837–854.

Baltes, P. B., & Smith, J. (1990). Toward a psychology of wisdom and its ontogenesis. In R. J. Sternberg (Ed.), *Wisdom: Its nature, origins, and development* (pp. 87–120). New York: Cambridge University Press.

Baltes, P. B., Smith, J., & Staudinger, U. M. (1992). Wisdom and successful aging. In T. B. Sonderegger (Ed.), *Nebraska Symposium on Motivation: Vol. 39. Psychology and aging* (pp. 123–167). Lincoln: University of Nebraska Press.

Baron, J. (1985). *Rationality and intelligence*. Cambridge: Cambridge University Press.

Berger, C. E. (1988). Planning, affect, and social action generation. In L. Donohew, H. E. Sypher, & E. T. Higgins (Eds.), *Communications, social cognition, and affect* (pp. 93–116). Hillsdale, NJ: Erlbaum.

Berger, C. E. (1993). Goals, plans, and mutual understanding in relationships. In S. Duck (Ed.), *Individuals in relationships*. Newbury Park, CA: Sage.

Berger, P. L., Berger, B., & Kellner, H. (1967). *The homeless mind: Modernization and unconsciousness*. New York: Random Press.

Berscheid, E. (1985). Compatibility, interdependence, and emotion. In W. Ickes (Ed.), *Compatible and incompatible relationships*. New York: Springer.

Beutler, L. E., & Bergan, J. (1991). Value change in counseling and psychotherapy: A search for scientific credibility. *Journal of Counseling Psychology, 38*, 16–24.

Birren, J. F. (1980). Age and decision strategies. In A. T. Welford & J. E. Birren (Eds.), *Decision making and age* (pp. 23–26). New York: Arno.

Bradbury, T. N., & Fincham, F. D. (1991). A contextual model for advancing the study of marital interaction. In G. J. O. Fletcher & F. D. Fincham (Eds.), *Cognition in close relationships* (pp. 127–150). Hillsdale, NJ: Erlbaum.

Braithwaite, V. A., & Scott, W. A. (1991). Values. In J. P. Robinson, P. R. Shaver, & L. S. Wrightsman (Eds.), *Measures of personality and social psychological attitudes* (Vol. 1, pp. 661–753). New York: Academic.

Brandtstädter, J. (1993). Development, aging and control: Empirical and theoretical issues. In D. Magnusson & P. Casaer (Eds.), *Longitudinal research on individual development: Present status and future perspective* (pp. 194–216). Cambridge: Cambridge University Press.

Brandtstädter, J., Baltes-Götz, B., & Heil, F. E. (1990). Entwicklung in Partnerschaften: Analysen zur Partnerschaftsqualität bei Ehepaaren im mittleren Erwachsenenalter [Development of marital relations: Analyses of the quality of the relationship between middle-aged couples]. *Zeitschrift für Entwicklungspsychologie und Pädagogische Psychologie, 22,* 183–206.

Brandtstädter, J., & Greve, W. (1994). The aging self: Stabilizing and protective processes. *Developmental Review, 14,* 52–80.

Brandtstädter, J., & Renner, G. (1990). Tenacious goal pursuit and flexible goal adjustment: Explication and age-related analysis of assimilative and accommodative strategies of coping. *Psychology and Aging, 5*(1), 58–67.

Brandtstädter, J., Renner, G., & Baltes-Götz, B. (1989). Entwicklung von Wertorientierungen im Erwachsenenalter: Quersequentielle Analysen [Development of value orientations in adulthood]. *Zeitschrift für Entwicklungspsychologie und Pädagogische Psychologie, 21,* 3–23.

Brandtstädter, J., & Wentura, D. (1994). Veränderungen der Zeit- und Zukunftsperspektive im Übergang zum höheren Erwachsenenalter: entwicklungspsychologische und differentielle Aspeckte [Changes in time perspectives and attitudes toward the future during the transition to later adulthood: Developmental and differential aspects]. *Zeitschrift für Entwicklungspsychologie und Pädagogische Psychologie, 26,* 2–21.

Brandtstädter, J., Wentura, D., & Greve, W. (1993). Adaptive resources of the aging self: Outlines of an emergent perspective. *International Journal of Behavioral Development, 16,* 323–349.

Brim, O. G. (1992). *Ambition: How we manage success and failure throughout our lives.* New York: Basic.

Bromley, D. B. (1969). Studies of intellectual function in relation to age and their significance for professional and managerial functions. *Interdisciplinary Topics of Gerontology, 4,* 103–126.

Brown, A., & DeLoache, J. (1978). Skills, plans, and self-regulation. In R. Siegler (Ed.), *Children's thinking: What develops?* (pp. 3–35). Hillsdale, NJ: Erlbaum.

Bruce, B., & Newman, D. (1978). Interacting plans. *Cognitive Science, 2,* 195–233.

Bühler, C. (1968). The developmental structure of goal setting in group and individual studies. In C. Bühler & F. Massarik (Eds.), *The course of human life: A study of goals in the humanistic perspective* (pp. 27—53). New York: Springer.

Byrne, R. (1977). Planning meals: Problem-solving on a real data-base. *Cognition, 5,* 287–332.

Cantor, N., & Fleeson, W. (1994). Social intelligence and intelligent goal pursuit: A cognitive slice of motivation. In W. D. Spaulding (Ed.), *Nebraska Symposium on Motivation: Vol. 41. Integrative views of motivation, cognition, and emotion* (pp. 125–179). Lincoln: University of Nebraska Press.

Cantor, N., & Kihlstrom, J. F. (1987). *Personality and social intelligence.* Englewood Cliffs, NJ: Prentice-Hall.

Cantor, N., & Kihlstrom, J. F. (1989). Social intelligence and cognitive assessments of personality. In R. S. Wyer & T. K. Srull (Eds.), *Advances in social cognition* (Vol. 2, pp. 1–59). Hillsdale, NJ: Erlbaum.

Cantor, N., Norem, J. K., Niedenthal, P. M., Langston, C. A., & Brower, A. M. (1987). Life tasks, self-concept ideals, and cognitive strategies in a life transition. *Journal of Personality and Social Psychology, 53*(6), 1178–1191.

Cantor, N., & Zirkel, S. (1990). Personality, cognition, and purposive behavior. In L. A. Pervin (Ed.), *Handbook of personality: Theory and research* (pp. 135–164). New York: Guilford.

Carstensen, L. L. (1992). Social and emotional patterns in adulthood: Support for socioeconomic selectivity theory. *Psychology and Aging, 7,* 331–338.

Carstensen, L. L. (1993). Motivation for social contact across the life span: A theory of socioemotional selectivity. In J. E. Jacobs (Ed.), *Nebraska Symposium on Motivation: Vol. 40. Developmental perspectives on motivation* (pp. 209–254). Lincoln: University of Nebraska Press.

Chalmers, D., & Lawrence, J. A. (1993). Investigating the effects of planning aids on adults' and adolescents' organization of a complex task. *International Journal of Behavioral Development, 16,* 191–214.

Denney, D. R., & Denney, N. W. (1973). The use of classification for problem solving: A comparison of middle and old age. *Developmental Psychology, 9,* 275–278.

Derr, C. B. (Ed.). (1980). *Work, family, and the career: New frontiers in theory and research.* New York: Praeger.

Dowie, J., & Elstein, A. (Eds.). (1988). *Professional judgement: A reader in clinical decision making.* Cambridge: Cambridge University Press.

Dreher, M., & Oerter, R. (1987). Action planning competencies during adolescence and early adulthood. In S. L. Friedman, E. K. Scholnick, & R. R. Cocking (Eds.), *Blueprints for thinking: The role of planning in cognitive development* (pp. 321–355). Cambridge: Cambridge University Press.

Duck, S. (Ed.). (1993). *Individuals in relationships.* Newbury Park, CA: Sage.

Duck, S., & Pond, K. (1989). Friends, romans, countryman, lend me your retrospective data: Rhetoric and reality in personal relationships. In C. Hendrick (Ed.), *Review of personality and social psychology: Vol. 10. Close relationships* (pp. 17–38). Newbury Park, CA: Sage.

Emmons, R. A. (1989). The personal striving approach to personality. In L. A. Pervin (Ed.), *Goal concepts in personality and social psychology* (pp. 87–126). Hillsdale, NJ: Erlbaum.

Emmons, R. A., & King, L. A. (1988). Conflict among personal strivings: Immediate and long-term implications for psychological and physical well-being. *Journal of Personality and Social Psychology, 54*(6), 1040–1048.

Engeström, Y. (1992). *Interactive expertise: Studies in distributed working intelligence.* Research Bulletin 83, University of Helsinki.

Erikson, E. H. (1959). *Identity and the life cycle.* New York: International Universities Press.

Evans, G., & Poole, M. (1991). *Young adults: Self-perceptions and life contexts.* London: Falmer.

Featherman, D. L., Smith, J., & Peterson, J. G. (1990). Successful aging in a post-retired society. In P. B. Baltes & M. M. Baltes (Eds.), *Successful aging: Perspectives from the behavioral sciences* (pp. 50–93). Cambridge: Cambridge University Press.

Flavell, J. H., & Ross, L. (1981). *Social cognitive development: Frontiers and possible futures.* Cambridge: Cambridge University Press.

Ford, M. E., & Nichols, C. W. (1987). A taxonomy of human goals and some possible applications. In M. E. Ford & D. H. Ford (Eds.), *Humans as self-constructing living systems: Putting the framework to work* (pp. 289–311). Hillsdale, NJ: Erlbaum.

Frese, M., & Sabini, J. (Eds.). (1985). *Goal-directed behavior: The concept of action in psychology.* Hillsdale, NJ: Erlbaum.

Frese, M., Stewart, J., & Hannover, B. (1987). Goal orientation and planfulness: Action styles as personality concepts. *Journal of Personality and Social Psychology, 52*(6), 1182–1194.

Friedman, S. L., Scholnick, E. K., & Cocking, R. R. (Eds.). (1987). *Blueprints for thinking.* New York: Cambridge University Press.

Galegher, J., Kraut, R. E., & Egido, C. (Eds.). (1990). *Intellectual teamwork: Social and technological foundations of cooperative work* (pp. 23–61). Hillsdale, NJ: Erlbaum.

Gardner, W., & Rogoff, B. (1990). Children's deliberateness of planning according to task circumstances. *Developmental Psychology, 26,* 480–487.

Gauvain, M. (1992). Social influences on the development of planning in advance and during action. *International Journal of Behavioral Development, 15*(3), 377–398.

Gauvain, M, & Rogoff, B. (1989). Collaborative problem solving and children's planning skills. *Developmental Psychology, 25,* 139–151.

Gollwitzer, P. M. (1990). Action phases and mind-sets. In E. T. Higgins & R. M. Sorrentino (Eds.), *Handbook of motivation and cognition: Foundations of social behavior* (Vol. 2, pp. 53–92). New York: Guilford.

Goodnow, J. J. (1987). Social aspects of planning. In S. L. Friedman, E. K. Scholnick, & R. R. Cocking (Eds.), *Blueprints for thinking: The role of planning in cognitive development* (pp. 179–201). Cambridge: Cambridge University Press.

Goodnow, J. J., & Collins, W. A. (1990). *Development according to parents: The nature, sources, and consequences of parents' ideas.* Hillsdale, NJ: Erlbaum.

Hagestad, G. O., & Neugarten, B. L. (1985). Age and the life course. In R. Binstock & L. George (Eds.), *Handbook of aging and the social sciences* (pp. 35–61). New York: Van Nostrand Reinhold.

Hammond, K. (1989). *Case-based planning: Viewing planning as a memory task*. Boston: Academic.

Havighurst, R. J. (1961). *Developmental tasks and education*. New York: McKay.

Hayes-Roth, B., & Hayes-Roth, F. (1979). A cognitive model of planning. *Cognitive Science, 3*, 275–310.

Heckhausen, J., Dixon, R. A., & Baltes, P. B. (1989). Gains and losses in development throughout adulthood as perceived by different adult age groups. *Developmental Psychology, 255*(1), 109–124.

Heckhausen, J., & Schulz, R. (1993). Optimization by selection and compensation: Balancing primary and secondary control in life-span development. *International Journal of Behavioral Development, 16*, 287–303.

Heckhausen, J., & Schulz, R. (1995). A life-span theory of control. *Psychological Review, 102*, 284–304.

Hickson, D. J. (1987). Decision-making at the top of organizations. *Annual Review of Sociology, 13*, 165–192.

Hudson, J. A., & Fivush, R. (1991). Planning in the preschool years: The emergence of plans from general event knowledge. *Cognitive Development, 6*, 393–415.

Ickes, W. J. (Ed.). (1985). *Compatible and incompatible relationships*. New York: Springer.

Janis, I. L., & Mann, L. (1977). *Decision making: Psychological analysis of conflict, choice and commitment*. New York: Free Press.

Johnson, M. K., & Sherman, S. J. (1990). Constructing and reconstructing the past and the future in the present. In E. T. Higgins & R. M. Sorrentino (Eds.), *Handbook of motivation and cognition: Foundations of social behavior* (Vol. 2, pp. 482–526). New York: Guilford.

Kelley, H. H., Berscheid, E., Christensen, A., Harvey, J. H., Huston, T. L., Levinger, G., McClintock, E., Peplau, L. A., & Peterson, D. R. (Eds.). (1983). *Close relationships*. New York: Freeman.

Klinger, E. (1977). *Meaning and void: Inner experience and the incentives in peoples' lives*. Minneapolis: University of Minnesota Press.

Klinger, E., Barta, S. G., & Maxeiner, M. E. (1980). Motivational correlates of thought content frequency and commitment. *Journal of Personality and Social Psychology, 39*(6), 1222–1237.

Kram, K. E. (1985). Phases of the mentor relationship. *Academy of Management Journal, 26*, 608–625.

Kram, K. E., & Isabella, L. A. (1985). Mentoring alternatives: The role of peer relationships in career development. *Academy of Management Journal, 28*, 110–132.

Kreitler, S., & Kreitler, H. (1987). Conceptions and processes of planning: The developmental perspective. In S. L. Friedman, E. K. Scholnick, & R. R. Cocking (Eds.), *Blueprints for thinking: The role of planning in cognitive development* (pp. 205–272). Cambridge: Cambridge University Press.

Kuhlen, R. G. (1959). Aging and life adjustment. In J. E. Birren (Ed.), *Handbook of aging and the individual: Psychological and biological aspects* (pp. 852–897). Chicago: Chicago University Press

Lachman, M. E., & Burack, O. R. (1993). Planning and control processes across the life span: An overview. *International Journal of Behavioral Development, 16*, 131–143.

Larson, J. R., & Christensen, C. (1993). Groups as problem-solving units: Toward a new meaning of social cognition. *British Journal of Social Psychology, 32*, 5–30.

Levine, J. M., & Moreland, R. L. (1991). Culture and socialization in work groups. In L. B. Resnick, J. M. Levine, & S. D. Teasley (Eds.), *Perspectives on socially shared cognition* (pp. 257–282). Washington, DC: American Psychological Association.

Levine, J. M., Resnick, L. B., & Higgins, E. T. (1993). Social foundations of cognition. *Annual Review of Psychology, 44*, 585–612.

LeVine, R. A. (1988). Human parental care: Universal goals, cultural strategies, individual behavior. In R. A. LeVine, P. M. Miller, & M. M. West (Eds.), *Parental behavior in diverse societies* (pp. 1–12). San Francisco: Jossey-Bass.

Levinson, D. J. (1978). *The seasons of a man's life*. New York: Knopf.

Little, B. R. (1983). Personal projects: A rationale and methods for investigation. *Environmental Behavior*, *15*, 273–309.

Locke, E. A. & Latham, G. (1984). *Goal setting for individuals, groups, and organizations.* Chicago: Research Associates.

Markus, H., & Cross, S. (1990). The interpersonal self. In L. A. Pervin (Ed.), *Handbook of personality: Theory and research* (pp. 576–608). New York: Guilford.

Markus, H., & Ruvolo, A. (1989). Possible selves: Personalized representations of goals. In L. A. Pervin (Ed.), *Goal concepts in personality and social psychology* (pp. 211–241). Hillsdale, NJ: Erlbaum.

Markus, H. R., & Nurius, P. (1986). Possible selves. *American Psychologist*, *41*, 954–969.

McAdams, D. P. (1985). The "Imago": A key narrative component of identity. In P. Shaver (Ed.), *Self, situations, and social behavior: Review of personality and social psychology* (Vol. 6, pp. 115–142). Beverley Hills, CA: Sage.

Maslow, A. (1943). A theory of human motivation. *Psychological Review*, *50*, 370–396.

Menaghan, E. G. (1991). Work experiences and family interaction processes: The long reach of the job. *Annual Review of Sociology*, *17*, 419–444.

Mintzberg, H. (1994). *The rise and fall of strategic planning: Reconceiving roles for planning, plans, and planners*. New York: Free Press.

Mischel, H. N., & Patterson, C. J. (1978). Effective plans for self-control in children. In W. A. Collins (Ed.), *Minnesota Symposium on Child Psychology* (Vol. 11, pp. 199–230). Hillsdale, NJ: Erlbaum.

Morris, C. (1956). *Varieties of human value*. Chicago: Chicago University Press.

Newell, A., & Simon, H. A. (1972). *Human problem solving*. Englewood Cliffs, NJ: Prentice-Hall.

Nurmi, J. E. (1989). Planning, motivation, and evaluation in orientation to the future: A latent structure analysis. *Scandinavian Journal of Psychology*, *30*, 64–71.

Nurmi, J. E. (1991). How do adolescents see their future? A review of the development of future orientation and planning. *Developmental Review*, *11*, 1–59.

Nurmi, J. E. (1993). Adolescent development in an age-graded context: The role of personal beliefs, goals, and strategies in the tackling of developmental tasks and standards. *International Journal of Behavioral Development*, *16*, 169–189.

Nurmi, J. E. Pulliainen, H., & Salmela-Aro, K. (1992). Age differences in adults' control beliefs related to life goals and concerns. *Psychology and Aging*, *7*(2), 194–196.

Palys, T. S., & Little, B. R. (1983). Perceived life satisfaction and the organization of personal project systems. *Journal of Personality and Social Psychology*, *44*(6), 1221–1230.

Pervin, L. A. (Ed.). (1989a). *Goal concepts in personality and social psychology*. Hillsdale, NJ: Erlbaum.

Pervin, L. A. (1989b). Goal concepts in personality and social psychology: A historical introduction. In L. A. Pervin (Ed.), *Goal concepts in personality and social psychology* (pp. 1–17). Hillsdale, NJ: Erlbaum.

Phillips-Jones, L. (1982). *Mentors and protégés*. New York: Arbor House.

Pulkkinen, L. (1982). Self-control and continuity from childhood to late adolescence. In P. B. Baltes & O. G. Brim, Jr. (Eds.), *Life-span development & behavior* (Vol. 4, pp. 63–105). Hillsdale, NJ: Erlbaum.

Radowski, W. (1979). Future time perspective in later adulthood: Review and research directions. *Experimental Aging Research*, *5*, 43–88.

Radziszewska, B., & Rogoff, B. (1988). Influence of adult and peer collaborators on children's planning skills. *Developmental Psychology*, *24*, 840–848.

Radziszewska, B., & Rogoff, B. (1991). Children's guided participation in planning imaginary errands with skilled adult or peer partners. *Developmental Psychology*, *27*, 381–389.

Rapkin, B. D., & Fischer, K. (1992a). Personal goals of older adults: Issues in assessment and prediction. *Psychology and Aging*, *7*(1), 127–137.

Rapkin, B. D., & Fischer, K. (1992b). Framing the concept of life satisfaction in terms of older adults' personal goals. *Psychology and Aging*, *7*(1), 138–149.

Rawls, J. (1971). *A theory of justice*. Cambridge: Cambridge University Press.

Raynor, J. O., & Entin, E. E. (1982). *Motivation, career striving, and aging*. London: Hemisphere.

Read, S. J., & Miller, L. C. (1989). Inter-personalism: Toward a goal-based theory of persons in relationships. In L. A. Pervin (Ed.), *Goal concepts in personality and social psychology* (pp. 413–472). Hillsdale, NJ: Erlbaum.

Rebok, G. W. (1989). Plans, actions, and transactions in solving everyday problems. In J. D. Sinnott (Ed.), *Everyday problem-solving* (pp. 100–122). New York: Praeger.

Resnick, L. B., Levine, J. M., & Teasley, S. D. (Eds.). (1991). *Perspectives on socially shared cognition*. Washington, DC: American Psychological Association.

Riesbeck, C. K., & Schank, R. C. (1989). *Inside case-based reasoning*. Hillsdale, NJ: Erlbaum.

Rogoff, B. (1991). Social interaction as apprenticeship in thinking: Guided participation in spatial planning. In L. B. Resnick, J. M. Levine, & S. D. Teasley (Eds.), *Perspectives on socially shared cognition* (pp, 349–364). Washington, DC: American Psychological Association.

Rokeach, M. (1968). *Beliefs, attitudes, and values: A theory of organization and change*. San Francisco: Jossey-Bass.

Russell, G. (1983). *The changing role of fathers*. St. Lucia, QLD: Queensland University Press.

Russell, G., & Smith, J. (1979). "Girls can be doctors can't they?": Sex differences in career aspirations. *Australian Journal of Social Issues, 14*, 91–102.

Schank, R., & Abelson, R. (1977). *Scripts, plans, goals, and understanding*. Hillsdale, NJ: Erlbaum.

Schegloff, E. A. (1991). Conversation analysis and socially shared cognition. In L. B. Resnick, J. M. Levine, & S. D. Teasley (Eds.), *Perspectives on socially shared cognition* (pp. 150–171). Washington, DC: American Psychological Association.

Schlenker, B. R., Britt, T. W., Pennington, J., Murphy, R., & Doherty, K. (1994). The triangle model of responsibility. *Psychological Review, 101*(4), 632–652.

Scholnick, E. K., & Friedman, S. L. (1987). The planning construct in the psychological literature. In S. L. Friedman, E. K. Scholnick, & R. R. Cocking (Eds.), *Blueprints for thinking: The role of planning in cognitive development* (pp. 3–38). Cambridge: Cambridge University Press.

Scholnick, E. K., & Friedman, S. L. (1993). Planning in context: Development and situational considerations. *International Journal of Behavioral Development, 16*, 143–167.

Smelser, N. J., & Erikson, E. H. (1980). *Themes of work and love in adulthood*. Cambridge: Cambridge University Press.

Smith, J. (in press). Perspectives on planning a life. In S. Friedman & M. K. Scholnick (Eds.), *Why, how and when do we plan? The developmental psychology of planning*. Hillsdale, NJ: Erlbaum.

Smith, J., & Baltes, P. B. (1990a). A life-span perspective on thinking and problem-solving. In M. Schwebel, C. A. Maher, & N. S. Fagley (Eds.), *Promoting cognitive growth over the life span* (pp. 47–70). Hillsdale, NJ: Erlbaum.

Smith, J., & Baltes, P. B. (1990b). Wisdom-related knowledge: Age/cohort differences in response to life-planning problems. *Developmental Psychology, 26*(3), 494–505.

Smith, J., Dixon, R. A., & Baltes, P. B. (1989). Expertise in life-planning: A new research approach to investigating aspects of wisdom. In M. L. Commons, J. D. Sinnott, F. A. Richards, & C. Armon (Eds.), *Adult development: Vol. 1. Comparisons and applications of developmental models* (pp, 307–331). New York: Praeger.

Smith, J., & Russell, G. (1984). Children's beliefs and sex differences. *Sex Roles, 11*, 1111–1115.

Smith, J., Staudinger, U. M., & Baltes, P. B. (1994). Occupational settings facilitating wisdom-related knowledge: The sample case of clinical psychologists. *Journal of Clinical and Counseling Psychology, 62*, 989–999.

Srull, T. K., & Wyer, R. S. (1986). The role of chronic and temporary goals in social information processing. In R. M. Sorrentino & E. T. Higgins (Eds.), *Handbook of motivation and cognition: Foundations of social behavior* (pp. 503–549). New York: Wiley.

Stein, N. L. (1988). The development of children's storytelling skill. In M. B. Franklin & S. Barten (Eds.), *Child language: A reader*. (pp. 282–297). New York: Oxford University Press.

Suchman, L. A. (1987). *Plans and situated actions: The problem of human–machine communication*. Cambridge: Cambridge University Press.

Tetlock, P. E. (1983). Accountability and complexity of thought. *Journal of Personality and Social Psychology, 45*, 74–83.

Tetlock, P. E. (1992). The impact of accountability on judgment and choice: Toward a social contingency model. In M. P. Zanna (Ed.), *Advances in experimental social psychology* (Vol. 25, pp. 331–376). San Diego: Academic.

Trabasso, T., Stein, N., Rodkin, P. C., Munger, M. P., & Baughn, C. R. (1992). Knowledge of goals and plans in the on-line narration of events. *Cognitive Development, 7*, 133-170.

Troll, L. E. (1994). Family connectedness of older women: Attachments in later life. In B. E. Turner & L. E. Troll (Eds.), *Women growing older: Psychological perspectives.* (pp. 169–201). Thousand Oaks, CA: Sage.

Tuckett, D., Boulton, M., Olson, C., & Williams, A. (1985). *Meetings between experts: An approach to sharing ideas in medical consultations.* London: Tavistock.

Turnbull, C. (1985). *The human cycle.* London: Triad/Paladin.

Wadsworth, M., & Ford, D. H. (1983). Assessment of personal goal hierarchies. *Journal of Counseling Psychology, 30*, 514–526.

Wilensky, R. (1983). *Planning and understanding.* Reading, MA: Addison-Wesley.

10 Wisdom and the social-interactive foundation of the mind

Ursula M. Staudinger

Abstract

This chapter examines the social-interactive nature of wisdom, which is defined by the importance of social interaction for (a) its cultural evolution as well as its ontogeny, (b) its activation and application, and (c) its identification and orientation. Earlier work within the Berlin wisdom paradigm has, to a certain degree, acknowledged the social-interactive nature of wisdom with regard to its ontogenesis and its identification. When it comes to the application and activation of wisdom, however, people have been studied using a traditional person-centered paradigm. Given the social-interactive nature of wisdom, this approach cannot be considered an optimal performance setting. On the basis of the extremely high demands that the elicitation of wisdom puts on knowledge and skill, one might even argue that wisdom by definition will hardly ever be found in an individual, but rather in cultural or social-interactive products. Drawing on research in the area of everyday problem solving and professional expertise, as well as the social psychology of group problem solving, a social-interactive wisdom paradigm was developed that gives credit to both individual and interactive cognition in their respective contributions to the activation of wisdom-related knowledge. The results of a first empirical study carried out within that paradigm indicated that indeed a delicate balance between individual and interactive cognition seems to characterize supportive wisdom-related performance settings.

Since the dawn of human culture, wisdom has been described as the ideal of human knowledge about life – an ideal always striven for but hardly ever

This chapter has developed, and some of the research reported here has been collected, as part of a larger research project, "Wisdom and Life-Span Development," conducted at the Max Planck Institute for Human Development and Education, jointly directed by Paul B. Baltes and Ursula M. Staudinger.

I would like to thank Petra Badke-Schaub, Paul B. Baltes, Cynthia Berg, Roger Dixon, David E. Lopez, Michael M. Marsiske, Fritz Oser, and an anonymous reviewer for very helpful comments on earlier versions of the chapter. In addition, I acknowledge the many valuable exchanges with colleagues from the Max Planck Institute for Human Development and Education, and the participants of the MPI conference "Interactive Minds." Last but not least, I thank Susanne Böhmig, Simone Elsing, Kerstin Haenel, Irmgard Pahl, and Xenia Peschel for their assistance in data collection and data organization.

276

reached by a single person. This chapter explores what social interaction may contribute and actually does contribute to the development, activation, and identification of wisdom. An imaginary conversation may serve to introduce the discussion. One person says, "I often wonder what life is all about." Another responds, "I always say two heads are better than one to figure it out."

Intuitively, one has a tendency to agree with the latter remark. In this chapter, it will be argued, however, that this statement is in need of differentiation. It is necessary to define what exactly *social-interactive* means, how it can be implemented and assessed, and under which conditions it is advantageous or detrimental to the manifestation (development, activation, identification) of wisdom-related knowledge and judgment.

The argument is presented in two parts. In the first part, a theoretical definition of wisdom and its social-interactive nature is offered. The second part centers on the role of social interaction with regard to the activation of wisdom-related knowledge in a given situation (microgenesis). Based on evidence reviewed in various areas of expertise research and in social-psychological research on group problem solving, a social-interactive paradigm for the measurement of wisdom-related performance is developed. Finally, first empirical evidence collected within this paradigm is reported.

The social-interactive nature of wisdom: toward a definition

In the following, three different approaches to the definition of wisdom are used to investigate the social-interactive nature of wisdom: (a) dictionary definitions, (b) implicit or lay theories of wisdom, and (c) an explicit theory of wisdom.

The reflection of the social-interactive nature of wisdom in dictionary definitions

No comprehensive review of dictionary definitions of wisdom is intended; these are available in the literature (for extensive reviews, see, e.g., Baltes, 1994a,b; Rudolph, 1987). Rather, available definitions are specifically analyzed with regard to indications of the social-interactive nature of wisdom.

The major German historical dictionary (Grimm & Grimm, 1854/1984), for instance, defines wisdom as "insight and knowledge about oneself and the world . . . and sound judgment in the case of difficult life problems." Similarly, the *Oxford Dictionary* includes in its definition of wisdom, "good judgment and advice in difficult and uncertain matters of life."

Both dictionary definitions support the notion of wisdom as an abstract entity that can find different manifestations. The *Oxford Dictionary* definition, for example, is "the quality or character of being wise *or* something in which this is exhibited" (*Oxford Dictionary of the English Language*, 1933, p. 191; emphasis added). In other words, wisdom may be exhibited by individuals, but this is not the only means of expression. Second, the definition of wisdom as the capacity to judge reflects the communicative, social-interactive aspect of wisdom. Finally, support for the social-interactive nature of wisdom is obtained in definitions with regard to its educational function in society.

The social-interactive nature of wisdom as reflected in implicit theories of wisdom

The communicative aspect of wisdom is emphasized even more strongly when we consider results from the research on people's subjective beliefs or implicit theories of wisdom. Table 10.1 compares the results of three major studies on implicit theories of wisdom. For example, one of the three dimensions that Clayton identified in a multidimensional scaling study of people's definitions of a wise person is directly related to the social-interactive nature of wisdom. She referred to this dimension as the *affective component of wisdom*, which captures adjectives such as *empathic* or *compassionate* (Clayton, 1976; Clayton & Birren, 1980). The other two dimensions, labeled *reflective* and *cognitive*, are more but not exclusively person-centered. For example, what she labeled the *cognitive dimension* includes characteristics such as exposure to experiential contexts that usually comprise interaction with other people.

Considering the results of Sternberg's (1985) study of implicit theories of wisdom also reveals that the social-interactive nature of wisdom is part of people's beliefs about wisdom. In his study, Sternberg (1985) identified six components (see Table 10.1): reasoning ability, sagacity, learning from ideas and the environment, judgment, expeditious use of information, and perspicacity. The components explicitly related to the social-interactive nature of wisdom are sagacity, perspicacity, and learning from ideas and the environment. They are defined by features such as the wise person showing concern for others or considering advice (sagacity), offering right and true solutions (perspicacity), and perceptive learning from mistakes (learning from ideas and the environment). The value of prior experience is also reflected in the component called expeditious use of information. Only two of the six components have an emphasis on the individual (reasoning ability, judgment).

In their studies of implicit theories of wisdom, Holliday and Chandler (1986) identified five factors: interpersonal skills, judgment and communicative skills, social unobtrusiveness, exceptional understanding, and general competence. Only general competence has an emphasis on the isolated individual. The other four are all related to the social-interactive nature of wisdom. The factor

Table 10.1. *Implicit theories of wisdom: a comparison of findings from three studies with sample items*

Clayton (1976)	Sternberg (1985)	Holliday and Chandler (1986)
Affective (1)	Sagacity (2)	Interpersonal skills (4)
Empathy	Concern for others	Sensitive
Compassion	Considers advice	Sociable˙
	Perspicacity (6)	Judgment and communication
	Intuition	skills (2)
	Offers right and	Is a good source of advice
	true solutions	Understands life
Reflective (2)	Judgment (4)	Social unobtrusiveness (5)
Intuition	Acts within own limitations	Discrete
Introspection	Is sensible	Nonjudgmental
	Learning from ideas and	Exceptional understanding as an
	environment (3)	ordinary experience (1)
	Perceptive	Has learned from experience
	Learns from mistakes	Sees things in a larger context
Cognitive (3)	Reasoning ability (1)	General competence (3)
Experience	Good problem-solving	Intelligent
Intelligence	ability	Educated
	Logical mind	
	Expeditious use of	
	information (5)	
	Experienced	
	Seeks out information	

Note: Sequence of factors or dimensions obtained in original research is given in parentheses. Studies are based on different methodologies (factor analysis, multi-dimensional scaling).
Source: After Staudinger & Baltes (1994).

called interpersonal skill, for example, is described by items like sensitive and sociable and the factor named judgment and communicative skill is characterized by items such as being a good source of advice.

Using a different data source, Baltes (1994a,b) deduced six characteristics of wisdom from his analysis of the cultural-historical wisdom literature: Wisdom (a) deals with important and/or difficult matters of life and the human condition; (b) is truly superior knowledge, judgment, and advice; (c) is knowledge with extraordinary scope, depth, and balance applicable to specific situations; (d) is used for one's own good or the good of others; (e) combines mind and character, and (f) is very difficult to achieve but more easily recognized. In sum, people's subjective beliefs about wisdom across both historical times and cultures reflect even more strongly than dictionary definitions the importance of social interaction for the development, activation, and intended consequence of wisdom.

The Berlin wisdom paradigm

Before attempting to define the social-interactive nature of wisdom, I will present a third approach to the definition of wisdom. It is an explicit theory of wisdom developed within the Berlin wisdom paradigm over the past 10 years (Baltes, Dittmann-Kohli, & Dixon, 1984; Baltes & Smith, 1990; Baltes, Smith, & Staudinger, 1992; Baltes & Staudinger, 1993; Dittmann-Kohli & Baltes, 1990). Applying an expertise paradigm, which originally evolved within cognitive psychology (e.g., Ericsson & Smith, 1991), *wisdom has been defined as an expert knowledge system in the fundamental pragmatics of life.* This is a body of knowledge and heuristics that concerns the mastery of difficult and uncertain problems related to life conduct and the meaning of life. Wisdom is defined as *superior knowledge* of how to act for one's own good, that of others, and that of society. Wisdom and wisdom-related knowledge become manifest in *sound judgment* and *exceptional insight* into difficult life problems. Note that the concept of wisdom is restricted to the expert-level products or performances in the domain "fundamental pragmatics of life." Any lower levels are denoted by the term *wisdom-related.*

The body of knowledge and heuristics called wisdom is a theoretical rather than an empirical object. Wisdom is conceived of as an "idea" in the sense that Plato developed in his early writings on geometry, aesthetics, and ethics (Mittelstraß, 1981). Reality by definition falls short of the ideal. In the very early wisdom literature, wisdom is described as an ideal that the individual or society can only strive for rather than attain (Adler, 1992).

The idea of wisdom, in this sense, can become manifest in an individual's judgment, behavior, and character, but it can also be displayed on a societal level in proverbs, tales, religious writings, constitutional texts, and law compendiums (see also Baltes & Smith, 1990). Given this conceptualization of wisdom as a *theoretical object*, it is *not* the specific carrier of wisdom (e.g., person or written product), but rather the structure and function of this body of knowledge associated with the fundamental matters of life and the human condition, that determines the essence of wisdom.

The core features of wisdom-related knowledge and heuristics, irrespective of whether they are instantiated in a written text or in the verbal or actual behavior of an individual, have been defined by a family of five criteria that are described in more detail elsewhere (cf. Baltes & Smith, 1990; Baltes & Staudinger, 1993): rich factual and procedural knowledge about life, life-span contextualism, value relativism, awareness, and management of uncertainty.

This conceptualization of wisdom as well as the dictionary definitions and implicit theories of wisdom suggest many ways in which wisdom may be social-interactive in nature. In the following, the three facets of the social-interactive nature of wisdom are outlined in more detail.

The three facets of the social-interactive nature of wisdom

Before I continue my argument, I will try to clarify some terminological issues in order to avoid misunderstandings. These issues concern the meaning of *social interaction*. Social interactions can be differentiated according to their degree of proximity. This dimension ranges from the immediate face-to-face interaction between two or more individuals on the proximal end to the interaction with what Cole (see Chapter 2, this volume) calls cultural artifacts of any kind on the distal end of the scale. I would like to maintain that human existence is inextricably related to social interaction; this certainly includes wisdom-related phenomena. However, beyond this "triviality," I will try to show that social interaction in the proximal sense also contributes to the development, activation, identification, and orientation of wisdom.

The social-interactive nature of wisdom in the distal sense, or the collective nature of wisdom, refers to social interactions within a given human community or society that have been aggregated over individuals and over time. One can also conceive of them as "depersonalized" social interactions, whereas *proximal social interaction* – which will be the focus of attention in this chapter – is defined as referring to any communicative exchange between two or more individuals that can be either *directly* or *symbolically mediated*. The members engaged in the interaction, however, still have to be identifiable.

Given these terminological specifications, three facets of the social-interactive nature of wisdom are distinguished: (a) the development of wisdom over time (cultural evolution, phylogenesis, ontogenesis), (b) the activation or application of wisdom in a given social situation (microgenesis), and (c) the identification and orientation of a given product (written, verbal, behavior) as wise. The agent or carrier of wisdom in all three cases can be either a culture or an individual.

Most of the fast-growing literature on social interaction and cognition (e.g., Bornstein & Bruner, 1989; Resnick, Levine, & Teasely, 1991; von Cranach, Doise, & Mugny, 1992; Wozniak & Fischer, 1993) does not distinguish among different facets of the relationship between social interaction and cognition. Especially, the distinction between ontogenesis and activation (microgenesis) of a given body of knowledge is often blurred. Thus, potential differences in the kind, amount, and function of social interaction involved in the ontogenesis as compared with the microgenesis (activation) of wisdom cannot be identified.

The distinction between ontogenesis and microgenesis becomes relevant, for example, when considering the question of whether the social-interactive nature of wisdom also implies that wisdom or something close to it cannot become manifest within an individual. With regard to the ontogenesis of wisdom, it seems that inasmuch as any human knowledge is mediated through proximal *and* distal social interaction, the development of wisdom-related knowledge is also influenced by it. In other words, a wise Kaspar Hauser, that is, a person growing up without almost any kind of social interaction, is difficult to imagine. Nevertheless, it is still an open issue whether a certain amount and a certain kind of proximal social interaction is indispensable for wisdom to emerge. When considering the microgenesis of wisdom, proximal social interaction is not absolutely necessary. I will argue, however, that proximal interaction increases the probability that higher levels of wisdom-related performance will be observed.

An illustration of some of the collective underpinnings of wisdom

In this section, I provide some examples of the threefold social-interactive nature of wisdom (development, activation, identification) as it becomes manifest on a cultural level. Of course, I am not a cultural anthropologist and therefore am not an expert in the field of cultural studies. Given our conceptualization of wisdom as a theoretical rather than an empirical object, it seems crucial, however, not only to concentrate on the individual as a carrier of wisdom, but also to pay attention to its cultural manifestations.

Social interaction and the cultural evolution of wisdom

Social interaction is constitutive for the cultural evolution of wisdom. The body of knowledge and heuristics indexed as wisdom can develop only in a community of people, only if and when people interact. According to cultural anthropology, culture can be defined as a collection of bodies of knowledge or a body of skills transmitted from one generation to the next (e.g., Boesch, 1991; Cole, 1990; D'Andrade, 1981; Shweder, 1991). It is further argued that whenever human beings form a community, a body of knowledge dealing with the conduct, interpretation, and meaning of life is constructed that in its highest elaboration is then called wisdom.

According to cultural-historical analyses, knowledge related to the conduct, interpretation, and meaning of life is one of the first bodies of knowledge to develop in any human community (e.g., J. Assmann, 1992; Baltes, 1994a,b; Rudolph, 1987). Especially in the early phases of cultural evolution, this collective knowledge (i.e., knowledge shared by members of a human community) becomes manifest in sayings, proverbs, and tales. The Egyptian and Mesopotamian cultures, as well as many current African cultures, are examples of this type of wisdom tradition. With cultural evolution proceeding – that is, with the increasing size and complexity of the human community – the number of proverbs increases, and proverbs subsequently become more and more detached from the concrete situations in which they were originally coined. At this later "stage" of cultural evolution, the key question then becomes when to apply a particular piece of that body of knowledge (Hahn,

1989). Wisdom then is contained not in the sayings and proverbs themselves, but rather in their insightful application to a given problem situation.

The study of proverbs further exemplifies the collective nature of the development of wisdom-related knowledge. Proverbs are defined as "a truth based on common sense or the practical experience of mankind" (*Oxford Dictionary of the English Language*, 1933). In this sense, proverbs seem to be prototypical examples of a product of the collective mind. At the same time, the investigation of proverbs also illustrates the delicate dialectic between the individual and the collective that is one of the underlying themes of this chapter. Taylor (1962), the doyen of proverb studies, has characterized this dialectic with a saying by Lord John Russell: "One man's wit and all men's wisdom." Proverbs become proverbs only by confirmation of recurrent action in a given community, by the experience of a community of people thinking and acting together over time (Goodwin & Wenzel, 1981). An individual's mind is needed, however, to integrate and transform this collective experience into a proper metaphor. The "socio-logic" (Goodwin & Wenzel, 1981) of certain events and relationships needs to be discovered and pinned down by an individual's mind.

The collective nature of the cultural activation and application of wisdom

When considering the second facet of the social-interactive nature of cultural wisdom, we find that wisdom has a central cultural function. The body of knowledge associated with wisdom is activated when successful solutions to difficult and uncertain problems of life are needed. Successful solutions to life problems, one can further assume, increase the likelihood of the survival or the prospering of a culture. This cultural function of wisdom as a body of knowledge dealing with life problems is well documented in cultural-historical analyses of the so-called wisdom literature of ancient societies and in psychological investigations on the evolutionary functions of aging (A. Assmann, 1991; J. Assmann, 1992; Baltes, 1994a,b; Brent, 1978; Brent & Watson, 1980; Mergler & Goldstein, 1983).

Taking the view of evolutionary hermeneutics, Csikszentmihalyi and Rathunde (1990) have argued that concepts such as wisdom, which have been used for many centuries under very different social and historical conditions to evaluate human behavior, are most likely to have adaptive value for humankind. Beyond the role of wisdom in cultural evolution, there is also an increasing literature that provides evidence for the effect of social interaction on even the evolution of certain cognitive processes (e.g., Barkow, Cosmides, & Tooby, 1992; Gigerenzer & Hug, 1992; Klix, 1993). Gigerenzer and Hug (1992), for example, showed that correct reasoning is facilitated when the task involves the detection of cheating.

Wisdom is also activated and asked for when the socialization and education of youth are concerned. In historical studies, wisdom is often described as crystallized in rules that were collected and put down in writing by certain societal subgroups such as priests. Such collections were then, among other purposes, used for the *education of youth* (J. Assmann, 1992; Rudolph, 1987). Another cultural use of wisdom – that is, the *exercise of power* – has been the topic of highly controversial discussions (e.g., Baltes, 1994a,b). It is often argued that full access to this body of knowledge was confined to certain societal elites, enabling them to seize and exercise power (Hahn, 1989; Rudolph, 1987).

Illustrations of the social-interactive nature of individual wisdom

In this section, we will consider illustrations of the social-interactive nature of individual wisdom – that is, when wisdom-related knowledge becomes manifest in an individual. The social-interactive facets involved in the ontogenesis, activation, and identification of wisdom and wisdom-related knowledge and heuristics will be discussed in turn.

Social interaction and the ontogenesis of wisdom-related knowledge

Like any knowledge acquisition, the *ontogenesis* of wisdom-related knowledge is highly dependent on social interaction and social context. Cultural anthropologists and sociologists of knowledge have argued that a good part (if not most) of what a person knows is learned from other people. A person's knowledge is very much influenced by his or her interactional history and social "fate" (e.g., Berger & Luckmann, 1967; Boesch, 1991; Schütz & Luckmann, 1979; Shweder, 1991). Along this line, wisdom researchers have argued that supportive interpersonal relationships are crucial for the development and maintenance of wisdom. Close relationships and friendships may provide for wisdom-conducive experiences and a conversational context that allows for the exploration of limits and doubts involved in knowing (Kramer, 1990; Meacham, 1990).

Within life-span developmental theory, several levels or territories of social influences are distinguished. Some of these developmental influences are socially interactive in the proximal sense defined earlier, and others are more distal and mediated through selective exposure to certain experiential settings (Lerner & von Eye, 1992). Underlying any development and "omnipresent" is the macrostructure of culture that has mediating and regulating power in shaping the content, level, and direction of development (Boesch, 1991; Cole, 1990; Schütz & Luckmann, 1979; Shweder, 1991). Being a member of a human community includes, for example, learning its language and its collectively defined rules of life. On a second level there is the society-driven production of individual differences by age, gender, educational level, and professional status, to name just a few (Dannefer, 1984; Featherman & Lerner, 1985).

Finally, there is the microenvironment in terms of the family in which we grow up and our educational or peer group settings. These settings often, by means of social interaction in the proximal sense, refine and specify the social influences exerted by the other two levels.

Social contexts as developmental influence in the Berlin model of the ontogenesis of wisdom. The Berlin model of the ontogenesis of wisdom (Baltes & Smith, 1990; Baltes & Staudinger, 1993) tries to consider these different levels and territories of social influence, although using a different logic of organization (see Figure 10.1). The logic of organization follows a hypothetical dimension ranging from wisdom-related developmental influences that are primarily person-related to those influences that are primarily linked to the social context. Variables that have been identified as relevant to the acquisition of expertise (e.g., Ericsson, Krampe, & Tesch-Römer, 1993) fill the middle ground between the two ends of this person–context dimension.

When applying the three-tiered model of social influences on development – introduced earlier – to this model of the ontogenesis of wisdom, the microenvironment of an individual or social interaction in its proximal sense becomes relevant – for instance, with regard to the experiential settings related to socialization, such as family background, schooling, peer groups, or later professional training. Society-driven interindividual differences like age and social class can be interpreted as allocating distinct bodies of wisdom-related experience by means of age-specific roles, expectations, and access to spheres of life (e.g., Riley, 1985). Finally, historical periods can be considered to be one concrete example of the cultural macrostructure. Besides, culture certainly provides the general framework (e.g., language, knowledge) within which wisdom-related development takes place.

Age by experience paradigms. As the majority of prior theoretical and empirical work within the Berlin wisdom paradigm relevant to the social foundation of the mind has been concerned with the ontogenesis of wisdom, those results will be summarized. Based on models of expertise development, and in contrast to the general wisdom stereotype, it was expected that chronological age per se is not a sufficient condition for acquiring wisdom-related knowledge. Living longer increases only the *probability of encountering* potentially wisdom-conducive experiences. Age is no guarantee for an actual increase of wisdom-related knowledge and skill. Instead, the accumulation of wisdom-related knowledge may depend on more than chance encounters with wisdom-facilitative life experiences. It may depend on a great number of experiences, guidance (having a mentor, i.e., social interaction) in dealing with those experiences, and on a certain personality makeup such as the interest in gaining insights into life. Furthermore, later in the development of wisdom-related

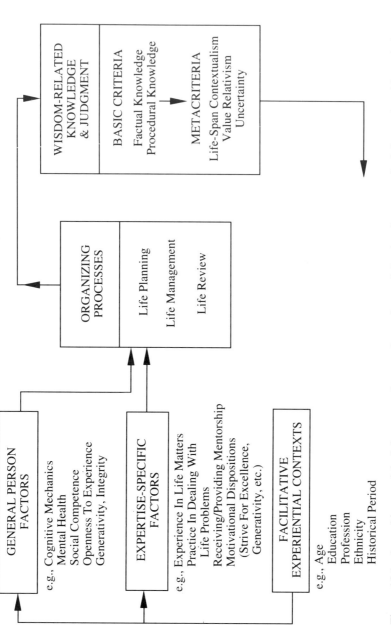

Figure 10.1. A working model of the antecedents and correlates of the development of wisdom-related knowledge and wisdom. Social context and social interaction as developmental influences form an integral part of this model. (After Baltes & Staudinger, 1993.)

knowledge, experiences with being a mentor become relevant. Given this relative importance of chronological age, it may also be possible for children to show wisdom. It is still an open issue as to what is the earliest possible point in time for wisdom to become evident. One can conceive of constellations of life events that may lead to an "accelerated" development of wisdom.

Thus, it was argued that the development of wisdom-related performance is best investigated within a design that examines age as well as exposure to wisdom-facilitative experiential settings and conditions. Within such a so-called age by experience paradigm (e.g., Charness, 1989; Salthouse, 1991), three developmental conditions have been specified as especially relevant: (a) extensive experience with a wide range of human conditions; (b) mentor-guided practice in dealing with difficult issues of life conduct and life interpretation, that is, social interaction with a more experienced person; and (c) a motivational disposition that would support the endurance of extended periods of "practice" in fundamental matters of life (see also Ericsson et al., 1993).

An empirical example of the investigation of the potential facilitative effect of certain experiential and social-interactive contexts is provided by the study of groups with specific professional training and practice. In one study, clinical psychology was selected as a profession that, in training and practice, is putatively characterized by an above average amount of exposure to fundamental matters of life and to ways of dealing with them, as well as the experience of mentorship in how to interpret and deal with such life issues. It was demonstrated that the experiential context of training and practice in clinical psychology indeed seems to be conducive to higher levels of wisdom-related performance. Clinical psychologists displayed higher levels of wisdom-related performance than comparison groups from other academic professions (Smith, Staudinger, & Baltes, 1994; Staudinger, Smith, & Baltes, 1992). At the same time, however, selection into the profession of clinical psychology because of a certain personality profile may account for some of the clinical psychologists' superiority.

Experiential settings and historical time. This finding of the wisdom-conducive effect of exposure to certain professional contexts was replicated and extended in a study that compared people nominated as wise with older clinical psychologists and control groups. People nominated as wise, among other things, were characterized by an average age of 64 years and by seemingly extraordinary biographies with regard to experiential settings and interpersonal relationships. Some 44% had published their autobiographies, 31% had been members of the resistance movement against the Nazi regime or had emigrated during the Third Reich, and 56% had been in leading positions in public administration, the church, the arts, and the sciences. The wisdom nominees, which had been designated independent of our definition of wisdom, outperformed both the clinical psychologists and the control groups on our measure of wisdom-related knowledge (Baltes, Staudinger, Maercker, & Smith, 1995). This finding seems to suggest that, besides professional contexts, historical times can also provide for experiential contexts that are – given a certain personality and intellectual profile – conducive to the development of wisdom-related knowledge.

Interacting with a mentor as part of the development of expertise. There is a large body of literature in educational and child psychology about the effect of social interaction on cognitive development (for a review see. e.g., Azmitia. Chapter 5, this volume; Azmitia & Perlmutter, 1989; Slavin, 1980). It is not the intention of this chapter to provide an extensive review of this literature. Rather, some more evidence will be provided concerning a small portion of this literature that concerns the role of mentorship in cognitive development. In conjunction with the conceptualization of wisdom as expertise, receiving as well as providing mentorship seems to play a crucial role in the accumulation of wisdom-related knowledge.

Within the expertise literature, Bloom (1985; see also Ericsson et al., 1993) has so far provided perhaps the most comprehensive overview of the attainment of exceptional performance in everyday domains of functioning. However, we are only beginning to gain insight into the external and internal support conditions that contribute to the development of expertise. Inspecting evidence across a variety of domains, Bloom distinguished three phases of expertise development. In all three phases, mentorship and social interaction play a crucial role. In the first phase, during the early years of childhood, it is the parents who provide encouragement and support. In the second and third phases, that is, in the middle and later years of training, it seems to be essential that the individual works with a teacher or coach who has also performed at an exceptional level or at least coached other exceptional performers.

Research on mentorship or apprenticeship in adult–child relationships has demonstrated that the *type* of guidance provided plays a critical role in the facilitation of development (e.g., Rogoff, 1993). It is not just any kind of social interaction with an adult or an individual with higher levels of knowledge that works; the interactional style has to fit the type of task, performance capacity, and motivational status of the individual in order to be profitable (see also Tudge, 1992). These findings emphasize how important it is to tailor social interaction to the individual and the task at hand if it is to be supportive.

The effect of social interaction on the life processes involved in the ontogenesis of wisdom: the sample case of life review. The ontogenetic model of wisdom presented in Figure 10.1 makes certain rudimentary assumptions about so-called life processes or organizing processes involved in the development of wisdom. Three such processes have been specified: life planning, life management, and life review. They may support the acquisition and refinement of personal as well as indirect life experiences (such as those mediated through conversations, observations, or the media). These life processes have also been employed to access and measure wisdom-related knowledge.

Life review – a more adequate term may be life (re)construction – will serve as a sample case to further illustrate the social-interactive nature of the ontogenesis of wisdom-related knowledge (Staudinger & Baltes, 1994; Staudinger & Dittmann-Kohli, 1994). Most of the life experiences that we collect are dependent on direct or indirect interaction with other people. Beyond this quite obvious fact, however, the process of life (re)construction itself, which organizes such experiences by means of selection, categorization, abstraction, and interpretation, is social-interactive in nature. With regard to knowledge about one's own life, we have known at least since James (1890) and later Mead (1934), that identity formation is mediated through feedback by others. This includes internal dialogue. In a similar vein, memory research has shown, for example, that the development of autobiographical memory is highly dependent on the development of the ability to communicate with others about what is happening or has happened (Nelson, 1992).

Let's consider some of the possible effects of social interaction on the process and product of life (re)construction (encompassing one's own life and life in general). Social interaction can facilitate as well as hamper this process. On the asset side, insights about life that we have arrived at individually may be tested by talking to other people about them. Or such insights may be gained only through communicative interaction with others. It may be the other who confronts us with undesirable observations about our own behavior, who points to contradictions in our construction of the world and prevents us from glossing over things. Certain kinds of communicative interaction may help us become more self-critical and gain distance from our own behavior. A look at the debit side of social interaction, however, reveals that social transactions may also be dysfunctional and may interfere with the individual's life (re)construction – for example, if a partner, by misusing his or her influence, "forces" interpretations on the person, or exclusively focuses on the strengths or the weaknesses of the person. The selection of the most suitable partner and the most suitable situation for a given piece of life (re)construction seems to be a crucial determinant of the utility of a given social interaction.

The role of social interaction with regard to the activation of individual wisdom

After the role of social interaction in the development of wisdom has been discussed, the social-interactive nature of the activation of individual wisdom-related knowledge will be considered. Whenever a situation calls for wisdom, most often more than one person is involved. Thus, wisdom very often is activated in situations of advice seeking or giving in view of difficult life

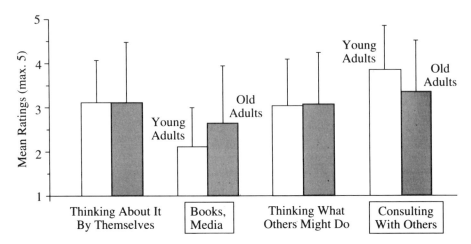

Figure 10.2. The everyday ecology of life-problem-solving behavior: consulting with others as the most important informational source. (From Staudinger & Baltes, 1994.)

problems. For example, when we consider how people deal with life problems, we find that very often they do consult with others, or perhaps also with books, before making a decision or coming up with a proper interpretation of events.

Such anecdotal evidence is supported by the findings from a study in which people were asked how they usually, that is, in everyday life, go about solving fundamental life problems. Specifically, a sample ($N = 140$) of differing social background, ranging in age from 19 to 80 years, was asked to which degree they dealt with life problems by (a) thinking about them by themselves, (b) "consulting" books or other media, (3) thinking what other people might say to the problem at hand, and, finally, (4) actually consulting with other people (Staudinger & Baltes, 1995).

Overall, subjects reported the highest degree of endorsement for the option of consulting with others. Significantly lower in rank were both the option of thinking about the problem by oneself and the option of taking into account what other people might say to this problem. Again, significantly lower (and last in the ranking) was the endorsement of "consulting" books and other media. This seems to indicate that on average people indeed value others' perspectives and advice when trying to solve fundamental life problems.

Age/cohort differences between these kinds of life-problem-solving behavior were also obtained (see Figure 10.2). Older subjects reported significantly more often than younger subjects that they consulted books and other media, while younger subjects reported more often than older adults that they consulted other people. Incidentally, no gender differences were obtained for any of these questions. Unfortunately, the cross-sectional design of the study does not allow us to distinguish between age and cohort effects. At least in Germany, there are likely cohort differences, with older cohorts favoring the opinion that one has to solve one's problem by oneself rather than including others in this problem-solving process. The demonstrated age differences in life-problem-solving behavior may also be due to older adults' need to fit the age stereotype, which says that the older you get the less you need to ask for advice.

Previous empirical efforts within the Berlin wisdom paradigm have generally neglected social interaction as part of the activation (microgenesis) of wisdom-related knowledge. The Berlin wisdom paradigm, like most other research efforts in this area, has been built around a person-centered experimental paradigm (see also the Prologue). That is, an individual subject had to respond to a given life dilemma. The social-interactive nature of wisdom, of course, was represented in the wisdom tasks, but not in the actual experimental performance setting. Therefore, most recent empirical efforts concentrated on developing a social-interactive paradigm for the activation of wisdom-related knowledge. Thus, the effect of social interaction on the activation of wisdom-related knowledge will be the focus of the second part of this chapter.

The role of social interaction with regard to the identification and orientation of wisdom

The third facet of the social-interactive nature of wisdom concerns its identification and orientation. Wisdom is usually attributed to others or by others, and is identified in social context (see also Sternberg, 1990). In an empirical study of the characteristics of wise nominees and their nominators, Orwoll and Perlmutter (1990) found, for example, that people hold a general belief that wisdom increases with age and that older people are more likely to be nominated as wise than young people. Subjects, however, did not rate their own wisdom in a manner that was consistent with this general belief in an age-related increase of wisdom. In fact, it is a well-established part of the wisdom literature that it is a characteristic of so-called wise persons not to attribute wisdom to themselves (e.g., Baltes, 1994a,b; Meacham, 1983). The classic Socratic citation "I know that I don't know" speaks to this point. With regard to the orientation of wisdom, the analysis of cultural-historical wisdom literature shows that wisdom is oriented toward the interests of others (Baltes, 1994a,b). In other words, the intention of wisdom is social-interactive in nature as well.

In the Berlin work on wisdom, the social-interactive nature of the identification and attribution of wisdom and its collective representation has been acknowledged by using a social consensus criterion of wisdom. This has been done in two ways. One way has been to have people nominated as wise by a group, which has to reach consensus concerning its choices, in order for the nominees to be included in the final sample (Baltes et al., 1995). Second, the usual procedure of measuring wisdom-related knowledge involves a panel of raters who are trained to assess the level of wisdom-related knowledge present in a subject's response to our life dilemmas (e.g., Baltes & Smith, 1990; Baltes & Staudinger, 1993). A rating of responses done according to the raters' own conceptions of wisdom, without the provision of a definition, resulted in interrater consistencies of about .7 and a correlation of .7 with a wisdom rating obtained through the application of the previously mentioned five wisdom-related criteria (Staudinger et al., 1992). Additional evidence to support the high social consensus with regard to the identification of wisdom was gained in a study of implicit theories of wisdom (Maciel, Sowarka, Smith, Staudinger, & Baltes, 1993). In this study there was a very high intersubject consistency on how a wise person was described.

Another result of this study of implicit theories of wisdom is relevant to the present topic. Although none of the subjects completing the questionnaire was found to be "wise" on the basis of their wisdom-related performance, all were very well able to describe and recognize a wise person. Following, for example, notions of production deficiency (Flavell, 1970), one could argue that people seem to have representations of the meaning and characteristics of wisdom and wise persons. They themselves are not able, however, to apply those characteristics (which they can recognize in others) to a given life dilemma and thereby generate a high-level wisdom-related performance.

The interesting question then becomes whether it is possible to identify support conditions that would help subjects to overcome this production deficiency and thus make them reach higher levels of wisdom-related performance (Overton & Newman, 1982). Without getting into the complexities of the distinction between competence and performance (e.g., Fischer, Bullock, Rotenberg, & Raya, 1993), it is possible to restrict the issue to the differentiation between baseline and optimal performance. This distinction makes it possible to specify a range of intraindividual performance levels associated with differences in the available internal and external resources. To be sure, baseline performance levels already comprise what we have called the influence of distal social interaction. Certain kinds of proximal social interaction, however, may be a means to support more optimal levels of performance. Within this frame of reference, the focus of investigation is on the range and limits of plasticity in performance (e.g., Baltes, 1987; Lerner, 1984).

Beyond person-centered paradigms: social interaction and performance in areas of the pragmatics of the mind

The second part of this chapter centers on social interaction as it contributes to the activation or microgenesis of wisdom-related knowledge. This is the facet most neglected in earlier work on wisdom and has therefore become the most recent focus of the Berlin work on wisdom (Staudinger & Baltes, 1994, 1995). The emphasis here will be on the facilitative and/or inhibitory role of proximal social interaction with regard to the activation and microgenesis of wisdom-related knowledge. First, literature in other areas of the pragmatics of the mind will be reviewed. This review will show that proximal interaction between two or more minds can be facilitative, inconsequential, or inhibitory for an individual's cognitive performance. Second, the initial results of the implementation of a social-interactive wisdom paradigm are presented. The paradigm is based on the general assumption that although not all social-interactive conditions of the proximal kind are facilitative, performance is likely to be the highest when a particular constellation of interactive minds is at least part of the performance setting.

Social interaction in research on professional expertise and adult thought

Contextualism, ecological validity, and social interaction: variations of one theme? Let us assume that there is some "truth" to the social-interactive nature of wisdom and, as has been argued elsewhere (e.g., Meacham, 1990; Resnick et al., 1991), to other cognitive phenomena involving the knowledge-based pragmatics of the mind. Consequently, traditional person-centered paradigms employed for the assessment of wisdom-related performance and other types of expertise would not present the best performance setting and thereby underestimate the potential level of performance. Person-centered paradigms refer to assessment settings in which individual persons are requested to perform on their own without proximal (immediate) social interactions taking place.

Here is perhaps an opportunity to link the present argument with other historical trends dealing with ecological validity and the importance of context for the study of the microgenesis as well as ontogenesis of performance and more specifically cognitive performance (e.g., Baltes & Willis, 1977; Bronfenbrenner, 1979; Dixon, 1992; Neisser, 1976; Poon, Rubin, & Wilson, 1989). The ecological movement can be characterized as having initiated a change in the content areas investigated. In memory research, we observed a shift from the study of memory for word lists to that of autobiographical memory and to that of everyday memory (e.g., Baddeley, 1981; Rubin, Wetzler, & Nebes, 1986); in problem-solving research, so-called everyday problem solving became prominent (e.g., Poon et al., 1989). Even in areas like analogical reasoning, researchers found that subjects were less error-prone if the reasoning task was not abstract but was put in an everyday context (e.g., Cheng & Holyoak, 1985; Cosmides, 1989; Gigerenzer & Hug, 1992). The same is true for research on intelligence, which moved into the study of practical intelligence and areas of cognitive functioning that were assumed to be more typical for the ecology of adults' daily lives (e.g., Sternberg & Wagner, 1986). The Berlin research on wisdom as a facet of the pragmatics of the mind, as well as the study of professional expertise (e.g., Ericsson & Smith, 1991), and the study of specific characteristics of adult thought in the Piagetian tradition are other examples of this movement (e.g., Alexander & Langer, 1990; Commons, Sinnott, Richards, & Armon, 1989; Sinnott & Cavanaugh, 1991).

About the same time, and most likely not unrelated, there was a movement to rejuvenate the study of social factors in their interaction with performance. Ideas on shared cognition and social interaction as performance context (e.g., Dixon, 1992; Resnick et al., 1991; Sternberg & Wagner, 1994; Wozniak & Fischer, 1993) have become increasingly prominent. This seems to indicate that the move to ecologically more "valid" content domains of cognitive functioning was paralleled by a search for additional supportive assessment conditions. In this vein, it is reasonable to argue that proximal social interaction may be one such component of a supportive performance setting, at least for certain types of cognitive functioning. I would like to argue that this is especially true for the pragmatics of the mind – that is, cognitive functioning that draws heavily on culturally transmitted bodies of knowledge such as wisdom. Tasks in that domain do not have one definite answer, sometimes even the problem to be solved is not clear at the beginning, and large but rather uncertain amounts of problem-related knowledge need to be identified and activated (cf. Simon, 1973). It seems that the large amount of knowledge involved in problem solving and also the uncertainty related to procedure and outcome make tasks in the domain of the fundamental pragmatics of life especially prone to profit from social-interactive performance contexts.

Social-interactive studies of professional expertise and complex problem solving: a rare event? The expertise paradigm that we have also adopted for the study of wisdom and wisdom-related knowledge is a quite prominent one in the study of the pragmatics of the mind. In their book on the prospects and limits of a general theory of expertise, Ericsson and Smith (1991) characterize three steps in the expertise approach. The first step consists of *capturing* superior, that is, expert, performance. The major challenge of this step consists of creating "a situation that is maximally simple and yet sufficiently similar to the real-life situation to allow the reproduction of the expertise under laboratory conditions" (Ericsson & Smith, 1991, p. 17). Given this statement, it is surprising that even in areas of expertise that in terms of ecological validity seem to depend on social interaction (e.g., medical diagnosis, managerial problem solving, complex and everyday problem solving), most of the empirical studies remain person-centered (for reviews, see, e.g., Chi, Glaser, & Farr, 1988; Ericsson & Smith, 1991; Sternberg & Frensch, 1991).

Social interaction, however, may play an important role in the development, application, and identification of a given expert-level performance. Expertise paradigms extensively acknowledge the role of social interaction in the acquisition of expertise (e.g., Ericsson et al., 1993) and in the identification or recognition of expertise (e.g., Reitman, 1965). Less often, social interaction has been considered as a resource for the activation of expert-level performance (see Strube, Janetzko, & Knauff, Chapter 13, this volume). While many elaborate statistical and communicative methods are discussed in the expertise literature, regarding the elicitation of expertise-related knowledge (e.g., Olson & Biolsi, 1991), none of these methods systematically includes the social context of experts.

Take, for instance, the extensive research done on computer-simulated complex problem solving, which was particularly popular in German-speaking countries in the late 1970s and 1980s and was introduced with a strong emphasis on ecological validity. Originally, the contextual approach was exclusively defined by the introduction of new domains of problem solving. Only lately have some researchers started to compare individual with group performance when working on the complex computer-simulated problems (e.g., Badke-Schaub, 1993; Putz-Osterloh, 1991). In her dissertation study dealing with the spread of AIDS, Badke-Schaub (1993) found, for example, that group problem solving (artificial groups) showed advantages but also disadvantages as compared with individual performance. On the one hand, it seemed that groups were able to prevent complete misdecisions. On the other hand, however, groups also seemed to prevent extremely successful problem solutions just as some individuals were able to produce them. Time seems to be one of the critical features in the group problem-solving process. The group needs more time than the individual because, besides dealing with the problem, it also needs to deal with the group dynamics. These are findings that – as will be documented later – correspond with results from the social psychology of group problem solving. To my knowledge, however, none of these approaches has so far studied natural groups or individual performance after social interaction, such as consultation or advice seeking, which would seem to be one of the ways that complex problems are solved in reality (e.g., Dörner, Kreuzig, Reither, & Stäudel, 1983; Funke, 1991; Putz-Osterloh, 1987).

Another area of expertise likely to profit from social interaction seems to be medical diagnosis. Again, in reviewing recent research in the field, we find very elaborate process models of the expert's judgment process but relatively little consideration of the interactive nature of the expertise (e.g., Lesgold et al., 1988; Patel & Groen, 1991). One exception was a study simulating the doctor–patient interaction in the laboratory, rather than working with written materials (Kaufman & Patel, 1988). Another more recent exception analyzes medical diagnosis as a case of complex problem solving that makes it necessary to integrate distributed knowledge (e.g., Cicourel, 1990). Medical diagnosis in such studies is indeed conceptualized as the product of a complex social process involving people who vary in status and area of expertise. The evaluation of the credibility of the informational source becomes very important in this process.

With regard to expert problem solving in the domain of politics, which by definition should be social-interactive in nature, we find consideration in the case studies of historical-political decision processes (e.g., Janis, 1972), but not in laboratory studies investigating political problem solving (Voss, Wolfe, Lawrence, & Engle, 1991). In his classical work on "victims of groupthink," Janis (1972) analyzed four cases of misdecisions with catastrophic consequences (the invasion of Cuba, the occupation of North Korea, the attack on Pearl Harbor, and the escalation of the Vietnam War) and two cases of good decisions (the response to the Cuban missile crisis, and the Marshall Plan). Janis identified what he called the groupthink phenomenon as the reason for the misdecisions. He defined *groupthink* by eight features that can be summarized under the heading of the social dynamics of group decision making. Groups that are characterized by high cohesion and that are isolated in their decision-making process are especially prone to engage in groupthink, whereas whenever multiple groups are involved in the decision-making process, as was true in the case of the Cuban missile crisis and the Marshall Plan, the probability of groupthink seemed to be reduced. Furthermore, the group leader's behavior has a strong influence on the decision-making process.

The area of managerial expertise seems to be one of the exceptions to the "neglect" of social interaction in expertise research. In this field of expertise, two approaches can be distinguished (Wagner, 1991). One has been called the rational approach. It views managers as rational technicians who apply the knowledge and procedures of managerial science. The other, which I will call the social-interactive approach, views management as an art that cannot be reduced to a set of scientific principles.

The rational approach essentially ignores the social context in which managerial expertise is applied or activated, whereas the approach that views management as an art at least acknowledges what has been termed "convoluted action" (McCall & Kaplan, 1985) as the best way of solving important managerial problems. Convoluted action refers to the cooperative effort of the many different parties involved in the problem at stake. Even when this time-consuming type of action is not applicable because quick action is necessary, a consultation and advice-seeking phase is still described as one step in the manager's problem-solving efforts (Wagner, 1991).

In conclusion, the field of research on expertise in managerial problem solving has identified the importance of social interaction as one component of the problem-solving process, with regard to both the group dynamics (or the motivational effect) and the cognitive effect. The motivational effect refers to the fact that people are more willing to carry out a decision if they participated in the decision-making process. The cognitive effect refers to, for example, the pooling of knowledge, the cross-checking for errors in reasoning. However, it is important to keep in mind that most often the final decision is made by the manager. Interactive cognition in this field of expertise is used as a resource for individual cognition and does not substitute for it.

Another area in the world of work that recognized the importance of group problem solving, and should at least be mentioned, is so-called distributed decision making (e.g., Rasmussen, Brehmer, & Leplat, 1991). Distributed decision making becomes necessary if a problem is too complex to be completely understood by one person. Related to the development of new (communication) technologies in industry and administration, a new area of research emerged dealing with distributed knowledge, distributed information, and the processes that may optimize their integration (e.g., Galegher, Kraut, & Egido, 1990; Greif, 1988).

Social interaction and the study of adult thought and everyday problem solving in the developmental literature. Most recently, research in the area of postformal reasoning seems to be concerned with social interaction (direct and indirect) and performance. A very recent example is a study by Kitchener, Lynch, Fischer, and Wood (1993). In this study, subjects between the ages of 14 and 28 years first completed the so-called Reflective Judgment Interview, by stating positions with regard to a series of dilemmas and explaining the bases for their positions. Afterward, subjects were presented with the same dilemmas but received what the authors called contextual support through the provision of answers prototypical for each stage and for each dilemma. In the language of this chapter, this condition can also be described as an indirect or mediated social interaction between the subject and the idealized person who produced the prototypical response. Subjects performed on a higher level of reflective judgment under the supportive than under the spontaneous condition. Performance increase also showed an interaction with age. With increasing age, the profit from support conditions doubled from about half a development stage for adolescents to one stage for those in their twenties. Two conclusions can be drawn from this study. First, even symbolically mediated social interaction, such as through written materials produced by others, seems to represent a condition supportive of higher levels of performance. Second, the supportive effect of any setting variation seems to depend on certain cognitive and socioemotional individual preconditions. As will be documented later, this finding corresponds to results from the social psychology of group problem solving.

Another example from research on adults' everyday problem solving is the work of Meacham and Emont (1989). The authors located the basis for everyday problem solving not within the mind of the individual, but within interpersonal relations. They contrasted traditional research on problem solving with their suggestion for an ecologically sound inquiry of everyday problem solving. They argued that it is "breaking out of a rut" that often contributes to successful problem solving, which is congruent with the perspective of proponents of the traditional problem-solving approach. Meacham and Emont (1989) did state, however, that they don't think that the individual mind, by using certain problem-solving routines, necessarily possesses the best resources to get out of the rut. Rather, they maintained that "mental sets are broken when friends offer a new way of thinking about situations, point to inconsistencies, provide a counterbalance to the individual's emotional attachments and probably may suggest new means of problem solving" (p. 10). However, no empirical paradigm is suggested to test such ideas.

In recent work on the development of everyday problem solving, Berg and Calderone (1994) have suggested that people's interpretations of everyday problems are central to understanding this development. Based on a contextual perspective to intellectual development, the authors view such interpretations as the outcome of the transaction of the individual with his or her context.

A further example of an area where the move to social-interactive paradigms has begun is jury decision making (Hastie & Pennington, 1991). Hastie and Pennington moved beyond the traditional person-centered approach of reconstructing the individual juror's decision making. They developed a model that tries to integrate cognitive and social processes involved in jury decision making. A first tentative result of their approach is the finding that jurors seem to form their opinions about what happened before they enter jury discussion. During group deliberation, they do not change their minds about what happened, but rather discuss how such events should be legally classified. This is interesting because it demonstrates that interactive cognition does not necessarily encompass all phases of the decision-making process.

Such findings concerning the distinct functions of both interactive and individual cognition, even if tentative, should guard us against overinterpreting the social-interactive approach to imply that individual cognitive activity is no longer a meaningful category of research. Rather, a social-interactive paradigm, in the sense suggested here, should be developed such that it allows an analysis of how individual and interactive cognition should be combined – concurrently and sequentially – in order to provide for optimal performance settings (see also the Prologue).

The effect of social context as documented in the social-psychological literature on group problem solving

An attempt will be made in this section to provide an overview of the considerable amount of research on group problem solving, in part to highlight the complexity of social influences, as well as the myriad possible constellations and outcomes. As one tries to understand the role of social interaction with regard to the activation of wisdom-related performance in adulthood, this review provides a helpful frame of reference for the study of the cognitive and socioemotional processes involved. Such evidence provides the kind of technical information necessary for the development of a social-interactive paradigm.

The social-psychological evidence concerning the effect of social context on cognitive performance can roughly be taxonomized into three categories: (a) studies analyzing the effect of the mere presence of others (historically, these were the first to be carried out), (b) studies in which individuals actually interact on a given task and produce a collective product, and (c) studies of individual performance after social interaction has taken place. The last category is the least investigated in the social-psychological literature. A literature search amounted to the identification of six studies. More evidence is available from learning research with children.

The effect of the mere presence of others on cognitive performance. Results concerning the effect of the mere presence of others on cognitive performance have been found to reflect both social facilitation and social inhibition. In his theory of social facilitation, Zajonc (1965) offered the level of task difficulty as a theoretical construct integrating divergent evidence. He argued that the mere presence of others – for evolutionary reasons – causes a higher level of arousal. This arousal energizes a performer's dominant response tendency, à la Hull, and therefore is helpful for routine tasks. The arousal is detrimental, however, in the case of new tasks that ask for reflection. His theory has since been criticized especially for its biologism, and alternative explanations have been advanced that offer explanatory constructs such as evaluation apprehension, self-awareness monitoring, or a distraction conflict.

A review article based on a meta-analysis of research on social facilitation by Bond and Titus (1982) pointed out that the theoretical discussions attempting to integrate the divergent findings may be much ado about nothing. In their meta-analysis of 241 studies, they found that the effect sizes of social facilitation and social inhibition were quite small. The central conclusion proffered in this article is one of conditioned evaluation apprehension. The presence of others creates uncertainty and arouses an individual's alertness. In this vein, Paulus (1983) has presented a model in which he argues that the direction of the effect depends on whether the performing individual holds positive or negative expectations related to the presence of others. In the case of positive expectations, like praise, both simple and complex tasks are facilitated, while in the case of negative expectations only simple tasks are facilitated.

The effect of social interaction on a group product. When considering studies that investigate the cognitive performance of interacting groups, the central question becomes whether $N + 1$ minds are better than one, as Hill asked in his 1982 review article. Intuitively, it seems to be clear that one would say yes. If one asks subjects who have participated in group problem solving, as well as in an individual performance condition, they are also convinced that the group performance was better than their individual performances. For research on brainstorming, Stroebe, Diehl, and Abakoumkin (1992) have called this the *illusion of group effectivity*. This illusion concerns not only the overestimation of the number of ideas generated by the group as a whole. In addition, individual group members also overestimate the amount of their individual contribution to the group product. Jokingly, Stroebe points out that everyone who has ever co-authored a paper should know this phenomenon.

The empirical evidence is certainly not as clear and obvious in favor of the group as subjects' evaluations would suggest. Group effectiveness varies according to a number of variables. As usual, various review articles (e.g., Hackman & Morris, 1975; Hoffman, 1965; Kelley & Thibaut, 1969; Lorge, Fox, Davitz & Brenner, 1958; Steiner, 1972) have suggested different concepts and models to systematize the enormous body of literature. In an attempt to integrate these different suggestions, an organizing scheme arose, which is depicted in Figure 10.3.

This is not the place to elaborate on this scheme in detail. The scheme is primarily meant to illustrate the complexity of the social and cognitive processes involved. The research evidence to be summarized here has been selected to provide insights into the conditions under which social-interactive and individual cognition seemed to be most profitable.

There is evidence that group performance is better than that of the *average* individual. Group performance, however, has often been found to be inferior to the *best* individual in a nominal group or the potential of the real group as suggested by a statistical pooling model (Hill, 1982). The distinction between a nominal and a real group is used in group problem-solving research as a control condition. The nominal group consists of as many individuals as the real group. Members of the nominal group, however, do not work together but alone.

Evidence from tasks requiring ideational fluency (e.g., brainstorming, creativity tests) has shown that with regard to quantity as a performance measure, real groups are worse than nominal groups. This is *not* true, however, if quality of solutions is considered (e.g., Lamm & Trommsdorff, 1973). The level of group productivity varies, among other things, as a function of performance criteria, task demands, member resources, and interactional process (see Figure 10.3). Group products seem to be superior if (a) qualitative performance criteria are applied, (b) tasks are of a medium to high difficulty, (c) group members are intelligent and sociable, and (d) the group operates problem-focused rather than solution-focused or has worked together before (cohesion).

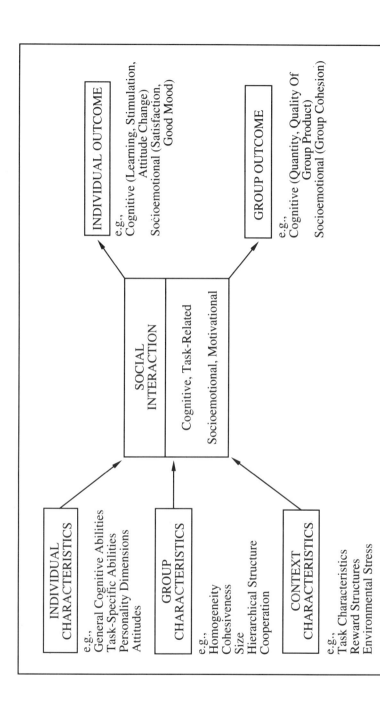

Figure 10.3. The process of group problem solving: overview of relevant constructs in the literature. (Adapted from Hackman & Morris, 1975.)

The disadvantage of the group with regard to quantity of production, especially in brainstorming tasks, is somewhat surprising. In numerous studies so-called coordination losses such as *blocking* or *interference* have been identified as underlying this disadvantage (e.g., Lamm & Trommsdorff, 1973). Blocking refers to the fact that, as long as one individual is talking, the other group members cannot talk. In addition, one member's utterance may interfere with the other members' cognitive processes. The latter interference effect is not unlike the interference reported in dual task conditions and its limiting effect on performance capacity. It has also been reported that idea generation within groups is quite *uniform*. Group members pursue a single line of thought for an unduly long time. Even if such coordination losses and strains on individual performance capacity are minimized by certain group-communication techniques, real group productivity in terms of quantity is still lower than nominal group activity (e.g., Hill, 1982).

Besides the effects on cognition, motivational processes have been suggested to account for some of the productivity loss of groups. For example, *social loafing*, or *free riding*, refers to the phenomenon whereby individuals in groups feel less responsible and motivated to contribute. They feel that their contribution is dispensable and that others will take care of it. Another socioemotional process loss may be due to *evaluation apprehension*; that is, group members may hesitate to contribute because they fear criticism. It has been demonstrated that these effects can be reduced by group conditions such as the identification of individual contributions, the provision of feedback on individual contributions, or the degree of group cohesion (e.g., Karau & Williams, 1993).

Studies of the effect of social interaction on individual performance. So far the focus has been on individual performance under social presence and group performance as an outcome after social interaction. What about *individual* performance following social interaction? As mentioned before, social-psychological research on this topic is scarce and often methodologically weak. Also mentioned earlier, there is more evidence available from the research on learning in childhood (e.g., Brown, Webber, & McGilly, 1992; Rogoff, 1993; Tudge, 1992).

To summarize, studies indicate that individual performance is indeed improved if it is preceded by social interaction. Unfortunately, the interpretation of most of these studies is hampered by the fact that, with a few exceptions, the experimental designs lack the important control condition that would make it possible to differentiate between the retest and the group effect. Osborn (1957), the father of brainstorming, has argued, for example, that the best product is arrived at if, first, subjects brainstorm individually, later in a group, and finally again individually. Laughlin and Adamopoulos (1980) have shown that individuals learned during group interaction. After participation in

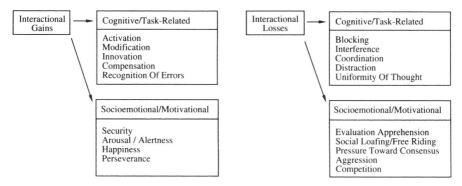

Figure 10.4. A summary of interactional gains and losses.

a group discussion, subjects were more likely to give a correct answer. In studies of facilitators of creativity, it was demonstrated that individuals showed higher levels of creativity after they had participated in group brainstorming sessions (e.g., Dunnette, Campbell, & Jaastad, 1963; Lindgren & Lindgren, 1965).

Social interaction: a summary of gains and losses. To summarize the research just reported, the group product is conceptualized as a function of the productivity of each individual member of the group, of interactional gains, and of interactional losses. Following Bales and Strodtbeck (1951), interactional gains and losses should be considered on a task-related or cognitive level of analysis, as well as on a socioemotional and motivational level. Figure 10.4 lists the gains and losses associated with social interaction.

First, *interactional losses* on the task-related or cognitive level of analysis are summarized. Group processes have been shown to be related to so-called coordination losses such as blocking or interference. Furthermore, thinking in groups results in a uniformity of cognitive operations among group members. Such coordination effects are especially critical if a group product is to be achieved. They play a lesser role if the individual performs alone afterward.

With regard to the socioemotional and motivational level of analysis, it has been found that individuals in a group tend to show social loafing or free riding. Another process discussed in the literature that may lead to interactional loss is evaluation apprehension. Furthermore, emotional hindrances such as aggression and competition have been demonstrated as a consequence of having to form a group decision (e.g., Kelley & Thibaut, 1969).

What about the potential of *interactional gains?* With respect to the motivational and socioemotional level of analysis, evidence for social facilitation can be cited which has demonstrated that the presence of another person increases arousal, alertness, and perseverance (Zajonc, 1965). Depending on group characteristics, such as cohesion, social interaction may also reduce anxiety, as well as increase happiness and positive mood.

The investigation of effects on cognitive component processes or on the level of cognitive efficacy is so far underrepresented in the social-psychological literature on group problem solving. Two sources have been suggested that may under certain conditions lead to interactional gains in cognitive processes: (a) the group members' capacity to learn in the course of group problem solving and (b) cognitive stimulation through social interaction (e.g., Hill, 1982; Lamm & Trommsdorff, 1973; Osborn, 1957).

Using a more cognitive and information-processing language, the following component processes are suggested. For instance, one could distinguish between processes of knowledge activation, modification, innovation, compensation, and error recognition (see Figure 10.4). The first three – knowledge activation, modification, and innovation – may become operative in an individual's knowledge system as a consequence of taking part in social interaction. In the language of network models of knowledge representation, activation would imply that ideas uttered by others in the group activate existing nodes in the individual's knowledge system. Taking part in a social exchange about a given problem may also result in the modification of one's own ideas; that is, existing interrelationships between nodes are revised. And finally with regard to innovation, social interaction may result in the development of new linkages between existing nodes. But also new ideas can emerge that are novel to all members of the group (Bos, 1937). This would imply, for example, that new nodes are added to the network.

The fourth process of compensation operates on a group level and refers to the division of labor idea. Group members contribute to the task depending on their respective abilities and thereby compensate for each others' weaknesses (e.g., Steiner, 1972). Finally, the recognition of errors refers to the greater ease in recognizing errors in other people's thinking than in one's own (e.g., Kelley & Thibaut, 1969).

To gain further insight into cognitive processes taking place during social interaction, effects of the *need to verbalize* on cognitive performance may also be helpful. Zajonc (1960) proposed a theoretical formulation that he called *cognitive tuning*. He showed that having to communicate certain information to others results in higher differentiation (breadth, number of categories), complexity (depth, subdivisions), unity (correlation between categories), and organization of one's own knowledge. Applying Zajonc's theory of cognitive tuning to a situation in which two people exchange ideas about a given problem, as compared with one in which an individual is left alone with a problem, one would expect that the knowledge system would be more widely activated and reorganized in terms of multilevel categories in the former case than in the latter. The idea of cognitive tuning has continued to instigate research in educational psychology and has evinced similar results (e.g., Benware & Deci, 1984).

Summary of review of relevant research in areas of expertise and social psychology

Reviewing some of the research on expertise and adult thought has demonstrated that (a) social interaction does not necessarily have to be direct (it can also be mediated) in order to be supportive of higher levels of performance, and (b) interactive as well as individual cognition can contribute to an optimal performance setting. The social-psychological evidence reported also indicates that superior levels of performance are mostly related to a combination of individual and interactive cognition rather than either one alone. Furthermore, the social-psychological evidence on group problem solving demonstrates that social interaction can have both positive (facilitative) and negative (debilitative) effects on cognitive as well as motivational and emotional processes of the individuals taking part in the interaction.

Social interaction and the assessment of wisdom-related performance

What has been presented so far? First, a theoretical argument has been provided that specifies the threefold social-interactive nature of wisdom. Second, a focus on the social-interactive nature of the application of wisdom-related knowledge has been introduced, and extant research relevant to this social-interactive facet of wisdom has been reviewed. In the following section, an experimental paradigm developed to assess the effect of a social-interactive context on wisdom-related performance will be presented.

The "traditional" person-centered assessment of wisdom-related performance

Before the social-interactive wisdom paradigm is introduced, the person-centered paradigm previously employed to assess wisdom-related knowledge will be summarized to provide a frame of reference. Although person-centered, this traditional paradigm can be considered as representing one aspect of an ecological approach to the assessment of adult cognition. It is *ecological* with respect to the selected domain, that is, the fundamental pragmatics of life.

To gain access to subjects' knowledge systems about the fundamental pragmatics of life, three areas of thinking about the conduct and meaning of life – life planning, life review, and existential life management – were selected (see Baltes, Smith, & Staudinger, 1992, for more details). Short problem vignettes describing scenarios covering these areas were developed. Such scenarios vary by age of problem character, by the typicality or normativeness of the problem, and by the targeted life domain.

In terms of experimental procedure, subjects first receive some training in thinking aloud (Ericsson & Simon, 1984) and in dealing with this type of task. Then they are handed the wisdom task, a problem vignette describing a difficult and uncertain life situation of a fictitious person, and are asked to spontaneously think aloud about the problem, such as what to consider and how to react when a friend calls and threatens to commit suicide. The think-aloud responses are tape-recorded and later transcribed. Verbatim transcripts are then evaluated on the five wisdom-related criteria using 7-point rating scales. The evaluation is carried out by an expert rater panel. Each rater evaluates only one of the five criteria to prevent halo effects. The scores obtained with this procedure demonstrate good interrater reliabilities, ranging from Cronbach alpha .7 to .98. Findings of past research were theory-consistent and also interesting, but they are characterized by two shortcomings: (a) the elicitation of low to average levels of wisdom-related performance and (b) the lack of ecological validity of the performance setting.

Development of a social-interactive paradigm for the assessment of wisdom-related performance

In the attempt to move beyond person-centered paradigms, the theoretical definition of the social-interactive nature of wisdom and the evidence provided by extant research in related fields was translated into a social-interactive paradigm for the assessment of wisdom-related performance. This attempt was guided by the goal of exploring under which assessment conditions – involving cognitive as well as emotional and motivational processes – social interaction would *support* or *hamper* the activation of wisdom-related knowledge.

As presented earlier, social-psychological research has provided an impressive list of potential interactional losses. Social interaction may, for example, create a cognitive overload that surpasses the individual's cognitive performance capacity, or it may create an interference problem by asking too much of the individual's attention. In addition, when considering emotional and motivational factors, social interaction may – based on controversial opinions – create strong negative emotions that again may hamper rather than support the activation of the individual's wisdom-related knowledge.

Furthermore, research has demonstrated that optimal performance settings often provide for both individual and interactive cognition. Finally, the review presented earlier highlighted the fact that social interaction can vary in directness. Performance increases were also found with settings involving symbolically mediated social interaction (i.e., written materials).

With such results in mind, the everyday ecology of life problem solving was the starting point of considerations. How do people usually deal with life problems? On the basis of our contention of the social-interactive nature of wisdom and the evidence reported earlier (see Figure 10.2), it was assumed that in most cases people have three ways of dealing with life problems: (a) consulting other people whom they consider potentially helpful *or* (b) taking into consideration what other people whose advice is usually sought might say to this problem *or* (c) "consulting" informational sources potentially helpful for the problem at hand, be it books or people's long-term memory. These three conditions vary among other ways along a dimension that may be labeled directness of social interaction – a dimension ranging from actual interactions between two people through symbolic interaction with mental representations of other people's ideas to interacting with crystallized written products of other people. The products of this "consultation phase," or this interactive cognitive activity, may then enter into individual cognition, which finally results in a solution to the problem.

A first study implementing a social-interactive paradigm. On the basis of such considerations, five experimental conditions were designed to help us gain initial insights into the effect of social interaction on wisdom-related perform-ance. The gains and losses involved in any social interaction have to form a positive balance in order to support the production of higher levels of wisdom-related knowledge. The experimental conditions were constructed such that they allowed us to start teasing apart the facilitative and inhibitory effects of interactive and individual cognition on wisdom-related performance (Stau-dinger & Baltes, 1995).

The five performance settings will be described in the order of predicted increase of wisdom-related performance. The greatest performance increase was expected for the experimental condition called "dialogue plus individual appraisal." This experimental condition first provides a natural dyad the op-portunity to discuss a wisdom task in any way they wish for 10 minutes. Afterward each member of the dyad has 5 minutes to think about the task and the discussion before each is asked to respond individually. This condition was expected to result in the greatest performance increase because it is character-ized by a combination of individual and interactive cognition. Considerable performance increase was also expected for the second condition, called "in-ner dialogue." This condition provided for a 10-minute period in which each subject was asked to think about the wisdom task by taking into consideration what other people whose advice he or she valued might have to say about this. Again, one can argue that this condition is characterized by a combination of interactive and individual cognition. A lower performance increase was ex-pected for two conditions of "dialogue" and "inner monologue." In the dia-logue condition, a natural dyad had 10 minutes to discuss a wisdom task in any way they wished. Immediately afterward each of the members had to respond individually. The inner monologue condition provided for 10 minutes of individual thinking after the subject had been presented with the wisdom task and before he or she had to respond. Finally, the lowest wisdom-related performance levels were expected of the traditional standard wisdom procedure, in which the subject was asked to think aloud immediately after being presented with the wisdom task.

These five experimental conditions were applied to a sample of 140 men and women from varied walks of life and covering an age range from 19 to 80 years of age. Two wisdom tasks were employed to access wisdom-related knowledge. One was a life review task that confronted a fictitious person with the meaning-of-life question, and the other was a non-normative life management problem that dealt with a young girl who wanted to move out of her parents' home.

Averaged across two wisdom-related tasks, the five performance conditions formed a linear trend in terms of level of performance with dialogue and individual appraisal being first, inner dialogue second, inner monologue third, dialogue fourth, and standard fifth in rank. No interactions with age or gender were obtained (Staudinger & Baltes, 1995).

This nascent research seems to offer some support for the usefulness of social-interactive paradigms in teasing apart the contribution of individual and interactive cognition to wisdom-related performance. The condition combining individual and actual interactive cognition, that is, dialogue and individual appraisal, increased performance levels as compared with the standard condition by *one standard deviation*, whereas the dialogue condition that gives primacy to actual interactive cognition did not result in a significant increase in performance as compared with traditional person-centered paradigms.

To offer a first tentative conclusion, it seems that performance settings, optimally facilitative of wisdom-related knowledge, may be characterized by a balance between interactive and individual cognition. According to the findings of this first study, it does not seem to make a difference whether two people actually interact with each other or whether this interaction is mediated through mental representations of other people's wisdom-related knowledge. Even stronger, one can hypothesize that symbolically mediated interaction provides for more individual freedom in terms of when to "access" another person's knowledge system. Thus, interactional losses due to a lack of coordination or to socioemotional discordances are minimized.

Conclusions

Dictionary definitions, as well as implicit and explicit theories, suggest that wisdom is social-interactive. This social-interactive nature has been conceptualized as having three facets, referring to the development (ontogenesis, evolution), application (microgenesis), and identification (recognition) of wisdom-related knowledge. Since wisdom can become manifest on an individual and a cultural level, all three facets can be identified on both levels as well. Proximal and distal forms of social interaction were distinguished. Wisdom cannot develop without distal and proximal social interaction. But when it comes to the activation of wisdom in a given situation, proximal interaction is not constitutive of, but rather optimizes, wisdom-related performance.

Focusing on the microgenesis or activation of wisdom-related performance in a social context, I conducted a selective review of the research on professional expertise and on group problem solving in the social psychology literature. The review can be summarized as follows. It is not social interaction per se that provides support for individual cognitive performance. The gains and losses involved in any given social-interactive performance setting need to be taken into account. Social interaction does not have to be direct in order to be supportive. The right combination of interactive and individual cognition seems to be a highly supportive performance setting for many cognitive tasks.

An empirical study applying for the first time an interactive-minds paradigm to the study of wisdom provided initial evidence to support the contention that optimal performance conditions for the activation of wisdom-related knowledge may involve a delicate balance between interactive and individual cognition rather than one or the other alone. Furthermore, the increase in performance by one standard deviation demonstrated that wisdom-related performance capacity seems to be quite rich given the right performance settings.

References

Adler, M. J. (1992). *The great ideas: One hundred two essays*. New York: Macmillan.

Alexander, C., & Langer, E. (Eds.). (1990). *Higher stages of human development: Perspectives on adult growth*. New York: Oxford University Press.

Assmann, A. (Ed.). (1991). *Weisheit* [Wisdom]. Munich: Fink.

Assmann, J. (1992). *Das kulturelle Gedächtnis. Schrift, Erinnerung und politische Identität in frühen Hochkulturen* [Cultural memory: Script, reminiscence and political identity in early cultures]. Munich: Beck.

Azmitia, M., & Perlmutter, M. (1989). Social influences on children's cognition: State of the art and future directions. *Advances in Child Development and Behavior, 22,* 89–144.

Baddeley, A. D. (1981). The cognitive psychology of everyday life. *British Journal of Psychology, 72,* 257–269.

Badke-Schaub, P. (1993). *Gruppen und komplexe Probleme* [Groups and complex problems]. Frankfurt (Main): Europäischer Verlag der Wissenschaften.

Bales, R. F., & Strodtbeck, F. L. (1951). Phases in group problem-solving. *Journal of Abnormal and Social Psychology, 46,* 485–495.

Baltes, P. B. (1987). Theoretical propositions of life-span developmental psychology: On the dynamics between growth and decline. *Developmental Psychology, 23,* 611–626.

Baltes, P. B. (1994a). *Wisdom* (Chapter 2: A glimpse at the ancient history of wisdom).

Unpublished manuscript. Berlin: Max Planck Institute for Human Development and Education.

Baltes, P. B. (1994b). *Wisdom* (Chapter 3: From cultural and religious beliefs to a philosophical [scientific] analysis of wisdom). Unpublished manuscript. Berlin: Max Planck Institute for Human Development and Education.

Baltes, P. B., Dittmann-Kohli, F., & Dixon, R. A. (1984). New perspectives on the development of intelligence in adulthood: Toward a dual process conception and a model of selective optimization with compensation. In P. B. Baltes & O. G. Brim (Eds.), *Life-span development and behavior* (Vol. 6, pp. 33–76). New York: Academic.

Baltes, P. B., & Smith, J. (1990). Toward a psychology of wisdom and its ontogenesis. In R. J. Sternberg (Ed.), *Wisdom: Its nature, origins, and development* (pp. 87–120). New York: Cambridge University Press.

Baltes, P. B., Smith, J., & Staudinger, U. M. (1992). Wisdom and successful aging. In T. B. Sonderegger (Ed.), *Nebraska Symposium on Motivation: Vol. 39. Psychology and aging* (pp. 123–167). Lincoln: University of Nebraska Press.

Baltes, P. B., & Staudinger, U. M. (1993). The search for a psychology of wisdom. *Current Directions in Psychological Science, 2,* 1–6.

Baltes, P. B., Staudinger, U. M., Maercker, A., & Smith J. (1995). People nominated as wise: A comparative study of wisdom-related knowledge. *Psychology and Aging, 10,* 155–166.

Baltes, P. B., & Willis, S. W. (1977). Toward psychological theories of aging and development. In J. E. Birren & K. W. Schaie (Eds.), *Handbook of the psychology of aging* (pp. 128–154). New York: Van Nostrand Reinhold.

Barkow, J. H., Cosmides, L., & Tooby, J. (Eds.). (1992). *The adapted mind: Evolutionary psychology and the generation of culture.* New York: Oxford University Press.

Benware, C. A., & Deci, E. L. (1984). Quality of learning with an active versus passive motivational set. *American Educational Research Journal, 21,* 755–765.

Berg, C. A., & Calderone, K. S. (1994). The role of problem interpretations in understanding the development of everyday problem solving. In R. J. Sternberg & R. K. Wagner (Eds.), *Mind in context* (pp. 105–132). New York: Cambridge University Press.

Berger, P. L., & Luckmann, T. (1967). *The social construction of reality.* Garden City, NY: Doubleday.

Bloom, B. S. (1985). Generalizations about talent development. In B. S. Bloom (Ed.), *Developing talent in young people* (pp. 507–549). New York: Ballantine.

Boesch, E. E. (1991). *Symbolic action theory and cultural psychology.* Heidelberg: Springer.

Bond, C. F., Jr., & Titus, L. J. (1982). Social facilitation: A meta-analysis of 241 studies. *Psychological Bulletin, 94,* 265–292.

Bornstein, M. H., & Bruner, J. S. (1989). On interaction. In M. H. Bornstein & J. S. Bruner (Eds.), *Interaction in human development* (pp. 1–14). Hillsdale, NJ: Erlbaum.

Bos, M. C. (1937). Experimental study of productive collaboration. *Acta Psychologica, 3,* 315–426.

Brent, S. B. (1978). Individual specialization, collective adaption and rate of environmental change. *Human Development, 21,* 21–33.

Brent, S. B., & Watson, D. (1980, November). *Aging and wisdom: Individual and collective aspects.* Paper presented at the annual meeting of the Gerontological Society of America, San Francisco, CA.

Bronfenbrenner, U. (1979). *The ecology of human development.* Cambridge, MA: Harvard University Press.

Brown, A. L., Campione, J. C., Webber, L. S., & McGilly, K. (1992). Interactive learning environments: A new look at assessment and instruction. In B. R. Gifford & M. C. O'Connor (Eds.), *Changing assessments: Alternative views of aptitude, achievement, and instruction* (pp. 121–211). Boston: Kluwer.

Charness, N. (1989). Expertise in chess and bridge. In D. Klahr & K. Kotovsky (Eds.), *Complex information processing: The impact of Herbert A. Simon* (pp. 183–289). Hillsdale, NJ: Erlbaum.

Cheng, P. W., & Holyoak, K. J. (1985). Pragmatic reasoning schemes. *Cognitive Psychology, 17,* 391–416.

Chi, M. T. H., Glaser, R., & Farr, M. J. (Eds.). (1988). *The nature of expertise.* Hillsdale, NJ: Erlbaum.

Cicourel, A. V. (1990). The integration of distributed knowledge in collaborative medical diagnosis. In J. Galegher, R. E. Kraut, & C. Egido (Eds.), *Intellectual teamwork* (pp. 221–242). Hillsdale, NJ: Erlbaum.

Clayton, V. P. (1976). *A multidimensional scaling analysis of the concept of wisdom.* Unpublished doctoral dissertation, University of California, Los Angeles.

Clayton, V. P., & Birren, J. E. (1980). The development of wisdom across the life-span: A reexamination of an ancient topic. In P. B. Baltes & O. G. Brim (Eds.), *Life-span development and behavior* (Vol. 3, pp. 103–135). New York: Academic.

Cole, M. (1990). Cultural psychology: A once and future discipline? *Nebraska Symposium on Motivation, 37,* 279–335.

Commons, M. L., Sinnott, J. D., Richards, F. A., & Armon, C. (Eds.). (1989). *Adult development: Comparisons and applications of developmental models* (Vol. 1). New York: Praeger.

Cosmides, L. (1989). The logic of social exchange: Has natural selection shaped how humans reason? Studies with the Wason selection task. *Cognition, 31,* 187–276.

Csikszentmihalyi, M., & Rathunde, K. (1990). The psychology of wisdom: An evolutionary interpretation. In R. J. Sternberg (Ed.), *Wisdom: Its nature, origins, and development* (pp. 25–51). New York: Cambridge University Press.

D'Andrade, R. G. (1981). The cultural part of cognition. *Cognitive Science, 5,* 179–195.

Dannefer, D. (1984). Adult development and social theory: A paradigmatic reappraisal. *American Sociological Review, 49,* 100–116.

Dittmann-Kohli, F., & Baltes, P. B. (1990). Toward a neofunctionalist conception of adult intellectual development. Wisdom as a prototypical case of intellectual growth. In C. Alexander & E. Langer (Eds.), *Higher stages of human development: Perspectives on adult growth* (pp. 54–78). New York: Oxford University Press.

Dixon, R. A. (1992). Contextual approaches to adult intellectual development. In R. J. Sternberg & C. A. Berg (Eds.), *Intellectual development* (pp. 350–380). New York: Cambridge University Press.

Dörner, D., Kreuzig, H., Reither, F., & Stäudel, T. (Eds.). (1983). *Lohausen. Vom Umgang mit Unbestimmtheit und Komplexität* [Lohausen: About dealing with uncertainty and complexity]. Bern: Huber.

Dunnette, M. D., Campbell, J., & Jaastad, K. (1963). The effect of group participation on brainstorming effectiveness for two industrial samples. *Journal of Applied Psychology, 47,* 30–37.

Ericsson, K. A., Krampe, R. Th., & Tesch-Römer, C. (1993). The role of deliberate practice in the acquisition of expert performance. *Psychological Review, 100,* 363–406.

Ericsson, K. A., & Simon, H. A. (1984). *Protocol analysis: Verbal reports as data.* Cambridge, MA: MIT Press.

Ericsson, K. A., & Smith, J. (Eds.). (1991). *Toward a general theory of expertise: Prospects and limits.* New York: Cambridge University Press.

Featherman, D. L., & Lerner, R. M. (1985). Ontogenesis and sociogenesis: Problematics for theory and research about development and socialization across the lifespan. *American Sociological Review, 50,* 659–676.

Fischer, K. W., Bullock, D. H., Rotenberg, E. J., & Raya, P. (1993). The dynamics of competence: How context contributes directly to skill. In R. H. Wozniak & K. W. Fischer (Eds.), *Development in context: Acting and thinking in specific environments* (pp. 93–117). Hillsdale, NJ: Erlbaum.

Flavell, J. H. (1970). Cognitive changes in adulthood. In L. R. Goulet & P. B. Baltes (Eds.), *Lifespan developmental psychology: Research and theory* (pp. 247–253). New York: Academic.

Funke, J. (1991). Solving complex problems: Exploration and control of complex social systems. In R. J. Sternberg & P. A. Frensch (Eds.), *Complex problem solving: Principles and mechanisms* (pp. 185–222). Hillsdale, NJ; Erlbaum.

Galegher, J., Kraut, R. E., & Egido, C. (Eds.). (1990). *Intellectual teamwork*. Hillsdale, NJ: Erlbaum.

Gigerenzer, G., & Hug, K. (1992). Domain-specific reasoning: Social contracts, cheating, and perspective change. *Cognition, 43*, 127–171.

Goodwin, P. D., & Wenzel, J. W. (1981). Proverbs and practical reasoning: A study in socio-logic. In W. Mieder & A. Dundes (Eds.), *The wisdom of many: Essays on the proverb* (pp. 140–159). New York: Garland.

Greif, I. (Ed.). (1988). *Computer-supported cooperative work: A book of readings*. San Mateo, CA: Morgan Kaufman.

Grimm, J., & Grimm, W. (1984). *Deutsches Wörterbuch* [German Dictionary]. Munich: Deutscher Taschenbuch-Verlag. (Original work published 1854)

Hackman, R. J., & Morris, C. G. (1975). Group tasks, group interaction process, and the group performance effectiveness: A review and proposed integration. In L. Berkowitz (Ed.), *Advances in experimental social psychology* (Vol. 8, pp. 46–99). New York: Academic.

Hahn, A. (1989). Zur Soziologie der Weisheit. [The sociology of wisdom]. In A. Assmann (Ed.), *Weisheit. Archäologie der literarischen Kommunikation* [Wisdom: Archeology of literary communication] (Vol. 3, pp. 47–58). Munich: Wilhelm Fink Verlag.

Hastie, R., & Pennington, S. (1991). Cognitive and social processes in decision making. In L. B. Resnick, J. M. Levine, & S. D. Teasley (Eds.), *Perspectives on socially shared cognition* (pp. 308–327). Washington, DC: American Psychological Association.

Hill, G. W. (1982). Group versus individual performance: Are $N + 1$ heads better than one? *Psychological Bulletin, 91*, 517–539.

Hoffman, R. L. (1965). Group problem solving. In L. Berkowitz (Ed.), *Advances in experimental psychology* (Vol. 2, pp. 99–131). New York: Academic.

Holliday, S. G., & Chandler, M. J. (1986). *Wisdom: Explorations in adult competence*. Basel: Karger.

James, W. (1890). *The principles of psychology*. New York: Henry Holt.

Janis, I. L. (1972). *Victims of groupthink*. Boston: Houghton Mifflin.

Karau, S. J., & Williams, K. D. (1993). Social loafing: A meta-analytic review and theoretical integration. *Journal of Personality and Social Psychology, 65*, 681–706.

Kaufman, D. R., & Patel, V. L. (1988). The nature of expertise in the clinical interview: Interactive medical problem solving. In *Proceedings of the Tenth Annual Conference of the Cognitive Science Society* (pp. 461–467). Hillsdale, NJ: Erlbaum.

Kelley, H. H., & Thibaut, J. W. (1969). Group problem solving. In G. Lindzey & E. Aronson (Eds.), *Handbook of social psychology* (3rd ed., pp. 1–101). Hillsdale, NJ: Erlbaum.

Kitchener, K. S., Lynch, C., Fischer, K. W., & Wood, P. (1993). Developmental range of reflective judgment: The effect of contextual support and practice on developmental stage. *Developmental Psychology, 29*, 893–906.

Klix, F. (1993). *Erwachendes Denken: Geistige Leistungen aus evolutions-psychologischer Sicht* [The awakening of thought: Cognitive performance from an evolutionary psychological perspective]. Heidelberg: Spektrum Akademischer Verlag.

Kramer, D. A. (1990). Conceptualizing wisdom: The primacy of affect–cognition relations. In R. J. Sternberg (Ed.), *Wisdom: Its nature, origins, and development* (pp. 279–313). New York: Cambridge University Press.

Lamm, H., & Trommsdorff, G. (1973). Group versus individual performance on tasks requiring ideational proficiency (brainstorming): A review. *European Journal of Social Psychology, 3*, 361–388.

Laughlin, P. R., & Adamopoulos, J. (1980). Social combination processes and individual learning for six-person cooperative groups on an intellective task. *Journal of Personality and Social Psychology, 38*, 941–947.

Lerner, R. M. (1984). *On the nature of human plasticity*. New York: Cambridge University Press.

Lerner, R. M., & von Eye, A. (1992). Sociobiology and human development: Arguments and evidence. *Human Development, 35*, 12–33.

Lesgold, A., Rubinson, H., Feltovich, P., Glaser, R., Klopfer, D., & Wang, Y. (1988). Expertise in a complex skill: Diagnosing x-ray pictures. In M. Chi, R. Glaser, & M. J. Farr (Eds.), *The nature of expertise* (pp. 311–342). Hillsdale, NJ: Erlbaum.

Lindgren, H. C., & Lindgren, F. (1965). Creativity, brainstormig, and orneriness: A cross-cultural study. *Journal of Social Psychology, 67,* 23–30.

Lorge, I., Fox, D., Davitz, J., & Brenner, M. (1958). A survey of studies contrasting the quality of group performance and individual performance, 1920–1957. *Psychological Bulletin, 55,* 337–372.

Maciel, A., Sowarka, D., Smith, J., Staudinger, U. M., & Baltes, P. B. (1993). *Dimensions of a wise person: Interrelating implicit and explicit theories of wisdom.* Unpublished manuscript. Berlin: Max Planck Institute for Human Development and Education.

McCall, M. W., & Kaplan, R. E. (1985). *Whatever it takes: Decision makers at work.* Englewood Cliffs, NJ: Prentice-Hall.

Meacham, J. A. (1983). Wisdom and the context of knowledge: Knowing that one doesn't know. In D. Kuhn & A. Meacham (Eds.), *On the development of developmental psychology* (pp. 111–134). Basel: Karger.

Meacham, J. A. (1990). The loss of wisdom. In R. J. Sternberg (Ed.), *Wisdom: Its nature, origins, and development* (pp. 181–211). New York: Cambridge University Press.

Meacham, J. A., & Emont, N. C. (1989). The interpersonal basis of everyday problem solving. In J. D. Sinnott (Ed.), *Everyday problem solving: Theory and applications* (pp. 7–23). New York: Praeger

Mead, G. H. (1934). *Mind, self, and society,* Chicago: Chicago University Press.

Mergler, N. L., & Goldstein, M. D. (1983). Why are there old people? *Human Development, 26,* 72–90.

Mittelstraß, J. (1981). Platon. In O. Höffe (Ed.), *Klassiker der Philosophie* [Classics of philosophy] (pp. 38–62). Munich: Beck.

Neisser, U. (1976). *Cognition and reality.* New York: Freeman.

Nelson, K. (1992). Emergence of autobiographical memory at age 4. *Human Development, 35,* 172–177.

Olson, J. R., & Biolsi, K. J. (1991). Techniques for representing expert knowledge. In K. A. Ericsson & J. Smith (Eds.), *Toward a general theory of expertise: Prospects and limits* (pp. 240–285). New York: Cambridge University Press.

Orwoll, L., & Perlmutter, M. (1990). The study of wise persons: Integrating a personality perspective. In R. J. Sternberg (Ed.), *Wisdom: Its nature, origins, and development* (pp. 160–177). New York: Cambridge University Press.

Osborn, A. F. (1957). *Applied imagination* (Revised edition). New York: Scribner.

Overton, W. F., & Newman, J. L. (1982). Cognitive development: A competence-activation/utilization approach. In T. Field, A. Houston, H. Quay, L. Troll, & G. Finlay (Eds.), *Review of human development* (pp. 217–241). New York: Wiley.

Oxford Dictionary of the English Language. (1933). Vol. 12. Oxford: Oxford University Press.

Patel, V. L., & Groen, G. J. (1991). The general and specific nature of medical expertise: A critical look. In K. A. Ericsson & J. Smith (Eds.), *Toward a general theory of expertise: Prospects and limits* (pp. 93–125). New York: Cambridge University Press.

Paulus, P. B. (1983). Group influence on task performance and informational processing. In P. B. Paulus (Ed.), *Basic group processes* (pp. 1–12). New York: Springer.

Poon, L. W., Rubin, D. C., & Wilson, B. A. (Eds.). (1989). *Everyday cognition in adulthood and late life.* New York: Cambridge University Press.

Putz-Osterloh, W. (1987). Gibt es Experten für komplexe Probleme [Are there experts for complex problems?]. *Zeitschrift für Psychologie, 195,* 63–84.

Putz-Osterloh, W. (1991). *Stärken und Schwächen der Entscheidungsbildung in Gruppen im Vergleich zu Einzelpersonen* [Strengths and weaknesses of decision making in groups as compared to individuals]. Vortrag, 33. Teap in Gießen, 24.–28.3.1991.

Rasmussen, J., Brehmer, B., & Leplat, J. (Eds.). (1991). *Distributed decision making.* Chichester: Wiley.

Reitman, W. (1965). *Cognition and thought.* New York: Wiley.

Resnick, L. B., Levine, J. M., & Teasley, S. D. (1991). *Perspectives on socially shared cognition.* Washington, DC: American Psychological Association.

Riley, M. W. (1985). Age strata in social systems. In R. H. Binstock & E. Shanas (Eds.), *Handbook of aging and the social sciences* (pp. 369–411). New York: Van Nostrand Reinhold.

Rogoff, B. (1993). Children's guided participation and participatory appropriation in sociocultural activity. In R. H. Wozniak & K. W. Fischer (Eds.), *Development in context: Acting and thinking in specific environments* (pp. 121–153). Hillsdale, NJ: Erlbaum.

Rubin, D. C., Wetzler, S. E., & Nebes, R. D. (1986). Autobiographical memory across the life-span. In D. C. Rubin (Ed.), *Autobiographical memory* (pp. 202–224). New York: Cambridge University Press.

Rudolph, K. (1987). Wisdom. In M. Eliade (Ed.), *Encyclopedia of religion: Wisdom* (Vol. 15, pp. 393–401). New York: Macmillan.

Salthouse, T. A. (1991). *Theoretical perspectives on cognitive aging.* Hillsdale, NJ: Erlbaum.

Schütz, A., & Luckmann, T. (1979). *Strukturen der Lebenswelt* [Structures of the everyday world, Vol. 1]. Frankfurt (Main): Suhrkamp.

Shweder, R. A. (1991). *Thinking through cultures.* Cambridge, MA: Harvard University Press.

Simon, H. A. (1973). The structure of ill-structured problems. *Artificial Intelligence, 4,* 181–201.

Sinnott, J. D., & Cavanaugh, J. C. (Eds.). (1991). Bridging paradigms: Positive development in adulthood and cognitive aging. New York: Praeger.

Slavin, R. (1980). Cooperative learning. *Review of Educational Research, 50,* 315–342.

Smith, J., Staudinger, U. M., & Baltes, P. B. (1994). Settings facilitating wisdom-related knowledge: The sample case of clinical psychologists. *Journal of Consulting and Clinical Psychology, 62,* 989–1000.

Staudinger, U. M., & Baltes, P. B. (1994). The psychology of wisdom. In R. J. Sternberg et al. (Eds.), *Encyclopedia of intelligence* (pp. 1143–1152). New York: Macmillan.

Staudinger, U. M., & Baltes, P. B. (1995). *Interactive minds: A facilitative setting for wisdom-related performance?* Unpublished manuscript. Berlin: Max Planck Institute for Human Development and Education.

Staudinger, U. M., & Dittmann-Kohli, F. (1994). Lebenserfahrung und Lebenssinn [Life experience and the meaning of life]. In P. B. Baltes, J. Mittelstraß, & U. M. Staudinger (Eds.), *Alter und Altern: Ein interdisziplinärer Studientext zur Gerontologie* [Old age and aging: An interdisciplinary reader in gerontology] (pp. 408–436). Berlin: de Gruyter.

Staudinger, U. M., Smith, J., & Baltes, P. B. (1992). Wisdom-related knowledge in a life review task: Age differences and the role of professional specialization. *Psychology and Aging, 7,* 271–281.

Steiner, I. D. (1972). *Group process and productivity.* New York: Academic.

Sternberg, R. J. (1985). Implicit theories of intelligence, creativity and wisdom. *Journal of Personality and Social Psychology, 49,* 607–627.

Sternberg, R. J. (1990). Understanding wisdom. In R. J. Sternberg (Ed.), *Wisdom: Its nature, origins, and development* (pp. 3–9). New York: Cambridge University Press.

Sternberg, R. J., & Frensch, P. A. (Eds.). (1991). *Complex problem solving: Principles and mechanisms.* Hillsdale, NJ: Erlbaum.

Sternberg, R. J., & Wagner, R. K. (1986). *Practical intelligence: Nature and origins of competence in the everyday world.* New York: Cambridge University Press.

Sternberg, R. J., & Wagner, R. K. (Eds.). (1994). *Mind in context.* New York: Cambridge University Press.

Stroebe W., Diehl, M., & Abakoumkin, G. (1992). The illusion of group effectivity. *Personality and Social Psychology Bulletin, 18,* 643–650.

Taylor, A. (1962). The wisdom of many and the wit of one. *Swarthmore College Bulletin, 54,* 4–7.

Tudge, J. R. (1992). Processes and consequences of peer collaboration: A Vygotskian analysis. *Child Development, 63,* 1364–1379.

von Cranach, M., Doise, W., & Mugny, G. (Eds.). (1992). *Social representations and the social bases of knowledge.* Lewiston, NY: Hogrefe & Huber.

Voss, J. F., Wolfe, C., Lawrence, J. A., & Engle, R. A. (1991). From representation to decision: An analysis of problem solving in international relations. In R. J. Sternberg & P. A. Frensch (Eds.), *Complex problem solving: Principles and mechanisms* (pp. 119–158). Hillsdale, NJ: Erlbaum.

Wagner, R. K. (1991). Managerial problem solving. In R. J. Sternberg & P. A. Frensch (Eds.), *Complex problem solving: Principles and mechanisms* (pp. 159–184). Hillsdale, NJ: Erlbaum.

Wozniak, R. H., & Fischer, K. W. (Eds.). (1993). *Development in context: Acting and thinking in specific environments*. Hillsdale, NJ: Erlbaum.

Zajonc, R. B. (1960). The process of cognitive tuning in communication. *Journal of Abnormal and Social Psychology, 61*, 159–167.

Zajonc, R. B. (1965). Social facilitation. *Science, 149*, 269–274.

Part III

Perspectives from cognitive and educational psychology

11   Rationality: why social context matters

Gerd Gigerenzer

Abstract

Rationality is commonly identified with axioms and rules, such as consistency, which are defined without reference to context, but are imposed in all contexts. In this chapter, I focus on the social context of rational behavior. My thesis is that traditional axioms and rules are incomplete as behavioral norms in the sense that their normative validity depends on the social context of the behavior, such as social objectives, values, and motivations. In the first part, I illustrate this thesis by showing that social context can determine whether an axiom or rule is satisfied or not. In the second part, I describe an alternative to context-independent rationality: a domain-specific theory of rational behavior derived from the evolutionary theory of cooperation.

I want to argue against an old and beautiful dream. It was Leibniz's dream, but not his alone. Leibniz (1677/1951) hoped to reduce rational reasoning to a universal calculus, which he termed the Universal Characteristic. The plan was simple: to establish characteristic numbers for all ideas, which would reduce every question to calculation. Such a rational calculus would put an end to scholarly bickering; if a dispute arose, the contending parties could settle it quickly and peacefully by sitting down and calculating. For some time, the Enlightenment probabilists believed that the mathematical theory of probability had made this dream a reality. Probability theory rather than logic became the flip side of the newly coined rationality of the Enlightenment, which acknowledged that humankind lives in the twilight of probability rather than the noontime sun of certainty, as John Locke expressed it. Leibniz guessed optimistically of the Universal Characteristic that "a few selected persons

I would like to thank Paul Baltes, Robert Boyd, Valerie Chase, Michael Cole, Lorraine Daston, Berna Eden, Bill Goldstein, Dan Goldstein, Wolfgang Hell, Ralph Hertwig, Amy Johnson, Elke Kurz, Peter Sedlmeier, Anna Senkevitch, Ursula Staudinger, Gerhard Strube, Zeno Swijtink, Elke Weber, and three anonymous reviewers for their helpful comments. I am grateful for the financial support provided by the UCSMP Fund for Research in Mathematics Education and by an NSF Grant SBR-9320797/GG.

might be able to do the whole thing in five years" (Leibniz, 1677/1951, p. 22). By around 1840, however, mathematicians had given up as thankless and even antimathematical the task of reducing rationality to a calculus (Daston, 1988). Psychologists and economists have not.

Contemporary theories embody Leibniz's dream in various forms. Piaget and Inhelder's (1951/1975) theory of cognitive development holds that, by roughly age 12, human beings begin to reason according to the laws of probability theory; Piaget and Inhelder thus echo the Enlightenment conviction that human rationality and probability theory are two sides of the same coin (Gigerenzer et al., 1989). Neoclassical economic theories center on the assumption that Jacob Bernoulli's expected utility maximization principle or its modern variants, such as subjective expected utility, define rationality in all contexts. Similarly, neo-Bayesians tend to claim that the formal machinery of Bayesian statistics defines rational inferences in all contexts. In cognitive psychology, formal axioms and rules – consistency, transitivity, and Bayes's theorem, for example, as well as entire statistical techniques – figure prominently in recent theories of mind and warrant the rationality of cognition (Gigerenzer, 1991a; Gigerenzer & Murray, 1987).

All these theories have been criticized as *descriptively* incomplete or inadequate, most often by showing that principles from logic or probability theory (such as consistency) are systematically violated in certain contexts. Piaget himself wondered why adults outside of Geneva seemed not to reach the level of formal operations. But even critics have generally retained the beautifully simple principles drawn from logic and probability theory as normative, albeit not descriptively valid – that is, as definitions of how we *should* reason. In this chapter, I will address the question of whether these principles are indeed normative: sufficient for defining rational behavior.

My discussion will challenge one central assumption in the modern variants of Leibniz's dream: that formal axioms and rules of choice can define rational behavior without referring to factors external to choice behavior. To the contrary, I will argue that these principles are incomplete as behavioral norms in the sense that their normative validity depends on the *social* context of the behavior, such as social objectives, values, and motivations.

The point I wish to defend in the first section is that formal axioms and rules cannot be *imposed* as universal yardsticks of rationality independent of social objectives, norms, and values; they can, however, be *entailed* by certain social objectives, norms, and values. Thus, I am not arguing against axioms and rules, only against their a priori imposition as context-independent yardsticks of rationality. In the second section, I will describe one alternative to context-independent rationality in some detail. This alternative account starts with the evolutionary theory of cooperation and puts objectives in social interaction first, formal rules second.

Challenges to a conception of rationality without social context

Leibniz's dream was of a formal calculus of reasonableness that could be applied to everything. Modern variants tend to go one step further and assume that the calculus of rationality has already been found and can be imposed in all contexts. I will focus only on the *social* context in this chapter, arguing that the idea of imposing a context-independent, general-purpose rationality is a limited and confused one. The several examples that follow seek to demonstrate that only by referring to something external to the rules or axioms, such as social objectives, values, and norms, can we decide whether an axiom or choice rule entails rational behavior.

Consistency: Property Alpha

Internal consistency of choice figures prominently as a basic requirement for human rationality in decision theory, behavioral economics, game theory, and cognitive theories. It is often seen as *the* requirement of rational choice. One basic condition of the internal consistency of choice is known as "Property Alpha," also called the "Chernoff condition" or "independence of irrelevant alternatives" (Sen, 1993). The symbols S and T denote two (nonempty) sets of alternatives, and $x(S)$ denotes that alternative x is chosen from the set S:

> *Property Alpha*:
> $x(S)$ and $x \,\varepsilon\, T \subseteq S \Rightarrow x(T)$.

Property Alpha demands that if x is chosen from S, and x belongs to a subset T of S, then x must be chosen from T as well. The following two choices would be inconsistent in the sense that they violate Property Alpha:

1. x is chosen given the options $\{x, y\}$.
2. y is chosen given the options $\{x, y, z\}$.

Property Alpha is violated here because x is chosen when the two alternatives $\{x, y\}$ are offered, but y is chosen when z is added to the menu. (Choosing x is interpreted here as a rejection of y, not as a choice that results from mere indifference.) It may indeed appear odd and irrational that someone who chooses x and rejects y when offered the choice set $\{x, y\}$ would choose y and reject x when offered the set $\{x, y, z\}$.

Property Alpha formulates consistency exclusively in terms of the internal consistency of choice behavior with respect to sets of alternatives. No reference is made to anything external to choice – for instance, intentional states such as people's social objectives, values, and motivations. This exclusion of everything psychological beyond behavior is in line with Samuelson's (1938) program of freeing theories of behavior from any traces of utility and from the priority of the notion of "preference." As Little (1949) commented on the underlying methodological program, Samuelson's "revealed preference" formulation "is scientifically more respectable [since] if an individual's behavior is consistent, then it must be possible to explain the behavior without reference to anything other than behavior" (p. 90). Sen (1993) has launched a forceful attack on internal consistency, as defined by Property Alpha and similar principles, and what follows is based on his ideas and examples.

The last apple. Consider Property Alpha in the context of the social politics at a dinner party. There is one apple left in the fruit basket. Dining alone, Mr. Polite would face no dilemma; but now he must choose between taking the apple (y) or having nothing (x). He decides to behave decently and go without (x). If the basket had contained another apple (z), he could reasonably have chosen y over x without violating standards of good behavior. Choosing x over y from the choice set $\{x, y\}$ and choosing y over x from the choice set $\{x, y, z\}$ violates Property Alpha, even though there is nothing irrational about Mr. Polite's behavior given his scruples in social interaction. If he had not held to such values of politeness, then Property Alpha might have been entailed. But it cannot be imposed independent of his values.

Waiting for dinner. Consider a second example. Mr. Pleasant is invited to his colleague's home on Sunday at 9:00 p.m. Upon arriving, he takes a seat in the living room, and his host offers him crackers and nuts (y). Mr. Pleasant decides to take nothing (x), because he is hungry for a substantial meal and does not want to fill up before dinner. After a while, the colleague's wife comes in with tea and cake (z). The menu has thereby been extended to $\{x, y, z\}$, but there is a larger implication: The new option z also has destroyed an illusion about what the invitation included. Now Mr. Pleasant chooses the crackers and nuts (y) over nothing (x). Again, this preference reversal violates Property Alpha. Given the guest's expectations of what the invitation entailed, however, there is nothing irrational about his behavior.

Tea at night. Here is a final example similar to the last. Mr. Sociable has met a young artist at a party. When the party is over, she invites him to come back to her place for tea. He chooses to have tea with her (x) over returning home (y). The young lady then offers him a third choice – to share some cocaine at her apartment (z). This extension of the choice set may quite reasonably affect Mr. Sociable's ranking of x and y. Depending on his objectives and values, he may consequently choose to go home (y).

All three examples seek to illustrate the same point: Property Alpha will or will not be entailed depending on the social objectives, values, and expectations of the individual making the choice. To impose Property Alpha as a general yardstick of rational behavior independent of social objectives or other factors external to choice behavior seems fundamentally flawed.

The conclusion is not that consistency is an invalid principle; rather, consistency, as defined by Property Alpha or similar principles, is indeterminate. The preceding examples illustrate different kinds of indeterminateness. With respect to the last apple, social values define what the alternatives in the choice set are and, thereby, *what* consistency is about. If there are many apples in the basket, the choice is between "apple" and "nothing." If a single apple remains and one does not share the values of Mr. Polite, the alternatives are the same; for Mr. Polite, however, they become "last apple" and "nothing." In the dinner and tea example, one learns something new about the old alternatives when a new choice is introduced. The fresh option provides new information – that is, it reduces uncertainty about the old alternatives.

To summarize the argument: Consistency, as defined by Property Alpha, cannot be imposed on human behavior independent of something external to choice behavior, such as social objectives and expectations. Social concerns and moral views (e.g., politeness), as well as inferences from the menu offered (learning from one option as to what others may involve), determine whether internal consistency is or is not entailed.

Maximizing: choice under certainty

Maximizing expectation was the cornerstone of the new Enlightenment rationality. The Chevalier de Méré, a notorious gambler, posed the following problem: Can one expect to make more money by betting on the occurrence of at least one "six" in 4 throws of a fair die, or on that of at least one "double six" in 24 throws of a pair of dice? (The first gamble offers the higher expectation.) The correspondence between Blaise Pascal and Pierre Fermat in 1654 over this and similar problems marks the first casting of the calculus of probabilities in mathematical form.

I will turn first to a simpler situation, the choice between alternatives that have certain rather than uncertain monetary payoffs. The choice set is $\{x, y\}$, and the values of x and y are $V(x)$ and $V(y)$ – for instance, the option of either a guaranteed \$200 (x) or a guaranteed \$100 (y). In this simple situation, one can maximize the gain according to the rule:

> *Maximizing under certainty*:
> Choose x if $V(x) > V(y)$.

The monetary values V may be replaced by the utilities U, but for all monotone utility functions the outcome is the same. Like Property Alpha, this rule seems to be so trivial that anyone who violates it would appear odd or irrational. Who would choose \$100 instead of \$200?

In many situations, of course, we are quite right to interpret violations of maximization as peculiar. Nevertheless, I seek to make the same point with maximization as with consistency: It cannot be imposed independent of something external to choice behavior. In particular, maximization, like internal consistency, does not capture the distinction between the individual in isolation and the individual in a social context. The following anecdote illustrates my point (Gigerenzer, 1991b).

The village idiot. In a small town there lives a village idiot. He was once offered a choice between one pound (*x*) and one shilling (*y*). He took the shilling. Having heard about this phenomenon, all of the townspeople in turn offered him the choice between a pound and a shilling. He always took the shilling.

Seen as a singular choice (as the first time was intended to be), his taking the shilling seems irrational by all strictly monotone utility functions. Yet seen in a social context where that particular choice increases the probability of getting to choose again, the violation of maximization makes sense. Make a "stupid" choice and you may get another chance.

My point here is the same as with Property Alpha. The principle of maximizing under certainty is indeterminate, unless the social objectives, motivations, and expectations are analyzed in the first place.

Maximizing: choice under uncertainty

Now consider a choice between alternatives with uncertain outcomes. The choice set is $\{x, y\}$. Choosing *x* will lead to a reinforcement with a probability $p(x) = .80$, whereas choosing *y* will only lead to the same reinforcement with a probability $p(y) = .20$. That is, the utilities of the outcomes (reinforcements) are the same, but their probabilities differ. It is easy to see that when the choice is repeated *n* times, the expected number of reinforcements will be maximized if an organism always chooses *x*:

> *Maximizing with equal utilities*:
> Always choose *x* if $p(x) > p(y)$.

Consider a hungry rat in a T-maze where reinforcement is obtained at the left end in 80% of cases and at the right end in 20% of cases. The rat will maximize reinforcement if it always turns left. Imagine students who watch the rat running and predict which side the reinforcement will appear in each trial. They will also maximize their number of correct predictions by always saying "left." But neither rats nor students seem to maximize. Under a wide variety of experimental conditions, organisms choose both alternatives with relative frequencies that roughly match the probabilities (Gallistel, 1990):

Probability matching:
Choose x with probability $p(x)$;
choose y with probability $p(y)$.

In the preceding example, the expected rate of reinforcements is 80% for maximizing, but only 68% for probability matching (this value is calculated by $.80^2 + .20^2 = .68$). The conditions of the seemingly irrational behavior of probability matching are discussed in the literature (e.g., Brunswik, 1939; Estes, 1976; Gallistel, 1990).

Violations of maximizing by probability matching pose a problem for a context-independent account of rational behavior in animals and humans. What looks irrational for an individual, however, can be optimal for a group. Again, the maximizing principle does not capture the distinction between the individual in social isolation and in social interaction. Under natural conditions of foraging, there will not be just one rat but many who compete to exploit food resources. If all choose to forage in the spot where previous experience suggests food is to be found in greatest abundance, then each may get only a small share. The one mutant organism that sometimes chooses the spot with less food would be better off. Natural selection will favor those exceptional individuals who sometimes choose the less attractive alternative. Thus, maximizing is not always an evolutionarily stable strategy in situations of competition among individuals. Given certain assumptions, probability matching may in fact be an evolutionarily stable strategy, one that does not tend to create conditions that select against it (Fretwell, 1972; Gallistel, 1990).

To summarize the argument: The maximization rule cannot be imposed on behavior independent of social context. Whether an organism performs in isolation or in the context of other organisms can determine, among other things, whether maximization is entailed as an optimal choice rule.

Betting against the probabilities

Mr. Smart would like to invest the $10,000 in his savings account in the hope of increasing his capital. After some consideration, he opts to risk the amount in a single gamble with two possible outcomes, x and y. The outcomes are determined by a fair roulette wheel with 10 equal sections, 6 of them white (x) and 4 black (y). Thus, the probability $p(x)$ of obtaining white is .6, and the probability $p(y)$ of obtaining black is .4. The rules of the game are that he has to bet *all* his money ($10,000) either on black or on white. If Mr. Smart guesses the outcome correctly, his money will be doubled; otherwise, he will lose three-quarters of his investment. Could it ever be advantageous for Mr. Smart to bet on black?

If Mr. Smart bets on white, his expectation is $20,000 with a probability of .6, and $2,500 with a probability of .4. The expected value $E(x)$ is $(.6 \times \$20,000) + (.4 \times \$2,500) = \$13,000$. But if he bets on black, the expected value $E(y)$ is only $(.4 \times \$20,000) + (.6 \times \$2,500) = \$9,500$. Betting on white would give him an expectation larger than the sum he invests. Betting on black, on the other hand, would result in an expectation lower than the sum he invests. A maximization of the expected value implies betting on white:

> *Maximizing expected value*:
> Choose x if $E(x) > E(y)$,

where $E(x) = \Sigma\, p(x)V(x)$. The principle of maximizing the expected value (or subjective variants such as expected utility) is one of the cornerstones of classical definitions of rationality. Mr. Smart would be a fool to bet on black, wouldn't he?

Let me apply the same argument again. The principle of maximizing the expected value does not distinguish between the individual in social isolation and in social interaction. If many individuals face the same choice, could it be to the benefit of the whole group that some sacrifice themselves and bet on black? Let us first look at an example from biology.

Cooper (1989; Cooper & Kaplan, 1982) discussed conditions under which it is essential for the survival of the group that some individuals bet against the probabilities and do *not*, at the individual level, maximize their expected value. Consider a hypothetical population of organisms whose evolutionary fitness (measured simply by the finite rate of increase in their population) depends highly on protective coloration. Each winter predators pass through the region, decimating those within the population that can be spotted against the background terrain. If the black soil of the organisms' habitat happens to be covered with snow at the time, the best protective coloration is white; otherwise, it is black. The probability of snow when predators pass through is .6, and protectively colored individuals can expect to survive the winter in numbers sufficient to leave an average of two surviving offspring each, whereas the conspicuous ones can expect an average of only 0.25 offspring each. This example assumes a simple evolutionary model with asexual breeding (each offspring is genetically identical to its parent), seasonal breeding (offspring are produced only in spring), and semelparous breeding (each individual produces offspring only once in a lifetime at the age of exactly one year).

Adaptive coin-flipping. Suppose two genotypes, W and WB, are in competition within a large population. Individuals of genotype W always have white winter coloration; that is, W is a genotype with a uniquely determined phenotypic expression. Genotype WB, in contrast, gives rise to both white and black individuals, with a ratio of 5 to 3. Thus, 3 out of 8 individuals with genotype *WB* are "betting" on the low probability of no snow. Each of these individuals' expectation to survive and reproduce is smaller than that of all other individuals in both *W* and *WB*.

How will these two genotypes fare after 1,000 generations (1,000 years)? We can expect that there was snow cover in about 600 winters, exposed black soil in about 400 winters. Then, the number of individuals with genotype *W* will be doubled 600 times and reduced to one-fourth 400 times. If *n* is the original population size, the population size after 1,000 years is

$$n2^{600}(1/4)^{400} \approx 6n \times 10^{-61}.$$

That is, genotype *W* will have been wiped out with practical certainty after 1,000 years. How does genotype *WB* do? In the 600 snowy winters, 5/8 of the population will double in number and 3/8 will be reduced to 25 percent, with corresponding proportions for the 400 winters without snow. The number of individuals after 1,000 years is then

$$n\left(\frac{5}{8} \times 2 + \frac{3}{8} \times \frac{1}{4}\right)^{600} \left(\frac{5}{8} \times \frac{1}{4} + \frac{3}{8} \times 2\right)^{400} \approx 8n \times 10^{59}.$$

Thus, genotype *WB* is likely to win the evolutionary race easily.[1] (The large estimated number is certainly an overestimation, however, because it does not take account of such other constraints as food resources.) The reason why *WB* has so much better a chance of survival than *W* is that a considerable proportion of the *WB* individuals do not maximize their individual expectations, but "bet" on small probabilities.

This violation of individual maximization has been termed "adaptive coin-flipping" (Cooper & Kaplan, 1982), meaning that individuals are genetically programmed to "flip coins" to adopt phenotypic traits. Thus, the phenotype is ultimately determined by the nature of the coin-flipping process, rather than uniquely specified by the genotype.[2]

Back to Mr. Smart. Assume he won and wants to try again. So do his numerous brothers, sisters, and cousins, who all are willing to commit their entire investment capital to this gamble. The game is offered every week, and the rules are as before: Each person's choice is every week to bet *all* his or her investment capital either on black or on white (no hedging of bets). If every-one wanted solely to maximize his or her individual good, his or her money would be better invested in white than in black, since the chances to double one's assets are 60% for white compared with only 40% for black. Investing in black would appear irrational. But we know from our previous calculations that someone who invests all his or her money every week in white will, with a high probability, lose every dollar of assets in the long run.

If Mr. Smart and his extended family, however, acted as one community rather than as independent individuals – that is, create one investment capital fund in which they share equally – they can quickly increase their capital with a high probability. Every week they would need to instruct 3/8 of their members to invest in black, the rest in white. This social sharing is essentially the same situation as the "adaptive coin-flipping" example (Cooper, 1989). Thus, Mr. Smart's betting on black needs to be judged against his motivation: If he is cooperating with others for their common interest, then betting on the wrong side of a known probability is part of an optimal strategy. If he is not cooperating but, rather, investing for his own immediate benefit, then betting on black is the fastest way to ruin.

This example, like the preceding ones, attempts to illustrate that a rule such as maximizing the expected value cannot be imposed on behavior without consideration of the social context. Is this context a single individual wagering all his or her assets at once or a population that risks their collective assets or offspring at regular intervals? It makes all the difference, since individual maximization can lead to the extinction of the genotype.

Conclusions

These examples show that general principles such as consistency and maximizing are insufficient for capturing rationality. I have argued that there is no way of determining whether a behavioral pattern is consistent or maximizes without first referring to something external to choice behavior (Sen, 1993). The external factor investigated in this chapter is the *social context* of choice behavior, including objectives, motivations, and values. I am not arguing against consistency, maximization, or any given rule per se, but against the a priori imposition of a rule or axiom as a requirement for rationality, independent of the social context of judgment and decision and, likewise, of whether the individual operates in isolation or within a social context (Elster, 1990; Gigerenzer, 1991b).

One way to defend general principles against this argument would be to say that maximization poses no restrictions on what individuals maximize, be it their own good (utilities) or the fitness of their genotype. Switching from individual goals to genotypic fitness can save the concept of maximization. Such a defense would imply, however, that maximization cannot be imposed independent of the motivations and goals built into living systems, which is precisely the point I have asserted. By the same token, to claim that consistency poses no restrictions on whatever consistency is about would destroy the very idea of behavioral consistency, because Property Alpha would as a result be open to any external interpretation and would no longer impose any constraint on choice.

More generally, the formal principles of logic, probability theory, rational choice theory, and other context-independent principles of rationality are often rescued and defended by post hoc justifications. Post hoc reasoning typically uses the social objectives, values, and motivations of organisms to make room for exceptions or to reinterpret the alternatives in axioms or rules until they are compatible with the observed result. Contemporary neoclassical economics, for instance, provides little theoretical basis for specifying the content and shape of the utility function; it thus affords many degrees of freedom for fitting any phenomenon to the theory (Simon, 1986). In Elster's (1990) formulation, a theory of rationality can fail through indeterminacy (rather than through inadequacy) to the extent that it fails to yield unique predictions.

The challenge is to go beyond general-purpose principles of rationality that allow context to slip in through the back door. What would a theory of reasoning that lets social context in through the front door look like? In the second part of this chapter I will present and discuss one example of such a "front door" theory. Inspired by evolutionary theory, it appears to be the only theory so far to relate reciprocal altruism to human reasoning.

Toward models of social rationality

The psychological flip side of Leibniz's dream of a universal calculus of reasonableness is the assumption that there is one – or at most a few – universal mechanisms that govern all of reasoning, learning, memory, inference, imitation, imagery, and so on. I will call these assumed mechanisms *general-purpose* mechanisms, because they have no features specialized for processing particular kinds of content. For instance, when Piaget started to work on mental imagery and memory, he did not expect and search for processes different from logical thinking. Rather, he attempted to demonstrate that at each stage in development, imagery and memory express the same logical structure as the one he had found in his earlier studies on children's thinking (Gruber & Vonèche, 1977). Similarly, B. F. Skinner's laws of operant behavior were designed to be general-purpose: to hold true for all stimuli and responses (the assumption of the *equipotentiality* of stimuli).

John Garcia's anomalous findings (e.g., Garcia & Koelling, 1966) challenged not only the notion of the equipotentiality of stimuli, but also the law of contiguity, which postulates the necessity of immediate reinforcement, independent of the nature of the stimulus and response. For instance, when the taste of flavored water is repeatedly paired with an electric shock immediately after tasting, rats have great difficulty learning to avoid the flavored water. Yet in just one trial the rat can learn to avoid the flavored water when it is followed by experimentally induced nausea, even when the nausea occurs

2 hours later. "From the evolutionary view, the rat is a biased learning machine designed by natural selection to form certain CS–US [conditioned stimulus–unconditioned stimulus] associations rapidly but not others. From a traditional learning viewpoint, the rat was an unbiased learner able to make any association in accordance with the general principles of contiguity, effect, and similarity" (Garcia y Robertson & Garcia, 1985, p. 25). Garcia's evolutionary challenge, however, was not welcomed by mainstream neobehaviorists. In 1965, after 10 years of research, he openly pointed out the clash between the data and the ideal of general-purpose mechanisms – and his manuscripts suddenly began to be rejected by the editors of the APA (American Psychological Association) journals. This pattern continued for the next 13 years until, in 1979, Garcia was awarded the APA's Distinguished Scientific Contribution Award (Lubek & Apfelbaum, 1987). By then, stimulus equipotentiality was driven out of behaviorism, but had found new fertile ground in cognitive psychology.

The view that psychological mechanisms such as those described in the laws of operant behavior are designed for specific classes of stimuli rather than being general-purpose is known as *domain specificity* (e.g., Hirschfeld & Gelman, 1994), *biological preparedness* (Seligman & Hager, 1972), or, in biology, *special-design* theories (Williams, 1966).

Mainstream cognitive psychology, however, still tries to avoid domain specificity. The senses, language, and emotions have occasionally been accepted as domain-specific adaptations (Fodor, 1983). But the "central" cognitive processes that define the rationality of *Homo sapiens* – reasoning, inference, judgment, and decision making – have not. Even such vigorous advocates of domain specificity as Fodor (1983) have held so-called central processes to be general-purpose. Research on probabilistic, inductive, and deductive reasoning tends to define good reasoning exclusively in terms of formal axioms and rules similar to those discussed in the first section. Mental logic, Johnson-Laird's mental models, and Piaget's formal operations all are examples of the hope that reasoning can be understood without reference to its content.

Yet content-dependence is by no means denied; rather, it is generally acknowledged, but only for *behavior* and not for *cognitive processes*, and more as an annoyance than as a challenge to rethink the nature of our theorizing. For instance, in the last pages of their *Psychology of Reasoning: Structure and Content* (1972), Wason and Johnson-Laird conceded that "for some considerable time we cherished the illusion . . . that only the structural characteristics of the problem mattered," finally concluding that "content is crucial" (pp. 244–245). However, neither this classic nor subsequent work on mental models (Johnson-Laird, 1983; Johnson-Laird & Byrne, 1991) has found a way to deal effectively with content. A similarly unresolved tension exists in Kahneman and Tversky's work on judgment under uncertainty. They grant that "human reasoning cannot be adequately described in terms of content-independent rules" (Kahneman & Tversky, 1982, p. 499). Despite this insight, however, they continued to explain reasoning by general-purpose heuristics such as representativeness and availability. Note that the notion of availability assumes that behavior is dependent on the context (such as the ease with which particular examples come to mind), but as with Skinner's laws, the assumption is that the process is general-purpose. Similarly, current research on decision making generally acknowledges that behavior is dependent on content, but it refrains from the assumption that the cognitive processes themselves may be domain-specific (see Goldstein & Weber, in press). In the same vein, artificial intelligence systems and research that models expert knowledge usually reduce domain specificity to knowledge and assume a single unified inference system as a working hypothesis. Finally, exemplar models of categorization that posit categories as represented by memory traces of the specific instances experienced nevertheless portray the categorization process itself by employing content-independent, general-purpose laws (Barsalou, 1990).

A glance at textbooks on cognitive psychology reveals how we have bottle-fed our students on the idea that whenever reasoning is the object of our investigation, content does not matter. Typically, a chapter on "deductive reasoning" teaches propositional logic and violations thereof by human reasoning, while a chapter on "probabilistic reasoning" teaches the laws of probability theory and violations thereof by human reasoning. Similarly, "fallacies" of reasoning are defined against formal structure – the base rate fallacy, the conjunction fallacy, and so on. Content is merely illustrative and cosmetic, as it is in textbooks of logic. Whether a problem concerns white and black swans, blue and green taxicabs, or artists and beekeepers does not seem to matter. Content has not yet assumed a life of its own. For the most part, it is seen only as a disturbing factor that sometimes facilitates and sometimes hinders formal, rational reasoning.

Is there an alternative? In what follows, I shall describe a domain-specific theory of cognition that relates reasoning to the evolutionary theory of reciprocal altruism (Cosmides & Tooby, 1992). This theory turns the traditional approach upside down. It does not start out with a general-purpose principle from logic or probability theory or a variant thereof; it takes social objectives as fundamental, which in turn makes content fundamental, since social objectives have specific contents. Traditional formal principles of rationality are not imposed; they can be entailed or not, depending on the social objectives.

Cheating detection in social contracts

One feature that sets humans and some other primates apart from almost all animal species is the existence of cooperation among genetically unrelated individuals within the same species, known as *reciprocal altruism* or *cooperation* (see Hammerstein, Chapter 1, this volume). The thesis that such cooperation has been practiced by our ancestors since ancient times, possibly for at least several million years, is supported by evidence from several sources. First, our nearest relatives in the hominid line, chimpanzees, also engage in certain forms of sophisticated cooperation (de Waal & Luttrell, 1988), and in more distant relatives, such as macaques and baboons, cooperation can still be found (e.g., Packer, 1977). Second, cooperation is both universal and highly elaborated across human cultures, from hunter-gatherers to technologically advanced societies. Finally, paleoanthropological evidence also suggests that cooperation is extremely ancient (e.g., Tooby & DeVore, 1987).

Why altruism? Kin-related helping behavior, such as that by the sterile worker castes in insects, which so troubled Darwin, has been accounted for by generalizing "Darwinian fitness" to "inclusive fitness" – that is, to the number of surviving offspring an individual has *plus* the individual's effect on the number of offspring produced by its relatives (Hamilton, 1964). But why reciprocal altruism, which involves cooperation among two or more nonrelated individuals? The now-classic answer draws on the economic concept of trade and its analogy to game theory (Axelrod, 1984; Williams, 1966). If the reproductive benefit of being helped is greater than the cost of helping, then individuals who engage in reciprocal helping can outreproduce those who do not, causing the helping design to spread. A vampire bat, for instance, will die if it fails to find food for two consecutive nights, and there is high variance in food-gathering success. Food sharing allows the bats to reduce this variance, and the best predictor of whether a bat, having foraged successfully, will share its food with a hungry nonrelative is whether the nonrelative has shared food with the bat in the past (Wilkinson, 1990).

But "always cooperate" would not be an evolutionarily stable strategy. This can be seen using the analogy of the prisoner's dilemma (Axelrod, 1984). If a group of individuals always cooperates, then individuals who always defect – that is, who take the benefit but do not reciprocate – can invade and outreproduce the cooperators. Where the opportunity for defecting (or cheating) exists, indiscriminate cooperation would eventually be selected out. "Always defect" would not be an evolutionarily stable strategy, either. A group of individuals who always defect can be invaded by individuals who cooperate in a selective (rather than indiscriminate) way. A simple rule for selective cooperation is "Cooperate on the first move; for subsequent moves, do whatever your partner did on the preceding move" (a strategy known as tit for tat). There are several rules in addition to tit for tat that lead to cooperation with other "selective cooperators" and exclude or retaliate against cheaters (Axelrod, 1984).

The important point is that selective cooperation would not work without a cognitive program for detecting cheaters – or, more precisely, a program for directing an organism's attention to information that could reveal that it (or its group) is being cheated (Cosmides & Tooby, 1992). Neither indiscriminate cooperation nor indiscriminate cheating demands such a program. In vampire bats, who exchange only one thing – regurgitated blood – such a program can be restricted to a sole commodity. Cheating, or more generally noncooperation, would mean, "That other bat took my blood when it had nothing, but it did not share blood with me when I had nothing." In humans, who exchange many goods (including such abstract forms as money), a cheating-detection program needs to work on a more general level of representation – in terms, for example, of "benefits" and "costs." Human cooperation can have the form

If you take the benefit, then you must pay the cost.

Information that can reveal cheating is of the following kind:

The other party took the benefit, but did not pay the cost.

Benefits, by definition, evolve from cooperation; costs, however, may be but are not necessarily incurred. For instance, the other party may possess the exchanged item in such abundance that no cost is associated with satisfying the requirement. Here, "must pay the cost" can be replaced by the more general term "satisfy the requirement" (Cosmides, 1989). For simplicity, I do not make this distinction here.

To summarize, cooperation between two or more individuals for their mutual benefit is a solution to a class of important adaptive problems, such as the sharing of scarce food when foraging success is highly variable. Rather than being indiscriminate, cooperation needs to be selective, requiring a cognitive program that directs attention to information that can reveal cheating. This evolutionary account of cooperation, albeit still general, has been applied to a specific topic in the psychology of reasoning.

Reasoning about conditional statements

In 1966, Peter Wason invented the "selection task" to study reasoning about conditionals. This was to become one of the most extensively researched subjects in cognitive psychology during the following decades. The selection task involves four cards and a conditional statement in the form "If *P* then *Q*." One example is, "If there is a 'D' on one side of the card, then there is a '3' on the other side." The four cards are placed on a table so that the subject can read only the information on the side facing upward. For instance, the four cards may read "D," "E," "3," and "4." The subject's task is to indicate which

Table 11.1. *Three selection tasks*

Numbers-and-letters rule:

If there is a "D" on one side of the card, then there is a "3" on the other side.

Each of the following cards has a letter on one side and a number on the other. Indicate only the card(s) you definitely need to turn over to see if the rule has been violated.

D	E	3	4

Transportation rule:

If a person goes in to Boston, then he takes the subway.

The cards below have information about four Cambridge residents. Each card represents one person. One side of the card tells where the person went and the other side tells how the person got there.
Indicate only the card(s) you definitely need to turn over to see if the rule has been violated.

SUBWAY	ARLINGTON	CAB	BOSTON

Day-off rule:

If an employee works on the weekend, then that person gets a day off during the week.

The cards below have information about four employees. Each card represents one person. One side of the card tells whether the person worked on the weekend, and the other side tells whether the person got a day off during the week.
Indicate only the card(s) you definitely need to turn over to see if the rule has been violated.

WORKED ON THE WEEKEND	DID GET A DAY OFF	DID NOT WORK ON THE WEEKEND	DID NOT GET A DAY OFF

---

of the four cards need(s) to be turned over to find out whether the statement has been violated. Table 11.1 shows three examples of selection tasks, each with a different content: a numbers-and-letters rule, a transportation rule, and a "day-off" rule.

Because the dominant approach has been to impose propositional logic as a general-purpose standard of rational reasoning in the selection task (independent, of course, of the content of the conditional statements), it is crucial to recall that, according to propositional logic, a conditional "If P then Q" can be violated only by "*P* & not-*Q*." In general, that is, the logical falsity of a material conditional is defined within propositional logic in the following way:

> *Logical falsity*:
> "If *P* then *Q*" is logically false if and only if "*P* & not-*Q*."

Thus, the "*P*" and "not-*Q*" cards, and no others, must be selected, since only these can reveal "*P* & not-*Q*" instances. In the numbers-and-letters rule, these cards correspond to the "*D*" and "4" cards; in the transportation problem, to the "Boston" and "cab" cards; and in the "day-off" problem, to the "worked on the weekend" and "did not get a day off" cards.

Wason's results showed, however, that human inferences did not generally follow propositional logic. An avalanche of studies has since confirmed this, reporting that, with numbers-and-letters rules, only about 10% of the subjects select both the "*P*" and "not-*Q*" cards, while most select the "*P*" card and the "*Q*" card, or only the "*P*" card. It was soon found that the selections were highly dependent on the content of the conditional statement. This was labeled the "content effect." For instance, about 30% to 40% of subjects typically choose the "*P*" and "not-*Q*" cards in the transportation problem (Cosmides, 1989), but 75% in the day-off problem (Gigerenzer & Hug, 1992). These results are inconsistent with Piaget's claim that adults should have reached the stage of formal operations (Legrenzi & Murino, 1974; Wason, 1968; Wason & Johnson-Laird, 1970).

Within a decade it was clear that these results – a low overall proportion of "*P* & not-*Q*" answers and the content effect – contradicted the model of human reasoning provided by propositional logic. One might expect that propositional logic was then abandoned; but it was abandoned only as a *descriptive* model of reasoning. Propositional logic was, however, retained as the *normative*, content-independent yardstick of good reasoning, and actual human reasoning was blamed as irrational. The experimental manipulations were evaluated, as is still the case today, in terms of whether or not they "facilitated logical reasoning." Much effort was directed at explaining subjects' apparent irrationality, including their "incorrigible conviction that they are right when they are, in fact, wrong" (Wason, 1983, p. 356). It was proposed that the mind runs with deficient mental software – for example, confirmation bias, matching bias, and availability heuristic – rather than by propositional logic. Yet these proposals were as general-purpose as propositional logic; they could be applied to any content. It seems fair to say that these vague proposals have not led to an understanding of what subjects do in the selection task.

Only since the mid-1980s have a few dissidents dared to design theories that start with the *content* of the conditional statement rather than with propositional logic (Cheng & Holyoak, 1985; Cosmides, 1989; Light, Girotto, & Legrenzi, 1990; Over & Manktelow, 1993). I will concentrate here exclusively on Cosmides' proposal, which takes the evolutionary theory of cooperation as its starting point (for a different evolutionary account, see Klix, 1993).

Cosmides' (1989) central point is that selective cooperation demands the ability to detect cheaters. This ability presupposes several others, including that of distinguishing different individuals, recognizing when a reciprocation (social contract) is offered, and computing costs and benefits, all of which I ignore here (Cosmides & Tooby, 1992). Being cheated in a social contract of the type

> If you take the benefit, then you have to pay the cost

means that the other party has exhibited the following behavior:

> Benefit taken and cost not paid.

The evolutionary perspective suggests that humans, who belong to one of the few species practicing reciprocal altruism since time immemorial, have evolved a cognitive system for directing attention to information that could reveal cheaters. That is, once a cognitive system has classified a situation as one of cooperation, attention will be directed to information that could reveal "benefit taken and cost not paid." Note that cheating detection in social contracts is a domain-specific mechanism; it would not apply if a conditional statement is coded as a threat, such as "If you touch me, then I'll kill you." But how does this help us to understand the content effect in the selection task?

The thesis is that the cheating detection mechanism required by the theory of reciprocal altruism guides reasoning in the selection task:

> If the conditional statement is coded as a social contract, and the subject is cued in to the perspective of one party in the contract, then attention is directed to information that can reveal being cheated.

In other words, a subject should select those cards that correspond to "benefit taken" and "cost not paid," whatever the cards' logical status is. This application of the theory of reciprocal altruism to an unresolved issue in human reasoning is, of course, a bold thesis.

Experimental studies

Cosmides (1989) has shown that her results as well as earlier studies corroborated this thesis. If the conditional statement expressed a social contract, then the percentage of "benefit taken" *and* "cost not paid" selections was very high. For instance, in the day-off problem in Table 11.1, 75% of subjects selected the cards "worked on the weekend" and "did not get a day off" (Gigerenzer &

Hug, 1992). However, this result can also be consistent with competing accounts that do not invoke reciprocal altruism, so we need to look more closely at tests that differentiate between competing accounts. Below is a sample of tests with that aim.

What guides reasoning: availability or cheater detection? The major account of the content effect in the 1970s and 1980s was variously called "familiarity" and "availability" (Manktelow & Evans, 1979; Pollard, 1982), without ever being precisely defined. The underlying idea is that the more familiar a statement is, the more often a subject may have experienced associations between the two propositions in a conditional statement, including those that are violations ("benefit taken" and "cost not paid") of the conditional statement. In this view, familiarity makes violations more "available" in memory, and selections may simply reflect availability. According to this conjecture, therefore, familiarity and not social contracts accounts for selecting the "benefit taken" and "cost not paid" cards. If familiarity were indeed the guiding cognitive principle, then *unfamiliar* social contracts should not elicit the same results. However, Cosmides (1989) showed that social contracts with unfamiliar propositions elicit the same high number of "benefit taken" and "cost not paid" selections, in contradiction to the availability account. This result was independently replicated by both Gigerenzer and Hug (1992) and Platt and Griggs (1993).

Are people simply good at reasoning about social contracts? The game-theoretic models for the evolution of cooperation require, as argued earlier, some mechanism for detecting cheaters in order to exclude them from the benefits of cooperation. The second conjecture, however, rejects any role of cheating detection in the selection task, claiming that people are, for some reason, better at reasoning about social contracts than about numbers-and-letters problems. Social contracts may be more "interesting" or "motivating," or people may have some "mental model" for social contracts that affords "clear" thinking. Although this alternative is nebulous, it needs to be taken into account; in her tests, Cosmides (1989) never distinguished between social contracts and cheating detection.

But one can experimentally disentangle social contracts from cheating detection. Klaus Hug and I also used social contracts, but varied whether the search for violations constituted looking for cheaters or not (Gigerenzer & Hug, 1992). For instance, consider the following social contract: "If someone stays overnight in the cabin, then that person must bring along a bundle of wood from the valley." This was presented in one of two context stories.

The "cheating" version explained that a cabin high in the Swiss Alps serves as an overnight shelter for hikers. Since it is cold and firewood is not otherwise available at this altitude, the Swiss Alpine Club has made the rule that each hiker who stays overnight in the cabin must bring along a bundle of firewood from the valley. The subjects were cued to the perspective of a guard who checks whether any of four hikers has violated the rule. The four hikers were represented by four cards (similar to those in Table 11.1) that read "stays overnight in the cabin," "does not stay overnight," "carried wood," and "carried no wood." The instruction was to indicate only the card(s) you definitely need to turn over to see if any of these hikers have violated the rule.

In the "no-cheating" version, the subjects were cued to the perspective of a member of the German Alpine Association, visiting the same cabin in the Swiss Alps to find out how it is managed by the local Alpine Club. He observes people carrying firewood into the cabin, and a friend accompanying him suggests that the Swiss may have the same overnight rule as the Germans, namely, "If someone stays overnight in the cabin, then that person must bring along a bundle of wood from the valley." That this is also the Swiss Alpine Club's rule is not the only possible explanation; alternatively, only its members (who do not stay overnight in the cabin), and not the hikers, might bring firewood. The subjects were now in the position of an observer who checks information to find out whether the social contract suggested by his friend actually holds. This observer does not represent a party in a social contract. The subjects' instruction was the same as in the cheating version.

Thus, in the cheating scenario, the observation "benefit taken and cost not paid" means that the party represented by the guard is being cheated; in the no-cheating scenario, the same observation suggests only that the Swiss Alpine Club never made the supposed rule in the first place.

Assume as true the conjecture that what matters is only that the rule is a social contract, making the game-theoretic model (which requires a cheating mechanism) irrelevant. Since in both versions the rule is always the same social contract, such a conjecture implies that there should be no difference in the selections observed. In the overnight problem, however, 89% of the subjects selected "benefit taken" and "cost not paid" when cheating was at stake, compared with 53% in the no-cheating version. Similarly, the averages across all four test problems used were 83% and 45%, respectively, consistent with the game-theoretic account of cooperation (Gigerenzer & Hug, 1992).

Do social contracts simply facilitate logical reasoning?   In most of Cosmides' tests, the predicted "benefit taken" and "cost not paid" selections corresponded to the truth conditions of conditionals in propositional logic. Thus, a third conjecture would be that social contracts may somehow facilitate logical reasoning, which we tested by deducing predictions from the cheating-detection hypothesis that contradicted propositional logic (Gigerenzer & Hug, 1992). The key to these tests is that cheating detection is pragmatic and perspectival, whereas propositional logic is aperspectival. For instance, in the day-off problem in Table 11.1, subjects were originally cued to the perspective of an employee, in which case cheating detection and propositional logic indeed predict the same cards. We switched the perspective from employee to employer but held everything else constant (the conditional statement, the four cards, and the instruction shown in Table 11.1). For the employer, being cheated means "did not work on the weekend and did get a day off"; that is, in this perspective subjects should select the "did not work on the weekend" and the "did get a day off" cards, which correspond to the "not-P" and "Q" cards. (Note that "not-P & Q" selections have rarely been observed in selection tasks.) Thus, perspective change can play cheating detection against general-purpose logic. The two competing predictions are: If the cognitive system attempts to detect instances of "benefit taken and cost not paid" in the other party's behavior, then a perspective switch implies switching card selections; if the cognitive system reasons according to propositional logic, however, pragmatic perspectives are irrelevant and there should be no switch in card selections.

The results showed that when the perspective was changed, the cards selected also changed in the predicted direction. The effects were strong and robust across problems. For instance, in the employee perspective of the day-off problem, 75% of the subjects had selected "worked on the weekend" and "did not get a day off," but only 2% had selected the other pair of cards. In the employer perspective, this 2% (who had selected "did not work on the weekend" and "did get a day off") rose to 61% (Gigerenzer & Hug, 1992). The result is consistent with the thesis that attention is directed toward information that could reveal oneself (or one's group) as being cheated in a social contract, but is inconsistent with the claim that reasoning is directed by propositional logic independent of content.[3]

Thus, social contracts do not simply facilitate logical reasoning. I believe that the program of reducing context merely to an instrument for "facilitating" logical reasoning is misguided. My point is the same as for Property Alpha. Reasoning consistent with propositional logic is entailed by some perspectives (e.g., the employee's), but is not entailed by other perspectives (e.g., the employer's).

Two additional conjectures can be dealt with briefly. First, several authors have argued that the cheating detection thesis can be invalidated because "logical facilitation" (large proportions of "P & not-Q" selections) has also been found in some conditional statements that were not social contracts (e.g., Cheng & Holyoak, 1989; Politzer & Nguyen-Xuan, 1992). This conjecture misconstrues the thesis in two respects. The thesis is not about "logical facilitation"; the conjunction "benefit taken and cost not paid" is not the same as the logical conjunction "P & not-Q," as we have seen. Furthermore, a domain-specific theory makes, by definition, no prediction about performance outside its own domain; it can only be refuted within that domain.

The second conjecture also tries to reduce the findings to propositional logic, pointing out that a conditional that states a social contract is generally understood as a biconditional "if and only if." In this case all four cards can reveal logical violations and need to be turned over. However, it is not true that four-card selections are frequent when cheating detection is at stake. We found in about half of the social contract problems (12 problems, each answered by 93 students) that not a single subject had selected all four cards; for the remaining problems, the number was very small. Only when cheating detection was excluded (the no-cheating versions) did four-card selections increase to a proportion of about 10% (Gigerenzer & Hug, 1992). There is, then, no evidence that subjects follow propositional logic even if we assume that they interpret the implication as a biconditional.

Such logical reductionism cannot explain how the mind infers that a particular conditional should be understood as a material implication, a biconditional, or something else. This inference is accomplished, I believe, by coding the specific content of the conditional statement as an instance of a larger domain, such as social contract, threat, and warning (Fillenbaum, 1977).

Conclusions

The evolutionary theory of cooperation illustrates how to begin constructing a theory of cognition situated in social interaction. The idea is to begin with a specific design that a cognitive system requires for social interaction, rather than with a general-purpose, formal system – in other words, to start with the functional and see what logic it entails, rather than to impose some logic a priori. The virtues of this approach are as evident as its unresolved questions. Among these questions are: How can we precisely describe the "Darwinian algorithms" that determine when a social contract is in place? How does the mind infer that the conditional statement "If you touch me, then I'll kill you" does not imply a social contract, but a threat? What are the cues coding this specific statement into the domain of "threats" rather than "social contracts"? Once a statement is categorized into a particular domain, what distribution of attention is implicated by that domain? In a threat, for example, attention needs to be directed to information that can reveal being bluffed or double-crossed rather than cheated (Fillenbaum, 1977). The challenge is to design theoretical proposals for reasoning and inference processes in other domains of human interaction beyond cooperation in social contracts.

To approach reasoning as situated in social interaction is to assume that the cognitive system (a) generalizes a specific situation as an instance of a larger domain, and (b) reasons about the specific situation by applying a domain-specific cognitive module. This raises two questions about the nature of the domains and the design of the modules.

What are the domains and at what level of abstraction are they located? Imagine a vertical dimension of abstraction, in which the specific problem corresponds to the lowest level of abstraction, and some formal representation of the problem, stripped of any content and context, to the highest. Two diametrically opposed views correspond to the ends of this continuum of abstraction. First, it may be argued that the cognitive system operates at the lowest level of abstraction, guided by familiarity and availability of instances in memory (e.g., Griggs & Cox, 1982). Second, it may be argued that the cognitive system generalizes the specific problem to the highest level of abstraction (e.g., propositional logic), performs some logical operations on this formal representation, and translates the result back into application to the specific problem. Variants of the latter view include Piaget's theory of formal operations and mental logics.

The primary challenge of domain-specificity is to find a level of abstraction between the two extremes, where some content is stripped but an adequate amount retained. For instance, the level of social contracts and cheating detection could turn out to be too abstract, because cheating may assume different forms (e.g., in contracts in which both or only one side can be cheated; Gigerenzer & Hug, 1992), requiring different procedures of cheating detection. In contrast,the notions of social contracts and cheating detection may not be abstract enough, needing to be stripped of some content and placed at the more general level of social regulations, such as obligations, permissions, and other kinds of deontic reasoning (Cheng & Holyoak, 1985, 1989; Over & Manktelow, 1993). This focus on level of abstraction parallels Rosch's (1978) concern with "basic level objects."

What is the design of a domain-specific cognitive module? A cognitive module organizes the processes – such as inference, emotion, and the distribution of attention – that have been evolved and learned to handle a domain. To classify a specific situation as an instance of a given domain, a cognitive module must be connected to an inferential mechanism. For instance, David Premack and others assume that humans and primates first classify an encounter as an instance of either social interaction (in the broadest sense) or interaction with the nonliving world. There is evidence that the cues used for this inference involve motion patterns, analyzed by cognitive systems to classify objects in the world as "self-propelled" or not; this analysis is reminiscent of Fritz Heider's and Albert Michotte's work (Premack, 1990;

Sperber, 1994; Thinès, Costall, & Butterworth, 1991). Cognitive modules dealing with something external that has been coded as "self-propelled" attend to information such as whether it is friend or enemy, prey or predator. For a module that deals with inanimate things, no attention needs to be directed to information of this kind. Domain-specific modules can thus distribute attention in a more focused way than a domain-general mechanism. The challenge now before us is to come up with rich and testable models about the design of cognitive modules.

Toward a social rationality

Researchers in several disciplines are converging on a domain-specific program of studying reasoning and inference situated in social interaction. Primatologists have joined philosophers and psychologists in studying "social intelligence" (Kummer, Daston, Gigerenzer, & Silk, in press) and "Machiavellian intelligence" (Byrne & Whiten, 1988). Linguists and philosophers have begun to reinterpret the conclusions of experimental research, in particular the so-called fallacies and biases, by arguing that the interaction between subject and experimenter is constrained by conversational rather than formal axioms (e.g., Adler, 1991; Grice, 1975; Sperber & Wilson, 1986). Social psychologists have tested some of these proposals experimentally, concluding among other things that pervasive reasoning "biases" may not reflect universal shortcomings of the human mind, but instead the application of Gricean conversational principles that conflict with what formal logic seems to dictate (e.g., Schwarz, Strack, Hilton, & Naderer, 1991). Similarly, Tetlock's (1992) concept of "accountability" models the social side of decision making by emphasizing that people do not simply choose the better alternative, but in certain social interactions, choose the alternative they can better justify. Developmental psychologists have departed from Piaget's general-purpose processes and investigate the domain-specific processes and their change during development (Hirschfeld & Gelman, 1994). The convergence of these approaches promises a new vision of reasoning and rationality situated in social context.

I can only hope that this chapter will inspire some readers to rethink the imposition of formal axioms or rules as "rational," independent of context. In my opinion, the challenging alternative is to put the psychological and the social first – and then to examine what formal principles these entail. We need less Aristotle and more Darwin in order to understand the messy business of how to be rational in the uncertain world of interacting human beings. And we may have to abandon a dream. Leibniz's vision of a sovereign calculus, the Universal Characteristic, was a beautiful one. If only it had proved true.

Notes

1 I have reported the numbers only for the most likely event (i.e., 600 snowy winters out of 1,000 winters). If one looks at all possible events, one finds that those in which W would result in a larger population size than WB are extremely rare (Cooper, 1989). Nevertheless, the expected value is larger for W than for WB, due to the fact that in those very few cases where W results in a larger population size, this number is astronomically large. The reader who is familiar with the St. Petersburg paradox will see a parallel (Wolfgang Hell, in a personal communication, has drawn my attention to this fact). The parallel is best illustrated in Lopes's (1981) simulations of businesses selling the St. Petersburg gamble. Although these businesses sold the gamble far below its expected value, most nonetheless survived with great profits.
2 Adaptive coin-flipping is a special case of a general phenomenon: In variable environments (in which the time scale of variation is greater than the generation time of the organism, as in the example given), natural selection does not maximize expected individual fitness, but geometric mean fitness (Gillespie, 1977).
3 I should mention here that Platt and Griggs (1993) have claimed that they could not replicate Gigerenzer and Hug's (1992) effects of perspective change. Platt and Griggs, however, cued all subjects to the same perspective, *never* changing the perspective from one party in a social contract to the other. What they labeled a "cheating perspective manipulation" involved deleting from the story explicit hints that people might cheat in a social contract and that the contract would be reinforced. But there is no need for such hints, nor should these have any effect, since the thesis is that there is a cognitive program for cheating detection. Therefore, I am not surprised by their results – only by their conclusions.

References

Adler, J. (1991). An optimist's pessimism: Conversation and conjunction. In E. Eells & T. Maruszewski (Eds.), *Probability and rationality: Studies on L. Jonathan Cohen's philosophy of science* (pp. 251–282). Amsterdam: Rodopi.

Axelrod, R. (1984). *The evolution of cooperation.* New York: Basic.

Barsalou, L. W. (1990). On the indistinguishability of exemplar memory and abstraction in category representation. In T. K. Srull & R. S. Wyer (Eds.), *Advances in social cognition: Vol. 3. Content and process specificity in the effects of prior experiences* (pp. 61–88). Hillsdale, NJ: Erlbaum.

Brunswik, E. (1939). Probability as a determiner of rat behavior. *Journal of Experimental Psychology, 36,* 553.

Byrne, R., & Whiten, A. (Eds.). (1988). *Machiavellian intelligence.* Oxford: Oxford University Press.

Cheng, P. W., & Holyoak, K. J. (1985). Pragmatic reasoning schemas. *Cognitive Psychology, 17,* 391–416.

Cheng, P. W., & Holyoak, K. J. (1989). On the natural selection of reasoning theories. *Cognition, 33,* 285–313.

Cooper, W. S. (1989). How evolutionary biology challenges the classical theory of rational choice. *Biology and Philosophy, 4,* 457–481.

Cooper, W. S., & Kaplan, R. (1982). Adaptive "coin-flipping": A decision-theoretic examination of natural selection for random individual variation. *Journal of Theoretical Biology, 94,* 135–151.

Cosmides, L. (1989). The logic of social exchange: Has natural selection shaped how humans reason? *Cognition, 31,* 187–276.

Cosmides, L., & Tooby, J. (1992). Cognitive adaptations for social exchange. In J. H. Barkow, L. Cosmides, & J. Tooby (Eds.), *The adapted mind: Evolutionary psychology and the generation of culture* (pp. 163–228). Oxford: Oxford University Press.

Daston, L. J. (1988). *Classical probability in the Enlightenment*. Princeton, NJ: Princeton University Press.

de Waal, F. B. M., & Luttrell, L. M. (1988). Mechanisms of social reciprocity in three primate species: Symmetrical relationship characteristics or cognition? *Ethology and Sociobiology, 9*, 101–118.

Elster, J. (1990). When rationality fails. In K. S. Cook & M. Levi (Eds.), *The limits of rationality* (pp. 19–51). Chicago: University of Chicago Press.

Estes, W. (1976). The cognitive side of probability learning. *Psychological Review, 83*, 37–64.

Fillenbaum, S. (1977). Mind your *p*'s and *q*'s: The role of content and context in some uses of *and, or*, and *if. Psychology of Learning and Motivation, 11*, 41–100.

Fodor, J. A. (1983). *The modularity of mind*. Cambridge, MA: MIT Press.

Fretwell, S. D. (1972). *Populations in seasonal environments*. Princeton, NJ: Princeton University Press.

Gallistel, C. R. (1990). *The organization of learning*. Cambridge, MA: MIT Press.

Garcia, J., & Koelling, R. A. (1966). The relation of cue to consequence in avoidance learning. *Psychonomic Science, 4*, 123–124.

Garcia y Robertson, R., & Garcia, J. (1985). X-rays and learned taste aversions: Historical and psychological ramifications. In T. G. Burish, S. M. Levy, & B. E. Meyerowitz (Eds.), *Cancer, nutrition and eating behavior: A biobehavioral perspective* (pp. 11–41). Hillsdale, NJ: Erlbaum.

Gigerenzer, G. (1991a). From tools to theories: A heuristic of discovery in cognitive psychology. *Psychological Review, 98*, 254–267.

Gigerenzer, G. (1991b). How to make cognitive illusions disappear: Beyond "heuristics and biases." In W. Stroebe & M. Hewstone (Eds.), *European Review of Social Psychology* (Vol. 2, pp. 83–115). New York: Wiley.

Gigerenzer, G., & Hug, K. (1992). Domain-specific reasoning: Social contracts, cheating, and perspective change. *Cognition, 43*, 127–171.

Gigerenzer, G., & Murray, D. J. (1987). *Cognition as intuitive statistics*. Hillsdale, NJ: Erlbaum.

Gigerenzer, G., Swijtink, Z., Porter, T., Daston, L., Beatty, J., & Krüger, L. (1989). *The empire of chance: How probability changed science and everyday life*. Cambridge: Cambridge University Press.

Gillespie, J. H. (1977). Natural selection for variances in offspring numbers: A new evolutionary principle. *American Naturalist, 111*, 1010–1014.

Goldstein, W. M., & Weber, E. (in press). Content and discontent: Indications and implications of domain specificity in preferential decision making. In J. R. Busemeyer, R. Hastie, & D. L. Medin (Eds.), *The psychology of learning and motivation*. New York: Academic.

Grice, H. P. (1975). Logic and conversation. In P. Cole & J. L. Morgan (Eds.), *Syntax and semantics: Vol. 3. Speech acts* (pp. 41–58). New York: Academic.

Griggs, R. A., & Cox, J. R. (1982). The elusive thematic-materials effect in Wason's selection task. *British Journal of Psychology, 73*, 407–420.

Gruber, H. E., & Vonèche, J. J. (Eds.). (1977). *The essential Piaget*. New York: Basic.

Hamilton, W. D. (1964). The genetic evolution of social behavior. Parts 1 and 2. *Journal of Theoretical Biology, 7*, 1–52.

Hirschfeld, L. A., & Gelman, S. A. (Eds.). (1994). *Mapping the mind: Domain specificity in cognition and culture*. Cambridge: Cambridge University Press.

Johnson-Laird, P. N. (1983). *Mental Models*. Cambridge: Cambridge University Press.

Johnson-Laird, P. N., & Byrne, R. M. J. (1991). *Deduction*. Hillsdale, NJ: Erlbaum.

Kahneman, D., & Tversky, A. (1982). On the study of statistical intuitions. In D. Kahneman, P. Slovic, & A. Tversky (Eds.), *Judgment under uncertainty: Heuristics and biases* (pp. 493–508). Cambridge: Cambridge University Press.

Klix, F. (1993). Erwachendes Denken: Geistige Leistung aus evolutionspsychologischer Sicht [Thought coming to life: Cognitive performance from an evolutionary psychological perspective]. Heidelberg: Spektrum Akademischer Verlag.

Kummer, H., Daston, L., Gigerenzer, G., & Silk, J. (in press). The social intelligence hypothesis.

In P. Weingart, P. Richerson, S. Mitchell, & S. Maasen (Eds.), *Human by nature*. Hillsdale, NJ: Erlbaum.

Legrenzi, P., & Murino, M. (1974). Falsification at the pre-operational level. *Italian Journal of Psychology*, *1*, 363–368.

Leibniz, G. W. (1677/1951). Toward a universal characteristic. In G. W. Leibniz (Ed.), *Selections* (pp. 17–25). New York: Scribner's.

Light, P., Girotto, V., & Legrenzi, P. (1990). Children's reasoning on conditional promises and permissions. *Cognitive Development*, *5*, 369–383.

Little, I. M. D. (1949). A reformulation of the theory of consumers' behavior. *Oxford Economic Papers*, *1*, 90–99.

Lopes, L. L. (1981). Decision making in the short run. *Journal of Experimental Psychology: Human Learning and Memory*, *7*, 377–385.

Lubek, I., & Apfelbaum, E. (1987). Neo-behaviorism and the Garcia effect: A social psychology of science approach to the history of a paradigm clash. In M. Ash & W. Woodward (Eds.), *Psychology in twentieth-century thought and society* (pp. 59–92). Cambridge: Cambridge University Press.

Manktelow, K. I., & Evans, J. S. B. T. (1979). Facilitation of reasoning by realism: Effect or non-effect? *British Journal of Psychology*, *70*, 477–488.

Over, D. E., & Manktelow, K. I. (1993). Rationality, utility and deontic reasoning. In K. I. Manktelow & D. E. Over (Eds.), *Rationality: Psychological and philosophical perspectives* (pp. 231–259). London: Routledge.

Packer, C. (1977). Reciprocal altruism in *Papio annubis. Nature*, *265*, 441–443.

Piaget, J., & Inhelder, B. (1951/1975). *The origin of the idea of chance in children*. New York: Norton.

Platt, R., & Griggs, R. (1993). Darwinian algorithms and the Wason selection task: A factorial analysis of social contract selection task problems. *Cognition*, *48*, 163–192.

Politzer, G., & Nguyen-Xuan, A. (1992). Reasoning about promises and warnings: Darwinian algorithms, mental models, relevance judgments or pragmatic schemas? *Quarterly Journal of Experimental Psychology*, *44A*, 402–421.

Pollard, P. (1982). Human reasoning: Some possible effects of availability. *Cognition*, *12*, 65–96.

Premack, D. (1990). The infant's theory of self-propelled objects. *Cognition*, *36*, 1–16.

Rosch, E. (1978). Principles of categorization. In E. Rosch & B. B. Lloyd (Eds.), *Cognition and categorization* (pp. 27–48). Hillsdale, NJ: Erlbaum.

Samuelson, P. A. (1938). A note on the pure theory of consumers' behavior. *Economica*, *5*, 61–71.

Schwarz, N., Strack, F., Hilton, D., & Naderer, G. (1991). Base rates, representativeness and the logic of conversation: The contextual relevance of "irrelevant" information. *Social Cognition*, *9*(1), 67–84.

Seligman, M. E. P., & Hager, J. L. (Eds.). (1972). *Biological boundaries of learning*. New York: Appleton-Century-Crofts.

Sen, A. (1993). Internal consistency of choice. *Econometrica*, *61*(3), 495–521.

Simon, H. (1986). Rationality in psychology and economics. In R. Hogarth & M. Reder (Eds.), *Rational choice: The contrast between economics and psychology* (pp. 25–40). Chicago: University of Chicago Press.

Sperber, D. (1994). The modularity of thought and the epidemiology of representations. In L. Hirschfeld & S. Gelman (Eds.), *Mapping the mind: Domain-specificity in cognition and culture* (pp. 39–67). Cambridge: Cambridge University Press.

Sperber, D., & Wilson, D. (1986). *Relevance: Communication and cognition*. Oxford: Blackwell.

Tetlock, P. (1992). The impact of accountability on judgment and choice: Toward a social contingency model. *Advances in Experimental Social Psychology*, *25*, 331–357.

Thinès, G., Costall, A., & Butterworth, G. (Eds.). (1991). *Michotte's experimental phenomenology of perception*. Hillsdale, NJ: Erlbaum.

Tooby, J., & DeVore, I. (1987). The reconstruction of hominid behavioral evolution through strategic modeling. In W. G. Kinzey (Ed.), *The evolution of human behavior: Primate models* (pp. 183–237). Albany: State University of New York Press.

Wason, P. C. (1968). Reasoning about a rule. *Quarterly Journal of Experimental Psychology, 20,* 273–281.

Wason, P. C. (1983). Realism and rationality in the selection task. In J. S. B. T. Evans (Ed.), *Thinking and reasoning: Psychological approaches* (pp. 44–75). London: Routledge & Kegan Paul.

Wason, P. C., & Johnson-Laird, P. N. (1970). A conflict between selecting and evaluating information in an inferential task. *British Journal of Psychology, 61,* 509–515.

Wason, P. C., & Johnson-Laird, P. N. (1972). *Psychology of reasoning: Structure and content.* Cambridge, MA: Harvard University Press.

Wilkinson, G. S. (1990). Food sharing in vampire bats. *Scientific American* (February), 76–82.

Williams, G. C. (1966). *Adaptation and natural selection: A critique of some current evolutionary thought.* Princeton, NJ: Princeton University Press.

12   Styles of thinking

Robert J. Sternberg

Abstract

This chapter presents a theory of thinking styles – the theory of mental self-government – as well as data in support of the theory. The chapter explains why styles are important, discusses some general characteristics of styles, and offers some alternative theories of styles. A theory of mental self-government is presented and a measurement approach is introduced. This paradigm is then applied to investigate cognitive styles in the classroom. The argument is advanced that, in addition to abilities and achievement, we need to take thinking styles into account in considering the interaction of children with one another, with teachers, and with the school.

Why is it that some people think like lawyers and others like scientists? Why do some children consistently ace multiple-choice tests, whereas others find such tests well-nigh impossible to take? How can a teacher one year think that a child is brilliant and another teacher the next year think the same child is a dunce? All of these questions can be elucidated by the concept of styles of thought.

A style of thought is a preference for using abilities in certain ways. It is not an ability itself, but rather a way in which one likes to utilize abilities. Thus, when we speak of individual differences in thinking styles, we are referring only to differences, not to "better" or "worse."

In this chapter, I first describe why styles are important from several points of view. Second, I describe some general properties of styles. Third, I briefly describe some alternative theories of styles. Fourth, I summarize my own theory, the theory of mental self-government (Sternberg, 1988, 1990). Fifth, I briefly characterize some of the instruments we have used to measure these

The work reported herein was supported under the Javits Act program (Grant R206R00001) as administered by the office of Educational Research and Improvement, U.S. Department of Education. The findings and opinions expressed in this report do not reflect the positions or policies of the office of Educational Research and Improvement or the U.S. Department of Education.

347

styles, and discuss some psychometric properties of these instruments. Sixth, I present some data collected in educational settings showing properties of styles as posited by the theory of mental self-government. Seventh, I describe the relevance of styles to instruction and assessment. Finally, I draw some conclusions.

Why styles are important

Styles of thought are important from several points of view. I shall discuss three of them – psychology, education, and occupations.

From the standpoint of psychology, we know that tests of abilities weakly or moderately predict many things, but they strongly predict practically nothing (see Brody, 1992; Gardner, 1993; Sternberg, 1985). If abilities as we currently measure them account for only some of the individual differences in school and job performance, then we must ask what other kinds of constructs might account for what is not predicted. Thinking styles, I will argue, provide one such construct. Thinking styles may be able to supplement abilities as a basis for predicting various kinds of performance.

From the standpoint of education, styles are essential. For example, I entered college planning to be a psychology major. I received a grade of "C" in the introductory course. As a result, I concluded that I did not have the ability to pursue psychology as a career. Perhaps fortunately, I decided to major in math and did even worse in math than I had done in psychology. I switched back to psychology and did well in subsequent courses. In retrospect, I realize that my problem was not lack of ability, but a mismatch between my own preferred styles of learning and thinking and those of the teacher of the course. I was lucky: I returned to psychology. But had I decided to switch to literature, history, economics, or biology, I might be following a career in one of those fields today rather than in the field that interested me (and still interests me) most. How many students do we lose to various fields of endeavor because they think they don't have the ability, when in fact their only problem is stylistic mismatch with a teacher?

The same principle holds in other fields as well. I will argue that any course in any discipline can be taught and performance in it assessed in a variety of ways, some of which favor one stylistic pattern, others of which favor another. I believed (and my high school French teacher reinforced my belief) that I lacked the ability to learn foreign languages. Yet when I learned Spanish much later via the direct (learning from context) method rather than the mimic-and-memorize method through which I had learned French, all of a sudden I found myself with plenty of ability to learn a foreign language.

The lessons I have learned about styles apply as well to my life as a teacher as they did to my life as a student. When I started including independent projects as well as examinations in the math classes I teach, I discovered that many students who did not do particularly well on exams were nevertheless quite able to use the concepts I had taught in project work, whereas other students who had done well on exams had great difficulty applying what they had learned to their research work. The point is that styles of thinking matter across the disciplines, and for both learners and teachers.

Styles also matter for jobs. In vocational counseling, we tend to emphasize the importance of abilities and interests. But styles of thinking are at least as important. The kinds of thinking styles that lead to success in scientific research, for example, are rather different from those that lead to success in contract law. Two people of equal abilities and comparable interests might perform very differently in the two occupations solely as a result of the consistency of their styles of thought with the demands of their job. In turn, their happiness might well be affected by the match between their thinking styles and their work.

Even more importantly, I will argue, sometimes the pattern of styles that leads to success in a course in a given discipline is not the pattern of styles that leads to actual success later in a job in that discipline. As a result, we may give the best grades to students who will later not be particularly successful in a given field, and derail other students who might be very successful but will never have the chance to prove it because of low course grades. In the world of work as in the world of education, styles count, and they count a great deal.

Some general characteristics of styles

Before proceeding, I wish to outline some general characteristics of styles of thought:

1. *Styles are proclivities, not abilities.* We need to remember that styles are preferred ways of processing information, not abilities to process that information. For example, someone could have styles of thought that are often associated with creativity, and thus like to be creative, but not have much creative ability, and thus not have very good ideas; or vice versa.
2. *Styles are not "good" or "bad," but rather matters of fit.* Whereas one might say that it is "better" to have more than to have less of an ability, on the average, such a statement is meaningless in the context of styles. What is "good" is to have a style that fits a given task or situation, and the same style that fits certain tasks and situations may be a poor fit to others; hence, we cannot speak of styles as generally being better or worse.
3. *Styles can vary across tasks and situations.* Styles of thinking are not rigid or fixed, but rather usually vary across tasks and situations. For example, the same person who needs to be very detail-oriented and exacting when filling out income tax forms may need to be very global and holistic in his or her thinking when deciding on an interesting topic for a paper or a talk. Although people may have preferences, they usually recognize that to adapt to the demands of the world, they cannot expect their stylistic preferences always to be honored.
4. *People differ in strengths of stylistic preferences.* When people are given assess-

ments of styles (to be described later), some come out strongly toward certain styles, whereas others come out more nearly in the middle of the scale on a number of styles. Thus, some people tend to be more extreme, others less so.

5. *People differ in stylistic flexibility.* Some people can easily alter their styles to meet the demands of a given task or situation, whereas other people seem locked into a small set of stylistic preferences. In general, higher flexibility is associated with better adaptation. A major theme of this chapter is that whether a person is a student, teacher, manager, or spouse, for that matter, the person will generally find life easier if he or she can adapt flexibly to differing situational demands on thinking styles.

6. *Styles are socialized.* My collaborators and I have not done any studies directly addressing the heritability of styles. But we do have evidence suggesting that, to a large extent, styles are socialized in the environment. We come to our styles through role modeling and through actively engaging various styles of thought. At the same time, people do seem to have certain preferences that may start quite early and may, so far as we know, have some heritable component.

7. *Styles can vary across the life span – they are not fixed.* People do not have a fixed set of styles with which they are born that they must then maintain throughout their lives. Rather, styles can change as the demands of life change. Someone who becomes an accountant probably needs to become detail-oriented, whether that is a natural preference or not. Someone who sells merchandise on commission has to become people-oriented, or risk starving to death. No one is locked into any fixed pattern of styles.

8. *Styles are measurable.* Many constructs in psychological theory die on the vine because they are conceptually specified but never operationalized; others survive, but as operationalized constructs that are never well conceptualized. Styles can be conceptualized by the theory presented in this essay, and they can also be measured by the kinds of assessments to be described.

9. *Styles are modifiable.* As implied earlier, we can help individuals to modify their styles by role-modeling other styles for them and by giving them opportunities to use those styles. Parents and teachers thus can and do influence the styles of those with whose well-being they are charged.

10. *What is valued in one time and place may not be valued in another.* Environments almost invariably tend to favor certain styles over others. The very style that leads to success in one school or job may lead to failure in another. A major challenge in life is finding and then, to the extent possible, placing oneself in an environment that matches and rewards one's profile of styles.

Alternative theories of styles

Many alternative theories of styles have been proposed, and a number of those are reviewed in Grigorenko and Sternberg (1995). I will highlight here only a small subset of the important theories in the field of styles.

One such theory is that of Jung (1923) as filtered through the work of Myers (1980; Myers & McCaulley, 1988). According to this theory, people can be characterized as falling into either of two types along each of four dimensions: as emphasizing sensing or intuition, thinking or feeling, introversion or extraversion, and judgment or perception. In a second theory, that of Gregorc (1979, 1985), people are characterized as either concrete or abstract, and sequential or random. Still another theorist, Holland (1973), speaks of people as being realistic, investigative, artistic, social, enterprising, or conventional.

These theories overlap with each other and with the theory to be presented here. One might refer to them as occupying a roughly common "style space," where orientations of axes differ and thus depict differing ways of partitioning the same set of constructs. From this point of view, these theories probably vary not so much in terms of which is "right" or "wrong," but rather in terms of how differentially useful the theories are for various purposes.

The theory of mental self-government

Aspects of the theory

The theory to be presented, that of mental self-government (Sternberg, 1988, 1990), holds that styles can be understood in terms of constructs from our notions of government. On this view, the kinds of governments we have in the world are not merely coincidental, but rather are external reflections or mirrors of ways in which we can organize or govern ourselves. According to this theory, people can be understood in terms of the functions, forms, levels, scope, and leanings of government.

Functions. There are three functions of government in the theory: legislative, executive, and judicial, each to be described here. To elucidate each style further, three sample questions of statements we use in an inventory that assesses styles are shown in Table 12.1. Statements are rated on a 1 (low) to 9 (high) scale according to the extent to which they characterize the functioning of a given individual. Thus, readers can assess themselves (roughly) on the styles by rating each of the sets of three statements and computing an arithmetic average for the three. Of course, in actual stylistic assessment, people rate considerably more than three statements per style (and often, other kinds of assessments are used as well).

1. *Legislative.* The legislative person has a predilection for tasks, projects, and situations that require creation, formulation, plans of ideas, strategies, products, and the like. This kind of person likes to decide what to do and how to do it, rather than to be told. For example, the kind of person who likes to do creative writing, design experiments, come up with theories, do original artistic compositions, or invent new things would tend toward the legislative.

2. *Executive.* The executive person has a predilection for tasks, projects, and situations that provide structure, procedures, or rules to work with and, although modifiable, can serve as guidelines to measure progress. Whereas the legislative person likes to decide what to do and how to do it, the executive

Table 12.1. *Sample questions used to measure thinking styles*

Functions

Legislative
1. When I work on a project, I like to plan what to do and how to do it.
2. I like tasks that allow me to do things my own way.
3. I like to pursue tasks or problems that have little structure.

Executive
1. I like situations in which it is clear what role I must play or in what way I should participate.
2. I like to follow instructions when solving a problem.
3. I like projects that provide a series of steps to follow to get to a solution.

Judicial
1. I like to analyze people's behavior.
2. I like projects that allow me to evaluate the work of others.
3. I like tasks that allow me to express my opinions to others.

Forms

Monarchic
1. I prefer to finish one assignment before starting another.
2. I like to devote all my time and energy to one project, rather than dividing my time and attention among several projects.
3. I like to put in long hours of work on one thing without being distracted.

Hierarchic
1. When undertaking some task, I like first to come up with a list of things the task will require me to do and then to assign an order of priority to the items on the list.
2. Whenever I engage in a task, it is clear to me in what order of priority various parts of it need to get done.
3. When writing, I tend to emphasize the major points and to deemphasize the minor ones.

Oligarchic
1. When there are competing issues of importance to address in my work, I somehow try to address them all simultaneously.
2. I sometimes have trouble setting priorities for multiple things that I need to get done.
3. Usually when working on a project, I tend to view almost all aspects of it as equally important.

Anarchic
1. When I have to start some task, I usually do not organize my thoughts in advance.
2. When thinking about an issue that interests me, I like to let my mind wander with the ideas in whatever which way.
3. When talking about issues that interest me, I like to say things just as they occur to me, rather than waiting until I have organized or censored my thoughts.

Table 12.1. *(cont.)*

Levels

Global
1. I like to do projects in which I don't have to pay much attention to details.
2. In any written work I do, I like to emphasize the scope and context of my ideas, that is, the general picture.
3. Usually when I make a decision, I don't pay much attention to the details.

Local
1. I like problems that require engagement with details.
2. In carrying out a task, I am not satisfied unless even the nitty-gritty details are given close attention.
3. Usually when I make a decision, I don't pay much attention to the details.

Scope

Internal
1. I like to be alone when working on a problem.
2. I like to avoid situations in which I have to work in a group.
3. To learn about some topic, I would rather read a well-written book than participate in a group discussion.

External
1. Before I start on a project, I like discussing my ideas with some friends or peers.
2. I like to work with others rather than by myself.
3. I like talking to people about ideas that occur to me and listening to what they have to say.

Leaning

Liberal
1. I like to do things in new ways, even if I am not sure they are the best ways.
2. I like to avoid situations where I am expected to do things according to some established way.
3. I am comfortable with projects that allow me to try unconventional ways of doing things.

Conservative
1. I like to do things in ways that have been shown in the past to be correct.
2. When I am in charge of something, I like to make sure to follow the procedures that have been used before.
3. I like to participate in situations where I am expected to do things in a traditional way.

Note: Examinees rate each inventory statement on a scale from 1 (low) to 9 (high) according to the extent to which the statement characterizes themselves. Actual inventories of styles contain more than three items per style.

person will often prefer to be told what to do, and will then give it his or her best shot at doing it well. For example, the kind of person who likes to follow recipes, build models or design things according to instructions, write papers on assigned topics, be given problems to solve, or implement the orders of others would tend toward the executive.

I have a friend – a contract lawyer – who once described success in his work as writing a contract so airtight that if the parties wanted to change their own contract, they had to pay him to do it. He didn't decide on terms, but rather implemented their terms, not only to their advantage, but to his own. He capitalized well in his work on his executive style.

It is worth noting that traditional schooling generally rewards most strongly the executive type. Good students are often seen as those who do what they are told, and do it well. Legislative students may have the same abilities, but the abilities may not manifest themselves, and such students may actually be viewed as "pains in the neck." The executive type will take naturally to memorizing given material, taking multiple-choice or short-answer tests, and doing assignments in ways that teachers expect. Legislative students are less likely to take naturally to multiple-choice and short-answer tests, and would probably rather do work on projects than take exams. They may therefore be penalized by conventional instruction and assessments because of their preference for a creative way of thinking.

3. *Judicial*. The judicial person has a predilection for tasks, projects, and situations that require evaluation, analysis, comparison–contrast, and judgment of existing ideas, strategies, projects, and the like. This kind of person tends to evaluate others, sometimes on the basis of minimal information. The judicial person tends to like evaluative essays, writing critiques, commenting on other people's ideas, and assessing others' strengths and weaknesses.

Another friend of mine showed a judicial style even in college. He was responsible for evaluating all courses in the college, and when he went out on dates, he gave his dates a test of values, which was oral and which they did not know they were taking. Today he is a very successful psychotherapist, an occupation that is an excellent fit for someone with a judicial style. The man spends his time evaluating people's problems and prescribing treatments. He is still unmarried.

Forms. There are four forms of mental self-government in the theory: monarchic, hierarchic, oligarchic, and anarchic.

1. *Monarchic*. The monarchic person has a predilection for tasks, projects, and situations that allow focusing fully on one thing or aspect at a time and staying with that thing until it is complete. A monarchic person is single-minded and often driven, and likes to finish one thing before moving on to the next. This style is usually easy to recognize in superiors, co-workers, or

spouses, for that matter, because the person with this style tends to be so devoted to a single thing. For example, one of my own children is currently monarchic about computers and at times seems to think about little else.

2. *Hierarchic.* The hierarchic person has a predilection for tasks, projects, and situations that allow creation of a hierarchy of goals to fulfill. This person likes to do multiple things in a given time frame but to assign differential priorities for getting them done. He or she will often make lists, and sometimes even lists of lists. A hierarchic person tends to be adaptive in many settings where it is necessary to set priorities for getting certain things done before others, or where it is necessary to decide that some things are more worthy of attention than others.

3. *Oligarchic.* The oligarchic person has a predilection for tasks, projects, and situations that allow working with competing approaches, with multiple aspects or goals that are equally important. This person, like the hierarchic one, likes to do multiple things within a given time frame but has trouble setting priorities. The oligarchic person thus adapts well if the competing demands are of roughly equal priority but has more trouble if the things are of different priorities. Students who can't decide which assignments to do first or how much time to put into each assignment, or professors who can't decide how to budget their time, may fall into the oligarchic category.

4. *Anarchic.* The anarchic person has a predilection for tasks, projects, and situations that lend themselves to great flexibility of approaches and to trying anything when, where, and how he or she pleases. This type of person tends to be asystematic or even antisystematic. The individual tends to take a random approach to problems and sometimes is difficult for other people to understand. The anarchic person may have good potential for creativity, because the individual draws ideas from so many places, but in order to exploit this potential, the person usually needs somehow to discipline him- or herself.

Levels. There are two levels of mental self-government: global and local.

1. *Global.* The global person has a predilection for tasks, projects, and situations that require engagement with large, global, abstract ideas. This person likes to deal with big ideas but can sometimes lose touch with the details of what he or she is doing – the individual may see the forest but lose track of the trees.

2. *Local.* The person with a local style has a predilection for tasks, projects, and situations that require engagement with specific, concrete details. This person likes to work with the nitty-gritty but may lose the forest for the trees.

Scope. There are two scopes of mental self-government: internal and external.

1. *Internal.* The internal person has a predilection for tasks, projects, and situations that require activities that allow one to work as a unit, independ-

ently of others. This person prefers to work alone, is typically introverted, and often is uncomfortable in groups.

2. *External.* The external person has a predilection for tasks, projects, and situations that require activities that allow working with others in a group or interacting with others at different stages of progress. This person prefers to work with others, is typically extraverted, and is very comfortable in group settings. The person may not like working, or even being, alone.

Leanings. There are two leanings of mental self-government: liberal and conservative.

1. *Liberal.* The person with a liberal style has a predilection for tasks, projects, and situations that involve unfamiliarity, going beyond existing rules or procedures, and the maximization of change. Sometimes the person may prefer change simply for the sake of change, even when it is not ideal.

2. *Conservative.* The conservative person has a predilection for tasks, projects, and situations that require adherence to and observance of existing rules and procedures. This person likes to minimize change and avoid ambiguity.

Relation of styles to abilities

Although styles are not themselves abilities but rather ways of using abilities, one can see that there are various kinds of relations between styles and abilities. My own triarchic theory (Sternberg, 1985) distinguishes among analytic and creative-synthetic, as well as practical-contextual abilities. One could argue that there is a natural affinity between the judicial style (found in someone who likes to analyze and judge) and analytic ability (the ability to analyze and judge well), and between the legislative style (found in someone who likes to come up with his or her own ideas) and creative-synthetic ability (the ability to come up with one's own ideas). I have argued that there is a possible synergy in the performance of someone whose abilities and styles match (Sternberg, 1994). For example, in our investment theory of creativity, we argue that, to be creative, a person needs both creative-synthetic ability and a legislative style (Sternberg & Lubart, 1991, 1995).

The triarchic theory also states that people are practically intelligent to the extent that they are able to find ways of capitalizing on strengths and compensating for or remediating weaknesses. People whose styles match their abilities have found one means by which they can capitalize on their strengths.

A related notion, proposed by Baltes, Dittmann-Kohli, and Dixon (1984), is that of selective optimization with compensation. As a person ages, he or she is likely to lose some degree of fluid abilities but to gain certain kinds of crystallized abilities (Horn, 1968), especially in a domain of expertise. A person may actually be able to shape a career to match changes in abilities as well as styles. For example, mathematicians seem to reach the peak of their creative contributions at a relatively early age (Simonton, 1988). A legislative, global style might behoove the mathematician in the years that he or she is best able to make important contributions to knowledge. Later, the individual might still be able to contribute to the field, perhaps in part by editing a journal or reviewing grant proposals (both of which call for a judicial style). A lawyer who finds his or her style turning toward the judicial might seek a judgeship; a doctor might seek a term on a medical review board.

At times, styles that seem to lead to high levels of job performance at one point in a career may be less productive or even counterproductive later on. For example, a low-level manager may be viewed as an "able" manager in part as a result of having an executive, monarchic, local style. The manager does what he or she is told to do, focuses on a single problem at a time and brings it to resolution, and deals with the details of that problem. Such managers tend to succeed in their jobs and to be promoted. At the higher levels of manage-ment, however, one seeks someone who is more legislative, judicial, hierarchi-cal, and global. Such a person will be able to deal with the large problems that confront organizational leaders and to resolve them in a way that is creative (corresponding to the legislative style) and wise (corresponding to the judicial style). But such persons may have been derailed early in their careers because they did not fit the prototype of an able (i.e., pliable) lower-level manager.

Styles and interactive minds

Styles also relate in several ways to the concept of interactive minds. For one thing, the construct of compensation for weaknesses (Cronbach & Snow, 1977; Sternberg, 1985) applies to styles just as much as abilities. Suppose, for exam-ple, that a scientist, designer, historian, or whatever needs to complete a project that requires attention to details, but that he or she has a predomi-nantly global style. The sensible thing to do is to find a collaborator who has a local style and will attend to the details while the global individual attends to the big picture. Similarly, a legislative researcher may seek to pair up with an executive researcher, and vice versa, so that one person attends more to planning and the other to execution. The legislative or executive individual may seek out a judicial individual when seeking someone to provide detailed feedback regarding his or her work. Likewise, an internal person, who prefers to work on his or her own, may pair up with an external person, who is more comfortable interacting with others. In sum, complementarity can provide a means of compensation for styles that do not come naturally to a person.

Certain styles probably lend themselves more naturally to profiting from interaction than do others. For example, a person with an external style is likely to feel more comfortable in interaction than is a person with an internal style. In my own experience, individuals with an anarchic style tend to be poorly understood and often rejected by others, except for others with an anarchic style as well. These individuals can be difficult to interact with because they do not follow the more linear and systematic models of interaction, and of information processing in general, to which most people are accustomed.

As noted earlier, styles are at least partly socialized, which provides another link to the concept of interactive minds. Indeed, we form our styles in interaction with others – although a style is a personal attribute, its origins are interactive.

Although, in an absolute sense, styles are not better or worse, they are differentially valued by those with whom we need to interact. For example, a business that emphasizes teamwork might value an external style more than would a business that emphasizes people working on their own. Even in science, which has traditionally favored people working in isolation, the advent of "big science" has necessitated the development of styles that in the past would not have been important. Thus, styles occur, develop, and are evaluated in the context of interaction with others.

Measurement of thinking styles

We have used several converging operations to measure thinking styles (Sternberg, 1994; Sternberg & Wagner, 1991). One such measure is the Thinking Styles Inventory (see Table 12.1). Subjects are given a statement like "If I work on a project, I like to plan what to do and how to do it" (which measures the legislative style) and are asked to rate the statement on a scale of 1 to 9.

A second measure is the Set of Thinking Styles Tasks for Students, which assesses styles via performance rather than inventory format. In one item, a student is given as a prompt the opening "When I am studying literature, I prefer . . ." and then must choose either "to make up my own story with my own characters and my own plot" (legislative), "to follow the teacher's advice and interpretations of the author's positions, and to use the teacher's way of analyzing literature" (executive), "to evaluate the author's style, to criticize the author's ideas, and to evaluate characters' actions" (judicial), or "to do something else (please indicate)." This measure is scored according to actual response.

In another item from this assessment, students are presented with a scenario in which they are asked to imagine being the "mayor of a small northeastern city. You have a city budget this year of $1 million. Below is a list of problems currently facing your city. Your job is to decide how you will spend the $1 million available to improve your city." The students are given options such as "drug problem," "roads," "landfill," and "shelters for the homeless." Scoring is based on the allocation of funds. Students who allocate all funds to one project are classified as showing a monarchic tendency. Those who prioritize their distribution of funds are scored as hierarchic. Those who distribute money equally across projects are classified as oligarchic. And those who show no system at all are classified as anarchic.

A third measure, the Thinking Styles Questionnaire for Teachers, assesses teachers' styles. These may or may not correspond to the teachers' own preferred style or styles. For example, a legislative person may require students to accept his or her ideas, and thus have an executive style of teaching. Typical items on this scale are "I want my students to develop their own ways of solving problems" (legislative) and "I agree with people who call for more, harsher discipline, and a return to the 'good old ways'" (conservative).

A fourth and final measure is the Students' Thinking Styles Evaluated by Teachers. Here a teacher (or other person) evaluates the style of each student. Statements to be rated are ones such as "S/he prefers to solve problems in her/his own way" (legislative) and "S/he likes to evaluate her/his own opinions and those of others" (judicial).

By using a variety of assessments, we are able to cancel out the biases and errors of measurement inevitably associated with a single kind of measurement, and thus can better converge on a more informed assessment of a person's profile of thinking styles.

The various measures have demonstrated good psychometric properties. For example, the 13 scales of the Thinking Styles Inventory have internal-consistency reliabilities ranging from .57 to .88, with a median of .82. Only one reliability is in the .50s, two in the .60s, one in the .70s, and the rest in the .80s.

Typically, we obtain certain significant correlations, regardless of the method of measurement. The global and local scales are negatively correlated, as are the legislative and conservative scales and the liberal and conservative scales. In contrast, the liberal and legislative scales are positively correlated, as are the conservative and executive scales.

Several factor analyses have revealed similar factor structures. In one such analysis, we obtained five factors accounting for 77% of the variance in the data. Factor 1, Adherence to Structure, contrasted the liberal and legislative scales with the conservative and executive. Factor 2, Engagement, comprised two scales, the oligarchic and the judicial. Factor 3, Scope, contrasted the external and internal scales. Factor 4, Level, contrasted the local and global scales. And Factor 5, Distribution of Time, comprised only the hierarchic scale.

We have found scores on the mental self-government scales to be correlated with scores on other measures of styles. For example, 30 of 128 correlations with the Myers–Briggs were statistically significant, as were 22 of 52 correlations with Gregorc's measure. Thus, it does appear that the various measures of styles map a roughly common space.

Styles in the classroom

Elena Grigorenko and I have conducted several studies investigating styles in the classroom (Sternberg & Grigorenko, 1993; Sternberg, 1994). One of these studies focused on teachers, another on students, and a third on the interaction between teachers and students.

In a first study with 85 teachers (57 female, 28 male) in four schools of widely varying types (private and public, and socioeconomically diverse), we found several interesting effects with respect to grade taught, age of teachers, subject area taught, and ideology.

Teachers are more legislative but less executive at the lower grades than at the upper grades. These findings might suggest either that more legislative individuals are attracted to teaching at the lower grade levels, or that people teaching at the lower grade levels become more legislative (or that those teaching at the upper grade levels become more executive). The demands on teachers in the United States are consistent with this pattern of findings: Teachers in the upper grades are forced to follow a more rigidly prescribed curriculum than are teachers in the lower grades.

We also found older teachers to be more executive, local, and conservative than younger teachers. Again, there are two interpretations of these findings, either or both of which might be correct. One interpretation is that teachers become more executive, local, and conservative with age; the other is that the difference is due to a cohort effect.

Further, we found that science teachers tended to be more local than were teachers of the humanities, whereas the latter tended to be more liberal than the former. These results again are roughly consistent with our experience. With respect to science, the results unfortunately suggest that science teachers may concentrate substantially more on the local details of science than on the "big picture" of scientific research.

Finally, we did an analysis of the relation of school ideology to teachers' styles. We had a rater who was not familiar with the individual teachers in each school rate each school for its own profile of styles on the basis of catalogues, faculty and student handbooks, statements of goals and purposes, and curricula. We also evaluated teachers' styles, and then assessed contrasts by looking at the match between teachers and schools. For six of seven planned contrasts, we found significant effects. In other words, teachers tend to match the stylistic ideology of their schools. Either teachers tend to gravitate toward schools that fit them ideologically or else they tend to become like the place they are in, suggesting again the importance of socialization in the formation of styles, even at the adult level.

In a second study of 124 students between the ages of 12 and 16 distributed among four schools, we found some interesting demographic effects. Socioeconomic level related negatively to the judicial, local, conservative, and oligarchic styles. These results are consistent with a notion of greater authoritarianism in the styles of the individuals of lower socioeconomic class. We also found that later-born siblings tend to be more legislative than earlier-born siblings, consistent with the past finding that firstborns tend to be more accepting of societal dictates than are later-born siblings (Simonton, 1988). Finally, we found a significant degree of match between students' and teachers' styles. Whereas for the teachers, the similarity of their styles to the profile of their schools could be interpreted in terms of choice of school, such an explanation is implausible in the case of students, who rarely get to choose their school. The results suggest socialization of styles.

In a third study, we went back to one of the original questions that motivated this work: Do students do better in classrooms where their styles match rather than mismatch the styles of their teachers? We assessed students' and teachers' styles and found that, indeed, students performed better and were more positively evaluated by teachers when the students' styles matched rather than mismatched those of their teachers, independent of actual level of achievement.

Styles thus seem to be important in school settings. In the next section, I discuss how they can be utilized directly in instruction and assessment.

Styles of thinking in instruction and assessment

For those who teach and assess students at any level – young children, adolescents, or adults – the theory of mental self-government implies modes of rendering teaching more effective. The key principle is that for students to benefit maximally from instruction and assessment, at least some of each should match their styles of thinking. I would not advocate a perfect match all the time: Students need to learn, as does everyone, that the world does not always provide people with a perfect match to their preferred ways of doing things. Flexibility is as important for students as for teachers. But if we want students to show what they truly can do, the match between their styles and that of instruction and assessment is key.

Table 12.2 shows various methods of instruction and the styles that are most compatible with them. The major point of this table is that different methods work best for different styles of thought. If teachers want to reach and truly interact with students, they need the flexibility to vary their teaching style to suit students' styles of thought.

Table 12.3 presents several methods of assessment and the styles with which they are most compatible. Note that different methods of assessment tend to benefit different styles of thought. For example, multiple-choice testing is very much oriented toward executive and local thinkers, whereas projects tend to be oriented more toward legislative and judicial thinkers, as well as global

Table 12.2. *Thinking styles and methods of instruction*

Method of instruction	Style(s) most compatible with method of instruction
Lecture	Executive/hierarchical
Thought-based questioning	Judicial/legislative
Cooperative learning	External
Solving of given problems	Executive
Projects	Legislative
Small-group recitation	External/executive
Small-group discussion	External/judicial
Reading	Internal/hierarchical
For details	Local/executive
For main ideas	Global/executive
For analysis	Judicial
Memorization	Executive/local/ conservative

Table 12.3. *Thinking styles and forms of assessment*

Form of assessment	Main skills tapped	Most compatible thinking style(s)
Short answer/ multiple choice	Memory	Executive/local
	Analysis	Judicial/local
	Time allocation	Hierarchical
	Working alone	Internal
Essay	Memory	Executive/local
	Macroanalysis	Judicial/global
	Microanalysis	Judicial/local
	Creativity	Legislative
	Organization	Hierarchical
	Time allocation	Hierarchical
	Acceptance of teacher viewpoint	Conservative
	Working alone	Internal
Project/portfolio	Analysis	Judicial
	Creativity	Legislative
	Teamwork	External
	Working alone	Internal
	Organization	Hierarchical
	High commitment	Monarchic
Interview	Social ease	External

ones. Note also the importance not only of the method of assessment used, but of the way in which it is scored. For example, an essay can be scored for recall, in which case it benefits executive students, or for analysis, in which case it benefits judicial students, or for creativity, in which case it benefits legislative

Table 12.4. *Thinking styles emphasized by instructional/evaluational prompts*

Executive	Judicial	Legislative
Who said ... ?	Compare and contrast ...	Create ...
Summarize ...	Analyze ...	Invent ...
Who did ... ?	Evaluate ...	If you ...
When did ... ?	In your judgment ...	Imagine ...
What did ... ?	Why did ... ?	Design ...
How did ... ?	What caused ... ?	How would ... ?
Repeat back ...	What is assumed by ... ?	Suppose ...
Describe ...	Critique ...	Ideally ... ?

students. It is not the essay, per se, but how it is evaluated, that determines who benefits.

Finally, Table 12.4 depicts the ways in which different prompts in instructional and evaluational assignments can lead to varying levels of compatibility for different styles. Prompts like "Who said ... ?" and "Who did ... ?" benefit executive students; prompts like "Compare and contrast ..." and "Analyze ..." benefit judicial students; and prompts like "Create ..." and "Invent ..." benefit legislative students. By varying the kinds of prompts they use, teachers can equalize the benefits to all of the students whom they teach.

Conclusions

Styles matter. Moreover, they are often confused with abilities, so that students or others who are thought to be incompetent are assessed in this way not because they lack abilities, but because their styles of thinking do not match those of the people making the assessment. Especially in teaching, we need to take into account students' styles of thinking if we hope to reach them.

We need to consider carefully how our practices in educational settings may deprive able people of opportunities, while giving opportunities to those who are less able. For example, extensive use of multiple-choice testing in the United States clearly benefits executive thinkers. Many tests of scholastic and other aptitudes confound measurements of styles with measurements of abilities. But replacing all of those tests with projects and portfolios would simply result in a different group of students being benefited. Ideally, we need to teach to and assess a variety of styles.

We also should ensure that the ways in which we teach and assess subject matter correspond to the ways in which performance will be assessed on the job. For example, if courses for scientists emphasize executive local thinking, but we then most value scientists who show legislative global thinking, we may end up with scientists who did well in their courses, but who will not make especially good researchers. At the same time, some of the best potential researchers may be derailed. The same principle applies in other areas as well.

In occupational settings as well, we must take into account the fit between styles of individuals and their jobs. For example, lower-level managers are probably rewarded for having an executive, monarchic, local style. They do what they are told. They focus on some things and don't let anything else get in the way. They deal with matters that are relatively narrow in scope. The managers with these styles are likely to be promoted. But at the upper levels of management, we probably want people who are more legislative or judicial, hierarchic, and global. The result may be that the best potential upper-level managers are derailed early on, and some of the weaker ones are promoted into high positions.

Fortunately, some occupations allow flexibility in styles. For example, someone who wants to become a college professor might go into scientific research, which is more legislative, or literary criticism, which is more judicial. A professor who tires of being legislative or judicial might become an entry-level administrator, who can be more executive. Lawyers can go the opposite way, becoming judges and exercising a more judicial style. Thus, flexibility exists not only in people, but in some job streams as well. In sum, we need to take styles into account in the worlds of education and work, and I believe that the theory of mental self-government provides a useful way to do so.

References

Baltes, P. B., Dittmann-Kohli, F., & Dixon, R. A. (1984). New perspectives on the development of intelligence in adulthood. Toward a dual-process conception and a model of selective optimization with compensation. In P. B. Baltes & O. G. Brim, Jr. (Eds.), *Life-span development and behavior* (Vol. 6, pp. 33–76). New York: Academic.

Brody, N. (1992). *Intelligence*. New York: Academic.

Cronbach, L. J., & Snow, R. E. (1977). *Aptitudes and instructional methods*. New York: Irvington.

Gardner, H. (1993). *Frames of mind: A theory of multiple intelligences*. New York: Basic.

Gregorc, A. F. (1979). Learning/teaching styles: Potent forces behind them. *Educational Leadership, 36*(4), 234–236.

Gregorc, A. F. (1985). *Inside styles: Beyond the basics*. Maynard, MA: Gabriel Systems.

Grigorenko, E., & Sternberg, R. J. (1995). Thinking styles. In D. Saklofske & M. Zeidner (Eds.), *International handbook of personality and intelligence* (pp. 205–229). New York: Plenum.

Holland, J. L. (1973). *Making vocational choices: A theory of careers*. Englewood Cliffs, NJ: Prentice-Hall.

Horn, J. L. (1968). Organization of abilities and the development of intelligence. *Psychological Review, 75*, 242–259.

Jung, C. (1923). *Psychological types*. New York: Harcourt Brace.

Myers, I. B. (1980). *Gifts differing*. Palo Alto, CA: Consulting Psychologists Press.

Myers, I. B., & McCaulley, M. H. (1988). *Manual: A guide to the development and use of the Myers–Briggs type indicator*. Palo Alto, CA: Consulting Psychological Press.

Simonton, D. K. (1988). *Scientific genius: A psychology of science*. New York: Cambridge University Press.

Sternberg, R. J. (1985). *Beyond IQ: A triarchic theory of human intelligence*. New York: Cambridge University Press.

Sternberg, R. J. (1988). Mental self-government: A theory of intellectual styles and their development. *Human Development, 31*, 197–224.

Sternberg, R. J. (1990). Thinking styles: Keys to understanding student performance. *Phi Delta Kappan, 71*, 366–371.

Sternberg, R. J. (1994). Thinking styles: Theory and assessment at the interface between intelligence and personality. In R. J. Sternberg & P. Ruzgis (Eds.), *Intelligence and personality* (pp. 169–187). New York: Cambridge University Press.

Sternberg, R. J., & Grigorenko, E. L. (1993). Thinking styles and the gifted. *Roeper Review, 16*(2), 122–130.

Sternberg, R. J., & Lubart, T. I. (1991). An investment theory of creativity and its development. *Human Development, 34*, 1–31.

Sternberg, R. J., & Lubart, T. I. (1995). *Defying the crowd: Cultivating creativity in a culture of conformity*. New York: Free Press.

Sternberg, R. J., & Wagner, R. K. (1991). *Thinking styles inventory*. Tallahassee, FL: Star Mountain Projects.

13 Cooperative construction of expert knowledge: the case of knowledge engineering

Gerhard Strube, Dietmar Janetzko, and Markus Knauff

Abstract

Knowledge-based, or "expert," systems are the best-known product of artificial intelligence and have been applied to real-world problems, although with mixed success. An essential task in constructing an expert system application is to build the knowledge base. Early research (in the 1970s) focused on accessing experts' knowledge. A decade ago, attention shifted from experts to tasks. The goal became to model the knowledge necessary to accomplish a given task. Although many have experienced the practical importance, the social embedding of knowledge engineering has not been emphasized in the theory so far; still, it can provide a useful framework for both system development and knowledge engineering – that is, for devising the application, constructing the system, and integrating the system in the workplace.

This chapter reviews approaches to knowledge engineering, knowledge acquisition, and design philosophies for expert systems. Using examples from our current work on expert system development in the domain of architectural design, we set forth the notion of the cooperative construction of knowledge and demonstrate its usefulness. The analysis of experts and knowledge engineers as interactive minds during system construction is complemented by case-based techniques for knowledge acquisition and "knowledge-level debugging" as a method for knowledge engineering, both of which are illustrated with examples.

Knowledge is not acquired in empty space, but through interaction with the environment, the most important part of which is social interaction. This is the common ground for all the chapters in this volume and needs no further discussion here. Rather, our objective is to demonstrate the applicability of

This research was supported by the Federal Ministry of Education, Science, Research and Technology (BMBF) within the joint project FABEL under contract 01-IW-104-D7. Project partners in FABEL are the German National Research Center for Computer Science (GMD), Sankt Augustin, the BSR Consulting GmbH, Munich, the Technical University of Dresden, the HTWK Leipzig, the University of Freiburg, and the University of Karsruhe.

We thank Brigitte Bartsch-Spörl, Gerd Gigerenzer, Robert Hoffman, Bob Sternberg, and an anonymous reviewer for valuable comments.

366

this theoretical stance to real-world problems in a highly technical domain, the design and construction of knowledge-based systems (KBSs), better known as expert systems. Since we cannot assume that the reader is familiar with this domain of application, the first part of the chapter will provide an introduction to expert systems and knowledge engineering, to highlight the issue of social interaction and its recognition (or rather, lack thereof) in past research.

In the second part we present an approach to knowledge engineering that puts knowledge acquisition for expert system design firmly in its social context. For this reason we focus on two different aspects of cooperation in the context of the development of KBSs: First, we argue that traditional methods of knowledge acquisition underestimate the influence of the cooperation and social interaction between knowledge engineers and experts in each phase of the knowledge acquisition process, the output of which is mostly seen only as experts' individual knowledge. But we also present some methods of knowledge acquisition that take the cooperation of knowledge engineers and experts into account. Experts and knowledge engineers are both active and equal agents in a cooperative knowledge acquisition process. The cooperatively acquired knowledge must be seen as a combination of the knowledge engineer's know-how and the insights gained during the very process of cooperation. Second, we distinguish three kinds of cooperation that KBSs might support: The system can be seen as a tool for coordinating the problem-solving activities of the users; it can also take part as an active agent in the cooperative problem-solving process with users and technical systems; and finally only technical systems could be involved in the problem-solving process.

Expert systems and knowledge engineering

Expert systems are perhaps the best-known product of artificial intelligence (AI), yet their development actually marked the beginning of a new era of AI. From its inception around 1956 until well into the seventies, AI relied on "knowledge-lean" representations and exhaustive search. This technique of problem solving was also thought to qualify as a theory of human problem solving (e.g., Ernst & Newell, 1969; Newell & Simon, 1963, 1972). In the seventies, a new orientation appeared: the notion of domain-specific knowledge as the basis of intelligent behavior. This led to the study of human expertise in psychology (see Ericsson & Smith, 1991, or VanLehn, 1989, for an overview), as well as to the development of the first KBSs in AI and later to their marketing as "expert systems" (Feigenbaum, 1977). At about the same time (ca. 1975), an initiative of the Sloan Foundation gave rise to cognitive science as an integrative view of cognition in biological and technical systems.

The development of knowledge-based systems

The original concept of an expert system was that it should be able to substitute for a human expert in routine work within a narrowly limited domain of expertise, for example, the analysis of complex chemical molecules (DENDRAL):

> At Stanford, Lederberg and I chose reasoning in science as our task and began to work with Buchanan and Djerassi on building a program that would elucidate chemical structure at a high level of competence.... For DENDRAL, knowledge was power. Obvious? In retrospect, perhaps. But ... in the late 1960s the knowledge-is-power hypothesis stood as a counter hypothesis awaiting further tests and the accumulation of evidence. (Feigenbaum, 1990, p. 325)

After several more or less successful projects in bacteria diagnosis (MYCIN), computer configuration (R1), and diagnosis in internal medicine (INTERNIST), expert systems were soon proclaimed to be the AI product that would change the economy (Feigenbaum, 1977). Although these hopes are somewhat quenched nowadays, expert systems still remain the most visible AI products.

Expert systems are one kind of knowledge-based system. Traditionally, a KBS has two or three basic components: (a) the knowledge base, which contains a formal representation of generally domain-specific knowledge, usually in terms of rules and concepts, (b) a deductive component ("inference engine") for reasoning, which is not domain-specific, but specific to the formal characteristics of the knowledge representation (e.g., whether rules, frames, or logical clauses are used), and (c) some kind of interface to another program, in which both the knowledge base and the inference component are embedded, or a stand-alone user interface to provide access to the knowledge base and allow for consultations.

Building a knowledge base: knowledge engineering

Expert system technology is a part of computer science. But only the formal aspects of the construction of knowledge bases can be tackled with logical methods (and they have been tackled for many years now, which has yielded interesting results, e.g., about the computational complexity of certain well-defined conceptual hierarchies; Nebel, 1990). All aspects pertaining to the content of a knowledge base by definition fall outside the scope of computer science, and empirical work is required to assess and formalize domain-specific knowledge. This primarily psychological task, which relies heavily on interviewing and observational methods, spawned a new discipline, called knowledge engineering (KE). However, KE may also be seen as a specialization of software engineering, and has indeed inherited much of its methodology.

Although we keep our discussion here to the early stages of knowledge acquisition and representation, the reader should bear in mind that the life cycle of a system requires updating and other maintenance. The usual setting for KE involves two roles: a domain expert (or better, a group of experts) and one (or several) knowledge engineer(s). In addition, the system to be developed and the constraints that have to be obeyed for this objective also play a major role. Modern software engineering has introduced other roles that have largely been neglected in KE: the users, for instance, and also the task to be supported and its integration in the overall work organization (Floyd, Reisin, & Schmidt, 1989). Software engineering has also pointed to the importance of the more comprehensive social embedding of KE and the introduction of new technologies in general: KE takes place in a context of potential social conflict (i.e., in the workplace) and is affected by experts and other personnel, by the politics of the management as well as the labor unions, and so forth. Our point in this chapter, however, concerns the essential social nature of expert knowledge and the process of KE through which it is acquired, a process that we view as a collaborative and cooperative construction of knowledge.

Early knowledge engineering: the mining view

The original approach to KE envisaged expert knowledge as a substance that could be extracted from human experts by means of suitable tools (Feigenbaum, 1977). This view pervades even some of the more recent literature on KE:

> Knowledge can be thought of as a natural resource, but, like many other natural resources, it is not always easy to extract. Like surface-mined coal, some knowledge is easily picked up. . . . To continue with this mining metaphor: some knowledge is not easily available at the surface; it has to be dug out. However, when a vein is hit, out comes whole, shiny nuggets. (Bell & Hardiman, 1989, p. 52)

Here the expert appears as the passive object of the knowledge engineer's activities. Knowledge is seen like a material that could exist without the context of task and work organization. As a symptom of this narrowed perspective, the term *knowledge acquisition* has often been substituted by *knowledge elicitation*.

Recent evaluations of the practical applications of expert systems technology unanimously agree that there have been few successes and many failures, and that one, perhaps the main, reason for this failure has been the neglect of the social embedding of the systems to be designed (Bachmann, Malsch, & Ziegler, 1993; Becker, Herrmann, & Steven, 1992; Jonas, 1992). The reasons are manifold. Experts may fear losing status and influence. Workers may fear losing their jobs, or may refuse to use the system, if they did not participate in its design from the start. The executives, on the other hand, may worry about the high costs of good KE and enforce parsimony. Any party might be rightly worried about issues of system security and reliability. At a time when designing an expert system usually implies the introduction of such an expert system into a company, KE takes place in a field of social tension. These aspects are usually not addressed by the theory, but are treated as part of the practical experience of KE professionals. From that perspective, expert knowledge is one thing, and the social setting of the work is another. Step by step, we will approach a theoretical stance from which the connections between knowledge and the work environment become apparent.

Reconstructing knowledge, an interactive process

The "mining" view presents just one perspective on the KE process. Taken literally, it is subject to an error of category (i.e., misunderstanding knowledge as a kind of substance). As a metaphor (cf. LaFrance, 1992), it leads one to ignore the problems of assessment, which are so well known to psychologists. Indeed, the first point of departure from the mining view rests on the conviction that all we can get by means of interviews, repertory grids, and so forth are empirical data that have to be interpreted in order to arrive at a reconstruction of an expert's (or several experts') knowledge.

Knowledge diagnosis versus knowledge acquisition. Knowledge is a hypothetical construct that can serve to explain the accomplishments of experts in solving real-world problems, but it cannot be "dug out" directly. Therefore, the objective of KE is not to get, but to reconstruct, expert knowledge.

This is a task quite different from knowledge diagnosis (which means to assess, for example, a student's knowledge in the context of classroom teaching, tutoring, or intelligent tutoring systems; see, e.g., Brown & Burton, 1978). Knowledge diagnosis is much like psychological testing in that the relevant variables are known, while the individual values of those variables are to be measured. In KE, however, the variables themselves are unknown, because the domain itself has to be modeled – its concepts and their relations, as well as the procedural rules.

In practice, important differences exist between knowledge acquisition in AI and knowledge diagnosis in psychology. Knowledge acquisition

- is a methodology of eliciting, formalizing, and representing experts' knowledge in a computational model, and
- addresses the question of how a specific domain can be structured and implemented in an effective system.

Psychological knowledge diagnosis

- builds a valid model of an individual's (cooperatively constructed) knowledge, and
- focuses on the description of structure and characteristics of human beliefs that underlie behavior.

The interested reader is referred to Gaines and Boose (1988) or Hoffman (1992) for overviews about knowledge acquisition/elicitation methods in AI. The spectrum of these methods ranges from rather "free-style" interviews to repertory-grid techniques adapted from Kelly (1955). Much work has focused on developing systems for "automatic" acquisition of knowledge, which means that the expert directly interacts with an automatic KE system (see Boose & Gaines, 1990, for an overview). In our opinion, all these attempts to eliminate the knowledge engineer and make the expert feed information directly into the system have either failed or succeeded to only a very limited degree. To give but one reason, experts can forget to make explicit what is fairly obvious to them. Another approach is to use machine learning techniques to enable expert systems to gain knowledge directly from documents – for example, databases. However, problems regarding background knowledge remain. Furthermore, the current state of machine learning allows learning in only a limited sense and in thoroughly formalized domains.

Concepts, relations, and rules

After the initial steps of KE (familiarization with the domain, textbook and document analysis, discussion with experts, etc.), the reconstruction of expert knowledge starts with the basic concepts of a given domain. These concepts are usually represented in a strictly or approximately hierarchical manner – for example, an inheritance network like KL-ONE (Brachman & Schmolze, 1985) or a hierarchy of frames (e.g., Bobrow & Winograd, 1977). Relations between concepts are relevant, too. Concepts and relations together describe the fundamental facts and regularities of a domain. Domain-specific concepts and their relations may be combined with general inference rules, like "If X stands in a causal relation to Y and X is the case, then infer Y." Generally, the representational tools of semantic networks, schemas (frames), and production rules are combined; often, logic (e.g., Prolog-like Horn clauses) provides an alternative means of knowledge representation.

The idea of expert system shells, originating in the 1970s, is to take an expert system (e.g., MYCIN), empty it of the domain-specific knowledge and thus make it a shell (EMYCIN, for empty MYCIN). Afterward, new knowledge from a different domain (i.e., concepts and relations) is put in to arrive at another working expert system (van Melle, 1980). Many expert system shells have been marketed in the meantime. They all attempt to reduce what Feigenbaum (1977) called the "knowledge acquisition bottleneck," namely, the acquisition of domain concepts and relations. From a current viewpoint, the idea of expert system shells seems naive because it assumes that one model of inference (which may be appropriate for the task that it was originally developed to solve) should fit all kinds of tasks. (The second-generation shells, e.g., KEE, were rather general AI programming environments and are not relevant in the present context.)

Systematically interactive methods

To reconstruct an expert's knowledge, it would be hazardous for a knowledge engineer to use the expert as a passive source of data (as the mining view does) and rely on the data alone. Knowledge acquisition for expert systems is a process that can consume many months of collaboration, and is not a one-point-in-time measurement; therefore, it is bound to be reactive. Also for reasons of accuracy, it is preferable to feed the knowledge engineer's results back to the expert, discuss and refine them, and if necessary repeat the process (Hoffman, 1987). KE is then necessarily conceptualized as an interactive process (Shaw & Woodward, 1986).

A technique for assessing concepts and their relations in an interactive framework is the Heidelberger Strukturlegetechnik (SLT; Scheele & Groeben, 1984). SLT employs a strictly limited set of relations, which are conceived as being domain-independent and thus universally applicable. In KE practice, however, the repertoire of these relations usually needs some modification to account for domain specificity. The hallmark of the SLT technique is that the knowledge engineer (originally, the counselor or psychotherapist) attempts to model the relevant concepts and relations in a given domain on the basis of his or her understanding of the domain (based on interviews with experts). The expert(s) (originally, the client[s]) does the same independently. Afterward, both parties discuss their models to arrive at a consensus model (Scheele & Groeben, 1984). Bonato (1988) was the first to apply this method to KE, and SLT indeed constitutes the first KE technique to be based on a systematically interactive view of the KE process.

Modern knowledge engineering: constructing knowledge

The functional approach to knowledge

KE has moved away from the objective of eliciting, or reconstructing, the total of the expert's problem-solving knowledge. Much of what an expert knows is implicit or "common sense," and, of course, an expert knows much that is not applied (often, not even applicable) to the specific task that the expert system is designed to support. This shift in objectives is linked to yet another one – that expert systems should not be designed to replace, but to assist the expert (and, at least temporarily, the expert's clients) in the solution of routine problems. The result is that expert systems are designed for narrowly circumscribed tasks and that KE must construct the appropriate knowledge for those tasks rather than attempt to reconstruct one expert's knowledge completely.

Succinctly put, if the task demands can be identified and the problem-solving method of the expert ascertained, the required knowledge becomes identifiable (Shaw & Woodward, 1990). It is not an expert's knowledge, but expert knowledge for a specific task that KE attempts to construct. The knowledge needed for a given task is both less and more than what the expert knows: less because only part of the expert's knowledge is needed, and more because other sources of knowledge (especially data from cases, i.e., solutions to problems that have been derived in the past) may also be needed.

Knowledge construction also bears some resemblance to "the 'CREATION' metaphor for expertise transfer" (LaFrance, 1992, p. 147). However, LaFrance falls back on the idea that knowledge acquisition is just a kind of transfer of knowledge from the expert to a knowledge base, which is not consistent with the view taken here.

The modeling perspective has, in some sense, always been a tenet of KE, but only recently have task-oriented methodologies been centered around this issue (Karunananda, Nwana, & Brereton, 1994).

Models of expertise

Many researchers have contributed to the effort to make expert system design and KE more manageable. For instance, tasks have been classified for the identification of those that are generic (Aamodt, 1990; Chandrasekaran, 1986; Steels, 1990). Currently, the most popular and perhaps most systematized approach goes by the acronym KADS (Design Structuring Knowledge Acquisition; Breuker & Wielinga, 1989; Cap Gemini, 1990; Schreiber, Wielinga, & Breuker, 1993; Wielinga, Schreiber, & Breuker, 1992). Ford and Bradshaw (1993) have assembled important work on knowledge acquisition as modeling, and their position (as expressed in Ford, Bradshaw, Adams-Webber, & Agnew, 1993) rests on a foundation similar to our view of KE.

A short overview of KADS

The KADS methodology developed by the Amsterdam group of Bob Wielinga and his associates has been designed to link bottom-up and top-down approaches in knowledge acquisition. While in bottom-up knowledge acquisition the focus is on knowledge provided by the expert, top-down knowledge acquisition concentrates on the knowledge needed for the task to be supported by the system. Thus, in KADS task analysis is used to arrive at preliminary definitions of which knowledge to look for, and new knowledge acquired from the expert(s) is at once evaluated with respect to its possible functional role(s) in solving the task and its subtasks. KADS defines several strata, or layers, of knowledge, which differ in function and generality. The most specific is the domain layer (concepts and relations, as described earlier). Above this layer follow rulelike basic inference steps that reflect the functional roles of the domain-specific concepts. The third, or task, layer organizes inference steps for the solution of specific tasks, and the topmost or "strategic" layer (now called the problem-solving model in KADS-II) describes the general problem-solving technique used, which is rather general and supposedly no longer domain-specific. The important points to note here about KADS and related approaches are that they stress the constructive aspect of KE, and that they also attempt, more or less successfully, to integrate information about the social setting of expert consultations and the work-organization context of the task. Schreiber et al. (1993) give extensive examples of applications of the KADS methodology.

The work environment: new design philosophies for expert systems

Assessments of expert systems applications and their fate (Bachmann et al., 1993) have shown that many expert system projects in industry failed because the needs of users were ignored, or experts and users feared to lose social standing. Even though KADS addresses issues of the social setting of expert consultation, other approaches go much further, putting expert system development and KE in the context of participatory software development (Rademakers & Pfeifer, 1992). This fits well with changed views about what an expert system should be and which functions it should serve. Concepts of "expert assistants" or of expert systems as "media" have broadened our perspective (Becker, Hoschka, & Rapp, 1989) and help to discriminate between the knowledge of the human expert and the expert knowledge used to build a system for dedicated purposes.

Cooperative construction of knowledge

In preceding sections we have outlined the mining view, the modeling view, and their relative virtues and shortcomings in KE. We now introduce the cooperative construction view.

1. Cooperative construction of knowledge may be described as a process of complex group problem solving. At the beginning of a KE endeavor, the initial state, the operators, and the goal state are not sufficiently specified. The same holds for the roles of the problem solvers, that is, the expert and the knowledge engineer. Cooperative construction of knowledge is directed toward an elaboration of these key variables and characteristics.

2. Cooperative construction of knowledge involves the specification of and agreement on the goals to be achieved in KE. Goals play a paramount role, since they focus attention on those aspects of expertise that are valuable to the knowledge base. The task to be modeled and the degree of support the KBS should offer are among the most important goal specifications. Goals may differ with respect to the degree of specification, and some may be

changed in the course of KE. Goals cannot be "elicited," but have to be shaped cooperatively: The expert may not know what is required and the knowledge engineer may not know what is possible when building a knowledge base in a particular domain, but both have to agree on the goals. In addition, these goals have to be assessed, discussed, agreed upon, and defended in the larger social context that we have mentioned before.

3. Cooperative construction of knowledge involves identifying the initial state of the problem of building a knowledge base. To achieve this objective, knowledge engineers and experts jointly have to identify concepts, relations, and tasks required for attaining a particular KE goal. Usually, the knowledge engineer tries to redescribe the expert's descriptions and behaviors in terms of knowledge representation constructs, referring to rules, frames, cases, and so on. Discussions with the experts give rise to further attempts by the knowledge engineers to cast their understanding of the domain in terms of constructs of knowledge representation. Again, both the knowledge engineers and the experts play a much more active role than suggested by either the mining or the modeling view.

4. Cooperative construction of knowledge involves establishing the roles that the knowledge engineer and the expert take. Once an initial description of a particular domain and the problem solving within this domain have been established, both the knowledge engineer and the expert are concerned with checking the adequacy of the knowledge for the task(s) that are to be addressed.

5. The cooperative construction of knowledge involves model building. The ultimate goal in KE is to create an explicit model of problem solving that describes and produces the relevant part of the expert's problem solving. Two criteria must be fulfilled by such a model. First, it has to be accepted by the domain experts as a valid descriptive model of (part of) their expertise. Second, it has to be accepted by the knowledge engineer as a model capable of realizing a particular intelligent behavior. These criteria are not met if the model of problem solving is judged as incomplete, incorrect, or inconsistent by one of the partners. In this case, the contributions of one or both partners aim at changing the model. This process is cooperative in nature since both domain experts and knowledge engineers have to contribute to model formation until the model meets both sets of criteria (which implies that agreement is reached between experts and knowledge engineers).

6. Cooperative construction as a KE approach also bears some risks because – by definition – it depends on a successful communication between kinds of experts (i.e., domain experts and knowledge engineers). Impatience, in conjunction with a tendency to agree on toy versions of domain rationales, or drifting toward the least common denominator are among the potential pitfalls of the approach advocated here and of similar ones that rely strongly and systematically on the constructive and cooperative nature of knowledge.

The cooperative construction view originated from cooperation between domain experts and knowledge engineers. But it could also be applied to the cooperation among domain experts. Several potential pitfalls come to mind. For example, a rationale for settling disagreements and mechanisms to map the domain experts' cooperation to the knowledge engineers' understanding have to be part of the methodology (a part not well specified to date).

When applied to cooperation among domain experts, or among experts and systems, the cooperative construction view bears some similarities to "situated cognition" views as discussed in the KE literature (Clancey, 1989; Suchman, 1987).

Some methods for the cooperative construction of expert knowledge

Explanation of behavior protocols

A technique of KE that we like very much is based on the familiar methods of behavior observation and thinking-aloud protocols. First, the expert is given a preselected task that consists of one or several cases. The steps toward a solution are recorded either manually or by video (if data are gathered in a traditional work environment), or directly by the computer (when computer-aided design is used as in one of our current projects). Step by step, the problem-solving process is discussed and interpreted by the expert in retrospection. We feel that this procedure combines the strengths of observation and protocol analysis, without interference from thinking-aloud during problem solving, and without the hazards of unsupported retrospection.

Tutoring observation

Listening to experts when they give a lecture (M. Welbank, cited in Boose, 1989) or teach novices is a well-known method in KE. The knowledge made explicit by teaching and teaching-back provides a common platform for both the knowledge engineer and the expert. Such a common ground is indispensable for agreeing on a particular scope of the domain to be investigated. Although we do not now employ these techniques, they are mentioned here because of their cooperative aspects.

Expert discussions

Many actual expert system projects have suffered from the "single expert problem." Combining information from multiple experts can serve to broaden the scope, identify areas of disagreement, and eliminate errors (Mittal & Dym, 1985). Discussions among experts, usually together with knowledge engineers, may serve to pinpoint disagreements, arguments, and, finally, consensual or alternative ways to solve problems in the domain at stake. Obviously, this technique aims explicitly at social interaction to construct and refine domain-specific knowledge. Unfortunately, there is no general recipe for reaching consensus or for handling disagreements that could be applied across all cases. Disagreements may have beneficial or detrimental consequences for KE. The knowledge engineer may gain insight into which knowledge is agreed on and where the controversial issues in a domain are. Sometimes this technique results in different (but equally applicable) styles of problem solving, as we have observed in different groups of architects (see later). In addition, a controversy among experts may bring to the fore causal knowledge about the domain that might otherwise have passed unnoticed. If disagreements among experts cannot be settled, a decision must be reached on which problem-solving techniques to select; sometimes, considerations of the usefulness of the system under design may settle the controversy.

Some further ideas for cooperative variants of KE techniques

A standard KE method involves the observation of an expert solving a problem. This could also be done from a distance, for example, over the phone. An expert (in our case, an architect) has to tell a nondomain expert (e.g., the knowledge engineer) everything to put him or her in a position to solve the problem. Since the expert cannot see the problem (i.e., the relevant part of the layout) over the phone, he or she has to be more explicit, which helps to establish a common language – even if it is restricted to a particular task. However, this method should be used only in conjunction with other methods since expert problem solving is here investigated from a non-natural perspective, which may produce *artifactual* results.

Another idea is cooperative time-limited problem solving, a method of KE that could be used to slow an expert's problem solving down to the degree that cooperation with a nondomain expert, for example, the knowledge engineer, becomes possible. Both the domain expert and the knowledge engineer would take turns working at a complex problem for fixed time intervals. This method could be applied to problems that require a multistep and time-consuming process of finding the solution. Again, both the domain expert and the knowledge engineer would have to comment on their problem-solving behavior. Still further cooperative variations on KE methods of controlled observation could be envisaged.

Exploiting natural experience: knowledge acquisition for CBR systems

Everyone who has interviewed experts for reasons of knowledge acquisition is familiar with the phenomenon of experts coming up with recollections and stories, be those examples for general rules or illustrations of exceptions. Moreover, case-based reasoning (CBR) – that is, applying successful solutions from memory to new problems – seems to be a natural way of human problem solving. This reliance on previous experiences is a hallmark of CBR, and many researchers have adopted the belief that people often use cases to solve problems in their daily lives (Kolodner, 1993; Riesbeck & Schank, 1989; Schank, 1982). Klein (1992) emphasizes that stories (which can be seen as cases) support training better than other knowledge sources, because users with moderate experience can benefit from stories to upgrade their skills and knowledge.

Under these circumstances it is not surprising that CBR has been proposed as a psychologically more plausible model of reasoning than the more fashionable rule-based reasoning systems (Riesbeck & Schank, 1989). The main advantages of CBR, according to the literature, are first its efficiency, because problems do not have to be solved from scratch. Second, CBR provides solutions in domains that are not completely understood (in the sense that no logical theory can be constructed for the domain).

Cases have yet another important advantage. When experts cooperate in their daily working environment and explain ideas or suggest solutions to their colleagues, they rarely mention rules, concepts, or other kinds of generic knowledge. Mostly they make use of examples or develop new ideas by adopting past experiences. Therefore, CBR seems to be an approach to KE that takes the aspect of cooperative construction of knowledge into account. Episodic knowledge (Strube & Janetzko, 1990) is also one of the hallmarks of what has been called the "situatedness" of cognition (Suchman, 1987). In particular, the cooperation between user and system should be much easier if the system makes use of cases for problem solving and explanation.

Taking a case-based approach

The usefulness of episodes, examples, and cases for human and machine problem solving has been reported in a number of studies (for an overview, see Kolodner, 1993). We will now focus on another aspect: the role that cases play in generating and transferring knowledge. It is this aspect that makes cases an important entry point for a cooperative construction of knowledge among intelligent agents. In the interaction between experts and knowledge engineers, experts often cite examples spontaneously or fall back on past solutions. In KE, the cooperative character of this process becomes evident right from the start:

1. Cases are provided by experts to characterize or exemplify their domain of expertise and their way of solving problems.
2. The knowledge engineer tries to make sense out of those cases by analyzing the overall framework in which these problem-solving episodes occur.
3. The experts contribute to an understanding of the situatedness of a case by delineating the context in which a case is framed.
4. The knowledge engineer presents the experts with an account or even a formal description of the cases.
5. The experts accept, modify, or even reject the description of the cases.
6. The knowledge engineer's attention is attracted to the details of the domain or the problem-solving strategies that have raised objections.

In this way, knowledge is cooperatively shaped by experts and knowledge engineers. The ideal result of this process is an explicit rationale for task-specific problem solving that meets two goals: It is accepted by the experts as a valid description of their expertise, and it is accepted by the knowledge engineers as a model capable of realizing a particular problem-solving behavior.

An example: the cooperative construction of knowledge by linking cases and tasks in the domain of building design

We are currently engaged in an expert system project, FABEL (together with groups from Bonn, Dresden, Karlsruhe, Leipzig, and Munich, funded by the German Ministry of Research and Technology; see Voss, 1993, for an overview). Focusing on cases plays a major role in the type of knowledge acquisition pursued in this project. In the past 2 years, several hundred cases have been sampled from the design work of two groups of architects at Karlsruhe (Germany) and Solothurn (Switzerland). Extensive work flow and task analyses were done, and the cases were discussed and evaluated among experts and knowledge engineers. (Note that some of the more problematic social aspects of our work were alleviated by the fact that our experts will also be the users of the systems under construction.)

We will now present an example that sheds light on the way knowledge is cooperatively constructed (see also Janetzko, Börner, Jäschke, & Strube, 1994). The example is taken from the domain of architecture and is concerned with the planning and design of supply nets in buildings. For the example to be presented we have to describe the graphic representation schema employed (Hovestadt, 1993). By using this schema we represent all entities (e.g., walls, pipes) located in particular regions (e.g., ground floor, rooms), both of which are employed to plan and design supply nets in buildings. We also describe the entities and the regions in various degrees of abstraction, for example, as a sketch or very precisely. Usually, rectangles are used to mark regions in the technical drawings that architects use. If many rectangles are depicted, the readability and transparency of the drawings suffer due to overlapping lines. For this reason we use a representation schema that resorts to ellipses instead of rectangles. Each ellipse is internally represented by its spatial dimensions and nine further attributes. Examples of these attributes are the time at which an object was created, the subsystem (which stands for used air, fresh air, rooms, paths, electricity), and morphology (which refers to development, connection, etc.; Figure 13.1).

In our example, the expert begins by describing how he or she arrives at a partitioning of rough locations for supply air (zab4) such that more specific locations (zab6) are attained. The knowledge engineer tries to make sense of the cases by analyzing the overall framework in which these cases are embed-

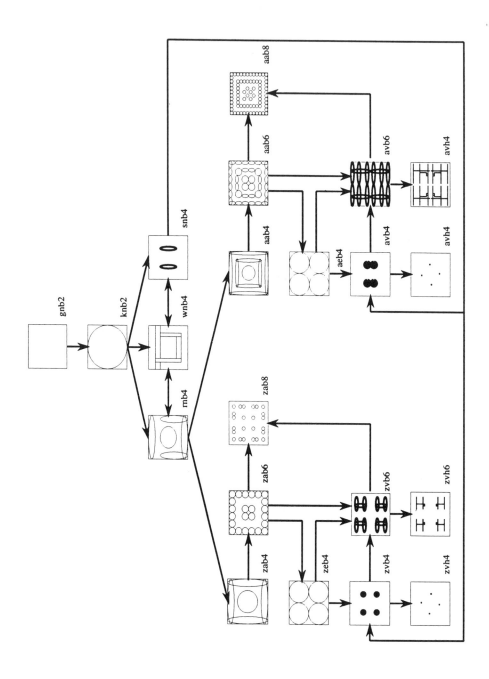

gnb2

knb2

snb4

wnb4

rnb4

aab8

aab6

aab4

avb6

avh4

aeb4

avb4

avh4

zab8

zab6

zab4

zvb6

zvh6

zeb4

zvb4

zvh4

ded, for example, the way the transition between zab4 and zab6 is embedded into the overall problem of planning and designing an air-conditioning system. The knowledge engineer introduces the notion of a task as an explanatory construct. A task is "something to be accomplished" (Steels, 1993).

The realizations of steps in problem solving are tasks that have to be identified in KE. Various methods have been developed to identify tasks (e.g., physical decomposition, analysis of requirements, etc.). If a domain can be partitioned into physical components, as is the case with buildings and floor plans, it is natural to take this way of partitioning as a rationale for identifying tasks. For example, "pipes to transport supply air" may refer to a set of physical components, as well as to the task of planning and designing these physical components. In addition, tasks have to be specified with respect to the knowledge and methods required, as well as the criteria to be met such that these tasks are successfully accomplished. The overall task of building an air-conditioning system may be decomposed into a number of tasks like "construct zab4" and "construct zab6" (Figure 13.1). Redescribing aspects of the domain in terms of tasks provides a common platform for the communication between expert and knowledge engineer. In addition, it offers a number of possibilities to extend and deepen the process of cooperative construction of knowledge. The expert contributes to an understanding of the situatedness of a case. For example, he or she tells the knowledge engineer which set of tasks has to be attained in order to accomplish the overall task, as well as the input and output specifications of each task, the interactions between tasks, and so on. The knowledge engineer in turn presents the expert

Figure 13.1. Task-decomposition schema used in planning and designing an air-conditioning system. Tasks are described by expressions made up of three letters and a number. The first letter relates to the subsystem of the building (e.g., a = used air, g = building, k = climate, r = rooms, w = paths, s = shaft, z = supply air). The second letter denotes the general function of the area addressed by the task (e.g., a = linkage, e = development, v = connection). The third letter specifies the kind of resolution that is employed (e.g., b = area, h = bounding box). The number relates to the part of the building that is envisaged (e.g., 2 = building, 4 = floor, 6 = room, 8 = areas within a room). For example, knb2 denotes the task of planning or designing the area of climate use that covers the whole building. The arrows indicate the standard sequence of tasks that are addressed while tackling the overall problem. The arrows neither point out the requirements to be fulfilled to complete a particular task nor exclude other sequences an architect may possibly choose when addressing these tasks. Single arrows refer to a transition between two adjacent tasks, with the former providing input to the latter. For example, the ground plan gnb2 provides input for the task of designing the areas of a building that are intended to have a homogeneous climate, knb2. The double arrows connect two adjacent tasks that interact strongly (loop), that is, provide input to each other. For example, the layout of the rooms rnb4 and the layout of the paths wnb4 in a building have to be attuned to each other.

with an account or even a formal description of the cases and tasks – for example, a flowchart that shows the sequence in which the tasks are tackled, as in Figure 13.1.

The expert then accepts, modifies, or even rejects the description of the cases and tasks. For example, the expert may object to flaws or failures of the knowledge engineer's redescription with respect to completeness, correctness, or consistency. The expert may recognize that the flowchart gives a valid account of a particular problem and its solution, but fails to give a general account of problem solving in the domain. Note that the process of cooperative construction of knowledge is considerably amplified once the knowledge engineer casts his or her understanding of the domain in terms of a written account, a flowchart, or a formal description. Objections by the expert cause the knowledge engineer's attention to be attracted to still underspecified details. For example, the knowledge engineer may add further subtasks or clarify the semantics of concepts or relations.

Validating knowledge-based systems

The computer science view on software evaluation focuses on the technical aspects and often ignores the application. The dominant theoretically oriented research tradition in AI attempts to apply techniques of program validation (i.e., logical proofs that a program is correct) to AI programs. This has not been successful with KBSs, for a variety of reasons (Hoenen, Kloth, & Steven, 1992). In contrast, practitioners of expert system development, especially in the early years of research on expert systems, took a "black box" approach to the evaluation of knowledge bases. If a system provided useful answers and the expert agreed with its contents, the system was assessed as usable. For testing the usability of a system, a number of problems were presented to both the expert and the system, and their solutions were compared (Golshani, 1990). Rapid prototyping, a technique often employed in building knowledge bases, aims to build a first working prototype, or demonstration system, as fast as possible. The main advantage is that, by executing this partial system, one can get information about the correctness and consistency of the represented concepts, relations, and rules early, and the knowledge engineer is likely to use this information as a focusing device in the later KE. The key idea is that it is faster to test pieces of a knowledge base rather than to be concerned with theoretical considerations. To summarize, in the traditional view of evaluation only the following questions were considered (e.g., Golshani, 1990; Hayes-Roth, Waterman, & Lenat, 1983):

1. Does the system solve problems from the domain?
2. Does the system provide right answers?
3. Is the content of the knowledge base consistent with the experts' knowledge?

4. Is the represented knowledge correct, complete, and consistent?
5. Is there a need for expansion or modification of the represented knowledge?
6. Is the knowledge representation format adequate or does it have to be changed?

This list of evaluation criteria demonstrates that the traditional view on the evaluation of KBSs rests on the idea of stand-alone systems. This does not invalidate the preceding criteria, but they need to be complemented by others. One of the most important problems has been called the cooperativity problem (Hickman et al., 1989). Interpersonal relations between experts and knowledge engineers have been ignored for a long time. The result has often been systems that did not fit into the working environment of the experts and could not support cooperative work. For this reason, more researchers now take social aspects into account. Some researchers like Shaw and Gaines (1986) have adopted theories from social psychology and different areas of applied psychology, in particular from industrial and organizational psychology, to gain more insight into the process of cooperative problem solving. However, progress has been slow to use those theories for the evaluation of knowledge bases. In the following section, some evaluation criteria will be introduced that address the social nature of expert knowledge.

Facets of cooperation and their evaluation

It might be helpful to distinguish various aspects of cooperation that a system usually has to support. Usually, the system has to support the cooperation of its users. We call this task user–user cooperation support. In this case the system is more or less a tool for coordinating the problem-solving activities of the users, like many current "groupware" programs do. But a KBS could also take part as an active agent in the cooperative problem-solving process. If the system contributes its special domain knowledge to the problem-solving process, this is user–system cooperation. The third (and, up to now, rare) possibility is that only technical systems are involved in the problem-solving process. In this case, there has to be system–system cooperation. This type of cooperation is the topic of distributed AI and beyond the scope of this paper, although the question of coordinating different problem solvers within one expert system has similar characteristics (Strube & Janetzko, 1990). For each of these types of cooperation, systems have to be evaluated in different ways. An explanation component, for example, one of the most important features of a system with respect to user–system cooperation, is less important when only technical systems are involved.

Another important aspect of system evaluation is how well it supports the cooperation between knowledge engineers and experts (e.g., for maintenance). Recent research on this topic has been done in the WISMOD project (Becker et al., 1989). From a cooperative view of knowledge base evaluation, the following questions have to be considered in addition to those listed earlier:

1. Does the system provide knowledge that is sufficient to support co-operation?
2. Does the system also support user–user cooperation?
3. How difficult is it for the user to interact with the system?
4. Is there a possibility of sharing the problem-solving process between users and system, for example, by dynamically allocating tasks?
5. How well does the system fit in the work environment of its users?

For some examples of criteria for user–system cooperation and regarding integration of the system into the work environment, we cite from a catalogue of criteria that has been compiled in the INRECA expert system project (Traphöner, Conruyt, Dittrich, & Manago, 1993, pp. 10–12):

1. "Is it possible to configure the consultation system's interface according to the current user's qualification and needs?" Here, flexibility and "cognitive adequacy" (Strube, 1992) of the system are addressed.
2. "Is the naive user guided during consultation?" Insofar as a system is not to be used by experts, who can be trusted to have the necessary background, knowledge, and judgment in the application domain. The system should enable its users to check the system's recommendations by means of explanations that the users can understand – still a field much in need of research.
3. "Does the consultation follow the logical flow expected by the domain expert; that is, is the system understandable for him?" This covers the same issue, but enhances the aspect that the visible mode of operation of the system has to be integrated into the normal work flow.
4. "Does the introduction of the system cause a reduction of routine work?" Reducing routine work (instead of qualified, expert work) should be a main objective, because it results in users doing more qualified work.
5. "Does the system cause new and/or higher qualification requirements?" Ideally, the system should also stimulate ongoing qualification of its users, as, in fact, has been done in the area of maintenance. Thus, expert systems provide a means to personnel development.

Clearly, these criteria focus on the integration of expert systems in the daily work environment of their users. The key idea is that a system alone cannot provide a satisfying way for dealing with problems from the domain. A system needs to be supported by its users, as well as the users by the system, and subtasks have to be delegated to both parties during the problem-solving process. These issues have to be taken into account in the design of expert systems, in the knowledge acquisition process, and in the evaluation of knowledge bases and systems.

In the following section, we present a cooperative approach to the elicitation and evaluation of knowledge in an early phase of the KE process. The evaluation process is organized as a cooperative process in which the model of expert knowledge commonly constructed by knowledge engineers and domain experts is evaluated at the knowledge level before it is implemented and subjected to the usual validation techniques.

Knowledge-level debugging

The concept of "knowledge level" was introduced by Alan Newell more than 10 years ago (Newell, 1982). Newell emphasized that knowledge of humans and AI processing systems have to be described not only on the symbol level (i.e., the level of abstraction that concepts of high-level programming languages employ), but also on a still more abstract level (comparable to what Marr, 1982, has called the "computational level"). Thus, on the knowledge level the granularity of the concepts and relations resembles very much the ontology of concepts and relations of a human problem solver. On the knowledge level, concepts referring, for example, to tasks, goals, physical components, and also various types of relations, such as causal relations, are represented. Newell postulates the knowledge level as a computer systems level that has to be studied in line with the other, lower levels. The knowledge level provides an explanation for human or system behavior – for example, in terms of goals. While the symbol level describes internal mechanisms of information processing, the knowledge level is more "world oriented" (Van de Velde, 1993).

Emphasis on the knowledge level has become the common denominator of the majority of approaches in the expert system community, particularly in the so-called modeling approach. To make use of the knowledge-level approach, further structuring is required. This means that the question that has to be answered is, which particular concepts and relations are taken to specify the knowledge level? There is, however, to date no general agreement concerning the structuring of knowledge on the knowledge level (Wielinga, Van de Velde, Schreiber, & Akkermanns, 1993). Clancey's model of heuristic classification can be seen as the first elaborated approach to expert systems on the knowledge level (Clancey, 1985). In recent years the KADS and CommonKADS groups (Schreiber et al., 1993; Wielinga & Breuker, 1986; Wielinga et al., 1992), the generic tasks theory (Chandrasekaran, 1986), and, especially, the components-of-expertise theory (Steels, 1990) are the most representative approaches to knowledge-level modeling in the KE literature. Given the popularity of the knowledge level in KE, it seems surprising that approaches to system evaluation have so far not attached much significance to the knowledge level. Knowledge-level approaches have relied on an implementation (usually in the "rapid prototyping" style) with specially designed high-level languages, often on top of Lisp interpreters (Linster, Karbach, Voss, & Walther, 1993). Our intention is to take the evaluation process one crucial step further by implementing evaluation directly at the knowledge level. The knowledge-level debugging that we propose is a kind of high-level "walk through." It is a method that integrates theories from cognitive psychology and KE and takes the cooperative character of expert system design and knowledge acquisition into account.

The key idea of knowledge-level debugging is to base the process of knowledge-base evaluation and debugging (i.e., spotting and correcting errors) on models of mental representations rather than on implementation. During knowledge acquisition, the knowledge engineer together with the expert build a model of the expert's task-relevant knowledge, a model that can be tested for correctness, completeness, consistency, and also for its functionality with regard to cooperative problem solving. If assessment by means of knowledge-level debugging credits the knowledge base to be sufficient for the task and usable by both the expert (and/or other intended users) and the knowledge engineer, implementation can start. Interim results of the debugging process provide a guideline and the framework for later phases of a cooperative knowledge acquisition process. Since KE does not strictly follow a sequence of knowledge acquisition–evaluation–implementation, but requires many cycles through the acquisition–evaluation loop, knowledge-level debugging has also the decisive economic advantage of spotting and repairing gross (and also many subtle) errors before implementation and reimplementation, when corrections are much more costly.

Knowledge-level debugging in practice

In this section, we introduce two methods developed by Dietmar Janetzko that allow for cooperative construction of knowledge and knowledge-level debugging. The methods are complementary in nature. The first method, *forced-choice card sorting* (not identical to the well-known hierarchical sorting of concepts), generates a problem-solving trace obtained from the observation of an expert who solves a problem. The second method, the *replay of cards*, tests and extends the results obtained by forced-choice card sorting. This is achieved by having another subject solve a similar problem and using (replaying) the cards produced by forced-choice card sorting.

Forced-choice card sorting. The leading principle behind forced-choice card sorting is to make explicit all the knowledge employed when approaching a problem. To allow for a well-structured procedure, two requirements have to be fulfilled. First, a problem that is nontrivial, but that can be solved irrespective of other problems, has to be selected. This is possible even in domains where cross-dependencies abound, because the necessary preconditions can be fixed experimentally, and codependencies may be neglected at that stage. Methods of task decomposition may be applied to isolate suitable problems

Table 13.1. *Cards used to generate a problem-solving trace*

Primitive cards	Compound cards
Concept card	Initial-state card
Rule cards	Goal-state cards
Constraint cards	Case cards
Relation cards	Frame cards
Instance-of	Problem cards
Part-of	Solution cards
Is-a	
Member-of	

(Janetzko, Börner, Jeschke, & Strube, 1994). Second, a set of cards that denote basic functional relations has to be provided to express the knowledge actually applied when solving a problem. This set is the result of theoretical considerations (cognitive theories of problem solving) and practical experience in KE. There are different types of cards that draw on central concepts of knowledge representation and problem solving. Primitive cards just express a single concept, relation, or rule. Compound cards combine a number of other cards (primitive or compound) so that a knowledge base can be constructed incrementally. Examples of linkage cards are initial state, goal state, case, and so forth. The set of cards is intended to bridge the gap between a structured interview and the representation of knowledge (see Table 13.1). The method proceeds as follows. The experts are given a preselected problem to solve. In particular, they are given the set of problem-solving cards through which they can express their way of solving the problem. The cards presented in the beginning are generic in nature. When the experts employ a domain concept, they take an empty concept card, write the name of the concept on the card, and place the card in the temporal sequence of other cards. In this way, a problem-solving trace is attained. The knowledge engineer has to watch that the trace actually covers all kinds of knowledge required for understanding the trace.

The experts may use each type of card and may even introduce new types of cards if required. However, they should use these cards to make their knowledge explicit. Forced-choice card sorting intervenes in the way experts solve a problem. To lessen the experts' burden of documenting each problem-solving step, two knowledge engineers are required to conduct forced-choice card sorting: One of them selects and writes cards, and the second one observes and interviews the expert. The result of the method of forced-choice card sorting is tested and cooperatively extended by the second method, the replay of cards.

Replay of cards. The leading principle behind the replay of cards is the reapplication of the problem-solving trace to similar problems by a different intelligent agent. The method proceeds as follows: A problem solver, for example, a knowledge engineer, is presented with a problem and the problem-solving trace produced by an expert who solved a similar problem using the forced-choice card-sorting technique. That expert is also present. The cards only provide expert knowledge that the nonexpert problem solver can use. Usually, the nonexpert quickly runs into difficulties when trying to solve the given problem. This situation is similar to forced-choice card sorting: The nonexpert has to ask the expert for the additional knowledge he or she needs to overcome the obstacle. This additional knowledge is also written on cards taken from the forced-choice card set. Additional cards are inserted into the trace. At times, a concept used by the expert as primitive turns out to be a compound one that has to be resolved into a number of primitive cards. This process leads to a cooperative change of the original problem-solving trace generated by the expert.

By using the replay of cards, the nonexpert slips into the role of the computer that is given a knowledge-based program to solve a problem. However, the replay of cards is more economical than the test of a program on the symbol level – for example, in rapid prototyping. When errors are detected, they can be alleviated on the spot. Applied in conjunction with forced-choice card sorting, the replay of cards supports and exploits the cooperative construction of knowledge and allows for knowledge-level debugging.

Effects of the social construction of knowledge

The effects of the social construction of knowledge in the KE process can be organized in three major parts:

1. Working with experts and users, modeling the task-relevant expert knowledge, and designing the complete system does not leave the knowledge engineer unchanged. Hoffman (1987, 1992) reports an extreme case of 4 years of KE in the domain of interpreting aerial photographs, where the knowledge engineer changed roles during those years, becoming an apprentice and practically an expert himself.
2. As investigations in the WISMOD project (Becker et al., 1989) have shown, domain experts also experience changes due to KE. Effects are, for example, that they reflect more on their knowledge and that knowledge becomes organized more systematically. This aspect certainly needs further research. Problems have been identified with respect to the discrepancies between expert knowledge (acquired for expert systems) and experts' knowledge (Becker, Steven, & Strohbach, 1991).
3. Users, such as former clients of the domain experts, experience changes as well. Ideally, the process can be viewed as one of personal development, or qualification, with regard to the employees that work with the system. The German research project TA-KI (1991) has emphasized the dangers of quali-

fied users (experts) being overcharged, or nonqualified users being under-charged by expert systems. Psychological evaluations of office workers using computer systems (e.g., Frese & Brodbeck, 1989) have also emphasized the need for user adaptation (Kobsa & Wahlster, 1989). As we have already mentioned, user participation (Floyd et al., 1989) is essential in expert systems design.

Summing up

Traditional KE largely ignores the social embedding of expert consultation, as well as the social foundations of expert knowledge, that is, the processes by which expertise is acquired. The result can be a naive conceptualization of KE that endorses the mining metaphor (i.e., eliciting knowledge from experts) and the diminishing belief that pieces of knowledge without an explicit organiza-tion (i.e., a model of the problem-solving process, which is often task-specific) provide a sufficient knowledge base for a working and useful expert system.

In contrast, modern KE has realized that it is neither feasible nor sensible to reconstruct expert knowledge as a complete model of an expert's knowledge, but that expert knowledge should be task-oriented (i.e., it must be complete for the task). Thus, KE views the modeling of knowledge as a process of construction, which is based on interaction and cooperation between knowl-edge engineers and experts. KE also concentrates on the use of knowledge in problem solving, that is, on the social side of expert consultation. This, in turn, leads to considering interactions between users, experts, and knowledge engi-neers in system design and application. (For the FABEL project, this work has been documented in Enzinger & Schmidt-Belz, 1994.) We believe that this might be a good way to arrive not only at software products, but also at working applications.

Considering the social foundations of KE has also enhanced our concept of knowledge. While knowledge in philosophy is constrained to true statements about the world, psychologists usually talk about knowledge as the set of beliefs a subject holds (Strube, 1988). But both disciplines, as well as the more recent one of cognitive science, have almost exclusively concentrated on knowledge as individual knowledge, that is, knowledge in the possession of a single agent, or system, while ignoring literature, traditions and social customs, or artifacts (see Cole, Chapter 2, this volume). Putting the emphasis on knowl-edge as shared knowledge, and on the social basis of knowledge acquisition and knowledge application, can help KE, AI, and cognitive science arrive at a more realistic and more useful theoretical stance.

References

Aamodt, A. (1990). A computational model of knowledge-intensive problem solving and learning: EKAW-90. *Proceedings of the Fourth European Knowledge Acquisition for Knowledge-Based Systems Workshop* (pp. 1–20). Amsterdam.

Bachmann, R., Malsch, T., & Ziegler, S. (1993). Success and failure of expert-systems in different fields of industrial applications. In H. J. Ohlbach (Ed.), *GWAI-92: Advances in artificial intelligence* (pp. 77–86). Berlin: Springer.

Becker, B., Herrmann, T., & Steven, E. (1992). *Zur Diskrepanz zwischen Expertensystementwicklung und -einsatz* [On the discrepancy between the development of expert systems and their implementation] (TA-KI Research report No. 23). Arbeitspapiere der Gesellschaft für Mathematik and Datenverarbeitung [Research papers of the German National Research Center for Information Technology] (GMD). St. Augustin: GMD, 641.

Becker, B., Hoschka, P., & Rapp, F. (1989). *Veränderung der Wissensproduktion und -verteilung durch Expertensysteme* [Change of production and distribution of knowledge by using expert systems] (WISMOD). St. Augustin: GMD; and Dortmund: Universität Dortmund.

Becker, B., Steven, E., & Strohback, S. (1991). *Verbundprojekt "Veränderungen der Wissensproduktion und -verteilung durch Expertensysteme"* [Joint project: Change of prodution and distribution of knowledge by using expert systems] (TA-KI Fachbericht Nr. 2). St. Augustin: GMD.

Bell, J., & Hardiman, R. J. (1989). The third role – The naturalistic knowledge engineer. In D. Diaper (Ed.), *Knowledge elicitation: Principles, techniques and applications* (pp. 49–85). Chichester: Horwood.

Bobrow, D. G., & Winograd, T. (1977). An overview of KRL, a knowledge representation language. *Cognitive Science, 1*, 3–46.

Bonato, M. (1988). Knowledge elicitation with structure formation techniques. In J. Diederich & T. Uthmann (Eds.), *Knowledge acquisition (Arbeitspapier 281 der GMD)*. St. Augustin: GMD.

Boose, J. H. (1989). A survey of knowledge acquisition techniques and tools. *Knowledge Acquisition, 1*, 3–37.

Boose, J. H., & Gaines, R. B. (Eds.). (1990). *The foundations of knowledge acquisition*. London: Academic.

Brachman, R. J., & Schmolze, J. G. (1985). An overview of the KL-ONE knowledge representation system. *Cognitive Science, 9*, 171–216.

Breuker, J. A., & Wielinga, B. J. (1989). Models of expertise in knowledge acquisition. In G. Guida & C. Tasso (Eds.), *Topics in expert system design* (pp. 265–295). Amsterdam: Elsevier.

Brown, J. S., & Burton, R. R. (1978). Diagnostic models for procedural bugs in basic mathematical skills. *Cognitive Science, 2*, 155–192.

Cap Gemini (1990). *KADS-II* (ESPRIT II technical annex for project P5248). Meylan: Cap Gemini Innovation.

Chandrasekaran, B. (1986). Generic tasks in knowledge-based reasoning: High-level building blocks for expert system design. *IEEE Expert, 1*, 23–30.

Clancey, W. J. (1985). Heuristic classification. *Artificial Intelligence, 27*, 289–350.

Clancey, W. (1989). The knowledge level reinterpreted: Modeling how systems interact. *Machine Learning, 4*, 285–291.

Enzinger, A., & Schmidt-Belz, B. (1994). *Methoden zur Analyse von Entwurfsprozessen in der Bauplanung* [Techniques for the analysis of design processes in architecture] (FABEL-Report). St. Augustin: GMD.

Ericsson, K. A., & Smith, J. (Eds.). (1991). *Toward a general theory of expertise: Prospects and limits*. Cambridge: Cambridge University Press.

Ernst, G., & Newell, A. (1969). *GPS: A case study in generality and problem solving*. New York: Academic.

Feigenbaum, E. A. (1977). The art of artificial intelligence: Part I. Themes and case studies of knowledge engineering. *Proceedings of the Fifth International Joint Conference on Artificial Intelligence* (Vol. 5, pp. 1014–1029). Cambridge, MA: IJCAI.

Feigenbaum, E. A. (1990). Knowledge processing: From file servers to knowledge servers. In R. Kurzweil (Ed.), *The age of intelligent machines* (pp. 324–329). Cambridge, MA: MIT Press.

Floyd, C., Reisin, F.-M., & Schmidt, G. (1989). STEPS to software development with users. In C. Ghezzi & J. A. McDermid (Eds.), *ESEC '89: 2nd European Software Engineering Conference* (Lecture notes in computer science, Vol. 387, pp. 48–64). Berlin: Springer.

Ford, K. M., & Bradshaw, J. M. (Eds.). (1993). Knowledge acquisition as modeling (special issue). *International Journal of Intelligent Systems, 8* (whole issues 1 and 2).

Ford, K. M., Bradshaw, J. M., Adams-Webber, J. R., & Agnew, N. M. (1993). Knowledge acquisition as a constructive modeling activity. *International Journal of Intelligent Systems, 8*(1), 9–32.

Frese, M., & Brodbeck, F. C. (1989). *Computer in Büro und Verwaltung* [Computer application in business and administration]. Berlin: Springer.

Gaines, B. R., & Boose, J. H. (Eds.). (1988). *Knowledge acquisition for knowledge-based systems.* London: Academic.

Golshani, F. (1990). Rule-based expert systems. In H. Adeli (Ed.), *Knowledge engineering* (Vol. 1, pp. 1–27). New York: McGraw-Hill.

Hayes-Roth, F., Waterman, D. A., & Lenat, D. B. (1983). *Building expert systems.* Reading, MA: Addison-Wesley.

Hickman, F. R., Killin, J. L., Land, L., Mulhall, T., Porter, D., & Taylor, R. M. (1989). *Analysis for knowledge-based systems: A practical guide to the KADS methodology.* Chichester: Horwood.

Hoenen, M., Kloth, M., & Steven, E. (1992). Verifikation oder Überprüfbarkeit? [Verification or validation?] *Künstliche Intelligenz, 4,* 67–70.

Hoffman, R. R. (1987). The problem of extracting the knowledge of experts from the perspective of experimental psychology. *AI Magazine, 8,* 53–67.

Hoffman, R. R. (Ed.). (1992). *The psychology of expertise.* New York: Springer.

Hovestadt, L. (1993). *A4 – Digital Building* (FABEL Report No. 13). St. Augustin: GMD.

Janetzko, D., Börner, K., & Jeschke, O., & Strube, G. (1994). Task-oriented knowledge acquisition for design support systems. *Proceedings of the First European Conference on Cognitive Science and Industry* (pp. 153–184). Eigenverlag der Universität Luxemburg.

Jonas, M. (1992). *Expertensysteme und konventionelle Informationssysteme in der chemischen Forschung und Entwicklung* [Expert systems and conventional information systems in chemical research and development] (3. Teilbericht). Dortmund: IUK-Institut für sozialwissenschaftliche Technikforschung.

Karunananda, A. S., Nwana, H. S., & Brereton, P. (1994). *Towards a domain analysis approach utilizing metaphors for knowledge acquisition* (Tech Report TR94-10). Keele, UK: University of Keele, Department of Computer Science.

Kelly, G. A. (1955). *The psychology of personal constructs.* New York: Norton.

Klein, G. A. (1992). Using knowledge engineering to preserve corporate memory. In R. R. Hoffman (Ed.), *The psychology of expertise* (pp. 170–187). New York: Springer.

Kobsa, A., & Wahlster, W. (Eds.). (1989). *User models in dialog systems.* Berlin: Springer.

Kolodner, J. (1993). *Case-based reasoning.* San Mateo, CA: Morgan Kaufman.

LaFrance, M. (1992). Excavation, capture, collection, and creation: Computer scientists' metaphors for eliciting human expertise. *Metaphor and Symbolic Activity, 7,* 135–156.

Linster, M., Karbach, W., Voss, A., & Walther, J. (1993). *An analysis of the role of operational modeling languages in the development of knowledge-based systems* (FABEL Report No. 3). St. Augustin: GMD.

Marr, D. (1982). *Vision: A computational investigation into the human representation and processing of visual information.* San Francisco: Freeman.

Mittal, S., & Dym, C. L. (1985). Knowledge acquisition from multiple experts. *AI Magazine, 6,* 32–36.

Nebel, B. (1990). *Reasoning and revision in hybrid representation systems.* Berlin: Springer.

Newell, A. (1982). The knowledge level. *Artificial Intelligence, 18,* 87–127.

Newell, A., & Simon, H. A. (1963). Computers in psychology. In R. D. Luce, R. R. Bush, & E. Galanter (Eds.), *Handbook of mathematical psychology* (Vol. 1, pp. 361–428). New York: Wiley.

Newell, A., & Simon, H. A. (1972). *Human problem solving*. Englewood Cliffs, NJ: Prentice-Hall.

Rademakers, P., & Pfeifer, R. (1992). The role of knowledge level models in situated adaptive design. In B. Neumann (Ed.), *ECAI 92: 10th European Conference on Artificial Intelligence* (pp. 601–602). Chichester: Wiley.

Riesbeck, C. K., & Schank, R. C. (1989). *Inside case-based reasoning*. Hillsdale, NJ: Erlbaum.

Schank, R. (1982). *Dynamic memory: A theory of reminding and learning in computers and people*. New York: Cambridge University Press.

Scheele, B., & Groeben, N. (1984). *Die Heidelberger Struktur-Legetechnik (SLT)* [The Heidelberger structure formation technique]. Weinheim: Beltz.

Schreiber, G., Wielinga, B. J., & Breuker, J. A. (1993). *KADS: A principled approach to knowledge-based systems development*. London: Academic.

Shaw, M. L. G., & Gaines, B. R. (1986). Interactive elicitation of knowledge from experts. *Future Computing Systems, 1*, 151–190.

Shaw, M. L. G., & Woodward, J. B. (1986). Validation of a knowledge support system. In J. H. Boose & B. R. Gaines (Eds.), *Proceedings of the Second AAAI Knowledge Acquisition for Knowledge-Based Systems Workshop* (pp. 1–18). Banff, Canada.

Shaw, M. L. G., & Woodward, J. B. (1990). Modeling expert knowledge. *Knowledge Acquisition, 2*, 179–206.

Steels, L. (1990, Summer). The components of expertise. *AI Magazine* (special issue). (Also Vrije Universitet Brüssel, VUB AI Lab Memo, 88–16.)

Steels, L. (1993). The componential framework and its use in reusability. In J. M. David, J. P. Krivine, & R. Simmons (Eds.), *Second generation expert systems* (pp. 273–298). Berlin: Springer.

Strube, G. (1988). Wissen und wissensbasierte Systeme: Was interessiert den Psychologen am Wissen? [Knowledge and knowledge-based systems: What is it about knowledge that interests psychologists?] *Forum für Interdisziplinäre Forschung, 1*, 42–44.

Strube, G. (1992). The role of cognitive science in knowledge engineering. In F. Schmalhofer, G. Strube, & T. Wetter (Eds.), *Contemporary knowledge engineering and cognition* (pp. 161–174). Berliń: Springer.

Strube, G., & Janetzko, D. (1990). Episodisches Wissen und fallbasiertes Schliessen [Episodic knowledge and case-based reasoning]. *Schweizerische Zeitschrift für Psychologie, 49*, 211–221.

Suchman, L. A. (1987). *Plans and situated actions: The problem of human–machine communication*. New York: Cambridge University Press.

TA-KI. (1991). *Restriktionen und Erweiterungsanforderungen bei Entwicklungs- und Nutzungsbedingungen von Expertensystemen unter der Perspektive integrierter Technik-folgenabschätzung* [Restricted and extended possibilities when developing and using expert systems: The perspective of integrated impact-assessment of technologies] (TA-KI Fachbericht Nr. 9). Bonn: University of Bonn, Institute of Computer Science.

Traphöner, R., Conruyt, N., Dittrich, S., & Manago, M. (1993). *Industrial criteria for comparing the technologies of INRECA* (ESPRIT project 6322 INRECA, Deliverable D4). Kaiserslautern: TecInno.

Van de Velde, W. (1993). Issues in knowledge-level modelling. In J. M. David, J. P. Krivine, & R. Simmons (Eds.), *Second generation expert systems* (pp. 211–231). Berlin: Springer.

VanLehn, K. (1989). Problem solving and cognitive skill acquisition. In M. I. Posner (Ed.), *Foundations of cognitive science* (pp. 527–579). Cambridge, MA: MIT Press.

van Melle, W. J. (1980). *System aids in constructing consultation programs*. Ann Arbor: University of Michigan Research Press.

Voss, A. (1993). *Survey of FABEL* (FABEL Report No. 2). St. Augustin: GMD.

Wielinga, B. J., & Breuker, J. A. (1986). Training of knowledge engineers using a structured methodology. In T. Bernold (Ed.), *Expert systems and knowledge engineering* (pp. 133-139). Amsterdam: Elsevier.

Wielinga, B. J., Schreiber, A. T., & Breuker, J. A. (1992). KADS: A modelling approach to knowledge engineering. *Knowledge Acquisition, 4* (special issue, "The KADS approach to knowledge engineering").

Wielinga, B. J., Van de Velde, W., Schreiber, G., & Akkermanns, H. (1993). Towards a unification of knowledge modelling approaches. In J. M. David, J. P. Krivine, & R. Simmons (Eds.), *Second generation expert systems* (pp. 299–335). Berlin: Springer.

14 Communities of practice toward expertise: social foundation of university instruction

Heinz Mandl, Hans Gruber, and Alexander Renkl

Abstract

Experts excel because of the outstanding flexibility they have in using their knowledge in many different problem situations. Instruction should provide the means to initiate students' growth toward expertise. In traditional forms of university instruction, however, students often acquire inert knowledge. Inert knowledge can be used in instructional settings, but cannot be transferred into complex problems typical of everyday or professional life. We review some studies to reveal specific deficits of university students with respect to knowledge application and to show that current forms of university instruction are not appropriate for students to gain flexible expertise, despite the fact that such students acquire much knowledge. Arguing along the theoretical lines of Lave and Rogoff, we conceive of the development of expertise as becoming a full participant in a community of practice by legitimate peripheral and guided participation. To prepare university students for this type of enculturation in later professional life, the cognitive apprenticeship approach seems to be a promising instructional method. We discuss some potential uses of this method in university education.

Introduction

A major function of university instruction is to equip students with basic competencies for later professional life, including some degree of expertise in their respective domains. In recent years, serious doubts have been expressed as to whether the common forms of instruction are well suited for this purpose. For example, Resnick (1987) and Gardner (1991) argue that learning and performance inside and outside instructional settings differ significantly. Thus, instruction hardly prepares students for the later lifelong learning demands that are posed by modern societies. This may be in part due to the fact that until now instructional research has not placed much emphasis on the nature of excellence in real-world domains.

It is also true that the psychology of expertise has neglected to investigate the development of expertise, which can be described as learning in complex domains (Gruber, 1994; Gruber, Renkl, & Schneider, 1994). Using the con-

394

trastive approach (Voss, Fincher-Kiefer, Green, & Post, 1986), it has dealt mainly with differences between experts and novices with respect to cognitive structures and processes. Many studies and models have investigated the memory performance (Chase & Simon, 1973) and problem-solving behavior (DeGroot, 1978) of experts, revealing that experts are not generally high-performing persons, but do have extensive knowledge and skills in their specific domains (for overviews of expertise, see Chi, Glaser, & Farr, 1988; Ericsson & Smith, 1991; Hoffman, 1992). We have argued elsewhere that beyond the domain-specific contextualization of expertise, the situational context also has to be taken into account when trying to explain cognitive processes of expert problem solving (Mandl, Gruber, & Renkl, 1993a). A major feature of experts is their tremendous flexibility in coping with new problem situations. This flexibility of experts is in contrast to transfer research that views the transferability of knowledge quite pessimistically (Detterman & Sternberg, 1993). To explain experts' extraordinary capacity to cope with various problem situations, it is necessary to analyze in more detail qualitative differences in the knowledge of experts and novices (Chi, Feltovich, & Glaser, 1981) and the mechanisms of knowledge application.

Research on expertise, which deals with high performance in complex, real-world domains, and research on learning and teaching, which aims to design effective learning settings, should get in far closer contact. In the following sections, we present some ideas on how this might be accomplished. First, however, it is necessary to analyze in more detail the deficits of traditional forms of instruction with respect to initiating the development of expertise.

Differences between learning within and outside instructional settings

Resnick (1987, p. 13) identified four major differences between these types of learning.

1. *Individual versus shared cognition.* The dominant form of learning in traditional forms of instruction and tests of performance is individual. Cooperation in exams is even condemned. In contrast, in professional life cooperation is very often necessary for coping with problems.
2. *Pure mentation versus tool manipulation.* In traditional instruction, pure "thought" activities are paramount. Students are required to perform without the support of tools such as books, notes, and calculators. Especially in exams, tools are mostly forbidden. In contrast, a common major component of professional expertise is the competent use of tools.
3. *Symbol manipulation versus contextualized reasoning.* The abstract manipulation of symbols is typical of traditional instruction. Students often fail to match symbols and symbolic processes to real-world entities and processes. In normal life, on the other hand, not only tools but also reasoning processes are an integral part of interaction. Real-world reasoning processes are typically situated in rich situational contexts.
4. *Generalized learning versus situation-specific competencies.* The rationale for

> the abstract character of traditional instruction is that it teaches general, widely usable skills and theoretical principles. Schools do not know in advance what professions the students will take up in later life. In professional life, in contrast, situation-specific skills must be acquired. Further learning is aimed primarily at gaining competencies for specific demands in working life.

Given these significant differences between learning within and outside instructional settings, it is not surprising that traditional instructional models lead to two major problems. First, university-acquired knowledge often remains bound to the very context of acquisition and cannot be used in solving problems of real-world complexity. This kind of knowledge is called inert (Bransford, Goldman, & Vye, 1991). Second, traditional university instruction provides little opportunity for students to acquire skills for the effective use of tools, as well as for cooperative learning and problem solving. Thus, students are not well prepared for the performance and learning demands of their later professional life.

Gardner (1991) supplemented Resnick's arguments with a more developmental perspective. Although somewhat simplifying, Gardner made a thought-provoking distinction between three types of learning. First, in their early years before going to school, children learn primarily by intuition. Thus, incidental learning processes without much effort predominate when learning, for example, the first language. Neurobiological and developmental factors play a major role in determining the learning processes. Second, when children enter school, a marked shift in learning takes place. The German *Reformpädagoge* Kerschensteiner (1907) nicely illustrated this point:

> Gone is all the activity that seized the child, gone is all the reality of the house, of the workshop, of the kitchen, of the cowshed, of the garden, and of the fields. Gone is the child's world. A new, strange world with hundreds of puzzles and curious demands and purposes imposes on the child. (p. 1; our translation)[1]

In instructional settings, explicit learning processes that focus on the mechanical and ritualized understanding necessary for passing exams are predominant. Gardner contrasts this type of understanding with real understanding that allows for flexible problem solving in new transfer situations. The third type is "expert learning." Expert learners (Glaser, 1993, created the expression "expert novice" to describe a similar phenomenon) can be of any age but in most cases are fully educated persons who possess knowledge that can be flexibly used in novel situations. They can also apply newly acquired knowledge in complex transfer situations. A notion similar to expert learning is used by Resnick (1987) in her claim that "school should focus its efforts on preparing people to be good adaptive learners, so that they can perform effectively when situations are unpredictable and task demands change" (p. 18). This argument is especially relevant to the perspective of lifelong learning, because in fast-developing societies in the West, knowledge and skills often become rapidly obsolete. Learning skills are thus essential for keeping up with changing demands.

Knowledge application problems of university students

Though the criticisms of traditional instruction originally focused on elementary and secondary education, they can analogously be applied to university instruction. Especially in Germany, the conventional models of instruction adopted in contemporary universities have been increasingly criticized. At first glance, there are several parallels between school instruction and university instruction. For example, the adoption of abstract instruction and the neglect of both cooperation and tool use are as prevalent in university education as they are in earlier education. Perhaps university students, in contrast to elementary and secondary school students, have already acquired enough of the prerequisites for learning (basic concepts, study skills, etc.) and are thus able to profit even from traditional forms of instruction with respect to applying their theoretical knowledge to the solution of practical problems. In the next section, we shall present empirical studies of our research group – in this case, studies of students of medicine and business management – in order to underline the assumption that knowledge application problems do occur in university instruction.

Studies in medicine

Our research project on medical instruction (Gräsel, Prenzel, & Mandl, 1993) analyzes the reasoning of students working with a case-based computer program (PlanAlyzer; Trustees of Dartmouth College, 1989) on the diagnosis of anemia. Expertise in an ill-defined domain like medical reasoning is considerably different from expertise in the well-defined domains that are usually considered in research on expertise (e.g., physics, chess; Spiro, Feltovich, Jacobson, & Coulson, 1991). Research on medical reasoning has shown that it is necessary to analyze the strategies used by diagnosticians (Groen & Patel, 1988; Patel, Groen, & Arocha, 1990) to get an adequate model of their medical expertise (Schmidt, Norman, & Boshuizen, 1990).

In our study, when working with the PlanAlyzer, the student adopts the role of a physician and must diagnose different types of anemia in simulated patients. The structure of the program simulates the examination of a patient in a clinical setting. Before making the final differential diagnosis, the student must analyze information about a patient's history, physical examinations, and blood smear to construct preliminary diagnostic hypotheses.

In studies with fourth-year medical students, think-aloud protocols were analyzed with regard to three indicators of the quality of knowledge construction and application processes; in each of these indicators, deficits were found even with advanced medical students.

Attention to salient data. Evidence indicated that medical students often selected from the presented data too narrowly and too prematurely for the
diagnostic process, instead of using all the findings and symptoms given. In
many cases, even the most salient symptoms were not adequately considered
during diagnosis, although the subjects could verbally acknowledge the importance of these symptoms.

Organization of concepts. It has often been shown that the degree of structure
and organization of concepts (e.g., symptoms and diagnoses) plays an important role in expert-like problem solving. The ability to sort symptoms and
diagnoses according to both their redundancy and their causal relations is
therefore crucial for being able to apply one's knowledge to diagnoses. Expert
ratings of the students' case representations extracted from verbal protocols
revealed that only a few students constructed well-organized representations;
most protocols, however, showed severe deficiencies in organization and structure. Obviously only a few medical students were able to organize their ample
knowledge of symptoms and diagnoses adequately. Poorly organized knowledge, however, cannot be applied.

Relations between symptoms and diagnoses. A central aspect of knowledge
application in medical reasoning is the degree of interrelatedness between
symptoms and possible diagnoses. Our subjects showed considerable deficits
in constructing causal explanations. Several subjects did not draw any relations
between symptoms and diagnoses, or established relations that narrowly connected a single symptom with a single diagnosis (parallel relations). Subjects
using such parallel relations constructed new diagnostic hypotheses whenever
new findings were presented to them. As a result, these subjects formulated
many different hypotheses, each of them being connected with only a single
symptom. Such problem solving, of course, proves to be unsuccessful. In sum,
the studies showed severe deficits in medical students' diagnostic skills.

Studies in business management

Like medicine, business management is an ill-defined domain. The problems
to be solved are complex and cannot be successfully approached by applying
simple algorithms. Voss, Blais, Means, Greene, and Ahwesh (1989) showed
that, in domains like economics, formal training does not play a major role
during the acquisition of expertise. Individuals develop accurate concepts of
the domain mainly through real-world experience, not through the pure accumulation of a large number of knowledge units. Dahlgren and Marton (1978)
similarly reported that university instruction in microeconomics often suffers
from the fact that knowledge is amassed without taking into account the later
application of that knowledge. The gathering of knowledge does not take

account of the problem that veridical concepts and misconceptions exist simultaneously in the subject's knowledge (Mandl, Gruber, & Renkl, 1993b). The result is often knowledge compartmentalization – one kind of knowledge to be used in university exams and another to be applied in real-world situations. Obviously, it would be preferable if both types of knowledge converged; to achieve this, instruction must be directed toward knowledge application and flexible expertise rather than toward the accumulation of knowledge. Similar views have recently been expressed by Miller and VanFossen (in press), VanFossen and Miller (1994), and VanSickle (1992).

In an investigation conducted by Mandl, Gruber, and Renkl (1994), graduate students of economics, who can be considered intermediate experts, participated in a computer-based simulation game in the domain of economics (JEANSFABRIK [jeans manufacturing]; Preiss, 1993). Their problem-solving processes and performance were compared with those of novices (students of psychology and education). The subjects' task was to maximize the profit of a computer-simulated jeans factory. The results showed that our graduate students of economics had enormous difficulties with knowledge utilization. This parallels the results of Voss et al. (1989), who found that their subjects with economic training could not use their corresponding knowledge in reasoning economics problems. In our study, however, even more striking results were obtained; students of psychology and education outperformed the intermediate experts in the computer-simulated business management task. All subjects had been given the opportunity to explore the simulation before working on it. The graduates were obviously hindered by their extensive knowledge base. We identified the following specific reasons for the relatively poor problem-solving performance of the intermediate experts as compared with the novices:

1. The intermediate experts put forward hypotheses that were too complicated. They had complex and correct mental models of the system, which, however, lacked adequate hierarchical organization. Thus, they took into account more aspects than they could integrate for making a sound decision.
2. The intermediate experts held assumptions that were theoretically true and consistent with economic theories but were not relevant to the actual problem-solving task.
3. The intermediate experts had difficulties in deducing appropriate operators (i.e., actions) from their declarative knowledge of domain rules. Knowing relevant rules did not necessarily lead to the selection of effective actions.
4. The intermediate experts were too cautious in manipulating the variables (selling price, production quantity) in the simulation. On the whole, even quite advanced students of economics showed serious deficits in knowledge application.

With respect to declarative knowledge, our intermediate experts outperformed the novices. They were more successful in constructing more differentiated and coherent mental models of the simulation JEANSFABRIK within the time allocated for problem solving (Renkl, Gruber, Mandl, & Hinkofer, 1994). Their expertise, however, seemed to be confined to declarative aspects. To put it simply, the graduate students of economics were not better at problem solving, but they were better at talking about the problem. One factor that might contribute to the difficulty of knowledge application is largely the abstract nature of university instruction.

Taken together, our studies in the domains of medicine and business management suggest that although university students learn much declarative knowledge, it is of little use in solving complex problems. The instruction therefore seems ill-suited to the development of flexible expertise in students. The specific reasons for the difficulties of knowledge application in the domains of economics and medicine are quite distinct and domain-specific. This fact supports the claim of many researchers (e.g., Mandl & Renkl, 1992) that it is necessary to take into account domain-specific factors when trying to explain learning and problem solving. General models (e.g., Holyoak, 1985) that analyze the transfer between well-defined but often very artificial tasks thus fail to provide guidelines for designing learning environments that support the acquisition of applicable knowledge. Nevertheless, research on transfer has identified many properties that may increase the transferability of a source problem solution to a target problem (Sternberg & Frensch, 1993). It is critical that relevant source problems be found and that relevant features of problems that serve to start mapping processes be identified. Elucidating the possibilities of transfer from source problems to target problems proved to be a central task of instruction (Gick & Holyoak, 1980, 1983). Holyoak and Koh (1987) showed that transfer can be facilitated by creating generalized high-quality schemata. Other components identified refer to the encoding and retrieval conditions: memory organization (Ross, 1989), multimodal presentation of information (Gick & Holyoak, 1983), visual support (Gick, 1985), and degree of expertise (Novick, 1988).

Despite these results, the overall impression given by research on transfer is rather pessimistic. This perhaps is not justified, as Pressley and Yokoi (1994) recently argued. They conclude that the picture might be more optimistic if not only basic cognitive processes but also more complex cognitive-behavioral aspects were considered. Transfer in the acquisition of complex skills may be different from transfer involved in solving simple analogy problems. However, more research is needed on the types of knowledge application that emerge in the typical problem-solving tasks of specific complex domains in order to clarify the role of transfer in the development of expertise.

Although the reasons for the difficulties of knowledge application vary across domains, there seems to be a common root: The lecture-like instruction formats that predominate in (German) higher education are not adequate to equip students with competencies for effective action; as Bransford, Franks, Vye, and Sherwood (1989) put it, "Wisdom can't be told" (p. 470). Students are not well prepared for later job demands or for the acquisition of the kind of domain-specific expertise that is typical of practitioners in their respective communities of practice (e.g., Lave, 1992). In the following discussion, we call the kind of competence demonstrated by successful practitioners *flexible expertise* (Hatano & Inagaki, 1986; Holyoak, 1991). In this context, the term *flexible* denotes the capacity of competent practitioners not only to cope with routine tasks but to solve complex, often ill-defined problems.

For many years, researchers on expertise have focused on subjects' performance in solving well-defined problems that frequently could be worked out by routines. Recently, models of expertise are increasingly concerned with the kind of flexible problem-solving capabilities typical of practicing professionals. If, as we have shown, this kind of expertise can hardly be acquired in instructional settings typical of the university, what is the usual way of acquiring it? In the following paragraph, we present two theoretical approaches that seem promising for analyzing the processes by which flexible expertise in real-world domains is acquired.

Expertise as full participation in a community of practice

Lave (1992; Lave & Wenger, 1991) has proposed a theoretical framework in which learning is conceived of as situated activity that has its central defining characteristic in a process called *legitimate peripheral participation*. She based her theoretical concept on the analysis of apprenticeship learning as it occurs, for example, among West African Vai and Gola tailors and Indian midwives, as well as in Alcoholics Anonymous. Legitimate peripheral participation pertains to the process by which learners or newcomers become enculturated into a *community of practice*.

Neither pivotal concept – legitimate peripheral participation or community of practice – has been precisely defined in Lave's work. They are merely illustrated by multiple examples. Nevertheless, these concepts provide an interesting theoretical perspective on learning, as we show later on.

The essential arrangements in a community of practice that influence learning are the relations between newcomers and old-timers, the relations among newcomers, the typical activities in the community, and the artifacts of the domain. The process by which a newcomer becomes, in Lave's terms, a full participant or – as we prefer to call it – an expert is fundamentally social. Newcomers as apprentices learn from the old-timers as well as from other newcomers. Even learning with physical or symbolic tools (e.g., books) is fundamentally social, because the tools as artifacts carry a substantial proportion of content knowledge developed historically in the respective communities (see Cole, Chapter 2, this volume). Finally, learning is viewed as not only the acquisition of knowledge, but also enculturation, involving as it does speaking, belief systems, social customs, and the like. In addition, from a radical constructivism viewpoint (Roth, 1991; von Foerster, 1985; von

Glasersfeld, 1985), knowledge is not a "representational copy" of reality or the ontological world. Thus, the body of knowledge held true in a community of practice is nothing more than a shared belief system. From this perspective, even the so-called cognitive aspect of learning – that is, the acquisition of knowledge – is nothing more than learning to accept socially shared beliefs and practices. The acquisition of expertise is thus not the acquisition of declarative and procedural knowledge, but more broadly the social process of enculturation. It means becoming a full participant in a community of practice, able to cope with the problems typical of the respective domain in a flexible manner.

Rogoff's (1990, 1991) theoretical approach shares some similarity with Lave's but puts more emphasis on cognitive development in childhood. Rogoff takes up the Vygotskian notion of the zone of proximal development and uses the term *guided participation* to describe the process by which children learn in the course of interaction with expert partners (e.g., parents or teachers). Children together with their more expert interactive partners build bridges from their present understanding to reach new understanding through communication (Rogoff, 1991). Guided participation may involve explicit face-to-face interactions that may be designed as instructional, but it can also rely on tacit forms of communication lacking any instructional intention on the part of the expert partner. The child, for example, merely observes or participates in everyday activities. The routine arrangements and interactions between children and their caregivers offer thousands of occasions to observe or participate in the skilled activities typical of the respective subculture or community. In the course of development, the child adopts an increasingly active role in the interaction. Rogoff (1991) underlines the importance of expert modeling, active observation, guidance by more able partners, and joint participation for the development of expertise.

On the whole, both approaches ascribe a novel role to learners as compared with more traditional models, which view learners as the recipients of predefined knowledge or as scientists learning by active exploration and hypothesis testing. On the contrary, guided approaches regard learners as apprentices. The learners are, from the beginning, active participants in authentic practices; learning and acquiring expertise are essentially viewed as processes of enculturation.

Acquiring expertise in the university

Do universities enculturate students into communities of practice?

As mentioned earlier, the learning arrangements described by Lave (1992) and Rogoff (1990) are apprenticeship models. Of course, in modern societies that need a substantial proportion of highly skilled personnel trained in scientific reasoning, it is not possible to abolish university teaching and send all students to apprenticeship training. At the university, however, students are not sufficiently enculturated into a community of practice, except that of researchers. In particular, students who begin an academic career typically start out as research assistants associated with some ongoing project. In this case, the learning process can be characterized by the concepts of legitimate peripheral participation and of guided participation within a community of practice. For other students less interested in research and, therefore, not in close contact with faculty members, apprenticeship-like learning is rare and typically confined to peer tutoring programs or project seminars. In Germany, however, participation in these activities is often voluntary, and therefore many students do not use these opportunities for apprenticeship learning.

Today's universities are no longer elitist institutions in which the scientific community trains highly talented students as potentially eminent scholars. Most students of our often overcrowded universities take jobs in applied fields and are not interested in the scientific aspects of their respective subjects. In addition, businesses frequently complain that after young professionals receive their formal university education, they know little of practical importance. Therefore, actual professional training often starts after university instruction, that is, on the job. Thus, acquiring professional expertise is again a matter of legitimate peripheral or guided participation within a community of practice. Given the deficits of university instruction with respect to preparing the students for later professional life, the crucial point is how the enculturation into a community of practice can at least be prepared in universities.

Cognitive apprenticeship learning in higher education

In contrast to the craft domains and the development of young children discussed so far, Collins, Brown, and Newman (1989) have proposed an instructional approach for the cognitive domains that seems suited for higher education. It is interesting to note that this approach recalls the work of Kerschensteiner (1912) and Dewey (1910).

The *cognitive apprenticeship* model of Collins et al. (1989) stresses the importance of explicating or reifying cognitive processes (e.g., strategies, heuristics) during learning. Thus, cognitive processes can be approximately as explicit as the more manual skills trained in traditional apprenticeship models.

The core of the cognitive apprenticeship model is a special instructional sequence employing authentic learning tasks. Cognitive processes are externalized by experts while applying their knowledge in authentic situations. Learning then leads the student to acquire knowledge that is applicable to a certain class of situations. Further learning takes place in sequenced environ-

ments of increasing complexity and diversity. At each stage of the apprenticeship approach, the expert is assigned an important role as a model and as a
coach providing scaffolding. However, the student has to increasingly take
over an active role, as the expert gradually decreases his or her role. In this
course, articulation and reflection are promoted by the expert; that is, the
normally internal, mental problem-solving processes are externalized. Thus,
the student's strategies can be compared with those of experts (and are then
negotiable), as well as with those of other students. In the course of interaction
with experts and other learners, students can also get to know different perspectives on the concepts and problems of the particular domain. As a result
of this instructional sequence, students increasingly work on their own (exploration) and may take over the role initially assumed by the expert. This
sequence resembles the development from legitimate peripheral participation
to full participation described by Lave (1992).

While the cognitive apprenticeship approach provides some stimulating
ideas for the reform or supplementation of current university instruction,
there are some theoretical shortcomings of this approach with respect to the
crucial learning processes that should be promoted by apprenticeship learning.
One of the pitfalls is that the specific boundary conditions for the application
of this approach are not delineated. For example, Collins et al. (1989) do not
specify what type of expert modeling is suited for what types of learning
objectives and for what types of students. In the following paragraphs, we
discuss these problems in some detail.

Problems of the cognitive apprenticeship approach

The cognitive apprenticeship approach favors an instructional sequence from
expert modeling to scaffolded practice and then finally to independent problem solving. This means that expert modeling is the starting point. However,
Gräsel and Mandl (1993) provided some empirical data indicating that this
may be too simple a rationale. Their study investigated the extent to which the
diagnostic reasoning of medical students could be improved by expert
modeling within a computer-supported, case-based learning program. A physician demonstrated a model solution of a case by thinking aloud, using an
efficient strategy of diagnostic reasoning. Subjects were assigned to two experimental groups and one control group. In the first experimental group,
subjects began working with the cognitive model, and then solved a similar
case by themselves. The second group of subjects initially solved one case by
themselves and were then shown the model solution of a similar case by the
physician. The subjects in the control group received no instructional support.
The results show that the expert modeling of an adequate strategy by an
experienced physician leads to the use of improved strategies by students
when solving a transfer case and, as a consequence, to greater diagnostic

success. The most interesting point in this study, however, was that the cognitive expert model proved to be more effective when students independently solved a case before receiving cognitive modeling. At least in diagnostic reasoning, it seems effective to have the students first experience their difficulties and problems in diagnosing. Hence, they can use the expert model more purposefully and focus their attention on those aspects of the modeled behavior that are especially important for them, given their personal difficulties. In contrast, one might not know what is important when observing an expert model initially. A cognitive overload, which inhibits learning, may result (Sweller, 1988).

The finding that expert modeling is not necessarily an optimal starting point raises more general questions of preparing students for apprenticeship learning. Especially in highly formalized domains, such as computer science or mathematics, apprenticeship learning without knowing the basic vocabulary, ideas, and purposes of a discipline may not be very effective. In these cases, a preparatory course of lectures on basic domain concepts might be helpful. Much research remains to be done on how to prepare students to profit effectively from apprenticeship learning.

Another important controversy regarding an effective expert model for apprenticeship learning is whether he or she is a mastery model or a coping model. There is some evidence that a model who initially has some problems with the tasks, but later copes with them successfully, is more effective than a smoothly performing mastery model (Gabrys, Weiner, & Lesgold, 1993; Schoenfeld, 1985; Schunk & Hanson, 1985). It seems plausible to assume that one can best learn how to overcome difficulties by observing models who demonstrate how to do so. In addition, employing top experts as models has the disadvantage that their diagnostic reasoning processes may have become automatized to the extent that they may not be able to explicate how they think (Dreyfus & Dreyfus, 1986).

Another critical point of the cognitive apprenticeship approach is how to make sure that the acquired knowledge does not remain bound to the very context of acquisition. Instructional models based on a constructivist philosophy propose several remedies. The expert should not only show how to solve problems, but also explicate the rationale behind his or her strategies. Thus, the behavior of the expert model in a given situation is connected with more general principles of the respective domain. Furthermore, students should articulate and reflect their problem-solving strategies and compare them with those of others. This implies that the acquired knowledge should also be "freed" from the very context of learning. Spiro and his colleagues (Spiro et al., 1991) propose to employ multiple perspectives to make knowledge more transferable: A student should deal with a concept at different times, in different contexts, with different purposes, and in different roles (e.g., as tutee and as tutor). Thus, oversimplification and narrow ties to a specific context are avoided. Interestingly, the claim for multiple perspectives as an effective means to foster transfer is consistent with experimental research on transfer (Catrambone & Holyoak, 1989).

In contrast to traditional instructional methods, according to the cognitive apprenticeship approach, transferability should not be attained by teaching *abstract* knowledge, but by fostering the *abstraction* of concrete knowledge (Adams, 1989).

To sum up, cognitive apprenticeship seems to be a promising instructional approach for higher education. However, the picture about the boundary conditions for its application has emerged only gradually. In addition to the didactic problems discussed earlier, there are theoretical questions that deserve further research. For example, no precise theory is available that can explain how the skills that are externalized by experts are internalized by students. It is surely too naive to assume a simple transmission of knowledge from expert to student (Azmitia, Chapter 5, this volume; Lawrence & Valsiner, 1993; Vygotsky, 1978). The specific steps of internal transformation of external processes are more or less unknown. These latter two aspects are, however, beyond the scope of this chapter.

Another important aspect of apprenticeship learning is the organizational framework of universities. This point is to be discussed in the next section.

Implementation of apprenticeship learning in universities

If instructional reforms such as the employment of cognitive apprenticeship are to become a part of everyday practice, the organizational framework has to be taken into account (Mandl, Gruber, & Renkl, 1993c; Shachar & Sharan, 1993). Otherwise, the implementation of new learning arrangements is likely to fail. The coaching of individuals or small learning groups, as proposed in the cognitive apprenticeship model, is both costly and difficult to implement in the often very overcrowded universities. However, there are some possible solutions:

1. Programs for employing advanced students as tutors should be fostered. In this way, younger students receive a more intensive coaching, and tutors profit from their teaching, as studies on learning by teaching have shown (Goodlad & Hirst, 1989).
2. Complex, realistic learning tasks for a large number of students might be provided by modern educational technology. For this purpose, computer-based simulation or case-based learning programs can be adopted. In fact, some very sophisticated computer-based learning environments for apprenticeship learning have already been developed. For example, Lesgold and his colleagues (Gabrys et al., 1993; Lajoie & Lesgold, 1990) developed the coached apprenticeship system SHERLOCK, which includes all essential features of the cognitive apprenticeship approach. It has proved to be highly effective with respect to acquisition of applicable knowledge (Gabrys et al., 1993).

3. To make learning through solving complex, authentic problems within social arrangements possible, we raise the old (at least in Germany) claim to clear out the curricula. The prevailing implicit notions of the university as a place for learning and of professional life as the application of what has been learned suggest that all important facets needed in a job should be covered by university instruction (Holzkamp, 1993). In modern industrial societies with their rapid social and technological changes, knowledge often becomes obsolete quickly. Many modern professions require continuous learning. Learning is thus a lifelong process.

Conclusion

The concept of learning as a social and lifelong task that does not cease with the end of formal university education implies that university instruction should take into account many of the features of what Resnick (1987) called out-of-school learning. In particular, the social character of out-of-school cognition has important theoretical implications. If out-of-school performances are achieved mainly by interactive minds, the idea that cognition is something residing in individual heads is too narrow. Under the label of distributed cognition (Salomon, 1993), it is increasingly acknowledged that important cognitive events emerge as social phenomena. Education has to take this into account. There is empirical evidence that learning from texts (Mandl, Stein, & Trabasso, 1983) and from worked-out examples (Chi & Bassok, 1989) requires certain skills. Other skills are needed for learning in social contexts. For this reason, university students should acquire the basic prerequisites for further lifelong learning such as social learning skills and competence for defining and solving complex problems. The new instructional approaches mentioned earlier attempt to design learning environments in which these demands can be met within university settings. In addition, learning is conceived of not only as the acquisition of facts and skills, but as enculturation. However, it is up to future research to provide empirical evidence that the cognitive apprenticeship approach can effectively prepare the student to acquire flexible expertise in communities of practice.

Note

1 "Weg ist alle Beschäftigung, die das ganze Kind erfaßte, weg alle Realität des Hauses, der Werkstatt, der Küche, des Stalles, des Gartens, des Feldes ... Weg ist die ganze Welt des Kindes. Eine neue, fremde Welt mit hundert Rätseln und unfaßbaren Forderungen und Zwecken steht vor ihm."

References

Adams, M. J. (1989) Thinking skills curricula: Their promise and progress. *Educational Psychologist, 24,* 25–77.

Bransford, J. D., Franks, J. J., Vye, N. J., & Sherwood, R. D. (1989). New approaches to learning and instruction: Because wisdom can't be told. In S. Vosniadou & A. Ortony (Eds.), *Similarity and analogical reasoning* (pp. 470–497). Cambridge: Cambridge University Press.

Bransford, J. D., Goldman, S. R., & Vye, N. J. (1991). Making a difference in people's ability to think: Reflections on a decade of work and some hopes for the future. In R. J. Sternberg & L. Okagaki (Eds.), *Influences on children* (pp. 147–180). Hillsdale, NJ: Erlbaum.

Catrambone, R., & Holyoak, K. J. (1989). Overcoming contextual limitations on problem-solving transfer. *Journal of Experimental Psychology: Learning, Memory, and Cognition, 15*, 1147–1156.

Chase, W. G., & Simon, H. A. (1973). Perception in chess. *Cognitive Psychology, 4*, 55–81.

Chi, M. T. H., & Bassok, M. (1989). Learning from examples via self-explanations. In L. B. Resnick (Ed.), *Knowing, learning, and instruction* (pp. 251–282). Hillsdale, NJ: Erlbaum.

Chi, M. T. H., Feltovich, P. J., & Glaser, R. (1981). Categorization and representation of physics problems by experts and novices. *Cognitive Science, 5*, 121–152.

Chi, M. T. H., Glaser, R., & Farr, M. J. (Eds.). (1988). *The nature of expertise*. Hillsdale, NJ: Erlbaum.

Collins, A., Brown, J. S., & Newman, S. E. (1989). Cognitive apprenticeship: Teaching the crafts of reading, writing, and mathematics. In L. B. Resnick (Ed.), *Knowing, learning, and instruction* (pp. 453–494). Hillsdale, NJ: Erlbaum.

Dahlgren, L. O., & Marton, F. (1978). Students' conceptions of subject matter: An aspect of learning and teaching in higher education. *Studies in Higher Education, 3*, 25–35.

DeGroot, A. D. (1978). *Thought and choice in chess* (2nd ed.). The Hague: Mouton.

Detterman, D. K., & Sternberg, R. J. (Eds.). (1993). *Transfer on trial: Intelligence, cognition, and instruction*. Norwood, NJ: Ablex.

Dewey, J. (1910). *How we think*. New York: Heath.

Dreyfus, H. L., & Dreyfus, S. E. (1986). *Mind over machine*. New York: Free Press.

Ericsson, K. A., & Smith, J. (Eds.). (1991). *Toward a general theory of expertise: Prospects and limits*. Cambridge: Cambridge University Press.

Gabrys, G., Weiner, A., & Lesgold, A. (1993). Learning by problem solving in a coached apprenticeship system. In M. Rabinowitz (Ed.), *Cognitive science foundations of instruction* (pp. 119–147). Hillsdale, NJ: Erlbaum.

Gardner, H. (1991). *The unschooled mind: How children think and how schools should teach*. New York: Basic.

Gick, M. L. (1985). The effect of a diagram retrieval cue on spontaneous analogical transfer. *Canadian Journal of Psychology, 39*, 460–466.

Gick, M. L., & Holyoak, K. J. (1980). Analogical problem solving. *Cognitive Psychology, 12*, 306–355.

Gick, M. L., & Holyoak, K. J. (1983). Schema induction and analogical transfer. *Cognitive Psychology, 15*, 1–38.

Glaser, R. (1993). Concluding remarks. In E. Ropo & R. Jaakola (Eds.), *Developing education for lifelong learning* (pp. 149–152). Tampere: University of Tampere.

Goodlad, S., & Hirst, B. (1989). *Peer tutoring: A guide to learning by teaching*. London: Kogan.

Gräsel, C., & Mandl, H. (1993). *Förderung des Erwerbs diagnostischer Strategien in fallbasierten Lernumgebungen* [Promoting the acquisition of diagnostic strategies in case-based learning environments] (Research Report No. 26). Munich: Ludwig-Maximilians-Universität, Lehrstuhl für Empirische Pädagogik und Pädagogische Psychologie.

Gräsel, C., Prenzel, M., & Mandl, H. (1993). Konstruktionsprozesse beim Bearbeiten eines fallbasierten Computerlernprogramms [Constructive processes in working with a case-based computer-based learning program]. In C. Tarnai (Ed.), *Beiträge zur empirischen pädagogischen Forschung* (pp. 55–66). Münster: Waxmann.

Groen, G. J., & Patel, V. L. (1988). The relationship between comprehension and reasoning in medical expertise. In M. T. H. Chi, R. Glaser, & M. J. Farr (Eds.), *The nature of expertise* (pp. 287–310). Hillsdale, NJ: Erlbaum.

Gruber, H. (1994). *Expertise. Modelle und empirische Untersuchungen* [Expertise: Models and empirical studies]. Opladen: Westdeutscher Verlag.

Gruber, H., Renkl, A., & Schneider, W. (1994). Expertise und Gedächtnisentwicklung: Längsschnittliche Befunde aus der Domäne Schach (Expertise and memory development: Longitudinal findings from the domain of chess). *Zeitschrift für Entwicklungspsychologie und Pädagogische Psychologie, 26,* 53–70.

Hatano, G., & Inagaki, K. (1986). Two courses of expertise. In H. Stevenson, H. Azuma, & K. Hakuta (Eds.), *Child development and education in Japan* (pp. 262–272). New York: Freeman.

Hoffman, R. R. (Ed.). (1992). *The psychology of expertise: Cognitive research and empirical AI.* New York: Springer.

Holyoak, K. J. (1985). The pragmatics of analogical transfer. In G. H. Bower (Ed.), *The psychology of learning and motivation* (Vol. 19, pp. 59–87). New York: Academic.

Holyoak, K. J. (1991). Symbolic connectionism: Toward third-generation theories of expertise. In K. A. Ericsson & J. Smith (Eds.), *Toward a general theory of expertise: Prospects and limits* (pp. 301–335). Cambridge: Cambridge University Press.

Holyoak, K. J., & Koh, K. (1987). Surface and structural similarity in analogical transfer. *Memory and Cognition, 15,* 332–340.

Holzkamp, K. (1993). *Lernen. Subjektwissenschaftliche Grundlegung* [Learning: Subject-oriented foundation]. Frankfurt (Main): Campus.

Kerschensteiner, G. (1907). *Grundfragen der Schulorganisation* [Basic questions of school organization]. Leipzig: Teubner.

Kerschensteiner, G. (1912). *Begriff der Arbeitsschule* [The concept of the working school]. Leipzig: Teubner.

Lajoie, S., & Lesgold, A. (1990). Apprenticeship training in the workplace: Computer coached practice environment as a new form of apprenticeship. *Machine-Mediated Learning, 3,* 7–28.

Lave, J. (1992). Situated learning in communities of practice. In L. B. Resnick, J. M. Levine, & S. D. Teasley (Eds.), *Perspectives on socially shared cognition* (pp. 63–82). Wasington, DC: American Psychological Association.

Lave, J., & Wenger, E. (1991). *Situated learning: Legitimate peripheral participation.* Cambridge: Cambridge University Press.

Lawrence, J. A., & Valsiner, J. (1993). Conceptual roots of internalization: From transmission to transformation. *Human Development, 36,* 150–167.

Mandl, H., Gruber, H., & Renkl, A. (1993a). Kontextualisierung von Expertise [Contextualization of expertise]. In H. Mandl, M. Dreher, & H. J. Kornadt (Eds.), *Entwicklung und Denken im kulturellen Konetext* (pp. 203–227). Göttingen: Hogrefe.

Mandl, H., Gruber, H., & Renkl, A.· (1993b). Misconceptions and knowledge compartmentalization. In G. Strube & F. Wender (Eds.), *The cognitive psychology of knowledge: The German Wissenspsychologie project* (pp. 161–176). Amsterdam: Elsevier.

Mandl, H., Gruber, H., & Renkl, A. (1993c). Neue Lernkonzepte für die Hochschule [New learning concepts for the university]. *Das Hochschulwesen, 41,* 126–130.

Mandl, H., Gruber, H., & Renkl, A. (1994). Problems of knowledge utilization in the development of expertise. In W. Nijhof & J. Streumer (Eds.), *Flexibility and cognitive structure in vocational education* (pp. 291 305). Utrecht: Lemma.

Mandl, H., & Renkl, A. (1992). A plea for "more local" theories of cooperative learning. *Learning and Instruction, 2,* 281–285.

Mandl, H., Stein, N. L., & Trabasso, T. (Eds.). (1983). *Learning and comprehension of text.* Hillsdale, NJ: Erlbaum.

Miller, S. L., & VanFossen, P. J. (in press). Assessing expertise in economic problem solving: A model. *Theory and Research in Social Education.*

Novick, L. R. (1988). Analogical transfer, problem similarity and expertise. *Journal of Experimental Psychology: Learning, Memory, and Cognition, 14,* 510–520.

Patel, V. L., Groen, G. J., & Arocha, J. F. (1990). Medical expertise as a function of task difficulty. *Memory and Cognition, 18,* 394–406.

Preiß, P. (1993). *Planspiel Jeansfabrik* [Simulation game Jeans Factory]. Wiesbaden: Gabler.

Pressley, M., & Yokoi, L. (1994). Motion for a new trial on transfer. *Educational Researcher,* *23*(5), 36–38.

Renkl, A., Gruber, H., Mandl, H., & Hinkofer, L. (1994). Hilft Wissen bei der Identifikation und Steuerung eines komplexen ökonomischen Systems? [Does knowledge support identification and control of a complex economical system?]. *Unterrichtswissenschaft, 22,* 195–202.

Resnick, L. B. (1987). Learning in school and out. *Educational Researcher, 16,* 13–20.

Rogoff, B. (1990). *Apprenticeship in thinking: Cognitive development in social context.* New York: Oxford University Press.

Rogoff, B. (1991). Social interaction as apprenticeship in thinking: Guidance and participation in spatial planning. In L. B. Resnick, J. M. Levine, & S. D. Teasley (Eds.), *Perspectives on socially shared cognition* (pp. 349–364). Washington, DC: American Psychological Association.

Ross, B. H. (1989). Distinguishing types of superficial similarities: Different effect on the access and use of earlier problems. *Journal of Experimental Psychology: Learning, Memory, and Cognition, 15,* 456–468.

Roth, G. (1991). Das konstruktive Gehirn: Neurobiologische Grundlagen von Wahrnehmung und Erkenntnis [The constructive brain: Neurobiological foundations of perception and knowledge]. In S. J. Schmidt (Ed.), *Kognition und Gesellschaft* (pp. 277–336). Frankfurt (Main): Suhrkamp.

Salomon, G. (Ed.). (1993). *Distributed cognitions: Psychological and educational considerations.* New York: Cambridge University Press.

Schmidt, H. G., Norman, G. R., & Boshuizen, H. P. (1990). A cognitive perspective on medical expertise: Theory and implications. *Academic Medicine, 65,* 611–621.

Schoenfeld, A. H. (1985). *Mathematical problem solving.* New York: Academic.

Schunk, D. H., & Hanson, A. R. (1985). Peer models: Influence on children's self-efficacy and achievement. *Journal of Educational Psychology, 77,* 313–322.

Shachar, H., & Sharan, S. (1993). Schulorganisation und kooperatives Lernen im Klassenzimmer: Eine Interdependenz [School organization and cooperative learning in the classroom]. In G. L. Huber (Ed.), *Neue Perspektiven der Kooperation* (pp. 54–70). Hohengehren: Schneider.

Spiro, R. J., Feltovich, P. J., Jacobson, M. J., & Coulson, R. L. (1991). Cognitive flexibility, constructivism, and hypertext: Random access instruction for advanced knowledge acquisition in ill-structured domains. *Educational Technology, 31,* 24–33.

Sternberg, R. J., & Frensch, P. A. (1993). Mechanisms of transfer. In D. K. Detterman & R. J. Sternberg (Eds.), *Transfer on trial: Intelligence, cognition, and instruction* (pp. 25–38). Norwood, NJ: Ablex.

Sweller, J. (1988). Cognitive load during problem solving: Effects on learning. *Cognitive Science, 12,* 257–285.

Trustees of Dartmouth College. (1989). *Program PlanAlyzer.* Hanover, NH: Dartmouth College.

VanFossen, P. L., & Miller, S. L. (1994, April). *The nature and constructs of relative expertise in economic problem solving.* Paper presented at the annual meeting of the American Educational Research Association, New Orleans.

VanSickle, R. L. (1992). Learning to reason with economics. *Journal of Economic Education,* Winter, 56–64.

von Foerster, H. (1985). Entdecken oder Erfinden. Wie läßt sich Verstehen verstehen? [Discovery or invention: How to understand understanding?] In H. Gumin & H. Meier (Eds.), *Einführung in den Konstruktivismus* (pp. 41–88). Munich: Piper.

von Glasersfeld, E. (1985). Konstruktion der Wirklichkeit und des Begriffes der Objekttivität [Construction of reality and of the notion of objectivity]. In H. Gumin & H. Meier (eds.), *Einführung in den Konstruktivismus* (pp. 9–40). Munich: Piper.

Voss, J. F., Blais, J., Means, M. L., Greene, T. R., & Ahwesh, E. (1989). Informal reasoning and subject matter knowledge in the solving of economics problems by naive and novice individuals. In L. B. Resnick (Ed.), *Knowing, learning, and instruction* (pp. 217–249). Hillsdale, NJ: Erlbaum.

Voss, J. F., Fincher-Kiefer, R. H., Green, T. R., & Post, T. A. (1986). Individual differences in performance: The contrastive approach to knowledge. In R. J. Sternberg (Ed.), *Advances in the psychology of human intelligence* (Vol. 3, pp. 297–334). Hillsdale, NJ: Erlbaum.

Vygotsky, L. S. (1978). *Mind in society: The development of higher psychological processes.* Cambridge, MA: Harvard University Press.

Epilogue: reflections and future perspectives

Peter Graf, Laura L. Carstensen, Franz E. Weinert, and Richard A. Shweder

This epilogue represents a collection of voices rather than one. In our own efforts to assess the impact of this book, we, the editors, were interested in the consequences and perspectives that might arise for the fields of cognitive psychology, developmental psychology, educational psychology, and cognitive anthropology. We consider these areas of specialization of paramount importance in advancing the use of theory and paradigms involving interactive minds. For this reason, we asked four noted scholars from these fields, Peter Graf (cognitive psychology), Laura Carstensen (developmental psychology), Franz Weinert (educational psychology), and Richard Shweder (cognitive anthropology), to reflect on the book as a whole, comment on the chapters of particular relevance to their work, and outline, if any, the kinds of perspectives and implications they envision for their own field of specialization.

Interactive minds from a cognitive psychologist's perspective (Peter Graf)

This volume explores a broad range of factors that shape the interactive human mind. The chapters vary, particularly in their breadth of perspective or level of analysis. At one extreme, the top level of analysis, are chapters like Hammerstein's (Chapter 1) and Cole's (Chapter 2), which addressed general, global factors that leave their "imprint" on the human mind, including evolution, culture, and ontogeny; at the other extreme, Dixon and Gould (Chapter 8) chose a much narrower focus for analysis and explored how minds interact when performing a specific kind of memory task. This focus on different levels of analysis has two consequences. On the one hand, each chapter offers only a selective view that is limited by its own theoretical-methodological vantage point, but on the other hand, a much fuller and broader portrait of the interactive mind emerges between or among the chapters.

I often teach a course in cognitive psychology designed to give graduate students a broad introduction to research issues, methods, and findings in the area. In this course, we construct the mind as an intelligent system that is

413

capable of learning and development, and we study the components of such systems, how systems or components interact with each other, and how they are physically instantiated in the brain (Baltes & Baltes, 1990; Martindale, 1991; Posner, 1989; Schacter & Tulving, 1994; Squire & Butters, 1992). Most texts in cognitive psychology, as well as in cognitive science and neuroscience, have the same emphasis as this course; they focus on component processes and structures, their coordinated normal and abnormal functioning, and their neural implementation (Anderson, 1985; Best, 1995; Eysenck & Keane, 1990; Martindale, 1991; Posner, 1989). It might be said, therefore, that the vista of cognitive psychology and cognitive science is the inside of the mind, and the goal is to "probe and read its entrails." By contrast, a very different point of view or theoretical perspective is reflected in the chapters of this volume (of course, the chapters differ from each other and many include a major cognitive component, especially those by Gigerenzer, Chapter 11; Klein, Chapter 3; Mandl, Gruber, & Renkl, Chapter 14; Sternberg, Chapter 12; and Strube, Janetzko, & Knauff, Chapter 13), which seem to consider the mind more as an external, plastic object that is shaped by its spatial-temporal-social-cultural context or setting, and the goal is to explore these settings and how they shape or constrain the mind's functions.

The contextualist view, the *portrait from the outside*, of the interactive mind that dominates this volume and the component processes view, the *portrait of the inside*, that guides cognitive science are clearly complementary, yin–yang related, the interlocking edges of the pieces of a puzzle. In the assembling of a puzzle, fitting two or three pieces together sometimes reveals their exact identity even though each of them is an enigma. Therefore, I proceeded to connect a few pieces from this volume with their complements from cognitive science, trusting that a more complete portrait of interactive minds will emerge from the exercise.

To begin, however, I shall first give a brief sketch of a component processes version of an interactive system of the kind that populates cognitive psychology. One of the first complete systems of this type, proposed nearly two decades ago by Rumelhart (1977), was concerned with fluent reading. A reading system must have sensory/perceptual processes (for gathering input from the page), working memory (for on-line construction or understanding of the plot), and knowledge of words and concepts (for making sense of ink marks on a page), and all of these components must function in a coordinated manner. The smooth and seamless interaction of all components is essential for fluent reading, which has been described as a psycholinguistic guessing game in which the reader generates hypotheses about the text (relying on knowledge and memory) and uses the written marks (those picked up by sensory-perceptual processes) to make decisions about them (Goodman, 1970). Analogous to the different levels of analysis that are reflected in the chapters of this volume, cognitive scientists also target their investigations at different levels of analysis. Some investigators apply their efforts to interactive systems of an intermediate scope, like that required for reading; by contrast, others prefer to focus their investigations more narrowly, at a lower level – for example, where there are subsystems for letter identification and for keeping in mind the ongoing sentence – and still others target a higher level – like the system involved in language and communication – and explore how reading, writing, hearing, and speaking interact with each other. Because different levels of analysis exist in both cognitive psychology and the contextualist view, they provide a convenient road map for seeking out parallels between cognitive science and the chapters in this volume.

One area of convergence between cognitive science and the chapters in this volume is immediately obvious when we focus on interactive minds as they function in the context of a specific, narrowly defined situation like the memory task used by Dixon and Gould (Chapter 8). Participants in Dixon and Gould's experiment were asked to listen to stories and then to use their own words to recollect as much information from them as possible. The critical manipulation was whether participants performed this task alone, together with one (and sometimes more than one) unknown other, or together with their spouse, and the primary research goal was to learn about the extent to which adults can and do use collaborators to perform a complex cognitive task. The experiments included participants from different age groups and also explored how collaborative recall changes with age. Dixon and Gould reported that cooperative remembering "works" for young and old participants, as well as between acquainted and unacquainted individuals; they also found qualitative differences in memory performance between acquainted and unacquainted older couples in terms of how they allocated their efforts toward the end of the task. To explain the findings, they (a) suggested that interactive minds perform better than noninteractive minds because they can pool resources or effort, and (b) speculated that performance may be more directly dependent on the effective pooling of resources in old age (Bäckman & Dixon, 1992; Bäckman, Mäntylä, & Herlitz, 1990; Baltes & Baltes, 1980, 1990; Schaie, 1990), which is accompanied by a general decline in attention and memory abilities (Kausler, 1982; Poon, 1986; Salthouse, 1985).

Dixon and Gould focused on only one aspect of the nature of interactive minds, that which emerges in a specific laboratory setting – the collaborative story recall task. To communicate their conception of a memory-task-specific interactive mind, the chapter first described the setting in which it functions (in a recall task, alone, or with a familiar or unfamiliar other), and then speculated about the kind of cognitive, social, and motivational resources that could be used to facilitate collaboration in this setting. By describing the interactive mind in this manner, in terms of its contextual constraints, Dixon and Gould hold up one piece of the puzzle, for which one can find many suitable complements in mainstream cognitive psychology. Of course (complementary to

Dixon and Gould), the emphasis of a typical cognitive psychology report is on component processes of interactive systems, on what specific sensory, perceptual, and conceptual processes and knowledge must be recruited for a particular tasks, and on what conditions are necessary for their efficient interactive functioning. What kind of cognitive/knowledge system is capable of relying more on collaboration with others in order to compensate for age-related selective declines in some input source or processing component? To me, this kind of question and this perspective of the interactive mind are already "programmed" as the default option that comes automatically to mind. But more important is that the puzzle pieces from the two domains fit together and, therefore more generally, that we systematically acknowledge the complementary nature of research efforts that are guided by a contextualist perspective or by a mainstream cognitive psychology approach.

The domain of social interactions has never been a major research focus in mainstream cognitive psychology (a few notable exceptions are reported by Staudinger in Chapter 10). Instead, in its investigations of the nature of interactive minds, cognitive psychology research has typically centered on situations with more static influences (relative to the dynamic situation created by the interaction between two individuals) – for example, the physical setting or environment, or the affective or pharmacological state (for reviews see Baddeley, 1982; Bjork & Richardson-Klavehn, 1989; Eich, 1985; Geiselman & Bjork, 1980; Godden & Baddeley, 1975; Smith, 1985, 1988) of the subjects in a memory experiment. To explain interaction effects that occur in these kinds of investigations, cognitive psychology has tended to concentrate on specific resources – for example the physical, emotional, and pharmacological cues – that are available to guide memory processing in each situation, and we speculate about how cues – one kind of resource – might be used to facilitate or inhibit the processing required for each target task (Bjork & Richardson-Klavehn, 1989; Eich, 1980, 1985; Graf, 1994; Graf & Ryan, 1990; Roediger & McDermott, 1993; Schacter & Tulving, 1994; Smith, 1988). Even more removed from the domain of social interactions, much of cognitive psychology is concerned with more basic and *abstract* situations that are defined without reference to a social or physical setting, and that differ mainly in terms of their distinctive performance requirements and the mental state induced by means of different instructions (Craik & Lockhart, 1972; Gardiner, 1988; Gardiner & Java, 1990; Graf & Schacter, 1985; Morris, Bransford, & Franks, 1977; Parkin, 1993; Parkin & Walter, 1992; Tulving, 1989). Investigations of such abstract situations have yielded insights into interactive systems at the level of specific sensory, perceptual, and conceptual processes.

What is underscored by these examples is that, to cognitive psychology, an interactive system is any entity (or construction) that uses (exploits) certain resources or inputs in order to adapt and respond appropriately to the demands of its context or setting. Therefore, working collaboratively with another person is regarded as implicating one such system, albeit one that is special by virtue of the fact that it operates in a highly complex setting with dynamically changing input, response, and monitoring requirements. More important, cognitive psychology assumes at least implicitly that the systems that are required for effective social interactions are the same, in principle, as those systems that we investigate under the much simplified conditions of our laboratory experiments. Consequently, if this assumption is valid, we are justified in proceeding with "business as usual," as if interactive systems differ mainly (or exclusively) in terms of cue availability, resource requirements, learning, and response strategies. Alternatively, if social interactions consti- tute a special kind of setting, with unique cues, resource requirements, and/or strategies for learning, future research should specifically compare similarities and differences between the systems required for social interactions versus those required for other kinds (e.g., nonsocial) of interactions.

Favoring more the latter possibility, Staudinger's (Chapter 10) description of the development of wisdom in adulthood highlights differences between a system that is required for a particular socially originated phenomenon versus systems that are designed for other, nonsocial types of interactions. The Berlin model of wisdom (Baltes & Smith, 1990; Baltes & Staudinger, 1993) postulates several avenues that might foster the growth of wisdom, including general personal factors – good health, cognitive skills, and interpersonal competence or expertise in a particular domain – in dealing with complex life problems, and the presence of facilitative learning contexts to allow for the practice of wisdom-relevant skills. General person factors do not seem specifically tied to social interactions, and thus, there may be no particular need to investigate them in complex social settings rather than under the much more controllable conditions of a single-person laboratory experiment. By contrast, however, the other two factors – acquisition of expertise in a particular domain and a context that facilitates the development of the relevant expertise – seem intrinsically linked with social interactions. Therefore, the minimal lesson that cognitive psychology might draw from Staudinger's discussion of the develop- ment of wisdom is that there arc complex interpersonal situations that reveal knowledge sources and skills that do not emerge in single-person laboratory investigations. It follows, therefore, that a complete cognitive psychology should consider the possibility of special domains like wisdom, which might differ from the domains tested in the typical laboratory experiment situations qualitatively and/or quantitatively on many dimensions, including the rate of learning and development across the life span, the focus on social and affectively laden as opposed to more "neutral" settings, and the requirement for adaptation to complex and dynamically changing circumstances.

Perhaps an even stronger message for cognitive psychology is delivered by Cole (Chapter 2), who focuses on the fundamental relation between our nature as social beings and the nature of interactive minds. Cole begins with a discussion of the social-cultural basis of human artifacts – the symbols that we use for communication – and discusses how understanding, communion, and interaction with another mind requires the finely coordinated use of artifact-mediated, joint symbolic activity. According to Cole, early in life children are "physically immature and have yet to accumulate a cultural-historical past," and thus, are dependent on adults who "structure children's experience in terms of their expectations for their future." Cole explains that culturally organized experience continues to accumulate, starting with a shared sleep–wake and feeding cycle, crying, the emergence of social smiling, social refer-encing, and then a major milestone – language. Vygotsky and his colleagues have described different kinds of signs, language, and counting systems and how they are used as "psychological tools," arguing that "like all other tools, by being included in the process of the behavior, psychological tools alter the entire flow and structure of mental functions" (Vygotsky, 1981, p. 137). The clear message for cognitive psychology that originates from this line of reason-ing, therefore, is that to the extent to which social-cultural influences are intrinsic to the nature of human cognition, they are part and parcel of all interactive symbol-processing systems, and thus they cannot be ignored or excluded from our investigations.

Most of the chapters in this volume (e.g., those of Staudinger, Cole, Klein, and Azmitia) focus on those aspects of interactive minds that seem to have emerged as a result of social interactions, and more specifically, in order to facilitate cooperation among individuals. By contrast to the cooperative inter-active minds that are revealed by such situations, cognitive psychology has focused on interactive systems that operate across a broader range of (or more basic) circumstances where the goal might be either collaboration or competi-tion between systems or component processes. In cognitive psychology, col-laboration and competition are regarded as having direct counterparts in basic neural processes that operate either in an activating or inhibiting manner – that is, processes that serve either to facilitate or to hinder the occurrence of certain neural states (Grossberg, 1980; Martindale, 1991; Tipper & Weaver, 1994). Consistent with such possibilities, it follows that to the extent that the social-interactive mind is like any other interactive system (i.e., like those investigated by cognitive science), we should also consider that this sytem has developed for the purpose not only of collaboration, but also of competing with other individuals. In other words, by highlighting the link between facili-tation and inhibition, a cognitive psychology perspective seems to complement in yet another manner the approach that dominates in this volume; it directs attention not only to the benefits but also to the specific costs (negative consequences) that can occur – for example, under the interactive story recall conditions of Dixon and Gould's experiments (Chapter 8). Similarly, in the context of the Berlin wisdom project (Staudinger, Chapter 10), focusing more on inhibition might direct attention to specific circumstances or personal factors that minimize or even prevent the occurrence of wise behavior in a particular situation. Finally, it is also possible that a bias in favor of considering only collaboration between minds might have even more far-reaching consequences and obscure the picture that emerges when we trace the phylogenetic evolution of interactive minds (Hammerstein, Chapter 1); it may prevent us from discovering interactive minds that might be able to compete, but not yet to cooperate with each other.

In the foregoing paragraphs, I have tried to demonstrate by example, that the systematic juxtaposing of research and theorizing from cognitive psychology and from the contextualist perspective represented in this volume might have considerable heuristic value and may be used to ferret out promising new avenues for research. Therefore, to conclude my commentary, I will outline one more point of convergence between these conceptions of the interactive mind, one that concerns the role of consciousness. In tracing the evolution of collaborative minds, Hammerstein (Chapter 1) explains the role of specific evolutionarily stable strategies that emerge in particular environments. More relevant for the present, he also explains that his use of the term *strategy* refers only to specific genetically transmitted behavioral programs that are noncognitive and do not implicate conscious choice and decision making. Even more important for the present, however, is a question raised by this discussion: Does the evolution of *conscious* (as opposed to unconsious) strategic processing, *conscious* decision making, and *conscious* communication play a specific role in the shaping of socially interactive minds? Hammerstein did not address this question, but an instructive case can be found in the memory literature.

In a widely cited article, Sherry and Schacter (1987) have traced the phylogenetic and ontogenetic evolution of two distinct memory systems – implicit/procedural memory and explicit/declarative memory – that differ primarily in that one can and the other cannot be consciously inspected and controlled (Graf & Schacter, 1985). They explored how the evolution of these two cognitive systems has shaped human beings (as well as some lower animals) and has enabled them to use their memory abilities more effectively and selectively to transfer learning across a broader range of circumstances. More critical, the distinction between two memory systems, one consciously controlled and the other not consciously controlled, has been exceedingly productive for researchers from cognitive and developmental psychology, as well as neuropsychology (see Graf & Masson, 1993), and it has been used to guide investigation into a variety of domains, including normal adult memory, the development of memory skills in early childhood, and the selective breakdown of memory functions in old age and in patients with anterograde amnesia. What is most relevant here, however, is that conscious and unconscious processes seem to make distinctive contributions to our memory performance, and therefore, it seems equally possible that conscious and unconscious processes might also exert distinctive influences of the functioning of a more complex system like the social-interactive mind. If we draw a generalization from the memory findings, we can pose the following question to guide future research: Is it possible that the emergence of the social-interactive mind is intrinsically linked with the evolution of specific conscious processes? Klein (Chapter 3) asks the same kind of question with respect to language and explores the possibility that language renders "possible all higher forms of cognition," especially the emergence of social-interactive minds. In the development of social-interactive minds, should we assign a less critical role to consciousness?

Interactive minds from a developmental perspective (Laura L. Carstensen)

The framing of a question often dictates its answer. By directing attention toward certain aspects and away from other aspects of a problem, a question imposes boundaries on the form and content of an answer. In science, theoretical paradigms serve a similar function. They facilitate the generation of hypotheses while simultaneously suppressing other lines of inquiry. Often theoretical paradigms become so ingrained that scientists fail to notice the extent to which new questions are limited by old paradigms. Imagining a new paradigm is much like imagining what one's thoughts and questions would be like had one been raised in another culture. Although it is easy to imagine the broad abstraction, it is extremely difficult, if not impossible, to imagine specific thoughts and questions that one might have had.

For me, reading this volume had the effect of bringing back into awareness the dominant paradigms of psychological science. In doing so, it served to reframe the questions that have traditionally surrounded the most central and enduring debate in developmental psychology – the role of nature versus nurture in human development. Taken together, the chapters point to a new way of considering this debate, at once critical of psychology's emphasis on the individual, with its implicit presumption that thought and action come from within, and the idea that social phenomena are external to the individual. The considered view suggests that "mind" is not only influenced by social phenomena; social phenomena are the "stuff" of mind. As Klein (Chapter 3) asserts, the distinction is not trivial, most importantly because this paradigmatic shift in focus leads to the generation of a fresh set of questions and unexplored answers. Thus, the collection steers the field in an importantly new direction.

Indeed, reviewing the chapters, I could not help but wonder what psychology would be like had it been established on the fundamental assumptions espoused by the authors of this volume. The very partitioning of psychology into subdisciplines of social, cognitive, developmental, personality, and so forth would be ironic. That is, what would psychology be like had it been premised on the assumption that "mind" or cognition is a social entity? What would we know, after a century of psychological research, if thoughts were considered to be derived from social processes rather than the precursors to social exchange? What questions would we have asked about language if language were not considered an intrinsic ability that can be used for social means, but fundamentally socially constituted? What woud we know that we do not know now if the unit of measurement was not the individual's response but the social interchange itself? I, for one, find it difficult to imagine answers to such questions, although the contributors to this volume offer glimmerings of both questions and answers that we might discover in the next hundred years of psychology as the field begins to pose such questions.

It is not by chance that the nature versus nurture debate was framed as it was in the beginning. Influenced by the early teachings of Christianity, the nativists, such as René Descartes and Immanuel Kant, believed that knowledge was God-given and, thus, innate. The antagonists included the likes of Jean Jacques Rousseau and, later, John Stuart Mill, who argued that knowledge was the product of associations among ideas and memories derived from experience. In the beginning the arguments were polarized, religiously influenced, and starkly black and white. And until the end of the nineteenth century, when Wilhelm Wundt established the first psychology laboratory and undertook the scientific study of the human mind, such debates about the human mind were solely philosophical.

There is little doubt that this philosophical history, combined with the sociocultural period that surrounded psychology's birth, framed the questions that the social sciences asked about the human mind. Psychological science originated during an era in which the natural sciences were making seemingly unbounded progress, shedding insights into the most elusive phenomena of the natural world. Very likely it was this intellectually fertile societal context, excited by the promise of the natural sciences, that allowed scholars to consider for the first time that the workings of the mind may also be susceptible to scientific analysis. This context most certainly influenced the paradigmatic approach that early experimentalists adopted. Wundt's structuralism was aimed at developing a kind of mental chemistry in which the structure of conscious experience would be reduced to its most basic elements. The experimental method of introspection, designed to study mental elements and their fusions, established the precedent of studying human subjects in isolation under highly controlled experimental conditions. The paradigm, despite its importance in so many ways, tacitly declared the social context "noise."

Developmental psychology followed this paradigmatic tradition. The early focus was on "the content of children's minds" (Hall, 1883). The infant was presumed to be born preprogrammed to develop language, form emotional attachments, and reason about the world in distinctive ways. Grounded in the nativist approach, developmental psychology took as its central task the description of the unfolding of the child over time.

So as not to build a straw case, I should add explicitly that the organismic approach does not ignore social interaction. Considerable research efforts have addressed the ways that external influences, such as parenting styles, aid or limit individual growth (H. E. Jones, Macfarlane, & Eichorn, 1960; M. C. Jones, 1967). Everyone agrees that the dominant culture determines which language the child will acquire, for example, and no linguist would disagree with the claim that there is "something deeply social about language" (Klein, Chapter 3). Yet, Klein's chapter illustrates well that even a process as basic and universal as language can be conceptualized as a social phenomenon and that this conceptualization leads to different questions about the subject matter and generates different answers.

Neither has the developmental field failed to consider social and environmental influences. On the contrary, over the years the field has been infused with spritely debates about the extent to which the environment influences development, many arguing that focus on the internal workings of the mind should be replaced entirely with attention to observable behavior. John B. Watson, credited with heralding the call to concentrate exclusively on observable subject matter and to ignore mental operations so that psychology could assume its place among the natural sciences, was not alone. Operant psychologists fueled the flames of this debate well into the 1950s and 1960s, shifting attention from the mind to reinforcement contingencies in the environment (see also Rogers & Skinner, 1956).

Unfortunately, however, arguments between the materialists and the organismics, and later the behaviorists and the cognitive counterrevolutionaries, centered primarily around mental control over behavior and the very existence of mind. More recently, arguments concerning the evolutionary influence on behavior have come to be debated in a similarly dichotomous way, as if "prepared" responses were responses that are uninfluenced by the social context. Gigerenzer (Chapter 11) eloquently illustrates the fallibility of this logic. Indeed, domain-specific processing is determined, albeit distally, by social forces. To me, a central message in this volume is that the framing of these debates may have obscured potential questions and shaped answers on both sides such that the dualism between mind and behavior was reified. That is, debating whether mind or environment controls behavior has obscured the consideration that mind is part of the environment and environment is part of mind.

Certainly some topics in developmental psychology have been considered more social than others. The acquisition of morality is believed to be derived from social relationships and social interaction. Freud would agree completely. Nevertheless, the bulk of the research on morality has focused on descriptions of individuals' acquired levels of morality rather than on the social nature of morality. Damon (Chapter 7) suggests that the interesting questions about morality concern the repeated social transformations of moral goals that are embedded in social interactions throughout life. Labouvie-Vief (Chapter 4) pursues a similar shift in focus by considering gender in terms of the social processes that indelibly shape the social scripts of men's and women's minds.

Similarly, life planning has certainly been viewed as a phenomenon that is socially influenced, but not as a social cognitive process (see Smith, Chapter 9). Few would argue that individuals plan their lives without noticing social norms and opportunities. Too often overlooked, however, is the insidious role that culture plays in determining the range of options people consider. Cole (Chapter 2) argues that the world is steeped in accumulated artifacts of past generations that provide representations of past achievements and values that influence later generations. The research literature has not considered planning life goals or negotiating the management of a household (see Goodnow, Chapter 6) as a continual social cognitive process. Thus, the concept of interactive minds applied to these domains once again points to new questions pertaining to the processes of both social and cognitive negotiation.

In contrast, some topics in life-span developmental psychology, such as memory, have been considered decidedly nonsocial. The vast majority of research on cognition follows a paradigm in which the performance of individuals is assessed. Individual subjects recount to experimenters their thinking about particular cognitive tasks from which experimenters infer mental phenomena. If a subject were to consult with another person during an experiment, the data would surely be discarded because the subject would have "cheated." Dixon and Gould (Chapter 8) maintain, however, that social collaboration occurs in much of everyday cognitive activity, and thus, as Vygotsky (1978) also argued, social interaction represents fertile ground for cognitive developmentalists. Dixon and Gould's work on cognitive collaboration contributes far more than specific empirical findings. It demonstrates the utility of a paradigm shift.

The cognitive benefits of social interchange in childhood and adulthood are also treated in very novel ways by Azmitia (Chapter 5) and Staudinger (Chapter 10). Azmitia considers peer influence in childhood and adolescence to go beyond motivational influences, as they are typically considered, to include improved comprehension and understanding of material – that is, improved mental processes.

Staudinger, in her discussion of wisdom, takes an even more radical position by suggesting that wisdom – a highly advanced way of thinking – is more likely to be found in the interchanges among individuals than in the responses of any one individual. Suddenly, the unit of measurement changes. Rather than tapping an internal feature of an individual, the social exchange becomes the focus. Thus, when an individual turns to others for input in considering a problem of everyday life, he or she participates in an exchange in which thousands of others – some dead, some living – also participate. Culture represented in the telling and retelling of stories (see also Dixon & Gould, Chapter 8) plays a central role in the generation of wise responses. Although a handful of individuals may have come to be expert retellers of wise responses, they are nevertheless carriers of a body of knowledge generated by multiple sources.

In closing, the collection of chapters embodied in this volume offers an important reframing of central conceptual and empirical issues that have captivated developmental psychologists for decades. The experimental findings reported throughout the volume are intriguing. In my opinion, the greater value lies in the way that the authors very effectively shift the focus from the consideration of individuals and social contexts as distinct entities to the inextricable interaction between the two. Paradigms are evaluated based on the degree to which they generate new questions and methods. In this regard the collection is impressive.

I add that it is not surprising that the life-span approach led to this profitable shift in perspective. Including the entire life-span in developmental psychology pushed the envelope of traditional paradigms and demanded that researchers consider the social context. It appears from this collection that such considerations have begun to move the mind into the public arena.

Educational psychology: study of the institutionalized genesis and formation of interactive minds (Franz E. Weinert)

In 1900, William Stern wrote of a typical phenomenon in the history of science:

> What had previously been viewed as a source of error and as something to be avoided at all costs suddenly proves to be an issue in its own right . . . a research program of its own. . . . Till now, practically all efforts of scientific psychology share the endeavour of conceiving of a problem in general terms. Research is focused on defining the constitutive elements of mental life, and theory is oriented towards establishing the general laws of mental processing. In order to concentrate on mental life in general, psychologists ignore – sometimes rightly, sometimes mistakenly – the infinite variety of different personalities, cultures, social classes, sexes, types, and so forth. Such an abstraction is justified as long as it is accompanied by the insight that it arises from a lack of scientific competence, but there is an immanent danger of forgetting the limitations of abstraction and believing that the general perspective can provide solutions for all the problems of scientific psychology. Perhaps psychology has been subject to this danger for a long time. But now we can assume that this danger has been overcome. (1900/1911, p. 1)

Although this early analysis of scientific psychology was remarkably clear-sighted, it was nevertheless mistaken in assuming that psychology had already achieved the mature status of a multiperspective discipline.

This volume represents evidence that Stern's high expectations came too early, because all of the contributions attempt to explode the classic paradigm of psychology and supplement or even replace it with a new approach. In retrospect, it is quite suprising how invariant the metatheoretical framework of psychological research has remained in the twentieth century, despite the temporary domination of such diverging approaches as functionalism, behaviorism, and cognitivism. Mainstream psychology was, and still is, concerned predominantly with the search for general, context-independent laws of the (causal) relationships between variables, the mechanisms responsible for these relationships, and their structural conditions and functional effects.

The majority of chapters in this volume contain good arguments. Authors describe social contents and contexts that are not intended to be viewed only as input, or mediating, variables in a general, functionally unchanging "if–then statement" model. Rather, there is a demand that the social world be integrated directly into psychological theories about the functioning of individual and interactive minds.

This demand for integration frequently emphasizes the fundamental antagonism between the "isolated individual" and the "individual within a social context." It appears to me that this is not the central problem because an understanding of the individual as a person is ignored by psychology almost as much as is the social embeddedness of human life and behavior. In mainstream research, the individual plays a role only as an experimental subject and as a theoretical unit of analysis in which the necessary species-specific preconditions for the functioning of particular psychological variables are localized.

What about the contribution of social psychology, which has also been around for more than a hundred years? Critics of this subdiscipline of psychology subscribe to the view that traditional social psychology is not really social, but primarily studies social attitudes of individuals, individual behavior in groups and institutions, cognitive processes with social contents, and so forth.

In contrast to the two-component scientific psychology program designed by Wundt, experimentally oriented physiological psychology and socially oriented developmental psychology did not develop into two research pillars of equal strength. Instead, experimental psychology exercised far greater influence on social psychology than vice versa.

This is also true of educational psychology. This subdiscipline is primarily concerned with learning and teaching in schools and in settings analogous to schools. Yet schools are, by definition, cultural institutions in which pupils are expected to acquire socially canonized knowledge, habits, values, and norms within the social context of the classroom. Nevertheless, educational research reveals a similar emphasis on the individual learner and general mechanisms of learning, rather than on the social conditions, processes, and effects of school acculturation of individuals, groups, and populations.

The theoretical assumption underlying and supporting the research program of educational psychology was described by Wilhelm Rein as early as 1893: "There is only one way of teaching that corresponds to nature: to follow carefully the laws of the human mind and to arrange everything according to these laws. The attainment of adequate instructional procedures follows from knowledge of, and insight into, these laws" (p. 107).

Even if, in the meantime, many doubts as to the implementation of such a scientific vision have surfaced, to this day the (sometimes desperate) hope has remained that psychological research can "help educators to improve the conditions of learning and the quality of learning of increasingly large numbers of students" (Anderson & Burns, 1985, p. ix).

In traditional schools (and critical observers believe most schools around the world to be of this kind) and in school-related psychological research, the learner has been conceptualized as an absorber and consumer of decontextualized knowledge; learning is viewed as the transmission of information. In other words, in educational practice and in psychological research "individuals leave their social status, history, beliefs, and values behind as they enter the laboratory (school). . . . By stripping behavior of its social context, psychologists rule out the study of socio-cultural and historical factors, and implicitly attribute causes to factors inside the individual" (Riger, 1992, p. 731).

Educational research inspired by social psychological concerns existed independently of the mainstream. To name a few examples: Lewin's work on the significance of the social climate for the behavior of individuals and groups (Lewin, Lippitt, & White, 1939), Barker and Gump's (1964) research about "behavior settings" in large and small schools, Jackson's *Life in Classroom* (1968), and studies on cooperative learning (Kagan, 1985). In comparison with these important but relatively marginal social psychological contributions to educational psychology, many models of permanent school reform proved to be a substantially richer source for new socially oriented educational ideas.

In 1900, the Swedish educator Ellen Key published her book *The Century of the Child*. This book included a massive critique of traditional school education, followed by suggestions for a radical reform of the school. To this day, Ellen Key's ideas can be recognized in a large number and variety of models for educational reform. These models include (a) the concept of learning as an unfettered mental activity in which students work according to their own needs to achieve self-selected goals in self-determined ways; (b) the facilitation of social learning through students' teams, teamwork, and reciprocal teaching; (c) the use of stimulating projects from the child's experiential world to provide meaningful learning activities; (d) the elimination of segregation by grade, the elimination of repetition of school years and of school marks; and (e) the orientation of school learning toward the natural development of the child and age-typical learning ativities.

In the past decade, the voice of science has made itself heard above the often confusing public discussion about the best ways to reform school education. Currently, findings from developmental psychology, cross-cultural research, and cognitive science facilitate access to theoretically rich and pragmatically useful information about meaningful learning and successful teaching. Research on social contexts for learning (Weinstein, 1991), on situated cognition (Greeno & Moore, 1993), on socially shared cognition (Resnick, Levine, & Behrend, 1991), and on interactive minds (this volume) are good examples of this new theoretical approach. With this research orientation, education is not only a field of application for theoretical insights, but also a rich base for personal experiences, systematic field studies, and experimental work that leads to the development and testing of new theoretical ideas.

Three sources of information play an important role in this new orientation: (a) development, learning, and teaching in non-Western cultures (Gay & Cole, 1967; Rogoff, 1990); (b) the acquisition of a variety of competencies and knowledge in the first years of life, that is, before the child enters school (Gardner, 1991); and (c) comparisons of learning within and outside of school (Resnick, 1987). Resnick (1987), for example, observed that a kind of learning and thinking dominates in schools that she describes as individualized, symbol-based, and pure (without the use of tools), and that aims at the acquisition of general, widely applicable knowledge and skills. Learning and problem-solving outside of school, in contrast, occur predominantly in social groups, depend on the embedding situational features, include the use of tools and materials, and primarily lead to the acquisition of situated, context-specific knowledge. These three sources of experience and research have recently contributed to a marked preference for situated cognition, apprenticeship, and interactive minds in the development of models of school education.

This volume provides good evidence for these tendencies. Although only one chapter deals with learning and instruction per se (Mandl, Gruber, & Renkl, Chapter 14), many of the chapters allow for making interesting references to educational issues. This is true of Cole's (Chapter 2) synopsis of the affinity between cultural-historical and life-span approaches to cognitive development, of Staudinger's (Chapter 10) conceptual view of the social-interactive nature of wisdom (with many analogies to concepts like creativity or intuitive thinking), of Damon's (Chapter 7) analysis of social influences on the lifelong transformation of moral goals, and of Smith's presentation (Chapter 9) on plans about life, a conception that is directly relevant for planning a school career or considering vocational choices.

Even more closely related to practice and research in education are the contributions of Azmitia (Chapter 5) on peer interactive minds, of Goodnow (Chapter 6) on collaborative rules in interactive situations, of Sternberg (Chapter 12) on styles of thinking, and of Klein (Chapter 3) on the determinants of language acquisition.

To clarify the genuine contribution of educational psychology to theories of situated cognition, socially shared knowledge, and interactive minds, it appears useful to list briefly some of the key concepts of this research field (although it should be noted that a considerable semantic overlap between concepts exists).

Classroom as a social context of learning (Weinstein, 1991). Studies of the significance of separate social factors (teacher–student interaction, student–student interaction, learning in teams, etc.) in school learning have been in circulation for a long time, but recently a tendency toward systematization of the influential factors (Salomon, 1992) and a greater concern with theoretical embeddedness have surfaced. From a social constructivist view, for example, learning is defined as the interactive re-creation of knowledge.

> In other words, social interaction is considered as essential for learning, with individual knowledge construction occurring through processes of interaction, negotiation and collaboration through which learners become acculturated members of a ... community and culture. ... As a result, common meanings, knowledge, and practices are developed by the community members. (DeCorte, Greer, & Verschaffel, in press)

Cooperative learning (Slavin, 1990). This is characterized by the cooperation of small groups of learners in order to achieve a common goal. Learning tasks and projects should be designed in a way that enables and necessitates cooperation between pupils. Typical methods include the "jigsaw" procedure (pupils divide up units of study and share responsibility for learning and teaching their piece of the puzzle to each other, or group investigations or student team learning methods; e.g., Slavin, 1990). Findings from these studies indicate

> that the classroom is not simply a social context in which students learn academic lessons. It is a social context in which students also learn social lessons – lessons about appropriate behavior in various contexts, about one's self as a learner and one's position in a status hierarchy, about relationships with students from other ethnic and racial groups, about the relative value of competition and cooperation, and about friendship. (Weinstein, 1991, p. 520)

Cognitive apprenticeship (Rogoff, 1990). This focuses on the application of principles, methods, and experiences of traditional craftsmanship to learning in schools. Authentic activities, social interactions, guided participation, and cognitive modeling are characteristic aspects. "Children participate as apprentices in structured and supported problem solving, contributing to decisions and actively observing others. Rather than receiving a packaged lesson to internalize as a result of this involvement, children's participation itself changes their understanding" (Rogoff, 1991, p. 363).

Community of practice (Lave, 1991; Mandl, Gruber, & Renkl, Chapter 14). The concept of cognitive apprenticeship shares many similarities with a process that Lave (1991) labels "legitimate peripheral participation." It entails "that newcomers become oldtimers through a social process of increasingly centripetal participation, which depends on legitimate access to ongoing community practice.... Knowledgeable skill is encompassed in the process of assuming an identity as a practitioner, of becoming a full participant, an oldtimer" (Lave, 1991, p. 68). Mandl et al. (Chapter 14) have applied this concept to the acquisition of expertise in universities. In accordance with the results of empirical studies about learning and teaching in medicine and business management, the possibilities and limitations of the apprenticeship model and the community of practice approach for learning in universities are extracted. Of course, it is an open question whether schools and universities are more aptly described as "communities of learners" (Brown, 1994) than as "communities of practice."

Reciprocal teaching (Palincsar & Brown, 1984). In this method, teachers and pupils alternate in adopting the role of instructor in order to improve reading comprehension by teaching cognitive strategies such as summarizing, generating questions, clarification, and prediction of what might appear in the next paragraph of the text. Particularly new and successful among the components of reciprocal teaching appears to be "the popularization of the idea of students providing support for each other within reading groups" (Rosenshine & Meister, 1994).

When looking for the common theoretical spirit of these and many other concepts of the "new learning theory" (Brown, 1994, p. 6), an understanding of learning as an active, constructive, situated, and social interactive process emerges. Learning is further seen as the acquisition of socially shared and distributed knowledge through guided participation and cooperative work in communities of learners and/or practitioners.

This position stands in direct opposition to traditional (information-processing-oriented) cognitive theories of learning. If science is considered to be a game between competing ideas, such a strategy seems appropriate. Empirical research can reap greater rewards from a theory if it is less eclectic and more focused. However, such a radical approach does not improve educational practice; nor does it help students and educators.

The general problem comes to mind when one reads a charming lampoon of the two theoretical approaches by Norman (1993):

> The caricature of the traditional information studies of symbolic processing is that they focus entirely upon the processing structures of the brain and the symbolic representations of mind. All the action is inside the head.... What could be more natural than to study the human by recognizing that the brain is the computational engine of thought, and thereby concentrating one's efforts upon understanding brain mechanisms and mental representations? Seems pretty obvious. Sure, there is a lot of action in the world at large and within sociocultural groups, but cognitive processing occurs within the heads of individuals.
>
> The caricature of the situated action approach to cognition is that these

> studies focus entirely upon the structures of the world and how they constrain
> and guide human behavior. Human knowledge and interaction cannot be
> divorced from the world. . . .
>   What really matters is the situation and the parts that people play.
>   The proponents of situated action – at least in caricature – tend to empha-
> size the importance of historical influences, social interaction, culture, and the
> environment and to minimize the importance of internal cognition.
>   Proponents of the traditional approach – at least in caricature – tend to
> downplay the importance of these external, social, and historical factors and
> to emphasize the importance of internal cognition. (pp. 3–4)

I believe that this caricature represents the core of the argument for the
necessity of combining the two theoretical approaches. Given the demands of
our scientific and technical world, it seems necessary to make sure that learners acquire both situational knowledge and general competencies, that they
avoid substantial knowledge deficits, as well as optimize vertical (within
knowledge domains) and horizontal (across domains and situations) transfer
of learning. Cognitive and social learning must be integrated in order to
promote the cognitive development of students and to help teachers to
optimize instruction (Weinert & Helmke, 1995).

Scientific prerequisites for this reform purpose are higher-order models of
learning that include and integrate the regularities of the individual mind and
the interactive minds – not in an eclectic way but in a theoretical perspective.
This represents an urgent need for psychology in general and for educational
psychology in particular.

The "mind" of cultural psychology (Richard A. Shweder)

Betwixt and between the monad and the receptacle

The essays in this volume range across quite disparate areas – gender development, wisdom, artificial intelligence, narrative, sociobiology, sociohistorical
psychology – yet amazingly they are unified by a common aim: to locate a
suitable intellectual space in between the Leibnizean conception of the human
mind as a *monad* and the Lockean conception of the human mind as a *receptacle*. That notional territory betwixt and between those two opposed ideas –
mind as monad versus mind as receptacle – is staked out by the editors of the
volume under the banner of "interactive minds." What Baltes and Staudinger
seek to achieve is a conception of the human mind that neither Leibniz nor
Locke thought credible.

Leibniz (the rationalist) conceptualized the human mind as a self-sufficient,
preformed, richly structured, asocial monad, which was fully equipped with
conceptual content (ideas) and was endowed with the capacity to cognize and
compute the implications of its own innate ideas. He imagined that everything
inside the mind – the "conceptual contents" cognized in thought plus their

computational implications – must have been there originally and all along. He supposed (as did Kant, Descartes, and Plato) that ideas (the conceptual contents of a mind) could not have their source in experience because to have an experience is to have an experience "of something," and for an experience to be an experience of something the mind must already know how to represent the experience as an experience of this or that or of such and so. This led Leibniz to reason that experience could not be the source of ideas because an outside experience (such as the visual or tactile perception of a chair) could have no impact on the mind unless its conceptual content (the this or that, the such and so, in this case the concept "chair") was already available to the mind in the form of an innate idea. According to the well-known image, the monad has no windows open to the outside world, but it does have a rich enough conceptual content and sophisticated enough computational ability to derive all the knowledge it needs.

One startling implication of this Leibnizean view of the mind is that minds cannot truly interact. A closely related implication is that the apparent fact of *negotiated* or *constructed* interactions between minds is an illusion. For if the mind is a monad then a "society of minds" (including apparent instances of social coordination, social communication, and responsive interactions between minds) must be merely the (centrally planned or locally accidental) by-product of the way separate self-contained minds derive and play out the implications of their own innate ideas. Leibniz introduced the theoretical notion of "God" as the choreographer or programmer (the central planner) who was in possession of a synoptic vision of a society of minds and had the power to write the innate scripts that produced the illusion of calibrated social interaction.[1] By Leibniz's account, the human mind is inherently active, but its conceptual content is not open to social programming; monads are animated but they run through the life course working out the necessary implications of ideas that are already there, as a matter of necessity.

In contrast, Locke (the empiricist) imagined that almost everything about the mind was a matter of contingency. He conceptualized the human mind as a dependent, unformed, minimally structured, socially dominated receptacle, relatively unendowed with conceptual content, passively responsive to the causal impact of exogenous experiences. Locke's receptacle is neither active nor interactive. It is, however, very social, or more accurately put, it is very socialized.[2]

Baltes's and Staudinger's phrase "interactive minds" is meant to point us in the direction of a possible middle ground between Leibniz and Locke. The slogan seems well designed as an invitation to the contributors to the volume to distance themselves theoretically from monads and receptacles and to formulate a coherent conception of a human mind that is inherently social yet free, spontaneous but receptive, responsive but contributory, already structured yet not fully formed.

Interactive minds: the unsteady middle ground

That invitation is, of course, a very hazardous one. Almost every attempt I know to actually occupy the middle ground or strike the proper balance between the idea of an a priori mental autonomy (Leibniz) and the idea of a fully socialized mental passivity (Locke) ultimately loses its equipoise and surreptitiously privileges one image of the mind (the monad) or the other (the receptacle). For example, the monad gets privileged by many sociobiologists, who try to explain social formations as the by-products of the egocentric choice behavior of self-interested individuals. (In contemporary secular social theory the "invisible hand" tends to replace the synoptic mind of God, as the "mastermind" of the social scene; see Hayek, 1973.) The monad also gets privileged by (those) infancy researchers and some developmental psycholinguists who argue that a young child's knowledge of conceptual content (e.g., of causation, mathematics, faces, and language) is far more complex than the inputs of early life experience and thus is best interpreted as the activation of mental representations (conceptual contents – ideas, rules, grammars, beliefs) that are already there.

On the other side of the balance scale, the receptacle gets privileged by social constructionists, who argue that a priori mental content (Platonic "intuitions" or innate ideas) does not exist, and who dismiss the notion of autonomous "agency" and "methodological individualism" as socially conditioned ideological illusions. The receptacle also gets privileged by many anthropologists and comparativists who argue that almost everything we know is impressed on us or handed over unidirectionally from one generation to the next. The most recent and in my view the very best book ever written in cognitive anthropology (D'Andrade, 1995) begins this way: "Most of what any human ever thinks has been thought before, and most of what any human ever thinks has been learned from other humans" (p. xiv). As appealing as I find that formulation, there is something about D'Andrade's way of stating that conception of cognitive anthropology that seems to favor receptivity over spontaneity.[3]

It is very hard to keep one's balance in the face of both Leibniz and Locke. In a world of academic discourse where things are either inside or outside, necessary or contingent, endogenous or exogenous, semantic or pragmatic, spontaneous or caused, intrinsic or extrinsic, innate or acquired, it is a Herculean task to give proper expression to the sought after middle realm of neither or both. Even the subtitle of this volume (*Life-Span Perspectives on the Social Foundations of Cognition*) unwittingly tilts (and thus slightly distorts) the intended meaning of the title (*Interactive Minds*) in the direction of Locke. No matter how bold or intelligent the claims put forward by an author about the middle ground, one almost always feels the need for some counterpoise.

Given the inherent difficulty of defining the middle ground, I am not surprised that the contributors to this volume interpret the idea of interactive minds in such diverse ways. Some authors interpret it as "cooperation." Others interpret it as "social interaction" or "joint activity." Still others interpret it as "social influence," "intersubjectivity," "collective representation," or "artifact." I take this as evidence that the quest for the promised land is still in progress and that no one is yet quite sure what it is going to look like. That only adds to the fascination of this particular collection of essays, which should be read as an exhilarating and historically significant multidirectional scouting expedition in search of the middle ground where spontaneity and receptivity can live together. (For a brilliant purely philosophical treatment of the tension between spontaneity and receptivity, see McDowell, 1994.)

In the remainder of this brief commentary I join in that exploratory spirit of things. Writing as a sympathetic and admiring fellow traveler I am going to point in one particular direction, and then just hope for the best. So here goes, a glimpse of the middle ground (interactive minds) from the perspective of cultural psychology (for more on cultural psychology, see Shweder 1991, 1993; Shweder & Sullivan, 1993).[4]

One mind, many mentalities: universalism without the uniformity

Mind is a dangerous and ambiguous word. For the sake of clarity (and safety) I want to define a few terms. I want to try to distinguish between mind, mental process, cognition, and mentality. Then I want to say something about psychic unity and two central tenets of cultural psychology, the principle of *universalism without the uniformity* and the principle of *original multiplicity*. Finally I want to briefly identify one of the ways the idea of the social might be used by cultural psychologists interested in the social foundations of human mentalities. The study of mentalities I shall suggest is not the same thing as the study of mind. Leibniz was right: Minds do not interact.

As part of this definitional exercise I will use the term *mind* in a Leibnizean sort of way to refer to the totality of the potential and actual conceptual contents of human cognitive processes. I will use the term *mental process* to refer to the capacity of human beings to sense, feel, remember, categorize, reason, deliberate, imagine, and so forth. I will use the term *cognitive* to refer to any process (including a mental process) that enables human beings to cognize (or represent) ideas (conceptual contents) and to attain knowledge by deriving (or computing) the implications of those ideas.

Please note that to cognize an idea or conceptual content is not the same as doing it slowly, deliberately, or with awareness. It is highly likely that there exist many processes (mental or otherwise) that enable human beings to cognize the conceptual contents of mind rapidly, nondeliberatively, and without awareness. It is also important for me to point out that to cognize an idea is not the same as stating that idea, although to state an idea is to cognize it, and any conceptual content of mind that can be cognized can (in principle) be stated in language.

Finally, I will use the term *mentality* to refer to the actual cognitive functioning of a particular person or people. To describe a mentality (e.g., the mentality of an Oriya Hindu Brahman) is to get specific about the particular conceptual contents (the ideas) that have actually been cognized by that person or people. It is a basic assumption of cultural psychology that the conceptual content of mental processes is not necessarily the same for all persons or peoples (e.g., concepts such as duty, loyalty, deference, respect, and sanctity do not play identical parts in the affective and moral lives of people around the world; see Menon & Shweder, 1994; Shweder, 1993; Shweder, Mahapatra, & Miller, 1990; Shweder, Much, Mahapatra, & Park, in press). To describe a mentality is also to get specific about the particular mental processes (the particular senses, feelings, memories, desires, inferences, imaginings, etc.) that have been recruited by this or that person or people to make their cognizing of ideas (conceptual contents) possible. It is a basic assumption of cultural psychology that the way mental processes are used to cognize the conceptual contents of mind is not the same way everywhere (e.g., see Markus & Kitayama, 1991, and Shweder, 1994, for a discussion of cross-cultural variations in the "emotionalization" of feelings and in the organization and functioning of self-processes).

If we stay for a moment within the terms and definitional logic of the argot just proposed, then it follows that there is only one mind and it is a universal mind. There can be a Hindu mentality, but not a Hindu mind. This is because by mind I mean the heterogeneous collection of all the conceptual contents that any human being might ever cognize or represent by means of some (mental or nonmental) process. Bits and pieces and whole domains of conceptual content, indeed everything that could ever be thought (cognized) is there in that universal mind. This universal mind then is broader and more encompassing than any one person or people's mentality. It is not the kind of thing that can be located in space (as, e.g., Eastern or Western) or in time (as, e.g., modern or premodern). Plato had his points.[5]

In contrast, a mentality is that cognized and activated subset of mind that has become the property of (and is invested in by) some designated person or people (e.g., a particular moral community or culture). Mentalities do exist in time and space, and (as a matter of empirical fact) they are not universal in their characteristics or in their spatial or temporal distributions.[6]

Viewed this way, psychic unity is not a description of human mentalities. It is a description of the symbolic capacity of human beings to make use of their mental processes to cognize (and thereby gain access to) any of the conceptual contents of the universal mind. Psychic unity is what makes anthropology and cultural psychology possible, for without it people with genuinely different mentalities could not conceptualize each other's lives. This co-existence of one mind with many mentalities is highlighted by two central tenets of cultural psychology, namely, the principle of original multiplicity and the principle of universalism without the uniformity. The basic idea is (a) that the universal mind contains diverse, heterogeneous, even contradictory conceptual content (hence, original multiplicity), and (b) only a subset of that conceptual content is cognized or brought on-line by any functioning mentality (hence, universalism without the uniformity).

Viewed this way, the cultural psychology of interactive minds is going to be a story about the way a universal mind gets transformed into many different mentalities. It is going to be the story of how an exuberant mind already rich and heterogeneous in conceptual content gets pruned and selectively brought on-line by means of some kind of process that is social, cultural, or interactive.

What is social about the "social foundations" of a mentality?

In the space of a short commentary it is not possible to catalogue the many types of social processes by which the mind is realized as a mentality. (For a discussion of the role of verbal and nonverbal social communication, see Goodnow et al., 1995; also Shweder, 1991). Like the term *mind,* the term *social* is also dangerous and ambiguous. The spectrum of senses of the social is broad. In light of the earlier definitional exercise in which mind was distinguished from mentality, I want to conclude by briefly mentioning the sense of the social that seems most relevant to the study of the social foundations of a mentality.

The sense of the social that I have in mind is often associated with the writings of Emile Durkheim (1953, 1965). That Durkheimian sense of the social is the idea of a "moral community," in which the individual members of the community act toward each other as though they were parties to an agreement to uphold a common moral order and to think, feel, and act in a special way (see Greenwood, n.d.). Durkheim's polysemous and ambiguous phrase "conscience collective" beautifully suggests the idea of a moral community in which the individual members of the community have both a conscience formed out of social interaction (a conscience collective) and a consciousness of the collectivity (a conscience collective) at the same time. Within the field of cultural psychology, the idea of culture as a reality, "lit up by a series of morally enforceable conceptual schemes that are expressed and instantiated in practice" (Shweder, Jensen, & Goldstein, 1995, pp. 26–27), incorporates this Durkheimian sense of the social. It is essential in the study of cultural psychology that one is able to identify the local moral community committed to enforcing some selective and hence restrictive conceptual scheme. In this sense, the conceptual content of any culture's practices is always a mere subset of mind.

The Durkheimian sense of the social as the moral community can be extended in various ways. It is compatible with the primary goal of cultural psychology to investigate the similarities and differences of human mentalities across groups or populations. Indeed, from this perspective, the common goal of both social and cultural psychology is to identify precisely those cognitive processes and cognized conceptual contents that are on-line in an individual's mental life by virtue of that person's membership in some particular group (i.e., moral community).

The Durkheimian sense of the social is also compatible with the recent emphasis in cultural psychology on the conceptual analysis of mundane practices (e.g., the design of a home, the arrangement of sleeping spaces, the structure of a meal, the analysis of conversation, and the social pragmatics of talk; see Shweder et al., 1995, and the essays in Goodnow et al., 1995). Social practices have conceptual content and they are the inputs for experience, which means that the social environment in which the individual development of a mentality takes place is already conceptually organized. Thus, when it comes to the question of interactive minds, the story of cultural psychology is going to be a story about precisely how the historically evolved (and hence restrictive) conceptual content of the social practices of particular moral communities selectively resonates or otherwise interacts with the unrestricted conceptual contents of a universal mind to form the particular mentality of a person or people. Question begging aside, if the story of cultural psychology is to have a happy ending, it will have to be a story about how the Leibnizean (Platonic, Cartesian, Kantian) conception of mind can be gotten to lie down with the other side. Remember, no question begging is allowed.

Notes

1 Leibniz's theoretical notion of "God" was a late-seventeenth- to early-eighteenth-century rationalist's way of talking about what others today might call "natural" design.

2 Strong echoes of the monad versus receptacle (or rationalist vs. empiricist) debate can be found in contemporary debates in the cognitive sciences between symbolists versus connectionists (see, e.g., D'Andrade, 1995; Fodor, 1983; Pinker & Mehler, 1988; Quinlan, 1991). This debate between contemporary rationalists versus empiricists (Leibnizeans vs. Lockeans) is not the same as another with which it is sometimes conflated, the debate over the domain-specificity of conceptual contents (language vs. mathematics; animals vs. inanimate objects) and over the degree of "modularity" of "cognitive" processes (e.g., memory). In my view, differences between contemporary Leibnizeans, who focus on the a priori conceptual contents of mind, and the contemporary Lockeans, who focus on experience-sensitive connectionist networks, will not be resolved by facts about the domain-specificity of the mind's conceptual contents or facts about the degree to which there is a modular or separate memory system or reasoning system for each conceptual domain. Whatever the facts, Leibnizeans and Lockeans will be able to explain them in their own terms. (For important discussions of domain-specificity and modularity, see, e.g., Chomsky, 1988; Fodor, 1983; Hirschfeld & Gelman, 1994.)

3 It is possible that I am reading more into D'Andrade's sentence than it is meant to imply. He may well intend to be perfectly neutral between Leibniz and Locke or to balance the two or to present a third alternative. And it is not impossible to generate a Leibnitzean interpretation of his formulation as well as a Lockean one. The fact that certain ideas or conceptual contents

recur over historical time is compatible with many different assumptions about the nature and source of those ideas – for example, those ideas might recur because they are innate. A Leibnizean might conceivably interpret the word *learning* in D'Andrade's sentence as "reminiscence" or retrieval (from inside out) rather than as "acquisition" or "internalization" (from outside in). Nevertheless the point holds: It is not easy for anyone to write about the mind without appearing to lean in one direction (the monad) or the other (the receptacle), and in this case D'Andrade appears to lean in the direction of Locke.

4 Of course, I cannot pretend to speak for all of cultural psychology, only from my particular version of it. For other voices see the various essays in Stigler, Shweder, and Herdt (1990), Kitayama and Markus (1994), and Goodnow, Miller, and Kessel (1995).

5 It is my assumption that the universal mind (all potentially cognizable conceptual contents) somehow inheres or subsists or has a physical parallel in the human brain, but in the context of this discussion I am going to sidestep all the mysteries of the mind–body problem.

6 For this reason it is valid to think of cultural psychologists as naturalists who go searching for mentalities, carefully describing their distribution and form.

References

Anderson, J. A. (1985). *Cognitive psychology and its implications* (2nd ed.). New York: Freeman.

Anderson, L.W., & Burns, R. B. (1985). *Research in classrooms*. Oxford: Pergamon.

Bäckman, L., & Dixon, R. A. (1992). Psychological compensation: A theoretical framework. *Psychological Bulletin, 112*, 259–283.

Bäckman, L., Mäntylä T., & Herlitz, A. (1990). The optimization of episodic remembering in old age. In P. B. Baltes & M. M. Baltes (Eds.), *Successful aging: Perspectives from the behavioral sciences* (pp. 118–163). New York: Cambridge University Press.

Baddeley, A. D. (1982). Domains of recollection. *Psychological Review, 89*, 708–729.

Baltes, P. B., & Baltes, M. M. (1980). Plasticity and variability in psychological aging: Methodological and theoretical issues. In G. E. Gurski (Ed.), *Determining the effects of aging on the central nervous system* (pp. 41–66). Berlin: Schering.

Baltes, P. B., & Baltes, M. M. (Eds.). (1990). *Successful aging: Perspectives from the behavioral sciences*. New York: Cambridge University Press.

Baltes, P. B., & Smith, J. (1990). Toward a psychology of wisdom and its ontogenesis. In R. J. Sternberg (Ed.), *Wisdom: Its nature, origins, and development* (pp. 87–120). New York: Cambridge University Press.

Baltes, P. B., & Staudinger, U. M. (1993). The search for a psychology of wisdom. *Current Directions in Psychological Science, 2*, 75–80.

Barker, R. G., & Gump, P. V. (1964). *Big school, small school*. Stanford, CA: Stanford University Press.

Best, J. B. (1995). *Cognitive Psychology* (4th ed). St. Paul, MN: West.

Bjork, R. A., & Richardson-Klavehn, A. (1989). On the puzzling relationship between environmental context and human memory. In C. Izawa (Ed.), *Current issues in cognitive processes: The Tulane Flowerree Symposium on Cognition* (pp. 313–344). Hillsdale, NJ: Erlbaum.

Brown, A. L. (1994). The advancement of learning. *Educational Researcher, 23*, 4–12.

Chomsky, N. (1988). *Language and problems of knowledge*. Cambridge, MA: MIT Press.

Craik, F. I. M., & Lockhart, R. S. (1972). Levels of processing: A framework for memory research. *Journal of Verbal Learning and Verbal Behavior, 11*, 671–684.

D'Andrade, R. (1995). *The development of cognitive anthropology*. Cambridge: Cambridge University Press.

De Corte, E., Greer, B., & Vershaffel, L. (in press). Mathematics teaching and learning. In D. Berliner & R. Calfee (Eds.), *Handbook of educational psychology*. New York: Macmillan.

Durkheim, E. (1953). *Sociology and philosophy* (D. F. Pocock, Trans.). London: Cohen & West.

Durkheim, E. (1965). *The elementary forms of the religious life: A study in religious sociology* (J. W. Swain, Trans.) New York: Free Press.

Eich, J. E. (1980). The cue-dependent nature of state-dependent retrieval. *Memory and Cognition*, *8*, 157–173.

Eich, J. E. (1985). Context, memory, and integrated item/context imagery. *Journal of Experimental Psychology: Learning, Memory and Cognition*, *11*, 764–770.

Eysenck, M. W., & Keane, M. T. (1990). *Cognitive psychology: A student's handbook*. Hove, UK: Erlbaum.

Fodor, J. A. (1983). *Modularity of mind*. Cambridge, MA: MIT Press.

Gardiner, J. M. (1988). Functional aspects of recollective experience. *Memory and Cognition*, *16*, 309–313.

Gardiner, J. M., & Java, R. I. (1990). Recollective experience in word and nonword recognition. *Memory and Cognition*, *18*, 23–30.

Gardner, H. (1991). *The unschooled mind: How children think and how schools should teach*. New York: Basic.

Gay, J., & Cole, M. (1967). *The new mathematics and an old culture*. New York: Holt, Rinehart, & Winston.

Geiselman, R. W., & Bjork, R. A. (1980). Primary versus secondary rehearsal in imagined voices: Differential effects on recognition. *Cognitive Psychology*, *12*, 188–205.

Godden, D. R., & Baddeley, A. (1975). Context-dependent memory in two natural environments: On land and underwater. *British Journal of Psychology*, *66*, 325–331.

Goodman, K. S. (1970). Reading: A psycholinguistic guessing game. In H. Singer & R. B. Ruddell (Eds.), *Theoretical models and processes in reading* (pp. 257–271). Newark, DE: International Reading Association.

Goodnow, J., Miller, P., & Kessel, F. (Eds.). (1995). *Cultural practices as contexts for development: New directions for child development*. San Francisco: Jossey-Bass.

Graf, P. (1994). Explicit and implicit memory: A decade of research. In C. Umilta & M. Moscovitch (Eds.), *Attention and performance: Vol. 15. Conscious and nonconscious information processing* (pp. 681–696). Cambridge, MA: Bradford.

Graf, P., & Masson, M. E. J. (Eds.). (1993). *Implicit memory: New directions in cognition, development and neuropsychology*. Hillsdale, NJ: Erlbaum.

Graf, P., & Ryan, L. (1990). Transfer-appropriate processing for implicit and explicit memory. *Journal of Experimental Psychology: Learning, Memory and Cognition*, *16*, 978–992.

Graf, P., & Schacter, D. L. (1985). Implicit and explicit memory for new associations in normal and amnesic subjects. *Journal of Experimental Psychology: Learning, Memory and Cognition*, *11*, 501–518.

Greeno, J. G., & Moore, J. L. (1993). Situativity and symbols: Response to Vera and Simon. *Cognitive Science*, *17*, 49–59.

Greenwood, J. D. (n.d.). *Durkheim, Weber and the demarcation of the social*. Unpublished manuscript, available from John D. Greenwood, 29 Sheppard Lane, Stony Brook, New York, 11790.

Grossberg, S. (1980). How does a brain build a cognitive code? *Psychological Review*, *87*, 1–51.

Hall, G. S. (1883). The contents of children's minds. *Princeton Review*, *11*, 249–272.

Hayek, F. A. (1973). *Law, legislation and liberty* (Vol. 1). Chicago: University of Chicago Press.

Hirschfeld, L. A., & Gelman, S. A. (Eds.). (1994). *Mapping the mind: Domain specificity in cognition and culture*. Cambridge: Cambridge University Press.

Jackson, P. W. (1968). *Life in classroom*. New York: Holt, Rinehart, & Winston.

Jones, H. E., Macfarlane, J. W., & Eichorn, D. (1960). Progress report on growth studies at the University of California. *Vita Humana*, *3*, 17–31.

Jones, M. C. (1967). A report on three growth studies at the University of California. *Gerontologist*, *7*, 49–54.

Kagan, S. (1985). Dimensions of cooperative classroom structures. In R. Slavin, S. Sharan, S. Kagan, R. Hertz Lazarowitz, C. Webb, & R. Schmuck (Eds.), *Learning to cooperate, cooperating to learn* (pp. 277–312). New York: Plenum.

Kausler, D. H. (1982). *Experimental psychology and human aging*. New York: Wiley.

Key, E. (1900). *Das Jahrhundert des Kindes* [The century of the child]. Berlin: S. Fischer.

Kitayama, S., & Markus, H. (Eds.). (1994). *Emotion and culture*. Washington, DC: American Psychological Association.

Lave, J. (1991). Situating learning in communities of practice. In L. B. Resnick, J. M. Levine, & S. D. Teasley (Eds.), *Perspectives on socially shared cognition* (pp. 63–82). Washington, DC: American Psychological Association.

Lewin, K., Lippitt, R., & White, R. K. (1939). Patterns of aggressive behavior in experimentally created "social climates." *Journal of Social Psychology, 10*, 271–299.

Markus, H., & Kitayama, S. (1991). Culture and the self: Implications for cognition, emotion and motivation. *Psychological Review, 98*, 224–253.

Martindale, C. (1991). *Cognitive psychology: A neural-network approach*. Belmont, CA: Wadsworth.

McDowell, J. (1994). *The mind and the world*. Cambridge, MA: Harvard University Press.

Menon, U., & Shweder, R. A. (1994). Kali's tongue: Cultural psychology and the power of "shame" in Orissa, India. In S. Kitayama & H. Markus (Eds.), *Emotion and culture* (pp. 242–284). Washington, DC: American Psychological Association.

Morris, C. D., Bransford, J. D., & Franks, J. J. (1977). Levels of processing versus transfer appropriate processing. *Journal of Verbal Learning and Verbal Behavior, 16*, 519–533.

Norman, D. A. (1993). Cognition in the head and in the world: An introduction to the special issue on situated action. *Cognitive Science, 17*, 1–6.

Palincsar, A. S., & Brown, A. L. (1984). Reciprocal teaching of comprehension-fostering and comprehension-monitoring activities. *Cognition and Instruction, 1*, 117–175.

Parkin, A. J. (1993). Implicit memory across the lifespan. In P. Graf & M. E. J. Masson (Eds.), *Implicit Memory: New directions in cognition, development and neuropsychology* (pp. 191–206). Hillsdale, NJ: Erlbaum.

Parkin, A. J., & Walter, B. M. (1992). Recollective experience, normal aging, and frontal dysfunction. *Psychology and Aging, 7*, 290–298.

Pinker, S., & Mehler, J. (Eds.). (1988). *Connections and symbols*. Cambridge, MA: MIT Press.

Poon, L. W. (Ed.). (1986). *Handbook for clinical memory assessment of older adults*. Washington, DC: American Psychological Association.

Posner, M. I. (Ed.). (1989). *Foundations of cognitive science*. Cambridge, MA: MIT Press.

Quinlan, P. (1991). *Connectionism and psychology*. Chicago: University of Chicago Press.

Rein, W. (1893). *Pädagogik im Grundriß* (A primer of education) (2nd ed.). Stuttgart: Göschen.

Resnick, L. B. (1987). Learning in school and out. *Educational Researcher, 16*, 13–20.

Resnick, L. B., Levine, R., & Behrend, A. (1991). *Perspectives on socially shared cognition*. Washington, DC: American Psychological Association.

Riger, S. (1992). Epistemological debates, feminist voices: Science, social values, and the study of women. *American Psychology, 47*, 730–740.

Roediger, H. L., & McDermott, K. L. (1993). Implicit memory in human subjects. In F. Boller & J. Grafman (Eds.), *Handbook of neuropsychology* (Vol. 8, pp. 63–131). Amsterdam: Elsevier.

Rogers, C. R., & Skinner, B. F. (1956). Some issues concerning the control of human behavior. *Science, 124*, 1057–1064.

Rogoff, B. (1990). *Apprenticeship in thinking: Cognitive development in social context*. New York: Oxford University Press.

Rogoff, B. (1991). Social interaction as apprenticeship in thinking: Guidance and participation in spatial planning. In L. B. Resnick, J. M. Levine, & S. D. Teasley (Eds.), *Perspectives on socially shared cognition* (pp. 349–364). Washington, DC: American Psychological Association.

Rosenshine, B., & Meister, C. (1994). Reciprocal teaching: A review of the research. *Review of Educational Research, 64*, 479–530.

Rumelhart, D. E. (1977). Toward an interactive model of reading. In S. Dornic (Ed.), *Attention and performance* (Vol. 6, pp. 573–603). Hillsdale, NJ: Erlbaum.

Salomon, G. (1992). New challenges for educational research: Studying the individual within learning environments. *Scandinavian Journal of Educational Research, 36*, 167–182.

Salthouse, T. A. (1985). *A theory of cognitive aging*. Amsterdam: North-Holland.

Schacter, D. L., & Tulving, E. (Eds.). (1994). *Memory systems, 1994.* Cambridge, MA: MIT Press.

Schaie, K. W. (1990). The optimization of cognitive functioning in old age: Predictions based on cohort-sequential and longitudinal data. In P. B. Baltes & M. M. Baltes (Eds.), *Successful aging: Perspectives from the behavioral sciences* (pp. 94–117). New York: Cambridge University Press.

Sherry, D. F., & Schacter, D. L. (1987). The evolution of multiple memory systems. *Psychological Review, 94,* 439–454.

Shweder, R. A. (1991). *Thinking through cultures: Expeditions in cultural psychology.* Cambridge, MA: Harvard Unviersity Press.

Shweder, R. A. (1993). The cultural psychology of the emotions. In M. Lewis & J. Haviland (Eds.), *The handbook of emotions* (pp. 417–43). New York: Guilford.

Shweder, R. A. (1994). You're not sick, you're just in love. In P. Ekman & R. Davidson (Eds.), *The nature of emotion: Fundamental questions* (pp. 32–44). New York: Oxford University Press.

Shweder, R. A., Jensen, L. A., & Goldstein, W. M. (1995). Who sleeps by whom revisited: A method for extracting the moral goods implicit in practice. In J. Goodnow, P. Miller, & F. Kessel (Eds.), *Cultural practices as contexts for development* (pp. 21–40). San Francisco: Jossey-Bass.

Shweder, R. A., Mahapatra, M., & Miller, J. G. (1990). Culture and moral development. In J. Stigler, R. A. Shweder, & G. Herdt (Eds.), *Cultural psychology: Essays on comparative human development* (pp. 130–204). New York: Cambridge University Press.

Shweder, R. A., Much, N. C., Mahapatra, M. M., & Park, L. (in press). The "big three" of morality (autonomy, community, divinity) and the "big three" explanations of suffering. In R. A. Shweder (Ed.), *Why do men barbecue?: And other recipes for cultural psychology.* Cambridge, MA: Harvard University Press.

Shweder, R. A., & Sullivan, M. (1993). Cultural psychology: Who needs it? *Annual Review of Psychology, 44,* 497–523.

Slavin, R. E. (1990). *Cooperative learning: Theory, research, and practice.* Englewood Cliffs, NJ.: Prentice-Hall.

Smith, S. M. (1985). Effects of number of study environments and learning instructions on free recall clustering and accuracy. *Bulletin of the Psychonomic Society, 23,* 440–442.

Smith, S. M. (1988). Environmental context-dependent memory. In G. M. Davies & D. M. Thomson (Eds.), *Memory in context: Context in memory* (pp. 13–34). New York: Wiley.

Squire, L. R., & Butters, N. (Eds.). (1992). *Neuropsychology of memory* (2nd ed.). New York: Guilford.

Stern, W. (1911). *Die differentielle Psychologie in ihren methodischen Grundlagen* [Differential psychology and its methodological foundations] (2nd ed.). Leipzig: Barth. (Original work published 1900).

Stigler, J., Shweder, R. A., & Herdt, G. (Eds.). (1990). *Cultural psychology: Essays on comparative human development.* New York: Cambridge University Press.

Tipper, S. P., & Weaver, B. (1994). Object-based and environmental-based inhibition of return of visual attention. *Journal of Experimental Psychology: Human Perception and Performance, 20,* 478–499.

Tulving, E. (1989). Memory: Performance, knowledge, and experience. *European Journal of Cognitive Psychology, 1,* 3–26.

Vygotsky, L. S. (1978). *Mind in society: The development of higher psychological processes.* Cambridge, MA: Harvard University Press.

Vygotsky, L. S. (1981). The development of higher forms of attention in children. In J. Wertsch (Ed.), *The concept of activity in Soviet psychology* (pp. 189–240). Armonk, NY: Sharpe.

Weinert, F. E., & Helmke, A. (1995). Learning from wise mother nature or big brother instructor: The wrong choice as seen from an educational perspective. *Educational Psychologist, 30,* 135–142.

Weinstein, C. S. (1991). The classroom as a social context for learning. *Annual Review of Psychology, 42,* 493–525.

Author index

The Author Index lists the names of all authors of publications included in the reference lists. The index does not include the names of editors if the reference is a chapter in an edited book. Page numbers refer to author names spelled out in the text. In the case of multiple author publications, the names of all authors are listed when the reference is mentioned for the first time. For subsequent "et al." citations, only the first author's name is listed in the index.

441

Subject index

LIBRARY, UNIVERSITY COLLEGE CHESTER